T0329994

Empirical Dynamic Asset Pricing

Empirical Dynamic Asset Pricing
Model Specification and Econometric Assessment

Kenneth J. Singleton

Princeton University Press
Princeton and Oxford

ISBN-13: 978-0-691-12297-7
ISBN-10: 0-691-12297-0

Library of Congress Control Number: 2005937679

British Library Cataloging-in-Publication Data is available

This book has been composed in New Baskerville by Princeton Editorial
Associates, Inc., Scottsdale, Arizona

pup.princeton.edu

10 9 8 7 6 5 4 3 2 1

For my mother, Estelle, and in memory of my father, Harold

Contents

Preface

THIS BOOK EXPLORES the interplay among financial economic theory, the availability of relevant data, and the choice of econometric methodology in the empirical study of dynamic asset pricing models. Given the central roles of all of these ingredients, I have had to compromise on the depth of treatment that could be given to each of them. The end result is a book that presumes readers have had some Ph.D.-level exposure to basic probability theory and econometrics, and to discrete- and continuous-time asset pricing theory.

This book is organized into three blocks of chapters that, to a large extent, can be treated as separate modules. Chapters 1 to 6 of Part I provide an in-depth treatment of the econometric theory that is called upon in our discussions of empirical studies of dynamic asset pricing models. Readers who are more interested in the analysis of pricing models and wish to skip over this material may nevertheless find it useful to read Chapters 1 and 5. The former introduces many of the estimators and associated notation used throughout the book, and the latter introduces affine processes, which are central to much of the literature covered in the last module. The final chapter of Part I, Chapter 7, introduces a variety of parametric descriptive models for asset prices that accommodate stochastic volatility and jumps. Some of the key properties of the implied conditional distributions of these models are discussed, with particular attention given to the second through fourth moments of security returns. This material serves as background for our discussion of the econometric analysis of dynamic asset pricing models.

Part II begins with a more formal introduction to the concept of a "pricing kernel" and relates this concept to both preference-based and no-arbitrage models of asset prices. Chapter 9 examines the linear asset pricing relations—restrictions on the conditional means of returns—derived by restricting agents' preferences or imposing distributional assumptions on the joint distributions of pricing kernels and asset returns. It is in this chapter that we discuss the vast literature on testing for serial correlation in asset returns.

Chapter 10 discusses the econometric analyses of pricing relations based directly on the first-order conditions associated with agents' intertemporal consumption and investment decisions. Chapter 11 examines so-called beta representations of conditional expected excess returns, covering both their economic foundations and the empirical evidence on their goodness-of-fit.

Part III covers the literature on no-arbitrage pricing models. Readers wishing to focus on this material will find Chapter 8 on pricing kernels to be useful background. Chapters 12 and 13 explore the specification and goodness-of-fit of dynamic term structure models for default-free bonds. Defaultable bonds, particularly corporate bonds and credit default swaps, are taken up in Chapter 14. Chapters 15 and 16 cover the empirical literature on equity and fixed-income option pricing models.

Acknowledgments

THIS BOOK IS an outgrowth of many years of teaching advanced econometrics and empirical finance to doctoral students at Carnegie Mellon and Stanford Universities. I am grateful to the students in these courses who have challenged my own thinking about econometric modeling of asset price behavior and thereby have influenced the scope and substance of this book.

My way of approaching the topics addressed here, and indeed my understanding of many of the issues, have been shaped to a large degree by discussions and collaborations with Lars Hansen and Darrell Duffie starting in the 1980s. Their guidance has been invaluable as I have wandered through the maze of dynamic asset pricing models.

More generally, readers will recognize that I draw heavily from published work with several co-authors. Chapters 3 and 4 on the properties of econometric estimators and statistical inference draw from joint work with Lars Hansen. Chapter 6 on simulation-based estimators draws from my joint work with Darrell Duffie on simulated method of moments estimation. Chapter 5 on affine processes draws from joint work with Qiang Dai, Darrell Duffie, Anh Le, and Jun Pan. Chapters 10 and 11 on preference-based pricing models and beta models for asset returns draw upon joint work with Lars Hansen, Scott Richard, and Marty Eichenbaum. Chapters 12 and 13 draw upon joint work with Qiang Dai, Anh Le, and Wei Yang. The discussion of defaultable security pricing in Chapter 14 draws upon joint work with Darrell Duffie, Lasse Pedersen, and Jun Pan. Portions of Chapter 16 are based on joint work with Qiang Dai and Len Umantsev. I am sincerely grateful to these colleagues for the opportunities to have worked with them and, through these collaborations, for their contributions to this effort. They are, of course, absolved of any responsibility for remaining confusion on my part.

I am also grateful to Mikhail Chernov, Michael Johannes, and Stefan Nagel for their helpful comments on drafts of this book, particularly on the chapters covering equity returns and option prices.

Throughout the past 20 years I have benefited from working with many conscientious research assistants. Their contributions are sprinkled throughout my research, and recent assistants have been helpful in preparing material for this book. In addition, I thank Linda Bethel for extensive assistance with the graphs and tables, and with related LaTeX issues that arose during the preparation of the manuscript.

Completing this project would not have been possible without the support of and encouragement from Fumi, Shauna, and Yuuta.

Empirical Dynamic Asset Pricing

1
Introduction

A DYNAMIC ASSET pricing model is refutable empirically if it restricts the joint distribution of the observable asset prices or returns under study. A wide variety of economic and statistical assumptions have been imposed to arrive at such testable restrictions, depending in part on the objectives and scope of a modeler's analysis. For instance, if the goal is to price a given cash-flow stream based on agents' optimal consumption and investment decisions, then a modeler typically needs a fully articulated specification of agents' preferences, the available production technologies, and the constraints under which agents optimize. On the other hand, if a modeler is concerned with the derivation of prices as discounted cash flows, subject only to the constraint that there be no "arbitrage" opportunities in the economy, then it may be sufficient to specify how the relevant discount factors depend on the underlying risk factors affecting security prices, along with the joint distribution of these factors.

An alternative, typically less ambitious, modeling objective is that of testing the restrictions implied by a particular "equilibrium" condition arising out of an agent's consumption/investment decision. Such tests can often proceed by specifying only portions of an agent's intertemporal portfolio problem and examining the implied restrictions on moments of subsets of variables in the model. With this narrower scope often comes some "robustness" to potential misspecification of components of the overall economy that are not directly of interest.

Yet a third case is one in which we do not have a well-developed theory for the joint distribution of prices and other variables and are simply attempting to learn about features of their joint behavior. This case arises, for example, when one finds evidence against a theory, is not sure about how to formulate a better-fitting, alternative theory, and, hence, is seeking a better understanding of the historical relations among key economic variables as guidance for future model construction.

As a practical matter, differences in model formulation and the decision to focus on a "preference-based" or "arbitrage-free" pricing model may also be influenced by the availability of data. A convenient feature of financial data is that it is sampled frequently, often daily and increasingly intraday as well. On the other hand, macroeconomic time series and other variables that may be viewed as determinants of asset prices may only be reported monthly or quarterly. For the purpose of studying the relation between asset prices and macroeconomic series, it is therefore necessary to formulate models and adopt econometric methods that accommodate these data limitations. In contrast, those attempting to understand the day-to-day movements in asset prices—traders or risk managers at financial institutions, for example—may wish to design models and select econometric methods that can be implemented with daily or intraday financial data alone.

Another important way in which data availability and model specification often interact is in the selection of the decision interval of economic agents. Though available data are sampled at discrete intervals of time— daily, weekly, and so on—it need not be the case that economic agents make their decisions at the same sampling frequency. Yet it is not uncommon for the available data, including their sampling frequency, to dictate a modeler's assumption about the decision interval of the economic agents in the model. Almost exclusively, two cases are considered: *discrete-time* models typically match the sampling and decision intervals—monthly sampled data mean monthly decision intervals, and so on—whereas *continuous-time* models assume that agents make decisions continuously in time and then implications are derived for discretely sampled data. There is often no sound economic justification for either the coincidence of timing in discrete-time models, or the convenience of continuous decision making in continuous-time models. As we will see, analytic tractability is often a driving force behind these timing assumptions.

Both of these considerations (the degree to which a complete economic environment is specified and data limitations), as well as the computational complexity of solving and estimating a model, may affect the choice of estimation strategy and, hence, the econometric properties of the estimator of a dynamic pricing model. When a model provides a full characterization of the joint distribution of its variables, a historical sample is available, and fully exploiting this information in estimation is computationally feasible, then the resulting estimators are "fully efficient" in the sense of exploiting all of the model-implied restrictions on the joint distribution of asset prices. On the other hand, when any one of these conditions is not met, researchers typically resort, by choice or necessity, to making compromises on the degree of model complexity (the richness of the economic environment) or the computational complexity of the estimation strategy (which often means less econometric efficiency in estimation).

With these differences in modelers' objectives, practical constraints on model implementation, and computational considerations in mind, this book: (1) characterizes the nature of the restrictions on the joint distributions of asset returns and other economic variables implied by dynamic asset pricing models (DAPMs); (2) discusses the interplay between model formulation and the choice of econometric estimation strategy and analyzes the large-sample properties of the feasible estimators; and (3) summarizes the existing, and presents some new, empirical evidence on the fit of various DAPMs.

We briefly expand on the interplay between model formulation and econometric analysis to set the stage for the remainder of the book.

1.1. Model Implied Restrictions

Let $\mathcal{P}_s$ denote the set of "payoffs" at date s that are to be priced at date t, for $s > t$, by an economic model (e.g., next period's cum-dividend stock price, cash flows on bonds, and so on),[1] and let $\pi_t : \mathcal{P}_s \to \mathbb{R}$ denote the pricing function, where $\mathbb{R}^n$ denotes the n-dimensional Euclidean space. Most DAPMs maintain the assumption of no arbitrage opportunities on the set of securities being studied: for any $q_{t+1} \in \mathcal{P}_{t+1}$ for which $\Pr\{q_{t+1} \geq 0\} = 1$, $\Pr(\{\pi_t(q_{t+1}) \leq 0\} \cap \{q_{t+1} > 0\}) = 0$.[2] In other words, nonnegative payoffs at $t+1$ that are positive with positive probability have positive prices at date t. A key insight underlying the construction of DAPMs is that the absence of arbitrage opportunities on a set of payoffs $\mathcal{P}_s$ is essentially equivalent to the existence of a special payoff, a *pricing kernel* q_s^*, that is strictly positive $(\Pr\{q_s^* > 0\} = 1)$ and represents the pricing function π_t as

$$\pi_t(q_s) = E\left[q_s q_s^* \mid \mathcal{I}_t\right], \tag{1.1}$$

for all $q_s \in \mathcal{P}_s$, where $\mathcal{I}_t$ denotes the information set upon which expectations are conditioned in computing prices.[3]

---

[1] At this introductory level we remain vague about the precise characteristics of the payoffs investors trade. See Harrison and Kreps (1979), Hansen and Richard (1987), and subsequent chapters herein for formal definitions of payoff spaces.

[2] We let $\Pr\{\cdot\}$ denote the probability of the event in brackets.

[3] The existence of a pricing kernel q^* that prices all payoffs according to (1.1) is equivalent to the assumption of no arbitrage opportunities when uncertainty is generated by discrete random variables (see, e.g., Duffie, 2001). More generally, when $\mathcal{I}_t$ is generated by continuous random variables, additional structure must be imposed on the payoff space and pricing function π_t for this equivalence (e.g., Harrison and Kreps, 1979, and Hansen and Richard, 1987). For now, we focus on the pricing relation (1.1), treating it as being equivalent to the absence of arbitrage. A more formal development of pricing kernels and the properties of q^* is taken up in Chapter 8 using the framework set forth in Hansen and Richard (1987).

This result by itself does not imply testable restrictions on the prices of payoffs in $\mathcal{P}_{t+1}$, since the theorem does not lead directly to an empirically observable counterpart to the benchmark payoff. Rather, overidentifying restrictions are obtained by restricting the functional form of the pricing kernel q_s^* or the joint distribution of the elements of the *pricing environment* $(\mathcal{P}_s, q_s^*, \mathcal{I}_t)$. It is natural, therefore, to classify DAPMs according to the types of restrictions they impose on the distributions of the elements of $(\mathcal{P}_s, q_s^*, \mathcal{I}_t)$. We organize our discussions of models and the associated estimation strategies under four headings: preference-based DAPMs, arbitrage-free pricing models, "beta" representations of excess portfolio returns, and linear asset pricing relations. This classification of DAPMs is not mutually exclusive. Therefore, the organization of our subsequent discussions of specific models is also influenced in part by the choice of econometric methods typically used to study these models.

1.1.1. Preference-Based DAPMs

The approach to pricing that is most closely linked to an investor's portfolio problem is that of the preference-based models that directly parameterize an agent's intertemporal consumption and investment decision problem. Specifically, suppose that the economy being studied is comprised of a finite number of infinitely lived agents who have identical endowments, information, and preferences in an uncertain environment. Moreover, suppose that $\mathcal{A}_t$ represents the agents' information set and that the representative consumer ranks consumption sequences using a von Neumann-Morgenstern utility functional

$$E\left[\sum_{t=0}^{\infty} \beta^t U(c_t) \,\Big|\, \mathcal{A}_0\right]. \tag{1.2}$$

In (1.2), preferences are assumed to be time separable with period utility function U and the subjective discount factor $\beta \in (0, 1)$. If the representative agent can trade the assets with payoffs $\mathcal{P}_s$ and their asset holdings are interior to the set of admissible portfolios, the prices of these payoffs in equilibrium are given by (Rubinstein, 1976; Lucas, 1978; Breeden, 1979)

$$\pi_t(q_s) = E\left[m_s^{s-t} q_s \mid A_t\right], \tag{1.3}$$

where $m_s^{s-t} = \beta U'(c_s)/U'(c_t)$ is the intertemporal marginal rate of substitution of consumption (MRS) between dates t and s. For a given parameterization of the utility function $U(c_t)$, a preference-based DAPM allows the association of the pricing kernel q_s^* with m_s^{s-t}.

To compute the prices $\pi_t(q_s)$ requires a parametric assumption about the agent's utility function $U(c_t)$ and sufficient economic structure to determine the joint, conditional distribution of m_s^{s-t} and q_s. Given that prices are set as part of the determination of an equilibrium in goods and securities markets, a modeler interested in pricing must specify a variety of features of an economy outside of securities markets in order to undertake preference-based pricing. Furthermore, limitations on available data may be such that some of the theoretical constructs appearing in utility functions or budget constraints do not have readily available, observable counterparts. Indeed, data on individual consumption levels are not generally available, and aggregate consumption data are available only for certain categories of goods and, at best, only at a monthly sampling frequency.

For these reasons, studies of preference-based models have often focused on the more modest goal of attempting to evaluate whether, for a particular choice of utility function $U(c_t)$, (1.3) does in fact "price" the payoffs in $\mathcal{P}_s$. Given observations on a candidate m_s^{s-t} and data on asset returns $\mathcal{R}_s \equiv \{q_s \in \mathcal{P}_s : \pi_t(q_s) = 1\}$, (1.3) implies testable restrictions on the joint distribution of $\mathcal{R}_s$, m_t^{s-t}, and elements of $\mathcal{A}_t$. Namely, for each s-period return r_s, $E[m_s^{s-t} r_s - 1 | \mathcal{A}_t] = 0$, for any $r_s \in \mathcal{R}_s$ (see, e.g., Hansen and Singleton, 1982). An immediate implication of this moment restriction is that $E[(m_s^{s-t} r_s - 1)x_t] = 0$, for any $x_t \in \mathcal{A}_t$.[4] These unconditional moment restrictions can be used to construct method-of-moments estimators of the parameters governing m_s^{s-t} and to test whether or not m_s^{s-t} prices the securities with payoffs in $\mathcal{P}_s$. This illustrates the use of restrictions on the moments of certain functions of the observed data for estimation and inference, when complete knowledge of the joint distribution of these variables is not available.

An important feature of preference-based models of frictionless markets is that, assuming agents optimize and rationally use their available information $\mathcal{A}_t$ in computing the expectation (1.3), there will be *no arbitrage opportunities* in equilibrium. That is, the absence of arbitrage opportunities is a consequence of the equilibrium price-setting process.

1.1.2. Arbitrage-Free Pricing Models

An alternative approach to pricing starts with the presumption of no arbitrage opportunities (i.e., this is not derived from equilibrium behavior). Using the principle of "no arbitrage" to develop pricing relations dates back at least to the key insights of Black and Scholes (1973), Merton (1973), Ross

---

[4] This is an implication of the "law of iterated expectations," which states that $E[y_s] = E[E(y_s|\mathcal{A}_t)]$, for any conditioning information set $\mathcal{A}_t$.

(1978), and Harrison and Kreps (1979). Central to this approach is the observation that, under weak regularity conditions, pricing can proceed "as if" agents are risk neutral. When time is measured continuously and agents can trade a default-free bond that matures an "instant" in the future and pays the (continuously compounded) rate of return r_t, discounting for risk-neutral pricing is done by the default-free "roll-over" return $e^{-\int_t^s r_u \, du}$. For example, if uncertainty about future prices and yields is generated by a continuous-time Markov process Y_t (so, in particular, the conditioning information set $\mathcal{I}_t$ is generated by Y_t), then the price of the payoff q_s is given equivalently by

$$\pi_t(q_s) = E\left[q_s^* q_s \mid Y_t\right] = E_t^{\mathbb{Q}}\left[e^{-\int_t^s r_u \, du} \, q_s \mid Y_t\right], \qquad (1.4)$$

where $E_t^{\mathbb{Q}}$ denotes expectation with regard to the "risk-neutral" conditional distribution of Y. The term risk-neutral is applied because prices in (1.4) are expressed as the expected value of the payoff q_s *as if agents are neutral toward financial risks*.

As we will see more formally in subsequent chapters, the risk attitudes of investors are implicit in the exogenous specification of the pricing kernel q^* as a function of the state Y_t and, hence, in the change of probability measure underlying the risk-neutral representation (1.4). Leaving preferences and technology in the "background" and proceeding to parameterize the distribution of q^* directly facilitates the computation of security prices. The parameterization of $(\mathcal{P}_s, q_s^*, Y_t)$ is chosen so that the expectation in (1.4) can be solved, either analytically or through tractable numerical methods, for $\pi_t(q_s)$ as a function of $Y_t : \pi_t(q_s) = P(Y_t)$. This is facilitated by the adoption of continuous time (continuous trading), special structure on the conditional distribution of Y, and constraints on the dependence of q^* on Y so that the second expectation in (1.4) is easily computed. However, similarly tractable models are increasingly being developed for economies specified in discrete time and with discrete decision/trading intervals.

Importantly, though knowledge of the risk-neutral distribution of Y_t is sufficient for pricing through (1.4), this knowledge is typically not sufficient for econometric estimation. For the purpose of estimation using historical price or return information associated with the payoffs $\mathcal{P}_s$, we also need information about the distribution of Y under its *data-generating* or *actual* measure. What lie between the actual and risk-neutral distributions of Y are adjustments for the "market prices of risk"—terms that capture agents' attitudes toward risk. It follows that, throughout this book, when discussing arbitrage-free pricing models, we typically find it necessary to specify the distributions of the state variables or risk factors under both measures.

If the conditional distribution of Y_t given Y_{t-1} is known (i.e., derivable from knowledge of the continuous-time specification of Y), then so typically is the conditional distribution of the observed market prices $\pi_t(q_s)$. The completeness of the specification of the pricing relations (both the distribution of Y and the functional form of P_s) in this case implies that one can in principle use "fully efficient" maximum likelihood methods to estimate the unknown parameters of interest, say θ_0. Moreover, this is feasible using market price data alone, even though the risk factors Y may be latent (unobserved) variables. This is a major strength of this modeling approach since, in terms of data requirements, one is constrained only by the availability of financial market data.

Key to this strategy for pricing is the presumption that the burden of computing $\pi_t(q_s) = P_s(Y_t)$ is low. For many specifications of the distribution of the state Y_t, the pricing relation $P_s(Y_t)$ must be determined by numerical methods. In this case, the computational burden of solving for P_s while simultaneously estimating θ_0 can be formidable, especially as the dimension of Y gets large. Have these considerations steered modelers to simpler data-generating processes (DGPs) for Y_t than they might otherwise have studied? Surely the answer is yes and one might reasonably be concerned that such compromises in the interest of computational tractability have introduced model misspecification.

We will see that, fortunately, in many cases there are alternative estimation strategies for studying arbitrage-free pricing relations that lessen the need for such compromises. In particular, one can often compute the moments of prices or returns implied by a pricing model, even though the model-implied likelihood function is unknown. In such cases, method-of-moments estimation is feasible. Early implementations of method-of-moments estimators typically sacrificed some econometric efficiency compared to the maximum likelihood estimator in order to achieve substantial computational simplification. More recently, however, various approximate maximum likelihood estimators have been developed that involve little or no loss in econometric efficiency, while preserving computational tractability.

1.1.3. Beta Representations of Excess Returns

One of the most celebrated and widely applied asset pricing models is the static capital-asset pricing model (CAPM), which expresses expected excess returns in terms of a security's beta with a benchmark portfolio (Sharpe, 1964; Mossin, 1968). The traditional CAPM is static in the sense that agents are assumed to solve one-period optimization problems instead of multi-period utility maximization problems. Additionally, the CAPM beta pricing relation holds only under special assumptions about either the distributions of asset returns or agents' preferences.

Nevertheless, the key insights of the CAPM carry over to richer stochastic environments in which agents optimize over multiple periods. There is an analogous "single-beta" representation of expected returns based on the representation (1.1) of prices in terms of a pricing kernel q^*, what we refer to as an *intertemporal* CAPM or ICAPM.[5] Specifically, setting $s = t + 1$, the benchmark return $r_{t+1}^* = q_{t+1}^*/\pi_t(q_{t+1}^*)$ satisfies[6]

$$E\big[r_{t+1}^*(r_{t+1} - r_{t+1}^*) \mid \mathcal{I}_t\big] = 0, \ r_{t+1} \in \mathcal{R}_{t+1}. \tag{1.5}$$

Equation (1.5) has several important implications for the role of r_{t+1}^* in asset return relations, one of which is that r_{t+1}^* is a benchmark return for a single-beta representation of excess returns (see Chapter 11):

$$E\big[r_{j,t+1} \mid \mathcal{I}_t\big] - r_t^f = \beta_{jt}\left(E\big[r_{t+1}^* \mid \mathcal{I}_t\big] - r_t^f\right), \tag{1.6}$$

where

$$\beta_{jt} = \frac{\mathrm{Cov}\big[r_{j,t+1}, r_{t+1}^* \mid \mathcal{I}_t\big]}{\mathrm{Var}\big[r_{t+1}^* \mid \mathcal{I}_t\big]}, \tag{1.7}$$

and r_t^f is the interest rate on one-period riskless loans issued at date t. In words, the excess return on a security is proportional to the excess return on the benchmark portfolio, $E[r_{t+1}^* - r_t^f \mid \mathcal{I}_t]$, with factor of proportionality β_{jt}, for all securities j with returns in $\mathcal{R}_{t+1}$.

It turns out that the beta representation (1.6), together with the representation of r^f in terms of q_{t+1}^*,[7] constitute exactly the same information as the basic pricing relation (1.1). Given one, we can derive the other, and vice versa. At first glance, this may seem surprising given that econometric tests of beta representations of asset returns are often not linked to pricing kernels. The reason for this is that most econometric tests of expressions like (1.6) are in fact *not* tests of the joint restriction that $r_t^f = 1/E[q_{t+1}^*|\mathcal{I}_t]$ and r_{t+1}^* satisfies (1.6). Rather tests of the ICAPM are tests of whether a proposed candidate benchmark return r_{t+1}^β satisfies (1.6) alone, for a given information set $\mathcal{I}_t$. There are an infinite number of returns r_t^β that satisfy (1.6) (see Chapter 11). The return r_{t+1}^*, on the other hand, is the unique

---

[5] By defining a benchmark return that is explicitly linked to the marginal rate of substitution, Breeden (1979) has shown how to obtain a single-beta representation of security returns that holds in continuous time. The following discussion is based on the analysis in Hansen and Richard (1987).

[6] Hansen and Richard (1987) show that when the pricing function π_t is nontrivial, $\Pr\{\pi_t(q_{t+1}^*) = 0\} = 0$, so that r_{t+1}^* is a well-defined return. Substituting r^* into (1.1) gives $E[r_{t+1}^* r_{t+1} \mid \mathcal{I}_t] = \{E[q_{t+1}^{*2} \mid \mathcal{I}_t]\}^{-1}$, for all $r_{t+1} \in \mathcal{R}_{t+1}$. Since r_{t+1}^* is one such return, (1.5) follows.

[7] The interest rate r_t^f can be expressed as $1/E[q_{t+1}^*|\mathcal{I}_t]$ by substituting the payoff $q_{t+1} = 1$ into (1.1) with $s = t + 1$.

return (within a set that is formally defined) satisfying (1.5). Thus, tests of single-beta ICAPMs are in fact tests of weaker restrictions on return distributions than tests of the pricing relation (1.1).

Focusing on a candidate benchmark return r_{t+1}^{β} and relation (1.6) (with r_{t+1}^{β} in place of r_{t+1}^*), once again the choices made regarding estimation and testing strategies typically involve trade-offs between the assumptions about return distributions and the robustness of the empirical analysis. Taken by itself, (1.6) is a restriction on the conditional first and second moments of returns. If one specifies a parametric family for the joint conditional distribution of the returns $r_{j,t+1}$ and r_{t+1}^{β} and the state Y_t, then estimation can proceed imposing the restriction (1.6). However, such tests may be compromised by misspecification of the higher moments of returns, even if the first two moments are correctly specified. There are alternative estimation strategies that exploit less information about the conditional distribution of returns and, in particular, that are based on the first two conditional moments for a given information set $\mathcal{I}_t$, of returns.

1.1.4. Linear Pricing Relations

Historically, much of the econometric analysis of DAPMs has focused on linear pricing relations. One important example of a linear DAPM is the version of the ICAPM obtained by assuming that β_{jt} in (1.6) is constant (not state dependent), say β_j. Under this additional assumption, β_j is the familiar "beta" of the jth common stock from the *CAPM*, extended to allow both expected returns on stocks and the riskless interest rate to change over time. The mean of

$$u_{j,t+1} \equiv \left(r_{j,t+1} - r_t^f \right) - \beta_j \left(r_{t+1}^{\beta} - r_t^f \right) \tag{1.8}$$

conditioned on $\mathcal{I}_t$ is zero for all admissible r_j. Therefore, the expression in (1.8) is uncorrelated with any variable in the information set $\mathcal{I}_t$; $E[u_{j,t+1} x_t] = 0$, $x_t \in \mathcal{I}_t$. Estimators of the β_j and tests of (1.6) can be constructed based on these moment restrictions.

This example illustrates how additional assumptions about one feature of a model can make an analysis more robust to misspecification of other features. In this case, the assumption that β_j is constant permits estimation of β_j and testing of the null hypothesis (1.6) without having to fully specify the information set $\mathcal{I}_t$ or the functional form of the conditional means of $r_{j,t+1}$ and r_{t+1}^{β}. All that is necessary is that the candidate elements x_t of $\mathcal{I}_t$ used to construct moment restrictions are indeed in $\mathcal{I}_t$.[8]

---

[8] We will see that this simplification does not obtain when the β_{jt} are state dependent. Indeed, in the latter case, we might not even have readily identifiable benchmark returns r_{t+1}^{β}.

Another widely studied linear pricing relation was derived under the presumption that in a well-functioning—some say *informationally efficient*—market, holding-period returns on assets must be unpredictable (see, e.g., Fama, 1970). It is now well understood that, in fact, the optimal processing of information by market participants is not sufficient to ensure unpredictable returns. Rather, we should expect returns to evidence some predictability, either because agents are risk averse or as a result of the presence of a wide variety of market frictions.

Absent market frictions, then, one sufficient condition for returns to be unpredictable is that agents are risk neutral in the sense of having linear utility functions, $U(c_t) = u_0 + u_c c_t$. Then the MRS is $m_s^{s-t} = \beta^s$, where β is the subjective discount factor, and it follows immediately from (1.3) that

$$E[r_s | I_t] = 1/\beta^s, \tag{1.9}$$

for an admissible return r_s. This, in turn, implies that r_s is unpredictable in the sense of having a constant conditional mean. The restrictions on returns implied by (1.9) are, in principle, easily tested under only minimal additional auxiliary assumptions about the distributions of returns. One simply checks to see whether $r_s - 1/\beta^s$ is uncorrelated with variables dated t or earlier that might be useful for forecasting future returns. However, as we discuss in depth in Chapter 9, there is an enormous literature examining this hypothesis. In spite of the simplicity of the restriction (1.9), whether or not it is true in financial markets remains an often debated question.

1.2. Econometric Estimation Strategies

While the specification of a DAPM logically precedes the selection of an estimation strategy for an empirical analysis, we begin Part I with an overview of econometric methods for analyzing DAPMs. Applications of these methods are then taken up in the context of the discussions of specific DAPMs. To set the stage for Part I, we start by viewing the model construction stage as leading to a family of models or pricing relations describing features of the distribution of an observed vector of variables z_t. This vector may include asset prices or returns, possibly other economic variables, as well as lagged values of these variables. Each model is indexed by a K-dimensional vector of parameters θ in an admissible parameter space $\Phi \in \mathbb{R}^K$. We introduce Φ

For instance, if I_t is taken to be agents' information set A_t, then the contents of I_t may not be known to the econometrician. In this case the set of returns that satisfy (1.6) may also be unknown. It is of interest to ask then whether or not there are similar risk-return relations with moments conditioned on an observable subset of A_t, say I_t, for which benchmark returns satisfying an analogue to (1.6) are observable. This is among the questions addressed in Chapter 11.

because, for each of the DAPMs indexed by θ to be well defined, it may be necessary to constrain certain parameters to be larger than some minimum value (e.g., variances or risk aversion parameters), or DAPMs may imply that certain parameters are functionally related. The basic premise of an econometric analysis of a DAPM is that there is a unique $\theta_0 \in \Phi$ (a unique pricing relation) consistent with the population distribution of z. A primary objective of the econometric analysis is to construct an estimator of θ_0.

More precisely, we view the selection of an *estimation strategy* for θ_0 as the choice of:

- A sample of size T on a vector z_t of observed variables, $\vec{z}_T \equiv (z_T, z_{T-1}, \ldots, z_1)'$.
- An *admissible* parameter space $\Phi \subseteq \mathbb{R}^K$ that includes θ_0.
- A K-vector of functions $\mathcal{D}(z_t; \theta)$ with the property that θ_0 is the unique element of Φ satisfying

$$E[\mathcal{D}(z_t; \theta_0)] = 0. \tag{1.10}$$

What ties an estimation strategy to the particular DAPM of interest is the requirement that θ_0 be the unique element of Φ that satisfies (1.10) for the chosen function $\mathcal{D}$. Thus, we view (1.10) as summarizing the implications of the DAPM that are being used directly in estimation. Note that, while the estimation strategy is premised on the economic theory of interest implying that (1.10) is satisfied, there is no presumption that this theory implies a unique $\mathcal{D}$ that has mean zero at θ_0. In fact, usually, there is an uncountable infinity of admissible choices of $\mathcal{D}$.

For many of the estimation strategies considered, $\mathcal{D}$ can be reinterpreted as the first-order condition for maximizing a nonstochastic *population estimation objective* or *criterion* function $Q_0(\theta) : \Phi \to \mathbb{R}$. That is, at θ_0,

$$\frac{\partial Q_0}{\partial \theta}(\theta_0) = E[\mathcal{D}(z_t; \theta_0)] = 0. \tag{1.11}$$

Thus, we often view a choice of estimation strategy as a choice of criterion function Q_0. For well-behaved Q_0, there is always a θ^* that is the global maximum (or minimum, depending on the estimation strategy) of the criterion function Q_0. Therefore, for Q_0 to be a sensible choice for the model at hand we require that θ^* be unique and equal to the population parameter vector of interest, θ_0. A necessary step in verifying that $\theta^* = \theta_0$ is verifying that $\mathcal{D}$ satisfies (1.10) at θ_0.

So far we have focused on constraints on the population moments of z derived from a DAPM. To construct an estimator of θ_0, we work with the sample counterpart of $Q_0(\theta)$, $Q_T(\theta)$, which is a known function of $\vec{z}_T$. (The subscript T is henceforth used to indicate dependence on the entire sample.)

The sample-dependent θ_T that minimizes $Q_T(\theta)$ over Φ is the *extremum* estimator of θ_0. When the first-order condition to the population optimum problem takes the form (1.11), the corresponding first-order condition for the sample estimation problem is[9]

$$\frac{\partial Q_T}{\partial \theta}(\theta_T) = \frac{1}{T}\sum_{t=1}^{T} \mathcal{D}(z_t; \theta_T) = 0. \tag{1.12}$$

The sample relation (1.12) is obtained by replacing the population moment in (1.11) by its sample counterpart and choosing θ_T to satisfy these sample moment equations. Since, under regularity, sample means converge to their population counterparts [in particular, $Q_T(\cdot)$ converges to $Q_0(\cdot)$], we expect θ_T to converge to θ_0 (the parameter vector of interest and the unique minimizer of Q_0) as $T \to \infty$.

As noted previously, DAPMs often give rise to moment restrictions of the form (1.10) for more than one $\mathcal{D}$, in which case there are multiple feasible estimation strategies. Under regularity, all of these choices of $\mathcal{D}$ have the property that the associated θ_T converge to θ_0 (they are *consistent* estimators of θ_0). Where they differ is in the variance-covariance matrices of the implied large-sample distributions of θ_T. One paradigm, then, for selecting among the feasible estimation strategies is to choose the $\mathcal{D}$ that gives the most econometrically efficient estimator in the sense of having the smallest asymptotic variance matrix. Intuitively, the later estimator is the one that exploits the most information about the distribution of $\vec{z}_T$ in estimating θ_0.

Once a DAPM has been selected for study and an estimation strategy has been chosen, one is ready to proceed with an empirical study. At this stage, the econometrician/modeler is faced with several new challenges, including:

1. The choice of computational method to find a global optimum to $Q_T(\theta)$.
2. The choice of statistics and derivation of their large-sample properties for testing hypotheses of interest.
3. An assessment of the actual small-sample distributions of the test statistics and, thus, of the reliability of the chosen inference procedures.

The computational demands of maximizing Q_T can be formidable. When the methods used by a particular empirical study are known, we occasionally comment on the approach taken. However, an in-depth exploration of

---

[9] In subsequent chapters we often find it convenient to define Q_T more generally as $1/T \sum_{t=1}^{T} \mathcal{D}_T(z_t; \theta_T) = 0$, where $\mathcal{D}_T(z_t; \theta)$ is chosen so that it converges (almost surely) to $\mathcal{D}(z_t; \theta)$, as $T \to \infty$, for all $\theta \in \Phi$.

alternative algorithms for finding the optimum of Q_T is beyond the scope of this book.

With regard to points (2) and (3), there are many approaches to testing hypotheses about the goodness-of-fit of a DAPM or the values of the parameters θ_0. The criteria for selecting a test procedure (within the classical statistical paradigm) are virtually all based on large-sample considerations. In practice, however, the actual distributions of estimators in finite samples may be quite different than their large-sample counterparts. To a limited degree, Monte Carlo methods have been used to assess the small-sample properties of estimators θ_T. We often draw upon this literature, when available, in discussing the empirical evidence.

Part I

Econometric Methods for Analyzing DAPMs

2

Model Specification and Estimation Strategies

A DAPM MAY: (1) provide a complete characterization of the joint distribution of all of the variables being studied; or (2) imply restrictions on some moments of these variables, but not reveal the form of their joint distribution. A third possibility is that there is not a well-developed theory for the joint distribution of the variables being studied. Which of these cases obtains for the particular DAPM being studied determines the feasible estimation strategies; that is, the feasible choices of $\mathcal{D}$ in the definition of an *estimation strategy*. This chapter introduces the maximum likelihood (ML), generalized method of moments (GMM), and linear least-squares projection (LLP) estimators and begins our development of the interplay between model formulation and the choice of an estimation strategy discussed in Chapter 1.

2.1. Full Information about Distributions

Suppose that a DAPM yields a complete characterization of the joint distribution of a sample of size T on a vector of variables y_t, $\vec{y}_T \equiv \{y_1, \ldots, y_T\}$. Let $L_T(\beta) = L(\vec{y}_T; \beta)$ denote the family of joint density functions of $\vec{y}_T$ implied by the DAPM and indexed by the K-dimensional parameter vector β. Suppose further that the admissible parameter space associated with this DAPM is $\Theta \subseteq \mathbb{R}^K$ and that there is a unique $\beta_0 \in \Theta$ that describes the true probability model generating the asset price data.

In this case, we can take $L_T(\beta)$ to be our sample criterion function— called the *likelihood function* of the data—and obtain the *maximum likelihood* (ML) estimator b_T^{ML} by maximizing $L_T(\beta)$. In ML estimation, we start with the joint density function of $\vec{y}_T$, evaluate the random variable $\vec{y}_T$ at the realization comprising the observed historical sample, and then maximize the value of this density over the choice of $\beta \in \Theta$. This amounts to maximizing, over all admissible β, the "likelihood" that the realized sample was drawn from the density $L_T(\beta)$. ML estimation, when feasible, is the most econometrically efficient estimator within a large class of consistent estimators (Chapter 3).

In practice, it turns out that studying L_T is less convenient than working with a closely related objective function based on the conditional density function of y_t. Many of the DAPMs that we examine in later chapters, for which ML estimation is feasible, lead directly to knowledge of the density function of y_t conditioned on $\vec{y}_{t-1}$, $f_t(y_t|\vec{y}_{t-1}; \beta)$ and imply that

$$f_t(y_t|\vec{y}_{t-1}; \beta) = f(y_t|\vec{y}_{t-1}^J; \beta), \tag{2.1}$$

where $\vec{y}_t^J \equiv (y_t, y_{t-1}, \ldots, y_{t-J+1})$, a J-history of y_t. The right-hand side of (2.1) is *not* indexed by t, implying that the conditional density function does not change with time.[1] In such cases, the likelihood function L_T becomes

$$L_T(\beta) = \prod_{t=J+1}^{T} f(y_t|\vec{y}_{t-1}^J; \beta) \times f_m(\vec{y}_J; \beta), \tag{2.2}$$

where $f_m(\vec{y}_J)$ is the marginal, joint density function of $\vec{y}_J$. Taking logarithms gives the *log-likelihood* function $l_T \equiv T^{-1} \log L_T$,

$$l_T(\beta) = \frac{1}{T} \sum_{t=J+1}^{T} \log f(y_t|\vec{y}_{t-1}^J; \beta) + \frac{1}{T} \log f_m(\vec{y}_J; \beta). \tag{2.3}$$

Since the logarithm is a monotonic transformation, maximizing l_T gives the same ML estimator b_T^{ML} as maximizing L_T.

The first-order conditions for the sample criterion function (2.3) are

$$\frac{\partial l_T}{\partial \beta}(b_T^{\text{ML}}) = \frac{1}{T} \sum_{t=J+1}^{T} \frac{\partial \log f}{\partial \beta}(y_t|\vec{y}_{t-1}^J; b_T^{\text{ML}}) + \frac{1}{T} \frac{\partial \log f_m}{\partial \beta}(\vec{y}_J; b_T^{\text{ML}}) = 0, \tag{2.4}$$

where it is presumed that, among all estimators satisfying (2.4), b_T^{ML} is the one that maximizes l_T.[2] Choosing $z_t' = (y_t', \vec{y}_{t-1}^{J}{}')$ and

---

[1] A sufficient condition for this to be true is that the time series $\{y_t\}$ is a strictly stationary process. Stationarity does not preclude time-varying conditional densities, but rather just that the functional form of these densities does not change over time.

[2] It turns out that b_T^{ML} need not be unique for fixed T, even though β_0 is the unique minimizer of the population objective function Q_0. However, this technical complication need not concern us in this introductory discussion.

$$\mathcal{D}(z_t; \beta) \equiv \frac{\partial \log f}{\partial \beta}(y_t|\vec{y}_{t-1}^{\,J}; \beta) \tag{2.5}$$

as the function defining the moment conditions to be used in estimation, it is seen that (2.4) gives first-order conditions of the form (1.12), except for the last term in (2.4).[3] For the purposes of large-sample arguments developed more formally in Chapter 3, we can safely ignore the last term in (2.3) since this term converges to zero as $T \to \infty$.[4] When the last term is omitted from (2.3), this objective function is referred to as the *approximate* log-likelihood function, whereas (2.3) is the *exact* log-likelihood function. Typically, there is no ambiguity as to which likelihood is being discussed and we refer simply to the log-likelihood function l.

Focusing on the approximate log-likelihood function, fixing $\beta \in \Theta$, and taking the limit as $T \to \infty$ gives, under the assumption that sample moments converge to their population counterparts, the associated population criterion function

$$Q_0(\beta) = E\left[\log f\left(y_t|\vec{y}_{t-1}^{\,J}; \beta\right)\right]. \tag{2.6}$$

To see that the β_0 generating the observed data is a maximizer of (2.6), and hence that this choice of Q_0 underlies a sensible estimation strategy, we observe that since the conditional density integrates to 1,

$$
\begin{aligned}
0 &= \frac{\partial}{\partial \beta} \int_{-\infty}^{\infty} f\left(y_t|\vec{y}_{t-1}^{\,J}; \beta_0\right) dy_t \\
&= \int_{-\infty}^{\infty} \frac{\partial \log f}{\partial \beta}\left(y_t|\vec{y}_{t-1}^{\,J}; \beta_0\right) f\left(y_t|\vec{y}_{t-1}^{\,J}; \beta_0\right) dy_t \\
&= E\left[\frac{\partial \log f}{\partial \beta}(y_t|\vec{y}_{t-1}^{\,J}; \beta_0) \,\bigg|\, \vec{y}_{t-1}^{\,J}\right],
\end{aligned}
\tag{2.7}
$$

which, by the law of iterated expectations, implies that

$$\frac{\partial Q_0}{\partial \beta}(\beta_0) = E\left[\frac{\partial \log f}{\partial \beta}(y_t|\vec{y}_{t-1}^{\,J}; \beta_0)\right] = E\left[\mathcal{D}(z_t; \beta_0)\right] = 0. \tag{2.8}$$

Thus, for ML estimation, (2.8) is the set of constraints on the joint distribution of $\vec{y}_T$ used in estimation, the ML version of (1.10). Critical to (2.8)

---

[3] The fact that the sum in (2.4) begins at $J+1$ is inconsequential, because we are focusing on the properties of b_T^{ML} (or θ_T) for large T, and J is fixed a priori by the asset pricing theory.

[4] There are circumstances where the small-sample properties of b_T^{ML} may be substantially affected by inclusion or omission of the term $\log f_m(\vec{y}_J; \beta)$ from the likelihood function. Some of these are explored in later chapters.

being satisfied by β_0 is the assumption that the conditional density f implied by the DAPM is in fact the density from which the data are drawn.

An important special case of this estimation problem is where $\{y_t\}$ is an independently and identically distributed (i.i.d.) process. In this case, if $f_m(y_t; \beta)$ denotes the density function of the vector y_t evaluated at β, then the log-likelihood function takes the simple form

$$l_T(\beta) \equiv T^{-1} \log L_T(\beta) = \frac{1}{T} \sum_{t=1}^{T} \log f_m(y_t; \beta). \qquad (2.9)$$

This is an immediate implication of the independence assumption, since the joint density function of $\vec{y}_T$ factors into the product of the marginal densities of the y_t. The ML estimator of β_0 is obtained by maximizing (2.9) over $\beta \in \Theta$. The corresponding population criterion function is $Q_0(\beta) = E[\log f_m(y_t; \beta)]$.

Though the simplicity of (2.9) is convenient, most dynamic asset pricing theories imply that at least some of the observed variables y are not independently distributed over time. Dependence might arise, for example, because of mean reversion in an asset return or persistence in the volatility of one or more variables (see the next example). Such time variation in conditional moments is accommodated in the formulation (2.1) of the conditional density of y_t, but not by (2.9).

Example 2.1.   *Cox, Ingersoll, and Ross [Cox et al., 1985b] (CIR) developed a theory of the term structure of interest rates in which the instantaneous short-term rate of interest, r, follows the mean reverting diffusion*

$$dr = \kappa(\bar{r} - r)\, dt + \sigma\sqrt{r}\, dB. \qquad (2.10)$$

An implication of (2.10) is that the conditional density of r_{t+1} given r_t is

$$f(r_{t+1}|r_t; \beta_0) = ce^{-u_t - v_{t+1}} \left(\frac{v_{t+1}}{u_t}\right)^{\frac{q}{2}} I_q\big(2(u_t v_{t+1})^{\frac{1}{2}}\big), \qquad (2.11)$$

where

$$c = \frac{2\kappa}{\sigma^2(1 - e^{-\kappa})}, \qquad (2.12)$$

$$u_t = \frac{2\kappa}{\sigma^2(1 - e^{-\kappa})} e^{-\kappa} r_t, \qquad (2.13)$$

$$v_{t+1} = \frac{2\kappa}{\sigma^2(1 - e^{-\kappa})} r_{t+1}, \qquad (2.14)$$

$q = 2\kappa \bar{r}/\sigma^2 - 1$, *and I_q is the modified Bessel function of the first kind of order q. This is the density function of a noncentral χ^2 with $2q + 2$ degrees of freedom and noncentrality parameter $2u_t$. For this example, ML estimation would proceed by substituting (1.11) into (2.4) and solving for b_T^{ML}. The short-rate process (2.10) is the continuous time version of an interest-rate process that is mean reverting to a long-run mean of $\bar{r}$ and that has a conditional volatility of $\sigma \sqrt{r}$. This process is Markovian and, therefore, $\vec{y}_t^J = y_t$, which explains the single lag in the conditioning information in (1.11).*

Though desirable for its efficiency, ML may not be, and indeed typically is not, a feasible estimation strategy for DAPMs, as often they do not provide us with complete knowledge of the relevant conditional distributions. Moreover, in some cases, even when these distributions are known, the computational burdens may be so great that one may want to choose an estimation strategy that uses only a portion of the available information. This is a consideration in the preceding example given the presence of the modified Bessel function in the conditional density of r. Later in this chapter we consider the case where only limited information about the conditional distribution is known or, for computational or other reasons, is used in estimation.

2.2. No Information about the Distribution

At the opposite end of the knowledge spectrum about the distribution of $\vec{y}_T$ is the case where we do not have a well-developed DAPM to describe the relationships among the variables of interest. In such circumstances, we may be interested in learning something about the joint distribution of the vector of variables z_t (which is presumed to include some asset prices or returns). For instance, we are often in a situation of wondering whether certain variables are correlated with each other or if one variable can predict another. Without knowledge of the joint distribution of the variables of interest, researchers typically proceed by *projecting* one variable onto another to see if they are related. The properties of the estimators in such projections are examined under this case of no information.[5] Additionally, there are occasions when we reject a theory and a replacement theory that explains the rejection has yet to be developed. On such occasions, many have resorted to projections of one variable onto others with the hope of learning more about the source of the initial rejection. Following is an example of this second situation.

---

[5] Projections, and in particular linear projections, are a simple and often informative first approach to examining statistical dependencies among variables. More complex, nonlinear relations can be explored with nonparametric statistical methods. The applications of nonparametric methods to asset pricing problems are explored in subsequent chapters.

Example 2.2. *Several scholars writing in the 1970s argued that, if foreign currency markets are informationally efficient, then the forward price for delivery of foreign exchange one period hence (F_t^1) should equal the market's best forecast of the spot exchange rate next period (S_{t+1}):*

$$F_t^1 = E[S_{t+1}|I_t], \tag{2.15}$$

where I_t denotes the market's information at date t. This theory of exchange rate determination was often evaluated by projecting $S_{t+1} - F_t^1$ onto a vector x_t and testing whether the coefficients on x_t are zero (e.g., Hansen and Hodrick, 1980). The evidence suggested that these coefficients are not zero, which was interpreted as evidence of a time-varying market risk premium $\lambda_t \equiv E[S_{t+1}|I_t] - F_t^1$ (see, e.g., Grauer et al., 1976, and Stockman, 1978). Theory has provided limited guidance as to which variables determine the risk premiums or the functional forms of premiums. Therefore, researchers have projected the spread $S_{t+1} - F_t^1$ onto a variety of variables known at date t and thought to potentially explain variation in the risk premium. The objective of the latter studies was to test for dependence of λ_t on the explanatory variables, say x_t.

To be more precise about what is meant by a *projection*, let L^2 denote the set of (scalar) random variables that have finite second moments:

$$L^2 = \{\text{random variables } x \text{ such that } Ex^2 < \infty\}. \tag{2.16}$$

We define an inner product on L^2 by

$$\langle x | y \rangle \equiv E(xy), \quad x, y \in L^2, \tag{2.17}$$

and a norm by

$$\| x \| = [\langle x | x \rangle]^{\frac{1}{2}} = \sqrt{E(x^2)}. \tag{2.18}$$

We say that two random variables x and y in L^2 are *orthogonal* to each other if $E(xy) = 0$. Note that being orthogonal is not equivalent to being uncorrelated as the means of the random variables may be nonzero.

Let A be the closed linear subspace of L^2 generated by all linear combinations of the K random variables $\{x_1, x_2, \ldots, x_K\}$. Suppose that we want to project the random variable $y \in L^2$ onto A in order to obtain its best linear predictor. Letting $\delta' \equiv (\delta_1, \ldots, \delta_K)$, the best linear predictor is that element of A that minimizes the distance between y and the linear space A:

$$\min_{z \in A} \| y - z \| \quad \Leftrightarrow \quad \min_{\delta \in \mathbb{R}^K} \| y - \delta_1 x_1 - \ldots - \delta_K x_K \|. \tag{2.19}$$

The *orthogonal projection theorem*[6] tells us that the *unique* solution to (2.19) is given by the $\delta_0 \in \mathbb{R}^K$ satisfying

$$E\left[(y - x'\delta_0)x\right] = 0, \quad x' = (x_1, \ldots, x_K); \tag{2.20}$$

that is, the forecast error $u \equiv (y - x'\delta_0)$ is orthogonal to all linear combinations of x. The solution to the first-order condition (2.20) is

$$\delta_0 = E[xx']^{-1}E[xy]. \tag{2.21}$$

In terms of our notation for criterion functions, the population criterion function associated with least-squares projection is

$$Q_0(\delta) = E\left[(y_t - x_t'\delta)^2\right], \tag{2.22}$$

and this choice is equivalent to choosing $z_t' = (y_t, x_t')$ and the function $\mathcal{D}$ as

$$\mathcal{D}(z_t; \delta) = (y_t - x_t'\delta)x_t. \tag{2.23}$$

The interpretation of this choice is a bit different than in most estimation problems, because our presumption is that one is proceeding with estimation in the absence of a DAPM from which restrictions on the distribution of (y_t, x_t) can be deduced. In the case of a least-squares projection, we view the moment equation

$$E\left[\mathcal{D}(y_t, x_t; \delta_0)\right] = E\left[(y_t - x_t'\delta_0)x_t\right] = 0 \tag{2.24}$$

as the moment restriction that *defines* δ_0.

The sample least-squares objective function is

$$Q_T(\delta) = \frac{1}{T}\sum_{t=1}^{T}(y_t - x_t'\delta)^2, \tag{2.25}$$

with minimizer

$$\delta_T = \left[\frac{1}{T}\sum_{t=1}^{T}x_t x_t'\right]^{-1}\frac{1}{T}\sum_{t=1}^{T}x_t y_t. \tag{2.26}$$

---

[6] The orthogonal projection theorem says that if L is an inner product space, M is a closed linear subspace of L, and y is an element of L, then $z^* \in M$ is the unique solution to

$$\min_{z \in M} \| y - z \|$$

if and only if $y - z^*$ is orthogonal to all elements of M. See, e.g., Luenberger (1969).

The estimator δ_T is also obtained directly by replacing the population moments in (2.21) by their sample counterparts.

In the context of the pricing model for foreign currency prices, researchers have projected $(S_{t+1} - F_t^1)$ onto a vector of explanatory variables x_t. The variable being predicted in such analyses, $(S_{t+1} - F_t^1)$, is not the risk premium, $\lambda_t = E[(S_{t+1} - F_t^1)|I_t]$. Nevertheless, the resulting predictor in the population, $x_t'\delta_0$, is the same regardless of whether λ_t or $(S_{t+1} - F_t^1)$ is the variable being forecast. To see this, we digress briefly to discuss the difference between *best linear* and *best* prediction.

The predictor $x_t'\delta_0$ is the best linear predictor, which is defined by the condition that the projection error $u_t = y_t - x_t'\delta_0$ is orthogonal to all linear combinations of x_t. Predicting y_t using linear combinations of x_t is only one of many possible approaches to prediction. In particular, we could also consider prediction based on both linear and nonlinear functions of the elements of x_t. Pursuing this idea, let V denote the closed linear subspace of L^2 generated by all random variables $g(x_t)$ with finite second moments:

$$V = \{g(x_t) : g : \mathbb{R}^K \to \mathbb{R}, \text{ and } g(x_t) \in L^2\}. \tag{2.27}$$

Consider the new minimization problem $\min_{z \in V} \| y_t - z_t \|$. By the orthogonal projection theorem, the unique solution z_t^* to this problem has the property that $(y_t - z_t^*)$ is orthogonal to all $z_t \in V$. One representation of z^* is the conditional expectation $E[y_t|x_t]$. This follows immediately from the properties of conditional expectations: the error $\epsilon_t = y_t - E[y_t|x_t]$ satisfies

$$E[\epsilon_t g(x_t)] = E\left[(y_t - E[y_t|x_t])g(x_t)\right] = 0, \tag{2.28}$$

for all $g(x_t) \in V$. Clearly, $A \subseteq V$ so the best predictor is at least as good as the best linear predictor. The precise sense in which best prediction is better is that, whereas ϵ_t is orthogonal to *all* functions of the conditioning information x_t, u_t is orthogonal to only linear combinations of x_t.

There are circumstances where best and best linear predictors coincide. This is true whenever the conditional expectation $E[y_t|x_t]$ is linear in x_t. One well-known case where this holds is when (y_t, x_t') is distributed as a multivariate normal random vector. However, normality is not necessary for best and best linear predictors to coincide. For instance, consider again Example 2.1. The conditional mean $E[r_{t+\Delta}|r_t]$ for positive time interval Δ is given by (Cox et al., 1985b)

$$\mu_{rt}(\Delta) \equiv E[r_{t+\Delta}|r_t] = r_t e^{-\Delta\kappa} + \bar{r}(1 - e^{-\Delta\kappa}), \tag{2.29}$$

which is linear in r_t, yet neither the joint distribution of $(r_t, r_{t-\Delta})$ nor the distribution of r_t conditioned on $r_{t-\Delta}$ is normal. (The latter is noncentral chi-square.)

With these observations in mind, we can now complete our argument that the properties of risk premiums can be studied by linearly projecting $(S_{t+1} - F_t^1)$ onto x_t. Letting $\text{Proj}[\cdot|x_t]$ denote linear least-squares projection onto x_t, we get

$$\text{Proj}[\lambda_t|x_t] = \text{Proj}\left[\left(S_{t+1} - F_t^1\right) - \epsilon_{t+1}\big|x_t\right]$$
$$= \text{Proj}\left[\left(S_{t+1} - F_t^1\right)\big|x_t\right], \tag{2.30}$$

where $\epsilon_{t+1} \equiv (S_{t+1} - F_t^1) - \lambda_t$. The first equality follows from the definition of the risk premium as $E[S_{t+1} - F_t^1|I_t]$ and the second follows from the fact that ϵ_{t+1} is orthogonal to all functions of x_t including linear functions.

2.3. Limited Information: GMM Estimators

In between the cases of full information and no information about the joint distribution of $\vec{y}_T$ are all of the intermediate cases of *limited information.* Suppose that estimation of a parameter vector θ_0 in the admissible parameter space $\Phi \subset \mathbb{R}^K$ is to be based on a sample $\vec{z}_T$, where z_t is a subvector of the complete set of variables y_t appearing in a DAPM.[7] The restrictions on the distribution of $\vec{z}_T$ to be used in estimating θ_0 are summarized as a set of restrictions on the moments of functions of z_t. These moment restrictions may be either *conditional* or *unconditional.*

2.3.1. Unconditional Moment Restrictions

Consider first the case where a DAPM implies that the unconditional moment restriction

$$E[h(z_t; \theta_0)] = 0 \tag{2.31}$$

is satisfied uniquely by θ_0, where h is an M-dimensional vector with $M \geq K$. The function h may define standard central or noncentral moments of asset returns, the orthogonality of forecast errors to variables in agents' information sets, and so on. Illustrations based on Example 2.1 are presented later in this section.

To develop an estimator of θ_0 based on (2.31), consider first the case of $K = M$; the number of moment restrictions equals the number of parameters to be estimated. The function $H_0 : \Phi \to \mathbb{R}^M$ defined by $H_0(\theta) =$

---

[7] There is no requirement that the dimension of Φ be as large as the dimension of the parameter space Θ considered in full information estimation; often Φ is a lower-dimensional subspace of Θ, just as z_t may be a subvector of y_t. However, for notational convenience, we always set the dimension of the parameter vector of interest to K, whether it is θ_0 or β_0.

$E[h(z_t; \theta)]$ satisfies $H_0(\theta_0) = 0$. Therefore, a natural estimation strategy for θ_0 is to replace H_0 by its sample counterpart,

$$H_T(\theta) = \frac{1}{T} \sum_{t=1}^{T} h(z_t; \theta), \qquad (2.32)$$

and choose the estimator θ_T to set (2.32) to zero. If H_T converges to its population counterpart as T gets large, $H_T(\theta) \to H_0(\theta)$, for all $\theta \in \Phi$, then under regularity conditions we should expect that $\theta_T \to \theta_0$. The estimator θ_T is an example of what Hansen (1982b) refers to as a generalized method-of-moments, or GMM, estimator of θ_0.

Next suppose that $M > K$. Then there is not in general a unique way of solving for the K unknowns using the M equations $H_T(\theta) = 0$, and our strategy for choosing θ_T must be modified. We proceed to form K linear combinations of the M moment equations to end up with K equations in the K unknown parameters. That is, letting $\bar{\mathcal{A}}$ denote the set of $K \times M$ (constant) matrices of rank K, we select an $A \in \bar{\mathcal{A}}$ and set

$$\mathcal{D}^A(z_t; \theta) = Ah(z_t; \theta), \qquad (2.33)$$

with this choice of $\mathcal{D}^A$ determining the estimation strategy. Different choices of $A \in \bar{\mathcal{A}}$ index (lead to) different estimation strategies. To arrive at a sample counterpart to (2.33), we select a possibly sample-dependent matrix A_T with the property that $A_T \to A$ (almost surely) as sample size gets large. Then the $K \times 1$ vector θ_T^A (the superscript A indicating that the estimator is A-dependent) is chosen to satisfy the K equations $\sum_t \mathcal{D}_T(z_t, \theta_T^A) = 0$, where $\mathcal{D}_T(z_t, \theta_T^A) = A_T h(z_t; \theta_T^A)$. Note that we are now allowing $\mathcal{D}_T$ to be sample dependent directly, and not only through its dependence on θ_T^A. This will frequently be the case in subsequent applications.

The construction of GMM estimators using this choice of $\mathcal{D}_T$ can be related to the approach to estimation involving a criterion function as follows: Let $\{a_T : T \geq 1\}$ be a sequence of $s \times M$ matrices of rank s, $K \leq s \leq M$, and consider the function

$$Q_T(\theta) = |a_T H_T(\theta)|, \qquad (2.34)$$

where $|\cdot|$ denotes the Euclidean norm. Then

$$\underset{\theta}{\text{argmin}} \, |a_T H_T(\theta)| = \underset{\theta}{\text{argmin}} \, |a_T H_T(\theta)|^2 = \underset{\theta}{\text{argmin}} \, H_T(\theta)' a_T' a_T H_T(\theta), \quad (2.35)$$

and we can think of our criterion function Q_T as being the quadratic form

$$Q_T(\theta) = H_T'(\theta) W_T H_T(\theta), \qquad (2.36)$$

where $W_T \equiv a'_T a_T$ is often referred to as the *distance matrix*. This is the GMM criterion function studied by Hansen (1982b). The first-order conditions for this minimization problem are

$$\frac{\partial H_T}{\partial \theta}(\theta_T)' W_T H_T(\theta_T) = 0. \qquad (2.37)$$

By setting

$$A_T = [\partial H_T(\theta_T)'/\partial \theta] W_T, \qquad (2.38)$$

we obtain the $\mathcal{D}_T(z_t; \theta)$ associated with Hansen's GMM estimator.

The population counterpart to Q_T in (2.36) is

$$Q_0(\theta) = E[h(z_t; \theta)]' W_0 E[h(z_t; \theta)]. \qquad (2.39)$$

The corresponding population $\mathcal{D}_0(z_t, \theta)$ is given by

$$\mathcal{D}_0(z_t, \theta) = E\left[\frac{\partial h}{\partial \theta}(z_t; \theta_0)'\right] W_0 h(z_t; \theta) \equiv A_0 h(z_t; \theta), \qquad (2.40)$$

where W_0 is the (almost sure) limit of W_T as T gets large. Here $\mathcal{D}_0$ is not sample dependent, possibly in contrast to $\mathcal{D}_T$.

Whereas the first-order conditions to (2.36) give an estimator in the class $\bar{\mathcal{A}}$ [with A defined by (2.40)], not all GMM estimators in $\bar{\mathcal{A}}$ are the first-order conditions from minimizing an objective function of the form (2.36). Nevertheless, it turns out that the *optimal* GMM estimators in $\bar{\mathcal{A}}$, in the sense of being asymptotically most efficient (see Chapter 3), can be represented as the solution to (2.36) for appropriate choice of W_T. Therefore, the large-sample properties of GMM estimators are henceforth discussed relative to the sequence of objective functions $\{Q_T(\cdot) : T \geq 1\}$ in (2.36).

2.3.2. Conditional Moment Restrictions

In some cases, a DAPM implies the stronger, conditional moment restrictions

$$E[h(z_{t+n}; \theta_0)|I_t] = 0, \qquad \text{for given } n \geq 1, \qquad (2.41)$$

where the possibility of $n > 1$ is introduced to allow the conditional moment restrictions to apply to asset prices or other variables more than one period in the future. Again, the dimension of h is M, and the information set I_t may be generated by variables other than the history of z_t.

To construct an estimator of θ_0 based on (2.41), we proceed as in the case of unconditional moment restrictions and choose K sample moment equations in the K unknowns θ. However, because $h(z_{t+n}; \theta_0)$ is orthogonal to any random variable in the information set I_t, we have much more flexibility in choosing these moment equations than in the preceding case. Specifically, we introduce a class of $K \times M$ full-rank "instrument" matrices A_t with each $A_t \in \mathcal{A}_t$ having elements in I_t. For any $A_t \in \mathcal{A}_t$, (2.41) implies that

$$E[A_t h(z_{t+n}; \theta_0)] = 0 \qquad (2.42)$$

at $\theta = \theta_0$. Therefore, we can define a family of GMM estimators indexed by $A \in \mathcal{A}$, θ_T^A, as the solutions to the corresponding sample moment equations,

$$\frac{1}{T} \sum_t A_t h(z_{t+n}; \theta_T^A) = 0. \qquad (2.43)$$

If the sample mean of $A_t h(z_{t+n}; \theta)$ in (2.43) converges to its population counterpart in (2.42), for all $\theta \in \Phi$, and A_t and h are chosen so that θ_0 is the unique element of Φ satisfying (2.42), then we might reasonably expect θ_T^A to converge to θ_0 as T gets large. The large-sample distribution of θ_T^A depends, in general, on the choice of A_t.[8]

The GMM estimator, as just defined, is not the extreme value of a specific criterion function. Rather, (2.42) defines θ_0 as the solution to K moment equations in K unknowns, and θ_T solves the sample counterpart of these equations. In this case, $\mathcal{D}_0$ is chosen directly as

$$\mathcal{D}_0(z_{t+n}, A_t; \theta) = \mathcal{D}_T(z_{t+n}, A_t; \theta) = A_t h(z_{t+n}; \theta). \qquad (2.44)$$

Once we have chosen an A_t in $\mathcal{A}_t$, we can view a GMM estimator constructed from (2.41) as, trivially, a special case of an estimator based on unconditional moment restrictions. Expression (2.42) is taken to be the basic K moment equations that we start with. However, the important distinguishing feature of the class of estimators $\mathcal{A}_t$, compared to the class $\bar{\mathcal{A}}$, is that the former class offers much more flexibility in choosing the weights on h. We will see in Chapter 3 that the most efficient estimator in the class $\mathcal{A}$ is often more efficient than its counterpart in $\bar{\mathcal{A}}$. That is, (2.41) allows one to exploit more information about the distribution of z_t than (2.31) in the estimation of θ_0.

---

[8] As is discussed more extensively in the context of subsequent applications, this GMM estimation strategy is a generalization of the instrumental variables estimators proposed for classical simultaneous equations models by Amemiya (1974) and Jorgenson and Laffont (1974), among others.

2.3.3. Linear Projection as a GMM Estimator

Perhaps the simplest example of a GMM estimator based on the moment restriction (2.31) is linear least-squares projection. Suppose that we project y_t onto x_t. Then the best linear predictor is defined by the moment equation (2.20). Thus, if we define

$$h\big(y_t, x_t; \delta\big) = \big(y_t - x_t'\delta\big)\, x_t, \tag{2.45}$$

then by construction δ_0 satisfies $E[h(y_t, x_t; \delta_0)] = 0$.

One might be tempted to view linear projection as special case of a GMM estimator in $\mathcal{A}_t$ by choosing $n = 0$,

$$A_t = x_t \quad \text{and} \quad h\big(y_t, x_t; \delta\big) = \big(y_t - x_t'\delta\big). \tag{2.46}$$

However, importantly, we are not free to select among other choices of $A_t \in \mathcal{A}_t$ in constructing a GMM estimator of the linear predictor $x_t'\delta_0$. Therefore, least-squares projection is appropriately viewed as a GMM estimator in $\bar{\mathcal{A}}$.

Circumstances change if a DAPM implies the stronger moment restriction

$$E\big[\big(y_t - x_t'\delta_0\big)\big|x_t\big] = 0. \tag{2.47}$$

Now we are no longer in an environment of complete ignorance about the distribution of (y_t, x_t), as it is being assumed that $x_t'\delta_0$ is the best, not just the best linear, predictor of y_t. In this case, we are free to choose

$$A_t = g(x_t) \quad \text{and} \quad h\big(y_t, x_t; \delta\big) = \big(y_t - x_t'\delta\big), \tag{2.48}$$

for any $g : \mathbb{R}^K \to \mathbb{R}^K$. Thus, the assumption that the best predictor is linear puts us in the case of conditional moment restrictions and opens up the possibility of selecting estimators in $\mathcal{A}$ defined by the functions g.

2.3.4. Quasi-Maximum Likelihood Estimation

Another important example of a limited information estimator that is a special case of a GMM estimator is the *quasi-maximum likelihood* (QML) estimator. Suppose that $n = 1$ and that I_t is generated by the J-history $\vec{y}_t^{\,J}$ of a vector of observed variables y_t.[9] Further, suppose that the functional

---

[9] We employ the usual, informal notation of letting I_t or $\vec{y}_t^{\,J}$ denote the σ-algebra (information set) used to construct conditional moments and distributions.

forms of the population mean and variance of y_{t+1}, conditioned on I_t, are known and let θ denote the vector of parameters governing these first two conditional moments. Then ML estimation of θ_0 based on the classical normal conditional likelihood function gives an estimator that converges to θ_0 and is normally distributed in large samples (see, e.g., Bollerslev and Wooldridge, 1992).

Referring back to the introductory remarks in Chapter 1, we see that the function $\mathcal{D}\,(=\mathcal{D}_0 = \mathcal{D}_T)$ determining the moments used in estimation in this case is

$$\mathcal{D}(z_t; \theta) = \frac{\partial \log f_N}{\partial \theta}\big(y_t \big| \vec{y}_{t-1}^{\,J}; \theta\big), \qquad (2.49)$$

where $z_t' = (y_t', \vec{y}_{t-1}^{\,J}{}')$ and f_N is the normal density function conditioned on $\vec{y}_{t-1}^{\,J}$. Thus, for QML to be an admissible estimation strategy for this DAPM it must be the case that θ_0 satisfies

$$E\left[\frac{\partial \log f_N}{\partial \theta}\big(y_t \big| \vec{y}_{t-1}^{\,J}; \theta_0\big) \right] = 0. \qquad (2.50)$$

The reason that θ_0 does in fact satisfy (2.50) is that the first two conditional moments of y_t are correctly specified and the normal distribution is fully characterized by its first two moments. This intuition is formalized in Chapter 3. The moment equation (2.50) defines a GMM estimator.

2.3.5. Illustrations Based on Interest Rate Models

Consider again the one-factor interest rate model presented in Example 2.1. Equation (2.29) implies that we can choose

$$h\big(\vec{z}_{t+1}^{\,1}; \theta_0\big) = \big[r_{t+1} - \bar{r}(1 - e^{-\kappa}) - e^{-\kappa} r_t\big], \qquad (2.51)$$

where $\vec{z}_{t+1}^{\,2} = (r_{t+1}, r_t)'$. Furthermore, for any 2×1 vector function $g(r_t) : \mathbb{R} \to \mathbb{R}^2$, we can set $A_t = g(r_t)$ and

$$E\big[(r_{t+1} - \bar{r}(1 - e^{-\kappa}) - e^{-\kappa} r_t)g(r_t)\big] = 0. \qquad (2.52)$$

Therefore, a GMM estimator $\theta_T^{A'} = (\bar{r}_T, \kappa_T)$ of $\theta_0' = (\bar{r}, \kappa)$ can be constructed from the sample moment equations

$$\frac{1}{T} \sum_t \big[r_{t+1} - \bar{r}_T(1 - e^{-\kappa_T}) - e^{-\kappa_T} r_t\big] g(r_t) = 0. \qquad (2.53)$$

Each choice of $g(r_t) \in \mathcal{A}_t$ gives rise to a different GMM estimator that in general has a different large-sample distribution. Linear projection of r_t onto r_{t-1} is obtained as the special case with $g(r_{t-1})' = (1, r_{t-1})$, $M = K = 2$, and $\theta' = (\kappa, \bar{r})$.

Turning to the implementation of QML estimation in this example, the mean of $r_{t+\Delta}$ conditioned on r_t is given by (2.29) and the conditional variance is given by (Cox et al., 1985b)

$$\sigma_{rt}^2(\Delta) \equiv Var[r_{t+\Delta}|r_t] = r_t \frac{\sigma^2}{\kappa}(e^{-\Delta\kappa} - e^{-2\Delta\kappa}) + \bar{r}\frac{\sigma^2}{2\kappa}(1 - e^{-\Delta\kappa})^2. \quad (2.54)$$

If we set $\Delta = 1$, it follows that discretely sampled returns $(r_t, r_{t-1}, \ldots)$ follow the model

$$r_{t+1} = \bar{r}(1 - e^{-\kappa}) + e^{-\kappa}r_t + \sqrt{\sigma_{rt}^2}\epsilon_{t+1}, \quad (2.55)$$

where the error term ϵ_{t+1} in (2.55) has (conditional) mean zero and variance one. For this model, $\theta_0 = (\bar{r}, \kappa, \sigma^2)' = \beta_0$ (the parameter vector that describes the entire distribution of r_t), though this is often not true in other applications of QML.

The conditional distribution of r_t is a noncentral χ^2. However, suppose we ignore this fact and proceed to construct a likelihood function based on our knowledge of (2.29) and (2.54), assuming that the return r_t is distributed as a normal conditional on r_{t-1}. Then the log-likelihood function is (l^q to indicate that this is QML)

$$l_T^q(\theta) \equiv \frac{1}{T}\sum_{t=2}^{T}\left(-\frac{1}{2}\log(2\pi) - \frac{1}{2}\log(\sigma_{rt-1}^2) - \frac{1}{2}\frac{(r_t - \mu_{rt-1})^2}{\sigma_{rt-1}^2}\right). \quad (2.56)$$

Computing first-order conditions gives

$$\frac{\partial l_T^q}{\partial \theta_j}(\theta_T^q) = \frac{1}{T}\sum_{t=2}^{T} -\frac{1}{2\hat{\sigma}_{rt-1}^2}\frac{\partial \hat{\sigma}_{rt-1}^2}{\partial \theta_j} + \frac{1}{2}\frac{(r_t - \hat{\mu}_{rt-1})^2}{\hat{\sigma}_{rt-1}^4}\frac{\partial \hat{\sigma}_{rt-1}^2}{\partial \theta_j}$$

$$+ \frac{(r_t - \hat{\mu}_{rt-1})}{\hat{\sigma}_{rt-1}^2}\frac{\partial \hat{\mu}_{rt-1}}{\partial \theta_j} = 0, \quad j = 1, 2, 3, \quad (2.57)$$

where θ_T^q denotes the QML estimator and $\hat{\mu}_{rt-1}$ and $\hat{\sigma}_{rt-1}^2$ are μ_{rt-1} and σ_{rt-1}^2 evaluated at θ_T^q. As suggested in the preceding section, this estimation strategy is admissible because the first two conditional moments are correctly specified.

Though one might want to pursue GMM or QML estimation for this interest rate example because of their computational simplicity, this is not the best illustration of a limited information problem because the true likelihood function is known. However, a slight modification of the interest rate process places us in an environment where GMM is a natural estimation strategy.

Example 2.3.   *Suppose we extend the one-factor model introduced in Example 2.1 to the following two-factor model:*

$$dr = \kappa(\bar{r} - r)\, dt + \sigma_r \sqrt{v}\, dB_r,$$
$$dv = \nu(\bar{v} - v)\, dt + \sigma_v \sqrt{v}\, dB_v. \tag{2.58}$$

In this two-factor model of the short rate, v plays the role of a stochastic volatility for r. Similar models have been studied by Anderson and Lund (1997a) and Dai and Singleton (2000). The volatility shock in this model is unobserved, so estimation and inference must be based on the sample $\vec{r}_T$ and r_t is no longer a Markov process conditioned on its own past history.

An implication of the assumptions that r mean reverts to the long-run value of $\bar{r}$ and that the conditional mean of r does not depend on v is that (2.29) is still satisfied in this two-factor model. However, the variance of r_t conditioned on r_{t-1} is not known in closed form, nor is the form of the density of r_t conditioned on $\vec{r}_{t-1}^{\,J}$. Thus, neither ML nor QML estimation strategies are easily pursued.[10] Faced with this limited information, one convenient strategy for estimating $\theta_0' \equiv (\bar{r}, \kappa)$ is to use the moment equations (2.52) implied by (2.29).

This GMM estimator of θ_0 ignores entirely the known structure of the volatility process and, indeed, σ_r^2 is not an element of θ_0. Thus, not only are we unable to recover any information about the parameters of the volatility equation using (2.52), but knowledge of the functional form of the volatility equation is ignored. It turns out that substantially more information about $f(r_t|r_{t-1}; \theta_0)$ can be used in estimation, but to accomplish this we have to extend the GMM estimation strategy to allow for unobserved state variables. This extension is explored in depth in Chapter 6.

2.3.6. GMM Estimation of Pricing Kernels

As a final illustration, suppose that the pricing kernel in a DAPM is a function of a state vector x_t and parameter vector θ_0. In preference-based DAPMs, the pricing kernel can be interpreted as an agent's intertemporal

---

[10] Asymptotically efficient estimation strategies based on approximations to the true conditional density function of r have been developed for this model. These are described in Chapter 7.

Table 2.1. Summary of Population and Sample Objective Functions for Various Estimators

	Maximum likelihood	GMM	Least-squares projection
Population objective function	$\max_{\beta\in\Theta} E\left[\log f\left(y_t \mid \vec{y}_{t-1}^J; \beta\right)\right]$	$\min_{\theta\in\Theta} E[h(z_t;\theta)]'W_0 E[h(z_t;\theta)]$	$\min_{\delta\in\mathbb{R}^K} E\left[\left(y_t - x_t'\delta\right)^2\right]$
Sample objective function	$\max_{\beta\in\Theta} \frac{1}{T}\sum_{t=J+1}^{T}\log f\left(y_t \mid \vec{y}_{t-1}^J; \beta\right)$	$\min_{\theta\in\Theta} H_T(\theta)'W_T H_T(\theta)$ $H_T(\theta)=\frac{1}{T}\sum_{t=1}^{T}h(z_t;\theta)$	$\min_{\delta\in\mathbb{R}^K} \frac{1}{T}\sum_{t=1}^{T}\left(y_t - x_t'\delta\right)^2$
Population F.O.C.	$E\left[\frac{\partial\log}{\partial\beta}f\left(y_t \mid \vec{y}_{t-1}^J; \beta_0\right)\right]=0$	$A_0 E[h(z_t;\theta_0)]=0$	$E\left[\left(y_t - x_t'\delta_0\right)x_t\right]=0$
Sample F.O.C.	$\frac{1}{T}\sum_{t=J+1}^{T}\frac{\partial\log}{\partial\beta}f\left(y_t \mid \vec{y}_{t-1}^J; b_T^{ML}\right)=0$	$A_T\frac{1}{T}\sum_{t=1}^{T}h(z_t;\theta_T)=0$	$\frac{1}{T}\sum_{t=1}^{T}\left(y_t - x_t'\delta_T\right)x_t=0$

marginal rate of substitution of consumption, in which case x_t might involve consumptions of goods and θ_0 is the vector of parameters describing the agent's preferences. Alternatively, q^* might simply be parameterized directly as a function of financial variables. In Chapter 1 it was noted that

$$E\big[\big(q^*_{t+n}(x_{t+n}; \theta_0)r_{t+n} - 1\big)\big|I_t\big] = 0, \tag{2.59}$$

for investment horizon n and the appropriate information set I_t. If r_{t+n} is chosen to be a vector of returns on M securities, $M \geq K$, then (2.59) represents M conditional moment restrictions that can be used to construct a GMM estimator of θ (Hansen and Singleton, 1982).

Typically, there are more than K securities at one's disposal for empirical work, in which case one may wish to select $M > K$. A $K \times M$ matrix $A_t \in \mathcal{A}_t$ can then be used to construct K unconditional moment equations to be used in estimation:

$$E\big[A_t\big(q^*_{t+n}(x_{t+n}; \theta_0)r_{t+n} - 1\big)\big] = 0. \tag{2.60}$$

Any $A_t \in I_t$ is an admissible choice for constructing a GMM estimator (subject to minimal regularity conditions).

2.4. Summary of Estimators

The estimators introduced in this chapter are summarized in Table 2.1, along with their respective first-order conditions. The large-sample properties of ML, GMM, and LLP estimators are explored in Chapter 3.

3

Large-Sample Properties of Extremum Estimators

EXTREMUM ESTIMATORS ARE estimators obtained by either maximizing or minimizing a criterion function over the admissible parameter space. In this chapter we introduce more formally the concept of an extremum estimator and discuss the large-sample properties of these estimators.[1] After briefly setting up notation and describing the probability environment within which we discuss estimation, we describe regularity conditions under which an estimator converges almost surely to its population counterpart.

We then turn to the large-sample distributions of extremum estimators. Throughout this discussion we maintain the assumption that θ_T is a consistent estimator of θ_0 and focus on properties of the distribution of θ_T as T gets large. Whereas discussions of consistency are often criterion-function specific, the large-sample analyses of most of the extremum estimators we will use subsequently can be treated concurrently. We formally define a family of estimators that encompasses the first-order conditions of the ML, standard GMM, and LLS estimators as special cases. Then, after we present a quite general central limit theorem, we establish the asymptotic normality of these estimators. Finally, we examine the relative asymptotic efficiencies of the GMM, LSS, and ML estimators and interpret their asymptotic efficiencies in terms of the restrictions on the joint distribution of the data used in estimation.

3.1. Basic Probability Model

Notationally, we let Ω denote the sample space, $\mathcal{F}$ the set of events about which we want to make probability statements (a "σ-algebra" of events), and

---

[1] The perspective on the large-sample properties of extremum estimators taken in this chapter has been shaped by my discussions and collaborations with Lars Hansen over the past 25 years. In particular, the approach to establishing consistency and asymptotic normality in Sections 3.2–3.4 follows that of Hansen (1982b, 2005).

Pr the probability measure.[2] Thus, we denote the probability space by $(\Omega,$ $\mathcal{F}, \text{Pr})$. Similarly, we let $\mathcal{B}^K$ denote the Borel algebra of events in $\mathbb{R}^K$, which is the smallest σ-algebra containing all open and closed rectangles in $\mathbb{R}^K$. A K-dimensional vector random variable X is a function from the sample space Ω to $\mathbb{R}^K$ with the property that for each $B \in \mathcal{B}^K$, $\{\omega : X(\omega) \in B\} \in \mathcal{F}$. Each random variable X induces a probability space $(\mathbb{R}^K, \mathcal{B}^K, \mu_X)$ by the correspondence $\mu_X(B) = \text{Pr}\{\omega : X(\omega) \in B\}$, for all $B \in \mathcal{B}^K$.

Two notions of convergence of sequences of random variables that we use extensively are as follows.

Definition 3.1. *The sequence of random variables $\{X_T\}$ is said to converge almost surely (a.s.) to the random variable X if and only if there exists a null set[3] $\mathcal{N}$ such that*

$$\forall \omega \in \Omega \setminus \mathcal{N} : \quad \lim_{T \to \infty} X_T(\omega) = X(\omega). \tag{3.1}$$

Definition 3.2. *The sequence of random variables $\{X_T\}$ is said to converge in probability to X if and only if, for every $\epsilon > 0$, we have*

$$\lim_{T \to \infty} \text{Pr}\{|X_T - X| > \epsilon\} = 0. \tag{3.2}$$

When the Tth element of the sequence is the estimator θ_T for sample size T and the limit is the population parameter vector of interest θ_0, then we call the estimator θ_T *consistent* for θ_0.

Definition 3.3. *A sequence of estimators $\{\theta_T\}$ is said to be strongly (weakly) consistent for a constant parameter vector θ_0 if and only if θ_T converges almost surely (in probability) to θ_0 as $T \to \infty$.*

There are many different sets of sufficient conditions on the structure of asset pricing models and the probability models generating uncertainty for extremum estimators to be consistent. In this chapter we follow closely the approach in Hansen (1982b), which assumes that the underlying random vector of interest, z_t, is a stationary and ergodic time series. Chapters 9 and 10 discuss how stochastic trends have been accommodated in DAPMs.

We let $\mathbb{R}^\infty$ denote the space consisting of all infinite sequences $x = (x_1, x_2, \ldots)$ of real numbers (lower case x indicates $x \in \mathbb{R}$). A T-dimensional rectangle is of the form $\{x \in \mathbb{R}^\infty : x_1 \in I_1, x_2 \in I_2, \ldots, x_T \in I_T\}$, where $I_1, \ldots, I_T$ are finite or infinite intervals in $\mathbb{R}$. If $\mathcal{B}^\infty$ denotes the smallest

---

[2] The topics discussed in this section are covered in more depth in most intermediate statistics books. See Chung (1974) and Billingsley (1979).

[3] A null set $\mathcal{N}$ for P is a set with the property that $\text{Pr}\{\mathcal{N}\} = 0$.

σ-algebra of subsets of $\mathbb{R}^\infty$ containing all finite dimensional rectangles, then $X = (X_1, X_2, \ldots)$ is a measurable mapping from Ω to $(\mathbb{R}^\infty, \mathcal{B}^\infty)$ (here the X's are random variables).

Definition 3.4. *A process $\{X_t\}$ is called stationary if, for every k, the process $\{X_t\}_{t=k}^\infty$ has the same distribution as $\{X_t\}_{t=1}^\infty$; that is,*

$$P\{(X_1, X_2, \ldots) \in \mathcal{B}^\infty\} = P\{(X_{k+1}, X_{k+2} \ldots) \in \mathcal{B}^\infty\}. \qquad (3.3)$$

In practical terms, a stationary process is one such that the functional forms of the joint distributions of collections $(X_k, X_{k-1}, \ldots, X_{k-\ell})$ do not change over time. An important property of a stationary process is that the process $\{Y_k\}$ defined by $Y_k = f(X_k, X_{k+1}, \ldots,)$ is also stationary for any f that is measurable relative to $\mathcal{B}^\infty$.

The assumption that $\{X_t\}$ is stationary is not sufficient to ensure that sample averages of the process converge to EX_1, a requirement that underlies our large-sample analysis of estimators. (Here we use EX_1, because all X_t have the same mean.) The reason is that the sample we observe is the realization $(X_1(\omega_0), X_2(\omega_0), \ldots)$ associated with a single ω_0 in the sample space Ω. If we are to learn about the distribution of the time series $\{X_t\}$ from this realization, then, as we move along the series $\{X_t(\omega_0)\}$, it must be as if we are observing realizations of $X_t(\omega)$ for fixed t as ω ranges over Ω.

To make this idea more precise,[4] suppose there is an event $A \in \mathcal{F}$ with the property that one can find a $B \in \mathcal{B}^\infty$ such that for every $t > 1$, $A = \{\omega : (X_t(\omega), X_{t+1}(\omega), \ldots) \in B\}$. Such an event A is called *invariant* because, for $\omega_0 \in A$, the information provided by $\{X_t(\omega_0), X_{t+1}(\omega_0), \ldots\}$ as t increases is essentially unchanged with t. On the other hand, if such a B does not exist, then

$$A = \{\omega : (X_1(\omega), X_2(\omega), \ldots) \in B\} \neq \{\omega : (X_t(\omega), X_{t+1}(\omega), \ldots) \in B\}, \qquad (3.4)$$

for some $t > 1$, and $\{X_t(\omega), X_{t+1}(\omega), \ldots\}$ conveys information about a different event in $\mathcal{F}$ (different part of Ω).

Definition 3.5. *A stationary process is ergodic if every invariant event has probability zero or one.*

If the process is ergodic, then a single realization conveys sufficient information about Ω for a strong law of large numbers (SLLN) to hold.

---

[4] For further discussion of stationary and ergodic stochastic processes see, e.g., Breiman (1968).

Theorem 3.1. *If $X_1 X_2, \ldots,$ is a stationary and ergodic process and $E|X_1| < \infty$,* *then*

$$\frac{1}{T} \sum_{t=1}^{T} X_t \rightarrow EX_1 \text{ a.s.} \tag{3.5}$$

One can relax the assumption of stationarity, thereby allowing the marginal distributions of z_t to change over time, and still obtain a SLLN. However, this is typically accomplished by replacing the relatively weak requirements implicit in the assumption of stationarity on the dependence between z_t and z_{t-s}, for $s \neq 0$, with stronger assumptions (see, e.g., Gallant and White, 1988).

Two considerations motivate our focus on the case of stationary and ergodic time series. First, in dynamic asset pricing models, the pricing relations are typically the solutions to a dynamic optimization problem by investors or a replication argument based on no-arbitrage opportunities. As we will see more formally in later chapters, both of these arguments involve optimal forecasts of future variables, and these optimal forecasting problems are typically solved under the assumption of stationary time series.[5] Indeed, these forecasting problems will generally not lend themselves to tractable solutions in the absence of stationarity. Second, the assumption that a time series is stationary does not preclude variation over time in the *conditional* distributions of z_t conditioned on its own history. In particular, the time variation in conditional means and variances that is often the focus of financial econometric modeling is easily accommodated within the framework of stationary and ergodic time series.

Of course, neither of these considerations rules out the possibility that the real world is one in which time series are in fact nonstationary. At a conceptual level, the economic argument for nonstationarity often comes down to the need to include additional conditioning variables. For example, the case of a change in operating procedures by a monetary authority, as we experienced in the United States in the early 1980s, could be handled by conditioning on variables that determine a monetary authority's operating procedures. However, many of the changes in a pricing environment that would lead us to be concerned about stationarity happen infrequently. Therefore, we do not have repeated observations on the changes that concern us the most. The pragmatic solution to this problem has often been to judiciously choose the sample period so that the state vector z_t in an asset pricing model can reasonably be assumed to be stationary. With these considerations in mind, we proceed under the formal assumption of stationary time series.

---

[5] An important exception is the case of nonstationarity induced by stochastic trends.

3.2. Consistency: General Considerations

Let $Q_T(\vec{z}_T, \theta)$ denote the function to be minimized by choice of the K-vector θ of unknown parameters within an admissible parameter space $\Theta \subset \mathbb{R}^K$, and let $Q_0(\theta)$ be its population counterpart. Throughout this chapter, it will be assumed that $Q_0(\theta)$ is uniquely minimized at θ_0, the model parameters that generate the data.

We begin by presenting a set of quite general sufficient conditions for θ_T to be a consistent estimator of θ_0. The discussion of these conditions is intended to illustrate the essential features of a probability model that lead to *strong* consistency (θ_T converges almost surely to θ_0). Without further assumptions, however, the general conditions proposed are not easily verified in practice. Therefore, we proceed to examine a more primitive set of conditions that imply the conditions of our initial consistency theorem.

One critical assumption underlying consistency is the uniform convergence of sample criterion functions to their population counterparts as T gets large. Following are definitions of two notions of uniform convergence.

Definition 3.6. *Let $g_T(\theta)$ be a nonnegative sequence of random variables depending on the parameter θ. Consider the two modes of uniform convergence of $g_T(\theta)$ to 0:*

$$P\left[\lim_{T \to \infty} \sup_{\theta \in \Theta} g_T(\theta) = 0\right] = 1, \qquad (3.6)$$

$$\lim_{T \to \infty} P\left[\sup_{\theta \in \Theta} g_T(\theta) < \epsilon\right] = 1 \quad \text{for any } \epsilon > 0. \qquad (3.7)$$

If (3.6) holds, then $g_T(\theta)$ is said to converge to 0 almost surely uniformly in $\theta \in \Theta$. If (3.7) holds, then $g_T(\theta)$ is said to converge to 0 in probability uniformly in $\theta \in \Theta$.

The following theorem presents a useful set of sufficient conditions for θ_T to converge almost surely to θ_0.

Theorem 3.2. *Suppose*

(i) *Θ is compact.*
(ii) *The nonnegative sample criterion function $Q_T(\vec{z}_T, \theta)$ is continuous in $\theta \in \Theta$ and is a measurable function of $\vec{z}_T$ for all θ.*
(iii) *$Q_T(\vec{z}_T, \theta)$ converges to a non-stochastic function $Q_0(\theta)$ almost surely uniformly in $\theta \in \Theta$ as $T \to \infty$; and $Q_0(\theta)$ attains a unique minimum at θ_0.*

Define θ_T as a value of θ that satisfies

$$Q_T(\vec{z}_T, \theta_T) = \min_{\theta \in \Theta} Q_T(\vec{z}_T, \theta). \qquad (3.8)$$

Then θ_T converges almost surely to θ_0.[6]

---

[6] In situations where θ_T is not unique, if we let Γ_T denote the set of minimizers, we can show that $\delta_T(\omega) = \sup\{|\theta_T - \theta_0| : \theta_T \in \Gamma_T\}$ converges almost surely to 0 as $T \to \infty$.

Proof (Theorem 3.2). *Define the function*

$$\rho(\epsilon) = \inf\{Q_0(\theta) - Q_0(\theta_0), \quad for \ |\theta - \theta_0| \geq \epsilon\}. \tag{3.9}$$

As long as $\epsilon > 0$, *Assumptions (i)–(iii) guarantee that* $\rho(\epsilon) > 0$. *(Continuity of* Q_0 *follows from our assumptions.) Assumption (iii) implies that there exists a set* Λ *with* $P(\Lambda) = 1$ *and a positive, finite function* $T(\omega, \epsilon)$, *such that*

$$\rho_T(\omega) \equiv \sup_{\theta \in \Theta} |Q_T(\omega, \theta) - Q_0(\theta)| < \rho(\epsilon)/2, \tag{3.10}$$

for all $\omega \in \Lambda$, $\epsilon > 0$, *and* $T \geq T(\omega, \epsilon)$. *This inequality guarantees that for all* $\omega \in \Lambda$, $\epsilon > 0$, *and* $T \geq T(\omega, \epsilon)$,

$$
\begin{aligned}
Q_0(\theta_T) - Q_0(\theta_0) &= Q_0(\theta_T) - Q_T(\omega, \theta_T) + Q_T(\omega, \theta_T) \\
&\quad - Q_T(\omega, \theta_0) + Q_T(\omega, \theta_0) - Q_0(\theta_0) \\
&\leq Q_0(\theta_T) - Q_T(\omega, \theta_T) + Q_T(\omega, \theta_0) - Q_0(\theta_0) \\
&\leq |Q_0(\theta_T) - Q_T(\omega, \theta_T)| + |Q_T(\omega, \theta_0) - Q_0(\theta_0)| \\
&\leq 2\rho_T(\omega) < \rho(\epsilon), \tag{3.11}
\end{aligned}
$$

which implies that $|\theta_T - \theta_0| < \epsilon$ *for all* $\omega \in \Lambda$, $\epsilon > 0$, *and* $T \geq T(\omega, \epsilon)$.

The assumptions of Theorem 3.2 are quite general. In particular, the z_t's need not be identically distributed or independent. However, this generality is of little practical value unless the assumptions of the theorem can be verified in actual applications. In practice, this amounts to verifying Assumption (iii). The regularity conditions imposed in the econometrics literature to assure that (iii) holds typically depend on the specification of Q_T and Q_0 and, thus, are often criterion function specific. We present a set of sufficient conditions to establish the almost sure uniform convergence of the sample mean

$$G_T(\vec{z}_T, \theta) = \frac{1}{T} \sum_{t=1}^{T} g(z_t, \theta) \tag{3.12}$$

to its population counterpart $G_0(\theta) = E[g(z_t, \theta)]$. This result then is used to establish the uniform convergence of Q_T to Q_0 for the cases of ML and GMM estimators for stationary processes.

To motivate the regularity conditions we impose on the time series $\{z_t\}$ and the function g, it is instructive to examine how far the assumption that

$\{z_t\}$ is stationary and ergodic takes us toward fulfilling the assumptions of Theorem 3.2. Therefore, we begin by assuming:

Assumption 3.1. $\{z_t : t \geq 1\}$ *is a stationary and ergodic stochastic process.*

As discussed in Chapter 2, the sample and population criterion functions for LLP are

$$Q_0(\delta) = E\left[\left(y_t - x_t'\delta\right)^2 \right], \quad Q_T(\delta) = \frac{1}{T}\sum_{t=1}^{T} \left(y_t - x_t'\delta\right)^2, \quad \delta \in \mathbb{R}^K. \quad (3.13)$$

For the LLP problem, $Q_0(\delta)$ is assured of having a unique minimizer δ_0 if the second-moment matrix $E[x_t x_t']$ has full rank. Thus, with this additional assumption, the second part of Condition (iii) of Theorem 3.2 is satisfied. Furthermore, under the assumption of ergodicity,

$$\frac{1}{T}\sum_{t=1}^{T} x_t x_t' \to E\left[x_t x_t'\right] \quad \text{and} \quad \frac{1}{T}\sum_{t=1}^{T} x_t y_t \to E\left[x_t y_t\right] \quad \text{a.s.} \quad (3.14)$$

It follows immediately that $\delta_T \to \delta_0$ a.s.

Though unnecessary in this case, we can also establish the strong consistency of δ_T for δ_0 from the observation that $Q_T(\delta) \to Q_0(\delta)$ a.s., for all $\delta \in \mathbb{R}^K$. From Figure 3.1 it is seen that the criterion functions are quadratic and eventually overlap (for large T), so the minimizers of $Q_T(\delta)$ and $Q_0(\delta)$ must eventually coincide. We conclude that the strong consistency of estimators in LLP problems is essentially implied by the assumption that $\{z_t\}$ is stationary and ergodic (and the rank condition on $E[x_t x_t']$).

More generally, the assumptions of ergodicity of $\{z_t\}$ and the continuity of $Q_T(\vec{z}_T, \theta)$ in its second argument do not imply the strong consistency of the minimizer θ_T of the criterion function $Q_T(\theta)$. The reason is that ergodicity guarantees only pointwise convergence, and the behavior in the "tails" of some nonlinear criterion functions may be problematic. To illustrate this

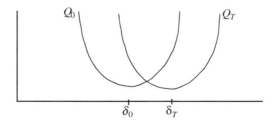

Figure 3.1. *Sample and population criterion functions for a least-squares projection.*

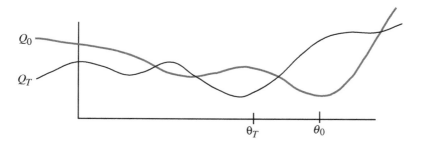

Figure 3.2.   *Well-behaved Q_0, Q_T.*

point, Figure 3.2 depicts a relatively well-behaved function Q_T that implies
the convergence of θ_T to θ_0. In contrast, although the function $Q_T(\theta)$ in
Figure 3.3 can be constructed to converge pointwise to $Q_0(\theta)$, θ_0 and θ_T
may grow increasingly far apart as T increases if the dip moves further out to
the right as T grows. This potential problem is ruled out by the assumptions
that $\{Q_T : T \geq 1\}$ converges almost surely uniformly in θ to a function Q_0
and that θ_0 is the unique minimizer of Q_0.

Even uniform convergence of Q_T to Q_0 combined with stationarity and
ergodicity are not sufficient to ensure that θ_T converges to θ_0, however. To
see why, consider the situation in Figure 3.4. If $Q_0(\theta)$ asymptotes to the
minimum of $Q_0(\theta)$ over $\mathbb{R}$ (but does not achieve this minimum) in the left
tail, then $Q_T(\theta_T)$ can get arbitrarily close to $Q_0(\theta_0)$, even though θ_T and θ_0
are growing infinitely far apart. To rule this case out, we need to impose a
restriction on the behavior of Q_0 in the "tails." This can be accomplished
either by imposing restrictions on the admissible parameter space Θ or by
restricting Q_0 directly. For example, if it is required that

$$\inf\{Q_0(\theta) - Q_0(\theta_0) : \theta \in \Theta, \ |\theta - \theta_0| > \rho\} > 0, \qquad (3.15)$$

then $Q_0(\theta)$ cannot asymptote to $Q_0(\theta_0)$, for θ far away from θ_0, and convergence of θ_T to θ_0 is ensured. This condition is satisfied by the least-squares

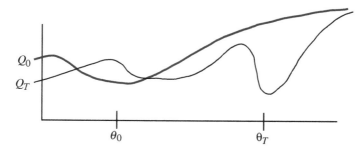

Figure 3.3.   *Poorly behaved Q_T.*

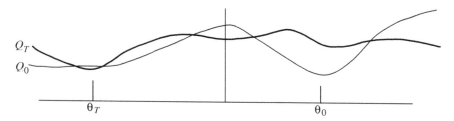

Figure 3.4. Q_T converging to asymptoting Q_0.

criterion function for linear models. For nonlinear models, potentially un-
desirable behavior in the tails is typically ruled out by assuming that Θ is
compact (the tails are "chopped off").

With these observations as background, we next provide a primitive set
of assumptions that assure the strong consistency of θ_T for θ_0. As noted in
Chapter 1, most of the criterion functions we will examine can be expressed
as sample means of functions $g(z_t, \theta)$, or are simple functions of such sample means (e.g., a quadratic form). Accordingly, we first present sufficient
conditions (beyond Assumption 3.1) for the convergence of

$$G_T(\theta) = \frac{1}{T} \sum_{t=1}^{T} g(z_t, \theta) \qquad (3.16)$$

to $E[g(z_t, \theta)]$ almost surely, uniformly in $\theta \in \Theta$. Our first assumption rules
out bad behavior in the tails and the second states that the function $g(z_t, \theta)$
has a finite mean for all θ:

Assumption 3.2. Θ *is a compact metric space.*

Assumption 3.3. *The function $g(\cdot, \theta)$ is Borel measurable for each θ in Θ;*
$Eg(z_t, \theta)$ exists and is finite for all θ in Θ.

We will also need a stronger notion of continuity of $g(z_t, \theta)$. Let[7]

$$\epsilon_t(\theta, \delta) = \sup\{|g(z_t, \theta) - g(z_t, \alpha)| \text{ for all } \alpha \text{ in } \Theta \text{ with } |\alpha - \theta| < \delta\}. \quad (3.17)$$

Definition 3.7. *The random function $g(z_t, \theta)$ is first-moment continuous at θ if*
$\lim_{\delta \downarrow 0} E[\epsilon_t(\theta, \delta)] = 0$.

---

[7] Assumption 3.2 guarantees that Θ has a countable dense subset. Hence, under Assumptions 3.2 and 3.3, the function $\epsilon_t(\theta, \delta)$ is Borel measurable (it can be represented as the almost
sure supremum of a countable collection of Borel measurable functions).

First-moment continuity of $g(z_t, \theta)$ is a joint property of the function g and the random vector z_t. Under Assumptions 3.1–3.3, if $g(z_t, \theta)$ is first-moment continuous at θ, then $g(z_t, \theta)$ is first-moment continuous for every $t \geq 1$.

Assumption 3.4.   *The random function $g(z_t, \theta)$ is first-moment continuous at all $\theta \in \Theta$.*

The measure of distance between G_T and $E[g(z_t, \cdot)]$ we are concerned with is

$$\rho_T = \sup_{\theta \in \Theta} \left| G_T(\theta) - Eg(z_t, \theta) \right|. \tag{3.18}$$

Using the compactness of Θ and the continuity of $g_t(\cdot)$, it can be shown that $\{\rho_T : T \geq 1\}$ converges almost surely to zero. The proof proceeds as follows: Let $\{\theta_i : i \geq 1\}$ be a countable dense subset of Θ. The distance between $G_T(\theta)$ and $Eg(z_t, \theta)$ satisfies the following inequality:

$$\left| G_T(\theta) - Eg(z_t, \theta) \right| \leq \left| G_T(\theta) - G_T(\theta_i) \right|$$
$$+ \left| G_T(\theta_i) - Eg(z_t, \theta_i) \right| + \left| Eg(z_t, \theta_i) - Eg(z_t, \theta) \right|. \tag{3.19}$$

For all $\theta \in \Theta$, the first term on the right-hand side of (3.19) can be made arbitrarily small by choosing θ_i such that $|\theta_i - \theta|$ is small (because the θ_i are a dense subset of Θ) and then using ergodicity and the uniform continuity of $g(z_t, \theta)$ (uniform continuity follows from Assumptions 3.2 and 3.4). The second term can be made arbitrarily small for large enough T by ergodicity. Finally, the last term can be made small by exploiting the uniform continuity of g. The following theorem summarizes this result, a formal proof of which is provided in Hansen (2005).

Theorem 3.3 (Hansen, 1982b). *Suppose Assumptions 3.1–3.4 are satisfied. Then $\{\rho_T : T \geq 1\}$ in (3.18) converges almost surely to zero.*

3.3. Consistency of Extremum Estimators

Equipped with Theorem 3.3, the strong consistency of the extremum estimators discussed in Chapter 2 can be established.

3.3.1. Maximum Likelihood Estimators

Suppose that the functional form of the density function of y_t conditioned on $\vec{y}_{t-1}, f(y_t | \vec{y}_{t-1}^J; \beta)$, is known for all t. Let $Q_0(\beta) = E[\log f(y_t | \vec{y}_{t-1}^J; \beta)]$

denote the population criterion function and suppose that β_0, the parameter vector of the data-generating process for y_t, is a maximizer of $Q_0(\beta)$.

To show the uniqueness of β_0 as a maximizer of $Q_0(\beta)$, required by Condition (iii) of Theorem 3.2, we use Jensen's inequality to obtain

$$E\left[\log \frac{f\left(y_t | \vec{y}_{t-1}^J; \beta\right)}{f\left(y_t | \vec{y}_{t-1}^J; \beta_0\right)}\right] < \log E\left[\frac{f\left(y_t | \vec{y}_{t-1}^J; \beta\right)}{f\left(y_t | \vec{y}_{t-1}^J; \beta_0\right)}\right], \quad \beta \neq \beta_0. \tag{3.20}$$

The right-hand side of (3.20) is zero (by the law of iterated expectations) because

$$\int_{-\infty}^{\infty} \frac{f\left(y_t | \vec{y}_{t-1}^J; \beta\right)}{f\left(y_t | \vec{y}_{t-1}^J; \beta_0\right)} f\left(y_t | \vec{y}_{t-1}^J; \beta_0\right) dy = 1. \tag{3.21}$$

Therefore,

$$E\left[\log f\left(y_t | \vec{y}_{t-1}^J; \beta\right)\right] < E\left[\log f\left(y_t | \vec{y}_{t-1}^J; \beta_0\right)\right], \quad \text{if} \quad \beta \neq \beta_0 \tag{3.22}$$

and β_0 is the unique solution to (2.6).

The approximate sample log-likelihood function is

$$l_T(\beta) = \frac{1}{T} \sum_{t=J+1}^{T} \log f\left(y_t | \vec{y}_{t-1}^J; \beta\right). \tag{3.23}$$

Thus, setting $z_t' \equiv (y_t', \vec{y}_{t-1}^{J}{}')$ and

$$g(z_t, \beta) = \log f\left(y_t | \vec{y}_{t-1}^J; \beta\right), \tag{3.24}$$

G_T in the preceding section becomes the log-likelihood function. If Assumptions 3.1–3.4 are satisfied, then Theorem 3.3 implies the almost sure, uniform convergence of the sample log-likelihood function to $Q_0(\beta)$.[8]

3.3.2. Generalized Method of Moment Estimators

The GMM criterion function is based on the model-implied M-vector of moment conditions $E[h(z_t, \theta_0)] = 0$. With use of the sample counterpart to this expectation, the sample and population criterion functions are constructed as quadratic forms with distance matrices W_T and W_0, respectively:

---

[8] See DeGroot (1970) for a discussion of the use of first-moment continuity of $\log f(y_t | y_{t-1}^J; \beta)$ in proving the strong consistency of ML estimators. DeGroot refers to first-moment continuity as "supercontinuity."

$$Q_T(\theta) = H_T(\vec{z}_T, \theta)' W_T H_T(\vec{z}_T, \theta), \tag{3.25}$$

$$Q_0(\theta) = H_0(\theta)' W_0 H_0(\theta), \tag{3.26}$$

where $H_T(\vec{z}_T, \theta) = T^{-1} \sum_{t=1}^{T} h(z_t, \theta)$ and $H_0(\theta) = E[h(z_t, \theta)]$. Since $H_0(\theta)$ is zero at θ_0, the function $Q_0(\cdot)$ achieves its minimum (zero) at θ_0.

To apply Theorem 3.3 to these criterion functions we impose an additional assumption.

Assumption 3.5. $\{W_T : T \geq 1\}$ *is a sequence of $M \times M$ positive semidefinite matrices of random variables with elements that converge almost surely to the corresponding elements of the $M \times M$ constant, positive semidefinite matrix W_0 with rank(W_0) $\geq K$.*

In addition, we let

$$\rho_T^* = \sup\{|Q_T(\theta) - Q_0(\theta)| : \theta \in \Theta\} \tag{3.27}$$

denote the maximum error in approximating Q_0 by its sample counterpart Q_T. The following lemma shows that Assumptions 3.1–3.5 are sufficient for this approximation error to converge almost surely to zero.

Lemma 3.1. *Suppose Assumptions 3.1–3.5 are satisfied. Then $\{\rho_T^* : T \geq 1\}$ converges almost surely to zero.*

Proof (Lemma 3.1). *Repeated application of the Triangle and Cauchy-Schwartz Inequalities gives*

$$\begin{aligned}
|Q_T(\theta) - Q_0(\theta)| &\leq |H_T(\theta) - H_0(\theta)| \quad |W_T| \quad |H_T(\theta)| \\
&+ |H_0(\theta)| \quad |W_T - W_0| \quad |H_T(\theta)| \\
&+ |H_0(\theta)| \quad |W_0| \quad |H_T(\theta) - H_0(\theta)|, \tag{3.28}
\end{aligned}$$

where $|W| = [\mathrm{Tr}\, WW']^{\frac{1}{2}}$. Therefore, letting $\phi_0 = \max\{|H_0(\theta)| : \theta \in \Theta\}$ and $\rho_T \equiv \sup\{|H_T(\theta) - H_0(\theta)| : \theta \in \Theta\}$,

$$0 \leq \rho_T^* \leq \rho_T|W_T|[\phi_0 + \rho_T] + \phi_0|W_T - W_0|[\phi_0 + \rho_T] + \phi_0|W_0|\rho_T. \tag{3.29}$$

Since $h(z_t, \theta)$ is first-moment continuous, $H_0(\theta)$ is a continuous function of θ. Therefore, ϕ_0 is finite because a continuous function on a compact set achieves its maximum. Theorem 3.3 implies that ρ_T converges almost surely to zero. Since each of the three terms on the right-hand side of (3.29) converges almost surely to zero, it follows that $\{\rho_T^* : T \geq 1\}$ converges almost surely to zero.

When this result is combined with Theorems 3.2 and 3.3, it follows that the GMM estimator $\{\theta_T : T \geq 1\}$ converges almost surely to θ_0.

3.3.3. QML Estimators

Key to consistency of QML estimators is verifying that the population moment equation (2.50) based on the normal likelihood function is satisfied at θ_0. As noted in Chapter 2, this is generally true if the functional forms of the conditional mean and variance of y_t are correctly specified (the moments implied by a DAPM are those in the probability model generating y_t). It is informative to verify that (2.50) is satisfied at θ_0 for the interest rate Example 2.1. This discussion is, in fact, generic to any one-dimensional state process y_t, since it does not depend on the functional forms of the conditional mean μ_{rt-1} or variance σ^2_{rt-1}. Extensions to the multivariate case, with some increase in notational complexity, are immediate (see, e.g., Bollerslev and Wooldridge, 1992).

Recalling the first-order conditions (2.57) shows the limit of the middle term on the right-hand-side to be

$$\frac{1}{T} \sum_{t=2}^{T} \left(\frac{(r_t - \hat{\mu}_{rt-1})^2}{\hat{\sigma}^4_{rt-1}} \frac{\partial \hat{\sigma}^2_{rt-1}}{\partial \theta_j} \right) \to E\left[\frac{(r_t - \mu_{rt-1})^2}{\sigma^4_{rt-1}} \frac{\partial \sigma^2_{rt-1}}{\partial \theta_j} \right]. \tag{3.30}$$

Using the law of iterated expectations, we find that this expectation simplifies as

$$E\left[\frac{(r_t - \mu_{rt-1})^2}{\sigma^4_{rt-1}} \frac{\partial \sigma^2_{rt-1}}{\partial \theta_j} \right] = E\left[E\left(\frac{(r_t - \mu_{rt-1})^2}{\sigma^4_{rt-1}} \,\Big|\, r_{t-1} \right) \frac{\partial \sigma^2_{rt-1}}{\partial \theta_j} \right]$$

$$= E\left[\frac{1}{\sigma^2_{rt-1}} \frac{\partial \sigma^2_{rt-1}}{\partial \theta_j} \right]. \tag{3.31}$$

The expectation (3.31) is seen to be minus the limit of the first term in (2.57), so the first and second terms cancel.

Thus, for the population first-order conditions associated with (2.57) to have a zero at θ_0, it remains to show that the limit of the last term in (2.57), evaluated at θ_0, is zero. This limit is

$$\frac{1}{T} \sum_{t=2}^{T} \left\{ \frac{(r_t - \hat{\mu}_{rt-1})}{\hat{\sigma}^2_{rt-1}} \frac{\partial \hat{\mu}_{rt-1}}{\partial \theta_j} \right\} \to E\left[\frac{(r_t - \mu_{rt-1})}{\sigma^2_{rt-1}} \frac{\partial \mu_{rt-1}}{\partial \theta_j} \right], \tag{3.32}$$

which is indeed zero, because $E[r_t - \mu_{rt-1}|r_{t-1}] = 0$ by construction and all of the other terms are constant conditional on r_{t-1}.

Consistency of the QML estimator then follows under the regularity conditions of Theorem 3.3.

3.4. Asymptotic Normality of Extremum Estimators

The consistency of θ_T for θ_0 implies that the limiting distribution of θ_T is degenerate at θ_0. For the purpose of conducting inference about the population value θ_0 of θ, we would like to know the distribution of θ_T for finite T. This distribution is generally not known, but often it can be reliably approximated using the limiting distribution of $\sqrt{T}(\theta_T - \theta_0)$ obtained by a central limit theorem. Applicable central limit theorems have been proven under a wide variety of regularity conditions. We continue our focus on stationary and ergodic economic environments.

Suppose that θ_T is strongly consistent for θ_0. To show the asymptotic normality of θ_T, we focus on the first-order conditions for the maximization or minimization of Q_T, the sample mean of the function $\mathcal{D}_0(z_t; \theta)$ first introduced in Chapter 1. More precisely, we let

$$
h(z_t, \theta) = \begin{cases}
\dfrac{\partial \log f}{\partial \theta}\left(y_t \mid \vec{y}_{t-1}^{\,J}; \theta\right) & \text{for the ML estimator,} \\[2ex]
h(z_t, \theta) & \text{for the GMM estimator,} \\[2ex]
\left(y_t - x_t'\theta\right) x_t & \text{for the LLP estimator.}
\end{cases} \tag{3.33}
$$

In each case, by appropriate choice of z_t and θ, $E[h(z_t, \theta_0)] = 0$. Thus, the function $\mathcal{D}_0(z_t; \theta)$, representing the first-order conditions for Q_0, is

$$
\mathcal{D}_0(z_t; \theta) = A_0 h(z_t; \theta), \tag{3.34}
$$

where the $K \times M$ matrix A_0 is

$$
A_0 = \begin{cases}
I_K & \text{for the ML estimator,} \\[1ex]
E[\partial h(z_t, \theta_0)'/\partial \theta]\, W_0 & \text{for the GMM estimator,} \\[1ex]
I_K & \text{for the LLP estimator,}
\end{cases} \tag{3.35}
$$

where I_K denotes the $K \times K$ identity matrix. The choice of A_0 for the GMM estimator is motivated subsequently as part of the proof of Theorem 3.5.

Using this notation and letting

$$
H_T(\theta) = \frac{1}{T} \sum_{t=1}^{T} h(z_t, \theta), \tag{3.36}
$$

we can view all of these estimators as special cases of the following definition of a GMM estimator (Hansen, 1982b).

Definition 3.8. *The GMM estimator $\{\theta_T : T \geq 1\}$ is a sequence of random vectors that converges in probability to θ_0 for which $\{\sqrt{T}A_T H_T(\theta_T) : T \geq 1\}$ converges in probability to zero, where $\{A_T\}$ is a sequence of $K \times M$ matrices converging in probability to the full-rank matrix A_0.*

For a sequence of random variables $\{X_T\}$, convergence in distribution is defined as follows.

Definition 3.9. *Let $F_1, F_2, \ldots$, be distribution functions of the random variables $X_1, X_2, \ldots$. Then the sequence $\{X_T\}$ converges in distribution to X (denoted $X_T \Rightarrow X$) if and only if $F_T(b) \rightarrow F_X(b)$ for all b at which F_X is continuous.*

The classical central limit theorem examines the partial sums $\sqrt{T}S_T = (1/\sqrt{T}) \sum_t X_t$ of an independently and identically distributed process $\{X_t\}$ with mean μ and finite variance. Under these assumptions, the distribution of $\sqrt{T}S_T$ converges to that of normal with mean μ and covariance matrix $\text{Var}[X_t]$. However, for the study of asset pricing models, the assumption of independence is typically too strong. It rules out, in particular, persistence in the state variables and time-varying conditional volatilities.

The assumption that $\{X_t\}$ is a stationary and ergodic time series, which is much weaker than the i.i.d. assumption in the classical model, is not sufficient to establish a central limit theorem. Essentially, the problem is that an ergodic time series can be highly persistent, so that the X_t and X_s, for $s \neq t$, are too highly correlated for $\sqrt{T}S_T$ to converge to a normal random vector. The assumption of independence in the classical central limit theorem avoids this problem by assuming away any temporal dependence. Instead, we will work with the much weaker assumption that $\{X_t\}$ is a Martingale Difference Sequence (MDS), meaning that

$$E[X_t | X_{t-1}, X_{t-2}, \ldots] = 0 \qquad (3.37)$$

with probability one. The assumption that X_t is mean-independent of its past imposes sufficient structure on the dependence of $\{X_t\}$ for the following central limit theorem to be true.

Theorem 3.4 (Billingsley, 1968). *Let $\{X_t\}_{t=-\infty}^{\infty}$ be a stationary and ergodic MDS such that $E\left[X_1^2\right]$ is finite. Then the distribution of $(1/\sqrt{T}) \sum_{t=1}^{T} X_t$ approaches the normal distribution with mean zero and variance $E\left[X_1^2\right]$.*

Though many financial time series are not MDSs, it will turn out that they can be expressed as moving averages of MDS, and this will be shown to be sufficient for our purposes.

Equipped with Billingsley's theorem, under the following conditions, we can prove that the GMM estimator is asymptotically normal.

Theorem 3.5 (Hansen, 1982b). *Suppose that*

    (i) $\{z_t\}$ is stationary and ergodic.

    (ii) Θ is an open subset of $\mathbb{R}^K$.

    (iii) h is a measurable function of z_t for all θ,

$$d_0 \equiv E\left[\frac{\partial h}{\partial \theta}(z_t, \theta_0)\right]$$

    is finite and has full rank, and $\partial h / \partial \theta$ is first moment continuous at all $\theta \in \Theta$.

    (iv) θ_T is a GMM estimator of θ_0.

    (v) $\sqrt{T}H_T(\vec{z}_T, \theta_0) \Rightarrow N(0, \Sigma_0)$, where $\Sigma_0 = \lim_{T \to \infty} TE[H_T(\theta_0)H_T(\theta_0)']$.

    (vi) A_T converges in probability to A_0, a constant matrix of full rank, and $A_0 d_0$ has full rank.

Then $\sqrt{T}(\theta_T - \theta_0) \Rightarrow N(0, \Omega_0)$, where

$$\Omega_0 = (A_0 d_0)^{-1} A_0 \Sigma_0 A_0' (d_0' A_0')^{-1}. \tag{3.38}$$

In proving Theorem 3.5, we will need the following very useful lemma.

Lemma 3.2. *Suppose that $\{z_t\}$ is stationary and ergodic and the function $g(z_t, \theta)$ satisfies: (a) $E[g(z_t, \theta_0)]$ exists and is finite, (b) g is first-moment continuous at θ_0, and suppose that θ_T converges to θ_0 in probability. Then $(1/T)\sum_{t=1}^{T} g(z_t, \theta_T)$ converges to $E[g(z_t, \theta_0)]$ in probability.*

Proof (Theorem 3.5). *When we apply Taylor's theorem on a coordinate by coordinate basis,*

$$H_T(\theta_T) = H_T(\theta_0) + G_T(\theta_T^*)(\theta_T - \theta_0), \tag{3.39}$$

where θ_T^* is a $K \times M$ matrix with the mth column, θ_{mT}^*, satisfying $|\theta_{mT}^* - \theta_0| \leq |\theta_T - \theta_0|$, for $m = 1, \ldots, M$, and the ijth element of the $M \times K$ matrix $G_T(\theta_T^*)$ is the jth *element of the* $1 \times K$ *vector* $\partial H_T^i(\theta_{iT}^*)/\partial \theta$. *The matrix* $G_T(\theta_T^*)$ *converges in probability to the matrix* d_0 *by Lemma 3.2. Furthermore, since* $\sqrt{T} A_T H_T(\theta_T)$ *converges in probability to zero,* $\sqrt{T}(\theta_T - \theta_0)$ *and* $[-(A_0 d_0)^{-1} A_0 \sqrt{T} H_T(\theta_0)]$ *have the same limiting distribution. Finally, from (v) it follows that* $\sqrt{T}(\theta_T - \theta_0)$ *is asymptotically normal with mean zero and covariance matrix* $(A_0 d_0)^{-1} A_0 \Sigma_0 A_0' (d_0' A_0')^{-1}$.

A key assumption of Theorem 3.5 is Condition (v), as it takes us a long way toward the desired result. Prior to discussing applications of this theorem, it will be instructive to discuss more primitive conditions for Condition (v) to hold and to characterize Σ_0. Letting I_t denote the information set generated by $\{z_t, z_{t-1}, \ldots\}$, and $h_t \equiv h(z_t; \theta_0)$, we begin with the special case (where ACh is shorthand for autocorrelation in h):

Case ACh(0). $E[h_t | I_{t-1}] = 0$.

Since I_{t-1} includes h_s, for $s \leq t-1$, $\{h_t\}$ is an MDS. Thus, Theorem 3.4, the central limit theorem (CLT), applies directly and implies Condition (v) with

$$\Sigma_0 = E\left[h_t h_t'\right]. \tag{3.40}$$

Case ACh($n-1$). $E[h_{t+n} | I_t] = 0$, *for some* $n \geq 1$. *When* $n > 1$, *this case allows for serial correlation in the process* h_t *up to order* $n-1$.

We cannot apply Theorem 3.4 directly in this case because it presumes that h_t is an MDS. However, it turns out that we can decompose h_t into a finite sum of terms that do follow an MDS and then Billingsley's CLT can be applied. Toward this end, h_t is written as

$$h_t = \sum_{j=0}^{n-1} u_{t,j}, \tag{3.41}$$

where $u_{t,j} \in I_{t-j}$ and satisfies the property that $E[u_{t,j} | I_{t-j-1}] = 0$. This representation follows from the observation that

$$h_t = E[h_t | I_{t-1}] + u_{t,0}$$

$$= E[h_t | I_{t-2}] + u_{t,0} + u_{t,1} = \ldots = \sum_{j=0}^{n-1} u_{t,j}, \tag{3.42}$$

where the law of iterated expectations has been used repeatedly. Thus,

$$\frac{1}{\sqrt{T}} \sum_{t=1}^{T} h_t = \frac{1}{\sqrt{T}} \sum_{t=1}^{T} \sum_{j=0}^{n-1} u_{t,j}. \tag{3.43}$$

Combining terms for which $t-j$ is the same (and, hence, that reside in the same information set) and defining

$$u_t^* = \sum_{j=0}^{n-1} u_{t+j,j}, \tag{3.44}$$

gives

$$\frac{1}{\sqrt{T}} \sum_{t=1}^{T} h_t = \frac{1}{\sqrt{T}} \sum_{t=0}^{T-n+1} u_t^* + V_T^n, \tag{3.45}$$

where V_T^n involves a fixed number of $u_{t,j}$ depending only on n, for all T. Since V_T^n converges to zero in probability as $T \to \infty$, we can focus on the sample mean of u_t^* in deriving the limiting distribution of the sample mean of h_t.

The series $\{u_t^*\}$ is an MDS. Thus, Billingsley's theorem implies that

$$\frac{1}{\sqrt{T}} \sum_{t=1}^{T-n+1} u_t^* \Rightarrow N(0, \Sigma_0), \quad \Sigma_0 = E[u_t^* u_t^{*\prime}]. \tag{3.46}$$

Moreover, substituting the left-hand side of (3.45) for the scaled average of the $u_t^{*\prime}$s in (3.46), gives

$$\Sigma_0 = \lim_{T \to \infty} E\left[\frac{1}{T}\left(\sum_{t=1}^{T} h_t\right)\left(\sum_{t=1}^{T} h_t'\right)\right]$$

$$= \lim_{T \to \infty} \sum_{j=-n+1}^{n-1} \left(\frac{T - |j|}{T}\right) E[h_t h_{t-j}'] = \sum_{j=-n+1}^{n-1} E[h_t h_{t-j}']. \tag{3.47}$$

In words, the asymptotic covariance matrix of the scaled sample mean of h_t is the sum of the autocovariances of h_t out to order $n - 1$.

Case AC$h(\infty)$. $E[h_t h_{t-s}'] \neq 0$, for all s.

Since, in case AC$h(n - 1)$, $n - 1$ is the number of nonzero autocovariances of h_t, (3.47) can be rewritten equivalently as

$$\Sigma_0 = \sum_{j=-\infty}^{\infty} E\big[h(z_t, \theta_0)h(z_{t-j}, \theta_0)'\big]. \tag{3.48}$$

This suggests that, for the case where $E[h_t h'_{t-s}] \neq 0$, for all s (i.e., $n = \infty$), (3.48) holds as well. Hansen (1982b) shows that this is indeed the case under the additional assumption that the autocovariance matrices of h_t are absolutely summable.

3.5. Distributions of Specific Estimators

In applying Theorem 3.5, it must be verified that the problem of interest satisfies Conditions (iii), (iv), and (v). We next discuss some of the implications of these conditions for the cases of the ML, GMM, and LLP criterion functions. In addition, we examine the form of the asymptotic covariance matrix Σ_0 implied by these criterion functions, and discuss consistent estimators of Σ_0.

3.5.1. Maximum Likelihood Estimation

In the case of ML estimation, we proved in Chapter 2 that

$$E\left[\mathcal{D}_0\big(y_t, \vec{y}_{t-1}^J, \beta_0\big)\big|\vec{y}_{t-1}^J\right] = 0,$$

where[9]

$$\mathcal{D}_0\big(y_t, \vec{y}_{t-1}^J, \beta\big) = \frac{\partial \log f}{\partial \beta}\big(y_t|\vec{y}_{t-1}^J; \beta\big). \tag{3.49}$$

Since the density of y_t conditioned on $\vec{y}_{t-1}^J$ is the same as the density conditioned on $\vec{y}_{t-1}$ by assumption, (2.7) implies that the "score" (3.49) is an MDS. Therefore, Theorem 3.4 and Case ACh(0) apply and

$$\sqrt{T}H_T(z_t, \theta_0) = \sqrt{T}\left(\frac{1}{T}\sum_{t=1}^{T}\frac{\partial \log f}{\partial \beta}\big(y_t|\vec{y}_{t-1}^J; \beta_0\big)\right) \tag{3.50}$$

---

[9] In deriving this result, we implicitly assumed that we could reverse the order of integration and differentiation. Formally, this is justified by the assumption that the partial derivative of $\log f(y_t|\vec{y}_{t-1}^J; \beta)$ is first-moment continuous at β_0. More precisely, consider a function $h(z, \theta)$. Suppose that for some $\delta > 0$, the partial derivative $\partial h(z, \theta)/\partial \theta$ exists for all values of z and all θ such that $|\theta - \theta_0| < \delta$, and suppose that this derivative is first-moment continuous at θ_0. If $E[h(z, \theta)]$ exists for all $|\theta - \theta_0| < \delta$ and if $E[|\partial h(z, \theta)/\partial \theta|] < \infty$, then

$$E\left[\frac{\partial h(z, \theta)}{\partial \theta}\bigg|_{\theta=\theta_0}\right] = \frac{\partial E[h(z, \theta)]}{\partial \theta}\bigg|_{\theta=\theta_0}.$$

converges in distribution to a normal random vector with asymptotic covariance matrix

$$\Sigma_0 = E\left[\frac{\partial \log f}{\partial \beta}\left(y_t \mid \vec{\mathbf{y}}_{t-1}^{\,J}; \beta_0\right) \frac{\partial \log f}{\partial \beta}\left(y_t \mid \vec{\mathbf{y}}_{t-1}^{\,J}; \beta_0\right)'\right]. \qquad (3.51)$$

Furthermore, the first-order conditions to the log-likelihood function give
K equations in the K unknowns (β), so A_T is I_K in this case and $\Omega_0^{\mathrm{ML}} = d_0^{-1}\Sigma_0(d_0')^{-1}$.

Thus, it remains to determine d_0. Since $E[\mathcal{D}_0(z_t, \beta_0)] = 0$, differentiating both sides of this expression with respect to β gives[10]

$$\begin{aligned}
d_0^{\mathrm{ML}} &= E\left[\frac{\partial^2 \log f}{\partial \beta \partial \beta'}\left(y_t \mid \vec{\mathbf{y}}_{t-1}^{\,J}; \beta_0\right)\right] \\
&= -E\left[\frac{\partial \log f}{\partial \beta}\left(y_t \mid \vec{\mathbf{y}}_{t-1}^{\,J}; \beta_0\right) \frac{\partial \log f}{\partial \beta}\left(y_t \mid \vec{\mathbf{y}}_{t-1}^{\,J}; \beta_0\right)'\right]. \qquad (3.52)
\end{aligned}$$

When we combine (3.38), (3.51), and (3.52) and use the fact that if $X \sim N(0, \Sigma_X)$, then $AX \sim N(0, A\Sigma_X A')$, it follows that

$$\sqrt{T}(b_T^{\mathrm{ML}} - \beta_0) \Rightarrow N\left(0, -E\left[\frac{\partial^2 \log f}{\partial \beta \partial \beta'}\left(y_t \mid \vec{\mathbf{y}}_{t-1}^{\,J}; \beta_0\right)\right]^{-1}\right). \qquad (3.53)$$

In actual implementations of ML estimation, the asymptotic covariance
in (3.53) is replaced by its sample counterpart. From (3.52) it follows that
this matrix can be estimated either as the inverse of the sample mean of
the "outer product" of the likelihood scores or as minus the inverse of the
sample mean of the second-derivative matrix evaluated at b_T^{ML},

$$\left(-\frac{1}{T}\sum_{t=1}^{T}\frac{\partial^2 \log f}{\partial \beta \partial \beta'}\left(y_t \mid \vec{\mathbf{y}}_{t-1}^{\,J}; b_T^{\mathrm{ML}}\right)\right)^{-1}. \qquad (3.54)$$

---

[10] The second equality in (3.52) is an important property of conditional density functions
that follows from (3.49). By definition, (3.49) can be rewritten as

$$0 = \int \frac{\partial \log f}{\partial \beta}\left(y_t \mid \vec{\mathbf{y}}_{t-1}^{\,J}; \beta_0\right) f\left(y_t \mid \vec{\mathbf{y}}_{t-1}^{\,J}; \beta_0\right) dy_t.$$

Differentiating under the integral sign and using the chain rule gives

$$0 = E\left[\frac{\partial^2 \log f}{\partial \beta \partial \beta'}\left(y_t \mid \vec{\mathbf{y}}_{t-1}^{\,J}; \beta_0\right)\right] + E\left[\frac{\partial \log f}{\partial \beta}\left(y_t \mid \vec{\mathbf{y}}_{t-1}^{\,J}; \beta_0\right) \frac{\partial \log f}{\partial \beta}\left(y_t \mid \vec{\mathbf{y}}_{t-1}^{\,J}; \beta_0\right)'\right].$$

Assuming that the regularity conditions for Lemma 3.2 are satisfied by the likelihood score, we see that (3.54) converges to the covariance matrix of b_T^{ML} as $T \to \infty$.

The asymptotic covariance matrix of b_T^{ML} is the Cramer-Rao lower bound, the inverse of the so-called Hessian matrix. This suggests that, even though the ML estimator may be biased in small samples, as T gets large, the ML estimator is the most efficient estimator in the sense of having the smallest asymptotic covariance matrix among all consistent estimators of β_0. This is indeed the case and we present a partial proof of this result in Section 3.6.

3.5.2. GMM Estimation

Theorem 3.5 applies directly to the case of GMM estimators. The GMM estimator minimizes (3.25) so the regularity conditions for Theorem 3.5 require that $h(z_t, \theta)$ be differentiable, $\partial h(z_t, \theta)/\partial \theta$ be first-moment continuous at θ_0, and that W_T converge in probability to a constant, positive-semidefinite matrix W_0.

The first-order conditions to the minimization problem (3.25) are

$$\frac{\partial H_T(\theta_T)'}{\partial \theta} W_T H_T(\theta_T) = 0. \tag{3.55}$$

Therefore, the A_T implied by the GMM criterion function (3.25) is

$$A_T = \frac{\partial H_T(\theta_T)'}{\partial \theta} W_T. \tag{3.56}$$

By Lemma 3.2 and the assumption that W_T converges to W_0, it follows that A_T converges in probability to $A_0 = d_0' W_0$. Substituting this expression into (3.38), we conclude that $\sqrt{T}(\theta_T - \theta_0)$ converges in distribution to a normal with mean zero and covariance matrix

$$\Omega_0^{GMM} = \left(d_0' W_0 d_0\right)^{-1} d_0' W_0 \Sigma_0 W_0' d_0 \left(d_0' W_0' d_0\right)^{-1}. \tag{3.57}$$

If the probability limit of the distance matrix defining the GMM criterion function is chosen to be $W_0 = \Sigma_0^{-1}$, then (3.57) simplifies to

$$\Omega_0^{GMM} = \left(d_0' \Sigma_0^{-1} d_0\right)^{-1}. \tag{3.58}$$

We show in Section 3.6 that this choice of distance matrix is the optimal choice among GMM estimators constructed from linear combinations of the moment equation $E[h(z_t, \theta_0)] = 0$.

A consistent estimator of Ω_0^{GMM} is constructed by replacing all of the matrices in (3.57) or (3.58) by their sample counterparts. The matrix W_0

is estimated by W_T, the matrix used to construct the GMM criterion function, and d_0 is replaced by $\partial H_T(\theta_T)/\partial\theta$. The construction of a consistent estimator of Σ_0 depends on the degree of autocorrelation in $h(z_t, \theta_0)$. In Case $ACh(n - 1)$, with finite n, the autocovariances of h comprising Σ_0 are replaced by their sample counterparts using fitted $h(z_t, \theta_T)$ in place of $h(z_t, \theta_0)$:

$$\frac{1}{T} \sum_{t=j+1}^{T} h(z_t, \theta_T) h(z_{t-j}, \theta_T)'. \tag{3.59}$$

An asymptotically equivalent estimator is obtained by subtracting the sample mean from $h(z_t, \theta_T)$ before computing the sample autocovariances.

If, on the other hand, $n = \infty$ or n is very large relative to the sample size T, then an alternative approach to estimating Σ_0 is required. In Case $ACh(\infty)$, Σ_0 is given by (3.48). Letting $\Gamma_{h0}(j) = E[h_t h'_{t-j}]$, we proceed by constructing an estimator Σ_T as a weighted sum of the autocovariances that can feasibly be estimated with a finite sample of length T:

$$\Sigma_T = \frac{T}{T - K} \sum_{j=-T+1}^{T-1} k\left(\frac{j}{B_T}\right) \Gamma_{hT}(j), \tag{3.60}$$

where the sample autocovariances are given by

$$\Gamma_{hT}(j) = \begin{cases} \dfrac{1}{T} \displaystyle\sum_{t=j+1}^{T} h(z_t, \theta_T) h(z_{t-j}, \theta_T)' & \text{for } j \geq 0, \\[2em] \dfrac{1}{T} \displaystyle\sum_{t=-j+1}^{T} h(z_{t+j}, \theta_T) h(z_t, \theta_T)' & \text{for } j < 0, \end{cases} \tag{3.61}$$

and B_T is a "bandwidth" parameter discussed later. The scaling factor $T/(T - K)$ is a small-sample adjustment for the estimation of θ.

The function $k(\cdot)$, called a *kernel*, determines the weight given to past sample autocovariances in constructing Σ_T. The basic idea of this estimation strategy is that, for fixed j, sample size must increase to infinity for $\Gamma_{hT}(j)$ to be a consistent estimator of $\Gamma_{h0}(j)$. At the same time, the number of nonzero autocovariances in (3.60) must increase without bound for Σ_T to be a consistent estimator of Σ_0. The potential problem is that if terms are added proportionately as T gets large, then the number of products $h_t h'_{t-j}$ in the sample estimate of $\Gamma_{hT}(j)$ stays small regardless of the size of T. To avoid this problem, the kernel must be chosen so that the number of autocovariances included grows, but at a slower rate than T, so that the number of terms in each sample estimate $\Gamma_{hT}(j)$ increases to infinity.

Two popular kernels for estimating Σ_0 are

$$\text{Truncated} \quad k(x) = \begin{cases} 1 & \text{for } |x| \leq 1, \\ 0 & \text{otherwise,} \end{cases} \tag{3.62}$$

$$\text{Bartlett} \quad k(x) = \begin{cases} 1 - |x| & \text{for } |x| \leq 1, \\ 0 & \text{otherwise.} \end{cases} \tag{3.63}$$

For both of these kernels, the bandwidth B_T determines the number of autocovariances included in the estimation of Σ_T. In the case of the truncated kernel, all lags out to order B_T are included with equal weight. This is the kernel studied by White (1984). In the case of the Bartlett kernel, the autocovariances are given declining weights out to order $j \leq B_T$. Newey and West (1987b) show that, by using declining weights, the Bartlett kernel guarantees that Σ_T is positive-semidefinite. This need not be the case in finite samples for the truncated kernel. The choice of the bandwidth parameter B_T is discussed in Andrews (1991).

3.5.3. *Quasi-Maximum Likelihood Estimation*

The QML estimator is a special case of the GMM estimator. Specifically, continuing our discussion of the scalar process r_t with conditional mean μ_{rt-1} and variance σ_{rt-1}^2 that depend on the parameter vector θ, let the jth component of $h(z_t, \theta)$ be the score associated with θ_j:

$$h_j(z_t, \theta) \equiv -\frac{1}{2\sigma_{rt-1}^2(\theta)} \frac{\partial \sigma_{rt-1}^2(\theta)}{\partial \theta_j} + \frac{1}{2} \frac{(r_t - \mu_{rt-1}(\theta))^2}{\sigma_{rt-1}^4(\theta)} \frac{\partial \sigma_{rt-1}^2(\theta)}{\partial \theta_j}$$

$$+ \frac{(r_t - \mu_{rt-1}(\theta))}{\sigma_{rt-1}^2(\theta)} \frac{\partial \mu_{rt-1}(\theta)}{\partial \theta_j}, \quad j = 1, \dots, K. \tag{3.64}$$

The asymptotic distribution of the QML estimator is thus determined by the properties of $h(z_t, \theta_0)$. From (3.64) it is seen that $E[h_j(z_t, \theta_0)|I_{t-1}] = 0$; that is, $\{h(z_t, \theta_0)\}$ is an MDS. This follows from the observations that, after taking conditional expectations, the first and second terms cancel and the third term has a conditional mean of zero.

Therefore, the QML estimator θ_T^{QML} falls under Case AC$h(0)$ with $M = K$ (the number of moment equations equals the number of parameters) and

$$\sqrt{T}\left(\theta_T^{\text{QML}} - \theta_0\right) \Rightarrow N\left(0, \left(d_0^{\text{QML}}\right)^{-1} \Sigma_0 \left(d_0^{\text{QML}}\right)^{-1}\right), \tag{3.65}$$

where $\Sigma_0 = E[h(z_t, \theta_0)h(z_t, \theta_0)']$, with h given by (3.64), and

$$d_0^{\mathrm{QML}} = E\left[\frac{\partial^2 \log f_N}{\partial\theta\partial\theta'}(r_t|I_{t-1}; \theta_0)\right]. \qquad (3.66)$$

Though these components are exactly the same as in the case of full-information ML estimation, d_0^{QML} and Σ_0 are not related by (3.52), so (3.65) does not simplify further.

3.5.4. Linear Least-Squares Projection

The LLP estimator is the special case of the GMM estimator with $z_t' = (y_t, x_t')$, $h(z_t, \delta) = (y_t - x_t'\delta)x_t$, $A_0 = I_K$. Also,

$$d_0^{\mathrm{LLP}} = -E[x_t x_t'] \qquad (3.67)$$

and with $u_t \equiv (y_t - x_t'\delta_0)$, where δ_0 is the probability limit of the least-squares estimator δ_T,

$$\Sigma_0 = \sum_{j=-\infty}^{\infty} E[x_t u_t u_{t-j} x_{t-j}']. \qquad (3.68)$$

It follows that

$$\Omega_0^{\mathrm{LLP}} = E[x_t x_t']^{-1} \sum_{j=-\infty}^{\infty} E[x_t u_t u_{t-j} x_{t-j}']E[x_t x_t']^{-1}. \qquad (3.69)$$

In order to examine several special cases of LLP for forecasting the future, we assume that the variable being forecasted is dated $t + n$, $n \geq 1$, and let x_t denote the vector of forecast variables observed at date t:

$$y_{t+n} = x_t'\delta_0 + u_{t+n}. \qquad (3.70)$$

We consider several different assumptions about the projection error u_{t+n}. Unless otherwise noted, throughout the following discussion, the information set I_t denotes the information generated by current and past x_t and u_t.

Consider first Case ACh(0) with $n = 1$ and $E[u_{t+1}|I_t] = 0$. One circumstance where this case arises is when a researcher is interested in testing whether y_{t+1} is unforecastable given information in I_t (see Chapter 1). For instance, if we assume that x_t includes the constant 1 as the first component, and partitioning x_t as $x_t' = (1, \tilde{x}_t')$ and δ_0 conformably as $\delta_0' = (\delta_c, \delta_{\tilde{x}}')$, then this case implies that $E[y_{t+1}|I_t] = \delta_c$, $\delta_{\tilde{x}} = 0$, and y_{t+1} is unforecastable given past information about $\tilde{x}_t$ and y_t. The alternative hypothesis is that

$$E[y_{t+1}|I_t] = \delta_c + x_t'\delta_{\tilde{x}}, \tag{3.71}$$

with the (typical) understanding that the projection error under this alternative satisfies $E[u_{t+1}|I_t] = 0$. A more general alternative would allow $\delta_{\tilde{x}} \neq 0$ and the projection error u_{t+1} to be correlated with other variables in I_t. We examine this case later.

Since $d_0 = -E[x_t x_t']$ and this case fits into Case AC$h(0)$,

$$\sqrt{T}(\delta_T - \delta_0) \Rightarrow N\left(0, \Omega_0^{\mathrm{LLP}}\right), \tag{3.72}$$

where

$$\Omega_0^{\mathrm{LLP}} = E\left[x_t x_t'\right]^{-1} E\left[u_{t+1}^2 x_t x_t'\right] E\left[x_t x_t'\right]^{-1}. \tag{3.73}$$

Without further assumptions, Ω_0^{LLP} does not simplify. One simplifying assumption that is sometimes made is that the variance of u_{t+1} conditioned on I_t is constant:

$$E\left[u_{t+1}^2|I_t\right] = \sigma_u^2, \text{ a constant.} \tag{3.74}$$

Under this assumption, Σ_0 in (3.73) simplifies to $\sigma_u^2 E[x_t x_t']$ and

$$\Omega_0^{\mathrm{LLP}} = \sigma_u^2 E\left[x_t x_t'\right]^{-1}. \tag{3.75}$$

These characterizations of Ω_0^{LLP} are not directly applicable because the asymptotic covariance matrices are unknown (are functions of unknown population moments). Therefore, we replace these unknown moments with their sample counterparts. Let $\hat{u}_{t+1} \equiv (y_{t+1} - x_t'\delta_T)$. With the homoskedasticity assumption (3.74), the distribution of δ_T used for inference is

$$\delta_T \approx N\left(\delta_0, \Omega_T^{\mathrm{LLP}}\right), \tag{3.76}$$

where

$$\Omega_T^{\mathrm{LLP}} = \hat{\sigma}_u^2 \left(\sum_{t=1}^{T} x_t x_t'\right)^{-1}, \tag{3.77}$$

with $\hat{\sigma}_u^2 = (1/T)\sum_{t=1}^{T} \hat{u}_t^2$. This is, of course, the usual distribution theory used in the classical linear least-squares estimation problem. Letting $\hat{\sigma}_{\delta^i}$ denote the ith diagonal element of (3.77), we can test the null hypothesis $H_0 : \delta_0^i = \delta_0^{i*}$ using the distribution

$$\frac{\delta_T^i - \delta_0^{i*}}{\hat\sigma_{\delta^i}} \approx N(0, 1). \tag{3.78}$$

Suppose that we relax assumption (3.74) and let the conditional variance of u_{t+1} be time varying. Then Ω_0^{LLP} is given by (3.73) and now Σ_0 is estimated by

$$\Sigma_T = \frac{1}{T} \sum_{t=1}^{T} \hat{u}_{t+1}^2 x_t x_t', \tag{3.79}$$

and

$$\Omega_T^{\text{LLP}} = \left(\sum_{t=1}^{T} x_t x_t' \right)^{-1} \Sigma_T \left(\sum_{t=1}^{T} x_t x_t' \right)^{-1}. \tag{3.80}$$

Testing proceeds as before, but with a different calculation of $\hat\sigma_{\delta^i}$.

Next, consider Case $ACh(n-1)$ which has $n > 1$ and $E[u_{t+n}|I_t] = 0$. This case would arise, for example, in asking the question whether y_{t+n} is forecastable given information in I_t. For this case, d_0 is unchanged, but the calculation of Σ_0 is modified so that

$$\Omega_0^{\text{LLP}} = E[x_t x_t']^{-1} \left(\sum_{j=-n+1}^{n-1} E[u_{t+n} u_{t+n-j} x_t x_{t-j}'] \right) E[x_t x_t']^{-1}. \tag{3.81}$$

Analogously to the case $ACh(0)$, this expression simplifies further if the conditional variances and autocorrelations of u_t are constants.

To estimate the asymptotic covariance matrix for this case, we replace $E[x_t x_t']$ by $(1/T) \sum_{t=1}^{T} x_t x_t'$ and Σ_0 by

$$\Sigma_T = \sum_{j=-n+1}^{n-1} \frac{1}{T} \sum_{t=1}^{T} \hat{u}_{t+n} \hat{u}_{t+n-j} x_t x_{t-j}'. \tag{3.82}$$

Testing proceeds in exactly the same way as before.

3.6. Relative Efficiency of Estimators

The efficiency of an estimator can only be judged relative to an a priori set of restrictions on the joint distribution of the z_t that are to be used in estimation. These restrictions enter the formulation of a GMM estimator in two ways: through the choices of the h function and the A_0. The form of the asymptotic covariance matrix Ω_0 in (3.38) shows the dependence of the limiting distribution on both of these choices. In many circumstances, a researcher will have considerable latitude in choosing either A_0 or $h(z_t, \theta)$ or both. Therefore, a natural question is: Which is the most *efficient* GMM estimator among all admissible estimators? In this section, we characterize the optimal GMM estimator, in the sense of being most efficient or, equivalently, having the smallest asymptotic covariance matrix among all estimators that exploit the same information about the distribution of $\vec{z}_T$.

3.6.1. GMM Estimators

To highlight the dependence of the distributions of GMM estimators on the information used in specifying the moment equations, it is instructive to start with the conditional version of the moment equations underlying the GMM estimation,

$$\frac{1}{T} \sum_{t=1}^{T} A_t h(z_t, \theta_T) = 0, \tag{3.83}$$

where A_t is a (possibly random) $K \times M$ matrix in the information set I_t, and $h(z_t, \theta)$ is an $M \times 1$ vector, with $K \leq M$, satisfying

$$E\big[h(z_t; \theta_0)\big|I_t\big] = 0. \tag{3.84}$$

In this section, we will treat z_t as a generic random vector that is not presumed to be in I_t and, indeed, in all of the examples considered subsequently $z_t \notin I_t$.

Initially, we treat $h(z_t; \theta)$ as given by the asset pricing theory and, as such, not subject to the choice of the researcher. We also let

$$\mathcal{A} = \left\{ A_t \in I_t, \text{ such that } E\left[A_t \frac{\partial h(z_t; \theta_0)}{\partial \theta} \right] \text{ has full rank} \right\} \tag{3.85}$$

denote the class of admissible GMM estimators, where each estimator is indexed by the (possibly random) weights A_t. The efficiency question at hand is: In estimating θ_0, what is the optimal choice of A_t? (Which choice of A_t gives the smallest asymptotic covariance matrix for θ_T among all estimators based on matrices in $\mathcal{A}$?) The following lemma, based on the analysis in Hansen (1985), provides a general characterization of the optimal $A^* \in \mathcal{A}$.

Lemma 3.3. *Suppose that the assumptions of Theorem 3.5 are satisfied and $\{A_t\} \in \mathcal{A}$ is a stationary and ergodic process (jointly with z_t). Then the optimal choice $A^* \in \mathcal{A}$ satisfies*

$$\lim_{T \to \infty} T E\left[\left(\frac{1}{T}\sum_{t=1}^{T} A_t h(z_t, \theta_0)\right)\left(\frac{1}{T}\sum_{t=1}^{T} A_t^* h(z_t, \theta_0)\right)'\right]$$

$$= E\left[A_t \frac{\partial h(z_t; \theta_0)}{\partial \theta}\right] \equiv d_A. \tag{3.86}$$

Proof (Lemma 3.3). *Using arguments analogous to those in Theorem 3.5, one can show the asymptotic covariance matrix of any estimator $A \in \mathcal{A}$ to be*

$$\Omega_0^A = E\left[A_t \frac{\partial h(z_t; \theta_0)}{\partial \theta}\right]^{-1} \Sigma_0^A E\left[\frac{\partial h(z_t; \theta_0)'}{\partial \theta} A_t'\right]^{-1}, \tag{3.87}$$

where

$$\Sigma_0^A = \sum_{j=-\infty}^{\infty} E\left[A_t h(z_t; \theta_0) h(z_{t-j}; \theta_0)' A_{t-j}'\right]. \tag{3.88}$$

Define

$$D_T^A \equiv E\left[A_t \frac{\partial h(z_t; \theta_0)}{\partial \theta}\right]^{-1} \frac{1}{\sqrt{T}}\sum A_t h(z_t; \theta_0)$$

$$- E\left[A_t^* \frac{\partial h(z_t; \theta_0)}{\partial \theta}\right]^{-1} \frac{1}{\sqrt{T}}\sum A_t^* h(z_t; \theta_0), \tag{3.89}$$

and note that under assumption (3.86),

$$\lim_{T \to \infty} E\left[D_T^A \left(\frac{1}{\sqrt{T}}\sum h(z_t; \theta_0)' A_t^{*'}\right)\right] = 0. \tag{3.90}$$

It follows immediately that

$$\Omega_0^A = \lim_{T \to \infty} E\left[D_T^A D_T^{A'}\right] + \Omega_0^{A*}. \tag{3.91}$$

Since $E\left[D_T^A D_T^{A'}\right]$ is positive-semidefinite for all T, the lemma follows.

In applying Lemma 3.3 to our various estimation environments, consider first our basic GMM problem, where an asset pricing theory implies that $E[h(z_t, \theta_0)] = 0$. In this case, all we know about the distribution of z_t is that the unconditional mean of h is zero. Therefore, in examining the optimality question we must restrict attention to constant $A_t = A_0$, for all

t. In other words, the optimality question in this case is simply the optimal choice of the $K \times M$ matrix of constants A_0. Optimality condition (3.86) in this case is

$$A_0 \Sigma_0 A_0^{*\prime} = A_0 d_0, \tag{3.92}$$

and substitution verifies that $A^* \equiv d_0' \Sigma_0^{-1}$. This is the "optimal" GMM estimator proposed by Hansen (1982b), which gives the asymptotic covariance matrix

$$\Omega_0^{\text{FGMM}} = \left(d_0' \Sigma_0^{-1} d_0\right)^{-1}. \tag{3.93}$$

The superscript FGMM indicates that this is the asymptotic covariance matrix for the optimal GMM estimator based on the fixed set of moment conditions $E[h(z_t, \theta_0)] = 0$.

To relate this observation back to the standard GMM criterion function, expressed as a quadratic form in $H_T(\theta)$, recall that $A_0 = d_0' W_0$, where W_0 is the distance matrix in the GMM criterion function. It follows immediately that the optimal GMM estimator is obtained by setting $W_0 = \Sigma_0^{-1}$. Intuitively, since Σ_0 is the asymptotic covariance matrix of the sample moment $H_T(\theta_0)$, this choice of W_0 gives the most weight to those moment conditions that are most precisely estimated in the sense of having a small (asymptotic) variance.

Next, suppose that the asset pricing theory under investigation provides the stronger restriction that

$$E[h(z_t; \theta_0) | I_{t-1}] = 0, \tag{3.94}$$

where I_{t-1} includes current and past values of z_{t-1}. Here we have changed notation to make precise the model's implication that $z_t \in I_t$ and, given the conditioning in (3.94) on I_{t-1}, the admissible weight matrices A_{t-1} must be in I_{t-1}. Once again, we presume that the function h is fixed by the theory. However, in contrast to the previous case, since any $A_{t-1} \in I_{t-1}$ satisfies $E[A_{t-1} h(z_t; \theta_0)] = 0$, we have considerable latitude in choosing $\{A_t\}$. A_{t-1} can be an essentially arbitrary function of z_{t-1} and its history, and possibly the history of other variables in I_{t-1}. In spite of this latitude, there is a solution to the problem of choosing the optimal A_{t-1}. Direct substitution into (3.86) shows that

$$A_{t-1}^* = E\left[\frac{\partial h(z_t; \theta_0)'}{\partial \theta} \bigg| I_{t-1}\right] \times E\left[h(z_t; \theta_0) h(z_t; \theta_0)' \big| I_{t-1}\right]^{-1}. \tag{3.95}$$

Substituting A_{t-1}^* into (3.87), using the simplified notation $h_t \equiv h(z_t, \theta_0)$, gives the asymptotic covariance matrix

$$\Omega_0^{\text{OGMM}} = E\left(E\left[\frac{\partial h_t'}{\partial \theta} \,\middle|\, I_{t-1}\right] E[h_t h_t' | I_{t-1}]^{-1} E\left[\frac{\partial h_t}{\partial \theta} \,\middle|\, I_{t-1}\right]\right)^{-1}. \qquad (3.96)$$

See Hansen (1985) and Hansen et al. (1988) for further discussions of this case.

3.6.2. LLP Estimators

When we set out to estimate the coefficients of the optimal linear forecast of y_{t+n} based on x_t, we proceeded using the sample counterpart to the moment equation

$$E[(y_{t+n} - x_t'\delta_0)x_t] = 0, \qquad (3.97)$$

which defines the LLP. If all we know about the relation between y_{t+n} and x_t is that (3.97) is satisfied (by construction), then essentially the only estimation strategy available to the econometrician is LLP and the sample counterpart to (3.97) is solved for the least-squares estimator δ_T.

However linear DAPMs often imply that $E[u_{t+n}|I_t] = 0$ and, hence, that u_{t+n} is orthogonal to any (measurable) function of x_t and not just x_t. This leads immediately to the question of whether there is a more efficient estimator of δ_0 that exploits additional orthogonality conditions beyond (3.97). Hansen (1985) shows that the answer to this question is yes. Using his results and those in several subsequent papers, we examine this optimality question for two special cases: (1) $n = 1$ and u_{t+1} is (possibly) conditionally heteroskedastic, and (2) $n > 1$ and u_{t+n} is conditionally homoskedastic.

If $n = 1$, then we set $u_{t+1} = h(z_{t+1}, \delta_0) = (y_{t+1} - \delta_0'x_t)$ and construct the optimal GMM estimator based on the moment equation $E[u_{t+1}|I_t] = 0$. Instead of using the orthogonality of u_{t+1} and x_t to define the LLP estimator, we consider the larger class of estimators based on the moment equation

$$\frac{1}{T}\sum_{t=1}^{T} A_t u_{t+1}, \qquad (3.98)$$

where A_t is a $K \times 1$ vector whose elements are in I_t. Least squares is the optimal estimator of δ_0 if the optimal choice of A_t is $A_t^* = x_t$. From (3.95) it is seen that the A_t^* for the conditional moment restriction $E[u_{t+1}|I_t] = 0$ is constructed from the two components,

$$E\left[\frac{\partial h(z_{t+1}, \delta_0)}{\partial \delta} \,\middle|\, I_t\right] = -x_t, \quad \sigma_{ut}^2 \equiv E[u_{t+1}^2 | I_t], \qquad (3.99)$$

which gives

$$A_t^* = x_t/\sigma_{ut}^2. \qquad (3.100)$$

Thus, instead of ordinary least squares, the optimal estimator is obtained by scaling the regressors by the inverse of the conditional variance of u_{t+1}. To interpret this result, note that the population orthogonality condition used in estimation with A^* can be rewritten as

$$E\left[\left(\frac{y_{t+1}}{\sigma_{ut}} - \frac{x_t'}{\sigma_{ut}}\delta_0\right)\frac{x_t}{\sigma_{ut}}\right] = 0. \tag{3.101}$$

This is the moment equation obtained from the population least-squares objective function for the projection equation that is scaled by $1/\sigma_{ut}$:

$$\frac{y_{t+1}}{\sigma_{ut}} = \frac{x_t'}{\sigma_{ut}}\delta_0 + \frac{u_{t+1}}{\sigma_{ut}}, \tag{3.102}$$

or what is commonly referred to as *generalized least squares*. In practice, the optimal estimator is obtained by first scaling each observation by a consistent estimator of σ_{ut}, $\hat{\sigma}_t^2$ constructed using fitted residuals, and then proceeding with a standard linear projection. The asymptotic covariance matrix of this estimator is

$$\Omega_0^{*\text{LLP}} = E\left[\frac{x_t x_t'}{\sigma_{ut}^2}\right]^{-1}. \tag{3.103}$$

The reason for scaling becomes clear when we recognize that, if $n = 1$ and $\sigma_{ut}^2 = \sigma_u^2$, a constant (homoskedasticity), then least squares is the optimal estimation strategy; $A_t^* = x_t$. Thus, in the presence of heteroskedasticity, we first scale the regression equation to arrive at a homoskedastic model and then implement the optimal estimator for this case, least-squares.

From a practical point of view, implementation of the optimal GMM estimator based on A_t^* requires an estimate of σ_{ut}^2 (i.e., an estimate of how σ_t^2 depends on I_t). Our point of departure in constructing the optimal GMM estimator was that all we know from our DAPM is that u_{t+1} is mean-independent of I_t. Thus this optimality result based on (3.94) alone is a "limited-information" result in that it holds using any consistent estimator of σ_{ut}^2, including a nonparametric estimator (that does not presume knowledge of the functional form of σ_{ut}^2).

Of course, if it is known that σ_{ut}^2 is given, say, by $g(x_t, \gamma_0)$, then this information can be used in constructing A^*. However, in this case, there is the additional moment equation

$$E\left[u_{t+1}^2 - g(x_t, \gamma_0)\big|I_t\right] = 0, \tag{3.104}$$

which can be used in estimation. Indeed, the moment equations (3.94) and (3.104) can be combined and, using similar arguments, the associated optimal GMM estimator can be derived. In general, this is a more efficient estimator than the optimal estimator based on (3.94) alone. The weights for the optimal estimator based on both (3.94) and (3.104) involve the fourth conditional moments of u_{t+1}, which are also unknown (without further assumptions). So, with knowledge of (3.104), the limited information is pushed back to fourth moments.

These observations suggest an intermediate, suboptimal estimation strategy that might lead to some efficiency gains over a naive GMM estimator that completely ignores the nature of the A^*. For instance, if the functional form of g in (3.104) is unknown, then reasonable efficiency might be achieved by projecting u_{t+1}^2 onto variables that are expected to influence σ_{ut}^2 and then scaling the model by the square root of the fitted values from this projection. If this strategy is pursued, then the asymptotic covariance matrix should be constructed without assuming that the conditional variance of the scaled u_t is 1, since knowledge of the correct functional form for σ_{ut}^2 has not been assumed.

Up to this point, we have been discussing best forecasts that are linear with forecast errors that are mean-independent of an information set I_t. So it is of interest to inquire how the preceding discussion is altered for the case of LLP of y_t onto x_t,

$$y_t = x_t'\delta_0 + u_t, \tag{3.105}$$

where $x_t'\delta_0$ is the best linear, not best, predictor. Without further assumptions on the properties of u_t, the asymptotic covariance matrix of the LLP estimator θ_T is given by (3.69). Analogously to the case of heteroskedasticity, one would expect that a more efficient estimator of δ_0 than the least-squares estimator could be obtained given some knowledge of the form of any serial correlation in u_t. To highlight one widely studied example of such an efficiency gain, we will focus on an example of serial correlation with homoskedastic errors.

Consider the case where it is known a priori that u_t follows an autoregressive process of order p $(AR(p))$:

$$u_t = \rho_1 u_{t-1} + \ldots + \rho_p u_{t-p} + \epsilon_t \tag{3.106}$$

or, equivalently, $\rho(L)u_t = \epsilon_t$, where L is the lag operator ($L^s x_t = x_{t-s}$), and $\rho(L)$ is the polynomial

$$\rho(L) = 1 - \rho_1 L - \ldots - \rho_p L^p. \tag{3.107}$$

The roots of the polynomial (3.107) are assumed to lie outside the unit circle in the complex plane. Consistent with most treatments of serial correlation in the classical setting, it is assumed that

$$E[u_t | J] = 0, \quad J = \{x_t, x_{t\pm1}, x_{t\pm2}, \ldots\}, \tag{3.108}$$

and that $E[\epsilon_t | J] = \sigma_\epsilon^2$, a constant. Finally, the assumption that u_t is correctly specified as an AR(p) process is captured in the assumption that $E[\epsilon_t | J_{t-1}^*] = 0$, where $J_{t-1}^* = \{J, \epsilon_{t-1}, \epsilon_{t-2}, \ldots\}$.

Under these assumptions, $\rho(L)u_t = \epsilon_t$ is an MDS relative to the information set J_{t-1}^*. Therefore, finding the optimal set of instruments amounts to finding the optimal $K \times 1$ vector $a_t \in J_t^*$ satisfying

$$E[a_t \epsilon_{t+1}] = E[a_t \rho(L) u_{t+1}] = 0. \tag{3.109}$$

If we use the same logic as before and assume homoskedasticity, the optimal instrument vector is given by[11]

$$a_t^* = E\left[\frac{\partial \epsilon_{t+1}}{\partial \theta} \,\Big|\, J_t^*\right] = -\rho(L)x_t. \tag{3.110}$$

An identical set of moment equations is obtained by first transforming the linear projection equation by $\rho(L)$,

$$\rho(L)y_t = \rho(L)x_t'\delta_0 + \epsilon_t, \tag{3.111}$$

and then examining the first-order conditions for least-squares estimation of this transformed equation. Not surprisingly, the optimal GMM estimator is the generalized least-squares estimator in the presence of autoregressive autocorrelation.

This result can be derived directly using Lemma 3.3. According to this lemma, the optimal weight vector A^* for weighting u_t (not ϵ_t) satisfies

$$
\begin{aligned}
E[A_t x_t'] &= \sum_{j=-\infty}^{\infty} E[A_t u_t u_{t-j}(A_{t-j}^*)'] \\
&= E[\rho(L)^{-1} A_t \rho(L)^{-1}(A_t^*)'] \\
&= E[A_t \rho(L^{-1})^{-1} \rho(L)^{-1}(A_t^*)'].
\end{aligned}
\tag{3.112}
$$

The second equality is obtained, under our assumption of homoskedasticity, by normalizing the variance of ϵ_t to be 1 (absorbing the variance into the definition of ρ) and using stationarity of the series. The last equality is also

---

[11] With constant conditional variance, the scaling constant $1/\sigma_\epsilon$ can be ignored in computing the optimal instruments.

an implication of stationarity. It follows immediately that the optimal GMM estimator in this case is characterized by the instrument matrix

$$A_t^* = \rho(L^{-1})\rho(L)x_t. \tag{3.113}$$

This result gives rise to exactly the same moment equation as (3.110) because

$$E[\rho(L^{-1})\rho(L)x_t u_t] = E[\rho(L)x_t\rho(L)u_t] = E[\rho(L)x_t\epsilon_t], \tag{3.114}$$

owing to the stationarity of the $\{x_t\}$ process.[12]

The weight vector A_t^* is a linear function of current, past, and future x_t. It is orthogonal to u_t because u_t is mean-independent of all elements of the information set J. Clearly, in this case, it is not enough to assume that u_t is mean-independent of current or current and past x_t in order for A^* to give a consistent estimator.

An important practical limitation of these results on models with serially correlated errors is that they maintain the "exogeneity" assumption (3.108). A more typical situation arising in the context of asset pricing is that of Case AC$h(n-1)$ where u_{t+n} is mean-dependent of an information set I_t that does not include future values of variables. Moreover, the implied autocorrelation structure of u is that of an MA$(n-1)$ and not the autoregressive structure (3.106).

Hayashi and Sims (1983) and Hansen and Singleton (1990, 1996) provide an analogous optimality result that applies to this more relevant situation. To illustrate their results, we focus on the case of a scalar u_t [see Hansen and Singleton (1996) for a treatment of the vector case] and let

$$u_t = \alpha(L)\epsilon_t, \quad \alpha(L) = 1 + \alpha_1 L + \ldots + \alpha_{n-1}L^{n-1}, \tag{3.115}$$

and proceed assuming the DAPM implies that $E[u_{t+n}|I_t] = 0$ and that $E[\epsilon_{t+1}^2|I_t] = \sigma_\epsilon^2$, a constant (conditional homoskedasticity). The reason that the A^* given by (3.113) is not optimal for this setting is that u_{t+n} is orthogonal to x_s for $s \leq t$, but not for $s > t$. Therefore, using A^* in (3.113) would lead to an inconsistent estimator.

Analogously to the classical treatment of serial correlation in GLS estimation, we would like to "filter" the error u_{t+n} to remove its autocorrelation, and then apply the known optimal A^* for this filtered model. The

---

[12] Suppose, e.g., that $\rho(L) = 1 + \rho_1 L$ and define $y_t \equiv \rho(L)x_t$. Then (3.114) states that $E[(y_t + \rho_1 y_{t+1})u_t] = E[y_t(u_t + \rho_1 u_{t-1})]$. This is an immediate implication of the joint stationarity of y_t and u_t. A very similar equality plays a central role in generating simplified moment equations and inference in Chapter 9.

added complication in this setting is that the filtering must be done in a manner that preserves the mean-independence of the filtered error from I_t. We accomplish this using the "forward filter" $\lambda(L^{-1}) \equiv \alpha(L^{-1})^{-1}$, since $\lambda(L^{-1})u_{t+n}$ is serially uncorrelated and

$$E\left[\lambda\left(L^{-1}\right)u_{t+n}\big|I_t\right] = 0. \tag{3.116}$$

Pursuing the example of linear projection of y_{t+n} onto x_t, under homoskedasticity, the optimal instruments for estimation based on the conditional moment restriction (3.116) are given by $E[\lambda(L^{-1})x_t]$. As shown in Hansen and Singleton (1990), this is equivalent to using the instruments

$$A_t^* = \lambda(L)E\left[\lambda\left(L^{-1}\right)x_t\big|I_t\right] \tag{3.117}$$

for the original projection error u_{t+n}.

3.6.3. ML Estimators

Maximum likelihood estimation does not, in general, fit into any of the optimality results obtained so far because we have taken h to be a given $M \times 1$ vector. ML estimation can be viewed as the solution to the problem of finding the optimal h function to use in estimation. To see this, we start by observing that if we are free to choose the function h, then we might as well set $M = K$ as this is the number of moment equations needed in estimation. Second, since the moment restriction $E[h(z_t, \theta_0)|I_{t-1}] = 0$ implies the moment restriction $E[h(z_{t+n}, \theta_0)|I_{t-1}] = 0$, we presume that our asset pricing theory implies the stronger condition $E[h(z_t, \theta_0)|I_{t-1}] = 0$. That is, if we are free to choose an $h(z_{t+n}; \theta_0)$ that is mean-independent of I_{t-1}, for any $n \geq 0$, then our search can be restricted to the case of $n = 1$. As we proved in Section 3.5.1, one candidate h satisfying this conditional moment restriction is $h^*(z_t; \beta_0) \equiv \partial \log f(y_t|\vec{y}_{1t-1}^J; \beta_0)/\partial\beta$. This choice is indeed optimal, as the following argument shows.

Since we have K equations in the K unknowns $\theta(=\beta)$ and our focus is on the selection of h, we set $A_t = I_K$, for all t. Given an arbitrary h satisfying (3.94), the GMM estimator based on the fact that the unconditional mean of h is zero satisfies

$$\frac{1}{T}\sum_{t=1}^{T} h(z_t; \theta_T) = 0. \tag{3.118}$$

Applying Theorem 3.5 and Theorem 3.4 [to establish Condition (v)], we get

$$\sqrt{T}(\theta_T - \theta_0) \Rightarrow N\left(0, d_0^{-1}\Sigma_0\left(d_0'\right)^{-1}\right), \tag{3.119}$$

where $\Sigma_0 = E[h(z_t; \theta_0)h(z_t; \theta_0)']$. Next, define $D \equiv d_0^{-1}h - d_0^{*-1}h^*$, where we have suppressed the arguments to conserve on notation and used "$*$" to indicate the terms associated with ML estimation. Consider the expectation

$$E[Dh^{*\prime}] = d_0^{-1}E[hh^{*\prime}] + d_0^{*-1}d_0^*. \tag{3.120}$$

The counterpart for h to the optimality condition (3.86) is $E[hh^{*\prime}] = -d_0$, which can be verified by direct calculation.[13] Thus, D is orthogonal to $h^{*\prime}$. It follows that, taking the expected value of $D + d_0^{*-1}h^*$ times its transpose,

$$d_0^{-1}\Sigma_0 d_0^{-1} = E[D(z_t)D(z_t)'] - d_0^{*-1}, \tag{3.121}$$

where the last matrix is the Cramer-Rao lower bound achieved by the ML estimator. Since $E[DD']$ is positive-semidefinite, we conclude that the optimal choice of h is the score of the log-likelihood, h^*.

---

[13] Using the fact that the mean of $h(z_t, \theta_0)$ is zero, we have

$$0 = \int \frac{\partial h}{\partial \theta} f \, dy + \int h \frac{\partial f}{\partial \theta} \, dy,$$

which implies that $-d_0 = E[hh^{*\prime}]$.

Goodness-of-Fit and Hypothesis Testing

IN THIS CHAPTER we explore in more depth the testing of hypotheses implied by a DAPM. The types of hypotheses considered are separated into two categories: (1) overall goodness-of-fit tests of whether a model is consistent with the data, in a sense that we make precise, and (2) tests of constraints on the parameters in a DAPM. For the purposes of this chapter we focus on classical testing in a stationary and ergodic statistical environment. The new problems induced by time trends and applications of Bayesian methods are discussed in the context of specific empirical issues.

4.1. GMM Tests of Goodness-of-Fit

In the context of GMM estimation, the sample criterion function is constructed from sample counterparts to the M moment conditions $E[h(z_t, \theta_0)] = 0$, namely $H_T(\theta_T) = (1/T) \sum_t h(z_t, \theta_T) = 0$. When $M > K$, there are more moment conditions than unknown parameters and, consequently, estimation proceeds by minimizing the GMM criterion function $Q_T(\theta) = H_T(\theta)' \Sigma_T^{-1} H_T(\theta)$, where the distance matrix has been chosen optimally as discussed in Chapter 3. In minimizing $Q_T(\theta)$ over the choice of $\theta \in \Theta$, the GMM estimator is chosen to set K linear combinations of the M sample moment conditions H_T to zero (the K first-order conditions):

$$\frac{\partial H_T(\theta_T)'}{\partial \theta} \Sigma_T^{-1} H_T(\theta_T) = 0. \tag{4.1}$$

Yet, if the model is correctly specified, all M sample moment equations $H_T(\theta_T)$ should be close to zero. This observation suggests that we can construct a goodness-of-fit test of the model by examining whether linear combinations of $H_T(\theta_T)$ that are not set to zero in estimation are in fact close to zero.

Conveniently, it turns out that the minimized value of the GMM criterion function, scaled by sample size, $TQ_T(\theta_T)$ is a goodness-of-fit test based on this observation. Under the null hypothesis that the model is correctly specified, $TQ_T(\theta_T)$ is asymptotically distributed as a chi-square distribution with $M-K$ degrees of freedom (Hansen, 1982b). To show this, we let d_T denote the partial derivative of $H_T(\theta_T)$ appearing in (4.1) and $\overset{a}{=}$ denote asymptotic equivalence, and note that, by a standard mean-value expansion,

$$\sqrt{T}H_T(\theta_T) \overset{a}{=} \sqrt{T}H_T(\theta_0) + d_T\sqrt{T}(\theta_T - \theta_0). \tag{4.2}$$

Furthermore, from the proof of Theorem 3.5, it follows that

$$\sqrt{T}(\theta_T - \theta_0) \overset{a}{=} -\left(d_T'\Sigma_T^{-1}d_T\right)^{-1}d_T'\Sigma_T^{-1}\sqrt{T}H_T(\theta_0). \tag{4.3}$$

Substituting (4.3) into (4.2) gives

$$\sqrt{T}H_T(\theta_T) \overset{a}{=} \left(I - d_0\left(d_0'\Sigma_0^{-1}d_0\right)^{-1}d_0'\Sigma_0^{-1}\right)\sqrt{T}H_T(\theta_0), \tag{4.4}$$

where d_0 is the probability limit of d_T.

Next, since Σ_0 is positive-definite, it can be factored as C_0C_0', with C_0 satisfying $C_0^{-1}\Sigma_0 C_0^{-1'} = I$. Letting $C_T C_T'$ denote the corresponding factorization of Σ_T, it follows from (4.4) that

$$\sqrt{T}C_T^{-1}H_T(\theta_T) \overset{a}{=} \left(I - C_0^{-1}d_0\left(d_0'\Sigma_0^{-1}d_0\right)^{-1}d_0'C_0^{-1'}\right)\sqrt{T}C_0^{-1}H_T(\theta_0). \tag{4.5}$$

By construction, the last term in (4.5), $\sqrt{T}C_0^{-1}H_T(\theta_0)$, converges in distribution to a $N(0, I)$. Furthermore, the matrix premultiplying this term, $[I - C_0^{-1}d_0(d_0'\Sigma_0^{-1}d_0)^{-1}d_0'C_0^{-1'}]$, is idempotent with rank $M-K$.[1] Therefore,[2]

$$TH_T(\theta_T)'\Sigma_T^{-1}H_T(\theta_T) \Rightarrow \chi^2_{M-K}, \tag{4.6}$$

where χ^2_{M-K} denotes the chi-square distribution with $M-K$ degrees of freedom.

The matrix $[I - C_0^{-1}d_0(d_0'\Sigma_0^{-1}d_0)^{-1}d_0'C_0^{-1'}]$ premultiplying $\sqrt{T}C_0^{-1}H_T(\theta_0)$ in (4.5) determines the linear combination of $C_0^{-1}H_T(\theta_0)$ that is being

---

[1] A matrix A is idempotent if $A^2 = A$. The rank of an idempotent matrix is equal to its trace. In this case,

$$\text{Tr}\left(I_M - C_0^{-1}d_0\left(d_0'\Sigma_0^{-1}d_0\right)^{-1}d_0'C_0^{-1'}\right) = M - \text{Tr}\left[\left(d_0'\Sigma_0^{-1}d_0\right)^{-1}\left(d_0'C_0^{-1'}C_0^{-1}d_0\right)\right]$$

$$= M - K.$$

[2] If the M-dimensional vector $x \sim N(0, I)$ and A is an idempotent matrix with rank K, then $x'Ax \sim \chi^2_K$.

tested. Premultiplying the left-hand side of (4.5) by $d'_T C'^{-1}_T$ gives the first-order conditions for the GMM estimator, while premultiplying the right-hand side of this expression by $\text{plim}(d'_T C'^{-1}_T) = d'_0 C'^{-1}_0$ gives zero. Thus, the matrix determining the linear combination of the moment conditions being tested is singular with rank equal to (at most) $M - K$. This is because K linear combinations of $H_T(\theta_T)$ are set to zero in estimation.

In assessing goodness-of-fit, there is typically no presumption that the most likely departures from the null hypothesis that the model is true are in the "direction" captured by the linear combination in (4.5). In particular, this statistic is not the most natural choice when one believes that a particular subset of the original M moment equations defined by $h(z_t, \theta)$ (or a specific linear combination of these moment equations) is the likely source of any model misspecification. In such circumstances, a direct test of these moment equations is of interest. There are several convenient test procedures for hypotheses about specific moment conditions, and the choice of which to implement often depends on whether the model is estimated under the null hypothesis, the alternative hypothesis, or both. We discuss each of these cases in turn.

Suppose we are interested in testing $H_0 : E[h_2(z_t, \theta_0)] = 0$,[3] where $h(z_t, \theta_0)$ factors as

$$h(z_t, \theta_0) = \begin{bmatrix} h_1(z_t, \theta_{10}) \\ h_2(z_t, \theta_0) \end{bmatrix}, \tag{4.7}$$

the subvectors h_1 and h_2 of h have dimensions M_1 and M_2, and $\theta'_0 = (\theta'_{10}, \theta'_{20})$ with θ_{10} and θ_{20} having dimensions K_1 and K_2, respectively. We proceed viewing the null hypothesis as $H_0 : E[h(z_t, \theta_0)] = 0$, and the alternative as $H_1 : E[h_1(z_t, \theta_{10})] = 0$; that is, in testing H_0, we maintain the assumption that h_1 has mean zero under both the null and alternative hypotheses.

For it to be feasible to estimate the parameters of the model under the alternative, it must be the case that $M_1 \geq K_1$. We let θ_{1T} denote the GMM estimator of θ_{10} based on the minimization of $H_{1T}(\theta_1)'(\Sigma_{11,T})^{-1}H_{1T}(\theta_1)$, where $H_{1T}(\theta_1) = (1/T)\sum_t h_1(z_t, \theta_1)$ and $\Sigma_{11,T}$ is a consistent estimator of the asymptotic covariance matrix of $\sqrt{T}H_{1T}(\theta_{10})$. Similarly, for the null hypothesis about h_2 to be interesting, it must be the case that $M_2 > K_2$. Were this not true, we would have a situation where the M_2 moment equations represented by h_2 were just sufficient or insufficient to estimate the K_2 parameters that appear in θ_0 but are distinct from θ_{10}. In this case, the knowledge that the mean of h_2 is zero does not lead to testable restrictions on

---

[3] This discussion of testing subsets of moment equations is based on Appendix C of Eichenbaum et al. (1988).

the data. Finally, we let θ_T denote the usual GMM estimator that minimizes $H_T(\theta)'\Sigma_T^{-1}H_T(\theta)$.

4.1.1. GMM Tests with Estimates under H_0 and H_1

A statistic for testing H_0, proposed by Eichenbaum et al. (1988), is[4]

$$TH_T(\theta_T)'\Sigma_T^{-1}H_T(\theta_T) - TH_{1T}(\theta_{1T})'\Sigma_{11,T}^{-1}H_{1T}(\theta_{1T}), \qquad (4.8)$$

where

$$\Sigma_0 = \begin{bmatrix} \Sigma_{11,0} & \Sigma_{12,0} \\ \Sigma_{21,0} & \Sigma_{22,0} \end{bmatrix} \qquad (4.9)$$

is a partition of Σ_0 conformable with the partition of h. The motivation for this statistic is that it is a measure of how much the GMM criterion function increases owing to imposition of H_0 over and above the assumption that $E[h_1(z_t, \theta_{10})] = 0$. In other words, maintaining the auxiliary assumption that h_1 has mean zero, one estimates the parameters with and without the moment conditions under H_0 imposed, and uses (4.8) as a measure of the degree to which imposing H_0 makes it difficult to get the criterion function close to zero.

Under H_0 the test statistic (4.8) is asymptotically distributed as $\chi^2_{(M_2 - K_2)}$. To see this, factor Σ_0^{-1} as $C_0'C_0$ and $\Sigma_{11,0}^{-1}$ as $C_1'C_1$. Then, using the same logic as before,

$$\sqrt{T}C_0H_T(\theta_0) \Rightarrow N(0, I_M); \quad \sqrt{T}C_1H_{1T}(\theta_{10}) \Rightarrow N(0, I_{M_1}). \qquad (4.10)$$

Define

$$\sqrt{T}\left(I_M - C_0 d_0(d_0'\Sigma_0^{-1} d_0)^{-1} d_0'C_0'\right) C_0 H_T(\theta_0) \equiv \sqrt{T}S_0 C_0 H_T(\theta_0), \qquad (4.11)$$

$$d_0 = E\left[\frac{\partial h(z_t, \theta_0)}{\partial \theta}\right], \qquad (4.12)$$

$$\sqrt{T}\left(I_{M_1} - C_1 d_{10}\left(d_{10}'\Sigma_{11,0}^{-1} d_{10}\right)^{-1} d_{10}'C_1'\right) C_1 H_{1T}(\theta_{10}) \equiv \sqrt{T}S_1 C_1 H_{1T}(\theta_{10}), \qquad (4.13)$$

$$d_{10} = E\left[\frac{\partial h_1(z_t, \theta_{10})}{\partial \theta_1}\right], \qquad (4.14)$$

---

[4] This is a GMM counterpart to a similar test of nonlinear restrictions on parameters proposed by Gallant and Jorgenson (1979) for instrumental variables estimators.

and note that the matrices S_0 and S_1 are idempotent with ranks $M - K$ and $M_1 - K_1$, respectively. When we use these intermediate results, it follows that (4.8) has the same limiting distribution as

$$TH_T(\theta_0)' C_0' \left(S_0 - (C_0')^{-1} \begin{bmatrix} I_{M_1} \\ 0 \end{bmatrix} C_1' S_{11,0} C_1 [I_{M_1} \, 0] \, C_0^{-1} \right) C_0 H_T(\theta_0), \quad (4.15)$$

where the center matrix in parentheses is idempotent with rank $M_2 - K_2 = (M - K) - (M_1 - K_1)$.[5] Thus, the proposed test statistic is asymptotically distributed as a $\chi^2_{M_2 - K_2}$.

At a practical level, it is important to choose the estimators of the two distance matrices in (4.8) so that this statistic is guaranteed to be nonnegative. This need not be the case if one proceeds with a standard two-step GMM procedure of computing consistent estimators of the parameters with a suboptimal distance matrix in the first step and then reoptimizing with an estimator of the optimal distance matrix. In this case, the matrices $\Sigma_{11,T}$ and Σ_T are evaluated at different values of θ_T, and (4.8) may be negative. To avoid this possibility, one can select $\Sigma_{11,T}$ to be the upper-left block of Σ_T. That is, the estimated distance matrix under the null is used in estimating the distance matrix under the alternative.

4.1.2. GMM Tests with Estimates under H_1

An alternative approach to testing a subset of moment restrictions is to introduce a set of auxiliary parameters that define the alternative of nonzero moments and test whether the values of these parameters are zeros. To illustrate this approach, suppose that the null hypothesis is that $E[h(z_t, \theta_{10})] = 0$, where now the entire vector h is assumed to be determined by the parameter vector θ_{10}. Under the alternative hypothesis, the augmented parameter vector is $\theta_0' = (\theta_{10}', \lambda_0')$, where $\dim(\lambda_0) = \dim(h_2) = M_2$, and

$$h(z_t, \theta_0) = \begin{bmatrix} h_1(z_t, \theta_{10}) \\ h_2(z_t, \theta_{10}) - \lambda_0 \end{bmatrix} \quad (4.16)$$

is assumed to satisfy $E[h(z_t, \theta_0)] = 0$. With the alternative specified in terms of (4.16), the null hypothesis can be expressed as $H_0 : \lambda_0 = 0$. In

---

[5] That the rank is $M_2 - K_2$ is verified as follows:

$$\text{Tr}(S_0) = M - K;$$

$$\text{Tr} \left[(C_0')^{-1} \begin{bmatrix} I_{M_1} \\ 0 \end{bmatrix} C_1' S_1 C_1 [I_{M_1} \, 0] \, C_0^{-1} \right] = \text{Tr} \left[C_1' S_1 C_1 \Sigma_{11,0} \right]$$

$$= \text{Tr}[S_1] = M_1 - K_1$$

constructing this test, the moment conditions are ordered in h so that the last M_2 moments comprising h_2 are those whose validity are in doubt.

A test of H_0 can be implemented by first computing GMM estimates of θ_0, θ_T, and then testing whether the subvector λ_0 is zero. Using the fact that $\sqrt{T}(\theta_T - \theta_0) \Rightarrow N(0, \Omega_0)$, we find that the limiting distribution of $\lambda_T = [0_{M_2 \times K} \, I_{M_2}] \theta_T$ is

$$\sqrt{T}(\lambda_T - \lambda_0) \Rightarrow N\left(0, \left[0 \, I_{M_2}\right]\Omega_0\left[0 \, I_{M_2}\right]'\right) \equiv N(0, \Omega_{\lambda 0}). \qquad (4.17)$$

It follows that, under H_0,[6]

$$T \lambda_T' \Omega_{\lambda T}^{-1} \lambda_T \Rightarrow \chi_{M_2}^2. \qquad (4.18)$$

The degrees of freedom in (4.15) and (4.18), $M_2 - K_2$ versus M_2, are different because of the way the alternatives have been formulated for these two testing problems. In the first case, we are testing whether the second M_2 moment equations are satisfied, but we lose K_2 degrees of freedom owing to the need to estimate the K_2 parameters θ_{20}. In the second approach, we presume that all K_1 model parameters in θ_{10} are estimable using the moment equations defined by h_1. This renders the entire set of M_2 moment constraints defined by h_2 testable. In the case of (4.15), if $K_2 = 0$ (equivalently, there are no parameters determining h_2 that do not determine h_1), then the degrees of freedom of these two tests are identical.

4.1.3. GMM Tests with Estimates under H_0

Pursuing the testing problem in the preceding subsection, we can also conduct a test based on estimates obtained under the null hypothesis. Specifically, let θ_T denote the GMM estimator of the K-dimensional vector θ_0 obtained based on minimization of the criterion function $H_{1T}(\theta)'(\Sigma_{11,T})^{-1} H_{1T}(\theta)$, where $\dim h_1(z_t, \theta) = M_1$. Suppose we are interested in testing the null hypothesis $H_0 : E[h_2(z_t, \theta_0)] = 0$, where $\dim h_2(z_t, \theta) = M_2$; that is, we wish to test whether the M_2 moment equations associated with h_2 are satisfied.

We can construct a test of H_0 by examining the distribution of $H_{2T}(\theta_T) = (1/T) \sum_t h_2(z_t, \theta_T)$. If we define

$$d_{20} = E\left[\frac{\partial h_2(z_t, \theta_0)}{\partial \theta}\right], \qquad (4.19)$$

---

[6] Here we use the result that, if the ℓ-dimensional vector $X \sim N(0, \Omega)$, and Ω is nonsingular, then $X'\Omega^{-1}X \sim \chi_\ell^2$.

a standard mean-value expansion of H_{2T} gives

$$\frac{1}{\sqrt{T}} \sum_{t=1}^{T} h_2(z_t, \theta_T) \stackrel{a}{=} \frac{1}{\sqrt{T}} \sum_{t=1}^{T} h_2(z_t, \theta_0) + d_{20}\sqrt{T}(\theta_T - \theta_0) \qquad (4.20)$$

$$\stackrel{a}{=} (C_1, I_{M_2}) \frac{1}{\sqrt{T}} \sum_{t=1}^{T} h(z_t, \theta_0) \equiv A \frac{1}{\sqrt{T}} \sum_{t=1}^{T} h(z_t, \theta_0), \qquad (4.21)$$

where $C_1 \equiv d_{20}(d_{10}' \Sigma_{11,0}^{-1} d_{10})^{-1} d_{10}' \Sigma_{11,0}^{-1}$ and $h' = (h_1', h_2')$. It follows that

$$\frac{1}{\sqrt{T}} \sum_{t=1}^{T} h_2(z_t, \theta_T) \Rightarrow N(0, A\Sigma_0 A') \qquad (4.22)$$

under the null hypothesis. This result can be used to construct a chi-square test of the M_2 moment equations defined by h_2 or of any subset of these moment restrictions.

A related circumstance where this testing problem arises is when a researcher has estimated the K parameters θ_0 using M moment equations defined by a function h and they wish to test, say, whether the mean of the ith component of h is zero: $H_0 : E[h_i(z_t, \theta_0)] = 0$. In general, the first-order conditions (4.1) to the GMM estimation problem do not set any of the individual sample moments $(1/T) \sum_t h_i(z_t, \theta_T)$ to zero. So a test based on this sample moment is in fact meaningful. Letting ι_i denote the selection vector with unity in the ith position and zeros elsewhere, we obtain the asymptotic distribution of this moment equation by premultiplying (4.4) by ι_i' and using the fact that the asymptotic distribution of $\sqrt{T}H_T(\theta_0)$ is $N(0, \Sigma_0)$.

4.2. Testing Restrictions on θ_0

Having settled on a model, researchers are often interested in testing hypotheses about the values of specific parameters. Depending on the criterion function used in estimation, a variety of procedures for testing hypotheses about θ_0 are available. In discussing these tests, it is again useful to classify tests according to whether they involve estimation of θ_0 under the null, the alternative, or both. Additional discussion of tests of parameter restrictions in a GMM setting can be found in Newey and West (1987a) and Eichenbaum et al. (1988).

4.2.1. Estimation under H_0 and H_1: LR-Style Tests

Suppose that the model provides a full characterization of the conditional density function $f(y_t|\vec{y}_{t-1}^J; \beta_0)$. Also, let b_T and $\tilde{b}_T$ denote the ML estimates of β_0 under the alternative and null hypotheses (the unconstrained and constrained estimates), respectively. Then a convenient statistic for testing constraints on a model's parameters is the *likelihood ratio* or LR statistic

$$\mathrm{LR}_T = -2\log\left(\frac{L(\tilde{b}_T)}{L(b_T)}\right). \tag{4.23}$$

The motivation for this measure of the fit of the constraints is that if the constraints are valid, then $L(\tilde{b}_T)$ and $L(b_T)$ should be approximately equal, whereas if the constraints are not valid then $L(\tilde{b}_T)$ is significantly smaller than $L(b_T)$.

For the case of LR tests, we suppose that the constraints can be written as $\beta_0 = R(\alpha_0)$, where $R : \mathbb{R}^{K-r} \to \mathbb{R}^K$ and $\dim \alpha_0 = K - r$. In other words, the unconstrained K-vector β_0 can be expressed as a function of $K - r$ parameters α_0. The number of constraints is then r.

From the mean-value expansion of the log-likelihood function,

$$l_T(b_T) = l_T(\beta_0) + \frac{\partial l_T}{\partial \beta}(b_0)(b_T - \beta_0) \tag{4.24}$$

$$+ \frac{1}{2}(b_T - \beta_0)'\frac{\partial^2 l_T}{\partial\beta\partial\beta'}\left(b_T^\#\right)(b_T - \beta_0),$$

for some intermediate value $b_T^\#$, it follows that

$$l_T(b_T) - l_T(\beta_0) \overset{a}{\approx} \frac{1}{2}(b_T - \beta_0)'\Omega_0^\beta(b_T - \beta_0), \tag{4.25}$$

where

$$\Omega_0^\beta = \mathrm{plim}_{T\to\infty}\frac{\partial^2 l_T}{\partial\beta\partial\beta'}(\beta_0).$$

Similarly, expanding under the constraints gives

$$l_T(\alpha_T) - l_T(\alpha_0) \overset{a}{\approx} \frac{1}{2}(\alpha_T - \alpha_0)'\Omega_0^\alpha(\alpha_T - \alpha_0). \tag{4.26}$$

The asymptotic distributions of $b_T - \beta_0$ and $\alpha_T - \alpha_0$ are derived from the mean-value expansions of the first-order conditions from maximizing the associated l_T,

$$\sqrt{T}(b_T - \beta_0) \overset{a}{\approx} \left(\Omega_0^\beta\right)^{-1}\frac{1}{\sqrt{T}}\sum_t\frac{\partial\log f}{\partial\beta}(y_t|\vec{y}_{t-1}^{\,J}, \beta_0), \tag{4.27}$$

$$\sqrt{T}(\alpha_T - \alpha_0) \overset{a}{\approx} \left(\Omega_0^\alpha\right)^{-1}\frac{\partial R(\alpha_0)'}{\partial\alpha}\frac{1}{\sqrt{T}}\sum_t\frac{\partial\log f}{\partial\theta}(y_t|\vec{y}_{t-1}^{\,J}, \alpha_0).$$

The term $\partial R(\alpha_0)/\partial \alpha$ comes from substituting $R(\alpha)$ for β and then maximizing $l_T(R(\alpha))$ by choice of α.

Combining these various expansions, and letting $\Omega = \Omega^{1/2}\Omega^{1/2\prime}$ denote the usual factorization of a positive-definite matrix, we can express $\text{LR}_T = 2T[l_T(b_T) - l_T(\alpha_T)]$ as

$$\text{LR}_T \overset{a}{\approx} T\frac{\partial l_T}{\partial \beta}(\beta_0)'\left[\left(\Omega_0^{\beta}\right)^{-1} - \frac{\partial R(\alpha_0)'}{\partial \alpha}\left(\Omega_0^{\alpha}\right)^{-1}\frac{\partial R(\alpha_0)'}{\partial \alpha}\right]\frac{\partial l_T}{\partial \beta}(\beta_0) \quad (4.28)$$

$$= T\frac{\partial l_T}{\partial \beta}(\beta_0)'\left(\Omega_0^{\beta}\right)^{-1/2}S\left(\Omega_0^{\beta'}\right)^{-1/2}\frac{\partial l_T}{\partial \beta}(\beta_0), \quad (4.29)$$

where the matrix

$$S \equiv \left[I - \left(\Omega_0^{\beta}\right)^{1/2}\frac{\partial R(\alpha_0)}{\partial \alpha}\left(\Omega_0^{\alpha}\right)^{-1}\frac{\partial R(\alpha_0)'}{\partial \alpha}\left(\Omega^{\beta'}\right)^{1/2}\right] \quad (4.30)$$

is idempotent with rank r.[7] Since $\sqrt{T}\partial l_T(\beta_0)/\partial \beta \Rightarrow N(0, \Omega_0^{\beta})$, it follows that $\text{LR}_T \Rightarrow \chi_r^2$.

When the conditional distribution of the variables in the model is not known, there is an analogous test based on the GMM criterion function (Eichenbaum et al., 1988). Suppose that the null and alternative hypotheses are[8]

$$H_0 : R(\theta_0) = 0, \quad H_1 : R(\theta_0) \neq 0, \quad (4.31)$$

where $R : \mathbb{R}^K \to \mathbb{R}^r$, $r < K$. Let θ_T denote the usual, unconstrained GMM estimator of θ_0 and let $\tilde{\theta}_T$ be the minimizer of

$$H_T(\theta)'\Sigma_T^{-1}H_T(\theta) \quad \text{such that} \quad R(\theta_T) = 0. \quad (4.32)$$

Then an immediate implication of our discussion of LR-style tests in a GMM setting is that

$$T\left[H_T(\tilde{\theta}_T)'\Sigma_T^{-1}H_T(\tilde{\theta}_T) - H_T(\theta_T)'\Sigma_T^{-1}H_T(\theta_T)\right] \Rightarrow \chi_r^2, \quad (4.33)$$

where $r = M - (K - r) - (M - K)$.

That this test procedure is a special case of the procedure for testing the validity of orthogonality conditions follows from the observation that the orthogonality conditions associated with the constraint $R(\theta_0) = 0$ are

---

[7] The rank of $\left((\Omega_0^{\beta})^{1/2\prime}S(\Omega_0^{\alpha})^{-1}S'(\Omega_0^{\beta})^{1/2}\right)$ is $K - r$.

[8] This is a slightly more general formulation of the testing problem than what we considered in discussing the LR statistic.

not random. Thus, in the notation of (4.9), we can partition a consistent estimator of the asymptotic covariance matrix of the moment equations as

$$\begin{bmatrix} \Sigma_T & 0 \\ 0 & 0 \end{bmatrix}, \tag{4.34}$$

where Σ_T is an estimator of the asymptotic covariance matrix of $\sqrt{T} H_T(\theta_0)$. Substitution of (4.34) into (4.8) leads to the statistic (4.33). The same practical considerations with regard to the estimation of the distance matrices in (4.33) apply as well.

Specializing to the classical linear regression model, $y_t = x_t' \delta_0 + u_t$, if $u_t \sim N(0, \sigma_u^2)$, then the likelihood function to be maximized is

$$L(\vec{y}_T \mid \vec{x}_T) = \left(\frac{1}{2\pi \sigma_u^2} \right)^{T/2} \exp \left\{ -\frac{1}{2\sigma_u^2} \sum_t (y_t - x_t' \delta)^2 \right\}. \tag{4.35}$$

The first-order condition for σ_u^2 is

$$\sigma_{uT}^2 = \frac{1}{T} \sum_t (y_t - x_t' \delta_T)^2. \tag{4.36}$$

Substituting this expression back into L gives the "concentrated" likelihood function

$$L(\vec{y}_T \mid \vec{x}_T) = (2\pi \sigma_{uT}^2)^{-T/2} \exp\{-T/2\}, \tag{4.37}$$

where σ_{uT}^2 is viewed as a function of δ. Therefore, the ratio of the constrained and unconstrained maximized likelihood functions is

$$\frac{(2\pi \tilde{\sigma}_{uT}^2)^{-T/2} e^{-T/2}}{(2\pi \sigma_{uT}^2)^{-T/2} e^{-T/2}} \tag{4.38}$$

and the LR statistic is

$$\text{LR}_T = T \log (\tilde{\sigma}_{uT}^2 / \sigma_{uT}^2). \tag{4.39}$$

4.2.2. Estimation Only under H_1: Wald Tests

Suppose a GMM estimator of θ_0, say θ_T, has been computed under the alternative, the unconstrained model, and one is interested in testing the null hypothesis $H_0 : R(\theta_0) = 0$, where $R : \mathbb{R}^K \to \mathbb{R}^r$. This can be accomplished by deriving the asymptotic distribution of $R(\theta_T)$ and checking to see whether $R(\theta_T)$ is close to zero. This test procedure is called a *Wald* test. As it is based on estimates obtained only under the alternative, it is a particularly convenient test statistic to use in circumstances where estimation under the null hypothesis is computationally demanding.

More precisely, a mean-value expansion gives

$$R(\theta_T) = R(\theta_0) + \frac{\partial R}{\partial \theta}\left(\theta_T^{\#}\right)(\theta_T - \theta_0) \tag{4.40}$$

for some intermediate value $\theta_T^{\#}$. If we assume that $\sqrt{T}(\theta_T - \theta_0) \Rightarrow N(0, \Omega_0)$, it follows that

$$\sqrt{T}\left[R(\theta_T) - R(\theta_0)\right] \Rightarrow N\left(0, \frac{\partial R}{\partial \theta}(\theta_0)\Omega_0\frac{\partial R}{\partial \theta}(\theta_0)'\right) \tag{4.41}$$

and, hence, that

$$TR(\theta_T)' \left(\frac{\partial R}{\partial \theta}(\theta_T)\Omega_T\frac{\partial R}{\partial \theta}(\theta_T)'\right)^{-1} R(\theta_T) \Rightarrow \chi_r^2. \tag{4.42}$$

An important special case is when the null hypothesis involves linear constraints on θ_0 for $r \times k$ matrix C and $r \times 1$ vector c,

$$R(\theta_0) = C\theta_0 - c. \tag{4.43}$$

The derivative of R with respect to θ is simply C, and (4.42) specializes to

$$T(C\theta_T - c)'\left[C\Omega_T C'\right]^{-1}(C\theta_T - c) \Rightarrow \chi_r^2. \tag{4.44}$$

Specializing further to the classical linear model, the Wald statistic becomes

$$\left[C\delta_T - c\right]'\left(\sigma_{uT}^2 C\left[\Sigma x_t x_t'\right]^{-1}C'\right)^{-1}\left[C\delta_T - c\right] \Rightarrow \chi_r^2. \tag{4.45}$$

If $u_t \sim N(0, \sigma_u^2)$, then (4.45) is distributed as an F distribution with degrees of freedom r and $T - K$, $F(r, T - K)$. As T gets large, this F statistic converges to a random variable distributed as χ_r^2. Our large-sample analysis provides a justification for using (4.45) even though u_t is not normally distributed. Furthermore, if $r = 1$, then the Wald statistic becomes

$$\frac{(C\delta_T - c)^2}{\sigma_{uT}^2 C\left(\Sigma x_t x_t'\right)^{-1}C'}, \tag{4.46}$$

which is the squared value of the usual t-statistic, $(C\delta_T - c)/\sqrt{\sigma_{uT}^2 C(\Sigma x_t x_t')^{-1}C'}$. For large T, a t_{T-K} approaches the standard normal distribution.

4.2.3. Estimation Only under H_0: LM Tests

There are circumstances where it is most convenient to estimate under the
null hypothesis and where one wants to test the null model against an alternative model that does not impose the constraints $R(\theta_0) = 0$. To derive a
test statistic for this situation, we begin by studying the properties of the sample Lagrange multiplier associated with minimization of the GMM objective
function under the constraint. The underlying principle of the Lagrange
multiplier (LM) test is that the multiplier should be small if the constraints
are not binding in the sample, and large if they are. Thus, the finding
that the sample multiplier is statistically larger than zero would be evidence
against the null hypothesis that the constraints hold.

Let λ denote the vector of Lagrange multipliers associated with the r
constraints under H_0 and consider the GMM criterion function

$$\min_{\theta,\lambda} \left[H_T(\theta)' \Sigma_T^{-1} H_T(\theta) + \lambda' R(\theta) \right]. \tag{4.47}$$

If we treat λ as part of the parameter vector to be estimated, the first-order
conditions to (4.47) are

$$\frac{\partial H_T}{\partial \theta}(\tilde{\theta}_T)' \Sigma_T^{-1} H_T(\tilde{\theta}_T) + \frac{\partial R}{\partial \theta}(\tilde{\theta}_T)' \lambda_T = 0, \tag{4.48}$$

$$R(\tilde{\theta}_T) = 0,$$

where $\tilde{\theta}_T$ denotes the estimator of θ_0 under the constraints. In order to solve
this system of equations for λ_T it suffices, from the perspective of asymptotic
analysis, to work with mean-value expansions of these nonlinear functions.
Specifically, letting $\tilde{\theta}_0 = \text{plim } \tilde{\theta}_T$, we have

$$H_T(\tilde{\theta}_T) = H_T(\tilde{\theta}_0) + \frac{\partial H_T}{\partial \theta}(\theta_T^{\#})(\tilde{\theta}_T - \tilde{\theta}_0), \tag{4.49}$$

$$0 = R(\tilde{\theta}_T) = R(\tilde{\theta}_0) + \frac{\partial R}{\partial \theta}(\theta_T^{\#})(\tilde{\theta}_T - \tilde{\theta}_0).$$

This leads to the following, asymptotically equivalent, system of equations:

$$\begin{bmatrix} (\tilde{d}_0' \Sigma_0^{-1} \tilde{d}_0) & \frac{\partial R'}{\partial \theta}(\tilde{\theta}_0) \\ \frac{\partial R}{\partial \theta}(\tilde{\theta}_0) & 0 \end{bmatrix} \begin{bmatrix} (\tilde{\theta}_T - \tilde{\theta}_0) \\ \lambda_T \end{bmatrix} = \begin{bmatrix} \tilde{d}_0' \Sigma_0^{-1} H_T(\tilde{\theta}_0) \\ 0 \end{bmatrix}, \tag{4.50}$$

where $\tilde{d}_0 = \text{plim } \partial H_T(\tilde{\theta}_T)/\partial \theta$. If we let $\tilde{D}_R \equiv \partial R(\tilde{\theta}_0)/\partial \theta$, it follows that

$$\lambda_T \stackrel{a}{=} - \left[\tilde{D}_R \left(\tilde{d}_0' \Sigma_0^{-1} \tilde{d}_0 \right)^{-1} \tilde{D}_R' \right]^{-1} \tilde{D}_R \left(\tilde{d}_0' \Sigma_0^{-1} \tilde{d}_0 \right)^{-1} \tilde{d}_0' \Sigma_0^{-1} H_T(\tilde{\theta}_0). \quad (4.51)$$

Since, under the null hypothesis, the asymptotic distribution of $\sqrt{T} H_T(\tilde{\theta}_0)$ is $N(0, \Sigma_0)$, the limiting distribution of $\sqrt{T} \lambda_T$ is $N(0, [\tilde{D}_R(\tilde{d}_0' \Sigma_0^{-1} \tilde{d}_0)^{-1} \tilde{D}_R']^{-1})$. Therefore,

$$\text{LM}_T = T \lambda_T' \tilde{D}_R (\tilde{d}_0' \Sigma_0^{-1} \tilde{d}_0)^{-1} \tilde{D}_R' \lambda_T \Rightarrow \chi_r^2. \quad (4.52)$$

To express this statistic in terms of the sample moment conditions, evaluated at $\tilde{\theta}_T$, we substitute (4.48) into (4.52) to obtain

$$\text{LM}_T = T H_T(\tilde{\theta}_T)' \Sigma_T^{-1} \tilde{d}_T \left[\tilde{d}_T' \Sigma_T^{-1} \tilde{d}_T \right]^{-1} \tilde{d}_T' \Sigma_T^{-1} H_T(\tilde{\theta}_T) \Rightarrow \chi_r^2. \quad (4.53)$$

Note that all of the components of this test statistic, including Σ_0, are estimated under H_0.

For the case of the classical linear regression model (possibly with non-normal disturbances)

$$H_T(\delta) = \frac{1}{T} \sum_t x_t u_t(\delta); \ \Sigma_T = \sigma_{uT}^2 \left(\frac{1}{T} \sum x_t x_t' \right)^{-1}; \ d_T = \frac{1}{T} \sum x_t x_t'. (4.54)$$

Therefore, for the constraint $R(\delta_0) = 0$, the LM statistic (4.53) simplifies to $H_T(\tilde{\theta}_T)' \Sigma_T^{-1} H(\tilde{\theta}_T)$ or, equivalently, to

$$\text{LM}_T = T \left(\frac{1}{T} \sum x_t u_t(\tilde{\delta}_T) \right)' \frac{1}{\tilde{\sigma}_{uT}^2} \left[\left(\frac{1}{T} \sum x_t x_t' \right)^{-1} \right] \left(\frac{1}{T} \sum x_t u_t(\tilde{\delta}_T) \right). (4.55)$$

An interesting and informative interpretation of this statistic comes from further inspection of its components. Let $\tilde{e}_t \equiv u_t(\tilde{\delta}_T)$ (the fitted residual under the constraint), and consider

$$\left(\frac{1}{T} \sum_t x_t \tilde{e}_t \right)' \left(\frac{1}{T} \sum_t x_t x_t' \right)^{-1} \left(\frac{1}{T} \sum_t x_t \tilde{e}_t \right). \quad (4.56)$$

A regression of $\tilde{e}_t$ on x_t gives the fitted values

$$x_t' \left(\frac{1}{T} \sum_t x_t x_t' \right)^{-1} \frac{1}{T} \sum_t x_t \tilde{e}_t. \quad (4.57)$$

It follows that the numerator of LM_T is the sum of squared fitted values from this regression,

$$\left(\frac{1}{T}\sum_t x_t \tilde{e}_t\right)' \left(\frac{1}{T}\sum_t x_t x_t'\right)^{-1} \left(\frac{1}{T}\sum_t x_t \tilde{e}_t\right). \qquad (4.58)$$

The denominator, $\tilde{\sigma}_{uT}^2$, of LM_T is the sample variance of $\tilde{e}_t$. Combining these observations, we see that LM_T is T times the R^2 from regression of $\tilde{e}_t$ on x_t.[9]

4.3. Comparing LR, Wald, and LM Tests

Consider the linear regression model with the linear constraints $R(\delta) = C\theta - c$, $H_0 : C\delta_0 = c$. In this section we compare the LR, LM, and Wald statistics given by (4.39), (4.55), and (4.45), respectively, for this null hypothesis.

The LM statistic is

$$\mathrm{LM}_T = T \left(\frac{1}{T}\sum_t x_t \tilde{e}_t\right)' \left(\frac{1}{T}\sum_t x_t x_t'\right)^{-1} \left(\frac{1}{T}\sum_t x_t \tilde{e}_t\right) \Big/ \tilde{\sigma}_{uT}^2. \qquad (4.59)$$

Using the definition of $\tilde{e}_t$, we set

$$\frac{1}{T}\sum_t x_t \tilde{e}_t = -\left(\frac{1}{T}\sum_t x_t x_t'\right)(\tilde{\delta}_T - \delta_T), \qquad (4.60)$$

and, therefore,

$$\mathrm{LM}_T = T\left(\tilde{\delta}_T - \delta_T\right)' \left(\frac{1}{T}\sum_t x_t x_t'\right)(\tilde{\delta}_T - \delta_T) \big/ \tilde{\sigma}_{uT}^2. \qquad (4.61)$$

If we use the fact that

$$\tilde{e}_t = y_t - x_t'\tilde{\delta}_T = e_t - x_t'(\tilde{\delta}_T - \delta_T), \qquad (4.62)$$

it follows that

$$\sum_t \tilde{e}_t^2 - \sum_t e_t^2 = (\tilde{\delta}_T - \delta_T)'\left(\sum_t x_t x_t'\right)(\tilde{\delta}_T - \delta_T). \qquad (4.63)$$

Substituting (4.63) into (4.61) gives

$$\mathrm{LM}_T = T(\tilde{\sigma}_{uT}^2 - \sigma_{uT}^2)\big/\tilde{\sigma}_{uT}^2. \qquad (4.64)$$

---

[9] These observations about the classical linear model, as well as those in the next section, date back to Savin (1976), Berndt and Savin (1977), and Breusch and Pagan (1980). A useful review is presented in Engle (1984).

Thus, the LM statistic measures the increase in the sum of squared residuals that arises from imposing the constraints, expressed as a percentage of the constrained sum of squared residuals. (Of course, this statistic still has an interpretation as an R^2 as well.)

Turning to the Wald test, note that $(\tilde{d}_T' \Sigma_T \tilde{d}_T)$ in (4.50) simplifies to $\sigma_{uT}^2 T^{-1} \sum_t x_t x_t'$ and $\tilde{d}_T' \Sigma_T^{-1} H_T(\tilde{\delta}_T)$ simplifies to $\sigma_{uT}^2 T^{-1} \sum_t x_t \tilde{e}_t$. Therefore,[10]

$$\tilde{\delta}_T = \delta_T - \left(\frac{1}{T} \sum_t x_t x_t' \right)^{-1} C' \left[C \left(\frac{1}{T} \sum_t x_t x_t' \right)^{-1} C' \right]^{-1} [C\delta_T - c]. \quad (4.65)$$

The numerator of the Wald statistic can thus be rewritten as

$$(\tilde{\delta}_T - \delta_T)' \left(\sum_t x_t x_t' \right) (\tilde{\delta}_T - \delta_T) = (C\delta_T - c)' \left[C \left(\sum_t x_t x_t' \right)^{-1} C' \right]^{-1} (C\delta_T - c). \quad (4.66)$$

This leads directly to

$$W_T = T(\tilde{\sigma}_{uT}^2 - \sigma_{uT}^2)/\sigma_{uT}^2. \quad (4.67)$$

The Wald statistic measures the increase in the sum of squared residuals owing to imposition of the constraints, expressed as a percentage of the unconstrained sum of squared residuals.

For this special case of linear constraints on the coefficients of linear projections, we can rank these three test statistics. Since $\tilde{\sigma}_T^2 \geq \sigma_T^2$, it follows from (4.64) and (4.67) that $W_T \geq LM_T$. Moreover, algebraic manipulation shows that

$$LR_T = T \log \left(\tilde{\sigma}_T^2 / \sigma_T^2 \right) = T \log(1 + W_T/T), \quad (4.68)$$

$$LM_T = W_T/(1 + W_T/T). \quad (4.69)$$

Therefore, these tests can be ordered as

$$W_T \geq LR_T \geq LM_T. \quad (4.70)$$

---

[10] The constrained estimator is obtained by minimizing $(1/T) \sum_t u_t^2 + 2\lambda'(C\delta - c)$, and the associated first-order conditions are $(1/T) \sum_t x_t(y_t - x_t'\tilde{\delta}_T) + C'\lambda_T = 0$ and $C\tilde{\delta}_T - c = 0$. For this case, it follows that

$$\begin{bmatrix} (1/T) \sum_t x_t x_t' & C' \\ C & 0 \end{bmatrix} \begin{bmatrix} \tilde{\delta}_T \\ \lambda_T \end{bmatrix} = \begin{bmatrix} (1/T) \sum_t x_t y_t \\ c \end{bmatrix}.$$

Solving for $\tilde{\delta}_T - \delta_T$ gives (4.65).

Under the null hypothesis H_0, the Wald, LM, and LR tests all have the same asymptotic χ^2 distribution. However, under this asymptotic paradigm, (4.70) implies that they have different sizes.

4.4. Inference for Sequential Estimators

A situation that commonly arises in practice is that the parameter vector of interest, $\beta_0' = (\theta_0', \lambda_0')$, is estimated in two stages. First, the subvector θ_0 is estimated using a subset of the available moment equations, and then the subvector λ_0 is estimated in a second stage using additional moment conditions *that also depend on θ_0*. An important issue with such sequential estimation is whether the asymptotic distribution of λ_T is affected by the first-stage estimation of θ_0. The answer is generally "yes." However, it is not always yes, and, fortunately, there is a simple way to check whether two-stage estimation affects the asymptotic distribution of λ_T.

A representative setup where these issues arise involves the moment equation $E[h(z_t, \beta_0)] = 0$, where

$$
h(z_t, \beta_0) = \begin{bmatrix} h_1(z_t, \theta_0) \\ h_2(z_t, \theta_0, \lambda_0) \end{bmatrix}, \tag{4.71}
$$

the subvector h_i has dimension M_i, θ_0 has dimension K_1 ($M_1 \geq K_1$), and λ_0 has dimension K_2 ($M_2 \geq K_2$). A first-stage estimator θ_T of θ_0 is obtained by solving the moment equation

$$
A_{1T} \frac{1}{T} \sum_t h_1(z_t, \theta_T) = 0, \tag{4.72}
$$

for some $K_1 \times M_1$ matrix A_{1T} with probability limit A_{10}. Similarly, the second-stage estimator λ_T of λ_0 is obtained as the solution to

$$
A_{2T} \frac{1}{T} \sum_t h_2(z_t, \theta_T, \lambda_T) = 0, \tag{4.73}
$$

for some $K_2 \times M_2$ matrix A_{2T} with probability limit A_{20}. What makes this a two-stage process is that λ_T is obtained by solving (4.73) with θ_T fixed at the solution to (4.72).

In determining the asymptotic distribution of λ_T we must account for the dependence of (4.73) on θ_T, a random variable. Specifically, taking mean-value expansions of (4.72) and (4.73) and solving for $(\theta_T - \theta_0)$ and $(\lambda_T - \lambda_0)$ gives

$$\sqrt{T}\begin{bmatrix}(\theta_T - \theta_0)\\(\lambda_T - \lambda_0)\end{bmatrix} = \begin{bmatrix} A_{1T}\dfrac{1}{T}\sum_t \dfrac{\partial h_1\left(z_t, \theta_T^*\right)}{\partial\theta} & 0 \\[2em] A_{2T}\dfrac{1}{T}\sum_t \dfrac{\partial h_2\left(z_t, \theta_T^*, \lambda_T^*\right)}{\partial\theta} & A_{2T}\dfrac{1}{T}\sum_t \dfrac{\partial h_2\left(z_t, \theta_T^*, \lambda_T^*\right)}{\partial\lambda} \end{bmatrix}^{-1}$$

$$\times \begin{bmatrix} \dfrac{1}{\sqrt{T}}\sum_t h_1(z_t, \theta_0) \\[1.5em] \dfrac{1}{\sqrt{T}}\sum_t h_2(z_t, \theta_0, \lambda_0) \end{bmatrix}, \tag{4.74}$$

where the θ_T^* and λ_T^* are suitably chosen intermediate vectors. The asymptotic distribution of λ_T is then obtained, jointly with the asymptotic distribution of θ_T, by determining the limiting distribution of the last vector in (4.74).

An interesting special case obtains when

$$\mathrm{plim}_{T\to\infty} A_{2T}\frac{1}{T}\sum_t \frac{\partial h_2\left(z_t, \theta_T^*, \lambda_T^*\right)}{\partial\theta} = A_{20}E\left[\frac{\partial h_2(z_t, \theta_0, \lambda_0)}{\partial\theta}\right] = 0. \tag{4.75}$$

As observed by Newey (1984), in this case the asymptotic distribution of λ_T that solves (4.73) is the same as that of the distribution of the λ_T that solves

$$A_{2T}\frac{1}{T}\sum_t h_2(z_t, \theta_0, \lambda_T) = 0. \tag{4.76}$$

In other words, the correct limiting distribution of λ_T is obtained by treating θ_0 as if it were known; there is no effect on the (limiting) distribution of λ_T of pre-estimation of θ_0 in a first stage.

The condition (4.75) is a very useful "test" for whether sequential estimation affects the inference in the second stage. To illustrate its application, consider the case of a regression model in which the conditional variance of the error u_t is given by

$$E\left[u_t^2 \big| x_t\right] = g(x_t, \lambda_0). \tag{4.77}$$

Common practice is to estimate the parameters of the underlying regression model (say θ_0), compute fitted residuals $u_t(\theta_T)$, and then to use these fitted residuals to estimate the parameters λ_0 governing the conditional heteroskedasticity. This second stage estimation is typically based on the moment equation (nonlinear least squares)

$$E\left[\left[u_t^2 - g(x_t, \lambda_0)\right]\frac{\partial g(x_t, \lambda_0)}{\partial \lambda}\right] = 0. \tag{4.78}$$

Thus, to check whether the asymptotic distribution of λ_T so obtained is affected by the first-stage estimation of θ_0, it is sufficient to check whether

$$E\left[2u_t\frac{\partial g(x_t, \lambda_0)}{\partial \lambda}\frac{\partial u_t'}{\partial \theta}\right] = 0. \tag{4.79}$$

So, for example, if u_t is the error term in the linear regression model $y_t = \theta_0' x_t + u_t$ and $E[u_t|x_t] = 0$, then $\partial u_t/\partial \theta = x_t$ and (4.79) is clearly satisfied.

On the other hand, if

$$E\left[u_t^2|I_{t-1}\right] = \lambda_1 + \lambda_2 u_{t-1}^2, \tag{4.80}$$

then the counterpart to (4.78) is

$$E\left[\begin{array}{c} u_t^2 - \lambda_1 - \lambda_2 u_{t-1}^2 \\ \left(u_t^2 - \lambda_1 - \lambda_2 u_{t-1}^2\right)u_{t-1}^2 \end{array}\right]. \tag{4.81}$$

Differentiating with respect to θ_0 shows that whether or not the asymptotic distribution of $\lambda_0' = (\lambda_1, \lambda_2)$ is unaffected by pre-estimation of θ_0 depends on whether third moments of u_t (e.g., $E[u_t^3]$) are zero. That is, on whether u_t has a symmetric distribution.

4.5. Inference with Unequal-Length Samples

Another practical problem that often arises in financial applications is that the data for the variables of interest are available over sample periods of different lengths. For example, the development of analytically tractable derivative pricing models and the increased availability of historical data on the prices of these derivatives have contributed to a rapid growth in empirical studies of dynamic option pricing models (see Chapter 15). A common feature of virtually all of these studies is that the available history of the relevant security prices in the underlying cash markets is longer, often substantially so, than that of the prices of the derivative securities being studied.

Faced with such mismatches, researchers often truncate their sample on the price of the underlying security so that the historical time periods of all of the security prices of interest are temporally aligned. Though convenient for the application of standard econometric estimation and inference procedures, by omitting historical information about the probability model for the underlying, this practice may lead to a substantial loss in econometric efficiency. Within the standard setting of GMM, this section develops inference procedures that exploit all of the information in mismatched histories of data.

There are many reasons that the relevant price series may be mismatched in the analysis of dynamic asset pricing models, and it is important at the outset to be precise about the case examined here. One reason is that the prices of a security of interest have not been collected and/or made available for academic research over the longer sample period for which other price series are available. For instance, in the empirical studies of S&P500 option prices in Bakshi et al. (1997), Chernov and Ghysels (2000), and Pan (2002), the option data cover only a subperiod of the total period for which S&P500 options have been trading, and their sample periods are, in turn, a small portion of the period for which S&P500 price indices have been compiled. Similarly, in their studies of credit spreads on defaultable bonds, Duffee (1999) and Duffie et al. (2003b) use data on corporate bond yield spreads that cover a much shorter period than the available data on treasury bond yields.

A very different case arises when the availability of data is determined by, or at least related to, the underlying economic processes being studied. For instance, if the recording of derivatives prices coincides with the introduction of a new derivative contract, and the introduction of this contract changes the distribution of the underlying on which the derivative is written, then there has effectively been a structural change in the economy. Another example of the economic environment affecting data availability is when sovereign entities temporarily suspend currency convertibility or payments on their debts and certain security prices are not available during this period. Dealing with these and similar cases is not simply an econometric issue; it seems necessary to model the reasons for the introduction of new contracts or for the temporary suspension of trading in markets. The subsequent discussion applies to the former, and not this second, reason for data sets of different lengths.

Consider the nonlinear model

$$h_1(x_{1t}, \beta_{10}) = u_{1t}, \tag{4.82}$$

$$h_2(x_t, \beta_{20}) = u_{2t}, \tag{4.83}$$

where, for notational ease, the u_{it} are assumed to be scalars and

$$x_t = \begin{pmatrix} x_{1t} \\ x_{2t} \end{pmatrix}, \quad \beta_{10} = \begin{pmatrix} \gamma_0 \\ \delta_{10} \end{pmatrix}, \quad \beta_{20} = \begin{pmatrix} \gamma_0 \\ \delta_{20} \end{pmatrix}. \tag{4.84}$$

The dimension of γ_0 is L and the dimensions of the δ_{i0} are K_i, $i = 1, 2$. We suppose that data are available on the subvector x_{1t} of x_t for T periods, whereas data on x_{2t} are available only for the last T_2 observation times.

The structure of the model presumes that the full sample (T observations) can be exploited in estimating the parameter vector β_{10}. However, data on both x_1 and x_2 are needed to estimate β_{20} governing h_2. Common practice in this situation is to omit the first $T_1 \equiv T - T_2$ observations on x_{1t} and estimate the model (4.82) and (4.83) using the last T_2 observations. Our objective is to design an estimator of $\beta_0' \equiv (\gamma_0', \delta_{10}', \delta_{20}')$ that fully exploits the available data (T observations on x_1 and T_2 observations on x_2) and, as such, is econometrically more efficient.

Suppose the asset pricing model implies the conditional moment restrictions

$$E[u_{1t}|I_t] = 0 \quad \text{and} \quad E[u_{2t}|I_t] = 0, \tag{4.85}$$

for some information set I_t. An implication of the moment restrictions (4.85) is that

$$E[z_{1t}u_{1t}] = 0, \tag{4.86}$$

$$E[z_{2t}u_{2t}] = 0, \tag{4.87}$$

for instrument matrices $z_{it} \epsilon I_t$ with $\dim(z_{it}) = n_i \times 1$, $i = 1, 2$. We assume that $n_1 \geq L + K_1$, and that $(n_1 + n_2) > (L + K_1 + K_2)$ so that there is a sufficient number of moment equations for estimation of the $\tilde{K} \equiv L + K_1 + K_2$ parameters.

Let

$$g_{1,T_1}(b_1) = \frac{1}{T_1} \sum_{t=1}^{T_1} z_{1t}u_{1t}(b_1), \tag{4.88}$$

$$g_{i,T_2}(b_i) = \frac{1}{T_2} \sum_{t=T_1+1}^{T} z_{it}u_{it}(b_i), \quad i = 1, 2, \tag{4.89}$$

be the sample counterparts of (4.86) and (4.87), where (4.88) is the sample version of (4.86) over the first sample period and (4.89) represents the moment conditions (4.87) over the second sample period. Then the GMM estimator $b_T' = (b_{1T}', b_{2T}')$ of $(\beta_{10}', \beta_{20}')$ that fully exploits the available information is based on the sample moment vector

$$G_T(b_1, b_2)' = [g_{1,T_1}(b_1)', g_{1,T_2}(b_1)', g_{2,T_2}(b_2)'] \tag{4.90}$$

and is obtained by minimizing

$$G_T(b_1, b_2)' W G_T(b_1, b_2) \tag{4.91}$$

by choice of γ, δ_1, and δ_2, where W is the weighting matrix. As discussed in Chapter 3, the optimal choice of W is the inverse of the asymptotic covariance matrix of $G_T(\beta_{10}, \beta_{20})$.

To derive the asymptotic distribution of b_T we must adopt a convention regarding the samples of lengths T_1 and T_2. If we let X denote the vector of variables in our models, our historical data appear as

$$\underbrace{X_1, X_2, \ldots, X_{T_1}}_{T_1 \text{ observations}}, \underbrace{X_{T_1+1}, X_{T_1+2}, \ldots, X_T}_{T_2 \text{ observations}}. \tag{4.92}$$

We assume that T_1, $T_2 \to \infty$, with

$$\lim_{T \to \infty} T_i/T = c_i, \, c_i > 0, \tag{4.93}$$

$c_1 + c_2 = 1$. Conceptually, we let both T_1 and T_2 get large as $T \to \infty$.[11]

Next, under this convention, we prove a lemma that establishes the asymptotic independence of functions of a stationary and ergodic time series $\{X_t\}$ over two nonoverlapping subsamples. Toward this end, let $h_{1t} \equiv h_1(X_t)$ and $h_{2t} \equiv h_2(X_t)$ be measurable functions with $E[h(X_t)] = 0$, $h_t' = (h_{1t}', h_{2t}')$. Introducing the sample means

$$G_{1,T_1} = \frac{1}{T_1} \sum_{t=1}^{T_1} h_{1t}, \quad \text{and} \quad G_{2,T_2} = \frac{1}{T_2} \sum_{t=T_1+1}^{T} h_{2t}, \tag{4.94}$$

we prove:

Lemma 4.1. *If* [12]

$$\sum_{j=0}^{\infty} \left| E[h_t' h_{t-j}] \right| < \infty, \tag{4.95}$$

then

$$\lim_{T \to \infty} \sqrt{T_1 T_2} E\left[G_{1,T_1} G_{2,T_2}'\right] = 0. \tag{4.96}$$

---

[11] The large-sample problem is uninteresting if, say, T_1 is fixed. For in this case the fact that we have an additional T_1 observations on x_1 has no effect on the asymptotic distribution of b_T obtained as $T_2 \to \infty$.

[12] See Hansen (1982b) for a discussion of sufficient conditions for (4.95) to hold; e.g., his assumptions 3.1 and 3.5 are sufficient.

Proof (Lemma 4.1). *To simplify notation, we prove this lemma for the special case where $T_2 = T_1 \equiv T$. Then*

$$\frac{1}{T} E\left[\sum_{t=1}^{T} h_{1t} \sum_{t=T+1}^{T} h_{2t}'\right] = \frac{1}{T} \sum_{m=1}^{T} (T - m + 1) E\left[h_{11} h_{2,T+m}'\right]. \qquad (4.97)$$

Taking absolute values gives

$$\left|\frac{1}{T} \sum_{m=1}^{T} (T - m + 1) E\left[h_{11} h_{2,T+m}'\right]\right| \leq \frac{1}{T} \sum_{m=1}^{T} (T - m + 1) \left|E\left[h_{11} h_{2,T+m}'\right]\right|. \qquad (4.98)$$

The last term in (4.98) converges to zero as $T \to \infty$ by assumption (4.95).

Under the regularity conditions adopted in Hansen (1982b) and Chapter 3, which are used to support use of a central limit theorem in Hannan (1973),

$$\sqrt{T_1} G_{1,T_1} \Rightarrow N(0, V), \quad V = \sum_{j=-\infty}^{\infty} E\left[h_{1t} h_{1,t-j}'\right], \qquad (4.99)$$

$$\sqrt{T_2} G_{2,T_2} \Rightarrow N(0, \Gamma), \quad \Gamma = \sum_{j=-\infty}^{\infty} E\left[h_{2t} h_{2,t-j}'\right]. \qquad (4.100)$$

In the light of Lemma 4.1, we conclude that the joint limiting distribution of (G_{1,T_1}, G_{2,T_2}) is normal with a block diagonal covariance matrix and, hence, there is asymptotic independence between the two sample means.

To apply these observations to the case of unequal sample lengths, we have, under regularity,

$$\sqrt{T_1} g_{1,T_1}(\beta_{10}) \Rightarrow N(0, V), \qquad (4.101)$$

$$\sqrt{T_2} (g_{1,T_2}(\beta_{10})', g_{2,T_2}(\beta_{20})')' \Rightarrow N(0, \Gamma), \qquad (4.102)$$

where the upper-left $n_1 \times n_1$ block of Γ is V owing to stationarity. Moreover, using the preceding reasoning, these limiting distributions are independent. It follows that the optimal distance matrix to use in GMM estimation is a consistent estimator of the matrix

$$W = \begin{pmatrix} V^{-1} & 0 \\ 0 & \Gamma^{-1} \end{pmatrix}. \qquad (4.103)$$

Though W is block diagonal, inclusion of the first T_1 observations improves the efficiency of the estimator of β_{10}. Furthermore, since u_{1t} and u_{2t} may be correlated and may both depend on γ_0, there is in general also a gain in efficiency in estimating β_{20} by inclusion of all T observations on x_{1t}.

An interesting special case, with further simplification, is when $K_2 = n_2$: the number of moment conditions associated with the second error u_2 is exactly equal to the number of additional distinct parameters introduced through h_2 (the dimension of δ_{20}). Intuitively, in this case, the moment conditions (4.86) are used to estimate all of the components of β_{10}, and in particular γ_0, while the moment conditions (4.87) are used to estimate the new parameters $\beta_{20} \equiv \delta_{20}$ introduced through h_2. The following proposition formalizes this intuition.

Proposition 4.1. *If $K_2 = n_2$, then the asymptotic distribution of b_{1T} obtained by minimization of (4.91) with the optimal distance matrix (4.103) is the same as the limiting distribution of the estimator b_{1T}^* that solves*

$$b_{1T}^* = \operatorname{argmin}_{b_1} g_{1,T}(b_1)' V_T^{-1} g_{1,T}(b_1). \qquad (4.104)$$

Proof (Proposition 4.1). *The first-order conditions for the GMM problem (4.91) are*

$$\frac{\partial G_T}{\partial \beta}(b_{1T}, b_{2T})' W G_T(b_{1T}, b_{2T}) = 0. \qquad (4.105)$$

The first matrix in (4.105), $\partial G_T(b_{1T}, b_{2T})'/\partial \beta$, is given by

$$\begin{pmatrix} \dfrac{1}{T_1} \displaystyle\sum_{t=1}^{T_1} \dfrac{\partial u_{1t}}{\partial \beta_{10}}(b_{1T})z_{1t}' & \dfrac{1}{T_2} \displaystyle\sum_{t=T_1+1}^{T} \dfrac{\partial u_{1t}}{\partial \beta_{10}}(b_{1T})z_{1t}' & \dfrac{1}{T_2} \displaystyle\sum_{t=T_1+1}^{T} \dfrac{\partial u_{2t}}{\partial \beta_{10}}(b_{2T})z_{2t}' \\[2em] 0 & 0 & \dfrac{1}{T_2} \displaystyle\sum_{t=T_1+1}^{T} \dfrac{\partial u_{2t}}{\partial \delta_{20}}(b_{2T})z_{2t}' \end{pmatrix}.$$

Let $D_{i,T_2}^{\delta_k} \equiv (1/T_2) \sum_{t=T_1+1}^{T} (\partial u_{it}(b_{iT})/\delta_{k0})z_{it}'$, a $K_i \times n_i$ matrix, and similarly define $D_{i,T_1}^{\delta_k}$ as the same expression with the sum going from 1 to T_1. Letting Γ_{ij}^{-1} denote the ij block of Γ^{-1} and solving the second set of K_2 equations gives

$$D_{2,T_2}^{\delta_2} \Gamma_{21}^{-1} g_{1,T_2}(b_{1T}) + D_{2,T_2}^{\delta_2} \Gamma_{22}^{-1} g_{2,T_2}(b_{2T}) = 0. \qquad (4.106)$$

If $K_2 = n_2$, then $D_{2,T_2}^{\delta_2}$ is square and nonsingular. Thus, (4.106) implies that

$$g_{2,T_2}(b_{2T}) = -\left(\Gamma_{22}^{-1}\right)^{-1} \Gamma_{21}^{-1} g_{1,T_2}(b_{1T}). \qquad (4.107)$$

The first $L + K_1$ equations in (4.105) give

$$D^{\beta_1}_{1,T_1} V^{-1} g_{1,T_1}(b_{1T}) + \left(D^{\beta_1}_{1,T_2}\Gamma^{-1}_{11} + D^{\beta_1}_{2,T_2}\Gamma^{-1}_{21}\right)g_{1,T_2}(b_{1T})$$

$$+ \left(D^{\beta_1}_{1,T_2}\Gamma^{-1}_{12} + D^{\beta_1}_{2,T_2}\Gamma^{-1}_{22}\right)g_{2,T_2}(b_{2T}) = 0. \qquad (4.108)$$

Substituting (4.107) into (4.108) and collecting terms premultiplied by $D^{\beta_1}_{1,T_2}$ gives the expression

$$D^{\beta_1}_{1,T_2}\left[\Gamma^{-1}_{11} - \Gamma^{-1}_{12}\left(\Gamma^{-1}_{22}\right)^{-1}\Gamma^{-1}_{21}\right]g_{1,T_2}(b_{1T}). \qquad (4.109)$$

Using the formulas for the partitioned inverse of a matrix, the matrix in square brackets in (4.109) can be shown to be equal to V^{-1}. Thus, (4.109) simplifies to $D^{\beta_1}_{1,T_2}V^{-1}g_{1,T_2}(b_{1T})$.
   Combining the terms in (4.108) premultiplied by $D^{\beta_1}_{2,T_2}$ gives

$$D^{\beta_1}_{2,T_2}\left[\Gamma^{-1}_{21} - \Gamma^{-1}_{22}\left(\Gamma^{-1}_{22}\right)^{-1}\Gamma^{-1}_{21}\right]g_{1,T_2}(b_{2T}) = 0. \qquad (4.110)$$

Substituting (4.109) and (4.110) into (4.108) gives

$$D^{\beta_1}_{1,T_1}V^{-1}g_{1,T_1}(b_{1T}) + D^{\beta_1}_{1,T_2}V^{-1}g_{1,T_2}(b_{1T}) = 0. \qquad (4.111)$$

Our proof is complete upon noting that

$$\mathrm{plim}_{T\to\infty}D^{\beta_1}_{1,T_1} = \mathrm{plim}_{T\to\infty}D^{\beta_1}_{1,T_2} \equiv D^{\beta_1}_{10}. \qquad (4.112)$$

Thus, b_{1T} is asymptotically equivalent to the estimator solving

$$D^{\beta_1}_{10}V^{-1}\frac{1}{T}\sum_{t=1}^{T}z_{1t}u_{1t}\left(b^*_{1T}\right) = 0. \qquad (4.113)$$

   The practical implication of Proposition 4.1 is that, when $K_2 = n_2$, we can proceed to estimate β_{10} using the full sample and the GMM criterion function (4.104), and then compute the δ_{2T} that solves the K_2 equations (4.107). This proposition generalizes the analysis in Stambaugh (1997) to a general GMM setting.

4.6. Underidentified Parameters under H_0

There are many important circumstances in the analysis of financial models where a subset of the parameters is not econometrically identified under the null hypothesis. This implies that the likelihood function is flat (with respect to these parameters) at its optimum. As such, it is not locally quadratic, contrary to what is typically presumed in standard large-sample asymptotic theory. Additionally, in some cases the score of the likelihood function with respect to the unidentified parameters is zero under the null hypothesis. This implies that the score does not have positive variance as required by most large-sample analyses. For either of these reasons, tests of the null hypothesis typically cannot proceed using standard large-sample distribution theory for likelihood estimators.

Solutions to the problem of testing in the presence of unidentified "nuisance" parameters have been proposed for several important cases. One such case is Hamilton's (1989) switching regime model for economic time series. Suppose that there are two regimes for a process y indexed by $s = 1, 2$. The conditional distribution of y_t in regime s_t is given by $f_i(y_t | \vec{y}_{t-1}^{J}, s_t = i; \beta_i)$, $i = 1, 2$. Further, suppose that the transition between these two regimes is governed by a Markov process that is independent of y and has transition probabilities

$$\Pr\{s_t = 1 | s_{t-1} = 1\} = P, \quad \Pr\{s_t = 2 | s_{t-1} = 2\} = Q. \quad (4.114)$$

This model captures the idea that, during state $s_t = 1$ of the economy, the evolution of y is governed by the distribution $f_1(y_t | \vec{y}_{t-1}^{J}, s_t = 1; \beta_1)$ with parameter vector β_1. At the same time, owing to cyclical developments or changes in policy, the distribution of y may change to $f_2(y_t | \vec{y}_{t-1}^{J}, s_t = 2; \beta_2)$ with probability $(1 - P)$, where the functional forms of f_1 and f_2 may be different. As we discuss more extensively in subsequent chapters, introducing switching of this form induces additional persistence, nonlinearity, and leptokurtosis (fat tails) into the distribution of y and this has proved useful for modeling financial time series.

The conditional density function $f(y_t | \vec{y}_{t-1}^{J})$ of the observed data for Hamilton's switching model is given by

$$f(y_t | \vec{y}_{t-1}^{J}) = \sum_{i=1}^{2} f_i(y_t | s_t = i, \vec{y}_{t-1}^{J}) p_{i, t-1}, \quad (4.115)$$

where $p_{i, t-1} = \Pr\{s_t = i | \vec{y}_{t-1}^{J}\}$.[13] Using Bayes's rule, we can express $p_{1, t-1}$ recursively as (see Gray, 1996)

---

[13] This follows from the observations that $f(y_t | \vec{y}_{t-1}^{J}) = \sum_{i=1}^{2} f(y_t, s_t = i | \vec{y}_{t-1}^{J})$ and $f(y_t, s_t = i | \vec{y}_{t-1}^{J}) = f(y_t, | s_t = i, \vec{y}_{t-1}^{J}) \Pr\{s_t = i | \vec{y}_{t-1}^{J}\}$. We maintain our convention of dating variables by the information set within which they reside and, hence, depart from Gray's notation of p_{it} for $\Pr\{s_t = i | \vec{y}_{t-1}^{J}\}$.

$$p_{1,t-1} = (1 - Q) \left[\frac{g_{2,t-1}(1 - p_{1,t-2})}{g_{1,t-1}p_{1,t-2} + g_{2,t-1}(1 - p_{1,t-2})} \right]$$

$$+ P \left[\frac{g_{1,t-1}p_{1,t-2}}{g_{1,t-1}p_{1,t-2} + g_{2,t-1}(1 - p_{1,t-2})} \right],$$

(4.116)

where $g_{i,t}$ is shorthand notation for $f_i(y_t | \vec{y}_{t-1}^{J}, s_t = i; \beta_i)$, $i = 1, 2$. Given initial values for p_{10} and $\vec{y}_0^{J}$, the likelihood function for the data can be constructed recursively using (4.115) and (4.116).

One potential hypothesis of interest in this setting is that $f_1(y_t | \vec{y}_{t-1}^{J}, s_t = 1; \beta_1)$ equals $f_2(y_t | \vec{y}_{t-1}^{J}, s_t = 2; \beta_2)$; that is, the conditional densities in the two regimes have the same functional form *and* $\beta_1 = \beta_2$. In cases where the modeler presumes that $f_1 = f_2$, the null hypothesis is simply $\beta_1 = \beta_2$. Under this null, it is easy to see that the density $f(y_t | \vec{y}_{t-1}^{J})$ does not depend on information about the regimes (since switching has no consequences for the evolution of y_t). Therefore, the parameters P and Q are not identified. Moreover, the null hypothesis yields a local optimum and higher-order derivatives may be zero as well. It follows that standard large-sample hypothesis testing does not apply. Hamilton recognized this problem, but did not address it formally.

Subsequently Hansen (1992) proposed a bound on a normalized likelihood ratio statistic that provides a conservative test of the null hypothesis $\beta_1 = \beta_2$ for switching regime models. To be consistent with his notation, we assume that $f_1 = f_2$ and reparameterize the model so that log-likelihood function depends on (β, γ, θ), the null hypothesis is $\beta = 0$ (the alternative is $\beta \neq 0$), θ is identified under both the null and alternative hypotheses, and γ is not identified under the null hypothesis. The first step in constructing Hansen's test statistic is "concentrating out" the nuisance parameter θ. Setting $\alpha \equiv (\beta', \gamma')$, we define $\hat{\theta}(\alpha) = \max_{\theta \in \Theta} l_T(\alpha, \theta)$, the ML estimates of θ for fixed α. The concentrated log-likelihood function is then $\hat{l}_T(\alpha) = l_T(\alpha, \hat{\theta}(\alpha))$. Next, we define $\hat{LR}_T(\alpha) \equiv \hat{l}_T(\alpha) - \hat{l}_T(0, \gamma)$, $LR_T(\alpha)$ to be the counterpart without the "hats" and $\hat{Q}_T(\alpha) \equiv \hat{LR}_T(\alpha) - E[LR_T(\alpha)]$. Note that $\hat{LR}_T(\alpha)$ is the likelihood ratio "surface," with the standard likelihood ratio statistic $\hat{LR}_T$ being the supremum of $\hat{LR}_T(\alpha)$ over α. Hansen shows that

$$\Pr\{\sqrt{T}\hat{LR}_T \geq x\} \leq \Pr\left\{\sup_{\alpha} \sqrt{T}\hat{Q}_T(\alpha) \geq x\right\},$$

(4.117)

which provides a bound on the likelihood ratio statistic. However, he argues that tests based on this bound will be overconservative in practice because the variance of $\hat{Q}_T$ depends on the value of α.

To circumvent this problem, Hansen proposes working with a standardized version of $\hat{Q}_T$. Specifically, let

$$V_T(\alpha, \hat{\theta}(\alpha)) = \sum_{t=1}^{T} q_t(\alpha, \hat{\theta}(\alpha))^2, \tag{4.118}$$

where

$$q_t(\alpha, \hat{\theta}(\alpha)) = \log f_t(\alpha, \hat{\theta}(\alpha)) - \log f_t(0, \gamma, \hat{\theta}(0, \gamma)) - \hat{LR}_T(\alpha), \tag{4.119}$$

with f_t denoting the conditional density at date t. Then, defining

$$\hat{Q}_T^*(\alpha) \equiv \frac{\hat{Q}_T(\alpha)}{V_T(\alpha)^{1/2}}, \quad \text{and} \quad \hat{LR}_T^*(\alpha) \equiv \frac{\hat{LR}_T(\alpha)}{V_T(\alpha)^{1/2}}, \tag{4.120}$$

he shows that

$$\Pr\{\hat{LR}_T^* \geq x\} \leq \Pr\left\{\sup_\alpha \sum_\alpha \hat{Q}_T^*(\alpha) \geq x\right\} \to \Pr\{\sup_\alpha Q^*(\alpha) \geq x\}, \tag{4.121}$$

where $Q^*(\alpha)$ is a Gaussian process and, as such, is completely characterized by its covariance function, the sample counterpart to which is

$$\hat{K}_T^*(\alpha_1, \alpha_2) = \frac{\sum_{t=1}^{T} q_t(\alpha_1, \hat{\theta}(\alpha_1)) q_t(\alpha_2, \hat{\theta}(\alpha_2))}{V_T(\alpha_1)^{1/2} V_T(\alpha_2)^{1/2}}. \tag{4.122}$$

Thus, to approximate the bound in (4.121), one can draw i.i.d. Gaussian processes with covariance function $\hat{K}_T^*$. Using the empirical distribution of $\sup Q^*$ one can then test the null hypothesis of interest. Hansen shows that, for the switching regime models examined empirically by Hamilton (1989), the small-sample reliability of using his bound as a test was high.

An interesting special case of this Markov switching model obtains with $P + Q = 1$. In this case there is no persistence in the Markov process (the probability that s_t takes on the value 1 or 2 is independent of the previous state) and the model reduces to the mixture-of-distributions model. In this setting, the conditional density of the data is given by

$$f(y_t | \vec{y}_{t-1}^J) = P f_1(y_t | \vec{y}_{t-1}^J, \beta_1) + (1 - P) f_2(y_t | \vec{y}_{t-1}^J, \beta_2), \tag{4.123}$$

and y_t is drawn from f_1 with probability P and from f_2 with probability $(1 - P)$. Once again we may have a nonstandard testing problem. For instance, under the null hypothesis that $P = 1$, not all of the parameters of β_2 are identified if $\beta_1 \neq \beta_2$.

We will see additional examples of this nuisance parameter problem, particularly in models with "jumps" in asset prices or returns.

5
Affine Processes

AMONG THE MOST widely studied time-series processes in the empirical finance literature is the family of *affine* processes. Their popularity is attributable to their accommodation of stochastic volatility, jumps, and correlations among the risk factors driving asset returns, while leading to computationally tractable pricing relations and moment equations that can be used in estimation. In this chapter we overview some of the key properties of affine processes, in both their discrete- and continuous-time formulations.

Intuitively, an affine process Y is one for which the conditional mean and variance are affine functions of Y. However, following Duffie et al. (2003a), it is convenient to characterize affine processes more formally in terms of their exponential-affine Fourier (for continuous-time) and Laplace (for discrete-time) transforms. We begin with the case of continuous time and present the family of affine-jump diffusions in their familiar form as a stochastic differential equation with affine drift and instantaneous conditional variance. This is followed by a discussion of the "admissibility" problem: the need to impose restrictions on the parameters of an affine process to ensure that it is well defined.

We then turn to the case of discrete-time affine models. While the special case of a Gaussian vector autoregression has been widely studied in the asset pricing literature, discrete-time affine models with stochastic volatility have received less attention. Drawing upon the work by Darolles et al. (2001) and Dai et al. (2005), among others, we present the discrete-time counterparts to a large subfamily of affine diffusions, including virtually all of the continuous-time models that have been examined in the empirical literature.

The popularity of affine representations of the state variables in DAPMs is in large part because they lead to tractable pricing relations. This tractability derives from the knowledge of closed-form solutions to several "transforms" of affine processes. Accordingly, we introduce two key transforms for affine diffusions from Duffie et al. (2000) and Bakshi and Madan (2000), and their counterparts for discrete-time affine processes, which will be used heavily in Part II of this book.

Finally, we review some of the more popular approaches to estimation of affine processes. Though we present this material outside of any pricing framework, it is instructive to bear in mind the interplay between model formulation and the choice of estimation strategy emphasized in Chapter 1. Many of the conceptual frameworks for pricing financial assets have been developed in continuous time under the assumption that the state variables (sources of uncertainty) follow diffusion or jump-diffusion models. Economically, the "short" decision intervals associated with continuous time might be justified by the relatively frictionless nature of financial markets relative to many other markets for goods and services—low transactions costs, fast communication of information, and trading mechanisms that allow frequent rebalancing of positions. However, even for financial markets, continuous decision making is perhaps better viewed as an approximation. This approximation brings considerable tractability when combined with the assumption that the state follows a diffusion process. In particular, the "change of measure" underlying risk-neutral pricing outlined in Chapter 1 is relatively tractable for diffusion models, typically amounting to a change in the drifts, but not the volatilities, of the state variables. Additionally, the distributional assumptions underlying jump-diffusion models often facilitate the derivation of moment conditions for use in estimation.

This last point is central to the estimation of continuous-time models in finance since, given a discretely sampled data set, the estimation problem for discrete- and continuous-time models is really the same: *derive a model-implied conditional likelihood function or population moment conditions of the discretely sampled data for use in estimation of the model parameters.* This chapter presents several approaches to the construction of such population moment conditions when $\{Y_t\}_{t=1}^{T}$ is an observed, discrete sample of length T. These approaches prove useful in the analysis of DAPMs where Y_t is a (possibly unobserved) state vector underlying the time-series properties of a vector of observed asset prices or returns.

Since diffusion models are Markov processes, the relevant conditional density for use in ML estimation is $f(Y_t|Y_{t-1}; \gamma_0)$. In rare cases, $f(Y_t|Y_{t-1}; \gamma_0)$ is known in closed form (see later). More generally, it can be shown that $f(Y_t|Y_{t-1}; \gamma_0)$ itself satisfies a partial differential equation (PDE) that could be solved numerically, much like we solve for asset prices in continuous-time models. In practice, the strategy of solving for f from its defining PDE is rarely pursued, however. The reason is the computational burden of simultaneously solving numerically for the density f and "climbing the hill" to maximize the likelihood function of $\{Y_t\}$. In fact, as we will see in subsequent chapters, in estimating a DAPM, the computational burden may be even greater because of the need to numerically solve for the model-implied prices or returns as functions of the state Y_t.

With these considerations in mind, most of the estimation strategies for continuous-time models exploit either approximations that reduce the computational burden or, for sufficiently specialized models, analytic representations of the implied conditional densities or moments of these conditional distributions. Rather than attempting a comprehensive review of the many approaches that have been proposed in the literature, we focus here on several that have proved to be particularly useful in the estimation of multivariate affine diffusion models.[1] Most of the methods covered in this chapter presume that Y is observed, and rely on the imposition of sufficient structure to obtain analytic representations of features of the relevant conditional distributions. In Chapter 6 we discuss alternative simulation-based methods that are applicable both to more general diffusions and to models in which some of the variables are latent (unobserved).

Estimation of the discrete-time affine processes presented subsequently is much more straightforward. By construction, the conditional densities of these processes are known in closed form. Therefore, the likelihood function of the data can be maximized directly.

5.1. Affine Processes: Overview

Fix a probability space $(\Omega, \mathcal{F}, P)$ and an information set $\mathcal{F}_t$. Initially we examine the case of a Markov (some say first-order Markov) process Y taking on values in a state space $D \subset \mathbb{R}^N$:

Definition 5.1.   *A process is Markov if, for any measurable function $g : D \to \mathbb{R}$ and for any fixed times t and $s > t$,*

$$E_t[g(Y_s)] = h(Y_t),$$

for some function $h : D \to \mathbb{R}$.

This means that the conditional distribution at time t of Y_s, given all available information, depends only on the current state Y_t. When the conditional distribution of Y depends on additional lags of Y, one can often

---

[1] Two of the approaches that we do not cover are the nonparametric methods proposed by Ait-Sahalia (1996), Stanton (1997), and Jiang and Knight (1997), applied to univariate models; and the GMM estimators proposed by Hansen and Scheinkman (1995) and Duffie and Glynn (2004), which exploit the special structure of diffusion models and certain moment equations derived from this structure.

expand the dimension of the state vector to obtain a new, first-order Markov process Y^*.[2]

The conditional characteristic function (CCF) of a Markov process Y_T, conditioned on current and lagged information about Y at date t, is given by the Fourier transform of its conditional density function:

$$\text{CCF}_t(\tau, u) \equiv E\left(e^{iu'Y_T} \mid Y_t\right), \quad u \in \mathbb{R}^N \tag{5.1}$$

$$= \int_{\mathbb{R}^N} f_Y(Y_T|Y_t; \gamma)e^{iu'Y_T} \, dY_T.$$

where $\tau = (T - t)$, $i = \sqrt{-1}$, and f_Y is the conditional density of Y. Similarly, the conditional moment-generating function (CMGF) is given by the Laplace transform of Y:

$$\text{CMGF}_t(\tau, u) \equiv E\left(e^{u'Y_T} \mid Y_t\right), \quad u \in \mathbb{R}^N \tag{5.2}$$

$$= \int_{\mathbb{R}^N} f_Y(Y_T|Y_t; \gamma)e^{u'Y_T} \, dY_T.$$

Definition 5.2. *A Markov process Y is said to be an affine process if either its CCF or CMGF has the exponential affine form*

$$\text{CCF}_t \text{ or } \text{CMGF}_t = e^{\phi_{0t} + \phi'_{Y_t} Y_t}, \tag{5.3}$$

where ϕ_{0t} and ϕ_{Y_t} are complex (real) coefficients in the case of the CCF (CMGF). They are indexed by t to allow for the possibility of time dependence of the moments of Y.

5.2. Continuous-Time Affine Processes

To relate this definition to standard formulations of affine processes, we focus first on the case of continuous time since it was in this context that affine models were popularized. A jump-diffusion process is a Markov process solving the stochastic differential equation

$$dY_t = \mu(Y_t, \gamma_0) \, dt + \sigma(Y_t, \gamma_0) \, dW_t + dZ_t, \tag{5.4}$$

---

[2] For the case of discrete time and dependence on a finite set of lagged Y's, the construction of Y^* is immediate. Even when, in continuous time, the conditional distribution of Y_s depends on a continuum of lagged values of Y_t, it is often possible to define a new state variable that captures this dependence. The expanded state vector Y^* that includes this function of past Y's may once again be Markovan.

where W is an $(\mathcal{F}_t)$-standard Brownian motion in $\mathbb{R}^N$; $\mu : D \to \mathbb{R}^N$, $\sigma :$ $D \to \mathbb{R}^{N \times N}$, Z is a pure-jump process whose jump amplitudes have a fixed probability distribution ν on $\mathbb{R}^N$ and arrive with intensity $\{\lambda(Y_t) : t \geq 0\}$, for some $\lambda : D \to [0, \infty)$, and $\gamma \in \mathbb{R}^K$ is the vector of unknown parameters governing the model for Y_t. We adopt the Cox process construction of jump arrivals in which, conditional on the path $\{Y_s : 0 \leq s \leq t\}$ to time t, the times of jumps during the interval $[0, t]$ are assumed to be the jump times of a Poisson process with time-varying intensity $\{\lambda(Y_s) : 0 \leq s \leq t\}$, and the size of the jump distribution ν is assumed to be independent of $\{Y_s : 0 \leq s < T\}$.

The special case of an affine-jump diffusion is obtained by requiring that μ, $\sigma\sigma'$, and λ all be affine functions on D. More precisely, Y_t follows an affine-jump diffusion if

$$dY_t = \mathcal{K}(\Theta - Y_t)\,dt + \Sigma\sqrt{S_t}\,dW_t + dZ_t, \tag{5.5}$$

where W_t is an N–dimensional independent standard Brownian motion, $\mathcal{K}$ and Σ are $N \times N$ matrices, which may be nondiagonal and asymmetric, and S_t is a diagonal matrix with the ith diagonal element given by

$$S_{ii,t} = \alpha_i + \beta_i' Y_t. \tag{5.6}$$

Both the drifts in (5.5) and the instantaneous conditional variances in (5.6) are affine in Y_t. When jumps are present, the jump intensity $\lambda(t)$ is assumed to be a positive, affine function of the state Y_t, $\lambda(t) = l_0 + l_Y' Y(t)$, and the jump-size distribution f_J is assumed to be determined by its characteristic function $\mathcal{J}(u) = \int \exp\{ius\} f_J(s)\,ds$.

An implication of the transform analysis in Duffie et al. (2000) [see also Singleton (2001) and Section 5.4] is that, under technical regularity conditions, $\mathrm{CCF}_t(\tau, u)$ is exponential-affine:

$$\mathrm{CCF}_t(\tau, u) = e^{\phi_{0t} + \phi_{Yt}' Y_t}, \tag{5.7}$$

with ϕ_0 and ϕ_Y satisfying the complex-valued ordinary differential equations (ODEs or Riccati equations),[3]

$$\dot{\phi}_{Yt} = \mathcal{K} \cdot \phi_{Yt} - \frac{1}{2}\phi_{Yt}' H_1 \phi_{Yt} - l_Y(\mathcal{J}(\phi_{Yt}) - 1), \tag{5.8}$$

$$\dot{\phi}_{0t} = -\mathcal{K}\Theta \cdot \phi_{Yt} - \frac{1}{2}\phi_{Yt}' H_0 \phi_{Yt} - l_0(\mathcal{J}(\phi_{Yt}) - 1), \tag{5.9}$$

with $H_0 \in \mathbb{R}^{N \times N}$ and $H_1 \in \mathbb{R}^{N \times N \times N}$ defined by $[\Sigma S_t \Sigma']_{ij} = [H_0]_{ij} + [H_1]_{ij} \cdot Y_t$, and boundary conditions $\phi_{YT} = iu$ and $\phi_{0T} = 0$. Thus affine diffusions,

---

[3] Here, for any $c \in \mathbb{C}^N$, $c'H_1 c$ denotes the vector in $\mathbb{C}^N$ with kth element $\sum_{i,j} c_i [H_1]_{ijk} c_j$.

as characterized by (5.5) and (5.6), are special cases of those covered by Definition 5.2. A complete characterization of the family of affine processes is given in Duffie et al. (2003a).

Focusing on the case of an affine diffusion (i.e., setting the jump term to zero), we see that the affine structure of the drift and instantaneous variance carries over to the conditional moments of $\{Y_t\}$ obtained by sampling Y at a fixed time interval (e.g., a day, week, and so on). This follows from the fact that the CCF is an exponential affine function, and $\phi_{0t}(u)$ and $\phi_{Yt}(u)$ are both zero at $u = 0$. Evaluating the nth derivative of the CCF with respect to u at zero gives the nth conditional moment of $Y_{t+\tau}$ as an affine function of Y_t for all $n > 0$. For instance, the conditional mean of $Y_{t+\tau}$ given Y_t (the optimal τ-period ahead forecast of the discretely sampled Y) is

$$E\big[Y_{t+\tau}\big|Y_t\big] = e^{-\mathcal{K}\tau}Y_t + (I - e^{-\mathcal{K}\tau})\Theta. \qquad (5.10)$$

It follows that $\mathcal{K}$ governs the degree of mean reversion in the process toward its "long-run" or unconditional mean $E[Y_t] = \Theta$.

In the case of univariate affine diffusions, one way of quantifying the degree of mean reversion of a series is with the "half-life" of the series, defined to be the number τ that sets $e^{-\mathcal{K}\tau} = 0.5$. Roughly speaking, τ is the mean time that must elapse before the effect of a current shock to Y of size 1 has an effect of 0.5 on $Y_{t+\tau}$.

Higher-order moments can also be derived in closed form for the case of affine diffusions (see Fisher and Gilles, 1996, and Liu, 1997). Focusing on the conditional variances, two special cases warrant particular mention. If the $\beta_i = 0$, for all i, then Y_t is a Gaussian process. Supposing that there exists an $N \times N$ matrix X such that $X\mathcal{K}(X')^{-1}$ is a diagonal matrix with elements $(\kappa_1, \kappa_2, \ldots, \kappa_N)$ along the diagonal, in this case the conditional covariance matrix is given by

$$\mathrm{Var}(Y_{t+\tau}|Y_t) = X^{-1}\Omega(\tau)\left(X^{-1}\right)', \qquad (5.11)$$

where

$$\Omega(\tau) = \left[V_{ij}\frac{1 - e^{-(\kappa_i+\kappa_j)\tau}}{\kappa_i + \kappa_j}\right]_{i,j=1}^{N}, \qquad (5.12)$$

and $V = X\Sigma^2 X'$. Alternatively, if $\mathcal{K}$ is diagonal with ith element κ_i, Σ is diagonal with ith element σ_i, β_i is zero except in the ith location (where it is unity), and $\alpha_i = 0$ for all i, then Y is a vector of N independent square-root diffusions. The conditional variance of Y_i is then given by (2.54) with $\kappa = \kappa_i$ and $\Delta = \tau$.

We stress that these moments are the true conditional moments of the discretely sampled Y_t from an affine diffusion. This is to be contrasted with the conditional moments implied by an Euler discretization of an affine diffusion,[4]

$$\Delta Y_t^n = \frac{1}{n} \mu \left(Y_{t-h}^n, \gamma_0 \right) + \sigma \left(Y_{t-h}^n, \gamma_0 \right) \frac{1}{\sqrt{n}} \epsilon_t^n, \tag{5.13}$$

where n indexes the number of intervals into which each unit of time is divided, $h = 1/n$, and $\epsilon_t^n \sim N(0, I)$. For large n (small h), under regularity, the distribution of the Y solving (5.4) and the Y_k^n following (5.13) are approximately the same. In particular,

$$\lim_{n \to \infty} n \left[E \left(Y_t^n | Y_{t-h}^n \right) - Y_{t-h}^n \right] = \mu(Y, \gamma_0), \tag{5.14}$$

$$\lim_{n \to \infty} n \mathrm{Var} \left[Y_t^n | Y_{t-h}^n \right] = \sigma(Y, \gamma_0). \tag{5.15}$$

However, for any fixed n, the distributions of Y_t^n and Y_t are not the same. This is clearly illustrated by Example 2.1 and its discretized counterpart.[5] From (2.54) it follows that the conditional variance of r_{t+1} is an affine function of r_t and not proportional to r_t, as is the case in the Euler approximation. Additionally, the shock driving r in the true discrete-time model is noncentral chi-square, not Gaussian.

For the CCF_t of an affine diffusion to be well defined, some structure must be imposed on the functions ϕ_0 and ϕ_Y. Implicit in the requirements for well defined CCF and CMGF are conditions that ensure that even-powered conditional moments of the distribution of Y are nonnegative (Duffie and Kan, 1996; Dai and Singleton, 2000; Dai et al., 2005). These functions are potentially also constrained by the supports of the distributions of the Y_i (Gourieroux et al., 2002). For instance if, for given i, $Y_i \geq 0$, then the CMGF_t is nondecreasing in u_i for given values of the other u's and Y's. This, in turn, may constrain the functional forms of ϕ_0 and ϕ_Y. Verifying that an affine process, as specified through its CCF or CMGF, is well defined may involve case-by-case analyses of the properties of the model. Fortunately, for a large subfamily of affine models built up from affine-jump diffusions, a complete characterization of the admissible parameterizations is available by inspection of the parameters of the diffusions directly.

Before formally treating the admissibility of affine parameterizations, it is instructive to develop further intuition for the issues by considering a

---

[4] The addition of jumps allows for the possibility that over the small interval h, with probability $\lambda(Y_{t-h}^n)h$, Y^n will experience a jump of amplitude v.
[5] See Sun (1992) and Backus et al. (1998b) for discussions of discrete-time models obtained as discretizations of affine diffusions.

specific example of a two-factor affine model. Suppose that the state vector $Y' = (Y_1, Y_2)$ follows the process

$$d\begin{pmatrix} Y_{1t} \\ Y_{2t} \end{pmatrix} = \begin{pmatrix} \kappa_{11} & 0 \\ 0 & \kappa_{22} \end{pmatrix}\left(\begin{pmatrix} \theta_1 \\ \theta_2 \end{pmatrix} - \begin{pmatrix} Y_{1t} \\ Y_{2t} \end{pmatrix}\right) dt$$
$$+ \begin{pmatrix} \sigma_1\sqrt{Y_{1t}} & 0 \\ 0 & \sqrt{\alpha_2 + \beta_{21}Y_{1t}} \end{pmatrix} dW_t. \tag{5.16}$$

Inspection of (5.16) reveals that, at a minimum, for (Y_1, Y_2) to be a well-defined process, the instantaneous conditional variances Y_{1t} and $\alpha_2 + \beta_{21}Y_{1t}$ must be nonnegative. For this case at hand, the constraints that Y_{2t} does not appear in the drift and volatility of Y_{1t} imply that the first state variable Y_1 is an autonomous square-root diffusion. As such, so long as $\sigma_1 > 0$ and $\kappa_{11}\theta_1 > 0$, Y_1 is guaranteed to be nonnegative. Further, this process is specified so that the volatility of Y_{2t} depends only on Y_{1t}. Therefore, upon imposing the additional constraints that $\alpha_2 > 0$ and $\beta_{21} > 0$, we are assured that $\alpha_2 + \beta_{21}Y_{1t} \geq 0$, and this parameterization is admissible. From this example we see that if the state vector is divided up into the subvector that drives the volatility of all state variables (in this example Y_{1t}) and the remaining state variables (Y_{2t}), and sufficient structure is imposed on the first subvector to ensure that it remains nonnegative, then we are assured admissibility up to the imposition of some sign restrictions.

This example illustrates the need to constrain the parameters γ_0 in order to ensure that the conditional variance of Y remains nonnegative. There is no admissibility problem if $\beta_i = 0$, for all i, because in this case the instantaneous conditional volatilities are all constants. However, outside of this special case, to ensure admissibility we find it necessary to constrain the drift parameters ($\mathcal{K}$ and Θ) and diffusion coefficients [Σ and $\mathcal{B} \equiv (\beta_1, \beta_2, \ldots, \beta_N)$]. Moreover, our requirements for admissibility become increasingly stringent as the number of state variables determining $S_{ii,t}$ increases.

To formalize this intuition we consider the case where there are M state variables (without loss of generality, the first M) driving the instantaneous conditional variances of the N-vector Y, so $M = \text{rank}(\mathcal{B})$. Then, following Dai and Singleton (2000), on the state space $\mathbb{R}_+^M \times \mathbb{R}^{N-M}$, we define a set of $N+1$ *benchmark* models $\mathbb{A}_M(N)$ as follows.

Definition 5.3 [Benchmark Model $\mathbb{A}_M(N)$]. *For each M, we partition Y_t as $Y' = (Y^{V'}, Y^{D'})$, where Y^V is $M \times 1$ and Y^D is $(N - M) \times 1$,[6] and define the benchmark model $\mathbb{A}_M(N)$ as the special case of equation (5.5) with*

---

[6] The superscripts V and D indicate source of volatility factors and dependent factors, respectively.

$$
\mathcal{K} = \begin{bmatrix} \mathcal{K}^{VV}_{M \times M} & 0_{M \times (N-M)} \\ \mathcal{K}^{DV}_{(N-M) \times M} & \mathcal{K}^{DD}_{(N-M) \times (N-M)} \end{bmatrix} \tag{5.17}
$$

for $M > 0$, and $\mathcal{K}$ is unconstrained for $M = 0$;

$$
\Sigma = \begin{bmatrix} \sigma I_{M \times M} & 0_{M \times (N-M)} \\ \Sigma^{DV}_{(N-M) \times M} & \Sigma^{DD}_{(N-M) \times (N-M)} \end{bmatrix}, \tag{5.18}
$$

where σI is a diagonal matrix with $\sigma_i > 0$ in the ith diagonal position;

$$
\alpha = \begin{bmatrix} 0_{M \times 1} \\ \alpha^{D}_{(N-M) \times 1} \end{bmatrix} \geq 0; \tag{5.19}
$$

$$
\mathcal{B} = \begin{bmatrix} I_{M \times M} & B^{VD}_{M \times (N-M)} \\ 0_{(N-M) \times M} & 0_{(N-M) \times (N-M)} \end{bmatrix}; \tag{5.20}
$$

with the following parametric restrictions imposed:

$$
\mathcal{K}_i \Theta \equiv \sum_{j=1}^{M} \mathcal{K}_{ij} \Theta_j > 0, \ 1 \leq i \leq M, \tag{5.21}
$$

$$
\mathcal{K}_{ij} \leq 0, \ 1 \leq j \leq M, \ j \neq i, \tag{5.22}
$$

$$
\mathcal{B}_{ij} \geq 0, \ 1 \leq i \leq M, \ M+1 \leq j \leq N. \tag{5.23}
$$

We refer to these special cases as benchmark models for two reasons. First, most of the empirical implementations of affine diffusion models are special cases of one of these benchmark models. By construction, a given model can be a special case of only one benchmark model because it must satisfy the defining rank condition $M = \text{rank}(\mathcal{B})$. Moreover, model $\mathbb{A}_M(N)$ satisfies this rank condition because of the structure of $\mathcal{B}$ in (5.20): the upper $M \times M$ block is the identity matrix and the last $(N - M)$ rows are zero. Second, in our discussion of dynamic term structure models in Chapter 12, the models $\mathbb{A}_M(N)$ serve as canonical representations of entire equivalence classes of DAPMs.

The benchmark model $\mathbb{A}_M(N)$ has the conditional variances of the state variables controlled by the first M state variables[7]:

---

[7] The notation β_{jk} means the kth element of the column vector β_j.

$$S_{ii,t} = Y_{it}, \quad 1 \leq i \leq M, \tag{5.24}$$

$$S_{jj,t} = \alpha_j + \sum_{k=1}^{M} \beta_{jk} Y_{kt}, \quad M+1 \leq j \leq N, \tag{5.25}$$

where $\alpha_j \geq 0$, $\beta_{ji} \geq 0$. Therefore, as long as $Y_t^V \equiv (Y_1, Y_2, \ldots, Y_M)'$ is nonnegative with probability one, the benchmark representation of $Y_t = (Y_t^{V'}, Y_t^{D'})'$, where $Y_t^D \equiv (Y_{M+1}, Y_{M+2}, \ldots, Y_N)$, is admissible. In general, Y^V follows the diffusion

$$dY_t^V = (\mathcal{K}^{VV} \; \mathcal{K}^{VD})(\Theta - Y_t)dt + (\Sigma^{VV} \; \Sigma^{VD})\sqrt{S_t} dW_t. \tag{5.26}$$

To ensure that Y_t^V is bounded at zero from below, the drift of Y_t^V must be nonnegative and its diffusion must vanish at the zero boundary. Necessary and sufficient conditions for this are: C1: $\mathcal{K}^{VD} = 0_{M \times (N-M)}$; C2: $\Sigma^{VD} = 0_{M \times (N-M)}$; C3: $\Sigma_{ij} = 0, 1 \leq i \neq j \leq M$; C4: $\mathcal{K}_{ij} \leq 0, 1 \leq i \neq j \leq M$; C5: $\mathcal{K}^{VV} \Theta^V > 0$.[8]

C1 is imposed because otherwise there would be a positive probability that the drift of Y^V at the zero boundary becomes negative since Y_t^D is not bounded from below. (Note that, conditional on the path of Y_t^V, Y_t^D follows a Gaussian diffusion.) C2 and C3 are imposed to prevent Y_t^V from diffusing across zero owing to nonzero correlation between Y_t^V and Y_t^D. Condition C4 [same as (5.22)] is imposed because otherwise, with $Y^V \geq 0$, there is a positive probability that large values of Y_{jt} induce a negative drift in Y_{it} at its zero boundary, for $1 \leq i \neq j \leq M$. Together, C4 and C5 ensure that the drift condition

$$\mathcal{K}_{ii} \Theta_i + \sum_{j=1; j \neq i}^{M} \mathcal{K}_{ij}(\Theta_j - Y_{jt}) \geq 0 \tag{5.27}$$

holds for all i, $1 \leq i \leq M$.[9]

Finally, C5 implies that the zero boundary of Y^V is at least reflecting. This is because, under C1–C3, the subvector Y_t^V is an *autonomous* multivariate correlated square-root process governed by

---

[8] Here, following Dai and Singleton (2000), we show sufficiency of these conditions. Their necessity follows from the analysis in Duffie et al. (2003a).

[9] Under C1–C5 the existence of an (almost surely) nonnegative and nonexplosive solution to our canonical representation in (5.5) is ensured because its drift and diffusion functions are continuous and satisfy a growth condition (see Ikeda and Watanabe, 1981: ch. IV, th. 2.4). The uniqueness of the solution is ensured if the drift satisfies a Lipschitz condition and the diffusion function satisfies the Yamada condition (see Yamada and Watanabe, 1971: th. 1). Sufficient for the latter condition to be satisfied is that $\Sigma = I$. As we will see in Chapter 12, setting $\Sigma = I$ is a normalization in the context of affine term structure models.

$$dY_t^V = \mathcal{K}^{VV}(\Theta^V - Y_t^V)dt + (\sigma I)\sqrt{S_t^{VV}}\,dW_t^V. \qquad (5.28)$$

If the off-diagonal elements of $\mathcal{K}^{VV}$ are zero, then Y^V is an M-dimensional vector of independent square-root processes. That the zero boundary is reflecting is trivial in this case. Under C4, the drift of the correlated square-root process dominates that of the independent square-root process. By appealing to Lemma A.3 of Duffie and Kan (1996), we conclude that the zero-boundary for the correlated square-root process is at least reflecting.[10]

Knowing that these $N + 1$ canonical models are admissible assures us that any nested special case is also admissible. However, not all affine models are specials cases of these canonical models. For models outside these subfamilies, admissibility should be verified, on a case-by-case basis as necessary.

5.3. Discrete-Time Affine Processes

As noted previously, a discretization of a continuous-time model typically does not lead to a well-defined discrete-time counterpart of an $A_1(1)$ model. To construct discrete-time affine models with many of the same features of the $A_M(N)$ families of models we follow Darolles et al. (2001), Gourieroux and Jasiak (2001), and Dai et al. (2005) and develop discrete-time affine processes from the primitive assumption that the CMGF of Y_{t+1} is an exponential-affine function of Y_t. Special cases include the (true) discrete-time models implied by Gaussian and square-root affine diffusions. However, importantly, starting with the CMGF may allow for richer formulations of the dynamics of Y than in standard affine diffusion models.[11]

A discrete-time affine process is obtained by positing a functional form for the ϕ_{0t} and ϕ_{Yt} that defines the CMGF_t. Perhaps the simplest example arises under the assumption that $Y_{t+1}|Y_t \sim N(\alpha+\beta Y_t, \sigma^2)$, the autoregressive Gaussian model. In this case, $\text{CMGF}_t(u) = e^{u(\alpha+\beta Y_t)+u^2\sigma^2/2}$, which is clearly exponential-affine in Y_t.

A more complex example arises under the assumption that the CMGF of a scalar Markov process Y is given by

$$E_t\left[e^{uY_{t+1}}\right] = e^{-\nu \ln(1-uc)-(\rho u/1-uc)Y_t}, \qquad (5.29)$$

---

[10] C5 may be replaced by the stronger condition $[\mathcal{K}^{VV}\Theta^V]_i \geq \sigma_i^2/2$, $i = 1, \ldots, M$, as in Duffie and Kan (1996). This stronger condition, under which the zero boundary for Y^V is entrance, is the multivariate generalization of the Feller condition.

[11] As discussed in subsequent chapters, whether or not a DAPM constructed from discrete-time affine process is richer than its counterpart based on an affine diffusion also depends on how investors' attitudes toward risk, as captured by the "market prices of risk," are parameterized. As shown by Dai et al. (2005), DAPMs based on discrete-time affine processes also offer more tractability in specifying the market prices of risk.

with $\rho > 0$, $c > 0$, and $v > 0$. As discussed in Gourieroux and Jasiak (2001), this is the CMGF of an autoregressive gamma (AG) process obtained by having $Y_{t+1}|(Z_{t+1}, Y_t) \sim c$ gamma $(v + Z_{t+1})$, where $Z_{t+1}|Y_t \sim$ Poisson $(\rho Y_t/c)$. Equivalently, Y_{t+1}/c follows a noncentral gamma distribution with noncentrality parameter ρY_t. The conditional density function of an AG$(v, \rho Y_t, c)$ process is obtained as a convolution of the standard gamma and Poisson distributions:

$$f(Y_{t+1}|Y_t) = \frac{1}{c} \sum_{n=0}^{\infty} p_n \left(\frac{\rho Y_t}{c}\right) \gamma \left(\frac{Y_{t+1}}{c}, v + n\right), \tag{5.30}$$

where

$$p_n(\lambda) = \frac{\lambda^n}{n!} e^{-\lambda} \quad \text{and} \quad \gamma(y, a) = \frac{y^{a-1}}{\Gamma(a)} e^{-y} \tag{5.31}$$

are, respectively, the probability of n jump arrivals from a Poisson process with parameter λ, and the probability density of a standard gamma distribution with parameter a. $\Gamma(\cdot)$ is the gamma function. The first two conditional moments of Y_{t+1} implied by this model are

$$E\left[Y_{t+1}|Y_t\right] = vc + \rho Y_t, \tag{5.32}$$

$$\text{Var}\left[Y_{t+1}|Y_t\right] = vc^2 + 2c\rho Y_t, \tag{5.33}$$

both of which are affine in Y_t. See Gourieroux and Jasiak (2001) for a more in-depth treatment of univariate AG processes.

Starting with the specification of the CMGF makes it clear that we can extend these discrete-time formulations beyond those directly linked to diffusion models, however. For instance, a higher-order Markov process is easily accommodated by changing the conditioning information to $\vec{Y}_t^{\,J}$ and replacing (5.29) with

$$E\left[e^{uY_{t+1}}|\vec{Y}_t^{\,J}\right] = e^{-v\ln(1-uc) - u\rho'\vec{Y}_t^{\,J}/(1-uc)}. \tag{5.34}$$

Note that in this construction the counterparts to both the conditional mean and variance are again affine in $\vec{Y}_t^{\,J}$. That the conditional variance is affine in $\vec{Y}_t^{\,J}$, and not simply Y_t, implies that all of the elements of ρ must be nonnegative. This, in turn, restricts the nature of the persistence in Y accommodated by the AG$(v, \rho\vec{Y}_t^{\,J}, c)$ process. Had we instead started with the CMGF of a conditional Gaussian process, with constant conditional variance, then the analogous ρ would be unconstrained.

All of these Laplace transforms describe well-defined discrete-time models in their own right. It also turns out that they can be interpreted as the discrete-time counterparts to continuous-time models in the sense that as the length of the sampling interval shrinks toward zero, they converge to affine diffusions. More precisely, in the case of the autoregressive Gaussian model, we let $\alpha = \kappa\theta\Delta t$, $\beta = 1 - \kappa\Delta t$, and $\sigma^2 = \tilde{\sigma}^2\Delta t$. Then, as $\Delta t \to 0$, Y_t converges to the Gaussian process: $dY_t = \kappa(\theta - Y_t)dt + \tilde{\sigma}\,dW_t$.

Similarly, for the AG($\nu, \rho Y_t, c$) process, let $\rho = 1 - \kappa\Delta t$, $c = (\sigma^2/2)\Delta t$, and $\nu = 2\kappa\theta/\sigma^2$. Then, as $\Delta t \to 0$,

$$\frac{E_t\,[Y_{t+\Delta t}] - Y_t}{\Delta t} \to \kappa(\theta - Y_t), \qquad \frac{\mathrm{Var}_t\,[Y_{t+\Delta t}]}{\Delta t} \to \sigma^2 Y_t, \qquad (5.35)$$

and Y_t converges to the square-root process: $dY_t = \kappa(\theta - Y_t)dt + \sigma\sqrt{Y_t}dW_t$.

The difference between the conditional density of the square-root diffusion and the AG process is illustrated in Figure 5.1 for the parameter values

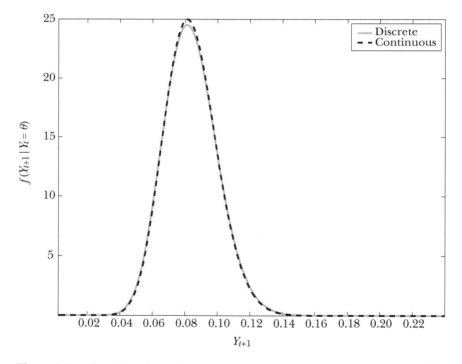

Figure 5.1. *Conditional density of an autoregressive gamma process: $\nu = 4$. The other parameter values are: $\rho = 0.917$, $c = 0.00167$, $\kappa = 1$, $\sigma = 0.2$, $\theta = 0.08$, and $\Delta t = 1/12$.*

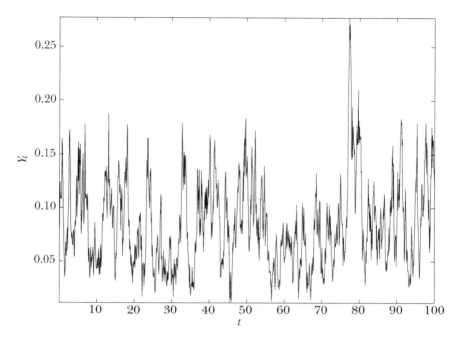

Figure 5.2. *Simulated time path of an autoregressive gamma process: $v = 4$.*

$v = 4$, $\rho = 0.917$, $c = 0.0017$, and with $\Delta t = 1/12$, indicating monthly data.[12] The distribution of the discrete process is somewhat fatter tailed than its continuous-time counterpart, but the two are very close in shape. An illustrative simulation from the AG process is presented in Figure 5.2. This simulated path is everywhere positive, fluctuates around the long-run mean of Y_t ($\theta = 0.08$), and never approaches zero.

The parameter v underlies the so-called Feller condition, named after W. Feller (1951), who proved that the condition $v > 1$ is sufficient to guarantee that the sample path of a square-root diffusion is strictly positive. A value of v between zero and one means that a square-root process hits zero and is absorbed there with probability one. Nevertheless, assuming that $\kappa > 0$, there exists a unique solution for $\{Y_t\}$ that is nonnegative for all finite t. To illustrate the different behavior of an AG process with $v > 1$ and $v < 1$, we display in Figures 5.3 and 5.4 the density and representative sample path for an AG process with $v = 0.4$. Note that, throughout this simulation, the process remains nonnegative. Moreover, it spends long periods near zero, which is well below its long-run mean of 0.08. This average is achieved

---

[12] I am grateful to Qiang Dai for providing these comparisons.

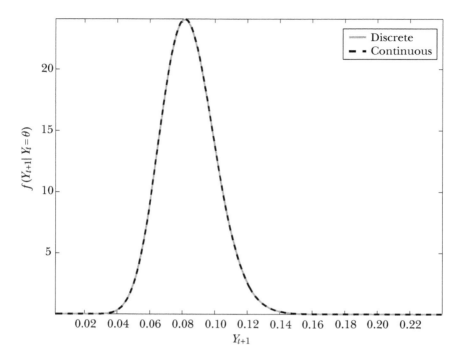

Figure 5.3   *Conditional density of an autoregressive gamma process:* $\nu = 0.4$. *The other parameter values are:* $\rho = 0.992$, $c = 0.00167$, $\kappa = 0.1$, $\sigma = 0.2$, $\theta = 0.08$, *and* $\Delta t = 1/12$.

through the relatively pronounced upward moves in Y_t, almost as if Y has a jump component with large positive amplitude.

To construct the discrete-time counterparts to many of the multivariate affine diffusions that have previously been examined in the literature, we need to combine multivariate Gaussian and AG processes. Following Dai et al. (2005), we refer to an $N \times 1$ vector of stochastic processes $X_t = (Z_t', Y_t')'$ as a $DA_M(N)$ process if: (i) Z_t is an autonomous $DA_M(M)$ process; and (ii) conditional on Y_t and Z_t, Y_{t+1} is normally distributed with a conditional variance that depends on Z_t. Elaborating, for the $M \times 1$ autonomous vector autoregressive gamma process Z_t, $f(Z_{t+1}|Z_t)$ is given by

$$f(Z_{t+1}|Z_t) = \prod_{i=1}^{M} \frac{1}{c_i} \sum_{n=0}^{\infty} \left[\frac{(\rho_i Z_t / c_i)^n}{n!} e^{-\frac{\rho_i Z_t}{c_i}} \times \frac{\left(Z_{t+1}^i / c_i\right)^{\nu_i + n - 1} e^{-(Z_{t+1}^i / c_i)}}{\Gamma(\nu_i + n)} \right], \quad (5.36)$$

where ρ_i is the ith row of an $M \times M$ nonsingular matrix $\rho = (I_{M \times M} - \varrho)$, so that $\rho_i Z_t = (1 - \varrho_{ii}) Z_t^i - \sum_{j \neq i} \varrho_{ij} Z_t^j$, with $0 < \varrho_{ii} < 1$, $\varrho_{ij} \leq 0$, $1 \leq i \leq M$.

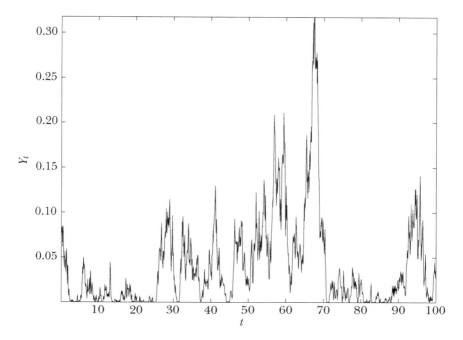

Figure 5.4 *Simulated time path of an autoregressive gamma process: $\nu = 0.4$.*

When the off-diagonal elements of the $M \times M$ matrix ρ are nonzero, the autoregressive gamma processes are correlated.

It follows that, for any u such that $u_i < (1/c_i)$, the conditional Laplace transform of Z has the exponential-affine form (5.2) with

$$\phi_{Z0}(u) = -\sum_{i=1}^{N} \nu_i \log (1 - u_i c_i), \quad \phi_{ZZ}(u) = \sum_{i=1}^{N} \frac{u_i}{1 - u_i c_i} \rho_i'.$$

Furthermore, the conditional mean m_{Zt} and the diagonal elements of the conditional covariance matrix V_{Zt} of Z_{t+1} given Z_t are

$$m_{Zt} = \nu_i c_i + \rho_i Z_t, \quad V_{Zt}(i, i) = \nu_i c_i^2 + 2c_i \rho_i Z_t.$$

The off-diagonal elements $V_{Zt}(i, j)$, $i \neq j$, are zero.

Conditional on X_t, Y_{t+1} is a $(N - M) \times 1$ autoregressive Gaussian process with the conditional density of Y_{t+1} given Y_t and Z_t given by

$$Y_{t+1} \sim \text{Normal} \left(\mu_{Yt}, \Omega_{Yt} \right),$$

where $\mu_{Yt} = \mu_{Y0} + \mu_{YX}X_t$ and $\Omega_{Yt} = \Sigma_Y S_t \Sigma_Y'$, with μ_{Y0} a $(N-M) \times 1$ vector, μ_{YX} an $(N-M) \times N$ matrix, Σ_Y an $(N-M) \times (N-M)$ matrix, and S_t a $(N-M) \times (N-M)$ diagonal matrix with ith diagonal given by $\alpha_i + \beta_i' Z_t$, $1 \le i \le N-M$. The conditional Laplace transform of Y takes the form $\exp\{\phi_{Y0}(u) + \phi_{YX}(u)'X_t\}$, with

$$\phi_{Y0}(u) = \mu_{Y0}'u + \frac{1}{2}u'\Omega_{Yt}u, \quad \phi_{YX}(u) = (\mu_{YX})'u.$$

It is easy to see that, conditional on Y_t, Y_{t+1} is normally distributed with conditional mean $\mu_{Y0} + \mu_{YX}X_t$ and conditional covariance matrix Ω_{Yt}.

To construct a joint density of X_{t+1} given X_t based on these observations, we exploit the fact that (by construction) $f(Z_{t+1}|X_t) = f(Z_{t+1}|Z_t)$. Additionally, we assume that, conditional on X_t, Z_{t+1} and Y_{t+1} are independent, so, in particular, $f(Y_{t+1}|Z_{t+1}, X_t) = f(Y_{t+1}|X_t)$. This assumption essentially amounts to assuming that within-period shocks to Z and Y are independent. In this regard, our construction of discrete-time affine processes is more restrictive than for the continuous-time models since the latter models allowed for nonzero (instantaneous) correlations across the Y^V and Y^D [see equation (5.18)]. While this added structure on the models $DA_M(N)$ may be restrictive in some settings, it turns out to be without loss of generality in dynamic term structure models (see Chapter 12).

Under these assumptions, it follows that the conditional Laplace transform of X_{t+1} given X_t is exponential-affine as in (5.2). In the continuous-time limit, X_t becomes the canonical model $\mathbb{A}_M(N)$ for the subfamily $A_M(N)$ of affine diffusions.

5.4. Transforms for Affine Processes

We noted earlier that the Fourier transform of the conditional density (the CCF) of Y_{t+1}, discretely sampled from an affine diffusion, is known in closed form as an exponential-affine function of Y_t. It turns out that related, more general transforms of affine processes are also known and these transforms turn out to play a central role in pricing bonds (Chapter 12) and options (Chapter 15). In anticipation of these analyses, we summarize the results on transforms for affine-jump diffusions from Duffie et al. (2000), and present some analogous results for discrete-time affine processes.

5.4.1. Transforms of Affine-Jump Diffusions

Discounting is an integral part of pricing so we first introduce a discount-rate function $R : D \to \mathbb{R}$ that is an affine function of the state

$$R(Y) = \rho_0 + \rho_1 \cdot Y, \tag{5.37}$$

for $\rho = (\rho_0, \rho_1) \in \mathbb{R} \times \mathbb{R}^N$. The affine dependence of the drift and diffusion coefficients of Y and the jump intensity λ are determined by coefficients (K, H, l) defined by[13]:

- $\mu(Y) = K_0 + K_1 Y$, for $K = (K_0, K_1) \in \mathbb{R}^N \times \mathbb{R}^{N \times N}$.
- $(\sigma(Y)\sigma(Y)')_{ij} = (H_0)_{ij} + (H_1)_{ij} \cdot Y$, for $H = (H_0, H_1) \in \mathbb{R}^{N \times N} \times \mathbb{R}^{N \times N \times N}$.
- $\lambda(x) = l_0 + l_1 \cdot x$, for $l = (l_0, l_1) \in \mathbb{R} \times \mathbb{R}^N$.

For $c \in \mathbb{C}^N$, the set of N-tuples of complex numbers, we let $\theta(c) = \int_{\mathbb{R}^N} \exp (c \cdot z) \, d\nu(z)$ whenever the integral is well defined. This jump transform determines the jump-size distribution. A "characteristic" $\chi = (K, H, l, \theta, \rho)$ captures both the distribution of Y as well as the effects of any discounting.

Using this notation, we define the transform $\mathbb{T}^\chi : \mathbb{C}^N \times D \times \mathbb{R}_+ \times \mathbb{R}_+ \to \mathbb{C}$ of Y_T conditional on $\mathcal{F}_t$, when well defined at $t \leq T$, by

$$\mathbb{T}^\chi (u, Y_t, t, T) = E^\chi \left(\exp \left(- \int_t^T R(Y_s)ds \right) e^{u \cdot Y_T} \, \bigg| \, \mathcal{F}_t \right), \qquad (5.38)$$

where E^χ denotes expectation under the distribution of Y determined by χ. [Here, $\mathbb{T}^\chi$ differs from the CCF of the distribution of Y_T because of the discounting at rate $R(Y_t)$.] Duffie et al. (2000) show that, under technical regularity conditions,

$$\mathbb{T}^\chi (u, y, t, T) = e^{\psi_{0t} + \psi_{Yt} \cdot y}, \qquad (5.39)$$

where ψ_0 and ψ_Y satisfy the complex-valued ODEs

$$\dot{\psi}_{Yt} = \rho_1 - K_1 \cdot \beta_t - \frac{1}{2}\psi'_{Yt}H_1\psi_{Yt} - l_1 \left(\theta(\psi_{Yt}) - 1\right), \qquad (5.40)$$

$$\dot{\psi}_{0t} = \rho_0 - K_0 \cdot \psi_t^Y - \frac{1}{2}\psi'_{Yt}H_0\psi_{0t} - l_0 \left(\theta(\psi_{Yt}) - 1\right), \qquad (5.41)$$

with boundary conditions $\psi_{YT} = u$ and $\psi_{0T} = 0$. The ODE (5.40) and (5.41) is easily conjectured from an application of Ito's formula to the candidate form (5.39) of $\mathbb{T}^\chi$. In some applications, explicit solutions for these ODEs are known (e.g., for square-root diffusions). In other cases, solutions are found numerically. This suggests a practical advantage to choosing jump distributions with an explicitly known or easily computed jump transform θ.

As we will see, certain pricing problems call for the calculation of the expected present value of the product of affine and exponential-affine

---

[13] Here we change notation from the previous section in order to conform with the notation in Duffie et al. (2000).

functions of Y_T. Accordingly, we define the "extended" transform $\tilde{\mathbb{T}}^\chi$: $\mathbb{R}^N \times \mathbb{C}^N \times D \times \mathbb{R}_+ \times \mathbb{R}_+ \to \mathbb{C}$ of Y_T conditional on $\mathcal{F}_t$, when well defined for $t \leq T$ by

$$\tilde{\mathbb{T}}^\chi(v, u, Y_t, t, T) = E\left(\exp\left(-\int_t^T R(Y_s)\, ds\right)(v \cdot Y_T) e^{u \cdot Y_T} \,\Big|\, \mathcal{F}_t\right). \quad (5.42)$$

The extended transform $\tilde{\mathbb{T}}^\chi$ can be computed by differentiation of the transform $\tilde{\mathbb{T}}^\chi$, just as moments can be computed from a moment-generating function (under technical conditions justifying differentiation through the expectation). Specifically, under technical conditions, including the differentiability of the jump transform θ, Duffie et al. (2000) show that

$$\tilde{\mathbb{T}}^\chi(v, u, y, t, T) = \tilde{\mathbb{T}}^\chi(u, y, t, T)(A_t + B_t \cdot y), \quad (5.43)$$

where $\tilde{\mathbb{T}}^\chi$ is given by (5.39) and B and A satisfy the linear ordinary differential equations

$$-\dot{B}_t = K_1' B_t + \beta_t' H_1 B_t + l_1 \nabla \theta(\beta_t) B_t, \quad (5.44)$$

$$-\dot{A}_t = K_0 \cdot B_t + \beta_t' H_0 B_t + l_0 \nabla \theta(\beta_t) B_t, \quad (5.45)$$

with the boundary conditions $B_T = v$ and $A_T = 0$, where $\nabla \theta(c)$ is the gradient of $\theta(c)$ with respect to $c \in \mathbb{C}^n$.

5.4.2. Transforms for Discrete-Time Affine Processes

An analogous extended transform that is useful for pricing in discrete-time models is

$$\mathbb{D}^\chi(v, u, Y_t) \equiv E\left[e^{u' Y_{t+1}}(v' Y_{t+1})\,\big|\, Y_t\right] = v' E\left[\nabla_u e^{u' Y_{t+1}} \,\big|\, Y_t\right], \quad (5.46)$$

where $\nabla_u f(u)$ is a $N \times 1$ column vector with ith element $\partial f(u)/\partial u_i$. Under exchange of expectation and differentiation we have

$$\mathbb{D}^\chi(v, u, Y_t) = v' \nabla_u E\left[e^{u' Y_{t+1}} \,\big|\, Y_t\right]$$
$$= e^{\phi_0(u) + \phi_Y(u)' Y_t} v'(\nabla_u \phi_0(u) + \nabla_u \phi_Y(u)' Y_t), \quad (5.47)$$

where $\phi_0(u)$ and $\phi_Y(u)$ are the coefficients from the conditional Laplace transform (5.2), $\nabla_u \phi_0(u)$ is a $N \times 1$ column vector with ith element $\partial \phi_0(u)/\partial u_i$ and $\nabla_u \phi_Y(u)$ is an $N \times N$ matrix with ijth element $\partial \phi_{Yj}(u)/\partial u_i$. Expression (5.47) simplifies further to

$$\mathbb{D}^\chi(v, u, Y_t) = e^{\phi_0(u)+\phi_Y(u)'Y_t}(c(u, v) + d(u, v)'Y_t), \qquad (5.48)$$

where $c(u, v) \equiv v'\nabla_u\phi_0(u)$ and $d(u, v)' \equiv v'\nabla_u\phi_Y(u)'$, for a scalar function $c(u, v)$ and an $N \times 1$ vector of functions $d(u, v)$.

5.5. GMM Estimation of Affine Processes

One straightforward, albeit often inefficient, approach to the estimation of affine processes is to construct GMM estimators based on knowledge of the conditional moments of Y_{t+1} given Y_t. These moments can be computed from the derivatives of the CCF (or CMGF when it exists) evaluated at $u = 0$. Therefore, given a particular conditional moment, say

$$\frac{\partial^{j+k}\mathrm{CCF}_t(u, \gamma_0)}{\partial u_{s_1}^j u_{s_2}^k}\Bigg|_{u=0} = i^{j+k}E\big[Y_{s_1,t+1}^j Y_{s_2,t+1}^k\big|Y_t\big], \qquad (5.49)$$

for $1 \leq s_1, s_2 \leq N$, orthogonality conditions for GMM estimation can be constructed from the moment restrictions

$$E\left(Y_{s_1,t+1}^j Y_{s_2,t+1}^k - \frac{\partial^{j+k}\mathrm{CCF}_t(u, \gamma_0)}{i^{j+k}\partial u_{s_1}^j u_{s_2}^k}\Bigg|_{u=0}\Bigg| Y_t\right) = 0. \qquad (5.50)$$

Special cases are the closed-form expressions for the conditional mean $E[Y_{t+1}|Y_t]$ and conditional variance $\mathrm{Var}[Y_{t+1}|Y_t]$ derived in Fisher and Gilles (1996) for affine diffusions. The corresponding moments for discrete-time affine processes can be derived directly off the CMGF.

With the first two conditional moments in hand, a standard QML estimator of ψ_0 with the normal likelihood function can be computed. This leads to consistent and asymptotically normal estimators that are generally less efficient than the density-based estimators discussed later. Indeed, apart from the case of Gaussian diffusions, the "innovations" in affine models are nonnormal (e.g., noncentral chi-square in the case of square-root diffusions). In a different, nonaffine setting, Sandmann and Koopman (1998) found that quasi-ML estimators of stochastic volatility models were relatively inefficient compared to full-information methods, because of the nonnormal innovations. One might expect that a similar result would emerge in the case of affine processes.

Additional efficiency may also be achieved by selection of a richer set of moments and implementing the simulated moments estimator introduced in Chapter 6. This estimation strategy is applicable to any model (not just affine models) as long as we can reliably simulate a discretely sampled Y_t from the model, so we defer discussion until the next chapter.

5.6. ML Estimation of Affine Processes

The special structure of affine models means that it is often possible to circumvent the use of simulation, while still achieving the efficiency of ML estimation. Whether this efficiency is actually or only approximately achieved depends on the specification of the model.

5.6.1. ML Estimation with Known Conditional Density

If the conditional density of Y_{t+1} given Y_t, $f(Y_{t+1}|Y_t; \gamma_0)$, is known in closed form, then we can proceed directly to write the conditional log-likelihood function of the sample $\{Y_t\}_{t=1}^T$, $l_T(\gamma)$, as in (2.3) of Chapter 2. Maximization of (2.3) proceeds in the usual way. Examples of affine diffusions with known conditional density functions are the cases where Y_t is a vector Gaussian process $(M = 0)$ and Y_t is a vector of independent square-root processes $(M = N$ and $\mathcal{K}$ is diagonal). In the Gaussian case, $Y_{t+\tau}$ conditional on Y_t is distributed as a normal with mean (5.10) and variance matrix (5.11). These moments lead immediately to the construction of the likelihood function for this model. The case of an independent square-root diffusion was covered in our discussion in Chapter 2, where it was noted that the distribution of each $Y_{i,t+1}$ conditional on Y_{it} is a noncentral chi-square. The relevant density for the multivariate case (under independence) is obtained by multiplying together the relevant conditional densities for the N elements of Y.

An example of a jump-diffusion model with a known likelihood function is the pure-jump diffusion

$$dY(t) = \mu_Y\,dt + \sigma_Y\,dW(t) + J(t)\,dZ(t), \tag{5.51}$$

where the jump amplitude $J(t)$ is distributed as $N(m_J, \delta^2)$. Focusing first on the moment of the nonjump component of (5.51), this model implies that $Y(t)$ follows a Gaussian diffusion model and, hence, that $Y_t - Y_{t-n}$ is distributed as $N(n\mu_Y, n\sigma_Y^2)$. This is an immediate consequence of the assumptions of constant instantaneous mean and variance and the independence over time of the increments (shocks) $dW(t)$. To this normal distribution, we add a Poisson jump process with the probability of a jump over any short time interval $[t, t + dt)$ of $\zeta\,dt$. Thus, within any discrete interval of length n there may be multiple jumps, with the number of jumps L being distributed as a Poisson process with intensity ζn. Combining these observations, we know that, conditional on the number of jumps $L = \ell$ over the sampling interval of the data (say one period so that $n = 1$), the distribution of ΔY_t is $f(\Delta Y_t|L = \ell) = N(\mu_Y + \ell\zeta, \eta^2 + \ell\delta^2)$. This is an implication of the assumption that the jump amplitudes J_t are normally distributed and that, conditional on L, ΔY_t is the sum of $L + 1$ independent normal random variables, $N(n\mu_Y, n\sigma_Y^2) + J_1 + \ldots + J_L$. The density of ΔY_t is then obtained by "integrating out" over the density of the number of jumps:

$$f(\Delta Y_t) = \sum_{\ell=0}^{\infty} \frac{e^{-\lambda}\lambda^{\ell}}{\ell!} \frac{1}{\sqrt{2\pi(\eta^2 + \ell\delta^2)}} e^{-\frac{1}{2}(\Delta Y_t - \mu_Y - \ell\psi)^2/(\eta^2 + \ell\delta^2)}. \qquad (5.52)$$

One of the major advantages of casting an affine model in discrete time is that the likelihood function of the data is known in closed form for a much larger class of models than in the case of continuous time. In particular, if Z_{t+1} conditional on Z_t follows an autoregressive gamma process with density function (5.36), Y_{t+1} conditional on $X_t' = (Z_t', Y_t')$ is Gaussian with density $f(Y_{t+1}|X_t)$, and (conditional on X_t) Z_{t+1} and Y_{t+1} are independent, then the conditional likelihood function for X can be constructed in closed form from the densities $f(X_{t+1}|X_t) = f(Z_{t+1}|Z_t) \times f(Y_{t+1}|X_t)$. Since this construction encompasses the discrete-time counterparts to a large fraction of the affine diffusions studied in the literature, having a closed-form likelihood is a very powerful result. Its practical importance becomes fully apparent upon review of the approximations developed in the literature to deal with our lack of knowledge of the conditional density functions for discretely sampled data from diffusion models.

5.6.2. Simulated ML Using Small Time Steps

Simulated ML estimators for diffusions have been proposed for general diffusion models by Pedersen (1995) and Brandt and Santa-Clara (2001), and for the special case of affine diffusions by Duffie et al. (2003b). This approach starts by dividing each sampling interval $[t, t+1]$ into n subintervals, say of equal length $h = (1/n)$, and expressing the density function of the data as

$$f(Y_{t+1}|Y_t) = \int_{\mathbb{R}^N} f(Y_{t+1}|Y_{t+1-h}) \times f(Y_{t+1-h}|Y_t) \, dY_{t+1-h}$$

$$= E[f(Y_{t+1}|Y_{t+1-h}; \gamma)|Y_t; \gamma]. \qquad (5.53)$$

From (5.53) we see that the density function $f(Y_{t+1}|Y_t)$ can be interpreted as an expectation of $f(Y_{t+1}|Y_{t+1-h})$, treated as a function of Y_{t+1-h}, and integrated against the conditional density $f(Y_{t+1-h}|Y_t)$. Therefore, if the density $f(Y_{t+1}|Y_{t+1-h})$ can be accurately approximated, and (given Y_t) Y_{t+1-h} can be simulated, then (5.53) can be computed by Monte Carlo integration.

Pedersen (1995) proposes working with the Euler approximation (5.13) and replacing the density $f(Y_{t+1}|Y_{t+1-h})$ in (5.53) with $f_N(Y_{t+1}|Y_{t+1-h}^{\gamma,n})$, the density function of a normal distribution with mean $(1/n)\mu(Y_{t+1-h}^{\gamma,n}; \gamma)$ and variance $\sigma^2(Y_{t+1-h}^{\gamma,n}; \gamma)/n$. Additionally, using the standard factorization of the conditional density $f(Y_{t+1}|Y_t)$,

$$
f(Y_{t+1}|Y_t) = \int_{\mathbb{R}^N} f(Y_{t+1}|Y_{t+1-h}) \times f(Y_{t+1-h}|Y_{t+1-2h}) \times
$$
$$
\cdots \times f(Y_{t+1-(n-1)h}|Y_t), \tag{5.54}
$$

Pedersen replaces each conditional density $f(Y_{t+1-jh}|Y_{t+1-(j+1)h})$ by the normal density $f_N(Y_{t+1-jh}|Y_{t+1-(j+1)h}^{\gamma,n})$. Then, fixing a t, to compute an approximation to the expectation in (5.53), he repeatedly simulates values of $Y_{t+1-h}^{\gamma,n}$, say $[Y_{t+1-h}^{\gamma,n}|Y_t]_j$ for the jth simulation, always starting from the same initial value Y_t. This is accomplished by recursively drawing from the distributions $f_N(Y_{t+1-jh}|Y_{t+1-(j+1)h}^{\gamma,n})$, after conditioning on the value of $Y_{t+1-(j+1)h}^{\gamma,n}$ from the previous step, starting with Y_t. Finally, Pedersen approximates the expectation in (5.53) as

$$
f(Y_{t+1}|Y_t) \approx \frac{1}{\mathcal{T}} \sum_{j=1}^{\mathcal{T}} f(Y_{t+1}|[Y_{t+1-h}^{\gamma,n}|Y_t]_j; \gamma), \tag{5.55}
$$

where $\mathcal{T}$ is the simulation size.

This approach relies on the Euler approximation multiple times to simulate $Y_{t+1-h}^{\gamma,n}$ given Y_t. Therefore, in establishing the large-sample properties of the resulting estimator, the nature of the inherent approximation errors have to be examined simultaneously with limiting distributions of sample moments. Pedersen (1995) shows, for the special case of a Gaussian diffusion, that there is a rate at which n can grow with T such that consistency and asymptotic normality are ensured. (Effectively, the approximation errors approach zero at a sufficiently fast rate relative to T that these errors can be ignored in the computation of the asymptotic distribution of the ML estimator for γ_0.) He does not provide a specific rate, however. Brandt and Santa-Clara (2001: th. 2) show that, if $T \to \infty$, $n \to \infty$, and $\mathcal{T} \to \infty$, with $\mathcal{T}^{1/2}/n \to 1$ and $T/\mathcal{T}^{1/4} \to 0$, then their simulated ML estimator is distributed asymptotically as a normal random vector.

Duffie et al. (2003b) propose a simulated ML estimator that shares certain features with estimators proposed by Pedersen (1995) and Brandt and Santa-Clara (2001) for general diffusions. However, importantly, it exploits the special structure of affine diffusions in order to avoid some of their approximations. To illustrate the basic idea of their approach, consider the bivariate affine diffusion

$$
dY_1 = (k_1 - K_{11}Y_1)dt + \sqrt{Y_1}\, dW_1, \tag{5.56}
$$

$$
dY_2 = (k_2 - K_{21}Y_1 - K_{22}Y_2)dt + \sqrt{1 + \beta Y_1}\, dW_2, \tag{5.57}
$$

and let $Y_t' = (Y_{1t}, Y_{2t})$. We are interested in computing the transition density of Y_{t+1} given Y_t implied by (5.56) and (5.57), where time is measured relative to the sampling interval of the available data.

Consider again the expression (5.53) and, in particular, the first density $f(Y_{t+1}|Y_{t+1-h})$. To simplify notation, we consider the generic case of $f(Y_t|Y_{t-h})$. The particular structure of this model, with no feedback from Y_2 to Y_1 as in our benchmark affine model with $M = 1$ and $N = 2$, implies that $f(Y_{1t}|Y_{t-h}) = f(Y_{1t}|Y_{1,t-h})$ and

$$f(Y_t|Y_{t-h}) = f(Y_{1t}|Y_{1,t-h}) \times f(Y_{2t}|Y_{1t}, Y_{t-h}). \tag{5.58}$$

The structure of (5.57) is such that $f(Y_{1t}|Y_{1,t-h})$ is known exactly to be a noncentral chi-square distribution; no approximation for its conditional density function is necessary (see the discussion of Example 2.1). In particular, Pedersen's Euler approximations are unnecessary. Thus, once we have determined a functional form for $f(Y_{2t}|Y_{1t}, Y_{t-h})$ we will have characterized $f(Y_t|Y_{t-h})$.

Now the conditional density of Y_{2t} given Y_{t-h} *and the entire path of Y_1 between dates $t - h$ and t* is known exactly to be a normal distribution,

$$f(Y_{2t}|Y_{1s}, s \in [t - h, t]; Y_{2,t-h}) \sim N(\mu_t, \sigma_t^2), \tag{5.59}$$

with

$$\mu_t = e^{-K_{22}h}\left[\int_{t-h}^{t} e^{K_{22}s}(k_2 - K_{11}Y_{1s})\, ds + Y_{2,t-h}\right], \tag{5.60}$$

$$\sigma_t^2 = e^{-K_{22}h}\left[\int_{t-h}^{t} e^{2K_{22}s}(1 + \beta Y_{1s})\, ds\right]. \tag{5.61}$$

We are interested in $f(Y_{2t}|Y_{1t}, Y_{t-h})$ and not (5.59). For small h, we approximate the former by the latter with Y_1 presumed to evolve deterministically between $t - h$ and t. That is, we assume that

$$f(Y_{2t}|Y_{1t}, Y_{t-h}) \sim N(\tilde{\mu}_t, \tilde{\sigma}_t^2), \tag{5.62}$$

with the moments $\tilde{\mu}_t$ and $\tilde{\sigma}_t^2$ given by

$$\tilde{\mu}_t = e^{-K_{22}h}\left[\int_{t-h}^{t} e^{K_{22}s}(k_2 - K_{11}\ell(Y_{1t}, Y_{1,t-h}, s))\, ds + Y_{2,t-h}\right], \tag{5.63}$$

$$\tilde{\sigma}_t^2 = e^{-K_{22}h}\left[\int_{t-h}^{t} e^{2K_{22}s}(1 + \beta\ell(Y_{1t}, Y_{1,t-h}, s))\, ds\right], \tag{5.64}$$

where $\ell(Y_{1t}, Y_{1,t-h}, s)$ is a deterministic scheme for interpolating between $Y_{1,t-h}$ and Y_{1t}. One simple version of ℓ is

$$\ell\left(Y_{1t}, Y_{1,t-h}, s\right) = Y_{1,t-h} + s\left(Y_{1t} - Y_{1,t-h}\right), \ s \in [0, 1]. \qquad (5.65)$$

Combining this approximation with the known density function for Y_1 gives $f(Y_t | Y_{t-h})$. With this approximation in hand, we can compute an approximate version, $\tilde{f}(Y_{t+1} | Y_{t+1-h}; \gamma)$, of the conditional density (5.53).

To compute the expectation in (5.53), Duffie et al. (2003b) also start with the factorization of $f(Y_{t+1} | Y_t)$ in (5.54). Like Pedersen, they compute the expectation by Monte Carlo integration, but in a manner that exploits the affine structure. Specifically, for the τth draw of Y_{t+1-h}, say Y_{t+1-h}^{τ}, they replace each of the densities $f(Y_{t+1-jh} | Y_{t+1-(j+1)h})$ with their approximate density $\tilde{f}(Y_{t+1-jh} | Y_{t+1-(j+1)h})$. Then, starting with the initial value Y_t, they sequentially draw Y_{t+1-jh}, $j = (n-1), \ldots, 1$, from the approximate densities with the previous draw used as the conditioning variable in the current draw, to obtain Y_{t+1-h}^{τ}. Finally, the desired expectation is computed as

$$f\left(Y_{t+1} | Y_t\right) \approx \frac{1}{\mathcal{T}} \sum_{\tau=1}^{\mathcal{T}} \tilde{f}\left(Y_{t+1} | Y_{t+1-h}^{\tau}\right), \qquad (5.66)$$

where $\mathcal{T}$ is the number of random draws.

Each draw from a representative conditional density $\tilde{f}(Y_{t+1-jh} | Y_{t+1-(j+1)h})$ is computed as follows. Given $Y_{t+1-(j+1)h}$, $Y_{1,t+1-jh}$ is drawn from the noncentral chi-square distribution with moments and a noncentrality parameter that are known functions of model parameters.[14] Then, given $Y_{t+1-(j+1)h}$ and $Y_{1,t+1-jh}$, they draw from the normal distribution (5.62), also with moments that are known functions of the model parameters. Having drawn Y_{t+1-jh}, they take this value as their initial condition for simulating $Y_{t+1-(j-1)h}$, and so on. These computations are repeated for every observation Y_t and for every trial set of parameters for the model. This approach would appear to use much more information than the one developed by Pedersen. Certainly this is true with regard to Y_1, since the noncentral chi-square is known exactly. However, even in the case of Y_2, they are exploiting the normality, conditional on the sample path of Y_1, in computing the conditional density.

5.6.3. Approximate Likelihood Functions

An alternative approach to ML estimation, based on polynomial approximations, has been proposed by Ait-Sahala (2001, 2002). To illustrate his

---

[14] Matlab, e.g., has a built-in random number generator for the noncentral chi-square. In multivariate cases, the square-root diffusions comprising $Y_{1,t+1-jh}$ are assumed to be independent. Therefore, drawing from the joint distribution can be accomplished using the marginals.

approach, suppose that Y follows a univariate diffusion with drift $\mu_Y(Y_t; \gamma)$ and instantaneous volatility $\sigma_Y(Y_t; \gamma)$. Ait-Sahalia's approximation begins by transforming Y to have unit volatility by means of the transformation

$$X_t \equiv \psi(Y_t; \gamma) = \int^{Y_t} \frac{du}{\sigma_Y(u; \gamma)}. \tag{5.67}$$

Using Ito's lemma, it follows that

$$dX_t = \mu_X(X_t; \gamma)dt + dW_t. \tag{5.68}$$

The basic idea then is to approximate the logarithm of the conditional density of X using Hermite polynomials, and then to use standard change-of-variable arguments to obtain the log-density of Y.

Specifically, letting Δ denote the time interval between discrete observations and assuming an expansion out to order K in powers of Δ gives Ait-Sahalia's approximation to $\ln f(\Delta, x|X_0)$ as

$$\ln f(\Delta, x|X_0) = -\frac{\ln(2\pi\Delta)}{2} - \frac{1}{2\Delta}(x - X_0)^2 + \sum_{k=0}^{K} C_X^{(k)}(x|X_0; \gamma)\frac{\Delta^k}{k!}, \tag{5.69}$$

where the $C_X^{(k)}$ are constructed recursively from integrals of μ_X and its derivatives. This form of an approximation is obtained by starting with a unit-variance Gaussian distribution for $\Delta^{-1/2}(X-X_0)$ scaled by a linear combination of Hermite polynomials in $\Delta^{-1/2}(X - X_0)$. [Note that the leading two terms in (5.69) are those of the log-density of a Gaussian distribution with unit variance.][15] The coefficients of the Hermite polynomials turn out to be conditional expectations of polynomials in $\Delta^{-1/2}(X - X_0)$; that is, linear combinations of conditional noncentral moments of X. The final step is approximating these conditional moments using Taylor expansions based on the infinitesimal generator of the process X.

The expansion of the conditional density of Y is obtained by a change of variable. The transition density of Y is

$$f_Y(\Delta, y|Y_0; \gamma) = \text{Det}[\nabla\psi(y; \gamma)]f_X(\Delta, \psi(y; \gamma)|\psi(Y_0); \gamma), \tag{5.70}$$

where $\nabla\psi(y; \gamma) = \sigma_Y^{-1}(y; \gamma)$ is the Jacobian of the transformation ψ. Taking logarithms gives the approximate log-likelihood function of Y:

---

[15] This expansion is reminiscent of the SNP approximate density used by Gallant and Tauchen (1996) (see Chapter 6). Both are approximations to an unknown conditional density of a discretely sample process from a diffusion model. However, Ait-Sahalia solves explicitly for the coefficients of the Hermite polynomials in terms of the fundamental model parameters.

$$\ln f_Y(\Delta, y|Y_0; \gamma) = -\frac{\ln(2\pi\Delta)}{2} + \ln \text{Det}[\nabla\psi(y; \gamma)]$$

$$-\frac{1}{2\Delta}(\psi(y; \gamma) - \psi(Y_0; \gamma))^2 + \sum_{k=0}^{K} C_X^{(k)}(\psi(y; \gamma)|\psi(Y_0; \gamma))\frac{\Delta^k}{k!}. \tag{5.71}$$

For the case of multivariate diffusions, whether the same approximation scheme works or not depends on the structure of the diffusion matrix σ_Y. Not every multivariate diffusion can be transformed to a new random variable X with unit diffusion, $\sigma_X = I$. A necessary and sufficient condition for such "reducibility" is that

$$\frac{\partial\sigma_{Y,ij}^{-1}(y; \gamma)}{\partial y_k} = \frac{\partial\sigma_{Y,ik}^{-1}(y; \gamma)}{\partial y_j}, \tag{5.72}$$

where $\sigma_{Y,ij}^{-1}$ is the ijth element of σ_Y^{-1}. Condition (5.71) is in fact not satisfied by many diffusions of interest. For example, it is not satisfied by the bivariate model (5.16) because Y_1 determines the conditional volatility of both factors. More generally, whenever a subset of the state variables determines the volatilities of other state variables, the diffusion is not likely to be reducible in this sense.

For irreducible diffusions, Ait-Sahalia starts with

$$\ln f_Y(\Delta, y|Y_0; \gamma) = -\frac{\ln(2\pi\Delta)}{2} - \frac{1}{2\Delta}(y - Y_0)^2$$

$$+ \sum_{k=0}^{K} C_Y^{(k)}(y|Y_0; \gamma)\frac{\Delta^k}{k!} + \ln \text{Det}[\sigma_Y^{-1}]. \tag{5.73}$$

Then the coefficients $C_Y^{(k)}(y|Y_0; \gamma)$ are expanded directly in Taylor series in $(y - Y_0)$. The computations are more involved, but he is nevertheless able to obtain analytic expressions for these coefficients (again, up to derivatives of the drift and diffusion coefficients of Y).

5.7. Characteristic Function-Based Estimators

Given that, by definition, the CCF and/or CMGF of an affine process is known (at least up to the solution of ODEs), estimation can in principle be based on these representations of the conditional distribution even when the functional form of the conditional density is unknown. This observation has been exploited by Chacko (1999), Jiang and Knight (1999), Singleton (2001), Das (2002), Knight and Yu (2002), and Chacko and Viceira (2005) among others, to construct estimators of affine diffusions, affine asset pricing models, or linear time-series models.

The case we focus on is that of $\tau = 1$, where time is measured in units of the sampling interval of the available data, so that CCF_t is the characteristic function of Y_{t+1} conditioned on Y_t. In this case, we suppress the dependence of CCF_t on τ and simply write $CCF_t(u)$. Adaptation of the proposed estimators to the case of $\tau > 1$ is immediate. To highlight the dependence of the CCF on the unknown parameter vector γ, we write $CCF_t(u, \gamma)$ and let γ_0 denote the true population value of γ.

5.7.1. ML Estimation by Fourier Inversion

Since the functional form of the CCF of an affine process is known, the conditional density function of Y_{t+1} is also known up to an inverse Fourier transform of $CCF_t(u, \gamma)$:

$$f_Y\left(Y_{t+1} \big| Y_t; \gamma\right) = \frac{1}{(2\pi)^N} \int_{\mathbb{R}^N} e^{-iu' Y_{t+1}} CCF_t(u, \gamma) \, du. \qquad (5.74)$$

Given (5.74), it follows that $l_T(\gamma)$ is

$$l_T(\gamma) = \frac{1}{T} \sum_{t=1}^{T} \log\left\{ \frac{1}{(2\pi)^N} \int_{\mathbb{R}^N} e^{-iu' Y_{t+1}} CCF_Y(u, \gamma) \, du \right\}. \qquad (5.75)$$

Maximization of (5.75) can proceed in the usual way, conjecturing a value for γ, computing the associated Fourier inversions, and so on. We refer to the resulting estimator as the ML-CCF estimator.

Singleton (2001) illustrates the ML-CCF estimator for a one-factor square-root diffusion process ($n = 1$ and $Y_t = r_t$ as in Example 2.1). Since the distribution of r_{t+1} conditioned on r_t is noncentral χ^2, the conditional characteristic function for r_{t+1} is

$$CCF_t(u) = (1 - iu/c)^{-(2\kappa\theta/\sigma^2)} \exp\left\{ \frac{iue^{-\kappa} r_t}{(1 - ui/c)} \right\}. \qquad (5.76)$$

To implement the ML-CCF estimator, with $\{r_t\}$ treated as an observed process, the conditional density of r_{t+1} given r_t was computed by Gauss-Legendre quadrature. With as few as twenty quadrature points the ML-CCF estimator was identical to those computed using the known noncentral chi-square distribution of r.

While these univariate results are encouraging, the computational demands of the ML-CCF estimator in the case of multivariate diffusions grow rapidly with the dimension of Y. For instance, using the basic product rule, the number of points in the grid for approximating the Fourier inversion increases with $(q_p)^N$, where N is the dimension of Y_t and q_p is the number of quadrature points used in numerical integration.

The computational burden of Fourier inversion of a multidimensional CCF can be avoided, at the cost of some econometric efficiency, by using the conditional density functions of the individual elements of Y.[16] Let ι_j denote the N-dimensional selection vector with 1 in the jth position and zeros elsewhere. Then the density of $Y_{j,t+1} = \iota_j \cdot Y_{t+1}$ conditioned on the *entire* Y_t is the inverse Fourier transform of $\mathrm{CCF}_t(\omega \iota_j, \gamma)$ viewed as a function of the scalar ω:

$$f_j\big(Y_{j,t+1}\big|Y_t; \gamma\big) = \frac{1}{(2\pi)} \int_{\mathbb{R}} e^{-i\omega\iota'_j Y_{t+1}} \mathrm{CCF}_t(\omega\iota_j, \gamma)\, d\omega. \qquad (5.77)$$

Estimation based on the densities (5.77) involves at most N one-dimensional integrations, instead of one N-dimensional integration. We refer to such estimators as partial-ML or PML-CCF estimators.

The PML-CCF estimator is most naturally implemented as a GMM estimator. Fixing j, if the model is correctly specified, we then get

$$E\left[\frac{\partial \log f_j}{\partial \gamma}\big(Y_{j,t+1}\big|Y_t, \gamma_0\big)\right] = 0 \qquad (5.78)$$

and hence, under regularity, maximization of the PML-CCF objective function

$$l_{jT}(\gamma) = \frac{1}{T}\sum_{t=1}^{T}\log\left\{\frac{1}{(2\pi)}\int_{\mathbb{R}} e^{-i\omega\iota'_j Y_{t+1}}\mathrm{CCF}_t(\omega\iota_j, \gamma)\, d\omega\right\} \qquad (5.79)$$

gives a consistent estimator of γ_0. One of the regularity conditions is that γ_0 is identified from knowledge of the conditional likelihood function of a single j, $f_j(Y_{j,t+1}|Y_t; \gamma)$.[17] The first-order conditions associated with (5.79) are

$$\frac{\partial l_{jT}}{\partial \gamma}(\gamma_T) = \frac{1}{T}\sum_{t=1}^{T}\frac{1}{f_j\big(Y_{j,t+1}\big|Y_t, \gamma_T\big)}$$

$$\times \frac{1}{(2\pi)}\int_{\mathbb{R}} e^{-i\omega\iota'_j Y_{t+1}}\frac{\partial \mathrm{CCF}_t}{\partial \gamma}(\omega\iota_j, \gamma_T)\, d\omega = 0. \qquad (5.80)$$

---

[16] The following is based on Singleton (2001). Chacko (1999) proposed a similar estimator for a single bond price (single component of Y_t).

[17] We take up the issue of econometric identification more systematically in later chapters when we consider specific asset pricing problems. Anticipating these discussions, γ_0 is identified from the pricing relations for a single bond in affine term structure models, for example. See Dai and Singleton (2000) and Chapter 12.

These K equations in the K unknowns γ_T can be solved to obtain a consistent and asymptotically normal GMM estimator of γ_0.

In general, the efficiency of this estimator increases with the number of the conditional densities (5.80) that are used in estimation. When multiple densities are used in constructing this GMM estimator, one introduces a distance matrix that exploits the fact that the moment conditions that underlie G_T are martingale difference sequences.

Though the PML-CCF estimator does not exploit any information about the conditional joint distribution,[18] information about the conditional covariances can be easily incorporated into the estimation by appending moments to the vector ϵ_{t+1}. For example, for an affine diffusion, the population conditional covariance between $Y_{j,t+1}$ and $Y_{k,t+1}$, say $\mathrm{Cov}_t(Y_{j,t+1}, Y_{k,t+1}; \gamma)$, is known to be an affine function of Y_t with coefficients that are known functions of γ. Thus, letting

$$\eta_{jk,t+1} \equiv \left(Y_{j,t+1} - E[Y_{j,t+1}|Y_t]\right)Y_{k,t+1} - \mathrm{Cov}_t\left(Y_{j,t+1}, Y_{k,t+1}; \gamma\right), \qquad (5.81)$$

we can add terms of the form $\eta_{jk,t+1}(\gamma)h(Y_t)$, where $h : \mathbb{R}^N \to \mathbb{R}$, to ϵ_{t+1}. The products $\eta_{jk,t+1}(\gamma_0)h(Y_t)$ are martingale difference sequences, so the optimal distance matrix is again computed from a consistent estimator of $E[\epsilon_{t+1}\epsilon'_{t+1}]$.

5.7.2. GMM Estimation Based on the CCF

Singleton (2001) and Carrasco et al. (2005) construct GMM-style estimators directly using the empirical characteristic function and show that certain versions of these estimators approximate, arbitrarily well, the efficiency of the ML estimator (are asymptotically equivalent to the ML-CCF estimator). Following Singleton, we introduce a set Z_T^∞ of "instrument" functions with elements $z_t(u) : \mathbb{R}^N \to \mathbb{C}^Q$, where $\mathbb{C}$ denotes the complex numbers, with $z_t(u) \in \mathcal{I}_t, z_t(u) = \bar{z}_t(-u), t = 1, \ldots, T$, where $\mathcal{I}_t$ is the σ-algebra generated by Y_t. Defining the "residual"

$$\epsilon_{t+1}(u, \gamma) \equiv e^{iu'Y_{t+1}} - \phi_t(u, \gamma), \qquad (5.82)$$

each $z \in Z_T^\infty$ indexes an estimator $\gamma_{\infty T}^z$ of γ_0 satisfying

$$\frac{1}{T}\sum_t \int_{\mathbb{R}^N} z_t(u)\epsilon_{t+1}\left(u, \gamma_{\infty T}^z\right)du = 0. \qquad (5.83)$$

---

[18] Estimation based on the conditional density functions $f(Y_{j,t+1}|Y_t)$ does, of course, exploit some information about the correlation among the state variables, since this density is conditional on Y_t. In particular, it exploits all of the information about the feedback among the variables through the conditional moments of each $Y_{j,t+1}, E[Y_{j,t+1}^m|Y_t]$.

Under the regularity conditions for GMM estimators outlined in Chapter 3, $\gamma_{\infty T}^z$ is consistent, and asymptotically normal with limiting covariance matrix

$$\mathcal{V}_0^\infty(z) = D(z)^{-1}\Sigma^\infty(z)(\bar{D}(z)')^{-1}, \tag{5.84}$$

where

$$D(z) = E\left[\int_{\mathbb{R}^N} z_t(u)\frac{\partial\phi_t(u)}{\partial\gamma}\,du\right], \tag{5.85}$$

$$\Sigma^\infty(z) = E\left[\int_{\mathbb{R}^N} z_t(u)\epsilon_{t+1}(u,\gamma_0)\,du\int_{\mathbb{R}^N}\bar{\epsilon}_{t+1}(u,\gamma_0)\bar{z}_t(u)'\,du\right]. \tag{5.86}$$

Extending the analyses by Feuerverger and McDunnough (1981) and Feuerverger (1990) for an i.i.d. environment to the case of Markov time-series models, Singleton (2001) shows that the optimal index in Z_T^∞, in the sense of giving the smallest asymptotic covariance matrix among empirical CCF estimators, is

$$z_{\infty t}^*(u) = \frac{1}{(2\pi)^N}\int_{\mathbb{R}^N}\frac{\partial\ln f}{\partial\gamma}\big(Y_{t+1}\big|Y_t,\gamma_0\big)'e^{-iu'Y_{t+1}}\,dY_{t+1}; \tag{5.87}$$

and, moreover, the limiting covariance matrix of the GMM estimator $\gamma_{\infty T}^*$ obtained using $z_{\infty t}^*(u)$ is the asymptotic Cramer-Rao lower bound, $I(\gamma_0)^{-1}$.

From a practical perspective, the ECCF estimator $z_{\infty t}^*$ has no computational advantages over the ML-CCF estimator, because the index z_∞^* cannot be computed without a priori knowledge of the conditional density function. Accordingly, Singleton developed a computationally tractable estimator that is consistent and "nearly" as efficient as these ML estimators. Setting $N=1$ for notational simplicity, the basic idea is to approximate the integral

$$\int_{\mathbb{R}} z_t(u)\big[e^{iuY_{t+1}} - \phi_{Yt}(u,\gamma)\big]du \tag{5.88}$$

underlying the construction of (5.83) with the sum over a finite grid in $\mathbb{R}$. For any finite grid, no matter how coarse, this GMM-CCF estimator is shown to be consistent and asymptotically normal with an easily computable asymptotic covariance matrix. Moreover, the asymptotic covariance matrix of the optimal GMM-CCF estimator is shown to converge to $I(\gamma_0)^{-1}$ as the range and fineness of the approximating grid in $\mathbb{R}$ increases.

This GMM-CCF estimator circumvents the need for multidimensional Fourier inversion. However, it introduces a new computational consideration. Namely, as the grid of u's is made increasingly fine, the correlations among the sample moments for "nearby" u's become increasingly large, so much so that the distance matrix often becomes ill conditioned (nearly singular). In practice, singularity problems may arise when as few as two or three u's are used in the approximating grid. Fortunately, as shown by Carrasco et al. (2005), there is a way around this problem. They construct a GMM-CCF estimator that exploits a continuum of moment equations simultaneously.

6

Simulation-Based Estimators of DAPMs

6.1. Introduction

For several reasons, the implementation of GMM and ML estimators in the analysis of DAPMs may be computationally demanding, if not essentially infeasible. One such circumstance is when there are unobserved state variables. For instance, the stochastic volatility model of the instantaneous return (Example 2.3) has

$$dr(t) = \kappa(\bar{r} - r(t)) \, dt + \sqrt{v(t)} \, dB_r(t), \tag{6.1}$$

$$dv(t) = \nu(\bar{v} - v(t)) \, dt + \sigma_v \sqrt{v(t)} \, dB_v(t), \tag{6.2}$$

where the volatility process $v(t)$ is assumed to be unobserved by the econometrician. Consequently, discretely sampled returns, $\{r_t\}$, are not Markov conditioned on their own history and the functional form of the conditional distribution of r_t is unknown. Moreover, apart from a few special cases, the moments of r_t, expressed as functions of the unknown parameters, are unknown.[1] The preceding estimation problem is, of course, rendered even more challenging by the presence of jumps in returns or volatility, possibly with state-dependent arrival intensities.

This chapter discusses two possible solutions to the problem of estimating DAPMs in the presence of jumps and latent time series: the simulated moments estimator (SME) and the Markov chain Monte Carlo (MCMC) estimator. Both of these estimators are applicable to DAPMs without latent variables. However, it is especially in situations where one or more variables are latent or the processes involve complex specifications of jumps that

---

[1] For this particular example approximate ML estimators have been developed, some of which were discussed in Chapter 5.

these methods often clearly dominate others, both in their tractability and potential econometric efficiency.

Much of this chapter is devoted to discussing conditions for the consistency and asymptotic normality of the SME.[2] We suppose that the state vector Y_t that determines asset prices follows a time-homogeneous Markov process whose transition function depends on an unknown parameter vector β_0. Asset prices, and possibly other relevant data, are observed as $g(Y_t, \beta_0)$ for some given function g of the underlying state and parameter vector. In parallel, a simulated state process $\{Y_s^\beta\}$ is generated (analytically or numerically) from the economic model and corresponding simulated observations $g(Y_s^\beta, \beta)$ are taken for a given parameter choice β. The parameter β is chosen so as to "match moments," that is, to minimize the distance between sample moments of the data, $g(Y_t, \beta_0)$, and those of the simulated series $g(Y_t^\beta, \beta)$, in a sense to be made precise. The SME extends the GMM estimator to a large class of asset pricing models for which the moment restrictions of interest do not have analytic representations in terms of observable variables and the unknown parameter vector.

For two reasons, the regularity conditions underlying GMM estimation for time-series models without simulation are not applicable to estimation problems involving simulation. First, in simulating time series, presample values of the series are typically required. In most circumstances, however, the stationary distribution of the simulated process, as a function of the parameter choice, is unknown. Hence, the initial conditions for the time series are not generally drawn from their stationary distribution and the simulated process is usually nonstationary. Second, functions of the current value of the simulated state depend on the unknown parameter vector both through the structure of the model (as in any GMM problem) and indirectly through the generation of data by simulation. The feedback effect of the latter dependence on the transition law of the simulated state process implies that the first-moment-continuity condition used in Chapter 3 in establishing the uniform convergence of the sample to the population criterion functions is not directly applicable to the SME. Furthermore, the nonstationarity of the simulated series must be accommodated in establishing the asymptotic normality of the SME.

The next three sections present a more formal definition of the SME and prove that it is consistent and asymptotically normal. Then we take up the important issue of moment selection or, equivalently, the choice of $g(Y_t, \beta)$. Specifically, we show how to construct moments using the scores of the log-likelihood function from an auxiliary time-series model that

---

[2] Portions of this chapter are taken from Duffie and Singleton (1993), copyright by the Econometric Society. Complementary discussions of simulated moment estimation are presented in McFadden (1987), Pakes and Pollard (1987), and Lee and Ingram (1991).

captures important features of the conditional distribution of the data. If the auxiliary model chosen is sufficiently flexible in capturing features of the conditional distribution of Y, then the resulting SME is asymptotically efficient (achieves the same efficiency as the unknown ML estimator).

The last section outlines the MCMC estimator as an alternative, one that in some circumstances has more attractive properties than the SME.

6.2. SME: The Estimation Problem

We assume that a given $\mathbb{R}^N$-valued *state* process $\{Y_t\}_{t=1}^{\infty}$ is generated by the difference equation

$$Y_{t+1} = H(Y_t, \epsilon_{t+1}, \beta_0), \tag{6.3}$$

where the parameter vector β_0 is to be estimated, and $\{\epsilon_t\}$ is an i.i.d. sequence of $\mathbb{R}^p$-valued random variables on a probability space $(\Omega, \mathcal{F}, P)$. The number of shocks, p, need not equal the dimension of the state vector, N. The probability distribution of ϵ_t is given a priori up to a possibly unknown parameter vector.

The parameter vector β_0 lies in the admissible parameter space $\Theta \subset \mathbb{R}^K$, Θ compact. In addition, letting $Z_t = (Y_t, Y_{t-1}, \ldots, Y_{t-\ell+1})$ for some positive integer $\ell < \infty$, we assume that estimation of β_0 is based on the moments of the *observation function* $g(Z_t, \beta)$, $g : \mathbb{R}^{N\ell} \times \Theta \to \mathbb{R}^M$, for positive integers ℓ and M, with $M \geq K$. Moments of the observed series are calculated as sample moments of the observed $g_t^* \equiv g(Z_t, \beta_0)$. Note that we do not require that all N of the state variables be observed by the econometrician. In the presence of unobserved state variables, it is implicit that g defines moments of those state variables for which historical observations are available.

The function H may be known or determined implicitly by the numerical solution of a discrete-time model for equilibrium asset prices or by a discrete-time approximation of a continuous-time model. For example, in the stochastic volatility diffusion model (6.1) and (6.2), with correlation $\mathrm{Corr}(dB_r, dB_v) = \rho$, the Euler discretization scheme leads to the bivariate data-generating process

$$\begin{pmatrix} \Delta r_k^n \\ \Delta v_k^n \end{pmatrix} = \frac{1}{n}\begin{pmatrix} \kappa(\bar{r} - r_{k-1}^n) \\ \nu(\bar{v} - v_{k-1}^n) \end{pmatrix} + \begin{pmatrix} \sqrt{v_{k-1}^n} & 0 \\ \rho\sigma_v\sqrt{v_{k-1}^n} & \sqrt{1-\rho^2}\sigma_v\sqrt{v_{k-1}^n} \end{pmatrix} \frac{1}{\sqrt{n}}\begin{pmatrix} \epsilon_{1k} \\ \epsilon_{2k} \end{pmatrix}, \tag{6.4}$$

where ϵ_k is a bivariate standard normal vector. According to this discretization, each discrete sampling interval (day, week, and so on) is divided up into n subintervals so every nth simulated observation from (6.4) corresponds to one observed data point. In deriving the asymptotic distribution of estimators based on this or other discretization schemes, one can either assume that discretization describes the true probability model for the state vector or, if the true model is a diffusion, then one can develop the asymptotics with $n \to \infty$ as sample size gets large. In this chapter we take n as fixed (the discretization is the truth). Chapters 5 and 7 discuss the asymptotic theory for the case of the true discrete-time process implied by a continuous-time model.

For certain special cases of (6.3) and g, the function mapping β to $E[g(Z_t, \beta)]$ is known and independent of t. In these cases, the GMM estimator

$$b_T = \operatorname{argmin}_{\beta \in \Theta} \left[\frac{1}{T} \sum_{t=1}^{T} g_t^* - E[g(Z_t, \beta)] \right]' W_T \left[\frac{1}{T} \sum_{t=1}^{T} g_t^* - E[g(Z_t, \beta)] \right],$$

$$(6.5)$$

for given "distance matrices" $\{W_T\}$ is consistent for β_0 and asymptotically normal under regularity conditions in Hansen (1982b) and Chapter 3. For instance, if the drift of r in (6.1) is the constant μ_r (no mean reversion), then the unconditional moments of discretely sampled r_t generated by the volatility specification (6.2), as well as the volatility model

$$d \log v(t) = v(\bar{v} - \log v(t)) \, dt + \sigma_v \, dB_v(t), \qquad (6.6)$$

are known in closed form.[3] However, essentially any deviation from these two basic specifications places one in an environment where the moments are not known.

The simulated moments estimator circumvents the requirement that $\beta \mapsto E[g(Z_t, \beta)]$ is known by making the much weaker assumption that the econometrician has access to an $\mathbb{R}^p$-valued sequence $\{\hat{\epsilon}_t\}$ of random variables that is identical in distribution to, and independent of, $\{\epsilon_t\}$. Then, for any $\mathbb{R}^N$-valued initial point $\widehat{Y}_1$ and any parameter vector $\beta \in \Theta$, the simulated state process $\{Y_t^\beta\}$ can be constructed inductively by letting $Y_1^\beta = \widehat{Y}_1$ and $Y_{t+1}^\beta = H(Y_t^\beta, \hat{\epsilon}_{t+1}, \beta)$. Likewise, the simulated observation process $\{g_t^\beta\}$ is constructed by $g_t^\beta = g(Z_t^\beta, \beta)$, where $Z_t^\beta = (Y_t^\beta, \ldots, Y_{t-\ell+1}^\beta)$. Finally, the SME of β_0 is the parameter vector b_T that best matches the sample moments of the actual and simulated observation processes, $\{g_t^*\}$ and $\{g_t^{b_T}\}$.

More precisely, let $\mathcal{T} : IN \to IN$ define the simulation sample size $\mathcal{T}(T)$ that is generated for a given sample size T of actual observations, where $\mathcal{T}(T) \to \infty$ as $T \to \infty$. For any parameter vector β, let

---

[3] See Das and Sundaram (1999) for a discussion of the moments of the square-root model and Melino and Turnbull (1990) for the moments of the log-volatility model.

$$G_T(\beta) = \frac{1}{T} \sum_{t=1}^{T} g_t^* - \frac{1}{T(T)} \sum_{s=1}^{T(T)} g_s^{\beta} \qquad (6.7)$$

denote the difference in sample moments. If $\{g_t^*\}$ and $\{g_s^{\beta}\}$ satisfy a law of large numbers, then $\lim_T G_T(\beta) = 0$ if $\beta = \beta_0$. With identification conditions, $\lim_T G_T(\beta) = 0$ if and only if $\beta = \beta_0$. We therefore introduce a sequence $W = \{W_T\}$ of $M \times M$ positive-semidefinite matrices and define the SME for β_0 given $(H, \epsilon, T, \widehat{Y}_1, W)$ to be the sequence $\{b_T\}$ given by

$$b_T = \operatorname*{argmin}_{\beta \in \Theta} G_T(\beta)' W_T G_T(\beta) \equiv \operatorname*{argmin}_{\beta \in \Theta} Q_T(\beta). \qquad (6.8)$$

The distance matrix W_T is chosen with rank at least K and may depend on the sample information $\{g_1^*, \dots, g_T^*\} \bigcup \{g_1^{\beta}, \dots, g_{T(T)}^{\beta} : \beta \in \Theta\}$.

Comparing (6.5) and (6.8) shows that the SME extends the method-of-moments approach to estimation by replacing the population moment $E[g(Z_t, \beta)]$ with its sample counterpart, calculated with simulated data. The latter sample moment can be calculated for a large class of asset pricing models for which $E[g(Z_t, \beta)]$ (treated as a function of β) is not known.

For several reasons, this estimation problem is not a special case of the estimation problem discussed in Chapter 3. The most important difference between the estimation problem with simulated time series and the standard GMM estimation problem lies in the parameter dependency of the simulated time series $\{g_t^{\beta}\}$. In a stationary, ergodic environment, one observes $g(Z_t, \beta_0)$, where the data-generation process $\{Y_t\}$ is fixed and β_0 is the parameter vector to be estimated. In contrast, $g_t^{\beta} = g(Z_t^{\beta}, \beta)$ depends on β not only directly, but indirectly through the dependence of the entire past history of the simulated process $\{Y_t^{\beta}\}$ on β.

Furthermore, in contrast to the simulated moments estimators for i.i.d. environments, the simulation of time series requires initial conditions for the forcing variables Y_t (r_t and v_t in our example). Even if the transition function of the Markov process $\{Y_t\}$ is stationary (i.e., has a stationary distribution), the simulated process $\{Y_t^{\beta}\}$ is not generally stationary since the initial simulated state Y_1^{β} is typically not drawn from the ergodic distribution of the process. In this case, the simulated process $\{g_t^{\beta}\}$ is nonstationary. At a practical level, one can leave out an initial portion of the simulated state variables $\{Y_t^{\beta}\}$ in order to mitigate transient effects. The formal justification for this approach to dealing with initial conditions problems comes with establishing that the effects of initial conditions die out in such a way as to not affect the asymptotic distribution of the SME.

A related initial conditions problem, common to the GMM and simulated moments estimation of equilibrium asset pricing models, occurs when one of the state variables, say Y_{jt}, is determined as a deterministic function of the history of Y_t. Examples include the GARCH model of stochastic volatility, where return volatility σ_t^2 is linear in σ_{t-1}^2 and $(r_{t-1} - \mu_{r,t-1})^2$ (see Chapter 7), and models with capital accumulation, where today's capital stock is linear in last period's stock and investment. In the former case, the initial volatility is unobserved, whereas in the second case one may wish to accommodate mis-measurement of the initial capital stock.[4] The regularity conditions introduced subsequently to address the initial conditions problem for simulation are also applicable to these other settings.

6.3. Consistency of the SME

The presence of simulation in the estimator pushes one to special lengths in justifying regularity conditions for the consistency of method-of-moments estimators that, without simulation, are often taken for granted. There are two particular problems. First, since the simulated state process is usually not initialized with a draw from its ergodic distribution, one needs a condition that allows the use of an arbitrary initial state, knowing that the state process converges rapidly to its stationary distribution. Second, one needs to justify the usual starting assumption of some form of uniform continuity of the observation as a function of the parameter choice. With simulation, a perturbation of the parameter choice affects not only the current observation, but also transitions between past states, a dependence that compounds over time.

Initially we describe the concept of geometric ergodicity, a condition ensuring that the simulated state process satisfies a law of large numbers with an asymptotic distribution that is invariant to the choice of initial conditions. Then ergodicity of the simulated series is used to prove a uniform weak law of large numbers for $G_T(\beta)$ and weak consistency of the SME (i.e., $b_T \to \beta_0$ in probability).[5]

6.3.1. Geometric Ergodicity

In order to define geometric ergodicity, let P_x^t denote the t-step transition probability for a time-homogeneous Markov process $\{X_t\}$; that is, P_x^t is the

---

[4] See Dunn and Singleton (1986) and Eichenbaum et al. (1988) for examples of studies of Euler equations using GMM estimators in which this type of initial condition problem arises.

[5] In our discussion of consistency for GMM estimators, we focused on strong consistency (almost sure convergence). Duffie and Singleton (1993) give conditions on the state transition function H that guarantee that the compounding effects of simulation on the properties of estimators damp out over time, and then use these conditions to prove strong consistency. However, their damping conditions are not satisfied by many of the diffusion models that make up DAPMs. Therefore, we focus on their conditions for weak consistency, which appear to place somewhat weaker requirements on H.

distribution of X_t given the initial point $X_0 = x$. The process $\{X_t\}$ is *ρ-ergodic*, for some $ρ \in (0, 1]$, if there is a probability measure $π$ on the state space of the process such that, for every initial point x,

$$ρ^{-t}\|P_x^t - π\|_v \to 0 \quad \text{as } t \to \infty, \tag{6.9}$$

where $\| \cdot \|_v$ is the total variation norm.[6] The measure $π$ is the ergodic distribution. If $\{X_t\}$ is $ρ$-ergodic for $ρ < 1$, then $\{X_t\}$ is *geometrically ergodic*. In calculating asymptotic distributions, geometric ergodicity can substitute for stationarity since it means that the process converges geometrically to its stationary distribution. Moreover, geometric ergodicity implies strong $(α)$ mixing in which the mixing coefficient $α(m)$ converges geometrically with m to zero (Rosenblatt, 1971; Mokkadem, 1985).

In what follows, for any ergodic process $\{X_t\}$, it is convenient for us to write X_∞ for any random variable with the corresponding ergodic distribution. We adopt the notation $\| X \|_q = [E(\| X \|^q)]^{1/q}$ for the L^q norm of any $\mathbb{R}^N$-valued random variable X, for any $q \in (0, \infty)$. We let L^q denote the space of such X with $\| X \|_q < \infty$, and let $\| x \|$ denote the usual Euclidean norm of a vector x.

A key ingredient for ergodicity is positive recurrence,[7] for which a key condition is irreducibility. For a finite Markov chain, irreducibility means essentially that each state is accessible from each state, obviously a sufficient condition in this case for both recurrence and geometric ergodicity. Mokkadem (1985) uses the following convenient sufficient condition of irreducibility of a time-homogeneous Markov chain $\{X_t\}$ valued in $\mathbb{R}^N$ with t-step transition probability P_x^t.[8]

CONDITION 6.3.1.   *For any measurable $A \subset \mathbb{R}^N$ of nonzero Lebesque measure and any compact $K \subset \mathbb{R}^N$, there exists some integer $t > 0$ such that*

$$\inf_{x \in K} P_x^t(A) > 0. \tag{6.10}$$

For Condition 6.3.1 to hold, it is obviously enough that $P_x(A)$ is continuous in x and supports all of $\mathbb{R}^N$ for each x. However, this single-period "full support" condition is too strong an assumption in a setting with endogenous state variables. To be more concrete, consider the equilibrium asset pricing

---

[6] The total variation of a signed measure $μ$ is $\| μ \|_v = \sup_{h:|h(y)|\leq 1} \int h(y)\, dμ(y)$.

[7] For a finite-state Markov chain, recurrence means essentially that each state occurs infinitely often from any given state. See, e.g., Doob (1953) for some general definitions.

[8] General criteria for the geometric ergodicity of a Markov chain have been obtained by Nummelin and Tuominen (1982) and Tweedie (1982).

model examined by Michner (1984) in which agents have logarithmic utility over a single consumption good. The production function is $z_t k_t^\phi$, $0 < \phi < 1$, where k_t is the capital stock and the technology shock follows the law of motion

$$\ln z_{t+1} = \varsigma_z + \rho \ln z_t + \epsilon_{t+1}, \tag{6.11}$$

for constants ς_z and ρ. Under these simplifying assumptions, the implied equilibrium asset pricing function and law of motion for the capital stock are:

$$p_t = \frac{\delta}{(1-\delta)}(1-\phi)z_t k_t^\phi, \tag{6.12}$$

$$d_t = (1-\phi)z_t k_t^\phi,$$

$$k_{t+1} = \delta\phi z_t k_t^\phi. \tag{6.13}$$

Clearly, the distribution of k_{t+1} given (k_t, z_t) is degenerate. Nevertheless, if $\{\epsilon_t\}$ is, say, i.i.d. normal, then $\{Y_t\}$ for this illustrative economy satisfies Condition 6.3.1. More generally, Condition 6.3.1 is not a strong condition on models with endogenous state variables provided that these variables do not move in such a way that renders some states inaccessible from others.[9]

A second key ingredient for ergodicity is aperiodicity. For example, the Markov chain that alternates deterministically from "heads" to "tails" to "heads" to "tails," and so on, is not ergodic, despite its recurrence.

With these definitions in hand, we can review Mokkadem's sufficient conditions for geometric ergodicity of what he calls "nonlinear AR(1) models," which includes our setting:

Lemma 6.1 (Mokkadem). *Suppose $\{Y_t\}$, as defined by (6.3), is aperiodic and satisfies Condition 6.3.1. Fix β and suppose there are constants $C > 0$, $\delta_\beta \in (0, 1)$, and $q > 0$ such that $H(\cdot, \epsilon_1, \beta) : \mathbb{R}^N \to L^q$ is well defined and continuous with*

$$\|H(y, \epsilon_1, \beta)\|_q < \delta_\beta \|y\|, \quad \|y\| > C. \tag{6.14}$$

Then $\{Y_t\}$ is geometrically ergodic. Moreover, $\{\|Y_t^\beta\|_q\}$ and $\|Y_\infty^\beta\|_q$ are uniformly bounded.

Condition (6.14), inspired by Tweedie (1982), means roughly that $\{Y_t\}$, once outside a sufficiently large ball, heads back into the ball at a uniform rate.

---

[9] If the state process $\{X_t\}$ is valued in a proper subset S of $\mathbb{R}^N$, Condition 6.3.1 obviously does not apply, but analogous results hold if Condition 6.3.1 applies when substituting S everywhere for $\mathbb{R}^N$ (and relatively open sets for sets of nonzero Lebesgue measure).

6.3.2. A Uniform Weak Law of Large Numbers

Since geometric ergodicity of $\{Y_t^\beta\}$ implies α-mixing, it also implies that $\{Y_t^\beta\}$ satisfies a strong (and hence weak) law of large numbers. For consistency of the SME, however, standard sufficient conditions require a strong or weak law to hold in a uniform sense over the parameter space Θ. For example, the family $\{\{g_t^\beta\} : \beta \in \Theta\}$ of processes satisfies the uniform weak law of large numbers if, for each $\delta > 0$,

$$\lim_{T \to \infty} P \left[\sup_{\beta \in \Theta} \left| E(g_\infty^\beta) - \frac{1}{T} \sum_{t=1}^T g_t^\beta \right| > \delta \right] = 0. \tag{6.15}$$

In our setting of simulated moments, $\{Z_t^\beta\}$ is simulated based on various choices of β, so continuity of $g(Z_t^\beta, \beta)$ in β (via both arguments) is useful in proving (6.15). We assume the following global modulus of continuity condition on $\{g_t^\beta\}$.

Definition 6.1.   *The family $\{g_t^\beta\}$ is Lipschitz, uniformly in probability, if there is a sequence $\{C_t\}$ such that for all t and all β and θ in Θ,*

$$\| g_t^\beta - g_t^\theta \| \leq C_t \| \beta - \theta \|,$$

where $C^T = T^{-1} \sum_{t=1}^T C_t$ is bounded (with T) in probability.

Lemma 6.2 (Uniform Weak Law of Large Numbers).   *Suppose, for each $\beta \in \Theta$, that $\{Y_t^\beta\}$ is ergodic and that $E(|g_\infty^\beta|) < \infty$. Suppose, in addition, that the map $\beta \mapsto E(g_\infty^\beta)$ is continuous and the family $\{g_t^\beta\}$ is Lipschitz, uniformly in probability. Then $\{\{g_t^\beta\} : \beta \in \Theta\}$ satisfies the uniform weak law of large numbers.*

Proof (Lemma 6.2).[10]   *Since Θ is compact it can be partitioned, for any n, into n disjoint neighborhoods $\Theta_1^n, \Theta_2^n, \ldots, \Theta_n^n$ in such a way that the distance between any two points in each Θ_i^n goes to zero as $n \to \infty$. Let $\beta_1, \beta_2, \ldots, \beta_n$ be an arbitrary sequence of vectors such that $\beta_i \in \Theta_i^n$, $i = 1, \ldots, n$. Then, for any $\epsilon > 0$,*

$$P \left[\sup_{\beta \in \Theta} \left| \frac{1}{T} \sum_{t=1}^T \left(g_t^\beta - E(g_\infty^\beta) \right) \right| > \epsilon \right]$$

$$\leq P \left[\bigcup_{i=1}^n \left\{ \sup_{\beta \in \Theta_i^n} \left| \frac{1}{T} \sum_{t=1}^T \left(g_t^\beta - E(g_\infty^\beta) \right) \right| > \epsilon \right\} \right]$$

---

[10] The strategy for proving this lemma, which was suggested by Whitney Newey, follows the proof strategies used by Jennrich (1969) and Amemiya (1985) to prove similar lemmas. Newey (1991) presents a more extensive discussion of sufficient conditions for uniform convergence in probability.

$$\leq \sum_{i=1}^{n} P\left[\sup_{\beta \in \Theta_i^n}\left|\frac{1}{T}\sum_{t=1}^{T}\left(g_t^{\beta} - E(g_{\infty}^{\beta})\right)\right| > \epsilon\right]$$

$$\leq \sum_{i=1}^{n} P\left[\left|\frac{1}{T}\sum_{t=1}^{T}\left(g_t^{\beta_i} - E(g_{\infty}^{\beta_i})\right)\right| > \frac{\epsilon}{2}\right] \tag{6.16}$$

$$+ \sum_{i=1}^{n} P\left[\frac{1}{T}\sum_{t=1}^{T}\sup_{\beta \in \Theta_i^n}\left|g_t^{\beta} - g_t^{\beta_i}\right| + \sup_{\beta \in \Theta_i^n}|E(g_{\infty}^{\beta}) - E(g_{\infty}^{\beta_i})| > \frac{\epsilon}{2}\right],$$

where the last inequality follows from the triangle inequality. For fixed n, since $\{Y_t^{\beta_i}\}$ is ergodic and $E(|g_t^{\beta_i}|) < \infty$, the first term on the right-hand side of (6.16) approaches zero as $T \to \infty$ by the weak law of large numbers for ergodic processes.

As for the second right-hand-side term in (6.16), the Lipschitz assumption on $\{g_t^{\beta}\}$ implies that there exist C_t such that

$$\sum_{i=1}^{n} P\left[\frac{1}{T}\sum_{t=1}^{T}\sup_{\beta \in \Theta_i^n}\left|g_t^{\beta} - g_t^{\beta_i}\right| + \sup_{\beta \in \Theta_i^n}|E(g_{\infty}^{\beta}) - E(g_{\infty}^{\beta_i})| > \frac{\epsilon}{2}\right]$$

$$\leq \sum_{i=1}^{n} P\left[\sup_{\beta \in \Theta_i^n}|\beta - \beta_i|\frac{1}{T}\sum_{t=1}^{T}C_t + \sup_{\beta \in \Theta_i^n}|E(g_{\infty}^{\beta}) - E(g_{\infty}^{\beta_i})| > \frac{\epsilon}{2}\right]. \tag{6.17}$$

The assumption that $C^T = T^{-1}\sum_{t=1}^{T}C_t$ is bounded in probability implies that there is a nonstochastic bounded sequence $\{A_T\}$ such that $\mathrm{plim}\left(C^T - A_T\right) = 0$. Thus, for T larger than some T^* and some bound B, the right-hand side of (6.17) is less than or equal to

$$\sum_{i=1}^{n} P\left[\sup_{\beta \in \Theta_i^n}|\beta - \beta_i|\left|C^T - A_T\right| + \sup_{\beta \in \Theta_i^n}|\beta - \beta_i|B\right.$$

$$\left. + \sup_{\beta \in \Theta_i^n}|E(g_{\infty}^{\beta}) - E(g_{\infty}^{\beta_i})| > \frac{\epsilon}{2}\right]. \tag{6.18}$$

By continuity of $\beta \mapsto E(g_{\infty}^{\beta})$, we can choose n once and for all so that $|\beta - \beta_i|B + |E(g_{\infty}^{\beta}) - E(g_{\infty}^{\beta_i})| < \epsilon/4$ for all β in Θ_i^n and all i. Thus, the limit of (6.18) as $T \to \infty$ is zero, and the result follows.   Q.E.D.

The ergodicity assumption on $\{Y_t^{\beta}\}$ in Lemma 6.2 can be replaced with Mokkadem's conditions for geometric ergodicity on the transition function H and disturbance ϵ_t, summarized in Lemma 6.1.

6.3.3. Weak Consistency

Next, we summarize several important assumptions that are used in our proofs of both consistency and asymptotic normality of the SME.

Assumption 6.1 *(Technical Conditions). For each $\beta \in \Theta$, $\{\| g_t^\beta \|_{2+\delta}: t = 1, 2, \ldots\}$ is bounded for some $\delta > 0$. The family $\{g_t^\beta\}$ is Lipschitz, uniformly in probability, and $\beta \mapsto E(g_\infty^\beta)$ is continuous.*

Assumption 6.2 *(Ergodicity). For all $\beta \in \Theta$, the process $\{Y_t^\beta\}$ is geometrically ergodic.*

The hypotheses of Lemmas 6.1 and 6.2 are sufficient for Assumptions 6.1 and 6.2 provided Mokkadem's conditions apply for some $q > 2$.

We impose the following condition on the distance matrices $\{W_T\}$ in (6.8).

Assumption 6.3 *(Convergence of Distance Matrices). Σ_0 is nonsingular and $W_T \to W_0 = \Sigma_0^{-1}$ almost surely, where (for any t)*

$$\Sigma_0 \equiv \sum_{j=-\infty}^{\infty} E\big([g_t^* - E(g_t^*)][g_{t-j}^* - E(g_{t-j}^*)]'\big). \tag{6.19}$$

For the second moments in this assumption to exist, and their sum to converge absolutely, the assumptions that $\{\| g_t^* \|_{2+\delta}: t = 1, 2, \ldots\}$ is bounded for some $\delta > 0$ and geometric ergodicity of $\{Y_t\}$ together suffice, as shown by Doob (1953: pp. 222–224). Further, as with GMM, the choice of W_0 in Assumption 6.3 leads to the most efficient SME within the class of SMEs with positive-definite distance matrices.

Note that Σ_0 in Assumption 6.3 is a function solely of the moments of $\{g_t^*\}$; in particular, Σ_0 depends neither on β nor on the moments of the simulated process $\{g_t^\beta\}$. Thus, Σ_0 can be estimated using, for instance, the sum of sample autocovariances of the data $\{g_t^*\}$, weighted as in Newey and West (1987b) and the discussion of Case AC$h(\infty)$ in Chapter 3.[11] Given the definition of Σ_0 and the fact that geometric ergodicity implies α-mixing, it follows that the Newey and West estimator is consistent for Σ_0 in our environment.

Alternatively, Σ_0 could be estimated using simulated data $\{g_t^\beta\}$. Since the rate of convergence of spectral estimators is slow and one has control

---

[11] Several estimators of Σ_0 have been proposed in the literature. See, e.g., Hansen and Singleton (1982), Newey and West (1987a), and Eichenbaum et al. (1988). In general, $E[(g_t^* - Eg_t^*)(g_{t-j}^* - Eg_{t-j}^*)']$ is nonzero for all j in (6.19) and the Newey and West estimator is appropriate.

over the size $\mathcal{T}(T)$ of the simulated sample, this alternative may be relatively advantageous. A two-step procedure for estimating Σ_0 is required, however, so in establishing consistency of a simulated estimator of Σ_0 one would need to account both for dependence of $\{g_t^\beta\}$ on an estimated value of β and the parameter dependence of simulated series. One approach to establishing consistency would be to extend the discussion of consistent estimation of spectral density functions using estimated residuals without simulation, found in Newey and West (1987a) and Andrews (1991), to the case of simulated residuals.

Under Assumptions 6.1–6.3, the criterion function $Q_T(\beta)$ converges to the asymptotic criterion function $Q_0 : \Theta \to \mathbb{R}$ defined by $Q_0(\beta) = G_\infty(\beta)' W_0 G_\infty(\beta)$ almost surely. We assume that Q_0 satisfies:

Assumption 6.4 (Uniqueness of Minimizer). $Q_0(\beta_0) < Q_0(\beta)$, $\beta \in \Theta$, $\beta \neq \beta_0$.

Our first theorem establishes the consistency of the SME $\{b_T : T \geq 1\}$ given by (6.8).

Theorem 6.1 (Consistency of SME). *Under Assumptions 6.1–6.4, the SME $\{b_T\}$ converges to β_0 in probability as $T \to \infty$.*

Proof (Theorem 6.1). *By the triangle inequality,*

$$\left| \left(\frac{1}{T} \sum_{t=1}^{T} g_t^* - \frac{1}{T} \sum_{s=1}^{T} g_s^\beta \right) - \left[E\big(g_\infty^*\big) - E\big(g_\infty^\beta\big) \right] \right|$$

$$\leq \left| E\big(g_\infty^*\big) - \frac{1}{T} \sum_{t=1}^{T} g_t^* \right| + \left| E\big(g_\infty^\beta\big) - \frac{1}{T} \sum_{s=1}^{T} g_s^\beta \right|. \qquad (6.20)$$

Assumption 6.2 implies that the first term on the right-hand side of (6.20) converges to zero in probability. By Lemma 6.2, the second term on the right-hand side of (6.20) converges in probability to zero uniformly in β. Now $\delta_T(\beta) \equiv | Q_T(\beta) - Q_0(\beta) |$ satisfies

$$\delta_T(\beta) = \left| G_T(\beta)' W_T G_T(\beta) - \left[E\big(g_\infty^*\big) - E\big(g_\infty^\beta\big) \right]' W_0 \left[E\big(g_\infty^*\big) - E\big(g_\infty^\beta\big) \right] \right|$$

$$\leq \left| G_T(\beta) - \left[E\big(g_\infty^*\big) - E\big(g_\infty^\beta\big) \right] \right|' | W_T | | G_T(\beta) |$$

$$+ | E\big(g_\infty^*\big) - E\big(g_\infty^\beta\big) |' | W_T - W_0 | | G_T(\beta) |$$

$$+ | E\big(g_\infty^*\big) - E\big(g_\infty^\beta\big) |' | W_0 | \left| G_T(\beta) - \left[E\big(g_\infty^*\big) - E\big(g_\infty^\beta\big) \right] \right|. \qquad (6.21)$$

Therefore, if we let $\ell_T = \sup_{\beta \in \Theta} | G_T(\beta) - [E(g_\infty^*) - E(g_\infty^\beta)] |$, then

$$\sup_{\beta \in \Theta} \delta_T(\beta) \le \ell_T \mid W_T \mid [\phi_0 + \ell_T] + \phi_0 \mid W_T - W_0 \mid [\phi_0 + \ell_T] + \phi_0 \mid W_0 \mid \ell_T,$$

$$(6.22)$$

where $\phi_0 \equiv \max\{|E(g_\infty^*) - E(g_\infty^\beta)| : \beta \in \Theta\}$ *exists by the continuity condition in Assumption 6.1. Since each of the terms on the right-hand side of (6.22) converges in probability to zero,* $\mathrm{plim}_T[\sup_{\beta \in \Theta} \delta_T(\beta)] = 0$. *This implies the convergence of* $\{b_T\}$ *to* β_0 *in probability as* $T \to \infty$, *as indicated, for example, in Amemiya (1985): p. 107.   Q.E.D.*

6.4. Asymptotic Normality of the SME

The regularity conditions used in Chapter 3 to prove the asymptotic normality of GMM estimators are no longer directly applicable because of the nonstationarity of $\{Y_t^\beta\}$. Therefore, in this section we extend our discussion of asymptotic normality to the case of geometrically ergodic forcing processes that may not be stationary.

In deriving the asymptotic distribution of $\{\sqrt{T}(b_T - \beta_0)\}$, we use an intermediate-value expansion of $G_T(\beta)$ about the point β_0. Accordingly, we adopt the following assumption.

Assumption 6.5.   *(1)* β_0 *and the estimators* $\{b_T\}$ *are interior to* Θ. *(2)* g_t^β *is continuously differentiable with respect to* β *for all* t. *(3)* $D_0 \equiv E[\partial g_\infty^{\beta_0}/\partial \beta]$ *exists, is finite, and has full rank.*

Expanding $G_T(b_T)$ about β_0 gives

$$G_T(b_T) = G_T(\beta_0) + \partial G^*(T)(b_T - \beta_0), \qquad (6.23)$$

where (using the intermediate value theorem) $\partial G^*(T)$ is the $M \times K$ matrix whose ith row is the ith row of $\partial G_T(b_T^i)/\partial \beta$, with b_T^i equal to some convex combination of β_0 and b_T.

Premultiplying (6.23) by $[\partial G_T(b_T)/\partial \beta]' W_T$, and applying the first-order conditions for the optimization problem defining b_T, we get

$$\left[\frac{\partial G_T(b_T)}{\partial \beta}\right]' W_T G_T(b_T) = 0 = \left[\frac{\partial G_T(b_T)}{\partial \beta}\right]' W_T G_T(\beta_0) + J_T(b_T - \beta_0), \quad (6.24)$$

where

$$J_T = \left[\frac{\partial G_T(b_T)}{\partial \beta}\right]' W_T \partial G^*(T).$$

Equation (6.24) can be solved for $(b_T - \beta_0)$ if J_T is invertible for sufficiently large T. This invertibility is given by Assumption 6.5(3) provided

$\partial G_T(b_T)/\partial\beta$ converges in probability to D_0. For notational ease, let $D_\beta f_t^\beta = df(Z_t^\beta, \beta)/d\beta$ (the total derivative). Under the following additional assumptions, Lemma 6.2 and Theorem 4.1.5 of Amemiya (1985) imply that $\plim_T \partial G_T(b_T)/\partial\beta = D_0$.

Assumption 6.6. *The family $\{D_\beta g_t^\beta : \beta \in \Theta, t = 1, 2, \ldots\}$ is Lipschitz, uniformly in probability. For all $\beta \in \Theta$, $E(|D_\beta g_\infty^\beta|) < \infty$, and $\beta \mapsto E(D_\beta g_\infty^\beta)$ is continuous.*

Under these assumptions, the asymptotic distribution of $\sqrt{T}(b_T - \beta_0)$ is equivalent to the asymptotic distribution of $(D_0' \Sigma_0^{-1} D_0)^{-1} D_0' \Sigma_0^{-1} \sqrt{T} G_T(\beta_0)$. The following theorem provides the limiting distribution of $\sqrt{T} G_T(\beta_0)$.

Theorem 6.2 *Suppose $T/\mathcal{T}(T) \to \tau$ as $T \to \infty$. Under Assumptions 6.1–6.6,*

$$\sqrt{T} G_T(\beta_0) \implies N\left[0, \Sigma_0(1 + \tau)\right]. \tag{6.25}$$

Proof (Theorem 6.2). *From the definition of G_T,*

$$\sqrt{T} G_T(\beta_0) = \left(\frac{1}{\sqrt{T}} \sum_{t=1}^{T} \left[g_t^* - E(g_\infty^*)\right]\right)$$

$$- \frac{\sqrt{T}}{\sqrt{\mathcal{T}(T)}} \left(\frac{1}{\sqrt{\mathcal{T}(T)}} \sum_{s=1}^{\mathcal{T}(T)} \left[g_s^{\beta_0} - E(g_\infty^{\beta_0})\right]\right). \tag{6.26}$$

We do not have stationarity, but the proof of asymptotic normality of each term on the right-hand side of (6.26) follows Doob's (1953) proof of a central limit theorem (Theorem 7.5), which uses instead the stronger geometric ergodicity condition. In particular, we are using the assumed bounds on $\| g_t^\beta \|_{2+\delta}$ to conclude that asymptotic normality of g_t^* and $g_t^{\beta_0}$ (suitably normalized) follows from the geometric ergodicity of $\{Y_t\}$ and $\{Y_t^{\beta_0}\}$. (Note that, although Doob's theorem 7.5 includes his condition D_0 as a hypothesis, the geometric ergodicity property is actually sufficient for its proof.) Our result then follows from the independence of the two terms in (6.26) and the convergence of $\sqrt{T}/\sqrt{\mathcal{T}(T)}$ to $\sqrt{\tau}$. Q.E.D.

The following corollary is an immediate implication of Theorem 6.2:

Corollary 6.4.1. *Under the assumptions of Theorem 6.2, $\sqrt{T}(b_T - \beta_0)$ converges in distribution as $T \to \infty$ to a normal random vector with mean zero and covariance matrix*

$$\Lambda_0 = (1 + \tau)\left(D_0' \Sigma_0^{-1} D_0\right)^{-1}. \tag{6.27}$$

As τ gets small, the asymptotic covariance matrix of $\{b_T\}$ approaches $[D_0' \Sigma_0^{-1} D_0]^{-1}$, the covariance matrix obtained when an analytic expression for $E(g_\infty^\beta)$ as a function of β is known a priori. The proposed SME uses a Monte Carlo generated estimate of this mean, which permits consistent estimation of β_0 for circumstances in which the functional form of $E(g_\infty^\beta)$ is not known. In general, knowledge of $E(f_\infty^\beta)$ increases the efficiency of the method-of-moments estimator of β_0. However, if the simulated sample size $\mathcal{T}(T)$ is chosen to be large relative to the size T of the sample of observed variables $\{g_t^*\}$, then there is essentially no loss in efficiency from ignorance of this population mean. Typically, in applications of the SME to asset pricing problems, it is assumed that $\mathcal{T}$ is large and $\tau \approx 0$.

These results presume that the model is identified. The rank condition for the class of models considered here is Assumption 6.5(3). In many GMM problems, verifying that the choice of moment conditions identifies the unknown parameters under plausible assumptions about the correlations among the variables in the model is straightforward. However, inspection of the moment conditions used in simultaneously solving and estimating dynamic asset pricing models may give little insight into whether Assumption 6.6(3) is satisfied. In the context of the stochastic volatility example, for instance, it might not be clear a priori which of the moments selected identify the correlation ρ between the diffusions. The identification problem is likely to be even more challenging when the model is solved numerically for some of the elements of $\{Y_t^\beta\}$ as functions of the state and parameter vectors. In Section 6.6 we discuss an approach to systematically selecting moments in such a way that many of the known features of the *conditional* distribution of Y_t are captured in the choice of g.

6.5. Extensions of the SME

The SME can be extended along a variety of different dimensions. One obvious extension is to let g_t^* be a function of β. In order to accommodate this extension, we need one additional primitive, a measurable observation function $\tilde{g} : \mathbb{R}^{N\bar{\ell}} \times \Theta \to \mathbb{R}^M$, where $\bar{\ell}$ is the number of periods of states entering into the observation $g[(Y_t, \ldots, Y_{t-\bar{\ell}+1}), \beta]$ at time t. We can always assume without loss of generality that $\bar{\ell} = \ell$. We replace the observation g_t^* on the actual state process used in the SME with the observation $\tilde{g}_t^{\beta_0} \equiv \tilde{g}(Z_t, \beta_0)$, and assume that $E[\tilde{g}_t^{\beta_0} - g_t^{\beta_0}] = 0$. This leads us to consider the difference in sample moments:

$$G_T(\beta) = \frac{1}{T} \sum_{t=1}^{T} \tilde{g}_t^\beta - \frac{1}{\mathcal{T}(T)} \sum_{s=1}^{\mathcal{T}(T)} g_t^\beta. \qquad (6.28)$$

We once again introduce a sequence $\{W_T\}$ of positive-semidefinite distance matrices and define the criterion function $Q_T(\beta) = G_T(\beta)'W_T G_T(\beta)$ as well as the extended SME $\{b_T\}$ of β_0, just as in (6.8).

In this case, we replace Σ_0 defined by (6.19) with the weighted covariance matrix, for the positive scalar weight $\tau \equiv \lim_{T \to \infty} T/T(T)$, $\Sigma_{\tilde{g},g,\tau} = \tau \Sigma_0 + \Sigma_1$, where

$$\Sigma_1 = \sum_{j=-\infty}^{\infty} E\Big(\big[\tilde{g}_t^{\beta_0} - E(\tilde{g}_t^{\beta_0})\big]\big[\tilde{g}_t^{\beta_0} - E(\tilde{g}_t^{\beta_0})\big]' \Big). \tag{6.29}$$

Assuming that the families $\{g_t^{\beta}\}$ and $\{\tilde{g}_t^{\beta}\}$ satisfy the technical conditions of Assumption 6.1[12] and that $W_T \to W_0 = \Sigma_{\tilde{g},g,\tau}^{-1}$ almost surely, the weak consistency of this extended SME follows from an argument almost identical to the proof of Theorem 6.1. Furthermore, under the same assumptions as in Theorem 6.2, $\sqrt{T}(b_T - \beta_0)$ converges in distribution to a normal random vector with mean zero and covariance matrix

$$\Lambda_{\tilde{g},g,\tau} = \big(D_0'\Sigma_{\tilde{g},g,\tau}^{-1}D_0\big)^{-1}. \tag{6.30}$$

In contrast to the matrix Λ_0 in (6.27), consistent estimation of $\Lambda_{\tilde{g},g,\tau}$ must typically be accomplished in two steps, using both simulated and observed data.

Allowing the observation function $\tilde{g}_t^{\beta}$ to depend on β is useful in many asset pricing problems. For instance, one may wish to compare the sample mean of the intertemporal marginal rate of substitution of consumption in the data to the mean of the corresponding simulated series.

A second example arises when one or more of the coordinate functions defining $\tilde{g}$, say $\tilde{g}_j$, has the property that $h_j(\beta) = E[\tilde{g}_j(Z_\infty, \beta)]$ defines a known function h_j of β. If this calculation cannot be made for every j, one can mix the use of calculated and simulated moments by letting $g_j(z, \beta) = h_j(\beta)$ for all z, for any j for which h_j is known. This substitution of calculated moments for sample moments improves the precision of the simulated moments estimator, in that the covariance matrix $\Lambda_{\tilde{g},g,\tau}$ is smaller than the covariance matrix Λ_0 obtained when all moments are simulated. Errors in measurement of g_t^* are accommodated by letting $\tilde{g}_t^{\beta_0} = g(Z_t, \beta_0) + u_t$, where $\{u_t\}$ is an ergodic, mean-zero $\mathbb{R}^M$-valued measurement error. Note that the asymptotic efficiency of the SME is increased by ignoring the measurement error in simulation and comparing sample moments of the simulated $\{g(Z_t^{\beta}, \beta)\}$ and $\{\tilde{g}_t^{\beta}\}$.

---

[12] Note that the uniform-in-probability Lipschitz condition for $\{\tilde{g}_t^{\beta}\}$ is qualitatively weaker than the same condition for $\{g_t^{\beta}\}$, since $\tilde{g}_t^{\beta}$ depends only directly on β (i.e., Y_t is not dependent on β).

6.6. Moment Selection with SME

A key issue faced in implementing the SME is the choice of the function g that describes the moments to be used in estimation. In principle, one would want to choose moment equations that capture some of the known features of the data, such as persistence, conditional heteroskedasticity, and nonnormality. Gallant and Tauchen (1996) have proposed a very clever application of the SME that allows one to easily capture these features of asset prices or returns.

Let $\mathcal{Y}_t$ denote the subvector of the state process Y_t that is observed. In the stochastic volatility model, for example, $\mathcal{Y}_t = r_t$ and $Y_t' = (r_t, v_t)$. Further, let $f(\mathcal{Y}_t | \vec{\mathcal{Y}}_{t-1}; \delta)$ denote a conditional density function of the data that captures parametrically the features of the data that one is interested in representing by g. Maximum likelihood estimation of δ gives the estimator δ_T that solves

$$\sum_t \frac{\partial \log f}{\partial \delta}(\mathcal{Y}_t | \vec{\mathcal{Y}}_{t-1}; \delta_T) = 0. \tag{6.31}$$

The estimator δ_T is a consistent estimator (under regularity conditions) of the δ_0 that satisfies

$$E\left[\frac{\partial \log f}{\partial \delta}(\mathcal{Y}_t | \vec{\mathcal{Y}}_{t-1}; \delta_0)\right] = 0. \tag{6.32}$$

Importantly, there is no presumption that the density f is the true conditional density of $\mathcal{Y}_t$ or that δ_T is a consistent estimator of any of the parameters of the true data-generating process for $\mathcal{Y}_t$. Rather, δ_T is a consistent estimator of the δ_0, the parameter vector that minimizes the *Kullback-Leibler* information criterion, $E[\log(p(\mathcal{Y}_t | \vec{\mathcal{Y}}_{t-1}; \beta_0)/f(\mathcal{Y}_t | \vec{\mathcal{Y}}_{t-1}; \delta))]$ by the choice of δ, where p is the density of the actual data-generating process for $\mathcal{Y}$. This information criterion can be interpreted as a measure of our ignorance about the true structure of the data-generating model.[13]

Having chosen f and estimated δ_T by the method of ML, we let the score of this log-likelihood function be the vector of moments used to estimate the parameters β_0 of the asset pricing model. That is, the function of the observed data is chosen to be

$$g(Z_t, \beta_0; \delta_T) = -\frac{\partial \log f}{\partial \delta}(\mathcal{Y}_t | \vec{\mathcal{Y}}_{t-1}; \delta_T), \tag{6.33}$$

---

[13] See Akaike (1973) for a discussion of the use of this information criterion in model selection, and White (1982) for a discussion of the properties of ML estimators of misspecified models.

and the corresponding function for simulated data with parameter vector β is

$$g\left(Z_t^\beta, \beta; \delta_T\right) = -\frac{\partial \log f}{\partial \delta}\left(\mathcal{Y}_t^\beta \big| \vec{\mathcal{Y}}_{t-1}^\beta; \delta_T\right). \tag{6.34}$$

In simulating $\mathcal{Y}_t^\beta$, it is generally necessary to simulate the entire state vector Y_t^β and then select out the subvector $\mathcal{Y}_t^\beta$ that enters these moment conditions.

Substituting these expressions into $G_T(\beta)$ in (6.7) gives

$$G_T(\beta) = -\frac{1}{T}\sum_t \frac{\partial \log f}{\partial \delta}\left(\mathcal{Y}_t \big| \vec{\mathcal{Y}}_{t-1}; \delta_T\right) + \frac{1}{T}\sum_s \frac{\partial \log f}{\partial \delta}\left(\mathcal{Y}_s^\beta \big| \vec{\mathcal{Y}}_{s-1}^\beta; \delta_T\right)$$

$$= \frac{1}{T}\sum_s \frac{\partial \log f}{\partial \delta}\left(\mathcal{Y}_s^\beta \big| \vec{\mathcal{Y}}_{s-1}^\beta; \delta_T\right), \tag{6.35}$$

where the last equality follows from the fact that δ_T is the ML estimator of the auxiliary model. Thus, the sample moments entering the GMM criterion function depend only on the simulated data. The sources of randomness in G_T are the estimator δ_T and shocks ϵ_t used in the simulation. However, if T is assumed to be large enough for the sample moments to have converged to their population counterparts, then we can interpret G_T as

$$G_T(\beta) = \iint \frac{\partial \log f}{\partial \delta}\left(\mathcal{Y}_t \big| \vec{\mathcal{Y}}_{t-1}; \delta_T\right) p\left(\mathcal{Y}_t \big| \vec{\mathcal{Y}}_{t-1}; \beta\right) d\mathcal{Y}_t \, p\left(\vec{\mathcal{Y}}_{t-1}; \beta\right) d\vec{\mathcal{Y}}_{t-1}, \tag{6.36}$$

where $p(\mathcal{Y}_t | \vec{\mathcal{Y}}_{t-1}; \beta)$ and $p(\vec{\mathcal{Y}}_{t-1}; \beta)$ are the true conditional and marginal distributions of the $\mathcal{Y}$ process generated by parameter vector β. In this case, the only source of randomness in $G_T(\beta)$ is δ_T. This "large T" assumption was made in Gallant and Tauchen (1996) and has been adopted implicitly in most applications of their approach to DAPMs.

For example, if $\mathcal{Y}_t$ is an observed scalar process and one is interested in capturing first-order serial correlation and conditional heteroskedasticity that depends on lagged squared projection errors, then one could set $\tilde{\mathcal{Y}}_t' = (1, \mathcal{Y}_t)$ and choose

$$\mathcal{Y}_t | \vec{\mathcal{Y}}_{t-1} \sim N\left(a_0'\tilde{\mathcal{Y}}_{t-1}, \gamma_0 + \gamma_1\epsilon_{t-1}^2\right), \quad \epsilon_t \equiv \mathcal{Y}_t - a_0'\tilde{\mathcal{Y}}_{t-1}. \tag{3.37}$$

The first-order conditions to maximizing the log-likelihood function over $\delta' = (a_0', \gamma_0, \gamma_1)$ are

$$\frac{1}{T}\sum_t \frac{\hat{\epsilon}_t \tilde{\mathcal{Y}}_{t-1}}{\hat{\sigma}_{t-1}^2} = 0, \tag{6.38}$$

$$\frac{1}{T} \sum_t \left(\frac{\hat{\epsilon}_t^2}{\hat{\sigma}_{t-1}^2} - 1 \right) \frac{\partial \hat{\sigma}_{t-1}^2}{\partial \gamma} \frac{1}{\hat{\sigma}_{t-1}^2} = 0, \tag{6.39}$$

where $\gamma_T' = (\gamma_{0T}, \gamma_{1T})$, and

$$\hat{\epsilon}_t \equiv \left(\mathcal{Y}_t - a_{0T}' \tilde{\mathcal{Y}}_{t-1} \right), \quad \hat{\sigma}_{t-1}^2 \equiv \gamma_{0T} + \gamma_{1T} \hat{\epsilon}_{t-1}^2. \tag{6.40}$$

Thus, the components of $G_T(\beta)$ are

$$\frac{1}{T} \sum_s \frac{\hat{\epsilon}_s^\beta \tilde{\mathcal{Y}}_{s-1}^\beta}{\hat{\sigma}_{s-1}^{\beta 2}}, \tag{6.41}$$

$$\frac{1}{T} \sum_s \left(\frac{\hat{\epsilon}_s^{\beta 2}}{\hat{\sigma}_{s-1}^{\beta 2}} - 1 \right) \frac{\partial \hat{\sigma}_{s-1}^{\beta 2}}{\partial \gamma} \frac{1}{\hat{\sigma}_{s-1}^{\beta 2}}, \tag{6.42}$$

where the hatted variables are evaluated at simulated Y_s^β and the ML estimator $\delta_T' = (a_T', \gamma_T')$.

More generally, as suggested in Gallant and Tauchen (1996), a tractable and flexible family of auxiliary models is constructed as follows. Let $\mu_{\tilde{y}, t-1}$ denote the linear projection of $\mathcal{Y}_t$ onto L_μ lags of $\mathcal{Y}$; that is, the fitted values from a standard vector autoregression with L_μ lags. Moreover, they allow for "ARCH"-like errors by transforming the innovations in this autoregression by the matrix $R_{\tilde{y}, t-1}$ with elements that are linear functions of the absolute values of L_r past values of the $\epsilon_{jt} = (\mathcal{Y}_t - \mu_{\tilde{Y}, t-1})_j$.[14] For example, with $L_r = 2$, the transformation $R_{y, t-1}$ has the form

$$R_{y, t-1} = \begin{bmatrix} \tau_1 + \tau_7 |\epsilon_{1, t-1}| \\ + \tau_{25} |\epsilon_{1, t-2}| & \tau_2 & \tau_4 \\ 0 & \tau_3 + \tau_{15} |\epsilon_{2, t-1}| \\ & + \tau_{33} |\epsilon_{2, t-2}| & \tau_5 \\ 0 & 0 & \tau_6 + \tau_{24} |\epsilon_{3, t-1}| \\ & & + \tau_{42} |\epsilon_{3, t-2}|, \end{bmatrix}. \tag{6.43}$$

We let z_t denote the standardized $\mathcal{Y}_t$:

---

[14] The computer code currently available from Gallant and Tauchen for implementing an SME using an auxiliary model of this type also allows one to specify the heteroskedasticity as being of the GARCH(1,1) type (Bollerslev, 1986). Andersen et al. (1999b) develop an auxiliary model based on Nelson's (1991) EGARCH model. All of these models of conditional heteroskedasticity are discussed in depth in Chapter 7.

$$z_t = R^{-1}_{\vec{y}, t-1}(\mathcal{Y} - \mu_{\vec{y}, -1}),\tag{6.44}$$

and approximate the conditional density function of X_t, as viewed through this auxiliary model, as

$$f(\mathcal{Y}_t | \vec{\mathcal{Y}}_{\ell, t-1}, \delta) = c(\vec{\mathcal{Y}}_{t-1})\Big[\varphi_0 + \big[h(z_t | \vec{\mathcal{Y}}_{t-1})\big]^2\Big]N(z_t),\tag{6.45}$$

where $N(\cdot)$ is the density function of the standard normal distribution, φ_0 is a small positive number, $h(z|\mathcal{Y})$ is a Hermite polynomial in z, $c(\vec{\mathcal{Y}}_{t-1})$ is a normalization constant, and $\vec{\mathcal{Y}}_{t-1}$ is the conditioning set. The Hermite polynomial h is given by

$$h(z_t | \vec{\mathcal{Y}}_{t-1}) = A_1 + \sum_{l=1}^{L_h}\sum_{i=1}^{n} A_{3(l-1)+1+i}\, z^l_{i,t}.\tag{6.46}$$

Its presence in (6.45) serves to introduce nonnormality in the conditional distribution of $\mathcal{Y}_t$ by scaling the conditional normal density by a polynomial in lagged values of $\mathcal{Y}_t$. This formulation is actually a special case of that in Gallant and Tauchen (1996) in that the coefficients in the Hermite polynomial $h(z_t | \vec{\mathcal{Y}}_{t-1})$ are assumed to be constants, independent of the conditioning information. This assumption can be relaxed to obtain a more general auxiliary model.

Returning to the general case, we still have to compute the large-sample distribution of the SME b_T of β_0. Toward this end, let

$$G_\infty(\beta) = \int\int \frac{\partial \log f}{\partial \delta}(\mathcal{Y}_t | \vec{\mathcal{Y}}_{t-1}; \delta_0)p(\mathcal{Y}_t | \vec{\mathcal{Y}}_{t-1}; \beta)d\mathcal{Y}_t\, p(\vec{\mathcal{Y}}_{t-1}; \beta)d\vec{\mathcal{Y}}_{t-1},\tag{6.47}$$

and note that $G_\infty(\beta_0) = 0$ if the DAPM is correctly specified, by definition of δ_0 in (6.32). Then, by the usual derivation of the large-sample distribution of ML estimators,

$$\sqrt{T}(\delta_T - \delta_0) \implies N\big(0, d_0^{-1}\Sigma_0(d_0')^{-1}\big),\tag{6.48}$$

where

$$d_0 = E\left[\frac{\partial^2 \log f}{\partial \delta \partial \delta'}(\mathcal{Y}_t | \vec{\mathcal{Y}}_{t-1}; \delta_0)\right].\tag{6.49}$$

The interpretation of Σ_0 depends on one's view of the auxiliary model. In standard ML theory,

$$\Sigma_0 = E\left[\frac{\partial \log f}{\partial \delta}(\mathcal{Y}_t | \vec{\mathcal{Y}}_{t-1}; \delta_0)\frac{\partial \log f}{\partial \delta}(\mathcal{Y}_t | \vec{\mathcal{Y}}_{t-1}; \delta_0)'\right].\tag{6.50}$$

Moreover, d_0^{ML} and Σ_0 cancel each other (up to signs), because of relation (3.52). If the chosen auxiliary model is assumed to be sufficiently rich to nest the true conditional density of the data-generating process, then these standard results apply and the asymptotic covariance matrix of δ_T is $d_0^{-1} = -\Sigma_0^{-1}$.

When selecting an auxiliary model, we do not require that the auxiliary density $f(\mathcal{Y}_t|\vec{\mathcal{Y}}_{t-1}; \delta)$ be the true density of the data-generating process for $\mathcal{Y}$, however. If not, then d_0^{-1} and Σ_0 do not cancel each other. Moreover, in general the score $\partial \log f(\mathcal{Y}_t|\vec{\mathcal{Y}}_{t-1}; \delta_0)/\partial\delta$ will not be a martingale difference sequence (does not satisfy the counterpart to (2.7)) and so will be serially correlated. Therefore, this SME falls under Case $\mathrm{AC}h(\infty)$ from Chapter 3 and

$$\Sigma_0 = \sum_{j=-\infty}^{\infty} E\left[\frac{\partial \log f}{\partial \delta}(\mathcal{Y}_t|\vec{\mathcal{Y}}_{t-1}; \delta_0) \frac{\partial \log f}{\partial \delta}(\mathcal{Y}_{t-j}|\vec{\mathcal{Y}}_{t-j-1}; \delta_0)' \right]. \qquad (6.51)$$

Using these observations, we see that

$$\sqrt{T}G_T(\beta_0) \stackrel{a}{=} \sqrt{T}G_\infty(\beta_0) + d_0\sqrt{T}(\delta_T - \delta_0)$$

$$= d_0\sqrt{T}(\delta_T - \delta_0) \implies N(0, \Sigma_0), \qquad (6.52)$$

where the $\stackrel{a}{=}$ denotes asymptotic equivalence. Therefore, the optimal distance matrix to use in constructing this score-based SME is Σ_0, and the optimal SME is

$$b_T = \operatorname*{argmin}_{\beta \in \Theta} G_T(\beta)' \Sigma_T^{-1} G_T(\beta), \qquad (6.53)$$

where Σ_T is a consistent estimator of Σ_0. This can be estimated using either the historical data on $\mathcal{Y}$ (just as the information matrix is estimated in conventional ML estimation), or using the simulated $\mathcal{Y}^{b_T}$. When using simulated data, a two-step estimation procedure is necessary in order to get a consistent estimator of β_0 to use in construction of Σ_T.

Finally, a standard mean-value expansion of the first-order conditions to this GMM problem implies that

$$0 \stackrel{a}{=} D_0'\Sigma_0^{-1}\sqrt{T}G_T(\beta_0) + D_0'\Sigma_0^{-1}D_0\sqrt{T}(b_T - \beta_0), \qquad (6.54)$$

where

$$D_0 \equiv \operatorname{plim}_{T\to\infty} \frac{\partial G_T(b_T)}{\partial \beta}. \qquad (6.55)$$

It follows that

$$\sqrt{T}(b_T - \beta_0) \Longrightarrow N\big(0, \big(D_0'\Sigma_0^{-1}D_0\big)^{-1}\big).$$ (6.56)

Typically, the number of parameters of the auxiliary model (equal to the dimension of the score vector), M, is much larger than the number of parameters of the DAPM, K. Therefore, a flexible choice of the auxiliary model leads naturally to a set of diagnostic tests of the fit of the model. Using (6.56) and the Wald test of an individual moment condition developed in Chapter 4, we can test the null hypotheses that elements of mean score vector from the auxiliary model, $G_\infty(\beta_0)$, are zero using the sample scores (6.35). In this setting, rejection of the null that a particular mean score is zero would suggest that the DAPM does not adequately describe the features of the conditional distribution of $\mathcal{Y}$ governed by the associated parameter in the auxiliary model. It is sometimes possible to group parameters according to, for example, whether they describe the conditional mean, variance, or higher-order moments of the distribution of $\mathcal{Y}$. In such cases, one can construct chi-square goodness-of-fit tests of a DAPM's fit to certain aspects of the distribution of $\mathcal{Y}$.

Several studies have examined the small-sample properties of the SME and compared them to the properties of standard GMM and (when feasible) ML estimators. Of particular interest is how the properties of the SME depend on the choice of auxiliary model (and hence number of moments chosen) and sample size. Chumacero (1997) compared the small-sample properties of the efficient SME and a GMM estimator using a more conventional selection of moments for a stochastic volatility model (see Chapter 7) and a consumption-based asset pricing model (see Chapter 10). He found that the SME was more efficient and often showed less bias than the GMM estimator. At the same time, tests of the overidentifying restrictions using the SME tended to reject the models too often under his null hypotheses.

Andersen et al. (1999a) also examine the finite-sample properties of estimators for a stochastic volatility model. They considered auxiliary models with ARCH (Engle, 1982), GARCH (Bollerslev, 1986), and EGARCH (Nelson, 1991) specifications of conditional volatility (see Chapter 7). Overall, the SME performed very well relative to GMM estimators based on a less systematic choice of instruments. In particular, they found that for their models and parameter choices the overall goodness-of-fit chi-square statistics from simulated moments estimation led to reliable inference.

Zhou (2001b) examines the finite-sample properties of GMM, ML and quasi-ML, and efficient SME of a univariate square-root diffusion model, motivated by the literature on interest rate modeling (see Example 2.1 and Chapter 12). He finds that the ML estimator is the most efficient. Quasi-ML estimation is second in efficiency, but it provides the most reliable results in testing overidentifying restrictions. GMM is the least efficient estimation method, based on the moments chosen. The efficient SME performs especially well in high-volatility environments. However, using this method leads to a substantial bias toward rejection of overidentifying restrictions.

6.7. Applications of SME to Diffusion Models

The application of SME to continuous-time models has been formally studied by Gallant and Long (1997) and Gallant and Tauchen (1997), and widely applied in subsequent studies. The basic idea is to discretize the process (5.4) describing the evolution of Y_t, simulate a long time series for the discretely sampled Y from this approximate model, and then compute method-of-moments estimators by comparing the model-implied sample moments to those computed using historical data.

More concretely, consider again the Euler approximation (5.13) to the diffusion (5.4). Starting with an initial value Y_0 of the state vector and a value for the parameter vector γ, a simulated time series $Y_t^{\gamma,n}$ can be constructed recursively using a standard normal random number generator to draw the ϵ_t^n. Every nth value of the $Y_t^{\gamma,n}$ is then sampled and assigned to the simulated, discretely sampled state, where we have indexed the simulation by the discretization size $1/n$.

Taken literally, for fixed n, the distribution of the simulated $Y_t^{\gamma,n}$ does not have the same distribution as Y_t because (5.13) is not the same as the original diffusion process. Whether or not this observation presents new econometric complications depends on one's view about the role of the discretization. One view—suggesting that there is a complication—is that when a discretization is used for simulation, it is not enough to take the limits as sample and simulation sizes go to infinity to derive the large-sample distribution of the resulting SME. We must also address what happens when the discretization interval goes to zero or, equivalently, when $n \to \infty$. The Euler scheme (5.13) has the property that, assuming μ and σ satisfy certain polynomial growth conditions (see Kloeden and Platen, 1992: th. 10.2.2),

$$E\big(\big|Y_t - Y_t^{\gamma,n}\big|\big) \leq K(1/n)^{1/2}, \tag{6.57}$$

for some constant K independent of n and for all $n \geq n^*$. In the sense of (6.57), the Euler approximate is said to converge strongly with order 0.5. However, strong convergence in this sense does not tell us directly at what rate n should be increased with sample size T to ensure the asymptotic normality of the SME. This issue is not avoided by the use of more "efficient" schemes with larger orders of strong convergence,[15] though such schemes may be preferred because of their faster convergence.

---

[15] The accuracy of the Euler scheme tends to deteriorate with increased variation in the drift and volatility of Y_t. See Kloeden and Platen (1992) for a theoretical treatment of

A second view is that discretization is a numerical or computational issue. With today's computers we are free to set n to a very large number and use approximation schemes that converge strongly with high order. Under this view, the approximation errors are not relevant to the derivation of the asymptotic distribution of γ_0, for which it is assumed that $n = \infty$. Furthermore, for high-order approximation schemes, they are also not material to the accuracy of the computation of parameter estimates. This second view is the one expressed most often [see, e.g., Gallant and Long (1997) and Gallant and Tauchen (1997)].

6.8. Markov Chain Monte Carlo Estimation

An alternative estimation strategy for diffusion models, including models with latent state variables, is the method of Markov chain Monte Carlo.[16] There are several features of this approach that may recommend it over alternatives, including SME. First, its conceptual foundations draw upon the Bayesian theory of inference. Additionally, as part of the estimation process, MCMC generates estimates not just of the parameters of the model, but also of the latent volatility, jump times, and jump sizes. From these estimates the historical residuals of the returns and volatility processes can be computed for use in diagnostic analyses, as we illustrate in Chapter 7. Thus, this approach may be particularly attractive for jump-diffusion models. Reliable estimation of these parameters using SME depends on the auxiliary model adequately capturing the fat-tailed nature of jump processes and, as we will see, ensuring that this richness is captured can be challenging. Finally, MCMC allows the separation and quantification of estimation risk and model specification risk, and infrequent observations or missing data are easily accommodated.

A classic example of a setting where MCMC is conveniently applied is the stochastic volatility model of equity returns in which that state vector is (S_t, v_t), where S_t is an observed stock price and v_t is a latent stock-price-volatility process (see, e.g., Jacquier et al., 1994, Eraker et al., 2003, and Eraker, 2004). A simplified version of this model has

$$d \ln S_t = \sqrt{v_t}\, dW_{St}, \tag{6.58}$$

$$d \ln v_t = (\bar{v} - \kappa \ln v_t)\, dt + \sigma_v dW_{vt}, \tag{6.59}$$

with $\mathrm{Corr}(dW_v, dW_S) = 0$. (The case of nonzero drift in $\ln S_t$ and nonzero correlation between return and volatility shocks are considered in Chapter 7.)

---

approximation schemes with higher orders of strong convergence and Gallant and Long (1997) for illustrations.

[16] A comprehensive survey of this method with applications to finance can be found in Johannes and Polson (2003). We largely follow their notation in the following overview of MCMC.

Whereas the stock price is observed, the stochastic volatility v is not. Moreover, $\ln S_t$ is not Markov given its past history (the only series that is observed) so the likelihood function of the sample $(\ln S_1, \ldots, \ln S_T)$ is not easily derived.

The parameters of this model can be estimated by the method of SME. In fact a very similar Example 2.3 was used as motivation of this estimation method. However, as a GMM estimator, SME is generally inefficient relative to MCMC since the latter exploits both information in the likelihood function and a researcher's priors. Moreover, SME does not provide an estimate of the latent state v. A time series on $\{v_t\}$ is usually computed after estimation using filtering methods.

The roots of MCMC estimation lie within the framework of Bayesian inference. The basic idea is to combine a prior distribution over the unknown parameter vector with the conditional density of the state vector to obtain a joint posterior distribution of the parameters and the state conditional on the observed asset prices (or any other observed data included in the analysis). From this joint posterior distribution the marginal posterior distributions of the states and parameters can be computed. In particular, the mean or median, standard deviation, quantiles, and so on, of the posterior distribution of the parameters can be computed. The mean of this posterior distribution is typically interpreted as the MCMC estimator of the unknown parameters.

Let Θ denote the parameter vector of interest, X be a vector of (possibly latent) state variables, and Y denote the vector of observed asset prices or yields. The MCMC algorithm constructs a Markov chain that converges to the joint distribution $p(\Theta, X|Y)$. From this distribution, one can determine both $p(\Theta|Y)$ (which gives the parameter estimates) and $p(X|Y)$ (which provides estimates of the unobserved states). Key to this construction is the Clifford-Hammersley theorem, which implies that under a positivity condition, knowing $p(\Theta|X, Y)$ and $p(X|\Theta, Y)$ is equivalent to knowing $p(X, \Theta|Y)$.[17] What gives the MCMC algorithm its traction is that the first two distributions are often much easier to characterize than the joint distribution $p(X, \Theta|Y)$.

When it is feasible to simulate from both of these densities, the MCMC algorithm uses the Gibbs sampler. Given realizations up to $g-1$, $X_t^{(g)}$ is drawn from $p(X_t|\Theta^{(g-1)}, Y)$; and $\Theta^{(g)}$ is drawn from $p(\Theta|X_t^{(g-1)}, \Theta^{(g-1)}, Y)$. When direct sampling from the joint density $p(X, \Theta|Y)$ is not feasible, researchers have replaced Gibbs sampling with Metropolis-Hastings sampling. Suppose, for example, that simulation from the conditional density $p(X|\Theta, Y)$ is not feasible and, to simplify notation, let X be a scalar and let

---

[17] This theorem brings comparable simplification when Θ or X is a vector. For instance, the conditional density $p(\Theta|X, Y)$ is determined by the densities $p(\Theta_j|\Theta^{(-j)}, X, Y)$, where $\Theta^{(-j)}$ is the set of Θ's excluding Θ_j. See Johannes and Polson (2003) for further discussion.

$\pi(X) = p(X|\Theta, Y)$. The basic idea is to start with a distribution $q(X^{(g+1)}|X^{(g)})$ that is known and from which samples can be easily drawn. Depending on the application, $q(\cdot)$ may depend on the parameters, other state variables, and previous draws of X. Then a single Gibbs sampling step is replaced by the two steps:

1. Draw $X^{(g+1)}$ from the proposal density $q(X^{(g+1)}|X^{(g)})$.
2. Accept $X^{(g+1)}$ with probability $\alpha(X^{(g)}, X^{(g+1)})$, where

$$\alpha(X^{(g)}, X^{(g+1)}) = \min\left(\frac{\pi(X^{(g+1)})/q(X^{(g+1)}|X^{(g)})}{\pi(X^{(g)})/q(X^{(g)}|X^{(g+1)})}, 1\right). \qquad (6.60)$$

Hence, instead of having to sample from the distribution $\pi(X)$, one needs to evaluate it at only two points. The reason this algorithm works is that the modified transition probability $q(X^{(g+1)}|X^{(g)})\,\alpha(X^{(g)}, X^{(g+1)})$ satisfies a *reversibility condition* that ensures that it converges to the stationary or invariant distribution of π. Note that the accept/reject decision depends only on the ratio $\pi(X^{(g+1)})/\pi(X^{(g)})$. This is an attractive feature since π is typically known only up to a constant of proportionality. Critical in practice to the success of this algorithm is the choice of the candidate density $q(\cdot)$, as this choice influences the rate of convergence to the invariant distribution.

Once a sample $\{\Theta^{(g)}, X^{(g)}\}_{g=1}^{G}$ is drawn, by either of these sampling methods, the moments of the joint distribution of (Θ, X) can be computed by Monte Carlo. This is because, under suitable regularity (see the papers cited previously for discussion),

$$\frac{1}{G}\sum_{g=1}^{G} h\big(\Theta^{(g)}, X^{(g)}\big) \underset{\text{a.s.}}{\rightarrow} \int h(\Theta, X)p(\Theta, X|Y)\, dX d\Theta. \qquad (6.61)$$

This convergence requires ergodicity or other similar conditions that ensure applicability of a strong law of large numbers, some regularity on the function h, and that the Markov chain generated by the sampling method converges in distribution to $p(\Theta, X|Y)$.

To gain some intuition for how MCMC works, consider again the stock price process (6.58) simplified to the case of constant volatility (while allowing for nonzero drift):

$$d\ln S_t = \mu_S\, dt + \sigma_S\, dW_t, \qquad (6.62)$$

for constants μ_S and σ_S. [See Johannes and Polson (2003) for further discussion of various perturbations of this example.] Given the Gaussian structure of this model, continuously compounded returns follow the discrete-time process

$$\Delta \ln S_t = \mu_S + \sigma_S \epsilon_t, \quad \epsilon_t \sim N(0, 1). \tag{6.63}$$

Though this model leads to a known, closed-form representation of the likelihood function for the data $(S_1, \ldots, S_T)$, it is nevertheless instructive to work through the MCMC algorithm to illustrate its use. The relevant distributions to be determined are $p(\mu_S | \sigma_S^2, \Delta \ln S)$ and $p(\sigma_S^2 | \mu_S, \Delta, \ln S)$. We can derive expressions for these densities using Bayes's rule and assumptions about the researcher's priors on (μ_S, σ_S^2).

For illustrative purposes, suppose that the researcher has independent priors. Then Bayes's rule allows us to write

$$p(\mu_S | \sigma_S^2, \Delta \ln S) = p(\Delta \ln S | \mu_S, \sigma_S^2) p(\mu_S), \tag{6.64}$$

$$p(\sigma_S^2 | \mu_S, \Delta \ln S) = p(\Delta \ln S | \mu_S, \sigma_S^2) p(\sigma_S^2), \tag{6.65}$$

where $p(\sigma_S^2)$ and $p(\mu_S)$ are the priors on these parameters. The density $p(\Delta \ln S | \mu_S, \sigma_S^2)$ is that of a normal, because ϵ is normally distributed. A common assumption is that $p(\mu_S)$ is normal and $p(\sigma_S^2)$ is inverted gamma. One motivation for this choice is that it gives rise to $p(\mu_S | \sigma_S^2, \Delta \ln S)$ and $p(\sigma_S^2 | \mu_S, \Delta \ln S)$ having the normal and inverted-gamma distributions, respectively. Therefore, the MCMC algorithm proceeds by drawing

$$\mu_S^{(g+1)} \sim p(\mu_S | (\sigma_S^2)^{(g)}, \Delta \ln S) \sim \text{Normal}, \tag{6.66}$$

$$(\sigma_S^2)^{(g+1)} \sim p(\sigma_S^2 | \mu_S^{(g)}, \Delta \ln S) \sim \text{Inverted Gamma}. \tag{6.67}$$

Since all of the relevant distributions are known, this is a Gibbs sampler. Note the key role of the researcher's priors in this implementation of MCMC.

The gains from application of MCMC become apparent when one or more of the state variables is unobserved. We encounter this situation when the preceding model of the stock price is extended to have stochastic volatility as in (6.58). For econometric analysis, the literature has often focused on the discrete-time counterpart of this model:

$$R_t = \sqrt{v_{t-1}} \epsilon_{St}, \tag{6.68}$$

$$\ln v_t = \alpha_v + \beta_v \ln v_{t-1} + \eta_v \epsilon_{vt}, \tag{6.69}$$

where $R_t \equiv \ln S_t - \ln S_{t-1}$ is the continuously compounded return. In applying the MCMC algorithm to this model, the Clifford-Hammersley theorem allows us to focus on the conditional densities

$$p(\alpha_v, \beta_v | \eta_v, v, R), \ p(\eta_v^2 | \alpha_v, \beta_v, v, R), \ \text{and} \ p(v | \alpha_v, \beta_v, \eta_v^2, R).$$

Jacquier et al. (1994) adopt normal priors on (α_v, β_v) and an inverted-gamma prior on η_v^2 so the densities $p(\alpha_v, \beta_v | \eta_v, v, R)$ and $p(\eta_v^2 | \alpha_v, \beta_v, v, R)$ are proportional to normal and inverted-gamma distributions, respectively.

However, simulating from the density $p(v | \alpha_v, \beta_v, \eta_v^2, S)$ is not easy even in this rather simplified model. Johannes and Polson (2003) show that

$$p(v|\Theta, R) \propto p(R|\Theta, v)p(v|\Theta) \propto \prod_{t=1}^{T} p(v_t|v_{t-1}, v_{t+1}, \Theta, R). \qquad (6.70)$$

Each term in the latter expression takes the form

$$p(v_t|v_{t-1}, v_{t+1}, \Theta, R) \propto v_t^{1/2} \times e^{-\ln R_t^2/2v_t} \times e^{-e_t^2/2\sigma_v^2} \times v_t^{-1} \times e^{-e_{t+1}^2/2\sigma_v^2}, \qquad (6.71)$$

were $e_t = \ln v_t - \alpha_v - \beta_v \ln v_{t-1}$. Expression (6.71) is clearly quite complicated and is not an immediately recognizable distribution. Therefore a Metropolis-Hastings algorithm is used in which the distribution $q(v_t)$ is chosen to be a gamma distribution.

Returning to the general MCMC estimation problem, within asset pricing settings, we can often exploit the Markov structure of the state variables to further simplify the relevant distributions. Additionally, some of the variables may be independent of each other, and jump times or sizes may be independent of the underlying asset prices. For instance, in the equity option pricing literature, jump amplitudes are usually assumed to be independent of the level of the stock price (see Chapter 15).

Some simplification was also achieved in the preceding examples through the choice of priors. The use of conjugate priors meant that some of the conditional densities for the parameters inherited the same functional forms as those of the priors. Should researchers prefer different priors, then determining these distributions might be a nontrivial task. It is also likely that in some applications of MCMC the results will be sensitive to the researcher's choice of priors.

Of course MCMC methods are not immune to all of the challenges we faced with likelihood estimation without unobserved states. In particular, we often do not have closed-form expressions for this density $p(Y|X, \Theta)$, so approximations may be involved. Another potential source of approximations in applications of MCMC methods is the discretization of a continuous-time process. For instance, in the stochastic volatility example, if (6.58) and (6.59) represent the true data-generating process, then (6.69) is not the exact representation of the implied discrete-time stock return process. Rather, the discrete-time model is more naturally thought of as a discretization of the continuous-time model.

7

Stochastic Volatility, Jumps, and Asset Returns

THIS CHAPTER EXPLORES the shapes of the conditional distributions of asset returns from two complementary perspectives. First, we present various descriptive statistics of the historical data that will be useful in assessing the goodness-of-fit of DAPMs. Second, we explore how alternative choices of probability models for the risk factors affect the model-implied shapes of return distributions.

That the distributions of most returns are "fat tailed" and often "skewed" has been extensively documented in the finance literature. We begin this chapter with some descriptive evidence on the nonzero skewness and excess kurtosis of the unconditional distributions of equity and bond market yields. Subsequently, we examine the *conditional* third and forth moments of return distributions and illustrate how these moments can be used to discriminate among alternative time-series models for returns.

Potentially important sources of these nonnormal shapes are recurrent periods of volatile and quiet financial markets. Accordingly, a central focus of this chapter is on how alternative parameterizations of time-varying volatility—"stochastic volatility"—and sudden infrequent price moves—"jumps"—affect the shapes of return distributions. Jumplike behavior can be induced by a classical jump process (e.g., a Poisson process), shocks that are drawn from a mixture of distributions, or a "switching-regime" process. Accordingly, we first highlight the conceptual differences among these alternative formulations and then add in stochastic volatility, all in discrete time.

This discussion is followed by a review of continuous-time models with stochastic volatility and jumps.[1] We also review some of the key empirical

---

[1] There is also a continuous-time counterpart to switching-regime models. See, e.g., Dai and Singleton (2003b) for a discussion of regime-switching versions of several popular continuous-time models of interest rates. Most of the empirical literature has focused on discrete-time versions of these models and we do as well.

findings in this literature as those results play a central role in our discussion of option pricing models in Chapter 15. Finally, we discuss the link between discrete- and continuous-time models by exploring the continuous-time limit of several discrete-time models as the sampling interval of the data becomes increasingly short.

7.1. Preliminary Observations about Shape

Beyond the first two moments (mean and volatility), we also examine the *skewness* and *kurtosis* of model-implied return distributions. The (unconditional) skewness of a random variable r, defined as Skew $= E[(r - E(r))^3]/\sigma^3$, is a measure of the degree to which positive deviations from its mean are larger than the negative ones. A second important feature of a distribution is the degree to which it is "thick" or "thin" tailed. A standard measure of tail fatness is kurtosis, Kurt $= E[(r - E(r))^4]/\sigma^4$. The kurtosis of a normal random variable is 3, so distributions with kurtoses larger than 3 are said to exhibit excess kurtosis.

To help in developing some intuition for the degree of departure from normality of actual market returns, Table 7.1 presents the sample mean (μ), standard deviation (σ, what we call "volatility"), skewness (Skew), and kurtosis (Kurt) of returns for various markets and instruments around the world. As an illustrative fixed-income instrument we used the 5-year swap rate, because data were available for a wider range of countries than was the case for intermediate-term government bonds. These instruments are defaultable, of course, and also implicitly reflect the sovereign risks associated with the currencies in which they were issued. The equity returns are constructed from MSCI price indices and the swap returns are approximate holding period returns on the 5-year swap rates, both over the sample period of January 1990 through June 2004.[2]

All of the returns exhibited substantial excess kurtosis. Hong Kong equity returns had the largest kurtosis, owing in part to the political turmoil surrounding the return of Hong Kong to Chinese control. In the case of swaps, the European currency crises and the consequent large interventions by monetary authorities are partially responsible for these kurtoses. In particular, the substantial increases in short-term rates in Sweden were reflected in a kurtosis of 23 for swap holding period returns.

Additionally, daily equity returns in developed markets tended to be negatively skewed (long tails in the direction of negative returns), whereas

---

[2] The sample period for the Hong Kong swap data is much shorter, starting in 2002, and some of the other swap yield series start in 1991, instead of 1990. Holding period returns on swaps were constructed using the linearized present value model discussed in Shiller (1979) and Singleton (1980).

Table 7.1. *Sample Unconditional Moments of 1-Day Holding Period Returns for Various Markets and Countries*

Equity returns (daily)

	Aust	Can	Fra	Ger	HK	Jap	Spain	Swe	UK	US
μ	0.019	0.024	0.021	−0.022	0.030	−0.022	0.030	0.035	0.017	0.032
σ	0.858	0.963	1.296	0.922	1.640	1.307	1.360	1.555	1.026	1.025
Skew	−0.237	−0.547	−0.134	0.549	−0.033	0.233	−0.157	0.170	−0.107	−0.114
Kurt	5.952	10.787	5.871	6.655	11.613	6.905	6.459	6.720	6.160	6.857

Swap holding-period returns (daily)

	Aust	Can	Fra	Ger	HK	Jap	Spain	Swe	UK	US
μ	0.035	0.034	0.030	0.028	0.025	0.019	0.041	0.037	0.038	0.030
σ	0.391	0.320	0.227	0.205	0.427	0.195	0.316	0.351	0.259	0.280
Skew	−0.306	−0.355	−0.025	−0.165	−0.547	−0.256	−0.075	0.009	0.580	−0.273
Kurt	8.180	8.232	6.303	6.817	28.270	8.138	17.144	23.319	14.263	5.298

Note: The countries are Aust = Australia, Can = Canada, Fra = France, Ger = Germany, HK = Hong Kong, Jap = Japan, Swe = Sweden, UK = United Kingdom, and US = United States.

several of the Asian markets exhibited positive skewness. This negative skewness is often attributed to the "leverage effect," because of Black's (1976) insight that declining stock prices tend to lead to a higher firm leverage ratio (higher debt/equity ratio) and, consequently, more risk for equity holders. While conceptually this relationship among prices, leverage, and volatility holds, subsequent research suggests that this particular economic mechanism may not account for the magnitude of skewness observed historically. Nevertheless, the basic empirical observation itself is frequently referred to as the *leverage effect*.

In summary, most holding period returns on securities exhibit excess kurtosis or fat tails. Equity returns tend to be negatively skewed, whereas the patterns of skewness for fixed-income instruments are more varied. These findings suggest that whatever the econometric model of returns adopted, it should imply nonnormal, fat-tailed marginal return distributions.

The nonnormality of the marginal distributions of returns need not imply the nonnormality of the conditional distributions. Moreover, Table 7.1 provides no information about the dependence of conditional moments of returns on the state of the economy. One simple "probability model" that characterizes the dependence of conditional moments on market conditions says that conditional moments of returns are well approximated by computing rolling historical sample moments over a fixed window of data, possibly with weighting of past observations to give more weight to the recent data. For instance, Figure 7.1 displays rolling estimates of the sample volatility, skewness, and kurtosis of returns on the S&P500 index using a geometric weighting of past observations with weight factor 0.98 and a 100-day window [see the discussion of (7.3) for a precise description of these calculations]. All of these estimates change over time. Moreover, there are notable periods of volatility clustering (quiet and turbulent times), with associated changes in rolling kurtosis and skewness statistics. The largest upward spikes in volatility are often accompanied by large increases in kurtosis.

As we will see, one potential source of time-varying skewness and kurtosis is the variation over time in the conditional volatilities of returns. Accordingly, it is also instructive to examine the rolling sample "standardized" returns, computed by subtracting off the rolling sample mean and dividing by the rolling sample standard deviation. The rolling sample skewness and excess kurtosis for these standardized returns are displayed in Figure 7.2. Standardizing does remove some of the large negative skewness in the levels of returns. However, those periods during which the skewness of returns was particularly large and negative remain, even in the standardized data. Similarly, though the excess kurtosis is notably smaller in the standardized data, there are coincident large excess kurtoses both in the levels and in the standardized series. That the standardized returns inherit the nonnormality of the unprocessed returns suggests, as we will see, that stochastic volatility

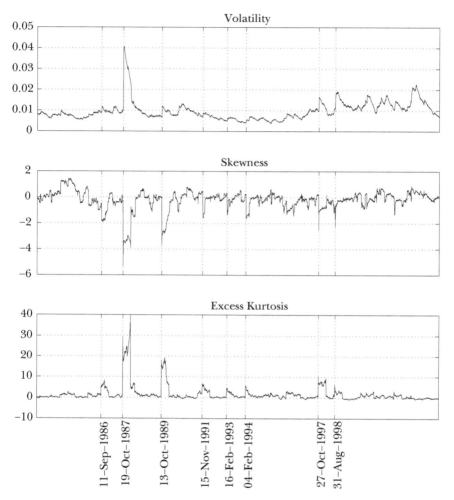

Figure 7.1. *Rolling sample moments of S&P500 returns. Daily continuously compounded returns on the S&P500 are used to construct rolling sample moments over 100-day windows. The sample period is October 1983 through December 2003.*

alone (or, at least, standard formulations of stochastic volatility) is not by itself sufficient to describe the conditional distributions of returns.

To explore the conditional distributions of returns more systematically, we turn next to an examination of the distributions implied by several popular time-series models of returns.[3]

---

[3] If our goal was solely to estimate the conditional distributions of returns, we could use nonparametric statistical methods to estimate the conditional densities and, from these

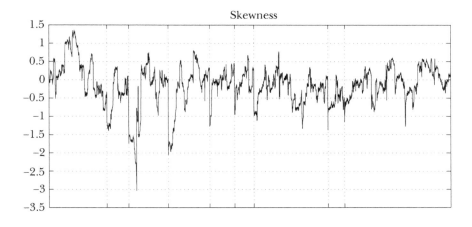

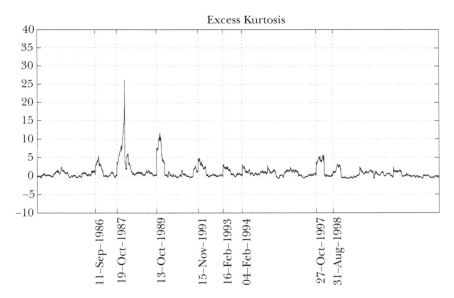

Figure 7.2. *Rolling sample moments of standardized S&P500 returns. The daily returns are standardized by subtracting off the sample mean and dividing by the rolling sample standard deviation. The sample period is October 1983 through December 2003.*

densities, the implied conditional moments. However, dynamic asset pricing models are typically constructed using parametric models of price/return behavior. Therefore, our primary focus is on how particular features of these parametric probability models translate into the shapes of return distributions.

7.2. Discrete-Time Models

A wide variety of discrete-time models for returns have been studied in the literature. Rather than attempting a comprehensive review of these models,[4] we focus on a small number of models that capture some of the key features of the more popular ones. We begin with an overview of models of stochastic volatility, and then discuss extensions of these to allow for jumps or switches in regimes.

7.2.1. Discrete-Time Stochastic Volatility Models

A widely studied formulation of stochastic volatility is the discrete-time GARCH(p,q) model proposed by Rosenberg (1972), Engle (1982), and Bollerslev (1986), which has returns following the process:

$$r_t = \mu_{t-1} + \sigma_{t-1}\epsilon_t, \tag{7.1}$$

$$\sigma_{t-1}^2 = \omega + \sum_{j=1}^{p} \alpha_j (r_{t-j} - \mu_{t-j-1})^2 + \sum_{i=1}^{q} \beta_i \sigma_{t-i-1}^2, \tag{7.2}$$

where μ_{t-1} is the mean of r_t conditioned on the history of returns at date $t-1$, $\{\epsilon_t\}$ is a sequence of i.i.d. $N(0, 1)$ shocks, and ω, $(\alpha_j : j = 1, \ldots, p)$, and $(\beta_i : i = 1, \ldots, q)$ are nonnegative.[5]

The special case with ($p = 1, q = 1$), the GARCH(1,1) model, is closely related to the so-called "rolling historical" volatility model that sets $\omega = 0$ and $\alpha = (1 - \beta)$[6]:

$$\hat{\sigma}_{t,\beta}^2 = (1 - \beta) \sum_{j=0}^{\infty} \beta^j (r_{t-j} - \mu_{t-j-1})^2. \tag{7.3}$$

This representation, which shows the geometric weighting of past squared return shocks implicit in GARCH models, underlies the plots in Figure 7.1. The geometric weighting serves to mitigate the sensitivity of estimated volatility to outliers relative to equally weighted, rolling finite histories.

Nevertheless, because the impact of the current return r_t on σ_t^2 (through $\sigma_{t-1}^2\epsilon_t^2$) is quadratic, outliers in the data may lead GARCH models to exaggerate the level of return volatility. In particular, a day of exceptionally large

---

[4] Excellent surveys of discrete-time models can be found in Bollerslev et al. (1992, 1994).

[5] This notation is nonstandard relative to the literature on GARCH and was chosen to reflect the fact that σ_t^2 resides in the information set I_t of returns dated t and before.

[6] This model is often used in market risk measurement systems. See, e.g., Litterman and Winkelmann (1998). RiskMetrics adopted a volatility model similar to (7.3) (Phelan, 1995) with μ_{t-1} constant and a horizon of 2 weeks, a history of 100 days, and a decay factor of $\beta = 0.96$.

absolute returns may cause an "overshooting" in forecasted volatility that dies out too slowly over time relative to actual market volatility. There are at least two ways to measure the implied persistence in volatility in GARCH models. One measure of persistence is the degree of autocorrelation of σ_t^2. Within the GARCH(1,1) model, the coefficient on σ_{t-1}^2 in the projection $E[\sigma_t^2|I_{t-1}]$ is $\alpha + \beta$. The condition $(\alpha + \beta) < 1$ ensures the covariance stationarity of the GARCH(1,1) process [Bollerslev (1986)].[7] Using this measure, a market crash or "jump" could imply an inappropriately sustained major impact on forecasted volatility if $(\beta + \alpha)$ is near unity.

An alternative measure of persistence is the median lag of past $(r_{t-j} - \mu_{t-j-1})^2$ in the conditional variance expression itself. Writing the conditional variance in a GARCH model as

$$\sigma_t^2 = \bar{\omega} + \sum_{j=0}^{\infty} \delta_j \left(r_{t-j} - \mu_{t-j-1} \right)^2, \qquad (7.4)$$

we define the median lag as the value of ν that satisfies $(\sum_{j=0}^{\nu-1} \delta_j)/(\sum_{j=0}^{\infty} \delta_j) = \frac{1}{2}$. For the GARCH(1,1) model $\nu = -\log 2/\log \beta$, which depends only on β as it is this parameter that governs the rate of geometric decay of the effect of past squared return shocks on σ_t^2 [see (7.3)]. With the median lag, as β gets larger a large return shock has a longer-term effect on volatility.

The dependence of σ_t^2 on ϵ_t^2 in all of these GARCH-style models implies that return shocks have a symmetric effect on volatility. A large positive or negative return shock of equal magnitude in absolute value has the same effect on volatility. For many markets, and in particular many equity markets, it has long been recognized that positive and negative shocks have asymmetric effects on volatility. Large negative shocks have a larger effect than correspondingly large positive shocks. Historical volatility measures, including GARCH models, do not capture this asymmetry.

Motivated by the evidence of asymmetry, several researchers have proposed "asymmetric" GARCH-like models. Nelson (1991) specified the logarithm of the conditional variance as

$$\ln \sigma_t^2 = \omega + \alpha(|\epsilon_t| - E|\epsilon_t| + \beta \epsilon_t), \qquad (7.5)$$

leading to the exponential or EGARCH model. By specifying the logarithm of σ_t^2 as a function of ϵ_t, he ensured that the conditional variance stays positive even if some of the coefficients in (7.5) are negative. Positive deviations of $|\epsilon_t|$ from its mean lead to increases in the conditional variance, similar to the GARCH model. However, unlike in the GARCH model, with nonzero β

---

[7] More generally, for a GARCH(p,q) process, we have covariance stationarity if the sum of α's and β's on lagged squared return shocks and variances is less than unity.

the effect of ϵ_t on σ_t^2 is asymmetric: if $-1 < \beta < 0$, then a negative surprise has a larger (positive) effect on volatility than a positive return surprise of the same absolute magnitude, for instance. Dependence on additional lagged deviations of $|\epsilon|$ from its mean is easily accommodated.

Modifications of the basic GARCH(1,1) model to allow for asymmetry have been proposed by Glosten et al. (1993) and Heston and Nandi (2000), among others. The GJR model has

$$\sigma_t^2 = \omega + \alpha \epsilon_t^2 + \gamma \epsilon_t^2 1_{\{\epsilon_t \geq 0\}} + \beta \sigma_{t-1}^2. \tag{7.6}$$

With $\gamma < 0$, positive return shocks increase volatility less than negative shocks, thereby inducing asymmetry. The conditional variance remains positive in this model as long as $\beta \geq 0$ and $\alpha + \gamma \geq 0$. Alternatively, the model proposed by Heston and Nandi has

$$r_t = \mu + \lambda \sigma_{t-1}^2 + \sigma_{t-1} \epsilon_t, \tag{7.7}$$

$$\sigma_t^2 = \omega + \alpha (\epsilon_t - \gamma \sigma_{t-1})^2 + \beta \sigma_{t-1}^2, \tag{7.8}$$

with $\epsilon_t \sim N(0, 1)$. The conditional covariance between r_t and σ_t implied by this model is $\text{Cov}_{t-1}(r_t, \sigma_t^2) = -2\alpha\gamma\sigma_{t-1}^2$. Hence, with $\gamma > 0$, a large negative return shock raises σ^2 more than a large positive shock.

Though volatility is time varying in these models, there is not an independent source of randomness to volatility over and above past return shocks. One can allow for "true" stochastic volatility in discrete-time models by introducing a random volatility shock to the process σ_t^2 or $\ln \sigma_t^2$. For instance, following Taylor (1986) (see also Jacquier et al., 1994, and Kim et al., 1998), one could assume that $\ln \sigma_t^2 = \omega + \beta \ln \sigma_{t-1}^2 + \sigma_v v_t$. By construction, in this model $\sigma_t^2 \geq 0$.

Alternatively, adapting our discussion of autoregressive-gamma models in Chapter 5, we could assume that σ_t^2 follows an $AG(a, b\sigma_{t-1}^2, c)$ process with

$$\sigma_t^2 = ca + b\sigma_{t-1}^2 + \eta_{v,t-1}v_t, \tag{7.9}$$

$$\eta_{vt}^2 = c^2 a + 2bc^2 \sigma_{t-1}^2, \tag{7.10}$$

where v_t is an error with mean zero and unit variance. A potential limitation of this model is that when combined with a model for returns, the construction of a $DA_1(2)$ model presumes that the return and variance shocks are independent, conditional on past returns and variances. That is, within a period return and volatility shocks are mutually independent. We will see that this is a counterfactual assumption, one that is not required for the preceding model of $\ln \sigma_t^2$.

More generally, when modeling the level σ_t^2 in discrete time, one must be careful to ensure that σ_t^2 remains nonnegative. While this can always be ensured by truncating the distribution of σ_t^2 at some lower bound $\bar{v}$, it may put positive probability mass on the variance $\bar{v}$ that should be accommodated when constructing the relevant likelihood function.

7.2.2. Jumps and Regime Switches in Discrete Time

Consistent with the preceding discussion, a common assumption in stochastic volatility models for returns is that ϵ in (7.1) is Gaussian (the conditional distribution of returns is a normal). As we have already seen, for many financial markets, the distributions of standardized returns $(r_t - \mu_{t-1})/\sigma_{t-1}$ over daily or weekly investment horizons exhibit substantial excess kurtoses and nonzero skewness. Thus, a Gaussian conditional distribution for r_t is typically counterfactual. To better match the higher-order moments of returns, we can extend the model by introducing fat-tailed shocks to r. Three tractable ways of introducing such shocks are: (1) let ϵ be drawn from a fatter-tailed distribution than a normal; (2) allow the conditional distribution of r to possibly change over time, with switching governed by a Markov "regime" process; or (3) add jumps to r. We discuss each of these modeling strategies in turn, initially in a setting with constant conditional volatility.

Several researchers have allowed the return shock ϵ to be drawn from a fat-tailed distribution. For example, Bollerslev (1987) assumes a t distribution and Baille and Bollerslev (1989) use a power exponential distribution for ϵ. Another approach is to have ϵ drawn from the "mixture-of-normals" model discussed briefly in Section 4.6. Specifically, suppose that

$$\epsilon_t \sim \begin{cases} N(0, \sigma_1^2) & \text{with probability } p \\ N(0, \sigma_2^2) & \text{with probability } (1-p) \end{cases}, \tag{7.11}$$

where $0 < p < 1$ is the mixing probability and $p\sigma_1^2 + (1-p)\sigma_2^2 = 1$ since ϵ_t has unit variance. The kurtosis of ϵ_t is[8]

$$\text{Kurt} = \frac{3[p\sigma_1^4 + (1-p)\sigma_2^4]}{[p\sigma_1^2 + (1-p)\sigma_2^2]^2} = 3[p\sigma_1^4 + (1-p)\sigma_2^4] \geq 3. \tag{7.12}$$

Thus, a mixture-of-normals shock induces excess kurtosis in returns.

Though this extension introduces fat tails, it preserves the zero conditional skewness of the basic stochastic volatility models, because the means of the normal distributions being mixed are zero. Similar models have been

---

[8] The last inequality follows from the fact that $p\sigma_1^4 + (1-p)\sigma_2^4$ is at least as large as $[p\sigma_1^2 + (1-p)\sigma_2^2]^2$.

studied by Jorion (1988) (a normal-Poisson mixture distribution) and Hsieh (1989) (a normal-log normal mixture distribution).

Alternatively, building on the work by Hamilton (1989) and Gray (1996), substantial attention has recently been devoted to switching-regime models. If we suppose that the economy can be in one of two regimes (extensions to more regimes are straightforward) and that the modeler does not observe which regime the economy is currently in, the information about the current state of the economy is summarized by I_t. As discussed in Section 4.6, the modeler is assumed to know the functional form of the conditional distribution of r_t given I_{t-1} and the *future* regime of the economy, $f(r_t|I_{t-1}, S_t = i; \theta_0)$, $i = 1, 2$. In general, both the functional forms of the conditional distributions and their associated parameter vectors may differ across regimes.

Under these assumptions, the conditional density of r_t,

$$
\begin{aligned}
f(r_t|I_{t-1}; \theta_0) = & f(r_t|I_{t-1}, S_t = 1; \theta_{10})p_{1,t-1} \\
& + f(r_t|I_{t-1}, S_t = 2; \theta_{20})(1 - p_{1,t-1}),
\end{aligned}
\tag{7.13}
$$

is known up to the conditional probability $p_{1,t-1} = \Pr\{S_t = 1|I_{t-1}\}$. This conditional probability is determined once the process governing switches in regimes is specified.

The transition between regimes in switching-regime models is typically assumed to be governed by a Markov switching process in which

$$
\Pr\{S_t = i|S_{t-1} = i, I_{t-1}\} = \begin{cases} P_{t-1} & i = 1 \\ Q_{t-1} & i = 2. \end{cases}
\tag{7.14}
$$

Hamilton (1989) assumed that P_{t-1} and Q_{t-1} were constant over time and many subsequent studies have retained this assumption.[9] On the other hand, Hamilton (1994) and Gray (1996) propose tractable models with time-dependent (I_{t-1}-dependent) switching probabilities. In particular, using Bayes's rule and letting $g_{i,t-2} \equiv f(r_{t-1}|I_{t-2}, S_{t-1} = i)$, the counterpart to (4.116) for state-dependent P and Q is

$$
\begin{aligned}
p_{1,t-1} = & (1 - Q_{t-1})\left[\frac{g_{2,t-2}(1 - p_{1,t-2})}{g_{1,t-2}p_{1,t-2} + g_{2,t-2}(1 - p_{1,t-2})}\right] \\
& + P_{t-1}\left[\frac{g_{1,t-2}p_{1,t-2}}{g_{1,t-2}p_{1,t-2} + g_{2,t-2}(1 - p_{1,t-2})}\right].
\end{aligned}
\tag{7.15}
$$

---

[9] This formulation generalizes the discussion in Section 4.6 by allowing state-dependent transition probabilities for the Markov process S_t.

Thus, once one expresses P_{t-1} and Q_{t-1} as functions of I_{t-1}, the conditional probabilities p_{1t} can be computed recursively using (7.15). Two possible specifications for P_{t-1} (similarly, Q_{t-1}) are $P_{t-1} = \Phi(\alpha_0 + \alpha_X X_{t-1})$, where Φ is the cumulative normal distribution function, and $1/(1 + e^{\alpha_0 + \alpha_X X_{t-1}})$, for some $X_{t-1} \in I_{t-1}$.

A key difference between a model based on a mixture of (not necessarily normal) distributions and a regime-switching model is that the latter introduces an additional source of persistence through the Markov process S_t governing changes in regimes. This can be seen formally by setting $P_t = (1 - Q_t)$, for all t. In this case,

$$\Pr\{S_t = i | S_{t-1} = i, I_{t-1}\} = \Pr\{S_t = i | S_{t-1} = j, I_{t-1}\},$$

for $\supset \neq i$, so the probabilities that S_t takes on the values of 1 or 2 are independent of the previous regime, S_{t-1}. Equivalently, the Markov process S_t exhibits no persistence. Substituting this constraint into (7.15) gives $p_{1,t-1} = P_{t-1}$. Therefore, in the absence of any persistence in the regime process S_t, the data-generating process for r_t simplifies to a mixture-of-distributions model with mixing probabilities P_t and $(1 - P_t)$.

A third means of introducing fat tails into return distributions is to add a jump process to the data-generating process. This can be accomplished by adding a Bernoulli random "jump" Z_t, taking on the values $\{0, 1\}$ and satisfying $\Pr\{Z_t = 1\} = \zeta$, with independent random amplitude ξ. A typical specification of the distribution of ξ is $N(m_J, \delta_J^2)$. With this addition,

$$r_t = \mu_{t-1} + \sigma \epsilon_t + \xi Z_t. \tag{7.16}$$

Note that the conditional mean of the error term, $E[\sigma \epsilon_t + \xi Z_t | I_{t-1}]$, is not zero, but rather is ζm_J, owing to the presence of the jump. By adjusting the mean of r_t by ζm_J, we can rewrite (7.16) in terms of the mean zero shock $(\xi Z_t - \zeta m_J)$.

This Bernoulli jump model has r_t jumping at most once between $t - 1$ and t. A convenient way of allowing for multiple jumps within a single time interval is to use a Poisson jump process. The Poisson formulation arises naturally when the discrete-time model of interest is derived from a continuous-time model. We discuss this model subsequently in our coverage of continuous-time models.

7.2.3. Reintroducing Stochastic Volatility

As will be apparent from our review of empirical work on continuous-time models, incorporating both jumps and stochastic volatility facilitates matching of the empirical distributions of stock returns. However, some care must be exercised in how this combination is achieved.

An issue that may arise in the case of jumps is that a jumpy random variable may take on inadmissible values. For instance, consider the model $AG(a, b\sigma_{t-1}^2, c)$ [see (7.9)] for the conditional variance σ_t^2. By construction, σ_t^2 is nonnegative in this model. However, if a jump in *volatility* is introduced by adding ξZ_t to this model,

$$\sigma_t^2 = ca + b\sigma_{t-1}^2 + \eta_{v,t-1}v_t + \xi Z_t, \tag{7.17}$$

$$\eta_{vt}^2 = c^2 a + 2bc\sigma_{t-1}^2, \tag{7.18}$$

then clearly the support of the distribution of ξ must be nonnegative. For otherwise, σ_t^2 may take on negative values. This problem does not arise in adding a jump to returns (which may be negative).

Computational tractability may also be compromised by the combination of stochastic volatility and regime switching. The reason is that the conditional variances of asset returns are often highly persistent. As such, σ_t^2 depends on lagged information that is itself regime dependent. In the case of an ARCH(p) model for r_t,

$$\sigma_{t-1}^2(S_t) = \sum_{j=1}^{p} \alpha_j \left(r_{t-j}(S_{t-j}) - \mu_{t-j-1}(S_{t-j-1}) \right)^2$$

so there is dependence not only on S_t, but also on $(S_{t-1}, \ldots, S_{t-p-1})$. This dependence can be handled by increasing the effective number of regimes. For example, if there are two regimes and p lagged squared residuals in an ARCH model, then the model can be recast as a standard regime-switching model with 2^{p+1} regimes (Cai, 1994; Hamilton and Susmel, 1994). The computational burden of estimation increases with p.

This problem is particularly acute in the case of a GARCH model, because σ_t^2 implicitly depends on the entire past history of the regimes. To circumvent the path dependence of GARCH volatilities, Gray (1996) proposed a modification of the literal implementation of a switching GARCH model. He examined the special case of (7.13) in which

$$f\left(r_t | I_{t-1}, S_t = i; \theta_{i0}\right) \sim N\left(\mu_{i,t-1}, \sigma_{i,t-1}^2\right)$$

with $\mu_{i,t-1}$ linear in r_{t-1} and $\sigma_{i,t-1}^2$ determined by a modified GARCH(1,1) process as follows. Letting

$$\epsilon_t = r_t - \left[p_{1,t-1}\mu_{1,t-1} + (1 - p_{1,t-1})\mu_{2,t-1} \right],$$

he assumed that

$$\sigma_{t-1}^2 = p_{1,t-1}\left(\mu_{1,t-1}^2 + \sigma_{1,t-1}^2\right) + \left(1 - p_{1,t-1}\right)\left(\mu_{2,t-1}^2 + \sigma_{2,t-1}^2\right) \quad (7.19)$$
$$- \left[p_{1,t-1}\mu_{1,t-1} + (1 - p_{1,t-1})\mu_{2,t-1}\right]^2$$

and

$$\sigma_{i,t-1}^2 = \omega_i + \alpha_i \epsilon_{t-1}^2 + \beta_i \sigma_{t-2}^2, \quad i = 1, 2. \quad (7.20)$$

In this manner, the σ_{it}^2 are dependent on a common, average lagged conditional variance that breaks the dependence of the likelihood on the entire history of regimes S_t, while keeping the key persistence property of a GARCH model.

7.3. Estimation of Discrete-Time Models

Given a parametric assumption about the distribution of ϵ_t conditional on the entire past history of returns at date $t-1$, and assuming that a Markov switching or jump process is independent of ϵ_t, then all of these discrete-time volatility models can be estimated by the method of maximum likelihood. (Here we have in mind Gray's version of the switching GARCH model.) In developing the relevant likelihood functions, we begin with models that exclude jumps.

Let μ_{t-1} and σ_{t-1} denote the conditional mean and volatility of r_t, and suppose that these moments may depend on finite J-histories of r_{t-1} and σ_{t-1}. This would be true, for example, in GARCH(p,q) models with $p \le J$ and $q \le J$. Then $r_t|I_{t-1} \sim N(\mu_{t-1}, \sigma_{t-1}^2)$, where I_{t-1} is the information set generated by past returns $r_{t-1}, r_{t-2}, \ldots, r_1$ and the presample values $\vec{r}_0^{\,J}$ and $\vec{\sigma}_0^{2J}$. This follows from the fact that σ_{t-1}^2 can be recursively built up in all of these models from past returns, given the initial presample values $\vec{\sigma}_0^{2J}$. Furthermore, if μ_{t-1} depends on $\vec{r}_{t-1}^{\,J}$, then the conditional mean of r_1 depends on $\vec{r}_0^{\,J}$, so we condition on these initial returns as well.

With this notation, the likelihood function of the data can be written as

$$L_T\left(r_T, \ldots, r_1 | \vec{r}_0^{\,J}, \vec{\sigma}_0^{2J}; \theta\right) = f\left(r_T, \ldots, r_1 | \vec{r}_0^{\,J}, \vec{\sigma}_0^{2J}; \theta\right) \quad (7.21)$$
$$= f\left(r_T | I_{T-1}; \theta\right) f\left(r_{T-1} | I_{T-2}; \theta\right) \ldots f\left(r_1 | \vec{r}_0^{\,J}, \vec{\sigma}_0^{2J}; \theta\right).$$

The functional form of the conditional density f, for a typical date t, depends on the model. In the case of GARCH models,

$$f\left(r_t | I_{t-1}; \theta\right) = \frac{1}{\sqrt{2\pi\sigma_{t-1}^2}} e^{-\frac{1}{2}(r_t - \mu_{t-1})^2/\sigma_{t-1}^2}. \quad (7.22)$$

Substituting this density into (7.21) and taking logarithms gives the log-likelihood function $l_T(\beta)$ used in estimation.

Alternatively, in the MixGARCH model, we have

$$
f(r_t|I_{t-1}; \theta) = p \times \frac{1}{\sqrt{2\pi\sigma_{t-1}^2\sigma_1^2}} e^{-\frac{1}{2}(r_t-\mu_{t-1})^2/(\sigma_{t-1}^2\sigma_1^2)}
$$

$$
+ (1-p) \times \frac{1}{\sqrt{2\pi\sigma_{t-1}^2\sigma_2^2}} e^{-\frac{1}{2}(r_t-\mu_{t-1})^2/(\sigma_{t-1}^2\sigma_2^2)}.
$$

$$(7.23)$$

This form arises because, in a given regime i, the conditional variance of r_t is $\sigma_{t-1}^2 \times \mathrm{Var}(\epsilon_t|\mathrm{Regime} = i)$, which is $\sigma_{t-1}^2\sigma_i^2$, $i = 1, 2$. The constraint $p\sigma_1^2 + (1-p)\sigma_2^2 = 1$ is imposed in estimation. Though easy to write down, the likelihood function of the MixGARCH model is globally unbounded, a well-known problem of mixture-of-normal models [e.g., Quandt and Ramsey (1978)]. This is illustrated by setting $\mu_0 = r_1$ and letting σ_1 approach zero, in which case (7.23) with $t = 1$ approaches infinity and, hence, so does the likelihood function. This is typically not a problem in practice, because numerical search routines find local optima, and one can search across local optima with bounded likelihood function values. Kiefer (1978) shows that there exists a consistent, asymptotically normal local optimum with the usual properties of ML estimators.

In Gray's formulation of a regime-switching GARCH model,

$$
f(r_t|I_{t-1}; \theta) = p_{1,t-1} \times \frac{1}{\sqrt{2\pi\sigma_{1,t-1}^2}} e^{-\frac{1}{2}(r_t-\mu_{1,t-1})^2/\sigma_{1,t-1}^2}
$$

$$
+ (1-p_{1,t-1}) \times \frac{1}{\sqrt{2\pi\sigma_{2,t-1}^2}} e^{-\frac{1}{2}(r_t-\mu_{2,t-1})^2/\sigma_{2,t-1}^2}.
$$

$$(7.24)$$

Owing to the mixture nature of the resulting likelihood function, this model also implies a globally unbounded likelihood function. Therefore, in general, it inherits the challenge of reliable numerical identification of the parameters of the global optimum to the likelihood function.

In maximizing l_T, it is necessary to choose an initial value of $\vec{\sigma}_0^{2J}$ and possibly of $\vec{r}_0^J$. The latter can be avoided by ignoring the conditional densities of the first J returns. However, the former is necessary, because σ_t^2 is a constructed series rather than one that is directly observed. To construct the time series of volatilities, Bollerslev (1986) suggests using the sample variance of r as the initial value of σ_t^2, and we do so here as well in our implementation of the GARCH(1,1) model. Intuitively, the use of this estimated initial condition should not affect the estimates if the dependence of

σ_t^2 on its own lagged values far in the past dies out over time, as is the case in the GARCH(1,1) model if $\alpha + \beta < 1$.

To formalize the argument that the asymptotic properties of ML estimators are insensitive to the choice of initial volatility, we can call upon the large-sample arguments used in Chapter 6. In GARCH models satisfying a "root condition" such as $\alpha + \beta < 1$, the effects of past $(r_{t-s} - \mu_{t-s-1})^2$ on σ_t^2, $s > 0$, die out geometrically fast. So we would expect that this "initial condition" problem, which gives rise to a nonstationarity, is transient and does not affect the asymptotic distribution of the estimators.

To highlight the key properties of alternative time-series models of returns, we focus on the classical GARCH(1,1) or "historical volatility" and MixGARCH discrete-time models. Table 7.2 shows the estimates for these reference models using daily data on continuously compounded S&P500 index returns. The data, which cover the sample period January 3, 1980, through December 31, 1996, are from the analysis by Andersen et al. (2002). In estimating the MixGARCH model we fixed p, somewhat arbitrarily, at 0.9. The intent was to avoid numerical indeterminacy associated with searching over p along with the other parameters of the model. The implied estimate of σ_2 in this model is 1.93, giving the plausible result that volatility is much higher in the infrequently occurring regime. The point estimates of $\alpha + \beta$ in both models (0.994, 0.996) show a high level of persistence in $(r_t - \mu)^2$, consistent with previous studies of equity return volatility (see, e.g., Bollerslev et al., 1992). Additionally, $\beta_T \gg \alpha_T$ so the median lag in the effect of past $(r_{t-j} - \mu)^2$ on σ_t^2 is also large.

Adding in jumps to these models does not introduce any new complications. For the case of a Bernoulli jump without regime switching, we end up with a mixture-of-distributions model. With probability ζ, r_t is drawn from the distribution $N(\mu_{t-1} + m_J, \sigma_{t-1}^2 + \delta_J^2)$, and with probability $(1 - \zeta)$ it is drawn from the distribution $N(\mu_{t-1}, \sigma_{t-1}^2)$. This mixture model was implemented, for example, by Das (2002) for interest-rate data.

Table 7.2. *ML Estimates of the Parameters of the GARCH(1,1) and MIXGARCH Models Using the S&P500 Equity Index*

Model	Parameters				
	μ	ω	α	β	σ_1
GARCH(1,1)	0.057	0.013	0.070	0.918	NA
	(0.012)	(0.002)	(0.002)	(0.004)	
MixGARCH	0.057	0.009	0.053	0.938	0.835
	(0.011)	(0.002)	(0.004)	(0.006)	(0.009)

Note: Standard errors of the estimates are given in parentheses.

When both regime switching and jumps are present, we effectively have two sources of mixing, one from jumps, which shows no persistence, and one from the persistent Markov regime-switching process. For the case of two regimes, and starting with (7.13), we write

$$
\begin{aligned}
f\big(r_t \big| I_{t-1}, S_t = i; \theta_{i0}\big) &= \zeta f\big(r_t \big| I_{t-1}, S_t = i, \text{ jump}; \theta_{i0}\big) \\
&+ \big(1 - \zeta\big) f\big(r_t | I_{t-1}, S_t = i, \text{no jump}; \theta_{i0}\big),
\end{aligned}
\tag{7.25}
$$

and proceed to parameterize the distributions of r_t conditional on both the regime and whether or not there was a jump. Then, substituting (7.25) into (7.13) gives the conditional density of r_t for use in constructing the likelihood function for the data.

Finally, throughout this discussion we have assumed that the likelihood of a jump, ζ, is constant. Replacing ζ by ζ_{t-1}, we see that a function of the information in I_{t-1} presents no new conceptual difficulties, though estimation of the resulting model may be more challenging in practice.

7.4. Continuous-Time Models

Many of the most widely studied continuous-time models are members of the affine family of models discussed in Chapter 5. Accordingly, our overview of these models here is relatively brief and focuses on the more widely adopted parameterizations in the literature. After this overview, we briefly discuss the nature of the continuous-time models implied by the discrete-time GARCH-style models as the sampling interval of the data approaches zero.

7.4.1. Continuous-Time Stochastic Volatility Models

Typical continuous-time models of equity returns[10] with stochastic volatility have the stock price S following the process

$$
d \ln S_t = (\mu_S + \eta_S v_t)\, dt + \sqrt{v_t}\, dW_{St},
\tag{7.26}
$$

and volatility v_t following either

$$
dv_t = \kappa_v(\bar{v} - v_t)\, dt + \sigma_v \sqrt{v_t}\, dW_{vt}
\tag{7.27}
$$

or

$$
d \ln v_t = (\bar{v} - \kappa \ln v_t)\, dt + \sigma_v dW_{vt}.
\tag{7.28}
$$

---

[10] Some of the continuous-time models of stochastic volatility are reviewed in Taylor (1994).

In both cases, the Brownian motions driving returns and volatility may be correlated with $\text{Cov}(dW_{St}, dW_{vt}) = \rho\, dt$. The specification (7.27) has v following a square-root diffusion and, thus, falls within the affine family discussed in Chapter 5. In contrast, $\ln v$ follows a Gaussian process in the specification (7.28). Though $\ln v$ follows an affine process, it is $\sqrt{v_t}$ that appears in (7.26), so the model (7.26)–(7.28) is not in the affine family.

Some researchers have chosen to model S instead of $\ln S$, in which case $d \ln S_t$ in (7.26) is replaced by dS_t/S_t. Using Ito's lemma, we can derive either of these specifications from the other by appropriate adjustments of the drifts. In some studies, the presence of volatility in the drift of S, $\eta_S v_t$, arises owing to such an adjustment. For instance, if the drift of dS_t/S_t is assumed to be the constant $\mu_S\, dt$, then the implied drift of $d \ln S_t$ is $(\mu_S - 0.5 v_t)\, dt$. In other cases, researchers have included v_t directly as a determinant of the drift of dS_t/S_t or $d \ln S_t$.

Jumps to either returns or volatility are easily added. As introduced in Chapter 5, we let Z^S be a Cox process with associated arrival intensity ζ_S and (possibly random) amplitude J_S, and then add the term dZ_{St} to (7.26). Just as in the discrete-time case, a typical specification has $J_S \sim N(m_{JS}, \delta_{JS}^2)$. When jumps in returns are present, we refer to the volatility model (7.27) as the *SVJ* model and to the model (7.28) as the *SLJ* model, and we omit the *J* when jumps in returns are not present.

Similarly, jumps in volatility are introduced through addition of the term dZ_{vt} to either (7.27) or (7.28). In the former case, J_v must have positive support to ensure that v stays positive. This is seen to, for example, by assuming that $J_v = e^{m_{Jv}}$ (constant positive amplitude for jumps in volatility) and imposing the Feller condition $(\sigma_v^2 - 2\kappa_v \bar{v}) < 0$ (see Chapter 5). Since $\ln v_t$ is Gaussian in the second specification of volatility, jumps with negative amplitude are admissible.

A model that is sometimes referred to as a "pure" jump-diffusion (PJ) model has

$$dx_t = \mu_S\, dt + \sigma_S\, dW_{St} + dZ_{St}, \qquad (7.29)$$

where $x(t) \equiv \ln [P(t)/P(0)]$ and J_S is distributed as $N(m_{JS}, \delta_{JS}^2)$. Focusing first on the nonjump component of (7.29), we note that this model implies that $x(t)$ follows a Gaussian diffusion model and, hence, that the continuously compounded return over any interval of length n, r_t^n, is distributed as $N(n\mu_S, n\sigma_S^2)$. This is an immediate consequence of the assumptions of constant instantaneous mean and variance and the independence over time of the increments (shocks) dW_{St}. To this normal distribution, we add a Poisson jump process with the probability of a jump over any short time interval $[t, t + dt)$ of $\zeta_S\, dt$. Within any discrete interval of length n there may be multiple jumps, with the number of jumps L being distributed as a Poisson process with intensity $\zeta_S n$. Combining these observations, we have

$$
r_t^n = \begin{cases} x \sim N\left(n\mu_S,\, n\sigma_S^2\right) & \text{if no jumps} \\ x + J_S^{(1)} + \ldots + J_S^{(L)} & \text{if L jumps} \end{cases}, \qquad (7.30)
$$

with $\Pr\{L = \ell\} = e^{-\zeta_S n}(\zeta_S n)^{\ell}/\ell!$ from the Poisson$(\zeta_S n)$ distribution.

All of these models have been studied in the financial literature. In particular, the PJ model was adopted in Das (2002) to model short-term interest rates. The SV model is similar to those used by Heston (1993) in his studies of equity and currency market volatility; and the SVJ model is similar to the models used by Bakshi et al. (1997) and Bates (2000) to study equity option prices (see Chapter 15). The SVJ and SLJ models are compared in Andersen et al. (2002). Eraker et al. (2003) study a model with jumps in both prices and volatility, with the jump in volatility added to (7.27).

7.4.2. Continuous-Time Limits of GARCH Models

The SV and SVJ models are "true" stochastic volatility models in that volatility may move independently of returns, in contrast to, say, the GARCH models, where volatility is driven by past return shocks. An interesting question raised by this difference is: How does the continuous-time limit of the GARCH model compare with these continuous-time, stochastic volatility models? Nelson (1990) was one of the first to examine the continuous-time limits of GARCH and EGARCH models. He obtained the result that the limit of the GARCH(1,1) process is the volatility process

$$
dv(t) = [\omega + \theta v(t)]\, dt + \eta \sigma^2(t)\, dW_v(t), \qquad (7.31)
$$

where $\theta < 0$ and the Brownian motion W_v is independent of the shock driving prices, W_S. Subsequently, Duan (1997) extended Nelson's arguments to a broader class of GARCH-type models.

What may seem striking about these results is that starting from a deterministic function of lagged information in a GARCH model (σ_t^2 is a deterministic function of past squared deviations of r_t from its conditional mean), Nelson obtains a limiting process in which v_t (the continuous-time limit of σ_t^2) is driven by a Brownian motion W_v that is not perfectly correlated with the price shock W_S. In particular, the fact that one shock drives prices in discrete time, whereas two shocks drive prices in continuous time, would seem to suggest that the financial theory underlying the pricing of securities with payoffs depending on $S(t)$ is fundamentally different in the discrete and limiting continuous-time economies.

A resolution of this apparent puzzle is provided by Corradi (2000), who showed that the nature of the limiting process obtained depends mathematically on how the limits are taken. She breaks each time interval into subintervals of length h and writes the GARCH$(1,1)$ process as

$$\ln S_{th} - \ln S_{(t-1)h} = \sigma_{(t-1)h}\epsilon_{th}, \tag{7.32}$$

$$\sigma_{th}^2 - \sigma_{(t-1)h}^2 = \omega_h + (\beta_h - 1)\sigma_{(t-1)h}^2 + h^{-1}\alpha_h\sigma_{(t-1)h}^2\epsilon_{th}^2, \tag{7.33}$$

where $\epsilon_{th} \sim$ i.i.d. $N(0, h)$. The coefficients are allowed to depend on h to reflect the fact that their magnitudes depend on the length of the discrete time interval over which data are (hypothetically) collected. The scaling by h^{-1} in the last term of (7.33) standardizes this term so that its expectation conditional on information at date $(t - 1)h$ is $\alpha_h\sigma_{(t-1)h}^2$ (as in the standard GARCH model). Starting from this approximation, Corradi assumes that

$$\lim_{h\to0} h^{-1}\omega_h = \omega, \quad \lim_{h\to0} h^{-1}(\alpha_h + \beta_h - 1) = \theta < 0 \tag{7.34}$$

and

$$\lim_{h\to0} h^{-\delta}\alpha_h = 0, \forall\delta < 1. \tag{7.35}$$

Under these assumptions she shows that, as $h \to 0$, the process (7.31)–(7.33) converges to

$$d \ln S(t) = \sqrt{v(t)}\, dW_S(t), \tag{7.36}$$

$$dv(t) = (\omega + \theta v(t))\, dt. \tag{7.37}$$

Thus, in her mathematical construction, $v(t)$, the continuous-time limit of $\sigma^2(t)$, is a deterministic process described by the ordinary differential equation (7.37).

The reason Corradi obtains a different limit than the one obtained by Nelson is explained by the different assumptions they make about the h-dependence of the coefficients in their discrete-time models. In particular, instead of (7.35), Nelson assumes that

$$\lim_{h\to0} 2h^{-1}\alpha_h^2 = \eta^2, \tag{7.38}$$

for a constant η. This assumption, together with (7.34), implies that the system (7.32)–(7.33) converges to the system (7.36) and (7.31), where W_S and W_v are independent Brownian motions.

To shed some light on the relative usefulness of these two (mathematically correct) limits of the discrete-time GARCH(1,1) model we use the conventional multiplication rules of stochastic calculus, $(d \ln S(t))^2 = v(t)(dW_S(t))^2 = v(t) \, dt$, to rewrite (7.37) as

$$dv(t) = (\omega + \theta_1 v(t)) \, dt + \theta_2 (d \ln S(t))^2, \qquad (7.39)$$

for any θ_1 and θ_2 satisfying $\theta_1 + \theta_2 = \theta$. Following Corradi (2000), if we take an Euler discrete approximation to (7.39) we get

$$v_{th} - v_{(t-1)h} = h\omega + \theta_1 h v_{(t-1)h} + \theta_2 v_{(t-1)h} \epsilon_{th}^2, \qquad (7.40)$$

with $\epsilon_{th} \sim$ i.i.d. $N(0, h)$. We see that setting $\omega_h = h\omega$, $\beta_h - 1 = \theta_1 h$, and $\alpha_h = \theta_2 h$ recovers the discrete-time GARCH(1,1) model (7.33). Moreover, the h-dependent parameters $(\omega_h, \beta_h, \alpha_h)$ satisfy Corradi's assumptions (7.34) and (7.35). This is not true of Nelson's limiting model. Indeed, an Euler approximation to (7.31) leads to a volatility process with its own independent source of uncertainty, contrary to the spirit of the GARCH model.

Similar intuition for why Corradi's assumptions seem natural is obtained by stepping outside these GARCH models and examining the true discrete-time model implied by the univariate square-root diffusion of Example 2.1. With (2.29) and (2.54) and the approximation $e^x \approx 1 + x$ for small x, the expressions for the mean and variance of the distribution of $r_{th} - r_{(t-1)h}$ conditional on $r_{(t-1)h}$ are approximately

$$E\left[r_{th} - r_{(t-1)h} \mid r_{(t-1)h}\right] \approx -\kappa h r_{(t-1)h} + \bar{r}\kappa h, \qquad (7.41)$$

$$\sigma_r^2(h) \approx \sigma^2 h r_{(t-1)h} + \bar{r}\frac{\sigma^2}{2}\kappa h^2. \qquad (7.42)$$

Focusing first on the conditional mean, we note that the parameters of the constant term, $\bar{r}\kappa h$, and slope coefficient, κh, are proportional to h. Therefore, when scaled by h^{-1}, these coefficients (trivially) converge to constants as $h \to 0$, consistent with the assumptions in Nelson and Corradi.

With regard to the conditional variance, the second term involves h^2 so it is approximately zero (for small h). Therefore, for fixed (small) h, the "shock" to r_{th} is $\sigma \sqrt{r_{(t-1)h} h} \epsilon_{th}$, where ϵ_{th} has conditional mean zero and conditional variance one. Equivalently, letting the conditional variance of ϵ_{th} be h, the shock term is $\sigma \sqrt{r_{(t-1)h}} \epsilon_{th}$. It follows that the coefficient (σ) does not depend on h. This is a special case of Corradi's assumption (7.33), with $h^{-1}\alpha_h = \alpha$, a constant. It does not match up naturally with Nelson's formulation, as he would have $h^{-1}\sigma^2$ converging to a nonzero constant as $h \to 0$.

7.5. Estimation of Continuous-Time Models

The discussion of estimation methods in Chapter 5 focused on the case where $\{Y_t\}$ is an observed, discretely sampled time series from a continuous-time model. This covers the case of the realized r_t from the (constant volatility) PJ model. However, in all of the other continuous-time models, stochastic volatility (v_t) is a latent process. Therefore, at least one component of Y is unobserved and estimation must be based on (observed) current and lagged prices or returns r_t alone. These particular latent variable models—the two stochastic volatility models for asset prices (7.27) and (7.28)—are rather special in that we know quite a bit about the conditional distribution of observed returns, even though volatility is latent. For some parameterizations of these models, analytic expressions for certain unconditional moments of r are known and, hence, GMM estimation is feasible (see, e.g., Melino and Turnbull, 1990). However, when v_t appears in the drift of r_t and/or there are jumps in returns or volatility, then the literature has typically turned to alternative estimation strategies.

As was discussed in Chapter 6, the SME estimator often remains a feasible estimator in the presence of latent variables. All one has to do is work with the moments of the subvector $\mathcal{y}_t$ of Y_t that is observed. This was the methodology used by Andersen, Benzoni, and Lund (ABL) (Andersen et al., 2002) to estimate several continuous-time, jump-diffusion models for the S&P500 equity index. They examined jump-diffusion models in which there were no jumps in volatility $(\zeta_v = 0)$ and the drift of dS_t/S_t was the constant $\mu_S\, dt$ (hence v entered the drift of $\ln S_t$ as $-0.5v_t$). The amplitude of jumps in $\ln S_t$, ξ_S, was distributed as $N(-0.5\delta^2, \delta^2)$, so they were assuming that the amplitude of jumps in dS_t/S_t had mean zero. Estimation was accomplished using the efficient selection of moments proposed by Gallant and Tauchen (1996) with an EGARCH-based auxiliary model to generate moments and data over the sample period 1980 through 1996.

Eraker, Johannes, and Polson (EJP) (Eraker et al., 2003) allowed for jumps in both $\ln S_t$ and v_t, with $J_S \sim N(m_{SJ}, \delta_{JS}^2)$. The drift in $\ln S_t$ was assumed to be $\mu_S\, dt$ $(\eta_S = 0)$. Their sample period was January 2, 1980, through December 31, 1999, and they used Markov Chain Monte Carlo (MCMC) methods to construct estimates of their parameters.[11] EJP considered two formulations of models with jumps in volatility, motivated by the specifications introduced in Duffie et al. (2000). Model SVIJ has independently arriving return and volatility jumps with $J_S \sim N(m_{JS}, \delta_{JS}^2)$ and $J_v = e^{m_{Jv}}$. Model SVCJ has perfectly correlated jump times (contemporaneously arriving jumps) with $J_v = e^{m_{Jv}}$ and $J_S | J_v \sim N(m_{JS} + \rho_J J_v, \delta_{JS}^2)$.

---

[11] See Chapter 5 for a brief overview of this estimation method, and Johannes and Polson (2005) for a more extensive discussion of the method and applications.

Table 7.3. Estimates of the Diffusion Parts of Several Stochastic Volatility Models Using the S&P500 Equity Index

Model	Parameters					
	μ_S	$\bar{v}$	κ	σ_v	η_S	ρ
Andersen et al. (2002: table 6)						
SV	0.050	0.660	0.016	0.077	$\equiv -0.5$	−0.380
	(0.010)	*	(0.005)	(0.014)		(0.083)
SVJ	0.055	0.664	0.013	0.068	$\equiv -0.5$	−0.323
	(0.011)	*	(0.002)	(0.011)		(0.027)
SL	0.050	−0.008	0.154	0.101	$\equiv -0.5$	−0.400
	(0.010)	(0.003)	(0.004)	(0.016)		(0.071)
SLJ	0.046	−0.010	0.021	0.114	$\equiv -0.5$	−0.386
	(0.008)	(.001)	(0.001)	(0.004)		(0.019)
Eraker et al. (2003: table 3)						
SV	0.044	0.905	0.023	0.143	$\equiv 0$	−0.397
	(0.011)	(0.108)	(0.007)	(0.013)		(0.052)
SVJ	0.050	0.814	0.013	0.095	$\equiv 0$	−0.467
	(.011)	(0.124)	(0.004)	(0.010)		(0.058)
SVCJ	0.055	0.538	0.026	0.079	$\equiv 0$	−0.484
	(0.011)	(0.054)	(0.004)	(0.007)		(0.062)
SVIJ	0.051	0.559	0.025	0.090	$\equiv 0$	−0.504
	(0.011)	(0.081)	(0.006)	(0.011)		(0.066)

Note: Standard errors of the estimates are given in parentheses.

Estimates for both the ABL and EJP models are shown in Tables 7.3 and 7.4, reported on a daily basis.[12]

 Within the SV and SL models, the magnitudes of κ_T reflect the highly persistent nature of volatilities in equity markets ($\kappa = 0$ would mean that the conditional variance is a random walk). For the parameterizations SVJ and SV, the estimated long-run mean of volatility ($\sqrt{\bar{v} * 252}$) ranges between about 13 and 15%, which is roughly consistent with historical sample volatility (15.9% for the EJP sample period).

 Particularly in the models studied by EJP, we see that the estimated values of σ_v fall with the addition of jumps. This suggests that, in the absence of jumps, the volatility of volatility has to be higher in order for this model to match the historical volatility in equity returns. Allowing for jumps facilitates matching the historical distribution of returns with relatively moderate volatility processes. As will be discussed more extensively in Chapter 15, this

---

[12] ABL parameterize the drift of v_t as $(\theta - \kappa v_t)\, dt$. We have computed the $\bar{v}$ implied by their estimates, but are unable to compute the associated standard errors from the information provided in their paper.

Table 7.4. *Estimates of the Jump Parts of Several*
Stochastic Volatility Models Using the S&P500 Equity Index

Model	$m_{SJ}(\%)$	$\delta_{JS}(\%)$	ζ_S	$m_{vJ}(\%)$	ζ_v	ρ_J
			Parameters			
Andersen et al. (2002: table 6)						
SVJ	NA	1.95	0.020	NA	NA	NA
		(0.06)	(0.003)			
SLJ	NA	2.17	0.019	NA	NA	NA
		(0.05)	(0.001)			
Eraker et al. (2003: table 3)						
SVJ	−2.59	4.07	0.006	NA	NA	NA
	(1.30)	(1.72)	(0.002)			
SVCJ	−1.75	2.89	0.007	1.48	NA	−0.601
	(1.56)	(0.568)	(0.002)	(0.340)		(0.992)
SVIJ	−3.09	2.99	0.005	1.80	0.006	NA
	(3.25)	(0.749)	(0.003)	(0.574)	(0.002)	
PJ	−0.01	0.80	0.767	NA	NA	NA
	(0.003)	(0.010)	(0.257)			

Note: Standard errors of the estimates are given in parentheses.

will be an important consideration in pricing options with related jump-diffusion models.

Turning to the jump parameters in Table 7.4, the estimated means of the jump amplitude distributions are negative; on average, jumps in prices are downward. (In the models of ABL, there is a negative mean induced by the Jensen's inequality adjustment to the mean of $\ln S_t$.) A negative mean jump size induces negative skewness in the implied return distribution because jumps in prices are on average downward. This is the only source of negative skewness in the PJ model.

In the other jump-diffusion models, there are two sources of nonzero skewness: a nonzero mean jump amplitude and negative correlation between the return and volatility shocks, ρ. Intuitively, $\rho < 0$ induces negative skewness because volatility increases when prices are declining and this makes it more likely that large negative returns will be realized.

The arrival intensity ζ_S measures the number of jumps per day. Therefore, annualized (using 252 days per year), the ABL models give an arrival rate of about five jumps per year, with the amplitude of each jump having a standard deviation of about 2%. Jumps in the EJP models are less frequent (on average 1.5 jumps per year), but when a jump occurs its amplitude is drawn from a distribution with a larger standard deviation (3–4%). This may in part reflect the priors imposed by EJP that jumps, by nature, should be relatively infrequent and large. When we estimated the PJ model using the same data (not reported here), we found its arrival rate was 190 jumps per year, with the amplitude of each jump being drawn from a distribution with a standard deviation of less than 1%. Since volatility in this model is constant, it appears that the likelihood function is using the jump process to capture day-to-day changes in volatility more than it is large jumps in returns. This finding provides a cautionary reminder that the likelihood function may use the parameters of the jump process to compensate for a misspecified (stochastic or constant) volatility process.

Particularly during periods of large market moves—"crashes"—EJP found that models SV and SVJ failed to describe return behavior adequately. In the former case, to achieve the observed market moves, a multiple-sigma draw from the diffusive shock would have to have occurred. Though jumps give model SVJ more flexibility in explaining crashes, given the average size of jumps, it appears as though multiple jumps—a clustering of jumps—within a short time period would have been required to match history. Such clustering is also counterfactual in the context of EJP's model with a constant arrival rate for jumps (ζ) and independent jump times for a given ζ.

The SVCJ and SVIJ models fit the data better than the SVJ model. Intuitively, this is because jumps in volatility have a more persistent effect on return distributions, owing to the highly persistent nature of volatility. The arrival rates of jumps in volatility in these models are also about 1.5 times per year (for both independent and perfectly correlated arrivals of return and volatility jumps). When a volatility jump does occur, its magnitude is about 1.5–2%. Equivalently, in annualized terms, starting from the mean level of volatility, an average sized jump in volatility increases volatility from 15 to 24%. EJP compute the percentage of total return volatility owing to jumps in returns and find that it is 14.7, 9.96, and 8.17% in the SVJ, SVCJ, and SVIJ models, respectively. Thus, allowing for jumps in volatility attenuates the role of jumps in returns in explaining overall return volatility. The added flexibility of the SVIJ model over the SVCJ leads to a slight reduction in the role of return jumps in the former. However, this flexibility comes with the added challenge of estimating additional jump parameters, and these parameters are relatively imprecisely estimated.

Figure 7.3 displays the time series of conditional volatilities of the S&P500 index, along with the posterior probabilities of jumps in volatility, implied by EJP's models SVJ and SVCJ.[13] The volatilities in the SVJ and SVCJ models track each other quite closely, except during periods when there is a high posterior probability of a jump in volatility. In the latter cases, the

---

[13] I am grateful to Michael Johannes for providing the background information used to construct this figure and for permission to reproduce it here.

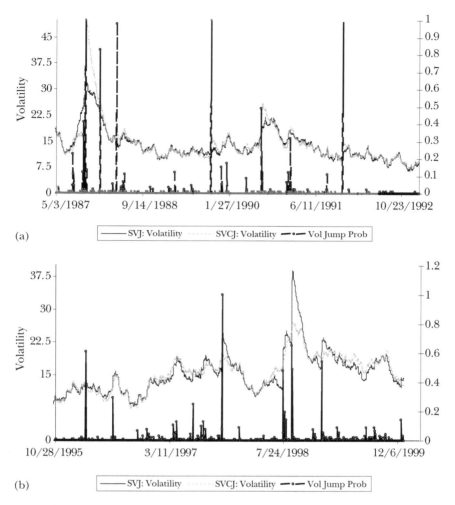

Figure 7.3. *Time series of volatilities implied by models SVJ and SVCJ as estimated in EJP. Vol Jump Prob is the time series of posterior probabilities computed from model SVCJ: (a) subperiod 1987–1992; (b) subperiod 1995–1999.*

volatility in SVCJ is higher than the volatility in SVJ. Furthermore, there are several periods during which the volatility in SVJ is systematically higher than in SVCJ. Such patterns are most likely attributable to the need for the SVJ model to overstate volatility in relatively quiet periods in order to better match volatility when it is relatively high.

An additional weakness of the SVJ model noted by EJP is that it calls for a clustering of jumps (in returns) in order to match historical patterns in the data. As noted earlier, such clustering is not a likely outcome of models with constant arrival rates of jumps. From Figure 7.3 it is seen that model SVCJ performs better in this regard. Focusing on the crash in 1987, as an extreme example, the posterior probability of a jump was 0.50 on October 16, the Friday before the crash. Other than October 19 itself, there were no other nearby days with posterior jump probabilities above 0.10.

An interesting question that emerges from these comparisons is whether or not a state-dependent intensity ζ is called for by the data. As we discuss in more depth in Chapter 15, the options data do suggest that ζ is state dependent. One common specification of a state-dependent intensity is to have ζ depend on volatility v. An alternative extension of the basic models considered so far is to allow for a persistent stochastic long-run mean of the volatility process; that is, allow for a two-factor model of volatility. It bears emphasis at this juncture that omission of either of these extensions may affect the conclusions drawn about the relative contributions of stochastic volatility versus jumps (in returns or volatility) to the volatility and kurtosis of returns. We revisit these issues (and the features of these jump-diffusion models more generally) in Chapter 15.

Two reasons for the differences across the point estimates in the studies by ABL and EJP are the different sample periods and the different estimation methods. The EJP study uses the additional data from 1997 through 1999. During the second half of 1998, in particular, the S&P500 index was quite volatile and experienced some relatively large 1-day moves. This may partially explain why EJP find a more pronounced role for jumps. The use of the MCMC estimator in EJP, versus the SME estimator in ABL, may also be playing a role. The relative performance of these estimation strategies in the presence of significant jumps is a largely unexplored topic.

Since the conditional second- and higher-order moments are state dependent in most of these models, in subsequent discussions we present evidence on the shapes of return distributions at various initial values of market volatility v_t. To put different models on an equal volatility footing, we compute conditional moments at an initial level of 14% volatility. This is approximately the median of the (unconditional) distribution of the VIX volatility index for our sample period.[14] As can be seen from Figure 7.4, the time pattern in the VIX index was similar to that of the fitted volatilities from the GARCH(1,1) model (evaluated at the estimated parameter values). (An explanation for the fact that the fitted GARCH estimate tended to lie below VIX is presented in Chapter 15.)

---

[14] This index is constructed as a weighted average of the implied volatilities on eight OEX calls and puts with an average time to maturity of 30 days.

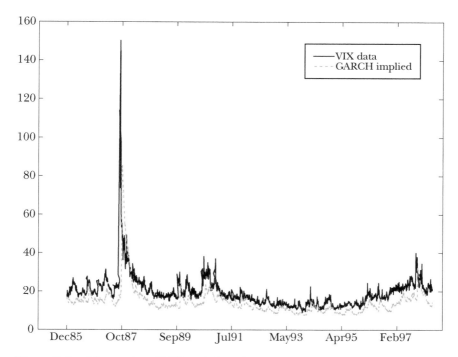

Figure 7.4. *Time series of VIX and GARCH-implied volatilities for the S&P500 index.*

7.6. Volatility Scaling

If asset returns are i.i.d. over time, then the conditional variance of the n-day holding period return r_{t+n}^n on a position,

$$\text{Var}_t(n) \equiv E\big[\big(r_{t+n}^n - E\big(r_{t+n}^n \big| \sigma_t^2\big)\big)^2 \big| \sigma_t^2\big], \tag{7.43}$$

is simply n times the conditional variance of the 1-day return, $\text{Var}_t(n) = n\text{Var}_t(1) = \sigma^2 n$. Accordingly, to gain some insight into the degree of temporal dependence in return distributions implied by our reference models, it is instructive to investigate the relative values of $\text{Var}_t(n)$ and $n\text{Var}_t(1)$. At this juncture, we undertake this investigation graphically, but in Chapter 9 we examine more formal tests of the autocorrelation of returns based on these relative variances.

Figure 7.5 displays the percentage errors,

$$\Big(\sqrt{n\text{Var}_t(1)} - \sqrt{\text{Var}_t(n)}\Big)\big/\sqrt{\text{Var}_t(n)} \times 100,$$

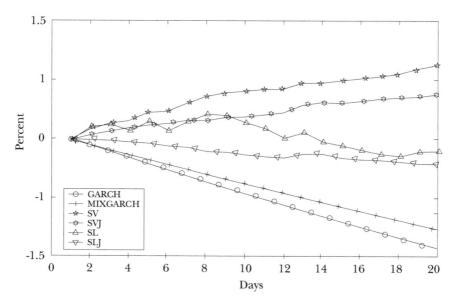

Figure 7.5. *Percentage errors from scaling 1-day variance to compute n-day variances computed at initial volatility of 14%.*

for various horizons and for the GARCH(1,1) and ABL reference models (we excluded model PJ because scaling holds exactly in this model—see below). For the GARCH-style models, the conditional variances are given by

$$\mathrm{Var}_t(n) = \omega \left(\sum_{j=1}^{n-1} \frac{1-(\alpha+\beta)^j}{1-(\alpha+\beta)} \right) + \sigma_t^2 \left(\sum_{j=1}^{n} \frac{1-(\alpha+\beta)^j}{1-(\alpha+\beta)} \right), \quad (7.44)$$

where it is understood that the first term is zero when $n = 1$. These errors are in fact very small for the GARCH and MixGARCH models. Thus, if portfolio returns are such that rolling historical volatility with normal or mixture-normal shocks is a valid probability model, then scaling volatilities leads to quite small errors.[15]

This finding is in sharp contrast to those in Diebold et al. (1998) and Christoffersen et al. (1998), for example. The explanation of the difference is that these authors answered a different question than the one we are addressing (with the latter being the one that is of most interest for pricing).

---

[15] How small these errors are depends, of course, on how the scaled volatilities are going to be used. Risk managers at financial institutions often compute multiday volatilities by scaling 1-day volatilities. The errors in Figure 7.5 are small relative to the error tolerance of most risk managers.

Specifically, using the results of Drost and Nijman (1993), they compare the conditional variances implied by the GARCH model for time series of 1-day and temporally aggregated n-day returns. In contrast, our comparison of volatilities involves $\mathrm{Var}_t(n)$ relative to $n\mathrm{Var}_t(1)$ *holding fixed the conditioning information set of 1-day returns.* By focusing on temporally aggregated returns, Diebold et al. effectively condition on the history of nonoverlapping n-day returns and, thereby, "throw away" the information in the past history of 1-day returns. In pricing securities, agents use the 1-day return information available to them, so the results from the literature on temporal aggregation are not the most relevant for agents' measurement problems.

Both of these discrete-time models have a single source of uncertainty; namely, return shocks. Therefore, it is of interest to examine the analogous plots for the continuous-time models with volatility shocks. The term structure of volatility in the SVJ model is given by

$$\mathrm{Var}_t(r_{t+n}^n) = \frac{\delta_{JS}^2 \kappa_v \zeta_S n + (-1 + e^{-\kappa_v n} + \kappa_v n)\kappa_v \bar{v} + v_t(1 - e^{-\kappa_v n})}{\kappa_v}, \quad (7.45)$$

with the special case of the SV model obtained from (7.45) by setting $\delta_{JS} = 0 = \zeta_S$. Note that the jump component adds a constant $\delta_{JS}^2 \zeta_S n$ to the n-day conditional variance and that this constant scales linearly with n. Consequently, jumps, as we have formulated them with constant intensities and moments of the jump amplitude distribution, satisfy the linear scaling rule. It is the presence of stochastic volatility v_t that potentially leads to mismeasurement of return volatility by scaling. The more important jumps are in determining $\mathrm{Var}_t(r_{t+n}^n)$, the better the approximation of the linear scaling rule.

The errors from scaling 1-day volatility to get long-horizon volatility in the SVJ and SLJ models are also displayed in Figure 7.5. Once again, the errors from scaling up volatility are less than 2% over the horizons examined.

7.7. Term Structures of Conditional Skewness and Kurtosis

To explore the implications of stochastic volatility and jumps for the shapes of return distributions in more depth, we examine the term structures of conditional skewness and kurtosis for the same six reference models (the GARCH models and the stochastic volatility models as estimated by ABL). For each model, the third and fourth moments of r_{t+n}^n, conditional on the level of volatility v_t, are computed for various holding periods n.[16]

---

[16] Formulas for these moments in the SV and PJ models are presented in Das and Sundaram (1999), where the implications of these models for the shapes of option-implied volatility smiles are investigated. The term structures of kurtosis for the GARCH and MixGARCH models were computed by Monte Carlo simulation. (The term structures of skewness for the latter models are zero by assumption.)

7.7.1. Term Structures of Skewness

A typical pattern for the term structure of skewness implied by a jump-diffusion model (with a fixed intensity of arrival of jumps) is for skewness to be large for small n and to decline (essentially exponentially) to zero as the length of the holding period increases (Das and Sundaram, 1999). In the PJ model, whether skewness approaches zero from above (positive skew) or below (negative skew) depends on whether the sign of the mean m_{JS} of the jump amplitude distribution is positive or negative. For the S&P500 data, $\hat{m}_{JS} < 0$, so the conditional distribution of r_t^n is negatively skewed for small n and the skew declines toward zero as n increases. The dissipation of skewness is often rapid in basic jump-diffusion models, approaching zero over horizons of just a few days. That is, the effect of jumps on the skewness of returns is often a short-horizon phenomenon.

The term structures of conditional skewnesses of the stochastic volatility models are displayed in Figure 7.6. The source of time variation in conditional skewness in these models is the presence of stochastic volatility—time variation in v_t—combined with the nonzero correlation ρ_T between return and volatility shocks. In the SVJ and SLJ models, the jump components could contribute an additional, state-independent skew to the distribution of returns (with characteristics much like in a pure-jump model). However,

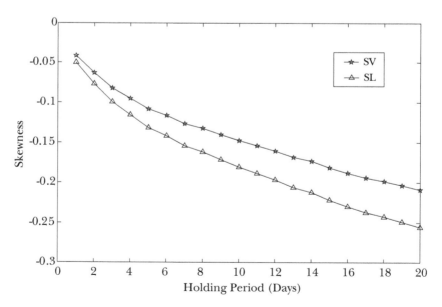

Figure 7.6.   *Term structures of skewness computed at 14% initial volatility.*

ABL set mu_{JS} to zero in their estimation, thereby removing this source of skewness.

Conditional skewness is negative in all of the ABL reference models because $\rho_T < 0$. As the length of the holding period is increased, skewness starts near zero and then increases with the length of the holding period. This pattern is what we would expect to see, because these models embody a diversification effect in the following sense: as $n \downarrow 0$ or $n \uparrow \infty$, skewness converges to zero (Das and Sundaram, 1999). An interesting question, then, for the purpose of our subsequent discussion of pricing is: Over what horizon does skewness build up, thereby invalidating an assumption of normal returns? From Figure 7.6 it is seen that for these models to fit historical S&P500 returns, skewness starts near zero and then builds up to a moderate magnitude in a matter of days (20 days is approximately 1 month). Inspection of similar plots over longer horizons shows that the skewness in S&P500 returns approaches zero (the temporal diversification effect) after about 1 year. However, the sample (daily) unconditional skewness of the S&P500 is -0.66, which is much larger in absolute value than the model-implied magnitudes displayed in Figure 7.6.

7.7.2. Term Structures of Kurtosis

The term structures of conditional kurtosis implied by the reference models are displayed in Figure 7.7. Focusing first on the SV and SL models, as with skewness, there is a temporal diversification effect: as $n \downarrow 0$ or $n \uparrow \infty$, conditional excess kurtosis tends to zero. Between these limits, excess kurtosis is positive for all $n > 0$. For the estimated reference models, excess kurtosis starts near zero and builds up, ever so gradually, over the 20-day horizon examined. However, after 20 days, the magnitude of the excess kurtosis is very small, certainly relative to the sample excess kurtosis of 7.93 for the S&P500 data.

The SVJ and SLJ models, with their added jump components, induce a different pattern for kurtosis than the SV and SL models. In the presence of jumps, kurtosis starts positive and converges to 3 as n tends to infinity. At the estimated parameter values, the jump effect is strong over horizons of a few days, but after about 2 weeks little excess kurtosis from jumps remains. This pattern is very much characteristic of a pure-jump model so, consistent with our earlier observations about kurtosis in the SV and SL models, it seems that the jump components are the primary determinants of excess kurtoses in the SVJ and SLJ models.

The temporal diversification effect within the SV model is quite intuitive. Over very short horizons, the shocks to returns are approximately normal by assumption, as would be true in any diffusion-based model with continuous sample paths. [This can be seen from the Euler approximation

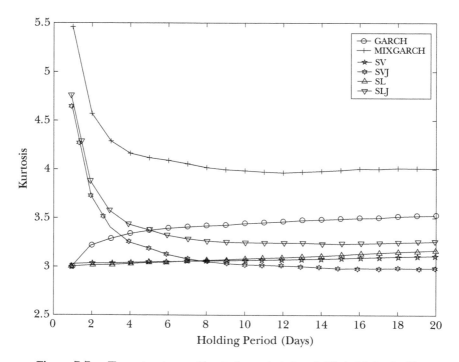

Figure 7.7.   *Term structures of kurtosis computed at 14% initial volatility.*

(6.4) of the SV model discussed in Chapter 6.] Since volatility is persistent, large shocks to volatility take time to die out. The SV model induces periods of high volatility followed by quiet periods, then periods of high volatility, and so on. Such volatility clustering induces negative skewness and excess kurtosis over intermediate horizons. Over long horizons, however, there is an averaging effect associated with the longer and longer holding periods and returns behave more like normally distributed variables for large n.

The nature of risk in pure-jump models is very different. Over short holding periods, the possibility of a jump with a given amplitude mean and variance may induce substantial skewness and excess kurtosis in return distributions. This is because the jump size may be large relative to the standard deviation of returns in the absence of jumps. However, as the holding period is lengthened, if the amplitude distribution of the jumps is held fixed, the effect of a jump on the cumulative holding period return is relatively small compared to the volatility of returns in the absence of jumps. This explains the convergence of both skewness and excess kurtosis to zero in the PJ model as n increases.

The discrete-time GARCH-style models also start with a conditionally normally distributed return over the sampling interval (by assumption) and then nonnormality builds up over time owing to the time-varying volatility. Recall that there are several ways of measuring persistence of volatility in a GARCH model and so an interesting question is which measure is more closely linked to nonnormality of returns as holding periods increase. Some guidance for answering this question comes from the expression for the unconditional kurtosis of returns implied by the GARCH(1,1) model (Bollerslev, 1986):

$$\text{Kurt}_{\text{GARCH}} = 3 + \frac{6\alpha^2}{\left(1 - \beta^2 - 2\alpha\beta - 3\alpha^2\right)}. \tag{7.46}$$

Fixing $(\alpha + \beta) < 1$, we see that excess kurtosis is not invariant to the relative size of α and β: increasing α increases the excess kurtosis of returns induced by stochastic volatility. So this sum, viewed as a measure of volatility persistence, is not directly relevant for assessing the degree of nonnormality.

The trade-offs are shown graphically in Figure 7.8 where the excess kurtosis (7.46) is graphed by fixing β and then ranging over the "admissible"

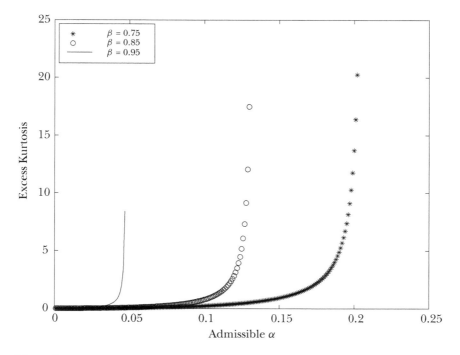

Figure 7.8. *Unconditional excess kurtosis of returns implied by the GARCH(1,1) model for various values of admissible α and β.*

values of α defined as those values that imply a finite fourth moment.[17] We see that, as β approaches unity, the range of admissible α's and the magnitudes of the model-implied excess kurtoses shrink substantially. Generally speaking, high persistence in volatility as measured by median lag length implies lower excess kurtoses of returns.

With an estimated $\hat{\beta}$ of around 0.96, it is clear that the GARCH model is theoretically incapable of generating excess kurtosis near the sample value unless $\hat{\beta} + \hat{\alpha} \approx 1$. This shows up in Figure 7.7 in the form of relatively small conditional kurtoses implied by the GARCH models. The MixGARCH circumvents this limitation of the GARCH model by introducing a marginal distribution of the return shock ϵ that inherently may exhibit substantial excess kurtosis. With volatility in the second regime (1.93) being roughly 2.3 times the level of volatility in the first regime (0.84), the mixture model generates substantial kurtosis. Indeed, from Figure 7.7 we see that the MixGARCH model generates more kurtosis over short horizons than any of the other reference models. The unconditional excess kurtosis implied by the MixGARCH model (at the ML estimates) is 13.11, which is even larger than the sample estimate.

---

[17] For the case of $\beta = 0.75$, there are somewhat larger admissible values of α that imply substantially larger excess kurtoses than those displayed in Figure 7.8. We omitted these values in order to show more clearly the behavior of the excess kurtosis for larger values of β.

Part II

Pricing Kernels, Preferences, and DAPMs

8
Pricing Kernels and DAPMs

VIRTUALLY ALL OF the DAPMs that we explore empirically can be character-ized in terms of the restrictions they impose on the joint distribution of a pricing kernel q^*, a vector of state variables or "risk factors" Y, and the securities with payoffs $\mathcal{P}$ that are being priced. In some cases q^* has a natural "structural" interpretation, in that it can be linked directly to agents' preferences or available technologies. In other cases, q^* is given as a "reduced-form" function of Y, in a manner that rules out arbitrage opportunities, but does not provide a direct link to preferences. This chapter outlines these approaches to modeling q^* in more detail, thereby setting the stage for in-depth analyses of the empirical fits of DAPMs.

We begin by expanding on the notion of a pricing kernel q^* introduced in Chapter 1 and, following Hansen and Richard (1987), present quite general conditions under which a payoff q_{t+1} is priced as $E[q_{t+1}^* q_{t+1}|\mathcal{I}_t]$ for an information set $\mathcal{I}_t$. Section 8.2 relates q^* to agents' marginal rate of substitu-tion of consumption and, thereby, presents the conceptual foundations for the consumption-based models examined in Chapter 10. This is followed by a discussion of conditional "beta" and factor models in Chapter 11. Though we derive a beta representation of asset returns starting from an arbitrary admissible pricing kernel q^*, we treat beta and factor models as part of our discussion of preference-based models, because this facilitates economic in-terpretation of the "benchmark" returns in beta/factor models. Finally, Sec-tion 8.3 presents an overview of the "no-arbitrage" approach to pricing risky securities, in which a reduced-form representation of q^* is combined with the assumption of no arbitrage opportunities to restrict the dynamic prop-erties of security prices. This formulation of the pricing kernel underlies the models covered in Chapters 12 through 16.

8.1. Pricing Kernels

To introduce the concept of a pricing kernel more formally, it is helpful to be more precise about the contents of the payoff spaces and information sets introduced in Chapter 1. Initially, we focus on agents' information set $\mathcal{A}$ and define the payoff space

$$\mathcal{P}_{t+1}^{+} = \left\{ q_{t+1} \in \mathcal{A}_{t+1} : E\left[q_{t+1}^{2} \middle| \mathcal{A}_{t} \right] < \infty \right\}; \qquad (8.1)$$

that is, $\mathcal{P}_{t+1}^{+}$ is the set of random variables in the information set $\mathcal{A}_{t+1}$ that have finite second moments conditioned on $\mathcal{A}_t$. This set can be interpreted as a set of payoffs that are contingent on the realizations of the variables in the information set $\mathcal{A}_{t+1}$ observed at date $t+1$. (We use the terminology "securities in $\mathcal{P}_t^{+}$" interchangeably with "securities whose payoffs are in $\mathcal{P}_t^{+}$.")

To describe the properties of $\mathcal{P}_t^{+}$, a notion of distance between payoffs is required. For any $q_{1,t+1}$ and $q_{2,t+1}$ in $\mathcal{P}_{t+1}^{+}$, let

$$\langle q_{1,t+1} \mid q_{2,t+1} \rangle_{\mathcal{A}} = E\left[q_{1,t+1} q_{2,t+1} \mid \mathcal{A}_t \right] \qquad (8.2)$$

denote a conditional inner product on $\mathcal{P}_{t+1}^{+}$, and define a conditional norm by $\| q_{t+1} \|_{\mathcal{A}} = [\langle q_{t+1} \mid q_{t+1} \rangle_{\mathcal{A}}]^{1/2}$. Using this notation, we define a payoff space $\mathcal{P}_t \subseteq \mathcal{P}_t^{+}$ to be *conditionally complete* if every conditionally Cauchy sequence in $\mathcal{P}_t$ converges conditionally to an element in $\mathcal{P}_t$.[1] Hansen and Richard (1987) show that $\mathcal{P}_{t+1}^{+}$ is a conditionally linear and complete payoff space.

We typically focus on the properties of conditionally complete subsets $\mathcal{P}_t$ of $\mathcal{P}_t^{+}$. The reference to a complete payoff space in the preceding mathematical (metric space) sense does not mean that we are assuming that markets are *economically* complete. If every element of $\mathcal{A}_{t+1}$ is the payoff on a tradable security, then markets are economically complete. However, if $\mathcal{P}_t$ is a proper subset of $\mathcal{P}_t^{+}$, then the payoff space $\mathcal{P}_t$ may be complete, but markets may not be economically complete. Examples of mathematically complete payoff spaces in settings of economically incomplete markets are those obtained by fixing a set of payoffs $x_{t+1} \in \mathcal{A}_{t+1}$ and letting $\mathcal{P}_{t+1}$ be the closure of the set of all payoffs of the form $\omega_t \cdot x_{t+1}$ with $\omega_t \in \mathcal{I}_t$, where $\mathcal{I}_t \subseteq \mathcal{A}_t$. A complete payoff space may be nested in or nest the set of tradable securities and, in either case, markets may be economically incomplete.

We do not presume that an econometrician's information set, say $\mathcal{J}$, is the same as $\mathcal{A}$. The typical situation faced by an econometrician is that market prices $\pi_t(q_{t+1})$ are available for a set of payoffs q_{t+1} in $\mathcal{P}_{t+1}$. Clearly, observing the payoffs and associated prices of these payoffs is not necessarily equivalent to observing $\mathcal{A}$. So as we proceed, we assess the prospects for

---

[1] More precisely, following Hansen and Richard (1987), a sequence $\{q_{j,t+1} : j = 1, 2, \ldots\}$ in $\mathcal{P}_{t+1}^{+}$ converges conditionally to $q_{0,t+1}$ if, for any $\epsilon > 0$, $\lim_{j \to \infty} \Pr\{\| q_{j,t+1} - q_{0,t+1} \|_{\mathcal{A}} > \epsilon\} = 0$. Additionally, a sequence $\{q_{j,t+1} : j = 1, 2, \ldots\}$ in $\mathcal{P}_{t+1}^{+}$ is conditionally Cauchy if, for any $\epsilon > 0$, $\lim_{j,k \to \infty} \Pr\{\| q_{j,t+1} - q_{k,t+1} \|_{\mathcal{A}} > \epsilon\} = 0$.

tractable empirical analysis by asking the question: Do analogous results hold if we condition on the smaller information set $\mathcal{J} \subset \mathcal{A}$?

In Chapter 1 we introduced the idea of an "inner product" representation of prices on a payoff space $\mathcal{P}$. Hansen and Richard (1987) formalize the existence of such an inner product representation of a *pricing function* $\pi_t : \mathcal{P}_{t+1} \to \mathcal{A}_t$ on a general payoff space under the assumption of value additivity—the value of the sum of two payoffs is the sum of their respective values. We henceforth refer to their underlying assumptions about $(\mathcal{P}_t, \pi_t, \mathcal{A}_t)$ as HR-regularity.[2] Under HR-regularity, Hansen and Richard show that there exists a unique payoff q_{t+1}^* in $\mathcal{P}_{t+1}$ that satisfies

$$\pi_t(q_{t+1}) = \langle q_{t+1} \mid q_{t+1}^* \rangle_{\mathcal{A}} = E\big[q_{t+1} q_{t+1}^* \mid \mathcal{A}_t\big], \text{ for all } q_{t+1} \text{ in } \mathcal{P}_{t+1}. \quad (8.3)$$

Furthermore, $\Pr\{\|q_{t+1}^*\|_{\mathcal{A}} > 0\} = 1$.

Importantly, the existence of a benchmark payoff q_t^* is not equivalent to the absence of arbitrage opportunities. A pricing function π_t on a payoff space $\mathcal{P}$ is said to have no arbitrage opportunities if, for any $q_{t+1} \in \mathcal{P}_{t+1}$ for which $\Pr\{q_{t+1} \geq 0\} = 1$, $\Pr(\{\pi_t(q_{t+1}) \leq 0\} \cap \{q_{t+1} > 0\}) = 0$. In other words, nonnegative payoffs that are positive with positive probability conditioned on $\mathcal{A}_t$ have positive prices.[3] If $\mathcal{P}_{t+1} = \mathcal{P}_{t+1}^+$, then Hansen and Richard (1987) show that, under HR-regularity, π_t has no arbitrage opportunities on $\mathcal{P}_{t+1}^+$ if and only if $\Pr\{q_{t+1}^* > 0\} = 1$. From the proof of their Lemma 2.3 it is immediate that, for any payoff space $\mathcal{P}_{t+1}$ satisfying HR-regularity (not necessarily $\mathcal{P}_{t+1}^+$), the assumption that $\Pr\{q_{t+1}^* > 0\} = 1$ implies the absence of arbitrage opportunities on $\mathcal{P}_{t+1}$. When there are no arbitrage opportunities, we will see in Section 8.3 that the pricing relation (8.3) can be transformed to one where pricing is as if agents are risk neutral.

Letting $r_{t+1} = q_{t+1}/\pi_t(q_{t+1})$ denote the (total) return on the security with payoff q_{t+1}, if $r_{t+1} \in \mathcal{P}_{t+1}$, then (8.3) implies that $\pi_t(r_{t+1}) = 1$; returns are those payoffs with unit price. We let $\mathcal{R}_{t+1}$ denote this set of returns:

$$\mathcal{R}_{t+1} = \{q_{t+1} \in \mathcal{P}_{t+1} : \pi_t(q_{t+1}) = 1\}. \quad (8.4)$$

Since $\|q^*\| > 0$ with probability one,

$$r_{t+1}^* = q_{t+1}^*/\pi_t(q_{t+1}^*) \in \mathcal{R}_{t+1}, \quad (8.5)$$

so the set of returns is nonempty.

---

[2] Specifically, their assumptions are: (i) $\mathcal{P}_{t+1}$ is a conditionally complete linear subspace of $\mathcal{P}_{t+1}^+$. (ii) (Value additivity) For any $q_{1,t+1}$ and $q_{2,t+1}$ and w_{1t} and w_{2t} in $\mathcal{A}_t$, $\pi_t(w_{1t}q_{1,t+1} + w_{2t}q_{2,t+1}) = w_{1t}\pi_t(q_{1,t+1}) + w_{2t}\pi_t(q_{2,t+1})$. (iii) (Conditional continuity) If $\{q_{j,t+1} : j = 1, 2, \ldots\}$ is a sequence of payoffs in $\mathcal{P}_{t+1}$ that converges conditionally to zero, then $\pi_t(q_{j,t+1})$ converges conditionally to zero: for any $\epsilon > 0$, $\lim_{j \to \infty} \Pr\{\| \pi_t(q_{j,t+1}) \|_{\mathcal{A}} > \epsilon\} = 0$. (iv) (Nondegenerate pricing) There exists a payoff $q_{0,t+1}$ in $\mathcal{P}_{t+1}$ for which $\Pr\{\pi_t(q_{0,t+1}) = 0\} = 0$.

[3] This is the conditional counterpart to Ross's (1978) no-arbitrage assumption.

The return $r_{t+1}^* \in \mathcal{R}_{t+1}$ is special in that it is the minimum second-moment return within the set $\mathcal{R}$. To see this, note that, for any $r_{t+1} \in \mathcal{R}_{t+1}$,

$$E\left[q_{t+1}^* r_{t+1} - 1 \mid \mathcal{A}_t\right] = 0. \tag{8.6}$$

Substituting (8.5) into (8.6) gives

$$E\left[r_{t+1}^* r_{t+1} \mid \mathcal{A}_t\right] = \left\{E\left[q_{t+1}^{*2} \mid \mathcal{A}_t\right]\right\}^{-1}, \qquad r_{t+1} \in \mathcal{R}_{t+1}. \tag{8.7}$$

Since $r_{t+1}^* \in R_t$, (8.7) implies that r_{t+1}^* satisfies

$$E\left[r_{t+1}^*\left(r_{t+1} - r_{t+1}^*\right) \mid \mathcal{A}_t\right] = 0, \text{ for all } r_{t+1} \in \mathcal{R}_{t+1}. \tag{8.8}$$

It follows that r_{t+1}^* is the global minimum second-moment return in $\mathcal{R}_{t+1}$:

$$E\left[r_{t+1}^{*2} \mid \mathcal{A}_t\right] \le E\left[r_{t+1}^{x2} \mid \mathcal{A}_t\right], \quad \text{for all } r_{t+1}^x \in \mathcal{R}_{t+1}. \tag{8.9}$$

This observation is central to the construction of beta representations of excess returns in Chapter 11.

8.2. Marginal Rates of Substitution as q^*

If agents are expected utility maximizers, then there is a direct link between agents' marginal rates of intertemporal substitution of consumption and q^*. Considering, for the moment, the case of a single consumption good c_t, we suppose that a representative agent chooses optimal consumption and investment plans to maximize (1.2). Then, following Rubinstein (1976) and Lucas (1978),

$$U'(c_t)\pi_t(q_{t+1}) = E\left[\beta U'(c_{t+1})q_{t+1} \mid \mathcal{A}_t\right]. \tag{8.10}$$

In words, agents choose their consumption/investment plans (which lead to equilibrium prices) so that the "utils" foregone by postponing consumption and investing in a risky security just equal the present value of the utils obtained from selling the security in the next period and consuming the proceeds. Dividing both sides of (8.10) by $U'(c_t)$ gives

$$\pi_t(q_{t+1}) = E\left[m_{t+1}^1 q_{t+1} \mid \mathcal{A}_t\right] = E\left[\beta \frac{U'(c_{t+1})}{U'(c_t)} q_{t+1} \,\Big|\, \mathcal{A}_t\right]. \tag{8.11}$$

Therefore, an agent's marginal rate of substitution $m_{t+1}^1 = \beta U'(c_{t+1})/U'(c_t)$, in equilibrium, prices all of the (potentially) tradable securities.

Since q_{t+1}^* is a *unique payoff in* $\mathcal{P}_{t+1}$ that prices all payoffs in $\mathcal{P}_{t+1}$, one may be tempted to conclude that $q_{t+1}^* = m_{t+1}^1$. However, in deriving the pricing relation (8.3), there was no presumption that the payoff space of interest, $\mathcal{P}_{t+1}$, contains the marginal rate of substitution of either a representative or an individual investor. Consequently we cannot conclude, and in general it is not the case, that q^*_{t+1} is equal to someone's marginal rate of substitution. Nevertheless, if $\mathcal{P}$ is a subspace of the payoffs on the traded securities available to agent j and the economic environment is such that $m^1_{j,t+1}$ prices all of these traded securities, then $\pi_t(q_{t+1}) = E[m^1_{t+1}q_{t+1}|\mathcal{A}_t]$, for $q_{t+1} \in \mathcal{P}_{t+1}$. That is, there are multiple pricing kernels that, when restricted to $\mathcal{P}$, give correct prices. This multiplicity goes away for the case $\mathcal{P} = \mathcal{P}^+$ where markets are economically complete and $q^*_{t+1} = m^1_{t+1}$.

This discussion extends immediately to richer parameterizations of preferences. In particular, a specification that encompasses many of the models that have been examined empirically (and that are discussed in Chapter 10) has

$$E\left[\sum_{t=0}^{\infty} \beta^t \left(\frac{U(s_t)^\gamma - 1}{\gamma} \right) \,\Big|\, \mathcal{A}_0 \right],\tag{8.12}$$

where $\gamma < 1$ and s_t is a vector of service flows from m goods and U is given by

$$U(s_t) = \prod_{i=1}^{m} [s_{it}]^{\delta_i}, \quad 0 < \delta_i < 1, \quad \sum_{i=1}^{m} \delta_i = 1,\tag{8.13}$$

and $\beta \in (0, 1)$ is the subjective discount factor. As in Eichenbaum et al. (1987), we assume that the dimension m of s_t is the same as the number of consumption goods in the economy. Further, the technology mapping acquisitions of goods to services is linear with

$$s_{it} = A(L)e_t,\tag{8.14}$$

where e_t is the m-dimensional vector of endowments of the m goods that agents consume, and $A(L)$ is a polynomial in the lag operator L ($Lx_t \equiv x_{t-1}$) given by

$$A(L) = \sum_{\tau=0}^{\infty} a_\tau L^\tau.\tag{8.15}$$

A positive value of the $i\ell$th entry of $a_\tau, \tau > 0$, implies that acquisition of the ℓth good in period $t - \tau$ contributes to the production of services from the ith good in period t, while a negative entry implies that the ℓth good contributes disservices to the service flow from good i.

Eichenbaum et al. (1987) and Schroder and Skiadas (2002) show that if there is a complete set of contingent claims to services from goods and agents have identical utility functions given by (8.12)–(8.13) with the service technology being given by (8.14), then equilibrium prices for securities in a representative consumer economy are identical to those of the underlying multiconsumer economy. Furthermore, if the polynomial $A(L)$ has a one-sided inverse and certain other regularity conditions are satisfied, then the existence of complete markets in claims to future services implies complete markets in claims to future goods and vice versa. Thus, for the purposes of empirical work, one can proceed with the use of aggregate per-capita data even though consumers are heterogeneous with regard to their endowments (e.g., "rich" and "poor"). In the light of this aggregation result, we henceforth interpret consumptions as aggregate numbers and speak of a "representative agent."

The choice variables in this model are the acquisitions of goods e_t that are inputs into the service technology. Assume, without loss of generality, that the numeraire consumption good—the good in which the payoffs in $\mathcal{P}_{t+1}$ are denominated—is good one. Also, let $U_1'(s_t)$ denote the marginal utility with respect to service flow s_{1t}. Then the marginal utility with respect to the numeraire good is

$$M_{1t} = E\big[A_{11}(L^{-1})U_1'(s_t)\big|\mathcal{A}_t\big]. \tag{8.16}$$

Therefore, agents' marginal rate of substitution is given by

$$m_{t+1}^1 = \beta \frac{M_{1,t+1}}{M_{1t}}. \tag{8.17}$$

Here m_{t+1}^1 is a ratio of conditional expectations, because goods acquired at date t provide services not only at date t, but also in future periods according to the technology (8.14). The present values of the future utils from these services affect an agent's decisions regarding current acquisitions of goods, with weights determined by the polynomial $A_{11}(L)$. It follows that the law of iterated expectations is not directly applicable to (8.3) with m_{t+1}^1 in (8.17) substituted for q_{t+1}^*. For the purposes of empirical analyses, it is therefore often more convenient to work with expressions of the form

$$M_{1t}\pi_t(q_{t+1}) = E_t\big[\beta M_{1,t+1}q_{t+1}\big|\mathcal{A}_t\big]. \tag{8.18}$$

Up to this point, all of the preference-based models examined have assumed that agents' maximize their expected utility that is additive across period utility functions. Several researchers have proposed alternative formulations of preferences that remain "recursive" (dynamically consistent), but depart from expected utility maximization. One of the most widely studied departures builds upon the work of Kreps and Porteus (1978), Johnsen and Donaldson (1985), and Epstein and Zin (1989).[4] These authors assume that utility U_t, based on information up to date t, is given by

$$U_t = V\left(u_t, E\left[U_{t+1}^\gamma \middle| \mathcal{A}_t\right]^{1/\gamma}\right).$$ (8.19)

The component u_t is the period utility function which measures the "utils" agents receive from consumption of goods and services at date t, and the time "aggregator" V is chosen so that preferences are dynamically consistent in the sense that agents' evaluations of consumption streams starting at a future date τ are consistent with U_τ. The most widely examined time aggregator is

$$V\left(u_t, E\left[U_{t+1}^\gamma \middle| \mathcal{A}_t\right]^{1/\gamma}\right) = \left((1-\beta)u_t^\rho + \beta E\left[U_{t+1}^\gamma \middle| \mathcal{A}_t\right]^{\rho/\gamma}\right)^{1/\rho},$$ (8.20)

where $\rho, \gamma < 1$. The special case of expected utility with constant relative risk averse (CRRA) preferences is obtained by setting $\rho = \gamma$.

Epstein and Zin (1989, 1991) stress the potential importance of relaxing the constraint that $\rho = \gamma$ when trying to resolve the asset pricing puzzles that arise in standard expected utility environments. The practical consequences of this extension are twofold. First, the coefficient of relative risk aversion, $1 - \gamma$, is no longer the reciprocal of the intertemporal elasticity of substitution of consumption, $1/(1 - \rho)$. As stressed by Hall (1988), the former measures agents' willingness to substitute across states of nature at a point in time, whereas the latter measures agents' willingness to substitute consumption over time in response to changes in macroeconomic conditions. Allowing for a separation of risk aversion from intertemporal substitution is shown in Chapter 10 to add considerable flexibility in matching the moments of the joint distribution of consumption and asset returns.

Second, agents care about the timing of the resolution of uncertainty (so, in particular, agents are no longer maximizers of expected utility). Early resolution of uncertainty is preferred if $\gamma < \rho$, whereas later resolution is preferred if $\gamma > \rho$.

As with the previous examples, if agents have homogeneous preferences and markets are economically complete, then there exists a representative agent. Furthermore, an intriguing feature of this model is that the associated pricing kernel involves the return on the aggregate wealth portfolio. For example, using the aggregator (8.20), m_{t+1}^1 is

$$m_{t+1}^1 = \beta^{\gamma/\rho}[c_{t+1}/c_t]^{\theta(\rho-1)} r_{M,t+1}^{\theta-1},$$ (8.21)

---

[4] See Backus et al. (2004) for a comprehensive survey of the use of nonexpected utility models in asset pricing models.

where $r_{M,t+1}$ is the return on the portfolio of aggregate wealth and $\theta \equiv \gamma/\rho$. The special case of logarithmic risk aversion is obtained as $\gamma \to 0$.

8.3. No Arbitrage and Risk-Neutral Pricing

Pricing kernels also play a central role in DAPMs built up from the premise of the absence of arbitrage opportunities. However, the interpretation of the pricing kernel in this case is often different, and its link to preferences is indirect. We first discuss the case of discrete time and then turn to continuous-time models.

At the outset of this discussion it bears re-emphasizing that a pricing kernel is typically defined relative to a space of payoffs $\mathcal{P}$ on the securities of interest. For term structure analysis, $\mathcal{P}$ typically includes a specific universe of bonds. For the pricing of options on common stocks, $\mathcal{P}$ may include the prices of both common stocks and options on these stocks. In these examples the pricing kernels discussed subsequently are in general not equal to any agent's marginal rate of substitution, in part because $\mathcal{P}$ does not encompass the universe of payoffs available to agents. Nor should we expect the pricing kernel for the term structure case to price options on common stocks. Particularly in the case of the no-arbitrage models specified in continuous time, the payoff space is often left implicit, though it can be inferred from the set of securities to which the kernel is applied in an econometric analysis.

8.3.1. Risk-Neutral Pricing in Discrete Time

We suppose that the state of the economy is described by a discrete-time Markovian process Y_t (see Definition 5.1) with conditional density function $f^{\mathbb{P}}(Y_{t+1}|Y_t)$, where $\mathbb{P}$ denotes the historical data-generating process of Y.[5] Additionally, we assume that the payoff space $\mathcal{P}_{t+1}$ satisfies HR-regularity, $\mathrm{Pr}^{\mathbb{P}}\{q_{t+1}^* > 0\} = 1$ (so there are no arbitrage opportunities), and $\mathcal{P}_{t+1}$ contains a unit payoff. Then a one-period riskless bond is traded with price $e^{-r_t} \equiv E^{\mathbb{P}}[q_{t+1}^*|Y_t]$, where r_t is the (continuously compounded) yield on this bond.

In this setting

$$\pi_t(q_{t+1}) = E^{\mathbb{P}}\left[q_{t+1} q_{t+1}^* | Y_t\right]$$

$$= e^{-r_t} \int q_{t+1} \frac{q_{t+1}^* f^{\mathbb{P}}(Y_{t+1}|Y_t)}{E^{\mathbb{P}}[q_{t+1}^*|Y_t]} \, dY_{t+1} \equiv e^{-r_t} E^{\mathbb{Q}}[q_{t+1}|Y_t], \quad (8.22)$$

---

[5] The measure $\mathbb{P}$ is sometimes referred to as the *physical* measure. At times we find it convenient to highlight the fact that probabilistic statements about historical distributions depend on $\mathbb{P}$ and we do so through the superscript $\mathbb{P}$. However, at other times, for notational simplicity, $\mathbb{P}$ is implicit. Note also that, in this context, the information set $\mathcal{I}_t$ is the σ-algebra generated by Y_t.

where $E^{\mathbb{Q}}$ denotes expectation under the *risk-neutral* probability distribution $f^{\mathbb{Q}}(Y_{t+1}|Y_t) \equiv q_{t+1}^* f^{\mathbb{P}}(Y_{t+1}|Y_t)/E^{\mathbb{P}}[q_{t+1}^*|Y_t]$. We see then that, formally, risk-neutral pricing is obtained by adjusting the $\mathbb{P}$ distribution $f^{\mathbb{P}}$ by $e^{r_t}q_{t+1}^*$. Equivalently, the pricing kernel is the transformation between the historical and risk-neutral measures:

$$q_{t+1}^* = e^{-r_t}\frac{f^{\mathbb{Q}}(Y_{t+1}|Y_t)}{f^{\mathbb{P}}(Y_{t+1}|Y_t)}. \tag{8.23}$$

In anticipation of discussions in subsequent chapters, it will also be useful to recognize that the Radon-Nikodym derivative of the $\mathbb{P}$ measure with respect to the $\mathbb{Q}$ measure—the $(d\mathbb{P}/d\mathbb{Q})_{t,t+1}^{\mathcal{D}}$ that satisfies

$$f^{\mathbb{P}}(Y_{t+1}|Y_t) = f^{\mathbb{Q}}(Y_{t+1}|Y_t) \times (d\mathbb{P}/d\mathbb{Q})_{t,t+1}^{\mathcal{D}} \tag{8.24}$$

and defines the transformation between $f^{\mathbb{P}}$ and $f^{\mathbb{Q}}$—is given by $(d\mathbb{P}/d\mathbb{Q})_{t,t+1}^{\mathcal{D}}$ $= 1/(e^{r_t}q_{t+1}^*)$. This follows immediately from (8.23).

The density $f^{\mathbb{Q}}$ is often referred to as the *state-price density*, because it represents the continuous-state counterpart to the so-called Arrow-Debreu state-contingent claims. Heuristically, this can be seen from consideration of a payoff q_{t+1} that is a Dirac delta function for the point $Y_{t+1}=y$—it pays one dollar if $Y_{t+1} = y$ and zero otherwise. From (8.22) the price of this security is $e^{-r_t}f^{\mathbb{Q}}(Y_{t+1} = y|Y_t)$. Note also that the scaling by $(d\mathbb{P}/d\mathbb{Q})_{t,t+1}^{\mathcal{D}}$ in (8.24) introduces the possibility that the $\mathbb{P}$ and $\mathbb{Q}$ distributions reside in different families of distributions. Even if they reside in the same family, typically all of the moments of the $\mathbb{P}$ distribution differ from the corresponding moments of the $\mathbb{Q}$ distribution.

Risk-neutral pricing—pricing as if agents are risk neutral—is potentially attractive because payoffs can be priced as discounted expected values and simple expectations are often easier to compute than the expectation of $q_{t+1}^* q_{t+1}$. However, inspection of (8.24) reveals that the derivation of the risk-neutral density $f^{\mathbb{Q}}$ requires, at least implicitly, some information about the pricing kernel and the density of the uncertainty under the actual probability measure, $f^{\mathbb{P}}$. Given q^* and $f^{\mathbb{P}}$, we can often derive $f^{\mathbb{Q}}$. On the other hand, positing $f^{\mathbb{Q}}$ directly, which may be convenient for pricing, leaves open the issues of the functional form of $f^{\mathbb{P}}$ and the nature of the dependence of q^* on Y_{t+1}. This "ignorance" is potentially problematic, because knowledge of $f^{\mathbb{Q}}$ alone is typically not sufficient for estimation (as contrasted with pricing) since estimation exploits knowledge of some aspects of the distribution of prices or returns under $\mathbb{P}$. Therefore, for both estimation and pricing, it is convenient to work with DAPMs for which the transformation between $f^{\mathbb{P}}$ and $f^{\mathbb{Q}}$ is given explicitly, $f^{\mathbb{P}}$ lends itself to tractable estimation, and $f^{\mathbb{Q}}$ leads to tractable pricing.

The same logic used to derive (8.22) can be used to price payoffs received multiple periods in the future. Consider, for example, the set of payoffs received at date $t + 2$, $\mathcal{P}_{t+2}$. From the vantage point of date $t + 1$, these are one-period-ahead payoffs and hence

$$\pi_{t+1}(q_{t+2}) = e^{-r_{t+1}} E_{t+1}^{\mathbb{Q}}[q_{t+2}], \quad q_{t+2} \in \mathcal{P}_{t+2}. \tag{8.25}$$

Moreover, for those payoffs in $\mathcal{P}_{t+2}$ for which $\pi_{t+1}(q_{t+2}) \in \mathcal{P}_{t+1}$, substitution of (8.25) into (8.22) gives

$$\pi_t(q_{t+2}) = E_t^{\mathbb{Q}}\left[e^{-(r_t + r_{t+1})} q_{t+2}\right], \quad q_{t+2} \in \mathcal{P}_{t+2}. \tag{8.26}$$

It follows more generally that, for similarly well-behaved payoffs at date T,

$$\pi_t(q_T) = E_t^{\mathbb{Q}}\left[e^{-\sum_{j=0}^{T-t-1} r_{t+j}} q_T\right], \quad q_T \in \mathcal{P}_T. \tag{8.27}$$

Under risk-neutral pricing, the price of a multi-period payoff is its expected present value, discounted by the sum of the one-period yields on zero-coupon bonds. Note that the latter yields are random variables from the vantage point of date t, and r_{t+j} ($j > 0$) may be correlated with q_T conditional on $\mathcal{I}_t$. Securities that involve a sequence of cash flows at different dates can typically be viewed as portfolios of securities with date-specific payoffs.[6] Under value additivity, the price of the portfolio is then the sum of the prices of the date-specific payoffs.

Whereas risk-neutral pricing starts with a one-period horizon and recursively constructs the prices of multiperiod payoffs, we could instead have started directly with the payoff space $\mathcal{P}_{t,T}$ defined as those payoffs at date T with finite second moments conditional on $\mathcal{I}_t$. Proceeding as before, letting $q_{t,T}^*$ denote the pricing kernel for this payoff space,

$$\pi_t(q_T) = E^{\mathbb{P}}\left[q_T q_{t,T}^* | Y_t\right]$$
$$= D(t, T) \int q_T \frac{q_{t,T}^* f^{\mathbb{P}}(Y_T | Y_t)}{D(t, T)} \, dY_T \equiv D(t, T) E^T[q_T | Y_t], \tag{8.28}$$

where $D(t, T)$ denotes the price of a riskless zero-coupon bond issued at date t with maturity T, and E^T denotes expectation under the *forward* probability distribution $f^T(Y_T | Y_t) \equiv q_{t,T}^* f^{\mathbb{P}}(Y_T | Y_t)/D(t, T)$. In this case, the terminology "forward measure" is used, because $\pi_t(q_T)/D(t, T)$ is the forward price (as of date T) of the payoff q_T. In words, (8.28) states that the for-

---

[6] As we discuss more extensively in Chapter 14, this portfolio approach to pricing is not always applicable to defaultable securities.

ward price of q_T, as of date t, is the expected value of the payoff q_T under the distribution f^T induced by the forward measure.

8.3.2. Risk-Neutral Pricing in Continuous Time

Suppose, in a continuous-time economy, the state is completely described by a Markovian process $Y(t)$ with

$$dY(t) = \mu_Y^{\mathbb{P}}(Y, t) \, dt + \sigma_Y(Y, t) \, dW(t), \qquad (8.29)$$

where $\mu_Y^{\mathbb{P}}$ is an $N \times 1$ vector of drifts under the historical measure $\mathbb{P}$ and σ_Y is an $N \times N$ state-dependent factor-volatility matrix. In this diffusion setting, the "pricing kernel" $\mathcal{M}_t$ is written generically as

$$\frac{d\mathcal{M}_t}{\mathcal{M}_t} = -r_t dt - \Lambda_t' dW(t), \qquad (8.30)$$

where $r_t = r(Y(t), t)$ is the instantaneous riskless rate, $W(t)$ is a vector of N independent Brownian motions, and $\Lambda_t = \Lambda(Y(t), t)$ is the N-vector of *market prices of risk*.[7] Furthermore, for a security with a dividend rate $h(Y(t), t)$ for $t \leq T$ and terminal payoff $g(Y(T))$ at date T, its price at date $t \leq T$ is expressed in terms of $\mathcal{M}$ as

$$P(Y(t), t) = E_t \left[\int_t^T \frac{\mathcal{M}(s)}{\mathcal{M}(t)} h(Y(s), s) ds \right] + E_t \left[\frac{\mathcal{M}(T)}{\mathcal{M}(t)} g(Y(T)) \right], \quad (8.31)$$

where E_t denotes expectation conditioned on $\mathcal{A}_t$.

Comparing (8.31) with (8.11), we see that the pricing kernel in continuous-time models is conceptually similar to agents' marginal utility. Since, in a discrete-time setting, q_{t+1}^* specializes to agents' marginal rate of substitution, $\mathcal{M}(t+1)/\mathcal{M}(t)$ is interpretable in an analogous manner to q_{t+1}^*. Of course a necessary condition for these associations with agents' preferences to hold is that the dividend rate $h(Y_t)$ and terminal payout $g(Y_T)$ be denominated in units of the numeraire consumption good. As in the discrete-time case, the pricing relation (8.31) does not require a direct link between $\mathcal{M}$ and preferences; it applies, for instance, to settings where all relevant cash flows and payoffs are nominal (denominated in units of a currency). Moreover, the pricing kernel $\mathcal{M}$ is often constructed to price a specific subset of traded securities (e.g., a set of bonds or a set of common stocks).

---

[7] For simplicity we take the risk factors driving $\mathcal{M}$ and Y to be one and the same. If this were not the case, then we would set one or more of the elements of σ_Y or Λ to zero.

Intuitively, the assumed drift for $\mathcal{M}$ is obtained by consideration of the price of a zero-coupon bond (denominated in the relevant numeraire) with short maturity of length Δ, $e^{-r_t\Delta}$,

$$E_t\left[\frac{\mathcal{M}_{t+\Delta}}{\mathcal{M}_t}\right] = e^{-r_t\Delta} \approx 1 - r_t\Delta. \qquad (8.32)$$

Subtracting one from both sides of (8.32) gives $E_t[(\mathcal{M}_{t+\Delta} - \mathcal{M}_t)/\mathcal{M}_t] = -r_t\Delta$, as in (8.30). Similarly, for small Δ, the diffusion component of $\mathcal{M}$ is approximately $-\sqrt{\Delta}\Lambda_t'\epsilon_{t+1}$, where $\epsilon_{t+1} \sim N(0, I)$. Therefore, the price of the security that pays off a (standardized) unit of the jth state variable driving M, $\epsilon_{j,t+1}$, is approximately

$$E_t\left[\frac{\mathcal{M}_{t+\Delta}}{\mathcal{M}_t}\epsilon_{j,t+1}\right] \approx \mathrm{Cov}_t\left(-\sqrt{\Delta}\Lambda_t'\epsilon_{t+1}, \epsilon_{j,t+1}\right) = -\sqrt{\Delta}\Lambda_{jt}. \qquad (8.33)$$

Thus, the market price of risk, $-\Lambda_{jt}$, of the jth risk factor can be thought of as the price, per unit of volatility, of shocks to the jth risk factor.

The practical problem faced by researchers pricing securities and their associated derivatives is one of computing the expectations in (8.31). A standard approach is to change from the historical ($\mathbb{P}$) to the risk-neutral ($\mathbb{Q}$) measure, just as with the discrete-time case. Paralleling our previous discussion, we start from (8.30) and note that the logarithm of $\mathcal{M}$ follows the process

$$d\log\mathcal{M}_t = \left(-r_t - \frac{1}{2}\Lambda(t)'\Lambda(t)\right)dt - \Lambda_t'dW(t). \qquad (8.34)$$

Therefore, the price of a generic payoff g_T that is in the date-T information set (generated by the stochastic process Y) can be expressed as

$$E_t^{\mathbb{P}}\left[e^{\log\mathcal{M}_T - \log\mathcal{M}_t}g_T\right] = E_t^{\mathbb{P}}\left[e^{-\int_t^T r(s)ds - \frac{1}{2}\int_t^T \Lambda(s)'\Lambda(s)ds - \int_t^T \Lambda(s)'dW(s)}g_T\right]. \qquad (8.35)$$

The term

$$\left(\frac{d\mathbb{Q}}{d\mathbb{P}}\right)^c_{t,T} \equiv e^{-\frac{1}{2}\int_t^T \Lambda(s)'\Lambda(s)ds - \int_t^T \Lambda(s)'dW(s)} \qquad (8.36)$$

that scales $e^{-\int_t^T r(s)ds}g_T$ is the continuous-time counterpart to the Radon-Nikodym derivative of $\mathbb{Q}$ with respect to $\mathbb{P}$, conditional on date t information. That is, we can rewrite (8.35) as

$$E_t^{\mathbb{Q}} \left[e^{-\int_t^T r(s)ds} g_T \right] = E_t^{\mathbb{P}} \left[e^{-\int_t^T r(s)ds} g_T \left(\frac{d\mathbb{Q}}{d\mathbb{P}} \right)_{t,T}^c \right]. \tag{8.37}$$

To arrive at a direct means of computing $E_t^{\mathbb{Q}}[\cdot]$ we can invoke Girsanov's theorem (see, e.g., Duffie, 2001) to conclude that

$$W_t^{\mathbb{Q}} = W_t + \int_0^t \Lambda(s) ds \tag{8.38}$$

is a Brownian motion under $\mathbb{Q}$. Therefore, differentiating (8.38) and substituting into (8.29) gives the following risk-neutral representation of the Y process:

$$dY(t) = \left[\mu_Y^{\mathbb{P}}(Y, t) - \sigma_Y(Y, t)\Lambda(t) \right] dt + \sigma_Y(Y, t) \, dW^{\mathbb{Q}}(t). \tag{8.39}$$

The risk-neutral drift of Y is

$$\mu_Y^{\mathbb{Q}}(Y, t) = \mu_Y^{\mathbb{P}}(Y, t) - \sigma_Y(Y, t)\Lambda(t), \tag{8.40}$$

and the volatility of Y is unchanged by the change of measure. This simplification (only the drift of Y is adjusted in the change in measure from $\mathbb{P}$ to $\mathbb{Q}$) is a convenient feature of continuous-time diffusion models. It is with respect to this $\mathbb{Q}$ process for Y that the expectation $E_t^{\mathbb{Q}}[\cdot]$ is evaluated. That is, with knowledge of $\mu^{\mathbb{Q}}$ and (8.39), the expectation $E^{\mathbb{Q}}[\cdot]$ can be computed without knowledge of or reference to the $\mathbb{P}$ distribution of Y.

An alternative construction of risk-neutral pricing starts with the observation that the price of a zero-coupon bond must satisfy

$$D(t, T)\mathcal{M}(t) = E_t^{\mathbb{P}} \left[D(s, T)\mathcal{M}(s) \right], \tag{8.41}$$

for any $t \leq s \leq T$. In other words, $\{D(t, T)\mathcal{M}(t)\}$ is a martingale and, as such, must have zero drift under $\mathbb{P}$. By Ito's lemma, $D(t, T)$ (for fixed T) satisfies the PDE

$$dD(t, T) = \mu_D^{\mathbb{P}}(Y_t, t; T) \, dt + \sigma_D(Y_t, t; T)' \, dW_t, \tag{8.42}$$

$$\mu_D(Y, t; T) = \left[\frac{\partial}{\partial t} + \mathcal{H} \right] D(t, T), \tag{8.43}$$

$$\sigma_D(Y, t; T) = \sigma_Y(Y, t)' \frac{\partial D(t, T)}{\partial Y}, \tag{8.44}$$

where $\mathcal{H}$ is the infinitesimal generator for the diffusion Y_t:

$$\mathcal{H} = \mu_Y^{\mathbb{P}}(Y, t)' \frac{\partial}{\partial Y} + \frac{1}{2}\mathrm{Tr}\left[\sigma_Y(Y, t)\sigma_Y(Y, t)' \frac{\partial^2}{\partial Y \partial Y'}\right]. \tag{8.45}$$

Therefore, the drift of $D(t, T)\mathcal{M}(t)$, $E_t^{\mathbb{P}}[d(D(t, T)\mathcal{M}(t))/dt]$, is

$$E_t^{\mathbb{P}}[dD(t, T)\mathcal{M}(t)] + E_t^{\mathbb{P}}[D(t, T)d\mathcal{M}(t)] + E_t^{\mathbb{P}}[dD(t, T)d\mathcal{M}(t)]$$

$$= \mu_D^{\mathbb{P}}(Y, t; T)D(t, T)\mathcal{M}(t) - r(t)\mathcal{M}(t)D(t, T) \tag{8.46}$$

$$- \mathcal{M}(t)D(t, T)\sigma_D(Y, t; T)'\Lambda(t) = 0.$$

Dividing through by $\mathcal{M}(t)$ (which is strictly positive), substituting for $\mu_D^{\mathbb{P}}$ and $\sigma_D(Y, t; T)$, and rearranging gives

$$\left[\frac{\partial}{\partial t} + \mathcal{G}\right]D(t, T) - r(t)D(t, T) = 0, \tag{8.47}$$

where $\mathcal{G}$ is the infinitesimal generator

$$\mathcal{G} = \left(\mu_{Yt}^{\mathbb{P}} - \sigma_{Yt}\Lambda_t\right)'\frac{\partial}{\partial Y_t} + \frac{1}{2}\mathrm{Tr}\left[\sigma_{Yt}\sigma_{Yt}'\frac{\partial^2}{\partial Y_t \partial Y_t'}\right]. \tag{8.48}$$

It is the drift $\mu_{Yt}^{\mathbb{Q}}$ that appears in (8.48). Thus, by the Feynman-Kac formula, the solution to this PDE is $E_t^{\mathbb{Q}}[e^{-\int_t^T r(s)ds}]$.

An analogous PDE is satisfied by the price of the fixed-income security with state-dependent continuous coupon stream $h(t)$ and payment $g(Y(T))$ at maturity, as in (8.31):

$$\left[\frac{\partial}{\partial t} + \mathcal{G}\right]P(t) - r(t)P(t) + h(t) = 0, \tag{8.49}$$

with terminal value $g(Y(T))$.

Returning to our discussion of market prices of risk, a more formal way of viewing Λ comes from inspection of the expected excess return from holding the security with price P satisfying (8.49):

$$e_P(t) \equiv E\left[\frac{dP(t) + h(t)dt}{P(t)dt} - r(t) \,\bigg|\, \mathcal{A}_t\right] = \frac{1}{P(t)}\frac{\partial P(t)}{\partial Y(t)'}\sigma_Y(t)\Lambda_t. \tag{8.50}$$

This expression is obtained by starting with the definition of $e_P(t)$ in (8.50) and using the fact that P, as the price of a traded security, follows the risk-neutral process

$$dP(t) + h(t)dt = r(t)P(t)dt + \sigma_P(t)dB^{\mathbb{Q}}(t)$$
$$= [r(t)P(t) + \sigma_P(t)\Lambda(t)] \, dt + \sigma_P(t)dB(t). \tag{8.51}$$

Consequently,

$$E\left[\frac{dP(t) + h(t)dt}{P(t)dt} - r(t) \,\bigg|\, \mathcal{A}_t\right] = \frac{\sigma_P(t)\Lambda(t)}{P(t)} = \frac{1}{P(t)}\frac{\partial P(t)}{\partial Y(t)'}\sigma_Y(t)\Lambda(t), \tag{8.52}$$

where in the last step we used Ito's lemma and the fact that $P(t) = P(Y(t))$ is a function of the state vector Y.

The term premultiplying $\Lambda(t)$ in (8.50) is the volatility of P induced by volatility in Y. Thus, Λ is the vector of risk premiums required for each unit of volatility of the N risk factors. It is independent of the cash-flow pattern of the security being priced and, hence, is common to all securities with payoffs that are functions of the risk factors Y.

Throughout this discussion we have focused on a change of measure to the risk-neutral measure $\mathbb{Q}$ because of its prominence in the pricing component of econometric studies of DAPMs. This change of measure is a special case of measure changes based on changing the numeraire in which value is measured. Particularly in Chapters 14 and 16 we have the need to price under alternative numeraires and, therefore, we briefly review the general case. We fix $T > 0$ and let $Z(t)$ and $P(t)$ denote the prices of two traded securities at date $t < T$, which, for simplicity, have no cash flows prior to date T. We view $P(t)$ as a numeraire price that defines an associated measure $m(P)$ in the following sense. If we let $V(t) = Z(t)/P(t)$, from the counterparts of (8.49) for $P(t)$ and $Z(t)$ it follows that

$$0 = V_t + \mu_Y^{m(P)'} V_Y + \frac{1}{2}\text{Tr}\left[\sigma_Y \sigma_Y' V_{YY'}\right], \tag{8.53}$$

where $\mu_Y^{m(P)} = \mu_Y^{\mathbb{P}} - \sigma_Y \left[\Lambda - \sigma_P\right]$ and $\sigma_P \equiv (\sigma_Y' \partial P/\partial Y)/P$. Under regularity, the Feynman-Kac theorem applied to (8.53) implies

$$V(t) = E_t^{m(P)} \left[V(T)\right] \Leftrightarrow \frac{Z(t)}{P(t)} = E_t^{m(P)}\left[\frac{Z(T)}{P(T)}\right], \tag{8.54}$$

where the conditional expectation is taken with respect to a measure $m(P)$ under which Y follows the process

$$dY(t) = \mu_Y^{m(P)}(t) \, dt + \sigma_Y(t) \, dW^{m(P)}(t),$$

with $W^{m(P)}$ a vector of standard Brownian motions under measure $m(P)$. Under the measure $m(P)$, the short rate r does not appear [in (8.53) and

(8.54)] and the relative price $V(t)$ follows a martingale. Different choices of $P(t)$ lead to different $\mu_Y^{m(P)}(t)$ and therefore different *pricing measures* $m(P)$.

Risk-neutral pricing is obtained by choosing $P(t)$ to be the price of a continuously compounded bank deposit, $P(t) = e^{\int_0^t r(s)ds}$, for which $\sigma_P = 0$ and the $\mathbb{Q}$-drift of Y is $\mu_Y^{\mathbb{Q}}(t) \equiv \mu_Y^{\mathbb{P}}(t) - \sigma_Y(t)\Lambda(t)$. Alternatively, we could choose $P(t) = D(t, T)$, the price of a zero-coupon bond issued at date t and maturing at date T. In this case, $V(t)$ is a "forward price" of security $Z(t)$, so $\mathbb{Q}^T$ is commonly referred to as the *forward measure*. Using the fact that $D(T, T) = 1$, we see that (8.54) becomes

$$Z(t) = D(t, T)E_t^T[Z(T)], \tag{8.55}$$

where $E_t^T[\cdot]$ denotes conditional expectation under the measure $\mathbb{Q}^T$.

9

Linear Asset Pricing Models

FROM THE VERY beginning of the application of statistical methods to financial market data, expected returns have occupied a central place in empirical finance. This is natural given the fundamental role of agents' expectations about future asset prices in portfolio theory. We begin our econometric analysis of DAPMs by examining the economic underpinnings of, and historical evidence for, two widely studied restrictions on expected returns: (1) expected holding-period returns on investments are constants (implying, among other things, that asset returns are unpredictable), and (2) the expected returns on two different investment strategies are equal. The former restriction is on the time-series properties of the return on a single asset. The latter is a restriction across securities and, by itself, it does not restrict the time-series properties of either return.

The interest in the first hypothesis of unpredictable returns has arisen primarily in the literature on returns on equity and currency positions, whereas the link between expected returns on different investment strategies has been the central issue in the literature on the term structure of interest rates. After briefly discussing the economic underpinnings of these two hypotheses, we turn to the empirical evidence from equity and bond markets.

9.1. Economic Motivations for Examining Asset Return Predictability

Early analyses of the conditional means of security returns (e.g., Fama, 1965) focused on the null hypothesis that expected holding-period returns on investments are constants. The economic motivation for this null hypothesis was that rational investors should use available information "efficiently" in predicting future stock prices and, as a consequence, stock returns (the changes in logarithms of prices) should be unpredictable.

Drawing upon the dynamic economic theory developed in the 1970s and 1980s, we now know that optimal use of available information does not, by itself, imply that stock returns will be serially uncorrelated. For instance, from the basic preference-based pricing relation (8.11), the conditional mean of the (total) return r_{t+1} from holding a security position for one period can be expressed (using the definition of the conditional covariance) as

$$E[r_{t+1}|\mathcal{I}_t] - r_t^f = -\frac{\text{Cov}[r_{t+1}, m_{t+1}^1|\mathcal{I}_t]}{E[m_{t+1}^1|\mathcal{I}_t]}, \tag{9.1}$$

where $r_t^f = 1/E[m_{t+1}^1|\mathcal{A}_t]$ is the total return on a one-period riskless bond and $\mathcal{I}_t$ is a subset of agents' information set $\mathcal{A}_t$ with the property that $r_t^f \in \mathcal{I}_t$. Intertemporal asset pricing theories, including standard neoclassical stochastic growth theory or life-cycle theories of consumer behavior (see Chapter 10), typically imply that the conditional second moment in (9.1) is serially correlated and, hence, that excess returns are predictable. By predictability here we mean best prediction, not best linear prediction, since there is no presumption that best predictors (conditional expectations) are linear in (9.1).

For a model to imply that expected excess returns are unforecastable, special assumptions about the risk preferences of agents or the distribution of the pricing kernel q^* are necessary. Perhaps the most widely cited rationale for the null hypothesis that security returns are unpredictable is the assumption that agents are risk neutral. To see the implications of risk neutrality in the context of the economic environment underlying (8.11), suppose that consumers have preferences over M consumption goods $(c^1, \ldots, c^M)$ and that c^1 is the numeraire good. In this case, we view returns and payoffs in the payoff space $\mathcal{P}$ as being real payoffs denominated in units of the numeraire consumption good. If agents are risk neutral in the sense that they have linear period utility functions for the numeraire consumption good,

$$U(c_t^1, c_t^2, \ldots, c_t^M) = ac_t^1 + \tilde{U}(c_t^2, \ldots, c_t^M), \tag{9.2}$$

then the marginal utility of the numeraire good is a and (8.11) simplifies to

$$\pi_t(q_{t+1}) = \beta E[q_{t+1} \mid I_t] \iff E[r_{t+1} \mid I_t] = 1/\beta. \tag{9.3}$$

Two key implications of (9.3) are: (1) the expected returns on all traded assets (assets with payoffs in $\mathcal{P}_{t+1}$) are constant and, hence, returns are serially uncorrelated; and (2) the expected returns on all admissible securities are the same. Importantly, (9.3) is silent about higher-order moments of the distributions of returns. In particular, the conditional variances are in general different across securities and they may be time varying.

These restrictions are on the means of *real* returns, as it is payoffs in terms of consumption that agents are concerned with. Nevertheless, empirical testing of (9.3) has often been based on returns on common stocks or bonds with nominal payoffs. Some researchers have deflated the nominal payoffs by a consumption deflator in order to get real returns, and then proceeded by assuming that these constructed real returns are in $\mathcal{P}_{t+1}$. Others have proceeded to study the implications of (9.3) using nominal returns directly. This presumes that one is using money as the numeraire and that the nominal pricing kernel q^* is constant. The exact form of the nominal q^* and whether or not it is constant depends on how money is introduced into a model. We address this issue in more depth in Chapter 10. At this juncture we simply remark that a nominal q^* would be constant if money appeared directly in agents' utility function and agents are risk neutral along the dimension of this particular good.[1]

Following Hansen and Singleton (1983), we can also derive restrictions on the conditional means of asset returns in economies populated by risk-averse agents. Starting with the fundamental pricing relation (8.3), in which q_t^* may be taken to be a generic pricing kernel and not necessarily agents' intertemporal marginal rate of substitution m_t^1, we assume that the pricing kernel and the holding-period returns on the securities of interest are jointly lognormally distributed. More precisely, assume that q_{t+1}^* prices the relevant universe of securities with payoffs at date $t + 1$ and let r_{t+1} denote the total return (payoff divided by initial price) on one of these securities. Also, let $x_{t+1}' = (\log q_{t+1}^*, \log r_{t+1})$ and ψ_t denote the information generated by $\{x_s : s \le t\}$. An immediate implication of (8.3) is that

$$E\left[q_{t+1}^* r_{t+1} \mid \psi_t\right] = 1. \tag{9.4}$$

Suppose we add the assumption that the distribution of x_{t+1} conditional on ψ_t is normal. Then (9.4) can be expressed equivalently as

$$
\begin{aligned}
1 = E[q_{t+1}^* r_{t+1} \mid \psi_t] = \exp \Big\{ & E\big[\log \left(q_{t+1}^* r_{t+1} \right) \mid \psi_t \big] \\
& + \frac{1}{2} \mathrm{Var}\big[\log \left(q_{t+1}^* r_{t+1} \right) \mid \psi_t \big] \Big\}.
\end{aligned}
\tag{9.5}
$$

Taking logarithms of (9.5) and rearranging gives

---

[1] One motivation for including money directly in U is that agents receive utility from the transactions services provided by money. Some have criticized this construction for being imprecise about the economic reasons that such transactions services are valued by consumers.

$$E\big[\log r_{t+1} \mid \psi_t\big] = -E\big[\log q^*_{t+1} \mid \psi_t\big] - \frac{1}{2}\text{Var}\big[\log\big(q^*_{t+1}r_{t+1}\big) \mid \psi_t\big]. \quad (9.6)$$

This expression has several potentially strong implications about the conditional mean of the return r. First, in this setting, the null hypothesis that returns are unpredictable (expected returns are constants) amounts to the hypothesis that the pricing kernel is unpredictable and the conditional second moments of q^* and r are constants. The former restriction implicitly imposes substantial structure on agents' marginal rates of substitution, as we discuss in depth in Chapter 10. The assumption that the conditional second moments are constant may also be strong in the light of the findings in Chapter 7. If the second moments in (9.6) are constant, as would be the case, for example, if the $\{x_t\}$ are jointly lognormal, then the returns on all securities that are priced by q^* and jointly lognormally distributed with this kernel all share the same degree of predictability. Put differently, the differences $(\log r^i_{t+1} - \log r^j_{t+1})$ between the returns on any two securities are unpredictable. This observation underlies some of our discussion of the conditional means of bond returns later in this chapter.

An alternative log-linear model is obtained by combining the assumptions of exponential utility, normally distributed endowments, and lognormal returns (Ferson, 1983).

As we proceed to explore the predictability of asset returns, we should bear in mind that the mean of an asset return is one of the most difficult moments to reliably "pin down," even with the large sample sizes that are sometimes available (e.g., a century of returns). Heuristically, this is a consequence of the fact that precision in estimation of means improves with the length of the sample period, and not so much with the frequency with which returns are measured over a given sample period (e.g., Merton, 1980). Though the effort expended over the past 40 years on estimating mean returns has been enormous, substantial disagreement remains about the temporal properties of this basic feature of return distributions. Moreover, in studying mean returns, one may reasonably be doubtful about the reliability of the large-sample paradigm underlying much of statistical inference. Not surprisingly, then, it is this literature that has devoted the most effort to exploration of the small-sample distributions of the tests being implemented. We review some of the findings regarding the small-sample properties of tests as part of our discussion.

9.2. Market Microstructure Effects

A direct way to explore the nature of serial correlation in returns is to examine projections of returns onto their own past histories and the histories of other economic variables that might have predictive content for returns. However, prior to undertaking such an analysis, it is desirable to assess whether measurement problems with the data might distort measured serial correlations and, thereby, lead to the spurious rejection of an economic hypothesis. One potentially important measurement issue, especially over short measurement intervals of 1 day or less, is that securities do not trade continuously in markets. Instead, trades take place at discrete intervals of time and the time between orders for trades is not perfectly predictable. Moreover, at the end of each day, when "closing prices" are being recorded, these prices often do not represent the prices of actual at-close trades, but rather of trades that took place some time before closing. Thirdly, trades take place at the "bid" or "ask" price, and not a single "true" price and the consequent "bid-ask bounce" can affect the predictability of measured returns.

Concern about "nonsynchronous" trading dates back at least to Fisher (1966). Subsequently Scholes and Williams (1977) and Lo and MacKinlay (1990), among others, have proposed statistical models of the trade arrival process and investigated the implications of these models for the autocorrelation of returns. The Scholes-Williams model provides an instructive environment for illustrating the implications of nonsynchronous trading for the autocorrelation of returns. Suppose that the logarithm of the price of the jth stock follows a Gaussian diffusion (see Chapter 5):

$$d \log P_j(t) = \mu_j \, dt + \sigma_j \, dB_p(t). \tag{9.7}$$

It follows that the (true) continuously compounded return over a time interval of length n on security j, r_{jt}^n, is distributed as $N(n\mu_j, n\sigma_j^2)$. However, with nonsynchronous trading, when measuring the price at date t, one is in fact recording the price for the last actual trade that took place at time $t-s_{jt}$, where s_{jt} measures the residual time before date t of the actual trade. Consequently, returns computed over one time interval ($n=1$) are not measured over the interval $[t-1, t]$, but rather over the interval $[t-1-s_{j,t-1}, t-s_{jt}]$.

This distinction between measurement time and trading time is illustrated in Figure 9.1 for two different securities j and k. The solid dots represent trade times of these securities. In recording the price at the end of a day, say date t, one is in fact recording the price at the last trade time before the close. In the case of security j, the mismeasurement gap is s_{jt}. A similar, though typically different, gap would occur for security k. These measurement errors induce biases in the population moments of the recorded returns r_{jt}^s compared to the moments of the returns r_{jt} implied by the model (9.7).

To explore these biases we suppose, following Scholes and Williams (1977), that the timing gap s_{jt} is stochastic and independently and identically distributed over time. Then the length of the time interval over which

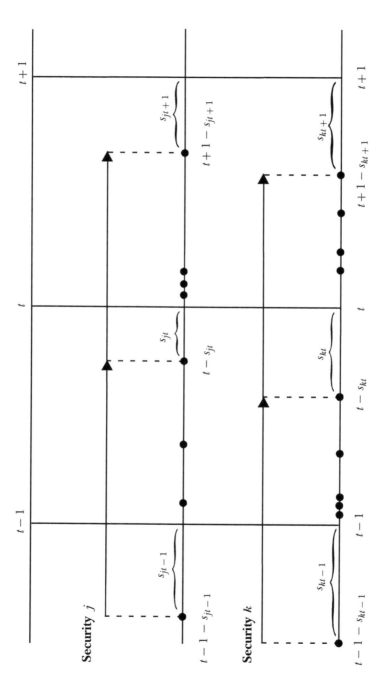

Figure 9.1. Nonsynchronous trading times of two securities. From Scholes and Williams (1977).

r_{jt}^s is being computed at date t is $(1 - s_{jt} + s_{jt-1})$. Therefore, the lognormal model for price implies that

$$E[r_{jt}^s] = E[E(r_{jt}^s|s_{jt}, s_{j,t-1})] = E[(1 - s_{jt} + s_{j,t-1})\mu_j] = \mu_j, \quad (9.8)$$

where the last equality follows from the assumption that $\{s_{jt}\}$ is an i.i.d. process. Nonsynchronous trading does not bias expected, continuously compounded returns.

Turning to the autocovariance of returns,

$$\begin{aligned}
\text{Cov}[r_{jt}^s, r_{j,t-1}^s] &= E[r_{jt}^s r_{j,t-1}^s] - (\mu_j)^2 \\
&= E[(1 - s_{jt} + s_{j,t-1})(1 - s_{j,t-1} + s_{j,t-2})(\mu_j)^2] - (\mu_j)^2 \\
&= -\frac{\text{Var}[s_j]}{(\sigma_j/\mu_j)^2}\sigma_j^2, \quad (9.9)
\end{aligned}$$

where the law of iterated expectations (conditioning on $\{s_{jt}, s_{j,t-1}, s_{j,t-2}\}$) has been used to get to the second line of (9.9). It follows that nonsynchronous trading induces *negative* serial correlation in returns over short measurement horizons. Similar reasoning can be used to show that variances computed from measured returns *overstate* the true variances of returns,

$$\text{Var}[r_{jt}^s] = \left(1 + \frac{2\text{Var}[s_j]}{(\sigma_j/\mu_j)^2}\right)\sigma_j^2. \quad (9.10)$$

However, a not atypical value of the coefficient of variation (σ_j/μ_j) for a common stock is in the range of 30+, so (9.9) and (9.10) imply that the biases in the measured autocorrelations and variances of individual common stocks are typically very small.

The implications for returns on portfolios of securities are somewhat different. The variance of the return on a portfolio is dominated by the covariances among the returns relative to the variances of the returns on the component securities. In the Scholes-Williams model, the covariance between two returns r_{jt}^s and r_{kt}^s is

$$\text{Cov}[r_{jt}^s, r_{kt}^s] = \left(1 - E[\max\{s_j, s_k\} - \min\{s_j, s_k\}] + 2\frac{\text{Cov}[s_j, s_k]}{\rho_{jk}(\sigma_j/\mu_j)(\sigma_k/\mu_k)}\right)\sigma_{jk},$$
$$(9.11)$$

where $\rho_{jk} = \sigma_{jk}/(\sigma_j\sigma_k)$ and, as shown by Scholes and Williams, the expected length of the period of overlap between r_{jt}^s and r_{kt}^s is $1 - (E[\max\{s_j, s_k\} -$

$\min\{s_j, s_k\}]$). For typical magnitudes of the coefficients of variation of the individual security returns the term involving $\text{Cov}[s_j, s_k]$ in (9.11) contributes a negligible amount to the covariance of returns and, therefore, one should typically expect that $\text{Cov}[r_{jt}^s, r_{kt}^s] < \text{Cov}[r_{jt}, r_{kt}]$. Combining these observations with the observation that the covariances are typically positive among returns in an aggregate portfolio, we expect measurement errors to imply that the variance of the measured market return understates the variance of the actual market return. Furthermore, the latter result suggests that the first-order autocorrelation of the measured return on the market portfolio tends to be positive, even if the return on each individual security is serially uncorrelated.

Lo and MacKinlay (1990), using a model of nonsynchronous trading with features similar to those of the Scholes-Williams model, reached the same conclusion about the signs of the biases in autocorrelations. They then calibrated their model to the distributions of stock returns and found that nonsynchronous trading does indeed lead to positive serial correlations in portfolio returns. However, the magnitudes of their positive autocorrelations were much smaller than what one sees in the data, unless they assumed an implausibly large probability that the individual stocks do not trade in a given period (probability of nontrading). They were led to conclude that nonsynchronous trading, by itself, cannot explain the magnitudes of the positive autocorrelations of portfolio returns.

Both the Scholes-Williams and Lo-MacKinlay models assume that the probability of trading within any given time interval is constant over time. Boudoukh et al. (1994) question the empirical plausibility of this assumption and propose an extension of the Scholes-Williams model that accommodates temporal variation in the probabilities of nontrading. By relaxing the Markov assumption in Lo-MacKinlay, Boudoukh et al. obtain autocorrelations that are approximately two-thirds higher than those implied by the model with time-independent probabilities. Based on these, and other extensions of the model, Boudoukh et al. (1994) argue that nonsynchronous trading can in principle explain the degree of positive estimated serial correlation in portfolio returns.

Another potential source of autocorrelation in short-horizon returns, explored by Niederhoffer and Osborne (1966), Blume and Stambaugh (1983), and Roll (1984), is the bid-ask bounce. Roll's model provides an intuitive illustration of why bid/ask spreads may induce serial correlation. Let P_t and P_t^* denote the measured and "fundamental" value of a common stock, respectively. Here fundamental value is interpreted as the economic value that would be achieved in a hypothetical economy where the costs of setting up a trading mechanism are zero. The prices of actual trades reflect a spread, say BA_t, earned by the market maker. Prices are assumed to differ from fundamental value by the rule:

$$P_t = P_t^* + \tau_t \frac{BA_t}{2}, \qquad (9.12)$$

where τ_t indicates the order type,

$$\tau_t = \begin{cases} +1 & \text{with probability } \frac{1}{2} \text{ buyer-initiated,} \\ -1 & \text{with probability } \frac{1}{2} \text{ seller-initiated.} \end{cases} \qquad (9.13)$$

It is assumed that $\{\tau_t\}$ is an i.i.d. process with $E[\tau_t] = 0$ so that, on average, P_t is equal to its fundamental value.

Price changes in this model are given by

$$\Delta P_t = \Delta P_t^* + (\tau_t - \tau_{t-1}) \frac{BA}{2}, \qquad (9.14)$$

under the assumption that the bid-ask spread is constant over time. It follows that

$$\text{Cov}[\Delta P_t, \Delta P_{t-1}] = \text{Cov}\left[\Delta P_t^*, \Delta P_{t-1}^*\right] - \frac{BA^2}{4} = -\frac{BA^2}{4}, \qquad (9.15)$$

with the last equality being an implication of the assumption that fundamental returns follow an i.i.d. process. Thus, bid-ask bounce induces negative serial correlation in returns. This is simply because if the last trade was at the ask, then the effect of the bid/ask spread on price is either zero or negative, whereas if the last trade was at the bid then this effect is zero or positive.

9.3. A Digression on Unit Roots in Time Series

For short holding periods (say a day or a week), stock returns have long been known to exhibit very little serial correlation and, when present, it is often attributed to the market-structure factors described in the previous section. Yet we do not expect these "short-horizon" correlations to reflect predictability resulting from business cycle factors. Such "long-horizon" dependence would, it seems, be more likely to show up in correlations of returns over longer holding periods. As we will see in the next section, it is indeed these long-horizon regressions that have received most of the attention in the literature.

One motivation for examining these correlations among long-horizon returns comes from a representation of asset prices in terms of permanent and transitory shocks (Summers, 1986; Fama and French, 1988). Suppose that $\log P_t$ can be represented as

$$\begin{aligned} \log P_t &= w_t + z_t, \\ w_t &= \mu + w_{t-1} + \epsilon_t, \end{aligned} \qquad (9.16)$$

where ϵ_t is a mean-zero i.i.d. process and z_t is any mean-zero stationary stochastic process. Though some have interpreted w_t as the "efficient markets" price and z_t as temporary deviations from this price, we have already seen that rational optimizing behavior of risk-averse agents may be consistent with the presence of both components. Accordingly, we view (9.16) as simply a convenient reduced-form means of capturing the possibility that there is a stochastic trend in asset prices.

In this permanent/transitory model, the continuously compounded return from purchasing a security at date t and holding the security for n periods, $r_{t+n}^n = \sum_{j=1}^n r_{t+j}^1$, can be expressed as

$$r_{t+n}^n = (w_{t+n} - w_t) + (z_{t+n} - z_t) = \sum_{j=1}^n \epsilon_{t+j} + (z_{t+n} - z_t). \qquad (9.17)$$

Thus, the variance of r_t^n is

$$\text{Var}\left[r_t^n\right] = n\sigma_\epsilon^2 + 2\rho_z(0) - 2\rho_z(n), \qquad (9.18)$$

where $\rho_z(n) = E[z_t z_{t+n}]$, and its autocorrelation is

$$\text{Corr}\left[r_t^n, r_{t-n}^n\right] = \frac{\text{Cov}[z_t - z_{t-n}, z_{t-n} - z_{t-2n}]}{\text{Var}[r_t^n]}. \qquad (9.19)$$

Whereas the random-walk component of $\log P_t$ does not induce serial correlation in r^n [see (9.17)], the stationary component does. So long as $\rho_z(n)$ approaches zero as $n \to \infty$ (a property that would hold for stationary autoregressive processes), the numerator of (9.19) approaches $-\sigma_z^2$ as n gets large.

Exactly how this negative serial correlation in $z_{t+n} - z_t$ shows up in returns depends on the horizon n. Summers (1986) noted that if z_t is itself highly persistent, then over short horizons $\text{Corr}[r_t^n, r_{t-n}^n]$ may be approximately zero. In other words, any persistence in r_t^n induced by the component z may be missed unless n is chosen to be sufficiently large. For intermediate horizons, it may well be that the autocorrelation in z shows up in (negatively) serially correlated returns. However, over long horizons (large n), the contribution of w_t to the variance of r^n ($n\sigma_\epsilon^2$) dominates the stationary component and the autocorrelations of returns approach zero.

Whether or not you feel that this permanent/transitory model provides sound conceptual motivation for studying long-horizon returns, it does raise a new, and as it turns out very important, econometric issue. Namely, stock returns (and other macroeconomic variables) may well embody a random-walk component. If so, or even if there is not literally a unit root component but one with very slow mean reversion, then the usual large-sample distribution theory underlying inference (see, e.g., Chapter 4) may be unreliable.

With these observations in mind, in this section we briefly digress and discuss some new econometric issues raised by the presence of a unit root in an economic time series.

9.3.1. Why Are Unit Roots a Problem?

By way of background, it is instructive at the outset of this discussion to deal briefly with the potential nature of time trends in time series. One possibility is that a process y_t evidences a *deterministic* trend and follows the trend-stationary (TrendS) process

$$y_t = \alpha_0 + \beta_0 t + u_t, \tag{9.20}$$

where u_t is a stationary stochastic process with mean zero. (The following observations extend immediately the case of a polynomial trend in t.) In this case, the unconditional mean of y_t is $\alpha_0 + \beta_0 t$ and, hence, the process is nonstationary with constant variance $\sigma_u^2 = \text{Var}(u_t)$.

Another possibility is that y_t embodies a *stochastic* trend, in which case we have the difference-stationary (DiffS) process

$$y_t = \alpha_0 + y_{t-1} + u_t, \tag{9.21}$$

where u_t is again a mean-zero, stationary process. This process is referred to as being difference-stationary, because Δy_t is a stationary time series. Recursive substitution of the expression corresponding to (9.21) for lagged y's gives

$$y_t = \alpha_0 t + y_0 + \sum_{i=0}^{t-1} u_{t-i}. \tag{9.22}$$

Therefore, as in the case of a TrendS process, the mean of y_t, $E[y_t] = \alpha_0 t + E[y_0]$, drifts with t. However, unlike in the case of a TrendS process, the variance of a DiffS y_t, $\text{Var}(y_t) = \text{Var}(y_0) + \text{Var}(\sum_{i=0}^{t-1} u_{t-i})$, grows with t without bound. For example, if $\{u_t\}$ is an i.i.d. process with variance σ_u^2, then $\text{Var}(y_t) = t\sigma_u^2$. This is in contrast to the variance of the stationary process $y_t = \alpha_0 + \rho_0 y_{t-1} + u_t$, with $|\rho_0| < 1$, which is $\text{Var}(y_t) = \sigma_u^2/(1 - \rho_0^2)$ when $\{u_t\}$ is an i.i.d. process.

Which (if any) form of trend is present may fundamentally affect the properties of tests of financial models. Most of standard testing theory carries over to the case of TrendS processes. All that is required is that the scaling factor $\sqrt{T}$ used to derive asymptotic distributions be adjusted to reflect the order of a polynomial trend. Similarly, the case of an exponential trend, $y_t e^{\beta_0 t}$, can typically be handled in the same manner as the case of polynomial deterministic trends by working with $\log y_t$. Even in this simple case, however, care must be taken to accommodate restrictions across the trends of different economic series that are linked by equilibrium relationships implied by a DAPM (see Chapter 10).

Similarly, if we know that we are dealing with a DiffS process, then one simply works with Δy_t in evaluating financial models.[2] Unfortunately, we are often not sure whether y is just highly persistent or whether the coefficient in the projection of y_t onto y_{t-1} is literally one. This world of ignorance brings with it numerous problems in inference. In particular, in the regression model

$$y_t = \rho_0 y_{t-1} + u_t, \qquad (9.23)$$

we cannot use the standard (asymptotic) t-test for the null hypothesis $\rho_0 = 1$. This is a consequence of the fact that, under the null, the variance of y_t is blowing up with t.

Equally important, working with the time difference of a process that is in fact TrendS leads to the "overdifferencing" problem (see, e.g., Plosser and Schwert, 1978). In (9.20), if u_t is an i.i.d. process for instance, then working with Δy_t induces a moving-average error $u_t - u_{t-1}$. This error structure should be accounted for in formal inference.

9.3.2. Testing for Unit Roots

Consider the problem of testing $H_0 : \rho_0 = 1$ in (9.23) with u_t an i.i.d., mean-zero process. Dickey and Fuller (1979) proposed working with the test statistic $T(\rho_T - \rho_0)$ and derived its small-sample distribution. Subsequently, Phillips (1987) showed that the limiting distribution of this statistic is[3]

$$T(\rho_T - \rho_0) = \frac{T^{-1} \sum_{t=1}^{T} y_{t-1} u_t}{\sum_{t=1}^{T} y_{t-1} y_t} \Rightarrow \frac{\int_0^1 B(r) dB(r)}{\int_0^1 B(r)^2 dr}, \qquad (9.24)$$

---

[2] In fact, the situation in practice is not this easy, because we are often interested in the relationships among several variables, not all of which may follow DiffS processes. This situation raises the issue of "co-integration" among time series. See Maddala and Kim (1998) for an overview of the literature on co-integration.

[3] The statistical theory required to derive Phillips's results is outside of the frameworks discussed in Chapters 3–6. What is typically involved is a functional central limit theorem (in particular, Donsker's theorem and the continuous mapping theorem). A useful overview of the relevant statistical theory as applied to the unit root problem is found in Maddala and Kim (1998).

where $B(r)$ is a standard Brownian motion. Alternatively, a test can be based on the usual t-statistic,

$$\frac{T(\rho_T - \rho_0)}{\sqrt{T}(1 - \rho_T^2)} \Rightarrow \frac{\int_0^1 B(r)\,dB(r)}{\left[\int_0^1 B(r)^2\,dr\right]^{1/2}}. \tag{9.25}$$

(If $|\rho_0| < 1$, then $\sqrt{T}(\rho_T - \rho_0)/(1 - \rho_0)^2 \Rightarrow N(0, 1)$, so (9.25) is in fact the usual t-statistic.) The numerators of these statistics can be rewritten as $(1/2)[B(1)^2 - 1]$, so they are a $\chi^2(1)$ random variable minus its degree of freedom. Though the numerator of (9.25) is skewed to the right, the t-ratio is skewed to the left. It follows that using conventional critical values for a t-test of $\rho_0 = 1$ may lead to overrejection of H_0. Phillip's results, as well as those discussed subsequently, are summarized in Table 9.1.

A richer regression setting in which to test for $\rho_0 = 1$ has

$$y_t = \alpha_0 + \beta_0 t + \rho_0 y_{t-1} + u_t \tag{9.26}$$

(again with i.i.d. errors). Small-sample critical values for testing $\rho = 1$ in (9.26)—the so-called Dickey-Fuller test—were tabulated in Fuller (1976) and Dickey and Fuller (1981). Its asymptotic distribution depends on whether the true data-generating process includes the deterministic component $\alpha_0 + \beta_0 t$ or not. If it does not, then the limiting distribution of the t-ratio (9.25) is again given by a ratio of functions of a Brownian motion $B(r)$. On the other hand, if $\alpha_0 \neq 0$ (β_0 may or may not be zero), then West (1988) proved the rather striking result that the limiting distribution of the t-ratio is $N(0, 1)$, just as in the classical case. The reason for this result is that the regressor y_t is dominated by the trend term $\beta_0 t$, for large t, so the estimator ρ_T behaves much as in the case of a least-squares estimator of the coefficient on a linear trend.

Table 9.1. *Asymptotic Distributions of t-Statistics for the Null Hypothesis that $\rho_0 = 1$ in Various Special Cases of the Time-Series Model (9.26)*

Regression	DGP	Asymptotic distribution
No deterministic trend $(\alpha_0 = \beta_0 = 0)$	$\alpha_0 = \beta_0 = 0$	FCLT: (Phillips)
Drift/no trend $(\alpha_0 \neq 0, \beta_0 = 0)$	$\alpha_0 = \beta_0 = 0$ $\alpha_0 \neq 0, \beta_0 = 0$	FCLT: (Phillips) $N(0,1)$ (West)
Deterministic trend $(\alpha_0 \neq 0, \beta_0 \neq 0)$	$\alpha_0 = \beta_0 = 0$ $\alpha_0 \neq 0, \beta_0 \neq 0$	FCLT: (Phillips) $N(0,1)$ (West)

Note: DGP is the true data-generating process and regression is the estimated model.

Not only does the presence of nonzero drift ($\alpha_0 \neq 0$) affect the limiting distribution of the statistic (9.25), but Perron (1988) has shown that omission of a trend from the regression model, when it is present in the DGP, leads to the power of the test going to zero as $T \to \infty$. His findings suggest that failing to specify the order of, say, a polynomial deterministic trend correctly may significantly affect the power of the test. This finding is somewhat discouraging, because we often have little a priori information about the exact nature of deterministic trends. Furthermore, specifying the order to be larger than the true order may also decrease the power of the test, owing to the inclusion of extraneous regressors.

The version of the Dickey-Fuller test discussed so far abstracts from any persistence in the time series y as, under $H_0 : \rho_0 = 1$, Δy_t is an i.i.d. process. Dickey and Fuller (1979) and Said and Dickey (1984) extended the testing framework to the case of autoregressive processes of order p:

$$y_t = \alpha_0 + \rho_0 y_{t-1} + \sum_{i=1}^{p} \beta_i \Delta y_{t-j} + u_t. \tag{9.27}$$

The t-statistic for $H_0 : \rho_0 = 0$ in (9.27) is often referred to as the augmented Dickey-Fuller test. This statistic has the same limiting distribution as the t-statistic in the simpler model with the $\beta_i = 0$, since ρ_T and $\{\beta_{iT}, i = 1, \ldots, p\}$ are asymptotically independent.

9.4. Tests for Serial Correlation in Returns

There is now a substantial body of evidence suggesting that stock returns exhibit some serial dependence, especially returns on portfolios of common stocks. Broadly speaking, evidence on the degree of serial correlation in stock returns has come from three different testing methodologies: (1) projections of stock returns on various candidate predictors measured at the same sampling interval as the holding period over which the return is computed; (2) prediction of long-horizon returns, sampled at daily or weekly intervals, using information variables also measured at daily or weekly intervals; and (3) comparison of the variance of a long-horizon return with the variance of the one-period return scaled up by the length of the long horizon. In this section we present an overview of the econometric methods underlying these tests.

Suppose that the null hypothesis is that

$$E\left[r_{t+1}^1 | I_t\right] = \mu, \tag{9.28}$$

with μ being a constant and I_t an information set that includes at least past values of the price of the security, P_t. This is a much weaker hypothesis than the hypothesis that returns are independent over time, though it is stronger than the hypothesis that r_{t+1}^1 is serially uncorrelated. Consideration of the stronger version is motivated by the economic discussions in Section 9.1.

Among the many possible strategies for testing (9.28), three have figured most prominently in the literature. Fama and French (1988) start with the implication of (9.28) that r_{t+n}^n satisfies

$$E\left[r_{t+n}^n \mid I_t\right] = n\mu, \quad n = 1, 2, \ldots. \tag{9.29}$$

This restriction can be tested by projecting r_{t+n}^n onto a vector of information variables $x_t \in I_t$ (including an intercept),

$$r_{t+n}^n = \delta_0(n) + \delta_x(n)'x_t + u_{t+n}^n, \tag{9.30}$$

and testing whether the slope coefficient $\delta_x(n)$ is zero. This inference problem was examined systematically in Hansen and Hodrick (1980) and falls under Case $ACh(n-1)$ of our discussion of asymptotic distributions in Chapter 3. Under our regularity conditions, the asymptotic covariance matrix of $\delta_T(n)' = (\delta_{0T}(n), \delta_{xT}(n)')$ is given by (3.81). This construction accommodates conditional heteroskedasticity of unknown form, consistent with the fact that the null hypothesis (9.28) does not restrict higher-order conditional moments. It maintains the assumption that under the alternative $\delta_x(n) \neq 0$, the projection error u_{t+n}^n continues to satisfy $E[u_{t+n}^n|I_t] = 0$.

In some economic settings (e.g., the economic environment studied by Hansen and Singleton (1983) and discussed in Chapter 10) (r_t^n, x_t) follow a joint lognormal distribution. In this case, the conditional second moments of the u_{t+n}^n are constants, and ML estimation is feasible and gives the most efficient estimator. However, in other settings, where the joint distribution of x_t and r_{t+n}^n is unknown, but the assumption of conditional homoskedasticity of u_{t+n}^n is maintained, least-squares projection is one feasible means of testing for serial correlation. Under conditional homoskedasticity, if we let $\tilde{x}_t' = (1, x_t')$, the asymptotic covariance matrix of $\delta_T(n)$ simplifies to

$$\Omega_0^{\text{LLP}} = E\left[\tilde{x}_t\tilde{x}_t'\right]^{-1}\left(\sum_{j=-n+1}^{n-1} \Gamma_u(j)E\left[\tilde{x}_t\tilde{x}_{t-j}'\right]\right)E\left[\tilde{x}_t\tilde{x}_t'\right]^{-1}, \tag{9.31}$$

where $\Gamma_u(j) = E[u_t^n u_{t-j}^n]$.

Fama and French (1988) investigated (9.28) by choosing x_t to be the long-horizon return r_t^n, the n-period return observed at date t. This amounted to examining the correlations

$$\gamma_T(n) = \frac{(1/T)\sum_t \left(r_{t+n}^n - n\hat{\mu}\right)\left(r_t^n - n\hat{\mu}\right)}{(1/T)\sum_t \left(r_t^n - n\hat{\mu}\right)^2}, \tag{9.32}$$

where $\hat{\mu} = (1/T)\sum_t r_t^1$.

The use of long-horizon returns means having to accommodate moving-average errors u_{t+n}^n of order $n-1$, and there is the possibility of small-sample biases, biases that may well increase with the forecast horizon. With this limitation of (9.30) in mind, Hodrick (1992) observed that, for scalar x_t,

$$\text{Cov}\left[r_{t+n}^n, x_t\right] = \text{Cov}\left[r_{t+1}^1, \sum_{j=0}^{n-1} x_{t-j}\right]. \tag{9.33}$$

Therefore, the same "economic" content of the long-horizon regression is achieved by estimating the projection

$$r_{t+1}^1 = \delta_0(1) + \delta_x(1)\left(\sum_{j=0}^{n-1} x_{t-j}\right) + u_{t+1}^1, \tag{9.34}$$

and testing the null hypothesis that $\delta_x(1) = 0$. Since this is a one-period-ahead projection, under the alternative of (9.34) it is reasonable to assume that $E[u_{t+1}^1 | I_t] = 0$. This falls under the simpler Case ACh(0) of Chapter 3 and the asymptotic covariance matrix of $(\delta_{0T}(1), \delta_{xT}(1))$ is given by (3.73).

In the context of projections of long-horizon returns on lagged returns, Jegadeesh (1991) computed the correlations among one-period returns and lagged n-period returns,

$$\gamma_T^*(n) = \frac{(1/T)\sum_t \left(r_{t+1}^1 - \hat{\mu}\right)\left(r_t^n - n\hat{\mu}\right)}{(1/T)\sum_t \left(r_t^n - n\hat{\mu}\right)^2}. \tag{9.35}$$

By analogy to Hodrick's analysis, this test can be reinterpreted as a Fama-French-like long-horizon projection of r_{t+n}^n onto r_t^1. It shares the property of (9.34) that the projection error is a martingale difference sequence, and hence (3.73) applies for inference.

An alternative test of (9.28) based on the variances of long-horizon returns was studied by Cochrane (1988), Lo and MacKinlay (1988, 1989), and Poterba and Summers (1988). As was discussed in Chapter 7, an implication of (9.28) is that

$$\text{Var}\left[r_{t+n}^n\right] = n\text{Var}\left[r_t^1\right]. \tag{9.36}$$

Therefore, a natural statistic to examine as a test of (9.36) is

$$\tau_T(n) = \frac{(1/T)\sum_t \left(r_{t+n}^n - n\hat{\mu}\right)^2}{n(1/T)\sum_t \left(r_t^1 - \hat{\mu}\right)^2} - 1. \tag{9.37}$$

Whether $\tau_T(n)$ is positive or negative depends on the alternative model and possibly on the value of n. For the permanent/transitory alternative model (9.16), the variance ratio can be written as

$$\frac{\text{Var}\left[r_t^n\right]}{n\text{Var}\left[r_t^1\right]} = \frac{n\sigma_\epsilon^2 + 2\rho_z(0) - 2\rho_z(n)}{n\left(\sigma_\epsilon^2 + 2\rho_z(0) - 2\rho_z(1)\right)}$$

$$\rightarrow 1 - \frac{\text{Var}[\Delta z_t]}{\text{Var}[\Delta \log P_t]}, \quad n \rightarrow \infty. \tag{9.38}$$

Thus, we would expect $\tau_T(n)$ to be negative for this alternative, at least for large enough n.

Richardson and Smith (1994) show that all three statistics $\gamma_T(n)$, $\gamma_T^*(n)$, and $\tau_T(n)$ can be expressed as linear combinations of the autocorrelations

$$\rho_T(i) = \frac{(1/T)\sum_t \left(r_t^1 - \hat{\mu}\right)\left(r_{t-i}^1 - \hat{\mu}\right)}{(1/T)\sum_t \left(r_t^1 - \hat{\mu}\right)^2} : \tag{9.39}$$

$$\gamma_T(n) = \sum_{i=1}^{2n-1} \min(i, 2n-i)\frac{\rho_T(i)}{n} \frac{(1/T)\sum_t \left(r_t^1 - \hat{\mu}\right)^2}{(1/T)\sum_t \left(r_t^n - n\hat{\mu}\right)^2/n}, \tag{9.40}$$

$$\gamma_T^*(n) = \sum_{i=1}^{n} \frac{\rho_T(i)}{n} \frac{(1/T)\sum_t \left(r_t^1 - \hat{\mu}\right)^2}{(1/T)\sum_t \left(r_t^n - n\hat{\mu}\right)^2/n}, \tag{9.41}$$

$$\tau_T(n) = 2\sum_{i=1}^{n-1} \left(\frac{n-i}{n}\right)\rho_T(i). \tag{9.42}$$

Under our regularity conditions and H_0,

$$\frac{(1/T)\sum_t \left(r_t^1 - \hat{\mu}\right)^2}{(1/T)\sum_t \left(r_t^n - n\hat{\mu}\right)^2/n} \rightarrow 1, \text{ as } T \rightarrow \infty. \tag{9.43}$$

It follows that the asymptotic distributions of these statistics (scaled by $\sqrt{T}$) depend only on the joint asymptotic distribution of the $\sqrt{T}\rho_T(i)$.

Pursuing this further, we let $y_t \equiv (r_t^1 - \mu)$ and suppose that $E[y_{t+1}|I_t] = 0$, where I_t is the information set generated by current and past y_t. The asymptotic distribution of interest is that of the

$$\sqrt{T}\rho_T(i) \overset{a}{=} \frac{(1/\sqrt{T})\sum_t y_t y_{t-i}}{\sigma_y^2}, \tag{9.44}$$

where $\sigma_y^2 = \text{Var}[y_t]$. For $|i| > 0, |j| > 0, i \neq j$, the limiting joint distribution of $\sqrt{T}\rho_T(i)$ and $\sqrt{T}\rho_T(j)$ is normal with mean zero (the null is no serial correlation) and

$$\text{Var}\left[\sqrt{T}\rho_T(i)\right] = \frac{E[y_t^2 y_{t-i}^2]}{(E[y_t^2])^2}, \tag{9.45}$$

$$\text{Cov}\left[\sqrt{T}\rho_T(i), \sqrt{T}\rho_T(j)\right] = \frac{E[y_t^2 y_{t-|i|} y_{t-|j|}]}{(E[y_t^2])^2}. \tag{9.46}$$

In deriving the asymptotic distribution of the γ and τ statistics, it has often been assumed that the covariance in (9.46) is zero for all i and j. To explore the plausibility of this assumption, suppose that $j > i > 0$ and consider the value of the numerator in (9.46) implied by the GARCH$(1,1)$ model [see (7.2) in Chapter 7]:

$$E\left[E[y_t^2|I_{t-i}]y_{t-i}y_{t-j}\right] = E\left\{\left[\omega\left(\sum_{k=0}^{i-2}(\alpha+\beta)^k\right) + (\alpha+\beta)^{i-1}\right.\right.$$
$$\left.\left. \times \left(\omega + \alpha y_{t-i}^2 + \beta\sigma_{t-i-1}^2\right)\right]y_{t-i}y_{t-j}\right\}$$
$$= (\alpha+\beta)^{i-1}\alpha E\left[E[y_{t-i}^3|I_{t-i-1}]y_{t-j}\right]. \tag{9.47}$$

Thus, in this model, if $E[y_{t-i}^3|I_{t-i-1}] = 0$—that is, if the conditional distribution of y_t is symmetric—then the covariance (9.46) is zero. While symmetry is a property of the formulation of the GARCH model in Bollerslev (1986), the empirical evidence reviewed in Chapter 7 suggests that equity return distributions are in fact skewed. This view was further supported by the fitted parameters of the continuous-time SV model with correlated return and volatility shocks applied to equity return data.

Proceeding under the assumption of symmetry, as in much of the literature on testing for serial correlation, we find that the three test statistics converge in distribution under the null to normals with mean zero and variances:

$$\Omega_\gamma = \sum_{i=1}^{2n-1}(\min(i, 2n-i))^2 \frac{E[y_t^2 y_{t-i}^2]}{n^2 E[y_t^2]^2}, \tag{9.48}$$

$$\Omega_{\gamma^*} = \sum_{i=1}^{n} \frac{E[y_t^2 y_{t-i}^2]}{n^2 E[y_t^2]^2}, \tag{9.49}$$

$$\Omega_\tau = \sum_{i=1}^{n-1} \left(\frac{2(n-i)}{n}\right)^2 \frac{E[y_t^2 y_{t-i}^2]}{E[y_t^2]^2}. \tag{9.50}$$

Lo and MacKinlay (1989) examined the small-sample properties of the statistic $\tau_T(n)$ for various values of T and n. They found that the performance of this test deteriorates as n/T becomes larger. Indeed, they showed that for $n = 2T/3$, $\tau_T(n)/\sqrt{\Omega_\tau}$ is never less than -1.73. Recall from the discussion of (9.38) that, for the alternative of the permanent-transitory components model, $\tau_T(n)$ is expected to be negative. Consequently, this lower bound implies that the statistic $\tau_T(n)/\sqrt{\Omega_\tau}$ has essentially no power against alternatives in which asset prices are driven by the sum of permanent and transitory components.

To accommodate a large n relative to T formally as part of the asymptotic analysis, Richardson and Stock (1989) examined the limiting distribution of $\tau_T(n)$ under the assumption that $n/T \to \delta$ as $T \to \infty$. Their idea is that researchers choose large n as sample size T grows in order to study autocorrelations over longer horizons. They show that

$$\tau_T(n) + 1 \Rightarrow \frac{1}{\delta} \int_\delta^1 Y_\delta(\lambda)^2 \, d\lambda, \tag{9.51}$$

where

$$Y_\delta(\lambda) = B(\lambda) - B(\lambda - \delta) - \delta B(1), \tag{9.52}$$

and $B(\lambda)$ is standard Brownian motion restricted to the unit interval. Note that the limiting distribution is nonnormal *even without scaling by* $\sqrt{T}$. Moreover, the mean of the limiting distribution is

$$E[\tau_T(n) + 1] \to (1 - \delta)^2, \tag{9.53}$$

as $T \to \infty$, $n/T \to \delta$. This may be very different from the value of 1 expected under H_0. For instance, if $\delta = 2/3$, then the mean is only $1/9$. Thus, inference based on standard asymptotic arguments may be very misleading when n is large relative to T.

Table 9.2 shows the asymptotic distributions of $\tau_T(n) + 1$ for conventional fixed-n asymptotic theory (first row), a fixed-n and bias-adjusted distribution proposed by Lo and MacKinlay (1989) (second row), and Monte Carlo derived small-sample distributions (remaining rows) under the assumption that $n/T \to \delta$. The large-sample, $n/T \to \delta$ distribution is approximately given by the row $T = 2880$. (It is obtained exactly by letting $T \to \infty$ while $n/T \to \delta$.) Clearly the fixed-n asymptotic distribution misrepresents both the upper and lower tails of the actual small-sample distribution of

Table 9.2. *Asymptotic Distributions of $\tau_T(n) + 1$ for $\delta = 1/3$ for Conventional Fixed-n Asymptotics, Bias-Adjusted Fixed-n Asymptotics, and Monte Carlo Results Obtained Assuming That $n/T \rightarrow \delta$*

| | Mean | \multicolumn{7}{c}{Percentile} |||||||
		2.5%	5%	10%	50%	90%	95%	97.5%
Not bias-adjusted fixed n	1.00	−0.31	−0.10	0.15	1.00	1.85	2.10	2.31
Bias-adjusted fixed n	0.44	−0.14	−0.04	0.06	0.44	0.82	0.93	1.03
Monte Carlo								
$T = 360$	0.44	0.09	0.11	0.14	0.35	0.86	1.09	1.29
$T = 720$	0.45	0.09	0.11	0.14	0.35	0.88	1.11	1.35
$T = 2880$	0.45	0.09	0.11	0.14	0.35	0.88	1.09	1.33

Source: Richardson and Stock (1989).

$\tau_T(n)$. The bias adjustment largely removes the distortion in the upper tail, but the distribution of this statistic remains skewed substantially to the left relative to the actual small-sample distribution of $\tau_T(n)$. Under the permanent/transitory shock model, for example, we expect small values of $\tau_T(n)$ if the alternative is true, so the bias in the fix-n tests would likely contribute to overrejection of H_0 of no serial correlation.

What is not fully clear from these Monte Carlo results is whether the small-sample biases in tests are due to the long forecast horizon per se, or whether they arise owing to the need to estimate the high-order autocorrelations underlying the standard errors in (9.48)–(9.50). Based on previous studies of the small-sample properties of tests in the presence of serially correlated errors, one may suspect that the latter plays a central role. Indeed, it appears as though the large-sample paradigm for testing is markedly more reliable (small- and large-sample distributions are more alike) when standard errors are computed using averages of past forecast variables, as proposed by Hodrick (1992), instead of averages of future forecast errors (Hodrick, 1992; Boudoukh and Richardson, 1993). More precisely, instead of using the asymptotic covariance matrix (3.81), the center matrix Σ_0 is replaced by

$$\Sigma_0 = E\left[\left(u_{t+1}^1\right)^2 \left(\sum_{j=0}^{n-1} x_{t-j}\right) \left(\sum_{j=0}^{n-1} x_{t-j}\right)' \right]. \qquad (9.54)$$

With these standard errors, an increase in the forecast horizon does not add complexity because the order of the MA error structure is effectively not changing.

*Table 9.3.   Empirical Sizes of Tests of Predictability of Excess Returns
on Common Stocks, for a Regression Test with Nominal Size of 5%,
Using Newey-West, Hansen-Hodrick, and Hodrick Standard Errors*

Horizon	Newey-West	Hansen-Hodrick	Hodrick
1	0.045	0.042	0.042
4	0.112	0.077	0.044
20	0.226	0.230	0.043

Note: The sample size is 200 (quarters).
Source: Ang and Bekaert (2003a).

The potential importance of this observation for the small-sample properties of regression tests is illustrated by the Monte Carlo analysis in Ang
and Bekaert (2003a) of the predictability of excess returns on stocks using
the dividend/price ratio. Using data generated from a simple present value
model, Ang and Bekaert compared the empirical sizes of regression tests
based on the "Hodrick," robust Hansen and Hodrick (1980), and Newey
and West (1987a) standard errors. A representative set of empirical sizes for
the case of a nominal size of 5% and sample size of 200 quarters is shown
in Table 9.3. Note that the empirical sizes of the tests based on Newey-West
and Hansen-Hodrick standard errors increase substantially with increasing
forecast horizon (given in the first column). That is, consistent with the
analysis in Richardson and Stock, regression tests tend to reject too often.
In contrast, the tests based on the Hodrick standard errors show no deterioration in test reliability as the forecast horizon increases. Thus, the need
to compute standard errors based on moving-average error structures of
increasingly large order does indeed appear to contribute to the poor small-
sample properties of conventional tests of return predictability.

9.5. Evidence on Stock-Return Predictability

The empirical evidence shows that both the degree of stock-return predictability and its statistical significance depend on the nature of the conditioning variables used for prediction. Focusing solely on the use of past
returns to forecast returns, Fama and French (1988) and Poterba and Summers (1988) regressed long-horizon returns on their historical counterparts
and found a pronounced U-shaped pattern to the first-order autocorrelation coefficients. For instance, using data on the value-weighted return on
the NYSE, Fama and French report autocorrelations near zero for small n
that reach about -0.35 at $n = 48$ months, and then decline toward zero
again as n increases.

Numerous studies have questioned the statistical reliability of these findings. Richardson (1993), for example, simulated stock price data under the
null hypothesis that stock returns are unpredictable (the logarithm of the

stock price follows a random walk) and generated U-shaped patterns in autocorrelations, much like those in Fama and French, as a consequence of small-sample bias. Additionally, he argued that the relevant test is not the t-test for each individual autocorrelation, but rather the test of the joint null hypothesis that all of the autocorrelations considered are zero. When he implemented this joint test for a variety of equity portfolio returns, he found little evidence against the random-walk hypothesis.

Lo and MacKinlay (1988) implemented the variance ratio test for small values of n with r_t^1 equal to the 1-week return on various stock portfolios. They found that the portfolio returns examined exhibited positive serial correlation and that $\tau(n)$ was often significantly different from zero at conventional significance levels. Evidence on whether their short-horizon results using variance ratio tests extend to long horizons is reported in Table 9.4, from Singleton (1990). The τ statistics displayed are calculated using the same y_t as in Lo and MacKinlay (1988) except with t indexing months (i.e., y_t^n denotes the n-month portfolio return deviated from its sample mean). Below each τ statistic in square brackets is the sample estimate of the corresponding $\text{Corr}[y_t^n, y_{t-n}^n]$. Consistent with the findings of Fama and French (1988), the sample autocorrelation of $\{y_t^{60}\}$ is negative and quite

Table 9.4. Tests of the Random-Walk Hypothesis
Based on the Variances of Multiperiod Stock Returns

Decile	$n = 3$	$n = 6$	$n = 12$	$n = 36$	$n = 60$
January 1926–December 1985					
1	1.870	1.026	0.877	0.371	0.194
	[−0.047]	[0.028]	[0.049]	[−0.121]	[−0.174]
4	1.830	0.816	0.712	−0.001	−0.394
	[−0.072]	[0.029]	[−0.032]	[−0.336]	[−0.527]
7	1.615	0.856	0.797	−0.270	−0.771
	[−0.036]	[0.041]	[−0.096]	[−0.432]	[−0.474]
10	1.097	0.235	0.428	−0.421	−0.867
	[−0.072]	[0.067]	[−0.099]	[−0.401]	[−0.291]
January 1936–December 1985					
1	0.469	0.454	−0.021	−0.169	−0.061
	[0.028]	[−0.057]	[0.004]	[0.012]	[−0.179]
4	0.930	1.100	0.422	−0.616	−0.758
	[0.074]	[−0.053]	[−0.139]	[−0.177]	[−0.418]
7	0.572	0.914	0.260	−1.014	−1.095
	[0.083]	[−0.064]	[−0.220]	[−0.169]	[−0.240]
10	−0.287	0.255	−0.085	−1.348	−1.275
	[0.062]	[−0.044]	[−0.245]	[−0.059]	[0.036]

Source: Singleton (1990).

large in absolute value for the sample period 1926–1985. However, the τ statistics do not lead to rejection at conventional significance levels of the null hypothesis of no autocorrelation in returns. On the other hand, the estimates of $\text{Corr}[y_t^3, y_{t-3}^3]$ are relatively small and yet the significance levels of the τ statistics are less than 6% for deciles 1, 4, and 7.

The sample period 1936–1985 does not include the Great Depression in the analysis. Interestingly, this omission results in much less evidence of serial correlation in the Fama-French data. In particular, the estimates of $|\text{Corr}[y_t^{60}, y_{t-60}^{60}]|$ are uniformly smaller than the corresponding estimates for the sample period 1926–1985. Moreover, the τ statistics provide much less evidence against the null hypothesis of serially uncorrelated returns when $n = 3$.

In addition to conditioning on past returns, the literature has explored the predictive content of several other conditioning variables including: short-term interest rates (Singleton, 1990; Campbell, 1991; Hodrick, 1992), the aggregate dividend yield (Campbell and Shiller, 1988; Fama and French, 1988), the spread between yields on long- and short-term bonds (Fama and French, 1989), and the credit spread between high- and low-grade corporate bonds (Keim and Stambaugh, 1986). The evidence that other conditioning variables predict returns together with the universal nature of these findings across OECD economies are often cited to reassure skeptics that predictability is not a spurious phenomenon.

Nevertheless, much of the evidence supporting predictive content for these variables comes from regressions in which long-horizon returns are the dependent variables. The Monte Carlo evidence in Richardson and Stock (1989), Richardson and Smith (1991), and Hodrick (1992) suggests that the small-sample distributions of the usual "t-tests" in these regressions are shifted substantially to the right, leading to overrejection of the null that returns are unpredictable. Motivated by this observation, Ang and Bekaert (2003a) reassessed the degree to which stock returns are predictable, using both U.S. and European stock returns and price/dividend ratios and interest rates as predictors. Their findings support the view that only short-term interest rates have predictive content for stock returns across countries. In particular, there was little evidence for predictability of earnings or dividend yields.

Stronger evidence that monthly returns are predictable using the dividend yield is reported in Lewellen (2004). He exploits the information in the auxiliary equation describing the autocorrelation of the predictor variable itself (in his case, the dividend yield) to show that, under certain circumstances, one can substantially increase the power of tests of stock return predictability.

Though not often exploited in the literature, these tests for predictability can be adapted to allow for conditioning information. Specifically, (9.28) implies not only that $(r_t^1 - \mu)$ is unpredictable, but also that $y_t^1 \equiv (r_t^1 - \mu)z_{t-1}$ satisfies $E[y_t^1 \mid I_{t-1}] = 0$ for any variable z_{t-1} in agents' information set at date $t-1$. We examined the predictability of returns using this stronger implication of (9.28) for three choices of z: the constant unity (i.e., the conventional approach), the 1-month U.S. Treasury bill rate (Tbill), and the monthly index of consumer sentiment (InConSent). The returns were industrywide indices for "consumer durables," "basic industries," "capital goods," and "services," and the sample period was July 1963 though December 1999.[4]

The panel labeled $\gamma_T(n)$ in Table 9.5 is the statistic (9.40). Three different standard errors are reported for this statistic: AsyUnc assumes that the sample correlations are asymptotically uncorrelated, giving rise to standard-based (9.48), GMM allows for asymptotic correlation among the sample correlations as described by (9.46), and Hodrick are the standard errors computed using the ideas in Hodrick (1992). The panel labeled $\gamma_T^*(n)$ is the statistic (9.41), and the standard errors given by (9.49) are for the asymptotically uncorrelated case.

With $z_{t-1} = 1$, there is little evidence for predictability of returns in the "basic" and "capital goods" industries. However, there is evidence of predictability for returns in the "consumer durables" and "services" industries. When Tbill is used as an instrument, there is stronger evidence of predictability, for basic industries over short horizons and the other three industry groupings over longer horizons. Finally, the instrument InConSent leads to evidence of predictability for all four industry groupings, with the evidence being particularly strong for consumer durables and services. All of these findings seem consistent with economic intuition.

Comparing the standard errors used in testing based on $\gamma_T(n)$ shows the GMM standard errors to be uniformly larger than the Hodrick standard errors. Though the differences are typically not large, this implies that there is more evidence against the null hypothesis of unpredictable returns using the Hodrick standard errors.

Instead of using regression tests, one can assess predictability by adapting the variance ratio tests to allow for conditioning information. By the same logic that underlies the tests reported in Table 9.5, it follows that the variance of $y_t^n = \sum_{j=0}^{n-1}(r_{t-j}^1 - \mu)z_{t-1-j}$ is n times the variance of y_t^1 and so the mean-independence of y_t^1 from past information can be examined using the $\tau(n)$ statistic. Table 9.6 displays the $\tau(n)$ statistics obtained with $z_{t-1} = \mathrm{DTB1}_{t-1}$ [$= (r_{t-1}^f - r_{t-2}^f)$, where r_t^f is the 1-month return on the bill issued at date $t-1$ and maturing at date t] and $z_{t-1} = 1$ for the sample period January 1959–December 1985. With $z_{t-1} = \mathrm{DTB1}_{t-1}$ there is a tendency for the value of the $\tau(n)$ statistics to increase as n increases from 2

---

[4] I am grateful to Joe Chen for providing these data.

Table 9.5. *Tests of Predictability of Stock Returns Based on the Statistics $\gamma_T(n)$ and $\gamma_T^*(n)$ Using Monthly Data on Industry Portfolio Returns and the Instruments 1-month Tbill and InConSent*

Statistic γ	None			Tbill			InConSent		
	$n=1$	$n=3$	$n=12$	$n=1$	$n=3$	$n=12$	$n=1$	$n=3$	$n=12$
Consumer durables	0.194	−0.045	−0.166	0.206	−0.109	−0.491	0.173	−0.180	−0.460
AsyUnc s.e.	(0.056)	(0.074)	(0.144)	(0.089)	(0.103)	(0.211)	(0.081)	(0.085)	(0.178)
GMM s.e.	(0.056)	(0.082)	(0.156)	(0.089)	(0.125)	(0.173)	(0.081)	(0.099)	(0.120)
Hodrick s.e.	(0.049)	(0.063)	(0.159)	(0.080)	(0.087)	(0.132)	(0.058)	(0.063)	(0.142)
Basic industries	−0.008	−0.002	−0.186	0.003	−0.207	−0.414	0.010	−0.186	−0.210
AsyUnc s.e.	(0.067)	(0.076)	(0.159)	(0.113)	(0.122)	(0.223)	(0.089)	(0.089)	(0.186)
GMM s.e.	(0.067)	(0.083)	(0.151)	(0.113)	(0.099)	(0.151)	(0.089)	(0.092)	(0.163)
Hodrick s.e.	(0.051)	(0.079)	(0.114)	(0.068)	(0.082)	(0.111)	(0.064)	(0.074)	(0.137)
Capital goods	−0.019	−0.047	−0.152	−0.047	−0.094	−0.330	−0.038	−0.131	−0.232
AsyUnc s.e.	(0.057)	(0.077)	(0.148)	(0.079)	(0.128)	(0.206)	(0.069)	(0.091)	(0.188)
GMM s.e.	(0.057)	(0.072)	(0.114)	(0.079)	(0.119)	(0.163)	(0.069)	(0.085)	(0.141)
Hodrick s.e.	(0.055)	(0.068)	(0.134)	(0.081)	(0.094)	(0.127)	(0.066)	(0.086)	(0.166)
Services	0.094	−0.015	−0.281	0.076	−0.069	−0.561	0.099	−0.118	−0.618
AsyUnc s.e.	(0.049)	(0.075)	(0.147)	(0.085)	(0.122)	(0.218)	(0.065)	(0.085)	(0.175)
GMM s.e.	(0.049)	(0.077)	(0.145)	(0.085)	(0.138)	(0.195)	(0.065)	(0.096)	(0.154)
Hodrick s.e.	(0.045)	(0.062)	(0.114)	(0.084)	(0.082)	(0.054)	(0.057)	(0.060)	(0.075)

Instrument

(continued)

Table 9.5. (*Continued*)

Statistic γ^*	Instrument								
	None			Tbill			InConSent		
	$n=1$	$n=3$	$n=12$	$n=1$	$n=3$	$n=12$	$n=1$	$n=3$	$n=12$
Consumer durables	0.194	0.021	−0.003	0.206	0.027	−0.030	0.173	−0.010	−0.034
AsyUnc s.e.	(0.056)	(0.030)	(0.015)	(0.088)	(0.044)	(0.022)	(0.081)	(0.038)	(0.019)
Basic industries	−0.008	−0.019	−0.001	0.003	−0.097	−0.044	0.010	−0.065	−0.016
AsyUnc s.e.	(0.067)	(0.034)	(0.017)	(0.111)	(0.052)	(0.024)	(0.089)	(0.042)	(0.020)
Capital goods	−0.019	0.028	−0.015	−0.047	−0.033	−0.017	−0.037	−0.056	−0.015
AsyUnc s.e.	(0.057)	(0.032)	(0.015)	(0.080)	(0.051)	(0.022)	(0.068)	(0.037)	(0.019)
Services	0.094	0.006	−0.012	0.076	0.023	−0.022	0.099	−0.001	−0.026
AsyUnc s.e.	(0.049)	(0.029)	(0.015)	(0.084)	(0.050)	(0.023)	(0.065)	(0.035)	(0.018)

Note: Standard errors (s.e.) are in parentheses.

Table 9.6. *Tests of the Random-Walk Hypothesis Based on the Variances of Products of Multiperiod Stock Returns and Treasury Bill Returns, December 1959–December 1985*

Decile	$z_{t-1} = 1$				$z_{t-1} = \mathrm{DTB1}_t$			
	$n=2$	$n=3$	$n=6$	$n=12$	$n=2$	$n=3$	$n=6$	$n=12$
1	1.365	1.037	0.443	−0.489	0.843	1.314	1.650	1.992
	[−0.001]	[−0.029]	[−0.177]	[−0.098]	[0.165]	[0.136]	[0.109]	[0.025]
4	2.462	1.854	1.471	0.628	1.115	1.621	1.791	2.074
	[0.020]	[0.049]	[−0.059]	[−0.077]	[0.261]	[0.184]	[0.114]	[−0.078]
7	2.394	1.868	1.612	0.674	1.118	1.376	1.624	1.837
	[0.039]	[0.073]	[−0.067]	[−0.211]	[0.183]	[0.165]	[0.101]	[−0.150]
10	0.107	−0.196	0.230	−0.155	0.895	0.932	1.324	1.467
	[−0.034]	[0.067]	[−0.070]	[−0.318]	[0.127]	[0.163]	[0.069]	[−0.177]

Source: Singleton (1990).

to 12, and the random-walk hypothesis is rejected at the 5% level for deciles 1, 4, and 7. In contrast, there is more evidence against the null hypothesis (9.28) with $z_t = 1$ when n is small.[5] Another difference between the results is that returns are more negatively autocorrelated than the products of returns and DTB1$_{t-1}$ for large values of n.

Taking all of this evidence together appears to support the view that stock returns are predictable, particularly when one incorporates information about the business cycle. Nevertheless, it is difficult to overlook the econometric challenges in assessing whether or not there is predictability. What one ultimately concludes may well depend on one's priors from economic or psychological studies of investor behavior.

Under risk neutrality, (9.3) must be satisfied for all securities with admissible payoffs. This observation is especially problematic for proponents of (9.3) when attention is focused on bonds, which we turn to next.

9.6. Time-Varying Expected Returns on Bonds

Fama (1984a,b) and Fama and Bliss (1987) present evidence of rich patterns of variation in expected returns across time and maturities that "stand as challenges or stylized facts" (Fama, 1984b: p. 545) to be explained by dynamic term structure models. A large literature subsequently elaborated on the inconsistency of these patterns with the implications of the traditional expectations hypothesis—there is compelling evidence from yield

---

[5] These tests are all based on standard large-sample distribution theory. It would be interesting to examine whether they inherit some of the small-sample biases of tests based on long-horizon regressions.

(Campbell and Shiller, 1991) and forward-rate (Backus et al., 2001) regressions for *time-varying* risk premiums. This section examines the economic underpinnings of the null hypothesis that expected *excess* returns on bonds should not be forecastable and reviews the evidence.[6]

To fix notation, we let $D(t, T)$ denote the price of a (default-free) zero-coupon bond issued at date t, with maturity date T. Its corresponding (continuously compounded) yield is $y_t^{T-t} \equiv -\log D(t, T)/(T - t)$; equivalently, $D(t, T) = e^{-y_t^{T-t}(T-t)}$. Letting $r_t \equiv y_t^1$, from this basic price-yield relation, we can express the conditional mean of the excess return

$$\mathrm{ER}_{t+1}^n = \ln(D(t + 1, t + n - 1)/D(t, t + n)) - r_t,$$

$e_t^n \equiv E_t[\mathrm{ER}_{t+1}^n]$, as

$$e_t^n = -(n - 1)E_t[y_{t+1}^{n-1} - y_t^n] + (y_t^n - r_t), \tag{9.55}$$

where E_t denotes expectation conditioned on date t information, $\mathcal{I}_t$. There is no economic content to (9.55) as it holds by definition. Economic content is added by linking e_t^n to the risk premiums implied by an economic model. Toward this end, we introduce two related notions of "term premiums" that have played prominent roles in the literature on expected bond returns: the yield term premium,

$$c_t^n \equiv y_t^n - \frac{1}{n} \sum_{i=0}^{n-1} E_t[r_{t+i}], \tag{9.56}$$

and the forward term premium,

$$p_t^n \equiv f_t^n - E_t[r_{t+n}], \tag{9.57}$$

where $f_t^n \equiv -\ln(D(t, t + n + 1)/D(t, t + n))$ denotes the forward rate for 1-month loans commencing at date $t+n$. Since $y_t^n \equiv (1/n) \sum_{i=0}^{n-1} f_t^i$, the term premiums p_t^n and c_t^n are linked by the simple relation

$$c_t^n \equiv \frac{1}{n} \sum_{i=0}^{n-1} p_t^i. \tag{9.58}$$

These variables are assumed to be stationary stochastic processes with finite first and second moments.

---

[6] This section draws heavily upon the analysis in Dai and Singleton (2002). This material is reprinted with permission from Elsevier.

The realized excess return ER_{t+1}^n can be decomposed into a pure "premium" part, ER_{t+1}^{*n}, and an "expectations" part[7]:

$$\text{ER}_{t+1}^n = \text{ER}_{t+1}^{*n} + \sum_{i=1}^{n-1}(E_t r_{t+i} - E_{t+1} r_{t+i}), \tag{9.59}$$

where

$$\text{ER}_{t+1}^{*n} = -(n-1)\big(c_{t+1}^{n-1} - c_t^{n-1}\big) + p_t^{n-1}. \tag{9.60}$$

Since the $(E_t r_{t+i} - E_{t+1} r_{t+i})$ have zero date-t conditional means, e_t^n depends only on the premium term ER_{t+1}^{*n}:

$$e_t^n = E_t\big[\text{ER}_{t+1}^{*n}\big] = -(n-1)E_t\big[c_{t+1}^{n-1} - c_t^{n-1}\big] + p_t^{n-1}. \tag{9.61}$$

Thus, expected excess returns on bonds are time varying (excess returns have a predictable component) if the term premiums c_t^n and p_t^n are time varying.

While numerous studies, going back at least to Fama (1984b), have examined the properties of term premia by studying excess returns, at least as much attention has been given to the following rearranged version of (9.55)[8]:

$$E_t\left[y_{t+1}^{n-1} - y_t^n + \frac{1}{n-1}\text{ER}_{t+1}^n\right] = \frac{1}{n-1}\left(y_t^n - r_t\right). \tag{9.62}$$

In light of (9.61), we can replace ER_{t+1}^n in (9.62) by ER_{t+1}^{*n} to obtain

$$E_t\left[y_{t+1}^{n-1} - y_t^n + \frac{1}{n-1}\text{ER}_{t+1}^{*n}\right] = \frac{1}{n-1}\left(y_t^n - r_t\right). \tag{9.63}$$

An immediate implication of (9.63) is that projections of the premium-adjusted changes in bond yields,

---

[7] Some of the intermediate steps in this derivation are: $\text{ER}_{t+1}^n \equiv n y_t^n - (n-1)y_{t+1}^{n-1} - r_t = n c_t^n - (n-1)c_{t+1}^{n-1} + \sum_{i=1}^{n-1}(E_t r_{t+i} - E_{t+1} r_{t+i}) = -(n-1)(c_{t+1}^{n-1} - c_t^{n-1}) + \sum_{j=0}^{n-1} p_t^j - \sum_{j=0}^{n-2} p_t^j + \sum_{i=1}^{n-1}(E_t r_{t+i} - E_{t+1} r_{t+i})$.

[8] Expression (9.62) is formally equivalent to equation (11) of Fama and Bliss (1987), which, in our notation, is

$$E_t\left[y_{t+1}^{n-1} - y_t^{n-1} + \frac{1}{n-1}\text{ER}_{t+1}^n\right] = \frac{1}{n-1}\left(f_t^{n-1} - r_t\right).$$

We focus on (9.62) because it is more directly linked to the yield regressions in Campbell and Shiller (1991).

$$y_{t+1}^{n-1} - y_t^n - (n-1)\left[c_{t+1}^{n-1} - c_t^{n-1}\right] + p_t^{n-1},$$

onto the scaled slope of the yield curve, $(y_t^n - r_t)/(n-1)$, should give coefficients of one (for all n). We exploit this observation in Chapter 13 to assess the goodness-of-fit of several term structure models by computing the premiums c and p implied by these models and estimating these projections.

One widely studied special case is that of the expectations hypothesis (EH), which maintains that term premiums are constant (or, in its strongest form, are zero). In this case, (9.63) implies that the projection of (conditional expectation of) $y_{t+1}^{n-1} - y_t^n$ onto $(y_t^n - r_t)/(n-1)$ gives a coefficient equal to one, for all n:

$$E_t\left[y_{t+1}^{n-1} - y_t^n\right] = \alpha_{n1} + \frac{1}{n-1}(y_t^n - r_t). \tag{9.64}$$

Defining $S_t^{(nm)} \equiv y_t^n - y_t^m$, Campbell and Shiller (1991) derived the following more general version of (9.64) under the EH:

$$E_t\left[y_{t+m}^{n-m} - y_t^n\right] = \alpha_{nm} + \frac{m}{n-m}S_t^{(nm)}. \tag{9.65}$$

While the assumption of constant term premia is surely strong, it does arise in equilibrium as a special case of the models examined in Hansen and Singleton (1983) and Breeden (1986) (see also Dunn and Singleton, 1986). To see this, we first note that $f_t^n = (n+1)y_t^{n+1} - ny_t^n$. Assuming that $\{q_{t+1}^*\}_{t=1}^T$ is a series of jointly lognormally distributed variables, we see that the kernel for pricing n-period-ahead payoffs, $q_{t+n}^{*n} = \prod_{j=1}^n q_{t+j}^{*1}$, is also lognormal. Therefore, using the fact that $y_t^n \in \mathcal{I}_t$, for all n, we have [analogously to (9.6)]

$$ny_t^n = -E_t\left[\ln q_{t+n}^{*n}\right] - \frac{1}{2}\mathrm{Var}_t\left[\ln q_{t+n}^{*n}\right]. \tag{9.66}$$

Subtracting the version of (9.66) for n from that for $n+1$ gives

$$\begin{aligned}
f_t^n &= -E_t\left[\ln q_{t+n+1}^{*,n+1}\right] + E_t\left[\ln q_{t+n}^{*n}\right] \\
&\quad - \frac{1}{2}\left(\mathrm{Var}_t\left[\ln q_{t+n+1}^{*,n+1}\right] - \mathrm{Var}_t\left[\ln q_{t+n}^{*n}\right]\right) \\
&= E_t[r_{t+n}] + p^n, \tag{9.67}
\end{aligned}$$

where the last equality follows from the fact that r_{t+n} satisfies a version of (9.66) with conditioning dated at $t+n$. The forward term premium p^n is constant in this setting because the conditional variances of the pricing kernels are constants under the conditional lognormality assumption. It follows that (from the definition of y_t^n in terms of forward rates) under this version of the EH

$$y_t^n = \frac{1}{n} E_t \left[\sum_{j=0}^{n-1} r_{t+j} \right] + \delta^n, \qquad (9.68)$$

where δ^n is a constant, and [from (9.63)]

$$E_t \left[y_{t+1}^{n-1} - y_t^n \right] = \alpha_{n1} + \frac{1}{n-1} \left(y_t^n - r_t \right). \qquad (9.69)$$

Projections of changes in bond yields onto the slope of the yield curve should give a coefficient of one, for all n.

Formally, this motivating argument pertains to returns on bonds with payoffs denominated in the numeraire good underlying q^*. If q^* is agents' marginal rate of substitution, then these expressions do not apply directly to the returns on nominal bonds (those we most often observe). Nevertheless, they are equally applicable to an economy with nominal bonds (bonds that pay off in the numeraire money), so long as they are priced by q_{t+n}^{*n} after dividing their nominal returns by the n-period inflation rate and, further, that the conditional second moments of inflation are constants. In this case, we can reinterpret y_t^n in (9.64) as the nominal yield, since the expected inflation rates implicit in the real returns cancel from this relation.[9]

Over the past decade, considerable attention has been focused on testing the null hypothesis that the coefficient in the projection of $y_{t+m}^{n-m} - y_t^n$ onto $(m/(n-m)) S_t^{(nm)}$, say ϕ_{nm}, is unity. Table 9.7 displays a representative set of projection coefficients from Backus et al. (2001), for the case of $m = 1$ (so we suppress the subscript m from ϕ_n). The data are U.S. Treasury zero-coupon bond yields computed monthly by Fama and Bliss for the sample period February 1970 through December 1995. Not only are the estimated ϕ_{nT} not unity, they are often statistically significantly negative, particularly for large n (measured in months). The basic intuition of the EH is that an increase in the slope of the yield curve ($y_t^n - r_t$) reflects expectations of rising short-term rates in the future. In order for the "buy an n-period bond and hold it to maturity" investment strategy to match, on average, the returns

---

[9] Expression (9.68) is not the traditional formulation of the EH, since y^n is the logarithm of the total return. If we instead define the yield as the y_t^n satisfying $D(t, t + n) = 1/(1 + y_t^n)^n$, then, under the approximation $\ln(1 + y_t^n) \approx y_t^n$,

$$y_t^n = \frac{1}{n} \sum_{j=0}^{n-1} E_t \left[y_{t+j}^1 \right] + \phi^n.$$

Table 9.7. Estimated Slope Coefficients ϕ_{nT} from the Indicated Linear Projections Using the Smoothed Fama-Bliss Data Set

$$y_{t+1}^{(n-1)} - y_t^n = \alpha_{nT} + \phi_{nT}\left(y_t^n - r_t\right)/(n-1) + \text{residual}$$

Maturity	6	9	12	24	36	48	60	84	120
ϕ_{nT}	−0.883	−1.228	−1.425	−1.705	−1.910	−2.147	−2.433	−3.096	−4.173
s.e.	(0.640)	(0.738)	(0.825)	(1.120)	(1.295)	(1.418)	(1.519)	(1.705)	(1.985)

$$f_{t+1}^{(n-1)} - r_t = \alpha_{fT} + \psi_{nT}\left(f_t^{(n)} - r_t\right) + \text{residual}$$

Maturity	6	9	12	24	36	48	60	84	120
ψ_{nT}	0.797	0.851	0.891	0.946	0.958	0.962	0.964	0.964	0.963
s.e.	(0.057)	(0.046)	(0.039)	(0.024)	(0.017)	(0.014)	(0.012)	(0.011)	(0.010)

Note: The maturities n are given in months. See also Backus et al. (2001), column 1 of Tables 1 and 5.

from rolling over short rates in a rising short-rate environment, the yield on the long bond must rise ($y_{t+1}^{n-1} - y_t^n$ must be positive). The projection coefficients suggest that the slope does not even get the direction of changes in the long-bond yield correct.

The analogous forward-rate projections computed by Backus et al. (2001) are also shown in Table 9.7. The coefficients ψ_{nT} are all less than one, their value predicted by the EH. Though the findings for the latter might seem to provide relatively less evidence against EH compared to the yield projections, Backus et al. (2001) show that under a simple one-factor AR(1) model for r, this is misleading. The small deviations from unity of ψ_{nT} translate into the large negative values of ϕ_{nT} in the yield projections.

Using U.S. data, we find that these violations of the EH are most pronounced (and statistically significant) for sample periods that include the change in monetary operating procedures during 1979–1983. However, notably, ϕ_{nT} is consistently negative across sample periods including prior and subsequent to this monetary "experiment," though (no doubt owing in part to the shorter sample period) the standard error bands are also larger (see Table 9.8). Looking outside the United States, the tendency for ϕ_{nT} to be substantially less than zero is not nearly so pronounced. Among the studies that document different patterns, primarily for European countries, are Hardouvelis (1994), Gerlach and Smets (1997), Kugler (1997), Evans (2000), and Bekaert and Hodrick (2001). Taken together, these findings suggest that the economic policy environment and investors' attitudes toward the associated risks may be key factors underlying cross-country and cross-time differences in the pattern of the ϕ_{nT}.

It is natural to inquire at this juncture whether small-sample biases explain these findings. After all, short-term interest rates are highly persistent

Table 9.8. The Estimated Slope Coefficients ϕ_{nT} in the Regression of $y_{t+1}^{(n-1)} - y_t^n$ on $(y_t^n - r_t)/(n - 1)$

	Slope coefficients					
Maturity:	12	24	36	48	60	120
Campbell-Shiller (1991)	−0.672	−1.031	−1.210	−1.272	−1.483	−2.263
1952–1978	(0.598)	(0.986)	(1.187)	(1.326)	(1.442)	(1.869)
Campbell-Shiller (1991)	−1.381	−1.815	−2.239	−2.665	−3.099	−5.024
1952–1987	(0.683)	(1.151)	(1.444)	(1.634)	(1.749)	(2.316)
Backus et al. (2001)	−1.425	−1.705	−1.910	−2.147	−2.433	−4.173
1970–1995	(0.825)	(1.120)	(1.295)	(1.418)	(1.519)	(1.985)
Backus et al. data	0.206	−0.001	−0.295	−0.478	−0.566	−0.683
1984–1995	(0.527)	(1.013)	(1.358)	(1.610)	(1.811)	(2.593)

Note: The maturities n are given in months, and estimated standard errors of the ϕ_{nT} are given in parentheses.

and, therefore, the asymptotic distributions may be poor approximations for the actual small-sample distributions. Bekaert et al. (1997) and Backus et al. (2001) examine this issue for the case of $m = 1$, under the assumption that

$$y_{t+1}^1 = \mu + \rho y_t^1 + v_{t+1}. \tag{9.70}$$

Citing Kendall (1954), they note that the least-squares estimate ρ_T of ρ is downward biased and that the bias is larger the larger the magnitude of ρ:

$$E[\rho_T] - \rho \approx -\frac{1 + 3\rho}{T}. \tag{9.71}$$

Moreover, they show these biases translate into a *positive* bias for ϕ_{nT}; $E[\phi_{nT}] - \phi_n > 0$. They conclude that taking account of small-sample biases and their effects on the small-sample distributions of standard test statistics for the null hypothesis $\phi_n = 1$ only heightens the puzzle related to the failure of the EH.

At the heart of this strong statistical evidence against the EH is the underlying predictability of excess returns. Equivalently, as seen by the expression (9.61) for e_t^n, there is evidently time variation in the term premiums c^n and p^n. Cochrane and Piazzesi (2005) have recently revisited the forecasting regressions of Fama and Bliss using the term structure of forward rates instead of just one forward rate. One of their most notable findings is that the coefficients in the projections of excess returns over 1-year holding periods on the 1-year forward rates, $f^{0 \to 1}$ (spot), $f^{1 \to 2}$, $f^{2 \to 3}$, $f^{3 \to 4}$, and $f^{4 \to 5}$, out to 5 years exhibit a tentlike pattern. This pattern is replicated in Figure 9.2a for the unsmoothed Fama-Bliss data (UFB), obtained from CRSP, over the sample period 1970–2000. The similarity in these tentlike responses suggests that there might a single common factor underlying the predictability of excess returns on bonds of all maturities.

However, as illustrated by Figure 9.2b for the smoothed Fama-Bliss data (SFB), this is not a robust feature of zero-coupon bond yields. For these data sets, a "wave" pattern emerges. In the case of the SFB data, for example, the wave pattern loads positively on the 2- and 4-year forward rates and negatively on the 3- and 5-year forward rates. The difference between the UFB and SFB data sets is in how the zero-coupon bond yields are extracted from the underlying observed coupon bond yields. The former method assumes a piecewise constant term structure of forward rates, whereas the SFB data are computed by smoothing out the UFB zero rates using a Nelson and Siegel (1987) exponential spline.

At a minimum, this comparison illustrates that some of the key properties of the spline-implied zero-coupon bond yields are not invariant to the spline method used to compute the zero yields. One interpretation of the

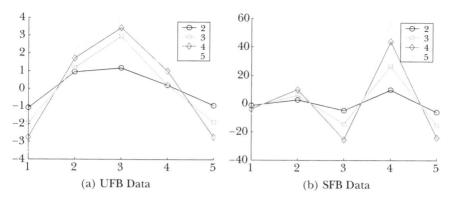

Figure 9.2. *Slope coefficients from the projections of 1-year excess returns on the 1-year forward rates over the sample period 1970–2000. The legend refers to the maturity of the zero-coupon bond used to compute excess returns.*

relatively choppy pattern for the SFB data is that the smoothing inherent in the construction of these data effectively amplifies the contribution of measurement errors. The UFB series also seems problematic in that almost surely the piecewise constant term structure of forward rates used to construct these data is counterfactual. In the light of these differences in results, it seems prudent to explain one's choice of spline methodology when studying zero-coupon bond yields.

Another intriguing feature of the results in Cochrane and Piazzesi (2005) is the relatively high degree of predictability of 1-year excess returns using the five annual forward rates. For the sample period 1970 through 2000, the R^2's from these regressions range between 36 and 39% for the UFB data. The R^2's are only slightly smaller for the smoothed SFB data, ranging between 30 and 32%. This is substantially more predictability than was originally obtained by Fama and Bliss using a single forward rate. It serves to underscore the failure of the EH, which presumes no predictability in excess returns.

The question of which economic models of interest rate behavior give rise to term premiums consistent with these empirical findings is addressed in depth in Chapter 13.

10
Consumption-Based DAPMs

THE CONCEPTUAL FOUNDATIONS for econometric analyses of preference-based, intertemporal asset pricing relations can be traced back to Rubinstein (1976), Lucas (1978), Breeden (1979), and Cox et al. (1985a). They deduced general equilibrium relations among consumption decisions, asset prices, and production decisions in the context of dynamic models under uncertainty. Typically, agents had common information sets and identical preferences, access to a complete set of contingent claims markets, and equal access to all production technologies.

Grossman and Shiller (1981) were the first to study empirically the relation between consumption and asset returns implied by the representative agent models of Rubinstein (1976), Lucas (1978), and Breeden (1979). They focused on the co-movements of consumption and returns in the context of a model in which consumers were risk averse and had perfect foresight about the future. Subsequently, Hansen and Singleton (1982, 1983) developed methods for estimating the parameters of asset pricing relations implied by stochastic dynamic models that incorporate fairly general specifications of concave preference functions.

The primary objectives of this chapter are to provide an overview of the specifications of preference-based DAPMs and to summarize the large body of empirical evidence on the goodness-of-fit of these models. We begin in Section 10.1 with a presentation of the key challenges facing preference-based models using a log-linear setting. This is followed in Section 10.2 by a discussion of alternative methodological approaches to assessing the fit of preference-based models.

The strengths and limitations of time-separable, single-good models in representing the historical co-movements of consumption and real returns on stocks and bonds are explored in Section 10.3. Among the issues addressed are the autocorrelation properties of the disturbances, the sensitivity of the results to the length of the holding period of the investments, and the relation between the average growth in consumption, the average real returns, and the estimated parameters for the postwar period. The findings from this analysis strongly suggest that the single-good, representative agent models are incapable of explaining several important features of asset return data.

A possible explanation for the poor performance of models based on a single nondurable consumption good is that utility is not separable over time with regard to the acquisition of goods. Two motivations for non-time-separability are: (1) some goods are durable in that they provide services over time, and (2) agents exhibit "habit formation" in their consumption choices. Section 10.4 discusses multigood models in which preferences are not separable across consumption goods and at least one of these goods is durable in character. Models based on habit formation, both of the "internal" and "external" varieties, are discussed in Section 10.5.

We then turn, in Section 10.6, to models in which agents are not maximizers of expected utility. The particular departure examined is one in which agents are not indifferent to the timing of the resolution of uncertainty in the economy (Kreps and Porteus, 1978). Section 10.7 briefly discusses recent efforts at assessing the consequences of loss or disappointment aversion, or different belief structures, into preference-based models.

Finally, Section 10.8 discusses bounds on the second moments of marginal rates of substitution proposed by Hansen and Jagannathan (1991) and others. These bounds provide an informative means of assessing the goodness-of-fit of consumption-based models, or indeed of any specification of a pricing kernel in a DAPM. We draw upon this material again in Chapter 11.

10.1. Empirical Challenges Facing DAPMs

We begin, following discussions in Hansen and Singleton (1983) and Campbell (1999), by using the log-linear model of marginal rates of substitution and returns to introduce some of the empirical challenges facing representative-agent, preference-based models, and to motivate some of the specifications that have been proposed in the literature to address these challenges.

Let m_{t+n}^n denote the marginal rate of substitution between consumption at date t and date $t + n$ and let $r_{\ell,t+n}^n$, $\ell = 1, \ldots, L$, denote L n-period holding-period returns on feasible investment strategies.[1] Further, let $x_{t+n}' = (\ln m_{t+n}^n, \ln r_{1,t+n}^n, \ldots, \ln r_{L,t+n}^n)$ and ψ_t denote the information generated by $\{x_s : s \leq t\}$, and suppose that the distribution of x_{t+n} given ψ_t is normal.

---

[1] Examples of investment strategies are: buy and hold an n'-period security for n periods ($n' > n$), or roll over a sequence of short-term securities for n periods.

Then, using reasoning similar to that in Section 9.1, the n-period version of (1.3) conditioned on ψ_t,

$$E\left[m_{t+n}^n r_{\ell,t+n}^n \mid \psi_t\right] = 1, \tag{10.1}$$

implies that

$$E\left[\ln r_{\ell,t+n}^n \mid \psi_t\right] = -E\left[\ln m_{t+n}^n \mid \psi_t\right] - \frac{1}{2}\mathrm{Var}\left[\ln \left(m_{t+n}^n r_{\ell,t+n}^n\right) \mid \psi_t\right]. \tag{10.2}$$

This derivation presumed lognormality without linking this assumption to more fundamental features of an economy. There are surely many economic environments that are consistent with the distributional assumptions underlying (10.2). Rubinstein (1976) and Brock (1980) provide examples, though under admittedly strong assumptions about individual endowment streams. We get a long ways toward rationalizing this setup by assuming that agents have constant relative risk-averse (CRRA) preferences for a single consumption good:

$$U(c_t) = \frac{c_t^\gamma - 1}{\gamma}, \quad \gamma < 1, \tag{10.3}$$

where c_t is the level of consumption and $\alpha \equiv 1 - \gamma$ is the coefficient of relative risk aversion. The marginal rate of substitution for the jth agent, $m_{j,t+n}^n$, is $\beta^n (c_{j,t+n}/c_{jt})^{-\alpha}$. If we are also in an endowment economy in which claims to the endowments of the consumers are traded assets, then in this economy prices are set such that m_{jt}^n can be replaced in (1.3) by the marginal rate of substitution expressed in terms of aggregate consumption, m_t^n (see Chapter 8). Furthermore, aggregate consumption equals the aggregate endowment ($\Sigma c_{jt} = \Sigma y_{jt}$), the price of a claim to the aggregate endowment flow from period t forward is proportional to $\Sigma_j y_{jt}$, and the price of an n-period pure discount bond is $E_t[m_{t+n}^n]$.[2] Therefore, the lognormality of m_t^n is implied by lognormality of the aggregate endowment.

For one-period ($n = 1$) returns:

$$
\begin{aligned}
E\left[\ln r_{t+1}^1 \mid \psi_t\right] = {} & -E\left[\ln m_{t+1}^1 \mid \psi_t\right] - \frac{1}{2}\mathrm{Var}\left[\ln m_{t+1}^1 \mid \psi_t\right] \\
& - \frac{1}{2}\mathrm{Var}\left[\ln r_{t+1}^1 \mid \psi_t\right] - \mathrm{Cov}\left[\ln m_{t+1}^1, \ln r_{t+1} \mid \psi_t\right].
\end{aligned} \tag{10.4}
$$

If we assume that there is a traded, one-period riskless asset with return r_t^f, a special case of (10.4) is

---

[2] The equilibrium prices for this economy can be derived using arguments similar to those in Brock's (1980) discussion of a production economy with log utility.

$$\ln r_t^f = -E\left[\ln m_{t+1}^1 \mid \psi_t\right] - \frac{1}{2}\mathrm{Var}\left[\ln m_{t+1}^1 \mid \psi_t\right]. \tag{10.5}$$

Subtracting (10.5) from (10.4) gives the following expression for the expected one-period excess returns on risky assets:

$$
\begin{aligned}
E\left[\ln r_{t+1}^1 - \ln r_t^f \mid \psi_t\right] + \frac{1}{2}\mathrm{Var}\left[\ln r_{t+1}^1 \mid \psi_t\right] = \\
- \mathrm{Cov}\left[\ln m_{t+1}^1, \ln r_{t+1}^1 \mid \psi_t\right].
\end{aligned}
\tag{10.6}
$$

According to (10.6), the expected (log) excess return on a risky asset is determined by the asset return's covariance with the representative agent's marginal rate of substitution. An asset is relatively risky when its return is high at the same time that an agent's ability to consume is high (owing to high financial wealth or labor income) and low when wealth is low.[3] That the signs in (10.6) support this interpretation is perhaps most easily seen by considering the special case of constant relative risk-averse preferences (10.3) for which

$$\ln m_{t+1}^1 = \ln \beta + (\gamma - 1)(\ln c_{t+1} - \ln c_t). \tag{10.7}$$

Since $\gamma < 1$, $(\gamma - 1) < 0$. Also, $\ln \beta < 0$. A larger value of $\ln c_{t+1}$ tends to make $\ln m_{t+1}^1$ smaller (and, typically, in a growing economy, more negative). If, at the same time, $\ln r_{t+1}^1$ is large, then there is a large negative covariance between $\ln m_{t+1}^1$ and $\ln r_{t+1}^1$. With the minus sign in (10.6), this pattern induces a relatively large positive excess return on the risky asset.

The challenge for preference-based models is to induce sufficient correlation between consumption growth and returns to generate the levels of excess returns observed on average in the risky financial markets. If this covariance is small, then we see from (10.6) and (10.7) that the risk-aversion parameter γ must be correspondingly large in order to match the expected excess return. As we will see, consumption growth and asset returns do indeed tend to have low correlations, so the requisite value of γ is typically (implausibly) large. This finding has come to be called the "equity premium puzzle" (e.g., Mehra and Prescott, 1985).

Hansen and Singleton (1983) tested the log-linear model with constant conditional variances by examining the implied restrictions on the bivariate vector-autoregressive representation of the logarithms of stock index returns and $\ln(c_{t+n}/c_t)$. These restrictions were tested for various combinations of returns and the results provided substantial evidence against

---

[3] The presence of the conditional variance of the return is due to Jensen's inequality and our expressing the Euler equation in logarithms.

their models using monthly data on real returns for aggregate and industry-average stock portfolios and Treasury bills. Ferson (1983) also provides evidence against this model using quarterly data. Together, these findings suggest that to explain the behavior of the conditional means of asset returns, we must relax some or all of the restrictions that: (1) agents have constant relative risk-averse preferences over a single good, (2) returns and consumption growth are jointly lognormal, or (3) conditional variances of returns and the pricing kernel are constants.

Note that within this lognormal setting, tests based on the difference between the logarithms of returns accommodate certain types of unobserved shocks to preferences. Let preferences be given by

$$U(c_t) = \frac{(c_t \varepsilon_t)^\gamma - 1}{\gamma}, \tag{10.8}$$

where ε_t is a taste shock that may be serially correlated. For this model, $m_{t+n}^n = \beta^n [(c_{t+n} \varepsilon_{t+n})/(c_t \varepsilon_t)]^{\gamma-1}$ is a nonlinear function of the unobserved taste shocks. However, under the assumption of lognormal shocks, $\ln m_{t+n}^n$ cancels from the difference $E[\ln r_{\ell,t+n}^n - \ln r_{k,t+n}^n \mid \psi_t]$. Therefore, the conclusions reached by Hansen and Singleton (1983) also apply to this model.

Corresponding to the equity premium puzzle is the "riskfree rate puzzle" first emphasized by Weil (1989). The logarithm of the riskless rate is

$$\ln r_t^f = -\ln \beta + (1-\gamma)E[\ln(c_{t+1}/c_t) \mid \psi_t]$$
$$- \frac{(1-\gamma)^2}{2} \mathrm{Var}[\ln(c_{t+1}/c_t) \mid \psi_t]. \tag{10.9}$$

In a growing economy, the expected (log) consumption growth is positive. Therefore, a high level of risk aversion is consistent with the historically observed low levels of the riskless interest rate only if either β is very near unity (agents are *unwilling* to substitute intertemporally) or, with large variability in consumption growth, the precautionary savings captured by the last term is high enough to offset the positive effects of expected growth on riskfree returns.

Campbell (1999) sheds further light on these issues by connecting this log-linear pricing relation with the linear present-value model of Campbell and Shiller (1988), obtained by linearizing the logarithm of the sum of the price P_t and dividend D_t of a common stock. Letting lower case letters represent the corresponding logarithms of these variables, Campbell and Shiller obtained

$$p_t - d_t = \frac{k}{1-\rho} + \sum_{j=0}^{\infty} \rho^j E_t [\Delta d_{t+1+j} - r_{t+1+j}], \tag{10.10}$$

where $r_t \equiv \ln[(P_t + D_t)/P_t]$ and k and ρ are constants with $1 > \rho > 0$, the latter being measured as the exponential of the difference between the average dividend growth rate and the stock return. Focusing on the "aggregate wealth" portfolio with dividend $d_t^c = \phi c_t$, substituting the corresponding version of (10.5) into (10.10), and using (10.7), gives

$$p_t^c - d_t^c = \frac{k^c}{1 - \rho} + (\phi - \alpha) \sum_{j=0}^{\infty} \rho^j E_t[\Delta c_{t+1+j}], \qquad (10.11)$$

where $\alpha \equiv (1 - \gamma)$ is the coefficient of relative risk aversion. From (10.11) we see that the volatility of the (logarithm of) the price-dividend ratio is induced, within this model, by volatility of a smoothed average of *expected* future consumption growth. Using the descriptive statistics in Campbell (1999), we find that postwar volatility in quarterly consumption growth in the United States has been about 0.005, and that volatility in expected consumption growth has necessarily been lower, perhaps much lower. By comparison, volatility of quarterly ($p_t - d_t$), as measured by the MSCI index, is 0.265. Clearly, in this model, to achieve this level of volatility in ($p_t - d_t$) requires either a very large multiplier ϕ (with low risk aversion) or a very high level of risk aversion (with a small multiplier). This observation is sometimes referred to as the "volatility puzzle."

10.2. Assessing Goodness-of-Fit

Researchers have pursued a variety of different approaches to testing the restrictions implied by consumption-based DAPMs. Among the differences in these approaches is the amount of information about the structure of the economy that is called upon to restrict the distribution of asset returns. To set up our subsequent discussion of the empirical literature we briefly introduce two of the most widely followed strategies.

10.2.1. Euler Equation-Based Tests

Perhaps the most widely used approach to testing preference-based models is to construct estimators and tests of overidentifying restrictions using the conditional moment restrictions (1.3) or (10.1) implied by the first-order conditions of agents' intertemporal optimization problems.

Assuming that m_t^n is specified parametrically as a function of observed state variables and an unknown parameter vector, GMM estimation is feasible. For instance, Hansen and Singleton (1982), Dunn and Singleton (1983), and Brown and Gibbons (1985) investigated single-good economies in which agents have CRRA preferences over a single consumption good as in (10.3). For an n-period investment horizon the stochastic Euler equation underlying these studies is

$$E\big[\beta^n(c_{t+n}/c_t)^{\gamma-1}r_{t+n}^n \mid \mathcal{A}_t\big] = 1. \tag{10.12}$$

Interpreting the variable

$$u_{t+n} = \beta^n(c_{t+n}/c_t)^{\gamma-1}r_{t+n}^n - 1 \tag{10.13}$$

as the disturbance for an econometric analysis, Hansen and Singleton (1982) show how to use the fact that $E[u_{t+n} \mid \mathcal{A}_t] = 0$ to construct instrumental variables estimators of the unknown parameters (β, σ) and to test overidentifying restrictions implied by (10.12).

Specifically, (10.12) implies that $E[u_{t+n}w_t] = 0$, for all $w_t \in \mathcal{I}_t$, and therefore elements of agents' information set at date t that are also observed by the econometrician (the information set $\mathcal{I}_t$) can be used as instrumental variables for the disturbance u_{t+n}. The dimension of the parameter space Θ in this case is $K = 2$ and $\theta_0' = (\beta_0, \gamma_0)$. After selecting an $s \times 1$ instrument vector w_t, $s \geq 2$, to be used in estimation, $h(z_t, \theta)$ in (2.32) is set to $h(z_t, \theta) = u_{t+n}w_t$ and θ_T is chosen by minimizing the quadratic form (2.36). The distance matrix W_T is typically chosen optimally as discussed in Chapter 3, in this case according to Case $\mathrm{AC}h(n)$. If $s > 2$, then there are $s-2$ independent linear combinations of the s orthogonality conditions that are not set to zero in estimation, but that should be close to zero if the model is true. These overidentifying restrictions can be tested using the chi-square goodness-of-fit statistic discussed in Section 4.1 and it is this test to which we refer when reporting test results later in this chapter.

These tests of (10.12) accommodate heterogeneity across consumers in the sense that agents may have different endowment processes, yet, so long as they have identical preferences, pricing can proceed as if there is a representative agent consuming aggregate consumption. (See the discussion of aggregation in Chapter 8.) These analyses are also robust to certain econometric difficulties. In particular, the model accommodates geometric growth in real per-capita consumption over time, since only the ratio (c_{t+n}/c_t) appears in (10.12). Moreover, the disturbance u_{t+n} may be conditionally heteroskedastic; that is, $\mathrm{Var}[u_{t+n} \mid \mathcal{A}_t]$ may be an essentially arbitrary function of the elements of agents' information set $\mathcal{A}_t$. Thus the model allows for the possibility that the volatilities of stock and bond returns vary across different stages of the business cycle.

Essentially the same steps can be followed to construct GMM-based tests of more complicated models, say in which m_t^n depends on multiple state variables, so long as there is an observable counterpart to the entire state vector. The resulting tests are robust in the important sense that very little structure is being imposed on the joint distribution of m_t^n and returns. One need only be certain that sufficient regularity is imposed to ensure consistency and asymptotic normality along the lines of the discussion in Chapter 3.

10.2.2. Toward a More Complete Model

Many researchers have gone beyond the Euler equations and imposed additional structure on the distributions of the exogenous forcing variables, the production process, or agents' budget constraints that underlie the determination of consumptions and asset returns. A primary goal in working with more fully specified models is to understand better how equilibrium consumptions and returns are affected by different assumptions about these features of an economy. There has been considerable interest, for example, in the implications of highly persistent components of exogenous factors for the joint distributions of consumptions and returns, particularly when agents are risk averse.

As we illustrated in Chapter 6, with a sufficiently completely specified economic model, SME estimation is feasible. Sample moments computed using data simulated from a DAPM can be compared to their counterparts computed using historical data to formally estimate and test the model of interest. Heaton (1995) and Bansal et al. (2004) are examples of studies that have used an SME to study preference-based models.

More often, however, those studies that have reached beyond Euler equations have stopped short of formal implementation of GMM or ML methods in estimation or testing. Rather, the parameters are often *calibrated* to the data by matching certain moments in the data to their counterparts in the model by choice of the model's parameters. Researchers have included many of the key moments underlying the empirical challenges outlined in Section 10.1. But they often stop short of matching the richer sets of moments that would emerge from standard auxiliary models underlying "efficient" SME estimation (see Section 6.6).

Furthermore, researchers have often worked with what are surely oversimplified specifications of the exogenous risk factors in the economies being examined. As a consequence, the co-dependence among key variables in the models may be exaggerated. An extreme example of this last point is a model with CRRA preferences (10.3) in which the nature of uncertainty impinging on the economy is such that the ratio of consumption to wealth is constant. [Parametric examples of such economies are examined in Brock (1980), Michner (1984), and Bakshi and Chen (1996).] In such an economy, the growth rate in aggregate consumption and the return on the aggregate wealth portfolio are perfectly correlated. Yet, as we discussed in Section 10.1, one of the major puzzles facing preference-based models is the relatively weak historical correlation between consumption growth and returns. A related recurring example is the tendency for there to be excessive volatility in some asset returns in models that do give rise to more plausibly low correlations between consumption growth and returns.

Regardless of how the unknown parameters are initially calibrated, an advantage of working with relatively completely specified models is that researchers can explore how changes in an economic environment affect the joint distributions of asset returns and consumptions. In particular, one can easily examine parameterizations that are outside those supported by available data. This may be particularly informative when the sample period available for empirical analysis is not fully representative of the cyclical or secular patterns in the economy being investigated. In such circumstances, dependence on formal, within-sample econometric tests alone may give rise to misleading conclusions about the joint distribution of m_t^n and returns.

Taken together, these observations point to strengths and weaknesses of both approaches to model assessment. Euler equation-based tests are in principle more robust but, by their nature, reliable inference is highly dependent on having a representative historical sample. More fully specified models allow experimentation with alternative formulations of economies and, perhaps, analysis of processes that are more representative of history for which data are not readily available. They also lead to more efficient estimators under the null hypothesis of a correctly specified model. On the more cautionary side, working with parametric specifications of the risk factors may lead to counterfactual co-dependence among the variables in a model. The oversimplification imposed by either the limitations of economic theory or the demands of computational tractability could leave researchers with misleading impressions about what economic factors are key to understanding the weaknesses of extant models.

Up to this point we have presumed that all of the state-dependent components of m_t^n are observed by the econometrician undertaking the empirical analysis. If in fact there are unobserved taste shocks, then Euler-equation methods for analyzing DTSMs are typically no longer feasible.[4] This is because the moment conditions that would be used in estimation involve unobserved variables. Estimation is nevertheless still feasible if one is willing to impose additional structure on the exogenous variables in the model, including the latest shocks to preferences. In particular, the SME estimator described in Chapter 6 is well suited to this estimation problem.

The empirical literature on preference-based DAPMs involving state-dependent preference shocks is quite limited. Most of the work that has been done has been based on calibrations or, even more commonly, on simulations from hypothetical economies. We briefly discuss this research in Section 10.7.

10.3. Time-Separable Single-Good Models

We begin our empirical assessment of preference-based DAPMs with the case of a single-good economy in which the consumption good is non-

---

[4] As we have already seen, there are exceptions to this statement. Such exceptions most often arise when sufficient structure is imposed on the joint distribution of consumptions and taste shocks to allow the researcher to substitute out for the latent variables.

durable. This environment is sufficiently rich to gain substantial insight into the degree to which representative agent models of intertemporal consumption and investment decisions are consistent with the historical time paths of aggregate consumption and real returns.

Assuming a representative agent with CRRA preferences, Hansen and Singleton (1984) found that relation (10.12) is generally not supported by the data on aggregate stock and Treasury bill returns for the period January 1959 through December 1978. When consumption was measured as National Income and Product Accounts (NIPA) "nondurables plus services" and the monthly return ($n = 1$) was either the value-weighted or equally weighted return on the NYSE, the probability values of the chi-square test statistics were typically larger than 0.1. However, for several return-instrument pairs, the estimate of the parameter γ was outside the concave region of the parameter space (i.e., $\gamma_T > 1$). Much more evidence against the model was found with combinations of returns (several stock returns or stock and bill returns). The probability values of the test statistics were typically less than 0.01 and γ_T was again greater than unity.

Similar findings are reported in Dunn and Singleton (1986) for real returns on several investment strategies using Treasury bills. The principal difference is that they also find substantial evidence against the model for individual returns on bills, as well as combinations of returns. Finally, using a different approach, Mehra and Prescott (1985) calculate the equity premiums implied by their equilibrium model for a range of plausible values for the riskfree rate and with the second moments of consumption fixed at the values of the sample second moments for the period 1889–1978. They find that their model does not produce an average excess return (over the riskfree return) on an equity-type security that is as large as the average excess returns observed historically in equity markets.

There are, of course, many possible explanations for these findings, including the misspecification of the agents' objective function and constraint set, mismeasurement of consumption, misspecification of the decision interval and associated problems with temporal aggregation, and the omission of taxes. If there is mismeasurement of aggregate consumption, then estimates of the autocorrelation function of nondurable goods and the correlations between consumptions and returns may be severely biased. This in turn may explain why sample versions of the orthogonality conditions $E[u_{t+n}w_t] = 0$, $w_t \in \mathcal{I}_t$, cannot be made close to zero for values of (β, γ) in the admissible region of the parameter space. This bias can be alleviated somewhat by working with monthly data point sampled at long intervals. That is, instead of using monthly returns one would use longer-term securities so that $m_{t+n}^n = \beta^n (c_{t+n}/c_t)^{\gamma-1}$ involves monthly consumptions sampled at widely separated points in time. Singleton (1990) explored this possibility for the returns VWRn and TBILLn, with the former computed by rolling over n 1-month investments in the value-weighted NYSE index and the latter being the (real) return on the n-month Treasury bill. He found that, for Treasury bill returns, the fit of the model tended to improve as the maturity was lengthened. Not only did the test statistics decline, but the coefficient of relative risk aversion increased to a value closer to logarithmic utility ($\gamma = 0$). In spite of this improvement in fit, the goodness-of-fit statistic remained large for TBILL12.

The pattern of results for the stock returns was altogether different. For the 1- and 6-month returns, γ_T was well outside the concave region of the parameter space. Correspondingly, the chi-square statistics were very small relative to their degrees of freedom. In contrast, for VWR12, γ_T was within the concave region of the parameter space, though again there was no strong evidence against the model. Overall, there was no systematic improvement in fit across stock and bill returns as n was increased, which suggests that mismeasurement that distorts primarily the low-order autocorrelations of consumption growth is not the explanation for previous findings.

This analysis does highlight several systematic differences in the estimates when either the holding period n or the type of security (stock or bond) is varied. In an attempt to gain some insight into these differences, we examine the autocorrelation properties of the variables comprising this single-good model. An immediate implication of (10.12) is that the disturbance (10.13) follows a moving average process of order $(n-1)$ [see Hansen and Singleton (1982) and the discussion of Case $ACh(n)$ in Chapter 3]. This is an implication of the fact that u_{t+n} is in agents' information set at date $t+n$ and $E[u_{t+n}|\mathcal{I}_t] = 0$. It follows that if the model is correct, then the autocorrelation properties of $\beta^n(c_{t+n}/c_t)^{\gamma-1}$ and r_{t+n} must interact in a manner that leads to an $MA(n-1)$ representation for their product.

The moving average representations of (c_{t+6}/c_t), TBILL6, VWR6, and the corresponding versions of the disturbance (10.13) (u_{t+6}^{T6} and u_{t+6}^{V6} for TBILL6 and VWR6, respectively) reported in Singleton (1990) are shown in Table 10.1. The coefficients in the MA representation for u_{t+6}^{T6} are significantly different from zero at the 2% level out to lag 7.[5] Thus, the implication of the theory that this disturbance follows an $MA(5)$ process seems contrary to the evidence. Moreover, disturbance u_{t+6}^{T6} is inheriting the autocorrelation properties of TBILL6; compare the coefficients in the third and fourth columns of Table 10.1 to each other and to those for the consumption ratio in the second column.

Next, consider the results for VWR6. Again, u_{t+6}^{V6} seems to be inheriting the autocorrelation properties of the return (in this case VWR6) and not

[5] The standard errors displayed in Table 10.1 should be interpreted with caution for at least two reasons. First, the disturbances u_{t+6}^{T6} and u_{t+6}^{V6} involve estimated parameters and the standard errors have not been adjusted for the randomness in the first-stage estimates. (See Section 4.4 for a discussion of this issue.) Second, the shocks underlying the MA representation may be conditionally heteroskedastic.

Table 10.1. *Moving Average Representations of Variables in the Single-Good Models (August 1963–December 1978)*

Lag	(c_{t+6}/c_t)	TBILL6	u^{T6}_{t+6}	VWR6	u^{V6}_{t+6}	u^{T12}_{t+12}
			Dependent variable			
1	0.7883^*	1.023^*	1.005^*	1.020^*	1.086^*	1.015^*
	(0.085)	(0.081)	(0.079)	(0.079)	(0.080)	(0.083)
2	0.7823^*	1.015^*	0.966^*	0.911^*	1.124^*	0.948^*
	(0.101)	(0.114)	(0.111)	(0.115)	(0.119)	(0.118)
3	1.118^*	1.114^*	1.062^*	0.209	0.430^*	1.052^*
	(0.129)	(0.137)	(0.131)	(0.137)	(0.150)	(0.141)
4	1.030^*	0.974^*	0.944^*	0.160	0.279	0.952^*
	(0.127)	(0.146)	(0.140)	(0.136)	(0.153)	(0.164)
5	0.072^*	0.932^*	0.891^*	0.265	0.319	0.919^*
	(0.131)	(0.146)	(0.140)	(0.138)	(0.153)	(0.179)
6	0.143	0.451^*	0.458^*	0.149	0.129	0.734^*
	(0.122)	(0.137)	(0.132)	(0.137)	(0.151)	(0.180)
7	0.336^*	0.284^{**}	0.279^{**}	-0.284	0.131	0.534^*
	(0.130)	(0.115)	(0.111)	(0.115)	(0.120)	(0.190)
8	0.252^*	0.067	0.087	-0.199^{**}	-0.167	0.446^{**}
	(0.085)	(0.081)	(0.079)	(0.080)	(0.082)	(0.179)
9						0.277
						(0.164)
10						0.244
						(0.141)
11						0.187
						(0.117)
12						0.013
						(0.082)
Constant	1.021	1.003	0.0015	1.003	0.0009	-0.0013
	(0.0017)	(0.0018)	(0.0016)	(0.012)	(0.016)	(0.0042)
R^2	0.724	0.847	0.851	0.678	0.732	0.877

Note: Standard errors are displayed in parentheses. A *($**$) denotes a coefficient that is significantly different from zero at the 1% (2%) level based on a two-sided test and the standard normal distribution. The variables u^{T6}_{t+6}, u^{V6}_{t+6}, and u^{T12}_{t+12} are the versions of the disturbance (10.12) for the returns TBILL6, VWR6, and TBILL12, respectively.
Source: Singleton (1990).

that of the consumption ratio. Though, in contrast to the results for TBILL6, the return VWR6 and u^{V6}_{t+6} exhibit only low-order serial correlation, much less correlation than is implied by an MA(5) process.

The findings that the disturbances are inheriting the autocorrelation properties of the returns may well explain why the probability value of the test statistic for TBILL6 is much larger than the test statistic for VWR6—the disturbance u^{T6}_{t+6} exhibits too much autocorrelation, whereas the disturbance u^{V6}_{t+6} exhibits less autocorrelation than might be expected from the theory. Additional evidence consistent with this interpretation appears in the last column of Table 10.1. The MA representation for the disturbance u_{t+12}^{T12} associated with TBILL12 indicates that there is not significant autocorrelation beyond lag 8, whereas the theory accommodates correlation out to lag 11. At the same time, the probability value of the chi-square statistic for TBILL12 is relatively small. In sum, it is the autocorrelation properties of the returns that largely explain the differences in test statistics both across maturity, holding fixed the type of security, and across types of securities. In part, this is a reflection of relatively low volatility of consumption growth and its low correlation with returns.

It is instructive to relate these findings to the consumption/return puzzles discussed in the context of Hansen and Singleton's (1983) log-linear DAPM. Recall that key to matching historical (conditionally) expected excess returns on risky securities is having sufficient covariation between the risky returns and agents' marginal rates of substitution [see (10.6)]. There is an analogous expression for the conditional mean of u_{t+n} given by (10.12). Specifically, we let y_t^n denote the yield to maturity on an n-period riskless zero-coupon bond, (10.12) can be rewritten as[6]

$$\left(1 + y_t^n\right)^n E_t[u_{t+n}] = \left(1 + y_t^n\right)^n \text{Cov}_t\left(\beta^n \left(\frac{c_{t+n}}{c_t}\right)^{\gamma - 1}, r_{t+n}^n\right)$$

$$+ E_t\left[r_{t+n}^n\right] - \left(1 + y_t^n\right)^n. \tag{10.14}$$

The finding that u_{t+n} is inheriting the autocorrelation of the return suggests that most of the variation on the right-hand side of (10.14) is due to variation in $E_t[r_{t+n}^n]$. In other words, the findings in Table 10.1 are evidently a manifestation of the failure of this single-good model to generate sufficient variation in m_{t+n}^n and covariation $\text{Cov}_t(m_{t+n}^n, r_{t+n}^n)$ to explain the mean excess returns on the securities examined.[7] For example, during the sample period August 1963 through December 1978, (c_{t+6}/c_t) showed little tendency to deviate from its average value. While in principle β and γ can be chosen to match the excess mean return on one particular portfolio, the evidence suggests that this model particularly has difficulty matching the excess returns on different equity portfolios simultaneously. The persistence in bond returns raises additional challenges for this single-good model.

Singleton (1990) also found striking differences in the point estimates of (β_0, γ_0) across bills and stocks. Whenever β_T exceeds unity, γ_T is less than

---

[6] Here we are using the fact that $E_t[m_{t+n}^n] = 1/(1+y_t^n)^n$ is the price of a riskless n-period zero-coupon bond.

[7] We formalize this intuition about insufficient volatility in m_t^n in Section 10.8, where we derive bounds on the volatility of m_t^n.

unity and vice versa. The results in the previous studies of this model display a similar pattern. Heuristically, this finding can be interpreted as follows. Taking the unconditional expectation of (10.12) gives

$$E\left[\beta^n (c_{t+n}/c_t)^{\gamma-1} r^n_{t+n}\right] = 1. \tag{10.15}$$

The estimation algorithm selects estimates of β_0 and γ_0 so as to make sample versions of the moment conditions, including (10.15), as close to zero as possible. Suppose then that estimates of β_0 and γ_0 are chosen as if (c_{t+n}/c_t) is fixed at its mean value, say μ_{cn}. Then, in order to satisfy (10.15), β and γ should be chosen such that $\delta_n = \beta^n (\mu_{cn})^{\gamma-1} E[r_{t+n}]$ approximately equals unity. For his sample period, $\mu_{c6} = 1.0133$. The mean of TBILL6 is 1.0035 and the estimated value of $\hat{\beta}^6 = 1.0012$. Thus, a value of γ_T less than unity is required to make δ_n close to unity. Similarly, the mean of VWR6 is 1.0047 and the estimated value of $\hat{\beta}^6$ is 0.9564, which is consistent with a value of γ_T that is much larger than unity.

These observations do not explain why there is a pattern of β_T being less than unity for the value-weighted return on the NYSE and β_T being greater than unity for returns on Treasury bills. The correlations between consumption growth and the log dividend-price ratio reported in Campbell and Shiller (1989) provide one possible explanation. In all of their vector autoregressions, a high log dividend-price ratio at the beginning of a year predicted low consumption growth over the year. The association of low consumption growth with a high one-period discount rate on common stocks requires γ to be larger than unity.

All of these studies presume that consumption is being reliably measured. With the imposition of some additional structure on agents' preferences, some of the potential measurement problems with consumption can be avoided.[8] Specifically, Rubinstein (1976) showed that if agents have logarithmic utility, then for certain production and exchange economies, the intertemporal marginal rate of substitution of consumption is proportional to the inverse of the total return on the aggregate wealth portfolio. In these economic environments, agents' first-order conditions for their optimal investments decisions include

$$E\left[r^n_{t+n}/r^{wn}_{t+n} \mid I_t\right] = k_n, \tag{10.16}$$

---

[8] An altogether different approach to avoiding the need for consumption data is to use a linearization of agents' intertemporal budget constraint to derive an expression for consumption in terms of wealth and the conditional moments of asset returns. In this manner Campbell (1993) obtained an (approximate) DAPM in which agents have CRRA preferences and the testable restrictions are expressed in terms of market returns.

where r_{t+n}^{wn} is the n-period return on the wealth portfolio and k_n is a constant that depends on n.[9] Conveniently, (10.16) depends on returns alone; in particular, a measure of consumption is not needed for estimation or inference.

Hansen et al. (1982) and Brown and Gibbons (1985) studied relation (10.16) empirically using the value-weighted return on the NYSE (VWRn) as a measure of r_{t+n}^{wn}. The former study tested the implication of (10.16) that the ratios of returns r_{t+n}^n / r_{t+n}^{wn} are serially uncorrelated using returns on individual stocks. For an economy in which there is a single nondurable good and VWRn is an accurate measure of the return r_{t+n}^{wn}, this test avoids the problems of temporal aggregation, and measurement of consumption or the deflator (to compute real returns) as $(r_{t+n}^n / r_{t+n}^{wn})$ can be formed as the ratio of two nominal returns. Their results also suggest that the model underlying (10.16) is not consistent with the data.

Another consideration is taxes. Their omission works in favor of, not against, the model. If r_{t+n}^n is replaced by an after-tax real return, then on average this return is lower than the unadjusted return. This in turn means that, for a given mean μ_{cn}, β has to exceed unity by an even wider margin for the condition (10.15) to be satisfied in the sample. In the context of a model with leisure, Eichenbaum et al. (1988) estimated the parameters of the corresponding Euler equations using before and after tax real returns on Treasury bills. Consistent with this discussion, they found that in both cases β_T exceeded unity and β_T was much larger when after tax real returns were used.

10.4. Models with Durable Goods

A potentially important source of misspecification in the models examined so far is the omission of goods that are durable (provide services over time). Durability may be an issue for two reasons. First, the misclassification of goods in the NIPA as being nondurable on a monthly basis is potentially important, because it may distort both the autocorrelation properties of consumption growth, as well as the mean and variance of consumption. In the NIPA, goods are classified as nondurable if they have a typical lifetime of less than 3 years. Clearly, many of the goods called nondurable should be considered durable for the purpose of analyses of models with monthly or quarterly decision intervals. Second, there is an important second category of goods labeled "durable" in the NIPA, and utility from these goods has so far been assumed to be separable from the utility from nondurable goods.

---

[9] The assumption of logarithmic utility can be replaced by the more general assumption of constant relative risk-averse utility, but at the expense of assuming independently and identically distributed growth rates in consumption over time.

The nonseparability of preferences across these two categories of goods may also affect the time-series properties of m_t^n.

10.4.1. Durability in Single-Good Models

A convenient parameterization of preferences that accommodates the possibility of durability is

$$U(s_t) = \left[s_t^\gamma - 1 \right] / \gamma, \qquad s_t = A(L)e_t, \quad \gamma < 1, \qquad (10.17)$$

where $A(L) = \sum_{\tau=0}^\infty a_\tau L^\tau$ is a scalar lag polynomial with $a_0 = 1$, and, in equilibrium, c_t equals the aggregate endowment of the good, e_t. Positive values of the a_τ imply that acquisitions of goods in the past continue to provide services in the current period; that is, the good is durable. Tests of the overidentifying restrictions implied by this model have been based on the Euler equation

$$E\left[\sum_{\tau=0}^\infty a_\tau \beta^\tau (s_{t+\tau})^{\gamma-1} \Big| \mathcal{A}_t \right] = E\left[\left(\sum_{\tau=0}^\infty a_\tau \beta^{\tau+1} (s_{t+\tau+1})^{\gamma-1} \right) r_{t+1} \Big| \mathcal{A}_t \right]. \quad (10.18)$$

Dunn and Singleton (1986) and Eichenbaum and Hansen (1990) considered the similar case of durable goods with $s_t = c_t + \psi c_{t-1}$. Consumption was measured as monthly NIPA nondurables plus services over the period 1959:1–1985:12. Exponential growth was accommodated in this economy by scaling both sides of (10.18) by $c_t^{\gamma-1}$, which led to the econometric MA(1) disturbance

$$u_{t+2} = \sum_{\tau=0}^1 a_\tau \beta^\tau (s_{t+\tau}/c_t)^{\gamma-1} - \left[\sum_{\tau=0}^1 a_\tau \beta^{\tau+1} (s_{t+\tau+1}/c_t)^{\gamma-1} \right] r_{t+1}^1. \quad (10.19)$$

The estimated value of a_1 was positive, consistent with the presumption that "nondurables plus services" provide consumption services over time. However, the probability value of the chi-square statistic for this model was 0.001 indicating that the introduction of nontime separability did not markedly improve the fit.

Additional evidence on the goodness-of-fit of single-good models with durability is presented in Gallant and Tauchen (1989). They considered a flexible approximation to a general, scaled period utility function of the form

$$U \left(c_t / c_{t-1}, \, c_{t-1} / c_{t-2}, \, \ldots, \, c_{t-\ell} / c_{t-\ell-1} \right). \qquad (10.20)$$

Their point estimates were consistent with a positive value of a_1 (durability of goods). However, as in previous studies, when stock and bond returns were studied simultaneously they found that the overidentifying restrictions implied by the Euler equations were not supported by the data.

10.4.2. Incorporating Durable and Nondurable Goods

There are notable co-movements in durable goods purchases and the levels of interest rates. Accordingly, if we introduce the services from durable goods into the model explicitly and assume that utility from the services of NIPA nondurable and durable goods are not separable, the model may better represent the "consumption risk" inherent in asset returns. Preference specifications that allow for this possibility were studied by Dunn and Singleton (1986), Eichenbaum and Hansen (1990), Ferson and Constantinides (1991), and Heaton (1995), among others. Their models are nested within the following specification of utility defined over two service flows:

$$U(s_{jt}) = \frac{\left(c_t^*\right)^{\gamma\delta}\left(d_t^*\right)^{\gamma(1-\delta)} - 1}{\gamma}, \tag{10.21}$$

where c^* and d^* are the service flows from nondurable and durable consumption goods, and the service technologies are given by

$$\begin{bmatrix} c_t^* \\ d_t^* \end{bmatrix} = \begin{bmatrix} A_{11}(L) & 0 \\ 0 & \theta(1-\theta L)^{-1} \end{bmatrix} \begin{bmatrix} c_t \\ d_t \end{bmatrix}, \tag{10.22}$$

where c_t and d_t are the endowments of nondurable goods plus services and durable goods, respectively, as defined in the NIPA of the United States, and $A_{11}(L)$ is a polynomial in the lag operator.

Substituting (10.22) into (10.21) gives an indirect period utility function defined over acquisitions of goods. Define the marginal utilities with respect to the services as

$$\text{MN}_t^* = \beta^t\delta\left(c_t^*\right)^{\gamma\delta-1}\left(d_t^*\right)^{\gamma(1-\delta)} \tag{10.23}$$

$$\text{MD}_t^* = \beta^t(1-\delta)\left(c_t^*\right)^{\gamma\delta}\left(d_t^*\right)^{\gamma(1-\delta)-1}. \tag{10.24}$$

Then the partial derivatives of $\sum_{t=0}^{\infty}\beta^t U(c_t^*, d_t^*)$ with respect to c_t and d_t, respectively, are given by

$$\text{MN}_t = E\left[A_{11}\left(L^{-1}\right)\text{MN}_t^* \mid \mathcal{A}_t\right], \tag{10.25}$$

$$\text{MD}_t = E\left[A_{22}\left(L^{-1}\right)\text{MD}_t^* \mid \mathcal{A}_t\right]. \tag{10.26}$$

The first-order conditions of the representative agent's intertemporal optimum problem imply that equilibrium acquisitions of goods and their relative price w_t (price of durables in terms of nondurable goods) satisfy

$$w_t \mathrm{MN}_t = \mathrm{MD}_t. \tag{10.27}$$

Substituting (10.25) and (10.26) into (10.27) and rearranging gives

$$
\begin{aligned}
E\Big[w_t \big\{ A_{11}\big(\beta L^{-1}\big)\big\{ \delta\big[A_{11}(L)c_t\big]^{\gamma\delta-1}\big[A_{22}(L)d_t\big]^{(1-\delta)\gamma}\big\}\big\} \\
- A_{22}\big(\beta L^{-1}\big)\big\{(1-\delta)\big[A_{11}(L)c_t\big]^{\gamma\delta}\big[A_{22}(L)d_t\big]^{(1-\delta)\gamma-1}\big\}\Big| \mathcal{A}_t \Big] = 0.
\end{aligned}
\tag{10.28}
$$

While versions of this intratemporal pricing relation have been studied in the literature on consumption-leisure choices,[10] this relation among optimal purchases of goods and their relative prices has received little attention in the asset pricing literature.

Most of the attention has been focused on the implied relations between consumptions and asset returns. If the consumer can trade an n-period asset with a price of one unit of c_t and with a random payoff of r_{t+n}^n units of c_{t+n} at date $t + n$, then utility maximization also implies that

$$E\big[r_{t+n}^n \mathrm{MN}_{t+n}\big| \mathcal{A}_t\big] = \mathrm{MN}_t. \tag{10.29}$$

Substituting for MN gives

$$
\begin{aligned}
E\Big[r_{t+n}^n \beta^n \big\{ A_{11}\big(\beta L^{-1}\big)\big\{ \delta\big[A_{11}(L)c_{t+n}\big]^{\gamma\delta-1}\big[A_{22}(L)d_{t+n}\big]^{(1-\delta)\gamma}\big\}\big\} \\
- A_{11}\big(\beta L^{-1}\big)\big\{\big[A_{11}(L)c_t\big]^{\gamma\delta-1}\big[A_{22}(L)d_t\big]^{(1-\delta)\gamma}\big\}\Big| \mathcal{A}_t \Big] = 0.
\end{aligned}
\tag{10.30}
$$

Focusing on (10.30) and assuming that $A_{11}(L) = 1 + \psi L$, to construct moment conditions to be used in constructing a GMM estimator of this model, we define

$$
\begin{aligned}
u_{t+n+1} = \Big[& c_t^{*\delta\gamma-1} d_t^{*(1-\delta)\gamma} + \psi\beta c_{t+1}^{*\delta\gamma-1} d_{t+1}^{*(1-\delta)\gamma} \\
& - \beta^n \Big(c_{t+n}^{*\delta\gamma-1} d_{t+n}^{*(1-\delta)\gamma} + \psi\beta c_{t+n+1}^{*\delta\gamma-1} d_{t+n+1}^{*(1-\delta)\gamma} \Big) r_{t+n}^n \Big] / c_t^{*\delta\gamma-1} d_t^{*(1-\delta)\gamma}.
\end{aligned}
\tag{10.31}
$$

The dating of u_{t+n+1} is due to the combination of the n-period investment horizon and the fact that agent's marginal utility of consumption of

---

[10] Mankiw et al. (1985) and Eichenbaum et al. (1988) examined models in which utility is represented as a nonseparable function of nondurable goods and leisure plus a separable function of the services from durable goods. The former study adopted a CES form of the utility function, while the latter adopted a version of the utility function (10.21) and (10.22) with c_t^* denoting services from NIPA nondurables plus services and d_t^* denoting leisure services (durable goods were excluded from the analysis). The empirical results from these studies show that many of the limitations of models with single or multiple consumption goods carry over to models that incorporate leisure in a nonseparable way.

the numeraire good involves consumption one period ahead owing to the short-term durability of c_t. An immediate implication of the Euler equation (10.30) is that $E[u_{t+n+1}|\mathcal{A}_t] = 0$. Following Dunn and Singleton (1986) and Eichenbaum et al. (1988), the scaling factor in (10.31) is included to control for possible trends in the acquisitions of goods.

To construct a GMM estimator of the parameters governing preferences and the service technologies, we suppose that there are J assets and interpret u_{t+n+1} as the J-dimensional vector of errors associated with these assets. Additionally, we let x_t denote a vector of instruments in $\mathcal{A}_t$ and base estimation on the M [equal to the product of J and $\dim(x_t)$] orthogonality conditions

$$E\big[u_{t+n+1} \otimes x_t\big] = 0. \tag{10.32}$$

The optimal distance matrix for GMM estimation is a consistent estimator of the inverse of

$$\Sigma_0 = \sum_{j=-n}^{n} E\big[u_{t+n+1}u'_{t+n+1-j} \otimes x_t x'_{t-j}\big]. \tag{10.33}$$

Dunn and Singleton (1986) and Eichenbaum and Hansen (1990) considered the special case of the service technology (10.22) with $A_{11}(L) = (1 + \psi L)$. Upon estimating the model for the period January 1959 through December 1978, they found that overidentifying restrictions were typically not rejected at conventional significance levels for individual returns. The returns considered were the 3-month real holding-period returns on U.S. Treasury bills for buy-and-hold and roll-over investment strategies (Dunn and Singleton) and 1-month holding-period returns on 1-month bills and an aggregate stock portfolio (Eichenbaum and Hansen). On the other hand, when the Euler equations for two different returns were examined simultaneously, there was substantial evidence against the overidentifying restrictions.

Eichenbaum and Hansen (1990) also investigated a quadratic utility function with the linear technology (10.22). Specifically, the function $U(s_{jt})$ was chosen to be

$$U(s_{jt}) = -\left\{\left[s_{jt}^1 - \frac{\alpha_1}{2}\left(s_{jt}^1\right)^2\right] + \left[\alpha_2 s_{jt}^2 - \frac{\alpha_3}{2}\left(s_{jt}^2\right)^2\right] + \alpha_4 s_{jt}^1 s_{jt}^2\right\}, \tag{10.34}$$

$\alpha_1, \alpha_2, \alpha_3 > 0$. A potentially important difference between the specifications (10.21) and (10.34) is that the quadratic model does not restrict the substitution elasticity between the service flows from nondurable and durable goods to unity. Eichenbaum and Hansen report substantial evidence against the null hypothesis that utility is separable across the two consumption services [$\alpha_4 = 0$ in (10.34)]. However, in spite of its more flexible substitution possibilities, chi-square statistics with probability values of 0.004 and 0.006 are obtained using TBILL1 (Eichenbaum and Hansen, 1990) and VWR1 (Singleton, 1985).

Three patterns of results emerge from these empirical studies of asset pricing models with multiple goods. First, for power utility, the introduction of durable goods seems to improve the fit of the models when individual returns are examined, perhaps with the exception of the 1-month Treasury bill. For quadratic utility, the *p*-values remain small for both TBILL1 and VWR1. Second, the fit of the consumption-based models is typically better for aggregate stock indexes and long-term bonds than for real Treasury bill returns. Third, there is substantial evidence against the overidentifying restrictions in models with and without durable goods, and for power and quadratic utility, when two or more returns are studied simultaneously.

To link these findings back to the opening remarks in this chapter, it is instructive to summarize the findings in Dunn and Singleton (1986) regarding the implications of changing γ for the "unconditional" risk premiums implied by the utility functions (10.21). The difference between the mean returns on any two *n*-period investment strategies can be written, using the Euler equation (10.29), as

$$E[r^1_{t+n}] - E[r^2_{t+n}] = -\text{Cov}[r^1_{t+n} - r^2_{t+n}, \hat{\text{MU}}_{t+n}]/E[\hat{\text{MU}}_{t+n}], \qquad (10.35)$$

where $\hat{\text{MU}}_t$ is the marginal utility MN_{t+n} scaled by $[(c^*_t)^{\delta\gamma-1}(d^*_t)^{(1-\delta)\gamma}]$ (in order to allow for real growth in acquisitions of goods). Letting $n = 3$ and choosing r^1_{t+3} and r^2_{t+3} to be the returns TBILL3 and the 3-month real return on a 6-month bill (TB6H3), Dunn and Singleton found that the sample estimate of $(E[r^1_{t+3}] - E[r^2_{t+3}])$ was -0.0012, whereas the estimate of the right-hand side of (10.35) (calculated at their point estimate $\gamma_T = -1.66$) was 1.37×10^{-7}. The estimated risk premium is much too small and has the wrong sign. Again, we find that consumption growth is not sufficiently correlated with historical returns to explain measured excess returns. Moreover, decreasing γ_T, holding all of the other parameters fixed at their estimated values, leads to a larger positive value of the sample unconditional premiums. Thus, as risk aversion is increased the difference between the sample excess return and the premium (which according to the theory should be equal to the excess return) actually *increases*.

10.5. Habit Formation

A quite different form in nonseparability of preferences over time arises when agents exhibit *habit* formation, by which we mean that an increase in consumption at date t increases the marginal utility of consumption at adjacent dates relative to the marginal utility of consumption at distant dates. Consumptions at adjacent dates are therefore complementary. Two quite different formulations of habit formation have been pursued in the literature: *internal* habit models in which the past *own* consumptions of an agent influence the marginal utility from current consumption, and *external* habit models in which the past *aggregate* consumptions influence today's consumption choice.

10.5.1. Models with Internal Habit Formation

The implications of internal habit formation for asset pricing has been explored by Sundaresan (1989), Constantinides (1990), Ferson and Constantinides (1991), and Heaton (1995). Referring once again to (10.17), we see that internal habit formation is present when the a_τ, for $\tau \geq 1$, are negative. The construct $-\sum_{\tau=1}^\infty a_\tau c_{t-\tau}$ can be interpreted as agent's subsistence level of consumption services, with large acquisitions of goods in the past increasing this subsistence level. Consumption is habitual in that, as c_t approaches $-\sum_{\tau=1}^\infty a_\tau c_{t-\tau}$, the marginal utility of s_t becomes infinite if $\gamma < 0$.

Ferson and Constantinides (1991) estimated the restricted version of (10.17) with $A(L) = 1 + a_1 L$, using postwar quarterly data and annual data for the period 1929–1986. To accommodate real growth they scaled (10.18) by one over $(c_t + a_1 c_{t-1})^{\gamma-1}$, which gives the econometric disturbance

$$
u_{t+2} = \sum_{\tau=0}^{1} a_\tau \beta^\tau \left(\frac{c_{t+\tau} + a_1 c_{t+\tau-1}}{c_t + a_1 c_{t-1}} \right)^{\gamma-1}
$$

$$
- \left[\sum_{\tau=0}^{1} a_\tau \beta^{\tau+1} \left(\frac{c_{t+\tau+1} + a_1 c_{t+\tau}}{c_t + a_1 c_{t-1}} \right)^{\gamma-1} \right] r_{t+1}.
$$

(10.36)

As instruments they used dividend yields, nominal Treasury bill returns, industrial production, and measures of nominal term and default premiums. The best fit of the model for real returns on Treasury bonds and NYSE decile portfolios was obtained with $a_1 < 0$, indicating that preferences exhibit internal habit formation. Furthermore, they did not reject the implied overidentifying restrictions at conventional significance levels. With quarterly data and c_t measured as nondurable consumption expenditures, the estimate of a_1 obtained by Ferson and Constantinides was -0.95, suggesting a very high level of habit formation. Moreover, when durable goods expenditures were substituted for nondurable expenditures, the estimates continued to suggest habit formation; $\hat{a}_1 = -0.65$.

Conceptually, the appeal of an internal habit is that the presence of the threshold habit level $x_t \equiv \sum_{j=1}^\infty a_j c_{t-j}$ increases the variability of agents' marginal rate of substitution, without necessarily increasing the variability of consumption growth. As argued by Constantinides (1990), it is in part this

Table 10.2. *Analysis of Single-Good Models with Habit Formation Using Quarterly Data from 1959:1 to 1986:4*

Returns	$\hat{\beta}$	$\hat{\gamma}$	$\hat{a}_1$	χ^2	DF
VWR3 and TBILL3	1.004	−0.2980	0.0	28.95	12
	(0.0021)	(0.4024)		(0.004)	
VWR3 and TBILL3	0.9906	0.4492	−0.5	10.66	12
	(0.0019)	(0.1426)		(0.559)	
VWR3 and TBILL3	0.9947	0.0274	−0.9	7.835	12
	(0.0025)	(0.0161)		(0.798)	

		Autocorrelations of $\{u_{t+2}\}$ in (10.36) with $\beta = 0.99$ and $\gamma = 0$					
$a_1 = -0.9$	u^{VWR}	−0.5864	−0.0477	0.1622	0.1296	−0.3312	0.1737
	u^{TB3}	−0.5836	−0.0565	0.1684	0.1254	−0.3447	0.2002
$a_1 = -0.5$	u^{VWR}	0.0896	−0.1420	−0.0683	−0.0062	−0.0307	−0.1445
	u^{TB3}	−0.4312	−0.0094	0.2082	−0.1286	−0.2539	0.2172
$a_1 = 0.0$	u^{VWR}	0.1323	−0.1677	−0.0612	−0.0250	−0.0451	−0.1056
	u^{TB3}	0.6512	0.5764	0.5577	0.4460	0.4104	0.4263
$a_1 = 0.5$	u^{VWR}	0.1316	−0.1696	−0.0588	−0.0261	−0.0493	−0.0990
	u^{TB3}	0.7824	0.6799	0.6098	0.5207	0.5194	0.4610
$a_1 = 0.9$	u^{VWR}	0.1315	−0.1698	−0.0585	−0.0262	−0.0499	−0.0983
	u^{TB3}	0.7819	0.6845	0.6109	0.5256	0.5137	0.4621

Source: Singleton (1993).

mechanism that allows the presence of internal habit to resolve the equity premium puzzle. Similarly, Dai (2001) shows that a generalized version of Constantinides's model with internal habit also resolves the expectations puzzles in the term structure literature (see Chapter 12).

Constantinides found that $x_t/c_t \approx -0.8$ for parameter values that resolved the equity premium puzzle. For models that set $x_t = a_1 c_{t-1}$, this means that a_1 must be a large negative number for the habit model to be consistent with historical return and consumption data. This was indeed what Ferson and Constantinides obtained with quarterly data.

Examination of the properties of the disturbances in a model with habit formation for various values of a_1 reveals why the goodness-of-fit improves as a_1 approaches -1. The top part of Table 10.2, from Singleton (1993), shows the estimates of the model (10.36) using quarterly data over the sample period 1959:1 through 1986:4. Estimates were obtained for the real return on 3-month Treasury bills and the real 3-month holding-period return on the value-weighted NYSE portfolio, using the constant unity and two lagged values of consumption growth and the real returns as instruments.[11] Estimates

[11] In choosing instruments, this analysis follows previous studies rather than Ferson and Constantinides. The model and instrument set correspond most closely to the model

were also obtained for three different fixed values of a_1 in order to evaluate the effects on the other preference parameters and test statistics of changes in a_1. When $a_1 = 0$, there is substantial evidence against the model, which is consistent with the results in Hansen and Singleton (1982) for the analogous monthly model. Consistent with the results in Ferson and Constantinides, the test statistic declines markedly as a_1 decreases to -0.9.

The second part of Table 10.2 shows the first six autocorrelations of $\{u_t^{VWR}\}$ and $\{u_t^{TB3}\}$ given by (10.36) with VWR3 and TBILL3 as returns, respectively, for various values of a_1. The disturbances were all computed with $\beta = 0.99$ and $\gamma = 0$ (log utility). Consider first the correlations for $a_1 = 0$. Though under the null hypothesis of this model the disturbances are serially uncorrelated, the autocorrelations of $\{u_t^{TB3}\}$ are in fact substantially larger than zero and decay relatively slowly. This is a manifestation of the positive persistence in TBILL3.

When $a_1 \neq 0$, the disturbances follow MA(1) processes under the null hypothesis. The computed autocorrelations of both $\{u_t^{VWR}\}$ and $\{u_t^{TB3}\}$ are much closer to an MA(1) autocorrelation structure for $a_1 = -0.5$ and -0.9. In particular, the second and third autocorrelations, which are aligned in time with the instruments, are quite small. On the other hand, positive values of a_1 tend to increase the autocorrelations of the disturbances and thereby lead to larger departures from the null of zero autocorrelations.

The reason for this pattern can be seen immediately from (10.36), in which terms of the form (c_{t+j}^*/c_j^*) are raised to the power $\gamma - 1$, where $c_t^* \equiv c_t + a_1 c_{t-1}$. As noted by Hansen and Jagannathan (1991) and Cochrane and Hansen (1992), when $a_1 < 0$, (c_{t+1}^*/c_t^*) is more volatile than (c_{t+1}/c_t). As a_1 approaches -1, the consumption term increasingly dominates the volatility of $\{u_t\}$, while the autocorrelation of $\{c_{t+1}^*/c_t^*\}$ declines. Thus, for a_1 near -1, $\{u_t\}$ is approximately a quasi-difference of a nearly serially uncorrelated process. As such, the time-series properties of $\{u_t\}$ are determined almost entirely by the terms involving (c_{t+1}^*/c_t^*) and not by r_{t+1}^1. As $\{u_t\}$ becomes increasingly dominated by the consumption term, the test statistics decline. This pattern is what would be expected from the discussion of Table 10.1. Positive values of a_1, on the other hand, increase the autocorrelation of $[(1+a_1\beta L)(c_{t+1}^*/c_t^*)^{\gamma-1}]$, but have relatively little effect on the volatility of the disturbances.

Further confirmation of this interpretation is provided by the correlation matrix of (u_t^{VWR}, u_t^{TB3}): when $a_1 = -0.9$, the correlation between u_t^{VWR} and u_t^{TB3} is 0.994 and the corresponding standard deviations and autocorrelations of these shocks are essentially equal. In contrast, when $a_1 = 0$,

---

underlying the second part of Table 4, Panel 3 in Ferson and Constantinides (1991). They used the return on the largest decile portfolio instead of VWR3 and the 3-month return from rolling over the 1-month Treasury bill instead of TBILL3.

$\text{Corr}(u_t^{\text{VWR}}, u_t^{\text{TB3}}) = 0.04$, the standard deviation of u_t^{VWR} is more than ten times larger than the standard deviation of u_t^{TB3}, and as in Table 10.1, the properties of these disturbances are determined largely by the returns.

The role of (internal) habit formation was examined in more depth by Heaton (1995) using the following special case of (10.17) in which goods are durable in character and agents' preferences exhibit habit persistence:

$$A(L) = \frac{1 - \phi L}{(1 - \psi L)(1 - \theta L)}, \tag{10.37}$$

where $\phi = \theta + \varphi(1 - \theta)$. If $\psi = 0$, then this model exhibits pure (internal) habit persistence in that

$$s_t = c_t - \varphi(1 - \theta) \sum_{k=0}^{\infty} \theta^k c_{t-1-k}, \quad 0 < \varphi < 1, \quad 0 < \theta < 1. \tag{10.38}$$

If in addition $\theta = 0$, then the one-period habit persistence model of Ferson and Constantinides (1991) is obtained with $s_t = c_t - \varphi c_{t-1}$. If, on the other hand, $\varphi = 0$, then

$$s_t = \sum_{k=0}^{\infty} \psi^k c_{t-k}, \quad 0 < \psi < 1, \tag{10.39}$$

with c acting like a durable good in that it provides positive utility over time.

To implement this model, consumption and dividend growths were assumed to follow a bivariate autoregressive process, and the parameters were estimated using the simulated method of moments (Chapter 6). Among other things, the SME allowed Heaton to accommodate time aggregation in measured consumption. He found that goods are locally durable, but that over long horizons there is evidence of significant habit formation. Furthermore, allowing for both local durability and habit persistence over longer horizons substantially improved the fit of the model compared to both the simple time-additive model and the nested special case of pure habit persistence (no local durability).

Heaton also documents the fact that the high level of volatility in m_t^n induced by the pure habit persistence model [$\psi = 0$ in (10.37)] gives rise to implausibly large standard deviations of the riskfree rate. This result, along with the preceding observation that the correlation between u_t^{VWR} and u_t^{TB3} approaches unity for high degrees of habit persistence, suggests that the good fit of pure-habit models along some dimensions comes at the expense of notable counterfactual implications along other dimensions. We revisit the implications of these models for the second moments of m_t^n and returns in Section 10.8.

10.5.2. Models with External Habit Formation

An alternative, external form of habit has been explored by Abel (1990), Campbell and Cochrane (1999, 2000), and Wachter (2005), among others. Habit is external in these models in the sense that each agent's subsistence level x_t is a function of aggregate quantities that are not directly under the agent's control. Abel specifies preferences as $U(c_t/x_t)$ so that it is consumption relative to the habit that affects preferences, whereas Campbell and Cochrane assume that the difference matters, $U(c_t - x_t)$. The choice makes a difference and, in particular, with Abel's ratio formulation the excess returns on equities (the equity risk premiums) are unaffected by the presence of an external habit (Campbell, 1999). Accordingly, we follow Campbell and Cochrane and focus on the difference formulation.

Campbell and Cochrane (1999) assume an economy of identical agents each with preferences given by

$$E\left[\sum_{t=0}^{\infty} \beta^t \frac{(c_t - x_t)^\gamma - 1}{\gamma}\right], \tag{10.40}$$

where x_t is the external habit. Letting $s_t = (c_t - x_t)/c_t$ denote the proportional distance between current consumption and the external habit gives the local curvature of the utility function as

$$-\frac{c_t U_{cc}(c_t, x_t)}{U_c(c_t, x_t)} = \frac{1 - \gamma}{s_t}. \tag{10.41}$$

Thus, the smaller $c_t - x_t$ (the closer the current consumption is to the habit subsistence level), the larger the curvature in preferences.

To close the model, the habit is assumed to depend on aggregate consumption,

$$s_t^a = \frac{c_t^a - x_t}{c_t^a}, \tag{10.42}$$

so, in particular, x_t is not affected by the decision of any individual agent. Since identical agents choose the same level of consumption, we can drop the superscript a in the following discussion, bearing in mind that x_t is taken as fixed when computing marginal utilities.

The underlying technology is chosen such that

$$\Delta \ln c_{t+1} = g + v_{t+1}, \quad v_{t+1} \sim \text{i.i.d. } N(0, \sigma^2). \tag{10.43}$$

Viewing this economy as an endowment economy, we can interpret c_t as aggregate consumption that equals the aggregate endowment.

The surplus ratio s_t is assumed to evolve according to the process

$$\ln s_{t+1} = (1 - \phi) \ln \bar{s} + \phi \ln s_t + \lambda(\ln s_t)(\ln c_{t+1} - \ln c_t - g), \quad (10.44)$$

where $\lambda(\ln s_t)$ is a sensitivity function. So that s_t "behaves like a habit," the sensitivity function was chosen so that x_t is predetermined at and near the steady state $s_t = \bar{s}$ and increases in consumption do not lead to declines in the habit x_t.

Additionally, in order avoid a riskfree rate puzzle, Campbell and Cochrane fixed the riskless rate at a constant. The marginal rate of substitution of consumption is given by

$$m^1_{t+1} = \beta \left(\frac{s_{t+1}}{s_t} \frac{c_{t+1}}{c_t} \right)^{\gamma - 1}. \quad (10.45)$$

Therefore, the logarithm of the riskless interest rate is

$$\ln r_t^f = -\ln \beta + (1 - \gamma)g - (1 - \gamma)(1 - \phi)(\ln s_t - \bar{s})$$
$$- \frac{(1 - \gamma)^2 \sigma^2}{2} [1 + \lambda(\ln s_t)]^2. \quad (10.46)$$

They chose $\lambda(\cdot)$ to set the left-hand side of (10.46) to a historically plausible constant. Risky assets are priced by substituting (10.45) into the standard intertemporal Euler equation.

To complete their specification, parameter values were chosen to match several moments of the distributions of historical macroeconomic data. In particular, the parameters of the consumption process were chosen to match the mean and volatility of consumption growth. Serial correlation in $\ln s_t$, governed by ϕ, was chosen to match the serial correlation in the logarithm of the price/dividend ratio.[12] Finally, the risk-aversion parameter γ was chosen to match the ratio of the unconditional mean excess return on equities to its standard deviation.

Figure 10.1 displays the model-implied expected returns on claims to the future aggregate consumption and dividend streams, as well as the riskless interest rate. As s_t declines (consumption approaches the level of external habit), the equity premium grows substantially. (The behavior of the return on the consumption and dividends claims is similar.) Underlying this resolution of the equity premium puzzle is the fact that the Sharpe ratios on risky claims are proportional to the curvature of utility. The relative risk-aversion parameter (γ) and the steady-state surplus ratio ($\bar{s}$) are chosen to

---

[12] This involves solving numerically for the price/dividend ratio implied by agents' Euler equation and the laws of motion of the state variables in their economy.

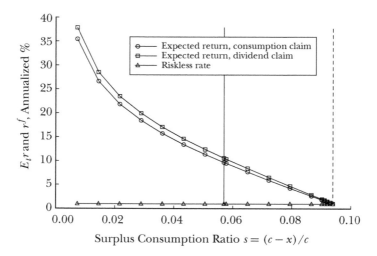

Figure 10.1. *Expected returns and the riskless rate. Source: Campbell and Cochrane (1999), copyright by the University of Chicago.*

be -1.0 and 0.057, respectively. Therefore, utility curvature at the steady state [from (10.41)] is 35, and it becomes much larger at low values of s_t. Put differently, low values of surplus consumption lead to large Sharpe ratios for risky claims in their model.

What makes this high level of curvature in utility less problematic (from the perspective of the puzzles outlined at the beginning of this chapter) is that the constant interest rate in the Campbell-Cochrane model is $r_t^f = -\ln\beta + (1-\gamma)g - [(1-\gamma)/\bar{s}]^2\sigma^2/2$. By keeping relative risk aversion $(1-\gamma)$ at the moderate value of 2, a high level of the curvature in utility does not distort the level of the short rate in the same way that it would in a model with constant relative risk-averse preferences. In the latter case, the equity premium puzzle is resolved by a large γ and this inflates the term γg, thereby introducing the "riskfree rate puzzle."

From Figure 10.2 it is seen that the standard deviations of returns also increase with declining surplus consumption. Since s_t, as parameterized in their model, is highly persistent, so is the conditional variance of returns. This is consistent with the empirical evidence reported in Chapter 7. Moreover, a declining s is associated with a simultaneous decline in the prices of risky securities (increase in expected returns) and increase in volatility. So the model reproduces the "leverage" effect that was also discussed in Chapter 7. Finally, this figure suggests that volatility is countercyclical.

Another implication of Figures 10.1 and 10.2 together is that the means and standard deviations of returns respond differently to changes in s. This

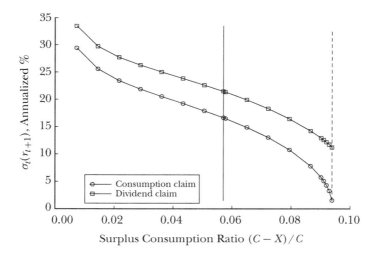

Figure 10.2. *Stock return volatility and the surplus consumption ratio. Source: Campbell and Cochrane (1999), copyright by the University of Chicago.*

implies a time-varying Sharpe ratio (expected excess return per unit of standard deviation), indeed a ratio that moves countercyclically.

Wachter (2005) extends this framework to allow for stochastic interest rates in order to investigate some of the expectations puzzles related to holding-period returns on bonds (see Section 13.2.1). This is accomplished by relaxing the constraint imposed by Campbell and Cochrane that the intertemporal substitution and precautionary savings effects offset each other to get a constant riskless rate. Wachter lets the data determine the effect of s_t on r_t^f. We explore the economic mechanisms underlying her analysis in more depth in Chapter 13.

A formal econometric implementation of an extended Campbell-Cochrane habit model is undertaken in Bansal et al. (2004). Agents' endowment followed the process (10.43), and dividends were assumed to be co-integrated with consumption: $d_t = \mu_{dc} + c_t + \eta_t$, where η_t is a stationary ergodic process. This representation of dividends, which extends that in Campbell and Cochrane, implies that consumption and dividends share a common stochastic trend (see Section 9.3) and, hence, that $(d_t - c_t)$ is a stationary process. Their goal in letting d_t and c_t share a common trend, while being less than perfectly correlated, is an empirical analysis of the effects of long-run "macro" risks on asset prices. The model is estimated using a simulated method-of-moments (Chapter 6) based on an auxiliary model constructed from a vector autoregressive model of the exogenous shocks. Using annual data for the period 1929–2001, the authors find that this model does a good job of matching the moments of consumption and dividend growth. However, it does not resolve the volatility puzzle—the price/dividend ratio is more volatile historically than what is implied by this formulation of habit formation (and long-run risks). Further, there is excessive co-dependence (Section 10.2.2) in that the model predicts a much tighter link between the price/dividend ratio and consumption growth than is seen in the data.

10.6. Non-State-Separable Preferences

The preferences examined so far are in the class of von Neuman-Morgenstern preferences. Epstein and Zin (1989) and Weil (1989) proposed a particular class of non-state-separable preferences for which agents are not indifferent to the timing of the temporal resolution of uncertainty (see Section 8.2). The Euler equations implied by their models may be fundamentally different than those, for example, implied by state-separable preferences, say of the CRRA form, in that the representative agent's marginal rate of substitution is a function of the return on the aggregate wealth portfolio. In this section we briefly describe the models in these papers and then assess the extent to which they fit the consumption and return data better than state-separable models.

Following Epstein and Zin (1989), we assume that agents maximize the recursive utility function leading to the pricing kernel (8.23) and associated pricing relations

$$\beta^\theta E\left\{ [c_{t+1}/c_t]^{-(\theta/\psi)}\, r_{M,t+1}^\theta \,\middle|\, \mathcal{A}_t \right\} = 1, \tag{10.47}$$

$$\beta^\theta E_t\left\{ [c_{t+1}/c_t]^{-(\theta/\psi)}\, r_{M,t+1}^{\theta-1} r_{t+1} \,\middle|\, \mathcal{A}_t \right\} = 1, \tag{10.48}$$

where $r_{M,t+1}$ and r_{t+1} are the one-period holding-period returns on the wealth portfolio and any security in the agent's choice set, respectively.[13] Note that the return on the wealth portfolio appears in (10.47) and (10.48) as part of the pricing kernel. In light of the significant correlation between the returns on common stocks and typical measures of the return r_M, the marginal rate of substitution in (10.48) may have very different properties than those that are functions of consumption variables alone.

The empirical results in Epstein and Zin (1991) for this model were mixed, however. The nested expected utility model [$\alpha \equiv (1 - \gamma) = 1/\psi \Rightarrow$ CRRA preferences] was strongly rejected. At the same time, Euler equation-based tests indicated rejecting the overidentifying restrictions for the unconstrained model for most instrument sets when returns on a common

---

[13] In practice, the budget constraint is often expressed as $w_{t+1} = r_{M,t+1}(w_t - c_t)$, where w denotes wealth. Therefore, r_M is the return on a claim to the aggregate consumption stream.

stock and a U.S. Treasury bond were studied simultaneously. There was less evidence against the model when common stock returns were studied individually. (Recall that in state-separable CRRA models, the test statistics exhibited a similar pattern.)

The point estimate of γ indicated that risk preferences were close to logarithmic. With logarithmic risk preferences, the asset return equations (10.48) reduce to those tested by Hansen et al. (1982) and Brown and Gibbons (1985), which were generally not supported by the data. Furthermore, (10.47) simplifies to a log-linear version of the Euler equation for the return on the wealth portfolio (Epstein and Zin, 1991):

$$E\left[-\frac{1}{\psi}\ln(c_{t+1}/c_t) + \ln r_{\mathcal{M},t+1} + \ln\beta \,\Big|\, \mathcal{A}_t\right] = 0. \tag{10.49}$$

This equation is nearly identical to the log-linear relation studied by Hansen and Singleton (1983), but here it is obtained without assuming lognormality of returns or consumption growth. The difference is in the constant term; in the expected utility models under lognormality, a constant conditional variance term also appears in the intercept. After freeing up this constraint, there is still substantial evidence against the log-linear model (Hansen and Singleton, 1996). Moreover, (10.49) holds only for the return on the wealth portfolio, so these two models are not observationally equivalent for all returns.

Though these Euler equation-based tests cast doubt on the view that a representative agent with Epstein-Zin preferences determines asset prices, the recursive structure of (8.22) and its separation into risk aversion and intertemporal substitution make it an attractive construct for exploring how exogenous shocks affect asset returns. For instance, Bansal and Yaron (2004) introduce a small (i.e., low conditional volatility) but persistent expected growth component in the consumption and dividend growth series into a model in which agents have Epstein-Zin preferences. In the presence of this persistent component, shocks to future expected growth rates lead to large changes in equity returns. Under the assumptions that the intertemporal elasticity of substitution ψ is greater than one and the risk aversion parameter $\alpha = 10$, they show that the model can generate an equity premium roughly consistent with its historical value.

Bansal et al. (2004) undertake a more formal econometric analysis of the Bansal-Yaron model, generalized to accommodate somewhat richer state dynamics. Fixing $\psi = 2$ and with an estimated $\alpha_T = 7.1$, they show that the model is capable of matching the first and second moments of a variety of macroeconomic time series as well as the equity premium. Importantly, when they examined the special case of CRRA preferences ($\theta = 1$), the overidentifying restrictions were strongly rejected at conventional significance levels. Thus, critical to the success of this model is the balancing of intertemporal substitution and risk aversion with $\alpha \neq 1/\psi$ and $\psi > 1$. Both of these studies focus primarily on the moments of macroeconomic aggregates and an equity index return. So the overidentifying restrictions implied by the models' pricing of multiple equity indices and bond yields examined by Epstein and Zin (which were found to challenge the model) are not being tested.

10.7. Other Preference-Based Models

A wide variety of other models have been explored for their potential to resolve the asset pricing puzzles outlined in Section 10.1. These include models with state-dependent preferences, heterogeneity across agents with limited access to financial markets, and preferences that exhibit loss or disappointment aversion. Most of the studies exploring these issues rely on calibration to certain moments, including in some cases microeconomic data on individual consumptions and incomes, rather than a formal analysis of the conditional distribution of asset returns. This is in part because of the limited available information about asset holdings and investment decisions at the micro level.

Within the first group of models are those with state-dependent risk preferences (e.g., Gordon and St-Amour, 2004, and Kogan et al., 2006), unforeseen contingencies (Kraus and Sagi, 2004), and time-varying subjective probability assessments (e.g., Mulligan, 2004). A representative pricing kernel from these models with state-dependent preferences has a discrete state space with S possible realizations of returns and Epstein-Zin preferences:

$$q_{t+1}^*(s) = \frac{\alpha_t(s)}{\pi(s)} \beta^\theta \left[c_{t+1}(s)/c_t\right]^{-(\theta/\psi)} r_{M,t+1}^{\theta-1}(s), \quad s = 1, \ldots, S, \quad (10.50)$$

where $\alpha_t(s)/\pi(s)$ is the ratio of the agents' subjective to the objective probability. This term adds sufficient flexibility so that essentially any pattern of asset returns can be matched after imposing no-arbitrage restrictions. Mulligan (2004) explores a particular parametric model with the implication that the volatility of asset returns may be largely driven by $\alpha_t(s)/\pi(s)$, in which case these returns may show little correlation with consumption growth. Thus, these models provide a potential explanation for the failings of standard time-separable models that depend on this correlation to explain excess returns.

Pursuing a different generalization of representative agent models, Telmer (1993), Heaton and Lucas (1995), and Marcet and Singleton (1999), among others, explored the implications of models with heterogeneous agents and incomplete markets for asset prices. Of particular interest was the issue of whether market incompleteness, transaction costs, or limitations on borrowing can explain the magnitude of the equity premium. Overall, these models were largely unable to fit the historical magnitude of the equity premium, at least without introducing implausibly large frictions through the transaction and borrowing technologies. Essentially, through trading in a limited number of securities, agents are able to nearly replicate the first-best consumption plan. In a related paper, Alvarez and Jermann (2001) assume complete markets but, unlike the preceding papers, the solvency constraints are derived endogenously in the model. They are able to generate equity premia that are more in line with the historical magnitudes.

Finally, researchers have recently been exploring different departures from the standard expected utility model that draws upon the literature in psychology on human behavior. Barberis and Huang (2001) explore the implications of loss aversion and narrow framing for asset returns. Under loss aversion, agents get utility from gains and losses in wealth and, in particular, are more sensitive to their losses than to their gains (Kahneman and Tversky, 1979). Narrow framing is the behavioral trait of paying attention to narrowly defined gains and losses. Barberis and Huang show that their model matches many of the empirical observations in Section 10.1 and Chapter 9, including a high mean and volatility of equity returns in the presence of a low interest rate and a moderately predictable aggregate stock index return. In a complementary study, Ang et al. (2005a) argue that disappointment aversion (Gul, 1991) is another motivation for agents to give more weight in their portfolio decisions to outcomes that are relatively bad. Their model can generate sizable equity premia and the phenomenon of investors with sufficiently strong disappointment aversion choosing not to invest in equity portfolios.

10.8. Bounds on the Volatility of m_t^n

We conclude this chapter with a brief overview of a bound on the volatility of a pricing kernel q^*. By way of motivation, we refer back to the puzzle introduced at the outset of this chapter, namely that marginal rates of substitution do not co-vary sufficiently with returns on risky assets to explain their historical returns. Intuitively, it seems that there must be a minimal level of the volatility of m_t^n in order for m_t^n to have sufficient co-variability with risky returns. Indeed, this is the case, and derivations of such bounds date back at least to the work of Shiller (1982) and Hansen (1982a), and the empirical applications in Dunn and Singleton (1986). However, the focus on volatility bounds on m_t^n as a diagnostic tool for examining DAPMs blossomed with the formalization of these bounds in Hansen and Jagannathan (1991), leading to the HJ bound. Consistent with the preceding motivation, we use the notation m_t to denote the pricing kernel in the following discussion. However, nothing in the subsequent derivations requires that the pricing kernel be a marginal rate of substitution from a preference-based model. The bounds apply to any conjectured pricing kernel.

We begin by selecting a set of N asset payoffs at date $t + 1$, $\mathbf{x}_{t+1}$, from among those that are priced by our candidate pricing kernel m. In general the larger the set $\mathbf{x}_{t+1}$, the more demanding the derived lower bound on the volatility of m. The reason for fixing $\mathbf{x}_{t+1}$ is that we seek an observable bound on the volatility of any m that prices $\mathbf{x}$, and this is accomplished by using the observed payoffs $\mathbf{x}$. We define the associated payoff space $\mathcal{P}_{t+1} \equiv \{\mathbf{c} \cdot \mathbf{x}_{t+1} : \mathbf{c} \in \mathbb{R}^N\}$, and, for now, assume that $\mathbf{x}$ includes the riskless payoff equal to one with probability one.

An implication of (8.11) is that any pricing kernel $m_{t+1}(\equiv m_{t+1}^1)$ that prices the payoffs $\mathbf{x}_{t+1}$ satisfies

$$E[m_{t+1}\mathbf{x}_{t+1}] = E[\pi_t(\mathbf{x}_{t+1})], \tag{10.51}$$

where $\pi_t(\mathbf{x}_{t+1})$ is an N-dimensional vector of prices of the payoffs $\mathbf{x}_{t+1}$. We refer to (10.51) as *Restriction UP*.

A lower bound on $\sigma(m_{t+1})$, the (unconditional) volatility of any candidate m_{t+1}, is obtained by projecting the family of pricing kernels satisfying Restriction UP onto $\mathcal{P}_{t+1}$, and then examining the volatility of this projection. The payoff $m_{t+1}^* = \mathbf{x}_{t+1} \cdot \alpha_0 \in \mathcal{P}_{t+1}$ satisfies (10.51) for the payoffs $\mathbf{x}_{t+1}$ if

$$E[\mathbf{x}_{t+1}\mathbf{x}_{t+1}']\alpha_0 = E[\pi_t(\mathbf{x}_{t+1})]. \tag{10.52}$$

Solving (10.52) gives $\alpha_0 = E[\mathbf{x}_{t+1}\mathbf{x}_{t+1}']^{-1}E[\pi_t(\mathbf{x})]$. Furthermore, any m_{t+1} (not necessarily in $\mathcal{P}_{t+1}$) satisfying Restriction UP satisfies $E[m_{t+1}] = E[\pi_t(1)] = E[m_{t+1}^*]$, and $E[\mathbf{x}_{t+1}(m_{t+1} - m_{t+1}^*)] = 0$. It follows that m^* is the least-squares projection of m_{t+1} onto $\mathcal{P}_{t+1}$ and

$$\sigma(m_{t+1}) \geq \sigma(m_{t+1}^*), \quad E[m_{t+1}] = E[m_{t+1}^*]. \tag{10.53}$$

As noted by Hansen and Jagannathan (1991), this lower bound is as tight as possible, because m^* satisfies Restriction UP. That is, m^* represents the best (in the sense of least-squares projection) approximation to m by random variables in $\mathcal{P}_{t+1}$.

When the payoff space does not include a unit payoff (a riskless return is not among the set of returns considered), then we no longer know $E[m_{t+1}]$. Accordingly, Hansen and Jagannathan proceed by augmenting the payoff vector to $\mathbf{x}_{t+1}^a$, which includes $\mathbf{x}_{t+1}$ and 1, and defining the corresponding payoff space $\mathcal{P}_{t+1}^a$ in terms of this $\mathbf{x}^a$. In this augmented payoff space, we can assign the value ν to the $\pi_t(1)$, an unknown number in circumstances where $\mathcal{P}$ does not include a unit payoff. Then, replicating the preceding discussion, we can construct an $m_{t+1}^\nu \in \mathcal{P}_{t+1}^a$ that satisfies

$$E[\mathbf{x}_{t+1} m_{t+1}^v] = E[\pi_t(\mathbf{x}_{t+1})], \quad E[m_{t+1}^v] = v. \tag{10.54}$$

The volatility bound is then

$$\sigma(m_{t+1}) \geq \sigma(m_{t+1}^v), \tag{10.55}$$

for any m that satisfies Restriction UP and has mean v.

The region

$$S \equiv \{(v, \omega) \in \mathbb{R}^2 : \omega \geq \sigma(m_{t+1}^v)\} \tag{10.56}$$

summarizes the implications of Restriction UP for the volatility of agents' m. To derive a simple expression for $\sigma(m_{t+1}^v)$, note that

$$E\left[(\mathbf{x}_{t+1} - E[\mathbf{x}_{t+1}])(m_{t+1}^v - v)\right] = E[\pi_t(\mathbf{x}_{t+1})] - vE[\mathbf{x}_{t+1}], \tag{10.57}$$

and m_{t+1}^v can be expressed as

$$m_{t+1}^v = (\mathbf{x}_{t+1} - E[\mathbf{x}_{t+1}])' \beta_v + v, \quad \beta_v \in \mathbb{R}^N. \tag{10.58}$$

This last expression follows from the fact that m^v is the projection of m onto $\mathcal{P}^a$ and the mean of m^v is v. Substituting (10.58) into (10.57) and solving for β_v gives

$$\beta_v = \Sigma_\mathbf{x}^{-1} \left(E[\pi_t(\mathbf{x}_{t+1})] - vE[\mathbf{x}_{t+1}]\right), \tag{10.59}$$

where $\Sigma_\mathbf{x}$ is the variance/covariance matrix of $\mathbf{x}_{t+1}$. Using this expression, we obtain

$$\sigma(m_{t+1}^v) = \left[\beta_v' \Sigma_\mathbf{x} \beta_v\right]^{1/2}. \tag{10.60}$$

Drawing upon Gallant et al. (1990), Hansen and Jagannathan (1991) report the region S, along with the mean/standard deviation pairs implied by the single-good model (10.17) with $A(L) = 1 + \theta L$ for various values of γ and θ (Figure 10.3).[14] Thus, the candidate m is given by

$$m_{t+1} = \frac{s_{t+1}^{\gamma-1} + \beta\theta E_{t+1}[s_{t+2}^{\gamma-1} \mid \mathcal{A}_{t+1}]}{s_t^{\gamma-1} + \beta\theta E_t[s_{t+1}^{\gamma-1} \mid \mathcal{A}_t]}. \tag{10.61}$$

The specification of $\mathcal{A}$ is based on an underlying time-series model for aggregate consumption of nondurables plus services, as discussed in Gallant et al. (1990).

---

[14] This figure actually displays a region S^+ that is derived under the additional restriction that $E[m_{t+1}]$ is strictly positive. However, Hansen and Jagannathan (1991) note that the regions S and S^+ are nearly identical for this example.

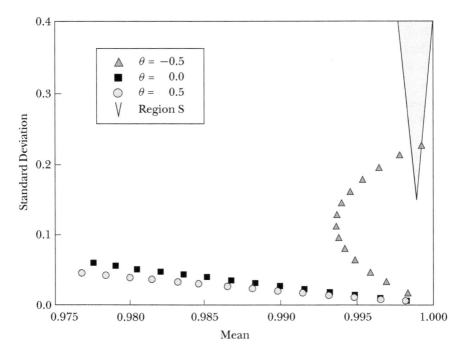

Figure 10.3.   *Hansen-Jagannathan bounds for a single-good model with* $U(s_t) =$ $[(c_t + \theta c_{t-1})^\gamma - 1]/\gamma$. *Source: Hansen and Jagannathan (1991), copyright by the University of Chicago.*

The region S is displayed as a shaded cone, and was computed using the same data as in Hansen and Singleton (1982), revised and updated to cover the period March 1959 through December 1986. For a fixed value of θ, the entries—starting from left to right—represent the means and volatilities of m, computed from (10.61), for values of γ ranging from 2 to 15. This figure captures, in mean-variance space for m, the essence of much of our preceding discussion of the goodness-of-fit of models with durability or (internal) habit formation. When $\theta > 0$, increasing agents' relative risk aversion gradually increases the volatility of m, but at the expense of introducing a riskfree rate puzzle (a mean of m that is too low). Even for very large γ, the mean/volatility pair for m is far from the region S. On the other hand, when $\theta < 0$, large values of γ induce sufficient variability in m [as given by (10.61)], while keeping the mean of m sufficiently large for the mean/volatility pair to satisfy the HJ bound (fall within the region S).

We can incorporate conditioning information by using "scaled payoffs" as follows. Define a new payoff space

$$\mathcal{P}_{t+1}^Z \equiv \left\{ \mathbf{c} \cdot Z_t \mathbf{x}_{t+1} : \mathbf{c} \in \mathbb{R}^N \right\}, \tag{10.62}$$

where Z_t is an $N \times N$ matrix with elements in an information set $\mathcal{I}_t$. Since $E[m_{t+1}Z_t\mathbf{x}_{t+1}|\mathcal{I}_t] = Z_t\pi_t(\mathbf{x}_{t+1})$, we can replicate our preceding discussion and obtain a new bound by replacing $E[\pi_t(\mathbf{x}_{t+1})]$ with $E[Z_t\pi_t(\mathbf{x}_{t+1})]$ and defining β_v^Z accordingly:

$$\sigma\left(m_{t+1}^v\right) = \left[\beta_v^{Z'} \Sigma_{\mathbf{x}} \beta_v^Z \right]^{1/2}. \tag{10.63}$$

Gallant et al. (1990), Ferson and Siegel (2003), and Bekaert and Liu (2004) have examined related "optimal instrument" problems. Following Bekaert and Liu, we consider the case of an $N \times 1$ vector $\mathbf{z}_t \in \mathbb{R}^N$ and the payoff space

$$\mathcal{P}_{t+1}^z \equiv \left\{ c\mathbf{z}_t'\mathbf{x}_{t+1} : N \times 1, \ c \in \mathbb{R} \right\}, \tag{10.64}$$

with an associated HJ volatility bound on m_{t+1} with $E[m_{t+1}] = v$, say $\sigma(v, \mathbf{z}_t'\mathbf{x}_{t+1})$. The question of interest is which $\mathbf{z}_t$ in some given information set $\mathcal{I}_t$ gives the highest HJ bound; that is, which $\mathbf{z}$ solves the optimization problem

$$\sigma^2\left(v, \mathbf{z}_t^{*'}\mathbf{x}_{t+1}\right) = \sup_{\mathbf{z}_t \in \mathcal{I}_t} \sigma^2\left(v, \mathbf{z}_t'\mathbf{x}_{t+1}\right). \tag{10.65}$$

Letting $\Sigma_{xt} \equiv E[\mathbf{x}_{t+1}\mathbf{x}_{t+1}'|\mathcal{I}_t]$ and $\mu_{xt} \equiv E[\mathbf{x}_{t+1}|\mathcal{I}_t]$, we arrive at the solution

$$\mathbf{z}_t^* = \Sigma_{xt}^{-1}(\pi_t(\mathbf{x}_{t+1}) - \omega\mu_{xt}), \tag{10.66}$$

where $\omega = (v - b)/(1 - d)$, $b = E[\mu_{xt}'(\mu_{xt}\mu_{xt}' + \Sigma_{xt})^{-1}\pi_t(\mathbf{x}_{t+1})]$, and $d = E[\mu_{xt}'(\mu_{xt}\mu_{xt}' + \Sigma_{xt})^{-1}\mu_{xt}]$. When the relevant conditional moments are known, this bound coincides with that derived by Gallant et al. (1990). A potential advantage of the bound $\sigma^2(v, \mathbf{z}_t^{*'}\mathbf{x}_{t+1})$ derived by Bekaert and Liu over the one derived by Gallant et al. is that the former is robust to misspecification of the conditional moments Σ_{xt} and μ_{xt}. That is, even if we use an incorrect model in estimating these moments, a valid HJ bound is obtained.

Hansen et al. (1995) discuss the large-sample properties of the conditional HJ bound derived in Gallant et al. (1990). Ferson and Siegel (2003) examine the small-sample properties of HJ bounds that use conditioning information and find that, typically, there is a small-sample bias toward overstating the bound (rejecting specifications of pricing kernels too often). The bias was found to be relatively small for the optimal bound based on $\mathbf{z}^*$.

11

Pricing Kernels and Factor Models

WHAT IS THE RELATIONSHIP between the DAPMs that start from an expression like $E[m^1_{t+1} r_{t+1} | \mathcal{A}_t] = 1$ [see, e.g., (10.1) in Chapter 10] and those that focus on beta relations that express expected returns in terms of covariances of these returns with a benchmark return? Such a beta relation is implied by the celebrated static capital asset pricing model (CAPM) of Sharpe (1964) and Lintner (1965), where the return on a "market portfolio" serves as a benchmark. However, from Merton (1973) and Long (1974), we know that the market return is not in general a benchmark return in intertemporal asset pricing models. This chapter explores in depth the nature of beta or factor models for excess returns implied by DAPMs.[1]

Starting from a general DAPM with pricing in terms of a pricing kernel q^* (see Chapter 8), we derive a "single-beta" representation of expected excess returns on traded assets. Among the aims of this chapter are: (1) linking the beta relations with time-varying betas studied in the literature to the preference-based DAPMs reviewed in Chapter 10, (2) characterizing the set of returns that can serve as benchmarks for beta relations, (3) identifying, where possible, observable members of this set, and (4) assessing the empirical support for factor models.

In addressing these issues, we answer the questions: (1) What is the link between conditional mean-variance efficiency and conditional single-beta models? (2) How does reducing the conditioning information set from agents' set to that of an econometrician affect the set of admissible benchmark returns for beta representations? (3) Do single-beta representations capture all of the restrictions on returns implied by DAPMs? (4) What are the implications of the answers to these questions for recent econometric studies of CAPMs with time-varying conditional moments? The answer to the second question, in particular, is central to the feasibility of econometric

---

[1] The approach to beta models taken in this chapter is based on Hansen et al. (1982).

analysis of beta relations implied by preference-based models because of the inherent difficulty of constructing empirical counterparts to benchmark returns.

11.1. A Single-Beta Representation of Returns

Given the central role of q^* in pricing, it is natural to inquire whether the associated benchmark return $r_t^* = q_t^*/E[(q_t^*)^2|\mathcal{A}_{t-1}]$ [see (8.5)] plays a role analogous to the role of the market return in the CAPM. The answer is yes in that a single-beta representation of the conditional moment restriction (8.6) can be derived using the fact that r^* is the globally minimum second-moment return.

To proceed with this construction we return to the concept of a payoff space $(\mathcal{P}_t, \pi_{t-1}, \mathcal{A}_{t-1})$ discussed in Chapter 8, and suppose that there is a unit payoff in $\mathcal{P}_t$ and that the pricing operator π_{t-1} does not admit arbitrage opportunities on $\mathcal{P}_t$. Under these assumptions, we conclude that the associated return space $\mathcal{R}_t$ (of payoffs with unit prices) contains the riskfree return $r_{t-1}^f = 1/E[q_t^*|\mathcal{A}_{t-1}]$.[2] From (8.8) it follows that

$$E[r_t^* r_t \mid \mathcal{A}_{t-1}] = r_{t-1}^f E[r_t^* \mid \mathcal{A}_{t-1}], \qquad r_t \in \mathcal{R}_t, \tag{11.1}$$

where

$$r_{t-1}^f = E[r_t^{*2} \mid \mathcal{A}_{t-1}]/E[r_t^* \mid \mathcal{A}_{t-1}] = 1/E[q_t^* \mid \mathcal{A}_{t-1}]. \tag{11.2}$$

Expanding (11.1) in terms of conditional means and covariances gives

$$E[r_t \mid \mathcal{A}_{t-1}] - r_{t-1}^f = \frac{-\text{Cov}[r_t, r_t^* \mid \mathcal{A}_{t-1}]}{E[r_t^* \mid \mathcal{A}_{t-1}]}, \qquad r_t \in \mathcal{R}_t. \tag{11.3}$$

Finally, evaluating (11.3) at $r_t = r_t^*$ and substituting back into (11.3) gives rise to the single-beta pricing relation

$$E[r_t^x \mid \mathcal{A}_{t-1}] - r_{t-1}^f = \beta_{x,t-1}\{E[r_t^* \mid \mathcal{A}_{t-1}] - r_{t-1}^f\}, \tag{11.4}$$

where

$$\beta_{x,t-1} = \frac{\text{Cov}(r_t^x, r_t^* \mid \mathcal{A}_{t-1})}{\text{Var}(r_t^* \mid \mathcal{A}_{t-1})}, \tag{11.5}$$

for all $r_t^x \in \mathcal{R}_t$.

---

[2] Adding these assumptions is not necessary to derive a beta representation for returns, but we nevertheless make them so that the resulting excess returns can be expressed relative to r_{t-1}^f. Also, the ensumption of no arbitrage opportunities is used here to ensure that $\Pr\{\pi_t(1) > 0\} = 1$; the price of the unit payoff is positive.

The beta representation (11.4) is equivalent to the inner product pricing relation (8.3)—just retrace the steps backward. There are, however, important practical and conceptual differences between these two representations as they are commonly studied in the literature. Suppose we have a candidate q^* to use in pricing (e.g., a model of q^* we want to test). Even if the econometrician does not observe all of the variables generating $\mathcal{A}$, the law of iterated expectations can be used to construct tests based on the relation

$$E\big[q^*_{t+1} r_{t+1} \mid \mathcal{J}_t\big] = 1, \quad r_{t+1} \in \mathcal{R}_t, \tag{11.6}$$

for an information set $\mathcal{J}_t$ observed by the econometrician. Given a candidate q^* for pricing returns in $\mathcal{R}_{t+1}$, we can test (11.6) using the methods outlined in Chapter 10.

In contrast, we cannot simply "condition down" the beta representation (11.4), since the law of iterated expectations does not apply to central second moments. (Later we explore whether a similar beta representation conditioned on $\mathcal{J} \subset \mathcal{A}$ obtains.) Equally importantly, in empirical studies of beta representations, researchers often focus on (11.4) and (11.5), but ignore (11.2); they do not impose the pricing relation $r^j_{t-1} = 1/E[q^*_t \mid \mathcal{A}_{t-1}]$. This is because the goal in studying beta relations is typically to express excess returns in terms of a benchmark return, without having to take a stand on the nature of the underlying pricing kernel q^*. A practical implication of this observation is that, whereas the return r^*_t is the unique element of $\mathcal{R}_t$ satisfying (8.8), there are an infinite number of returns that can substitute for r^* in (11.4) and (11.5) with this beta relation continuing to hold. It follows that tests of intertemporal CAPMs (ICAPMs) based on beta representations focus on a subset of the restrictions on the joint distributions of returns implied by equilibrium DAPMs.

While the goals in studying pricing relations based on pricing kernels versus benchmark returns may be different, they share the common challenge of identifying a pricing kernel q^* that satisfies (11.6) or a benchmark return that satisfies a beta relation like (11.4) and (11.5). In preference-based models, one candidate for q^* is an agent's marginal rate of substitution. The associated minimum conditional second moment, and candidate benchmark, return is $r^*_t = m^1_t/E[(m^1_t)^2 \mid \mathcal{A}_{t-1}]$. To implement tests based on these constructs requires knowledge of both the functional dependence of m^1_t on the state of the economy and the conditional distribution of the state. When such information is available, tests based on the pricing relations expressed in terms of q^* allow the incorporation of more of this known economic structure. For Euler-equation-based tests, there is also the convenience of conditioning down to the econometrician's information set. These considerations motivate in part the continued focus on pricing kernels in the empirical analysis of consumption-based DAPMs.

On the other hand, when exploring beta relations, there is a long-standing tradition of positing a candidate benchmark return r_t^β and then testing the conditional moment restrictions

$$E[r_t^x | \mathcal{A}_{t-1}] - r_{t-1}^f = \beta_{x,t-1} \left(E[r_t^\beta | \mathcal{A}_{t-1}] - r_{t-1}^f \right), \qquad r_t^x \in \mathcal{R}_t, \quad (11.7)$$

where $\beta_{x,t-1} = \mathrm{Cov}(r_t^x, r_t^\beta | \mathcal{A}_{t-1}) / \mathrm{Var}(r_t^\beta | \mathcal{A}_{t-1})$. While (11.7) looks like a conditional version of the static CAPM, neither that nor standard preference-based DAPMs provides concrete guidance as to which benchmark returns r^β should satisfy (11.7), other than $r_t^* = m_t^1 / E[(m_t^1)^2 | \mathcal{A}_{t-1}]$.

Given the attention received by the market return r_t^M—the return on a broadly diversified set of equities like the NYSE securities—in the static CAPM, one might conjecture that it is a benchmark for a conditional beta relation. However, this choice does not have the same economic underpinnings as it does in the static environment of the CAPM. In particular, we cannot set $r^* = r^M$, because then (11.7) is not an economically meaningful model. The reason is that from substitution of r_t^* for r_t in (11.3) and using the fact that $\mathrm{Var}(r_t^* | \mathcal{I}_{t-1}) > 0$, we set

$$E[r_t^* | \mathcal{A}_{t-1}] - r_{t-1}^f = -\frac{\mathrm{Var}(r_t^* | \mathcal{A}_{t-1})}{E[r_t^* | \mathcal{A}_{t-1}]} \Rightarrow E[r_t^* | \mathcal{A}_{t-1}] < r_{t-1}^f; \quad (11.8)$$

and r^* must have a lower mean than the riskless interest rate. In light of the substantial magnitude of the "equity premium" on diversified equity portfolios (see Chapter 10), clearly we cannot have r^* and r^M as the same return. This observation does not rule out a more flexible model, say, with $r_t^* = \phi_{0,t-1} + \phi_{M,t-1} r_t^M$, for $\phi_{0,t-1}$ and $\phi_{M,t-1}$ in $\mathcal{A}$. However, we see no simple way of imposing the requirement (11.8) outside of the derivation of ϕ_0 and ϕ_M from an equilibrium economic model.

Of course, the fact that $r^* \neq r^M$ does not mean that r^M cannot serve as one of the risk factors comprising an admissible benchmark return for a conditional beta relation. Indeed, such beta relations have been studied by Jagannathan and Wang (1996) and Ferson and Harvey (1999), among others. Rather, these observations are intended simply to highlight the challenge in providing an economic foundation for this or any other choice of r^β that is not r^*.

11.2. Beta Representations of Excess Returns

With these observations in mind, we turn next to a more general discussion of beta representations and the concept of conditional mean-variance efficiency (MVE). For the purpose of this discussion, we continue our focus on a conditionally complete payoff space $\mathcal{P} \subset \mathcal{P}^+$, defined relative to agents' information set $\mathcal{A}$, satisfying HR regularity. A return $r_t^\beta \in \mathcal{R}_t$ is said to be on the mean-variance frontier conditioned on $\mathcal{A}$ if it satisfies the following property:

Property 11.1: MVE. $r_t^\beta \in \mathcal{R}_t$ *satisfies*

$$\text{Var}\big(r_t^\beta \mid \mathcal{A}_{t-1}\big) \leq \text{Var}\big(r_t^x \mid \mathcal{A}_{t-1}\big), \tag{11.9}$$

for all $r_t^x \in \mathcal{R}_t$ such that $E(r_t^x \mid \mathcal{A}_{t-1}) = E(r_t^\beta \mid \mathcal{A}_{t-1})$.

Note that r_t^* in (8.5) (constructed with $\mathcal{A}$) satisfies Property MVE, because it is the global minimum second-moment return among all returns in $\mathcal{R}_t$ and, as such, its conditional variance is at least as small as that of any other return in $\mathcal{R}_t$ with the same mean. In representative agent, consumption-based models r^* is the return on security that pays off the representative agent's marginal rate of substitution. Though mean-variance efficient, for the reasons outlined earlier, this return must lie on the lower portion of the conditional mean-variance frontier.

A key result in the literature on mean-variance efficiency is that the set of all returns satisfying Property MVE is a two-dimensional set in the sense that two returns span all of the returns with this property. More precisely, suppose (P, π) is HR-regular and that there exist returns r_t^x and r_t^y in $\mathcal{R}_t$ such that $Pr\{E(r_t^x - r_t^y \mid \mathcal{A}_{t-1}) = 0\} = 0$ (which rules out risk-neutral pricing on $\mathcal{P}_t$). Then there exists a return $r_t^\#$ in $\mathcal{R}_t$ satisfying Property MVE such that every $r_t^\beta \in \mathcal{R}_t$ satisfying Property MVE can be represented as

$$r_t^\beta = \big(1 - \omega_{t-1}^\beta\big)r_t^* + \omega_{t-1}^\beta r_t^\#, \tag{11.10}$$

for some $\omega_{t-1}^\beta \in \mathcal{A}_{t-1}$, where $r_t^* = q_t^*/\pi_{t-1}(q_t^*)$. This result is the conditional counterpart of Roll's (1977) two-fund theorem.[3] It allows us to characterize completely the mean-variance frontier conditioned on $\mathcal{A}$ by characterizing two returns that are on the frontier. The return r_t^* is one such return.

If $\mathcal{P}_t$ contains a unit payoff and there are no arbitrage opportunities on $\mathcal{P}_t$, then $\mathcal{R}_t$ contains the riskfree return $r_{t-1}^f = 1/E(q_t^* \mid \mathcal{A}_{t-1})$. In this case, $r_t^\#$ can be shown to be[4]

$$r_t^\# = \left(1 - \frac{1}{r_{t-1}^f}\right)r_t^* + \left(\frac{1}{r_{t-1}^f}\right)r_{t-1}^f. \tag{11.11}$$

---

[3] It follows immediately from Lemma 3.3 in Hansen and Richard (1987), which implies that $r_t^\beta = r_t^* + \omega_{t-1}^* z_t^*$, where z_t^* satisfies $\pi_{t-1}(z_t^*) = 0$. Their expression is equivalent to (11.10) with $r_t^\# = r_t^* + z_t^* \in \mathcal{R}_t$.

[4] When there is a unit payoff in $\mathcal{P}_t$, z^* in the preceding footnote is given by $z_t^* = 1 - r_t^*/r_{t-1}^f$. Substituting into $r_t^\# = r_t^* + z_t^*$ and rearranging gives (11.11).

This return is in R_t since it is a weighted average of r_t^* and r_{t-1}^f with weights in $\mathcal{A}_{t-1}$. Substituting (11.11) into (11.10) leads to the following alternative characterization of the mean-variance frontier in R_t:

$$r_t^\beta = \left(1 - \frac{\omega_{t-1}^\beta}{r_{t-1}^f}\right) r_t^* + \left(\frac{\omega_{t-1}^\beta}{r_{t-1}^f}\right) r_{t-1}^f, \quad \omega_{t-1}^\beta \in \mathcal{A}_{t-1}. \qquad (11.12)$$

Hence, when there is a unit payoff in $\mathcal{P}_t$, the mean-variance frontier is spanned by r_t^* and r_{t-1}^f.

In practice, tests of mean-variance efficiency of a portfolio are typically conducted in the context of a beta representation of returns. Accordingly, we next explore the relation between the property of being on the conditional mean-variance frontier and the property of being a benchmark return for a single-beta representation of returns, which follows:

Property 11.2: SβB. $r_t^\beta \in R_t$ *satisfies* $\Pr\{\mathrm{Var}(r_t^\beta \mid \mathcal{A}_{t-1}) > 0\} = 1$ *and*

$$E\left[r_t^x \mid \mathcal{A}_{t-1}\right] - \mu_{t-1} = \beta_{x,t-1}\left\{E\left[r_t^\beta \mid \mathcal{A}_{t-1}\right] - \mu_{t-1}\right\}, \qquad (11.13)$$

where

$$\beta_{x,t-1} = \frac{\mathrm{Cov}\left(r_t^x, r_t^\beta \mid \mathcal{A}_{t-1}\right)}{\mathrm{Var}\left(r_t^\beta \mid \mathcal{A}_{t-1}\right)},$$

for some $\mu_{t-1} \in \mathcal{A}_{t-1}$ *and all* $r_t^x \in R_t$.

Suppose $(\mathcal{P}, \pi)$ is HR regular, π has no arbitrage opportunities on $\mathcal{P}$, $\mathcal{P}_t$ does not admit risk-neutral pricing, and $\mathcal{P}$ contains a unit payoff. Let r_t^β be the frontier return in (11.10). Then r_t^β satisfies Property SβB if and only if $r_t^\beta = (1 - \omega_{t-1}^\beta) r_t^* + \omega_{t-1}^\beta r_{t-1}^f$, where $\omega_{t-1}^\beta \in \mathcal{A}_{t-1}$, and there exists a return r_t^0 such that $\mathrm{Var}(r_t^0 \mid \mathcal{A}_{t-1}) < \mathrm{Var}(r_t^\beta \mid \mathcal{A}_{t-1})$. This result, which is a conditional counterpart to Roll's (1977) Corollary 6, is an immediate implication of Lemma 3.5 in Hansen and Richard (1987). The assumption that there is a return $r_t^0 \in R_t$ with smaller variance than r_t^β guarantees that there is zero probability that r_t^β is the minimum conditional variance return.

It follows that the entire mean-variance frontier conditioned on $\mathcal{A}$ can be characterized in terms of the pricing kernel for this economy. If there is a representative agent, then $q^* = m^1$, and the frontier can be characterized in terms of agents' marginal rate of substitution.

11.3. Conditioning Down and Beta Relations

On the other hand, a primary motivation for testing CAPMs using beta representations is that the restrictions are expressed entirely in terms of returns. In this manner, possibly serious measurement problems with such macroeconomic variables as consumption may be avoided. This reason alone may be sufficient motivation for imposing only a subset of the restrictions implied by an ICAPM. However, tests based on beta representations in environments where conditioning information is important also present challenging measurement problems. Specifically, the set of returns on mean-variance frontiers conditioned on the econometrician's information set $\mathcal{J}$ must be characterized. In particular, specific benchmark returns that are in the information set $\mathcal{J}_t$ must be identified for use in econometric analyses. Following Hansen and Richard (1987), we next address this issue of conditioning down to a smaller information set.[5]

Let

$$P_t^{\mathcal{J}} = \left\{ q_t \in \mathcal{P}_t : E\left[q_t^2 \mid \mathcal{J}_{t-1}\right] < \infty \right\}, \qquad (11.14)$$

where $\mathcal{J}_t \subseteq \mathcal{A}_t$, and let

$$\mathcal{R}_t^{\mathcal{J}} = \mathcal{R}_t \cap P_t^{\mathcal{J}}. \qquad (11.15)$$

If we assume that there exists a return r_t^0 in $\mathcal{R}_t^{\mathcal{J}}$, the return $r_t^* \in \mathcal{R}_t$ is in $\mathcal{R}_t^{\mathcal{J}}$ since r_t^* is the minimum conditional second-moment return in $\mathcal{R}_t$.[6] Hence, r_t^* satisfies Property MVE in any return space $\mathcal{R}_t^{\mathcal{J}}$ with $\mathcal{J}_t \subseteq \mathcal{A}_t$. It turns out that the returns r_t^* and $r_t^{\#}$ underlying (11.10) continue to span the mean-variance frontier conditioned on $\mathcal{J}_{t-1}$, with the weights being in $\mathcal{J}_{t-1}$.

More precisely, under HR regularity of $P^{\mathcal{J}}$, if r_t^{β} satisfies Property MVE in the return space $\mathcal{R}_t^{\mathcal{J}}$, then[7]

$$r_t^{\beta} = \left(1 - \omega_{t-1}^{\beta}\right)r_t^* + \omega_t^{\beta} r_t^{\#}, \quad \omega_{t-1}^{\beta} \in \mathcal{J}_{t-1}. \qquad (11.16)$$

It follows immediately that returns on the mean-variance frontier conditioned on $\mathcal{J}$ are on the mean-variance frontier conditioned on $\mathcal{A}$. The converse is not true in general, however.

More generally, using arguments similar to those in the preceding section, for any information set $\mathcal{J}$ and conditionally complete payoff space $\mathcal{P}^{\mathcal{J}}$, under HR regularity, we can conclude that the family of benchmark returns in $\mathcal{R}^{\mathcal{J}}$ satisfies the beta relation

$$E\left[r_t^x \mid \mathcal{J}_{t-1}\right] - \mu_{t-1}^{\mathcal{J}} = \beta_{x,t-1}^{\mathcal{J}}\left\{E\left[r_t^{\beta\mathcal{J}} \mid \mathcal{J}_{t-1}\right] - \mu_{t-1}\right\}, \qquad (11.17)$$

---

[5] Hansen and Richard (1987) provide the conceptual foundations for this section. The presentation here draws upon their analysis and the analysis in Hansen et al. (1982).

[6] If $E[r_t^{*2} \mid \mathcal{A}_{t-1}] \leq E[r_t^2 \mid \mathcal{A}_{t-1}]$, for all $r_t \in \mathcal{R}_t$, then $E[r_t^{*2} \mid \mathcal{J}_{t-1}] \leq E[r_t^2 \mid \mathcal{J}_{t-1}]$, for all $r_t \in \mathcal{R}_t^{\mathcal{J}}$, by the law of iterated expectations.

[7] This result is an implication of the law of iterated expectations and the arguments used to prove Lemma 3.3 in Hansen and Richard (1987).

where

$$\beta_{x,t-1}^{\mathcal{J}} = \frac{\mathrm{Cov}\left(r_t^x, r_t^{\beta\mathcal{J}} \mid \mathcal{J}_{t-1}\right)}{\mathrm{Var}\left(r_t^{\beta\mathcal{J}} \mid \mathcal{J}_{t-1}\right)}$$

for some $\mu_{t-1}^{\mathcal{J}} \in \mathcal{J}_{t-1}$ and all $r_t^x \in \mathcal{R}_t^{\mathcal{J}}$. The construct $\mu_{t-1}^{\mathcal{J}}$ is often interpreted as the expected return (conditioned on $\mathcal{J}$) of the "zero-beta" portfolio (see Black, 1972). The reason is that any $r_t^x \in \mathcal{R}_t^{\mathcal{J}}$ that has a zero beta with $r_t^{\beta\mathcal{J}}$ has mean $\mu_{t-1}^{\mathcal{J}}$.

In the context of the ICAPM with $q^* = m_t^1$, r_t^* is on the frontier for the return space $\mathcal{R}_t^{\mathcal{A}}$, and hence remains on the frontier for all return spaces $\mathcal{R}_t^{\mathcal{J}}$, as long as $\mathcal{J}_{t-1} \subseteq \mathcal{A}_{t-1}$. The analogous statement cannot be made with respect to r_{t-1}^f. If r_{t-1}^f is not in the information set $\mathcal{J}_{t-1}$, then r_{t-1}^f is not in general on the frontier conditioned on $\mathcal{J}_{t-1}$ and, hence, this frontier cannot be represented as in (11.12) with $\omega_{t-1}^{\beta} \in \mathcal{J}_{t-1}$. Nevertheless, in this case, there is a return that is a function of r_t^* and r_{t-1}^f that does remain on the frontier for $\mathcal{R}_t^{\mathcal{J}}$. Specifically, consider the counterpart to $r_t^\#$ in (11.11) for the ICAPM:

$$r_t^\# = \left(1 - \frac{1}{r_{t-1}^f}\right) r_t^* + \left(\frac{1}{r_{t-1}^f}\right) r_{t-1}^f. \tag{11.18}$$

The assumption that $E[(r_t^*)^2 \mid \mathcal{J}_{t-1}] < \infty$ implies that $r_t^\# \in \mathcal{R}_t^{\mathcal{J}}$. Furthermore, $r_t^\#$ satisfies Property MVE in $\mathcal{R}_t^{\mathcal{J}}$.[8]

This discussion leads to a useful characterization of the mean-variance frontier for $\mathcal{R}_t^{\mathcal{J}}$ implied by the ICAPM. Yet we have not avoided measurement of the representative agent's marginal rate of substitution as r_t^* and $r_t^\#$ both depend on m_t^1 and its conditional moments. Can we identify other returns on the mean-variance frontier that are admissible benchmark returns for single-beta representations conditioned on the econometrician's information set? The ICAPM does not provide an answer to this question.

If we define the payoff space analogously to the payoff space implicitly used in many formulations of the CAPM, then there is a constructive solution to the problem of finding a benchmark return. Let $\bar{r}_t$ denote an n-dimensional vector of returns in $\mathcal{R}_t^{\mathcal{J}}$, ι_n denote an n-dimensional vector of ones, and consider the return space:

$$\mathcal{C}_t^{\mathcal{J}} = \left\{ r_t \in \mathcal{R}_t^{\mathcal{J}} : r_t = \omega_{t-1} \cdot \bar{r}_t; \quad \omega_{t-1} \cdot \iota_n = 1, \quad \omega_{t-1} \in \mathcal{J}_{t-1} \right\}. \tag{11.19}$$

The space $\mathcal{C}_t^{\mathcal{J}}$ is the set of returns on portfolios of the n assets underlying $\bar{r}_t$ with portfolio weights in $\mathcal{J}_{t-1}$. If, for example, $\bar{r}$ includes returns on all

---

[8] See Hansen et al. (1982) for details.

stocks listed on the NYSE and the values of the outstanding shares for these firms are in the information set $\mathcal{J}$, then the equally- and value-weighted returns on the NYSE are in $\mathcal{C}_t^{\mathcal{J}}$.

An implication of HR regularity is that there exists an element $\tilde{r}_t^{\mathcal{J}}$ of $\mathcal{C}_t^{\mathcal{J}}$ of the form $\tilde{r}_t^{\mathcal{J}} = \tilde{\omega}_{t-1} \cdot \tilde{r}_t$ satisfying

$$E[(\iota_n\tilde{\omega}_{t-1} \cdot \tilde{r}_t - \tilde{r}_t)\tilde{r}_t \cdot \tilde{\omega}_{t-1} \mid \mathcal{J}_{t-1}] = 0. \tag{11.20}$$

Suppose $\Omega_{t-1} \equiv E[\tilde{r}_t\tilde{r}_t' \mid \mathcal{J}_{t-1}]$ is nonsingular almost surely. Then the unique choice of $\tilde{\omega}_{t-1}$ that satisfies (11.20) is

$$\tilde{\omega}_{t-1} = \Omega_{t-1}^{-1}\iota_n / (\iota_n'\Omega_{t-1}^{-1}\iota_n). \tag{11.21}$$

By construction the return $\tilde{r}_t^{\mathcal{J}} = \tilde{\omega}_{t-1} \cdot \tilde{r}_t$, with $\tilde{\omega}_{t-1}$ given in (11.21), is on the conditional mean-variance frontier in the space $\mathcal{C}_t^{\mathcal{J}}$ and hence serves as a benchmark return for this space. Therefore, using the definition of $\tilde{r}^{\mathcal{J}}$ in terms of the pricing kernel $\tilde{q}$ for $\mathcal{P}^{\mathcal{J}}$, it follows that

$$\tilde{q}_t = \iota_n'\Omega_{t-1}^{-1}\tilde{r}_t. \tag{11.22}$$

Of course, there are no testable restrictions implied by this analysis as $\tilde{r}^{\mathcal{J}}$ satisfies a beta relation by construction.

This discussion leaves us with the following practical dilemma: we can condition down to an econometrician's information set $\mathcal{J}$ and fully characterize the family of returns that serve as benchmarks for single-beta representations of excess returns (conditional on $\mathcal{J}$). However, in the absence of guidance from an economic model, the only known candidate for a benchmark return is the marginal rate of substitution return, because it remains on the conditional mean-variance frontier as we condition down from the agents' to the econometrician's information set. Faced with this dilemma, several researchers have proposed the imposition of a "factor structure" on the pricing kernel q^* as a means of deriving testable multibeta representations of excess returns. Depending on the context, these factor models are sometimes interpreted as reduced-form representations of agents' marginal rate of substitution, and sometimes viewed more restrictively as a representation of the pricing kernel for a subset of payoffs on tradable securities. We turn next to a discussion of this modeling strategy.

11.4. From Pricing Kernels to Factor Models

We have already seen that specifying r^* as a weighted sum of portfolio returns leads to potential inconsistencies in that r^* is on the lower, inefficient part of the mean-variance frontier, whereas the portfolios that researchers have used as benchmarks are on or closer to the efficient part of the frontier. In an alternative modeling approach, which preserves the tradition of working with a finite set of risk factors and ensures that (11.8) is satisfied, we can work directly with a factor representation of q^*. Such factor models have been discussed by Dybvig and Ingersoll (1982) and Cochrane (1996) (based on unconditional moments) and by Lettau and Ludvigson (2001b) (using conditioning), among others. Initially, we proceed with our general conditional framework, starting with a payoff space $\mathcal{P}$ defined relative to agents' information set $\mathcal{A}$.

We suppose that q_t^* has the "factor" representation

$$q_t^* = \phi_{t-1}^0 + \phi_{t-1}^{f\,'} f_t, \tag{11.23}$$

where $\tilde{\phi}_{t-1}' = (\phi_{t-1}^0, \phi_{t-1}^{f\,'}) \in \mathcal{A}_{t-1}$ and f_t is a vector of K risk factors. Letting $\tilde{f}_t' = (1, f_t')$, in this case, we get

$$r_{t-1}^f = \frac{1}{E[q_t^* | \mathcal{A}_{t-1}]} = \frac{1}{E[\tilde{f}_t | \mathcal{A}_{t-1}]' \tilde{\phi}_{t-1}}, \tag{11.24}$$

and, from (11.3) and the definition of r^*,

$$E[r_t^x | \mathcal{A}_{t-1}] - r_{t-1}^f = \frac{-\mathrm{Cov}[r_t^x, q_t^* \,|\, \mathcal{A}_{t-1}]}{E[q_t^* \,|\, \mathcal{A}_{t-1}]}, \qquad r_t^x \in \mathcal{R}_t. \tag{11.25}$$

Substituting (11.23) into (11.25) and rearranging gives

$$
\begin{aligned}
E[r_t^x | \mathcal{A}_{t-1}] &= \frac{1 - \mathrm{Cov}(r_t^x, f_t' | \mathcal{A}_{t-1}) \mathrm{Cov}(f_t, f_t' | \mathcal{A}_{t-1})^{-1} \mathrm{Cov}(f_t, f_t' | \mathcal{A}_{t-1}) \phi_{t-1}^f}{E[\tilde{f}_t' | \mathcal{A}_{t-1}] \tilde{\phi}_{t-1}} \\
&= r_{t-1}^f + \beta_{x,t-1}' \lambda_{t-1}, \tag{11.26}
\end{aligned}
$$

where $r_t^x \in \mathcal{R}_t$ and

$$\beta_{x,t-1} = \mathrm{Cov}(f_t, f_t' | \mathcal{A}_{t-1})^{-1} \times \mathrm{Cov}(f_t, r_t^x | \mathcal{A}_{t-1}), \tag{11.27}$$

$$\lambda_{t-1} = -r_{t-1}^f E[q_t^*(f_t - E[f_t | \mathcal{A}_{t-1}]) | \mathcal{A}_{t-1}]. \tag{11.28}$$

As discussed previously, the conditional moment restrictions (11.26) and (11.24), together, are equivalent to the moment condition $E[q_t^* r_t^x | \mathcal{A}_{t-1}] = 1$.

The jth element of λ_{t-1} is

$$
\begin{aligned}
\lambda_{j,t-1} &= -r_{t-1}^f \big(E[q_t^* f_{jt} | \mathcal{A}_{t-1}] - E[q_t^* | \mathcal{A}_{t-1}] E[f_{jt} | \mathcal{A}_{t-1}] \big) \\
&= E[f_{jt} | \mathcal{A}_{t-1}] - r_{t-1}^f E[q_t^* f_{jt} | \mathcal{A}_{t-1}]. \tag{11.29}
\end{aligned}
$$

If f_j is an excess return, then $E[q_t^* f_{jt} | \mathcal{A}_{t-1}] = 0$ and $\lambda_{j,t-1}$ is the conditional mean of the excess return factor f_j. Alternatively, if f_j is a return, then $E[q_t^* f_{jt} | \mathcal{A}_{t-1}] = 1$ and (11.29) gives the expected excess return on the jth factor. Common terminology is that "factor j is priced" if $\lambda_{j,t-1}$ is nonzero, the idea being that the risks from this factor are reflected in excess returns according to (11.26). From (11.29) we see that $\lambda_{j,t-1} = 0$ when q_t^* and f_{jt} are uncorrelated or, equivalently, when the price of the payoff ($f_{jt} - E[f_{jt} | \mathcal{A}_{t-1}]$) is zero (hence we say that factor j is not priced).

As noted by Cochrane (1996), whether a factor is priced is distinct from whether the jth factor f_j is useful in pricing other assets; that is, whether $\phi_{j,t}^f = 0$, for all t. Substituting (11.23) into (11.28) gives

$$\lambda_{t-1} = -r_{t-1}^f \text{Cov}(f_t, \tilde{f}_t' | \mathcal{A}_{t-1}) \tilde{\phi}_{t-1}. \tag{11.30}$$

Therefore, the hypotheses $\phi_{j,t-1}^f = 0$ and $\lambda_{j,t-1} = 0$ are equivalent only if the factors are uncorrelated.

To illustrate the ideas behind these calculations, suppose that $K = 1$ and $q_t^* = \phi_{t-1}^0 + \phi_{t-1}^M (r_t^M - r_{t-1}^f)$, where r_t^M is the return on some market portfolio (analogously to the static CAPM). Then substitution first into (11.29) and then into (11.26) gives (11.7) with $r_t^\beta = r_t^M$.

More generally, if q^* is a conditional affine function of a vector of excess returns, constructed from the factor benchmark returns ($r^{p_1}, \ldots, r^{p_N}$), then we get multifactor models such as those studied by Ferson and Harvey (1999) and Moskowitz (2003): for any $r_t^x \in \mathcal{R}_t$,

$$E[r_t^x | \mathcal{A}_{t-1}] - r_{t-1}^f = \beta_{x,t-1}^1 \left(E[r_t^{p_1} | \mathcal{A}_{t-1}] - r_{t-1}^f \right)$$
$$+ \ldots + \beta_{x,t-1}^N \left(E[r_t^{p_N} | \mathcal{A}_{t-1}] - r_{t-1}^f \right). \tag{11.31}$$

Note that the weights on the underlying risk factors, the ϕ_{t-1}^f in (11.23), do not appear in (11.31). Therefore, when the factors are returns or excess returns we can, in principle, study (11.31) without having to model the dependence of ϕ_{t-1}^f on the state vector for this economy (on elements of $\mathcal{A}_{t-1}$).

There are two important qualifications to this observation. First, not needing to know ϕ_{t-1}^f does not overcome the need to know agents' information set $\mathcal{A}$. This is because all of the moments in (11.31) depend on $\mathcal{A}$. Second, in studying (11.31), we are not imposing the relation $r_{t-1}^f = 1/(E[\tilde{f}_t' | \mathcal{A}_{t-1}] \tilde{\phi}_{t-1})$, so (11.31) does not embody the same economic content as (8.3).

The former of these qualifications in particular generally makes the study of (11.31) infeasible without further simplifying assumptions. Substantial simplification is achieved if we impose the additional assumption that

$\tilde{\phi}_{t-1} \in \mathcal{J}_{t-1}$, where $\mathcal{J}$ is the econometrician's information set. This assumption has been made (explicitly or implicitly) in most studies of time-varying beta models in the literature on dynamic CAPMs. Proceeding under this assumption we begin again with the supposition that

$$q_t^* = \tilde{\phi}_{t-1}' \tilde{f}_t, \quad \tilde{\phi}_{t-1} \in \mathcal{J}_{t-1}. \tag{11.32}$$

Retracing our steps we get the following beta relation conditioned on $\mathcal{J}$[9]:

$$E[r_t^x \mid \mathcal{J}_{t-1}] = \mu_{t-1}^{0\mathcal{J}} + \beta_{x,t-1}^{\mathcal{J}'} \lambda_{t-1}^{\mathcal{J}}, \tag{11.33}$$

$$\mu_{t-1}^{0\mathcal{J}} = 1/E[q_t^* \mid \mathcal{J}_{t-1}], \tag{11.34}$$

$$\beta_{x,t-1}^{\mathcal{J}} = \text{Cov}(f_t, f_t' \mid \mathcal{J}_{t-1})^{-1} \times \text{Cov}(f_t, r_t^x \mid \mathcal{J}_{t-1}), \tag{11.35}$$

$$\lambda_{t-1}^{\mathcal{J}} = -\mu_{t-1}^{0\mathcal{J}} \text{Cov}(f_t, \tilde{f}_t' \mid \mathcal{J}_{t-1}) \tilde{\phi}_{t-1}. \tag{11.36}$$

If $r_{t-1}^f \in \mathcal{J}_{t-1}$, then $\mu_{t-1}^{0\mathcal{J}} = r_{t-1}^f$ and excess returns are relative to the riskfree rate. More generally, $\mu_{t-1}^{0\mathcal{J}}$ is the return on a zero-beta (conditional on $\mathcal{J}$) portfolio.

There are at least two views on the scope of the applicability of the beta model (11.36) to returns r_t^x. One view is that $q_t^* = \tilde{\phi}_{t-1}' \tilde{f}_t$, with $\tilde{\phi}_{t-1} \in \mathcal{J}_{t-1}$, is the pricing kernel for a payoff space $\mathcal{P}_t^{\mathcal{A}}$ conditioned on $\mathcal{A}$ (where $\mathcal{J}_t \subset \mathcal{A}_t$ and $f_t \in \mathcal{A}_t$). In this case q_t^* must price all of the payoffs (and in particular all returns) in $\mathcal{P}^{\mathcal{A}}$. It seems that pricing kernels with this special property are what some researchers had in mind when studying factor specifications of q^*. For instance, Lettau and Ludvigson (2001b) motivate their factor model by starting with constant relative risk-averse preferences for a representative agent [see (10.3)] and then linearizing the implied marginal rate of substitution $m_t^1 = \beta(c_t/c_{t-1})^{\gamma-1}$ to obtain

$$q_t^* = m_t^1 \approx \phi_{t-1}^0 + \phi_{t-1}^m \Delta \ln c_t. \tag{11.37}$$

Furthermore, they presume that $\tilde{\phi}_{t-1}' = (\phi_{t-1}^0, \phi_{t-1}^m)$ is a known function of a vector $z_{t-1} \in \mathcal{J}_{t-1}$. Since the representative agent's marginal rate of substitution is fully characterized, if we maintain an economic environment that admits aggregation (see Chapter 10), then all securities that agents trade and that are priced by their marginal rates of substitution are priced by this q^*.

In cases like this, we can define $\mathcal{J}_t$ to be the information set generated by the z_t that determines the factor weights defining q^*. The zero-beta return

---

[9] We use the assumption that $\tilde{\phi}_{t-1} \in \mathcal{J}_{t-1}$ to factor out $\tilde{\phi}_{t-1}$ in (11.38).

$\mu_{t-1}^{0\mathcal{J}}$ and the conditional betas $\beta_{x,t-1}^{\mathcal{J}}$ can then be computed relative to this narrowly defined information set $\mathcal{J}_{t-1}$. Of course, unless r_{t-1}^f is included explicitly in $\mathcal{J}_{t-1}$, $\mu_{t-1}^{0\mathcal{J}}$ is typically not equal to r_{t-1}^f. Therefore, excluding r_{t-1}^f from z_{t-1} and centering excess returns around r_{t-1}^f essentially amounts to assuming that r_{t-1}^f is redundant in $\tilde{\phi}_{t-1}$.

An alternative interpretation of a factor model for q^* with the factor weights $\tilde{\phi}_{t-1} \in \mathcal{J}$ is that q^* is the pricing kernel for $(\mathcal{P}^{\mathcal{J}}, \mathcal{R}^{\mathcal{J}})$ and it is hypothesized to have the form (11.32). Once one parameterizes the weights $\tilde{\phi}_{t-1}$ as functions of elements of $\mathcal{J}_{t-1}$, then econometric analysis can proceed as discussed later. However, left unspecified in this approach is the connection between the "reduced-form" representation of q^* and any specific economic model.

Finally, before turning to empirical analyses of factor models, we examine when conditional factor models imply a corresponding unconditional formulation. As we set out to address this issue, it is instructive to distinguish between two, very different, interpretations of an implied unconditional model. First, we inquire under what circumstances a K-factor conditional beta model specializes to a K-factor unconditional beta model of expected excess returns. Second, we show that any conditional model in which the factors f are excess returns and the factor weights $\tilde{\phi}_{t-1}$ in the definition of q_t^* are affine functions of a state vector z_{t-1} naturally leads to an unconditional beta representation of unconditional expected returns. No additional assumptions are required; the unconditional model represents a subset of the restrictions implied by the conditional model. We elaborate on each of these versions in turn. To simplify notation, we focus on the case of a single factor $(K = 1)$ that is the excess return on a benchmark portfolio, $f_t = r_t^\beta - r_{t-1}^f$.

One special case that gives rise to an unconditional single-beta model is when $\tilde{\phi}$, the factor weights determining q_t^*, are constant (state independent). In this case we can again retrace the steps followed to derive (11.32)–(11.36), but now with $\mathcal{J}_t$ being the null information set. This leads to

$$E[r_t^x] - \mu_0 = \beta_x E[f_t], \tag{11.38}$$

where $\mu_0 = 1/E[q_t^*]$ and $\beta_x = \mathrm{Cov}[r_t^x, f_t]/\mathrm{Var}[f_t]$. Of course the assumption that the factor weights $\phi_{t-1} = \phi$ are state independent is not generally consistent with dynamic economies.

More generally, to examine the case of dynamic economies with state-dependent factor weights, we fix an information set $\mathcal{J}_t$ and assume that $r_{t-1}^f \in \mathcal{J}_{t-1}$ and $r_t^\beta \in \mathcal{J}_t$. Further suppose that, analogously to the development of (11.32)–(11.36),

$$E[r_t^x \mid \mathcal{J}_{t-1}] - r_{t-1}^f = \beta_{x,t-1}^{\mathcal{J}} \lambda_{t-1}^{\mathcal{J}}, \tag{11.39}$$

$$\lambda_{t-1}^{\mathcal{J}} = E\left[r_t^\beta - r_{t-1}^f \,\middle|\, \mathcal{J}_{t-1}\right], \tag{11.40}$$

where the last equality follows from the fact that the risk factor f_t is an excess return. Letting $R_t^x \equiv (r_t^x - r_{t-1}^f)$ denote the excess return for any security x, an implication of these equilibrium restrictions is that the $(\alpha_{x,t-1}, \beta_{x,t-1}^{\mathcal{J}})$ that solve the conditional least-squares minimization problem

$$\min_{\alpha_{x,t-1}, \beta_{x,t-1}^{\mathcal{J}}} E\left[\left(R_t^x - \alpha_{x,t-1} - \beta_{x,t-1}^{\mathcal{J}} R_t^\beta\right)^2 \,\middle|\, \mathcal{J}_{t-1}\right] \tag{11.41}$$

satisfy

$$\beta_{x,t-1}^{\mathcal{J}} = \frac{\text{Cov}\left[r_t^x, r_t^\beta \,\middle|\, \mathcal{J}_{t-1}\right]}{\text{Var}\left[r_t^\beta \,\middle|\, \mathcal{J}_{t-1}\right]}; \tag{11.42}$$

$$\alpha_{x,t-1} = E\left[R_t^x \,\middle|\, \mathcal{J}_{t-1}\right] - \beta_{x,t-1}^{\mathcal{J}} E\left[R_t^\beta \,\middle|\, \mathcal{J}_{t-1}\right] = 0. \tag{11.43}$$

The last expression is the economic content of this conditional beta model —the conditional beta model implies that conditional α's are zero.

Sufficient conditions for this model to condition down to an unconditional single-factor model obtain immediately from inspection of the first-order conditions to the optimum problem (11.41). Let $\beta_x \equiv E[\beta_{x,t-1}^{\mathcal{J}}]$ denote the mean of the conditional beta for security x, and let $\eta_{x,t-1}$ denote the mean-zero, stochastic component of $\beta_{x,t-1}^{\mathcal{J}}$; $\eta_{x,t-1} \equiv \beta_{x,t-1}^{\mathcal{J}} - \beta_x$. If we substitute for $\beta_{x,t-1}^{\mathcal{J}}$ into the first-order conditions to the minimization problem (11.41) and condition down to unconditional expectations, it is easy to verify that

$$E\left[\left(R_t^x - \beta_x R_t^\beta\right) R_t^\beta - \eta_{x,t-1}\left(R_t^\beta\right)^2\right] = 0, \tag{11.44}$$

$$E\left[\left(R_t^x - \beta_x R_t^\beta\right) - \eta_{x,t-1} R_t^\beta\right] = 0. \tag{11.45}$$

It follows immediately that if

$$E\left[\eta_{x,t-1}\left(R_t^\beta\right)^2\right] = 0 \text{ and } E\left[\eta_{x,t-1} R_t^\beta\right] = 0, \tag{11.46}$$

then (11.44) and (11.45) reduce to the normal equations for (unconditional) least-squares projection. That is,

$$\alpha_x = E\left[R_t^x\right] - \beta_x E\left[R_t^\beta\right] = 0, \tag{11.47}$$

and we obtain an unconditional beta model with $\beta_x = E[\beta_{x,t-1}^{\mathcal{J}}]$.

To interpret the sufficient conditions (11.46) for an unconditional beta model, note that they can be rewritten as[10]

$$E\left[\eta_{x,t-1}(R_t^\beta)^2\right] = \text{Cov}\left[\eta_{x,t-1}, \sigma_{\beta,t-1}^2\right] + \text{Cov}\left[\eta_{x,t-1}, (\lambda_{t-1}^{\mathcal{J}})^2\right] = 0, \quad (11.48)$$

$$E\left[\eta_{x,t-1} R_t^\beta\right] = \text{Cov}\left[\eta_{x,t-1}, \lambda_{t-1}^{\mathcal{J}}\right] = 0, \tag{11.49}$$

where $\sigma_{\beta,t-1}^2$ is the variance of R_t^β conditioned on $\mathcal{J}_{t-1}$. Thus, the conditional beta model implies a corresponding constant-beta model if the temporal variation in $\eta_{x,t-1}$ (which captures any variation in $\beta_{x,t-1}^{\mathcal{J}}$) is uncorrelated with the market price of the factor risk ($\lambda_{t-1}^{\mathcal{J}}$) and with ($\sigma_{\beta,t-1}^2 + (\lambda_{t-1}^{\mathcal{J}})^2$), the sum of the conditional variance of the benchmark return and the squared market price of risk. These conditions are a complementary representation of the sufficient conditions for a constant-beta model derived in Lewellen and Nagel (2005). We discuss their analysis in more depth when we take up the goodness-of-fit of conditional beta models.

A very different unconditional beta model has been the focal point of many econometric studies of conditional pricing models. Specifically, following Cochrane (1996), several researchers have assumed that the factor weights ϕ_{t-1} in the definition of q_t^* are affine functions of a state vector z_{t-1}. Continuing with our one-factor illustration, suppose that[11]

$$\phi_{t-1}^0 = a^0 + b^0 z_{t-1} \quad \text{and} \quad \phi_{t-1}^f = a^f + b^f z_{t-1}, \tag{11.50}$$

for observable $z_t \in \mathcal{J}_t$ and $K = 1$. Using this assumption we can condition down the pricing relation (11.6) to the unconditional moment equation

$$E\left[(a^0 + b^0 z_{t-1} + a^f f_t + b^f z_{t-1} f_t) r_t\right] = 1. \tag{11.51}$$

If we view $f_t^\# \equiv (f_t, z_{t-1}, f_t z_{t-1})$ as a set of risk factors and $q_t^\# \equiv a^0 + b^0 z_{t-1} + a^f f_t + b^f z_{t-1} f_t$ as a pricing kernel, then (11.51) can be treated (mechanically) as an unconditional version of (11.33), with $\mathcal{J}$ being the null information set. Exploiting this observation, we can write

$$E\left[r_t^x\right] = \mu + \beta_x' \lambda, \tag{11.52}$$

where μ is the (constant) average return on an unconditional zero-beta portfolio, $\beta_x = \text{Cov}(f_t^\#, f_t^{\#\prime})^{-1} \text{Cov}(f_t^\#, r_t^x)$, and $\lambda = -\mu \text{Cov}(f_t^\#, q_t^\#)$.

---

[10] In deriving the following we use the facts that $E[R_t^\beta | \mathcal{J}_{t-1}] = \lambda_{t-1}^{\mathcal{J}}$, from (11.40), and $\eta_{x,t-1}$ has mean zero.

[11] In the tradition of multibeta versions of CAPMs, this approach typically ignores the constraint $r_{t-1}^f = 1/(E[f_t' | \mathcal{J}_{t-1}] \tilde{\phi}(z_{t-1}))$.

That the one-factor conditional model we started with leads to a three-dimensional unconditional beta model illustrates a more general point. Factor risks are priced by agents conditioning on their information set $\mathcal{A}$. If there are K factor risks that are priced, a researcher testing a version of the CAPM conditional on $\mathcal{J} \subset \mathcal{A}$ may well be led to conclude that the number of priced factors is $K' > K$. In particular, if a researcher assumes that $\mathcal{J}$ is the null information set, then it may appear necessary to include additional risk factors in an unconditional CAPM regression to explain the cross section of historical means, even though these factors are not priced by agents. At the root of the appearance of additional factors in unconditional models is the correlation between risk premiums in the underlying conditional model and the state of the economy, as seen from (11.44) and (11.45). If the second terms in these relations are not zero (i.e., (11.46) does not hold), then state variables that are useful for predicting λ_t appear as additional factors.

11.5. Methods for Testing Beta Models

Fama and MacBeth (1973) test three implications of the unconditional beta model (11.38) with $f_t = (r_t^\beta - \mu_0)$ and r^β presumed to be the return on a marketwide stock index: (1) The expected return is linear in its risk in the efficient portfolio; (2) β_x is a complete measure of risk of security x in the efficient portfolio; and (3) the risk premium $E[r^\beta - \mu_0]$ is positive. Denoting an unrelated measure of risk as s_x, they use the following model to test these hypotheses:

$$r_t^x = \gamma_{0t} + \gamma_{1t}\beta_x + \gamma_{2t}\beta_x^2 + \gamma_{3t}s_x + u_{xt}. \tag{11.53}$$

They first estimated the β_x for individual securities or portfolios of securities, and then estimated the parameters in (11.53). Seven years of data were used to sort individual equities into portfolios, the next 5 years were used to compute the β's for these portfolios, and finally the subsequent 4 years were used to estimate the γ's in cross-sectional regressions, one for each month in the sample. As a measure of s_x, they used the standard error of the residual in the time-series regression of r^x onto r^β used to estimate β_x.

The reason for using nonoverlapping periods to estimate the β's and then the coefficients in (11.53) was to avoid the "errors-in-variables" problem associated with the use of estimated β_{xT} in the final stage of cross-sectional regressions. Under their maintained assumption of i.i.d. returns and factors, the use of nonoverlapping samples in implementing these stages leads to consistent estimators of the parameters. With the estimated γ's in hand, their null hypotheses were (1) $E(\gamma_{2t}) = 0$, (2) $E(\gamma_{3t}) = 0$, and (3) $E(\gamma_{1t}) = E(r_t^\beta) - \mu_0 > 0$.

Shanken (1992) examines the statistical properties of the Fama-Mac-Beth two-step estimation procedure in more depth. He notes that, though the Fama-MacBeth procedure leads to a consistent estimator of the γ's, the inference procedures they used are not asymptotically valid—they overstate the precision of the estimated γ's. This is a consequence of the fact that two-stage estimation affects the standard errors of the estimators in general, even if the estimators are consistent (see Section 4.4). Shanken proposed a two-stage estimator that corrected for both the effects of two stages on the asymptotic standard errors and for the heteroskedasticity owing to the fact that, in the cross-section, the portfolios have different residual variances—the variances of the u_{xt} in (11.53) vary with x. (Shanken maintained the assumption of i.i.d. returns and factors and conditionally homoskedastic errors in the time series.) He showed that his estimator is as efficient as the ML estimator of the unconditional beta model discussed in Gibbons (1982). The Fama-MacBeth approach, usually with the modifications suggested by Shanken, has been widely applied in testing unconditional factor models, when f represents the actual risk factors as well as when the vector $f^{\#}$ of pseudofactors is considered from conditioning down to an unconditional model.

Since the ML estimators discussed by Gibbons and Shanken are asymptotically efficient (under their maintained assumptions, including the additional assumption of normality), we briefly expand on this approach to testing beta models. The ML approach uses the time series and cross-section information simultaneously to avoid two-stage estimation. Specifically, Gibbons examines the restriction (11.47), rewritten for expected returns (versus excess returns): an implication of the unconditional one-factor model is that $\alpha_x = \mu_0(1 - \beta_x)$ in the relation $E[r_t^x] = \alpha_x + \beta_x E[r^\beta]$. For a collection of portfolios, this restriction on the α's amounts to a set of nonlinear cross-equation restrictions on the parameters that can be tested by a likelihood ratio statistic using a panel of time series on returns. He implemented this approach for the case of factors that are portfolio returns under the assumption that returns were i.i.d. normal with constant conditional variances.

As discussed by Shanken, this approach is easily adapted to the case where some or all of the factors are macroeconomic variables and not returns. (Though to preserve the assumption of temporal independence of the factors, Shanken interprets the macro factors as "innovations" in the underlying macro variables.) To see this, consider a multifactor version of the unconditional beta model (11.38), derived under the assumption that the pricing kernel is $q_t^* = \tilde{\phi}'\tilde{f}_t$ for constant weights $\tilde{\phi}$:

$$E[r_t^x] = \mu_0 + \beta_x'\lambda, \tag{11.54}$$

$$\beta_x = \text{Cov}[\,f_t, f_t\,]^{-1}\text{Cov}[\,f_t, r_t^x\,], \tag{11.55}$$

$$\lambda = E[f_t] - \mu_0 E[q_t^* f_t]. \tag{11.56}$$

Substituting (11.56) into (11.55) gives the following restriction on the mean of r_t^x:

$$E[r_t^x] = \mu_0 + \beta_x' E[f_t] - \beta_x' E[f_t \tilde{f}_t'] \tilde{\phi} \mu_0. \tag{11.57}$$

If f_t is a vector of excess returns, then we have seen that this expression simplifies to $E[r_t^x] = \mu_0 + \beta_x' E[f_t]$, the multifactor version of the restrictions tested by the likelihood ratio statistic in Gibbons (1982).

On the other hand, if f_t is a vector of, say, macro variables, and not returns, then (11.57) has to be considered in its entirety. Consistent estimators of the β_x are obtained using (11.55). Similarly, $E[f_t]$ and $E[f_t \tilde{f}_t']$ are estimable from the data (assuming that the risk factors f_t are observable to the modeler). Thus, the unknown parameters in (11.57) are μ_0 and $\tilde{\phi}$. Assuming that the dimension of the set of returns being studied $(x_1, \ldots, x_N)$ is larger than the dimension of f (i.e., $N > K$), then (11.57) implies a set of cross-equation nonlinear, overidentifying restrictions on the parameters.[12] These restrictions can be tested using either GMM or *ML* methods and the associated likelihood ratio statistic.

It warrants emphasis that this discussion applies to the special case of a q^* with constant factor weights ϕ. As we will see, this discussion nevertheless covers a large portion of the recent empirical literature on factor models, because the ϕ_t defining q_{t+1}^* have been assumed to be affine functions of a state vector z_t and, upon conditioning down to the null information set, this gives rise to an unconditional factor model. That is, starting from (11.51), we can derive counterparts to all of the expressions (11.54)–(11.57). Of course, for the pseudopricing kernel $q^\#$, the resulting λ in (11.56) is not interpretable as the market price of risk for priced factors. Moreover, the restrictions (11.57) are not all of the restrictions implied by the original pricing model with state-dependent ϕ_t because the restrictions implied by conditioning on agents' information set are being ignored [owing to taking unconditional expectations in (11.51)]. Additionally, as typically presented, there is no accommodation for conditional heteroskedasticity in the return or factor distributions. Thus, whether estimated by Fama-MacBeth or ML methods, the estimators obtained are in general asymptotically inefficient.

If, as in much of the literature on beta models for returns, the returns and factors are assumed to be i.i.d. processes, then testing can often proceed using the Gaussian likelihood function. The resulting estimators are either

---

[12] This assumes, implicitly, a rank condition that allows one to solve for the unknown ϕ from the estimates of the intercepts. Outside of special cases, the β's are typically such that this rank condition is satisfied.

efficient (if returns and factors are jointly normal) or are quasi-ML estimators otherwise. If the i.i.d. assumption is relaxed, then the use of GMM is a natural approach. We can illustrate the issues that arise using the testing approach in Gibbons et al. (1989) which focuses on unconditional factor models in which the factors are excess returns and returns are i.i.d. normal processes. For the regression model $r_t^i - r_{t-1}^f = \alpha_i + \beta_i' f_t + \epsilon_t^i$, for returns $i = 1, \ldots, N$, Gibbons et al. (1989) assume that the ϵ_t^i are jointly normally distributed with constant covariance matrix Σ. The relevant null hypothesis is that the vector $\alpha = (\alpha_1, \ldots, \alpha_N)'$ of intercepts is zero. They propose using the statistic

$$\text{GRS} = \frac{T}{N} \frac{(T - N - K)}{(T - K - 1)} \frac{\alpha_T' \Sigma_T^{-1} \alpha_T}{1 + \bar{f}_T' \Omega_T^{-1} \bar{f}_T} \sim F(N, T - N - K), \qquad (11.58)$$

where $\bar{f}_T$ is the sample mean of f_t and Ω_T is the sample covariance matrix of the factors; α_T is the vector of least-squares estimates of α; and Σ_T is an unbiased estimator of the residual covariance matrix. The associated Wald statistic, analogous to (4.45) from Chapter 4 but for multiple equations, is a monotone transformation of the statistic (11.58). These statistics have the same asymptotic χ^2 distribution under the maintained assumptions of normally distributed f_t with constant covariance matrix. Therefore, for small-sample inference, use of these statistics abstracts from the negative skewness and time-varying volatility that is prevalent in equity returns (Chapter 7). The large-sample distribution is also not robust to time-varying volatility.

To accommodate nonnormality and time-varying volatility, one can instead compute a robust GMM version of the Wald test as in (4.42). When constructing the matrix Ω_0 underlying this test one simply allows for conditional heteroskedasticity. Additionally, there may be grounds for allowing for serial correlation in the products $\epsilon_t^i f_t$. Least-squares estimation, by definition, chooses (α_i, β_i) so that $E[(\alpha_i + \beta_i' f_t) f_t] = 0$. These projections do not imply that the resulting population ϵ_t^i is orthogonal to past values of f or $r_t^i - r_t^f$. In general, this situation falls under Case $ACh(\infty)$ in Chapter 3. However, based on the review of the evidence in Chapter 9, it seems likely that excess equity returns exhibit only a mild degree of persistence so Case $ACh(n)$, for moderate n, might be the most relevant. Whatever one's preferred n, allowing for some nonzero autocorrelation is easily accommodated by appropriate choice of Ω_0.

While the cross-sectional Fama-MacBeth methods or the panel approach with GMM or ML are easily applied for given choices of risk factors, comparing the goodness-of-fits across models based on nonnested choices of f is often challenging. In order to assess the relative fits of nonnested models, Hodrick and Zhang (2001) proposed comparing the pricing errors across models using the notion of "maximum pricing error" from Hansen and

Jagannathan (1997). Consider the set of pricing kernels $\mathcal{M}_{t+1}$ that price a vector R of excess returns: $E[m^1_{t+1}R_{t+1}] = 0$, for any $m^1_{t+1} \in \mathcal{M}_{t+1}$. Suppose that a researcher conjectures that the pricing kernel q^*_{t+1} following the linear factor model $q^*_{t+1} = \tilde{\phi}' f_{t+1}$ is in $\mathcal{M}_{t+1}$. Here q^* can be interpreted either as the actual pricing kernel, under the assumption that the factor weights $\tilde{\phi}$ are state independent, or as a pseudopricing kernel arising from conditioning down in a dynamic model in which $\tilde{\phi}_t$ is an affine function of the state of the economy [as illustrated by (11.51)].

Hansen and Jagannathan show that, if this conjecture is false, then the distance δ between q^* and $\mathcal{M}$,

$$\delta = \min_{m \in L^2} \left\| q^*_{t+1} - m \right\|, \text{ such that } E[m_{t+1}R_{t+1}] = 0, \tag{11.59}$$

is nonzero. Furthermore, they show that δ can be expressed as

$$\delta = \left(E\left[q^*_{t+1}R_{t+1}\right] E\left[R_{t+1}R'_{t+1}\right]^{-1} E\left[q^*_{t+1}R_{t+1}\right] \right)^{1/2}, \tag{11.60}$$

and that δ has the intuitive interpretation as the maximum pricing error among the set of portfolios based on the basic assets underlying R with norm equal to one.

The factor weights $\tilde{\phi}$ can be estimated either by GMM exploiting the moment equations $E[q^*_{t+1}R_{t+1}] = 0$, or by minimizing δ by choice of $\tilde{\phi}$. In fact, either estimation strategy leads to a GMM estimator based on the same moment conditions. Where they differ is in the choice of the distance matrix. As was discussed in Chapter 3, Hansen's (1982b) optimal GMM estimator for the given set of moment conditions $E[q^*_{t+1}R_{t+1}] = 0$ involves the minimization of the quadratic form in (11.60), but with $E[R_{t+1}R'_{t+1}]^{-1}$ replaced by the inverse of the asymptotic covariance matrix of $(1/T)\sum_t q^*_t R_t$, S_0^{-1}. An attractive feature of the optimal GMM estimator is its relative efficiency. On the other hand, an advantage of minimizing δ to obtain an estimator $\tilde{\phi}_T$ is that the distance matrix used is invariant to the model being examined. As such, δ is a useful statistic for comparing the relative fits of different, nonnested pricing models. It is for this reason that Hodrick and Zhang focus on the relatively inefficient estimator that minimizes δ.

The asymptotic covariance matrix of $\tilde{\phi}_T$ obtained in this way is given by (3.57) with d_0 being the probability limit of $(1/T)\sum_t R_t f'_t$, $W_0 = E[R_t R'_t]^{-1}$, and S_0 being the inverse of the distance matrix for Hansen's optimal GMM estimator. Jagannathan and Wang (1996) show that the statistic δ_T, obtained by replacing the population moments in (11.60) by their sample counterparts and $\tilde{\phi}$ by $\tilde{\phi}_T$, can be expressed as a weighted sum of $\chi^2(1)$ random variables and they use this observation to derive its large-sample distribution.

11.6. Empirical Analyses of Factor Models

By the early 1990s a large body of evidence had accumulated supporting the view that the static CAPM, with a one-dimensional f being the excess return on a market portfolio, was not consistent with either the time-series or cross-sectional distribution of returns. Most notably, Banz (1981) documented a significant size effect: average returns on firms' equities with low market value of equity (ME) are too high given their β's, whereas average returns on large ME stocks are too low. Additionally, Rosenberg et al. (1985) and Chan et al. (1991) present evidence that the ratio of a firm's book value of common equity (BE) to ME has significant explanatory power for the cross section of equity returns (in the United States and Japan, respectively). Thirdly, Basu (1983) documents a significant role for earnings/price ratios in explaining the cross section of expected stock returns, even after accounting for size and market betas.

Fama and French (1992, 1993) captured the spirit of these findings by constructing two portfolios from a two-dimensional stratification of U.S. common stocks. Along one dimension stocks were sorted according to their values of BE/ME and then grouped into three portfolios (L, M, H) containing the firms with the smallest, middle, and largest ratios of book-to-market values (30, 40, and 30% of the firms, respectively). Along a second dimension, firms were stratified according to whether their ME was above (B = big) or below (S = small) the median value for all firms. Value-weighted portfolio returns were then computed within each of these six groups. Finally, the returns on the portfolios "small minus big" (SMB) and "high minus low" BE/ME (HML) were computed as

$$r_t^{\text{SMB}} = \frac{1}{3}\left(r_t^{\text{SL}} + r_t^{\text{SM}} + r_t^{\text{SH}}\right) - \frac{1}{3}\left(r_t^{\text{BL}} + r_t^{\text{BM}} + r_t^{\text{BH}}\right), \tag{11.61}$$

$$r_t^{\text{HML}} = \frac{1}{2}\left(r_t^{\text{SH}} + r_t^{\text{BH}}\right) - \frac{1}{2}\left(r_t^{\text{SL}} + r_t^{\text{BL}}\right). \tag{11.62}$$

Using these portfolio returns, they constructed a three-factor model with $f_t = (r_t^M - r_{t-1}^f, r_t^{\text{SMB}}, r_t^{\text{HML}})'$.[13]

Fama and French (1993) tested a three-factor model with constant conditional betas using the GRS statistic and twenty-five equity portfolios ($N = 25$). These portfolios were constructed by sorting stocks into quintiles of both the size and BE/ME distributions. While the three factors had substantial explanatory power for these equity portfolio returns, overall, the GRS

---

[13] Returns on the SMB and HML portfolios are not computed relative to r_{t-1}^f, because they are already excess returns; each is the difference between the returns on two different portfolios.

statistic indicated rejection of the null $\alpha = 0$ at conventional significance levels. The source of this rejection seems to be the stocks with the lowest BE/ME ratios—growth stocks. Among these stocks, the smallest stocks had returns that were too low relative to the predictions of the model, whereas the largest stocks had returns that were too high. In other words, statistical rejection of this constant-beta, three-factor model was linked to the absence of a size effect in the lowest BE/ME quintile.

Vassalou (2003) explores the informational content of the r^{SMB} and r^{HML} portfolios, over and above the market return, with particular emphasis on business cycle information. Using a technique for constructing mimicking portfolios proposed by Lamont (2001), Vassalou regresses GDP growth between t and $t + 4$, $\text{GDPGR}_{t,t+4}$, onto a set of portfolio returns measured over the interval $t - 1$ to t, $B_{t-1,t}$, and a vector of control variables $Z_{t-2,t-1}$ measured at date $t-1$:

$$\text{GDPGR}_{t,t+4} = cB_{t-1,t} + kZ_{t-2,t-1} + \eta_{t,t+4}. \tag{11.63}$$

This recovers the GDP mimicking portfolio $c_T B_{t-1,t}$ (the portfolio with an *unexpected* component that is maximally correlated with $\text{GDPGR}_{t,t+4}$) under the assumption that the control variables $Z_{t-2,t-1}$ determine expected returns $E_{t-1}[B_{t-1,t}]$. When this mimicking portfolio was used along with the return on the market to explain the cross section of excess returns on equities, Vassalou found that the model performed as well as the Fama-French three-factor model. Moreover, in the presence of $cB_{t-1,t}$ as a factor, r^{SMB} and r^{HML} had very little additional explanatory power.

Rather than presuming that betas (conditioned on the econometrician's information set $\mathcal{J}$) are constants, Jagannathan and Wang (1996) derive a regression model with constant betas from a conditional beta model. Starting from the conditional excess return relation (11.33), they assumed that $K = 1$, $f_t = r_t^M$ (the "market" return), and treated $\mu_{t-1}^{0\mathcal{J}}$ as a zero-beta return (so there was no presumption that $r_{t-1}^f \in \mathcal{J}_{t-1}$). These features of their model are reproduced by positing that $q_t^* = \phi_{t-1}^0 + \phi_{t-1}^M r_t^M$, which implies that $\lambda_{t-1}^{\mathcal{J}} = E[r_t^M - r_{t-1}^f | \mathcal{J}_{t-1}]$ (because the single factor is a portfolio return). Jagannathan and Wang further restrict their model by assuming that $\lambda_{t-1}^{\mathcal{J}} = \kappa_0 + \kappa_1 r_{t-1}^{\text{prem}}$, where r^{prem} is the yield spread between BAA- and AAA-rated bonds. This amounts to assuming that the market risk premium on equities is an affine function of the corporate bond credit spread. Empirical support for using a credit spread as a conditioning variable is provided by Stock and Watson (1989) and Bernanke (1990), who find that credit spreads are useful predictors of the U.S. business cycle.

Jagannathan and Wang complete their model by assuming that their single factor r_t^M is itself an affine function of two returns:

$$r_t^M = \gamma^0 + \gamma^{\text{VW}} r_t^{\text{VW}} + \gamma^L r_t^L, \tag{11.64}$$

where r^{VW} is the return on the value-weighted stock index portfolio and r^L is their measure of the return to human capital (labor). (Note that the weights in (11.64) are constants even though the model is formulated with conditioning.) Under these assumptions, they derive a three-factor *unconditional* CAPM in which

$$E[r_t^x] = c^0 + c^{\text{VW}} \beta_{x,\text{VW}} + c^{\text{prem}} \beta_{x,\text{prem}} + c^L \beta_{x,L}, \tag{11.65}$$

and all of the β's are constants. They find that their model fits the cross section of (unconditional) expected returns better than the conventional CAPM. Moreover, their model with the factors r^{VW} and r^L fit the data about as well as the Fama and French (1993) model. The size effect is again much weaker after allowing for multiple factors.

Lustig and Nieuwerburgh (2005) and Santos and Veronesi (2005) study similarly motivated conditional CAPMs in which factor betas depend on the ratios of housing to total wealth and the fraction of total income produced by labor income, respectively. In the former case, the economic mechanism underlying time-varying risks is the effect of changing house prices on the collateral value of housing and the associated exposure of agents to idiosyncratic risk. Changes in the ratio of housing wealth to human capital affect the market price of risk. In the latter study, the risk premium that investors require to hold stock varies with business cycle fluctuation in the fraction of total income produced by wages. As with Jagannathan and Wang, these studies end up examining multifactor unconditional beta models for the cross-sectional distribution of excess returns, in which the number of factors exceeds the number of (conditionally) priced risks. That is, all of these models are illustrations of the construction (11.50)–(11.52).

When working with a multifactor unconditional beta model derived from a conditional model there is always some ambiguity as to whether a factor is truly a priced risk factor or whether it enters owing to time-varying risk premiums. For instance, does r^{HML} in the Fama-French three-factor truly represent a priced distress factor? Or does it enter their model because firms that have recently experienced negative shocks to nondistress factors have their book-to-market ratios and expected returns increase because the risk premiums associated with these factors increase?

Daniel and Titman (1997) examine a third possibility: expected returns are determined by a set of time-varying "characteristics" or firm attributes θ_{t-1}, and θ_{t-1} is not equal to $\beta_{t-1}^{\mathcal{J}\prime} \lambda_{t-1}^{\mathcal{J}}$. Their point is that if characteristics determined expected returns, then there should be firms with these characteristics (say distress) that do not match up with their risk loadings—distressed firms have high expected returns irrespective of their risk loadings. Put differently, in the characteristics model, strong firms in distressed industries have low expected returns, but they can have high loadings on a distress factor like r^{HML}. Thus, it appears as if the returns on these firms are too low given their risk loadings.[14]

To test their model, Daniel and Titman triple sorted stocks according to size, BE/ME, and risk loadings. They concluded that the characteristics model described the cross section of expected returns more accurately than the risk model. Subsequently, Davis et al. (2000) used the same methodology, but studied a much longer sample period. They concluded that the Daniel-Titman findings are special to their chosen sample period; in the longer sample the risk explanation dominates the characteristics-based explanation for the cross-sectional patterns in expected returns.

There is a complementary empirical literature that has focused more directly on pricing kernels by deriving testable implications from parametric specifications of the dependence of the weights $\tilde{\phi}_{t-1}$ on $\mathcal{J}_{t-1}$. Lettau and Ludvigson (2001b) tested the moment restriction (11.54) implied by a model in which the factors were the value-weighted market return, the growth rate of labor income [as in Jagannathan and Wang (1996)], and the growth rate of nondurable consumption. The scaling variable z was "CAY," a measure of the consumption/aggregate wealth ratio constructed in Lettau and Ludvigson (2001a). Upon examining the cross section of expected excess returns associated with twenty-five size and book-to-market sorted portfolios, they found that their scaled consumption-CAPM performed about as well as the three-factor model of Fama and French. This finding, which is striking in the light of the limited success that previous studies have found using consumption-based models to explain excess returns, is attributed to the time-varying risk premiums implicitly captured by letting $\tilde{\phi}_{t-1}$ in the definition of the pricing kernel depend on CAY_{t-1}.

The excellent goodness-of-fit of these conditional CAPMs to the cross section of expected excess returns is striking in at least two aspects. First, even low-dimensional models seem to be able to match the cross section of returns quite well. Second, though the economic underpinnings and risk factors are quite different across some of these models, they appear to perform about equally well in matching the cross section of expected excess returns. Lewellen and Nagel (2005) argue that the conclusions of good fits to the cross sections of excess returns is misleading in these studies because there was a failure to impose critical economic restrictions when conducting the tests. In its simplest form, for the case of a single risk factor,

---

[14] As the authors note, their characteristics-based model potentially admits asymptotic arbitrage opportunities.

their argument is based on the observation that the relation $E[R_t^x|\mathcal{J}_{t-1}] = \beta_{x,t-1}^{\mathcal{J}}\lambda_{t-1}$ implies a strong restriction on the slope coefficients in the cross-sectional regressions that are often run. Specifically, taking unconditional expectations gives

$$E[R_t^x] = \beta_x E[\lambda_{t-1}] + \text{Cov}[\beta_{x,t-1}^{\mathcal{J}}, \lambda_{t-1}], \qquad (11.66)$$

where $\beta_x = E[\beta_{x,t-1}^{\mathcal{J}}]$ and λ_{t-1} is the market risk premium. Following Lewellen and Nagel and using the model of Lettau and Ludvigson as an example, λ_{t-1} becomes the consumption risk premium. In this formulation, $\beta_{x,t-1}^{\mathcal{J}}$ is assumed to be an affine function of CAY_{t-1} with coefficient δ_x and, therefore, (11.66) simplifies to

$$E[R_t^x] = \beta_x E[\lambda_{t-1}] + \delta_x \text{Cov}[\text{CAY}_{t-1}, \lambda_{t-1}]. \qquad (11.67)$$

Lettau and Ludvigson treat the coefficients $E[\lambda_{t-1}]$ and $\text{Cov}[\text{CAY}_{t-1}, \lambda_{t-1}]$ as free parameters in their cross-sectional regressions. However, these coefficients are tightly linked to the moments of macroeconomic variables that determine the factor and factor weights. Calculations in Lewellen and Nagel suggest that these overidentifying restrictions are unlikely to be satisfied by U.S. data. It remains an open question as to whether similar conditional beta models such as those developed in Lustig and Nieuwerburgh (2005) and Santos and Veronesi (2005) satisfy the analogous model-implied over-identifying restrictions.

Hodrick and Zhang (2001) computed their distance measure δ [see (11.59)] as a measure of goodness-of-fit for several models, including consumption CAPMs of the type studied by Lettau and Ludvigson, the model of Jagannathan and Wang, and versions of the Fama-French factor models. Their evidence suggests that none of these models fits the cross section of expected excess returns as measured by δ and several related diagnostic statistics. In addition, they examined the fit to returns scaled by the term premium. Since this premium, say TP_t, is in agents' information set at date t, the moment condition $E[q_{t+1}^* R_{t+1} \text{TP}_t] = 0$ can also be used to construct model diagnostics. All of the models also failed to adequately price these scaled excess returns.

Finally we note that substantial econometric efficiency is potentially lost in both estimation and inference in many of these studies of unconditional models, relative to the analysis of a parametric model of the dependence of the conditional mean and variance of $\{f_t\}$ on $\mathcal{J}_{t-1}$. In fact, if one is willing to parameterize the first two conditional moments of f_t, then there are several alternative approaches that can be pursued.

Consider first the case where f_t is a vector of observable excess returns on portfolios of securities, $\mathcal{J}$ includes the riskless interest rate, and $\phi_{t-1} \in \mathcal{J}_t$. In this case, we can derive a "conditioned down" version of (11.31),

$$E[r_t^x \mid \mathcal{J}_{t-1}] - r_{t-1}^f = \beta_{x,t-1}^{\mathcal{J}1} \Big(E[r_t^{p_1} \mid \mathcal{J}_{t-1}] - r_{t-1}^f \Big)$$

$$+ \dots + \beta_{x,t-1}^{\mathcal{J}N} \Big(E[r_t^{p_N} \mid \mathcal{J}_{t-1}] - r_{t-1}^f \Big),$$

(11.68)

where $\beta_{x,t-1}^{\mathcal{J}i}$ is the ith element of $\beta_{r,t-1}^{\mathcal{J}} = \operatorname{Cov}(\tilde{f}_t, \tilde{f}_t' \mid \mathcal{J}_{t-1})^{-1} \operatorname{Cov}(\tilde{f}_t, r_t^x \mid \mathcal{J}_{t-1})$
with $\tilde{f}_t$ being the vector of excess returns on the benchmark portfolios.
If a researcher is willing to parameterize the joint distribution of $(r_t^x, \tilde{f}_t')$
conditioned on $\mathcal{J}_{t-1}$, at least up through the first two conditional moments,
then (11.68) is easily tested using quasi- or full-information ML estimation.
This is the approach taken by Moskowitz (2003), where the factors were
the excess returns on the "market" and the size-factor and book-to-market
portfolios studied by Fama and French (1993). Moskowitz assumed that
the conditional second moments were well approximated by a multivariate
GARCH model. This formulation allows empirical analysis without having to
specify the functional dependence of ϕ_{t-1} on elements of $\mathcal{J}_{t-1}$. On the other
hand, it does not provide an economic explanation for why these factors,
which are themselves portfolio returns, explain the time-series properties
of excess returns on other portfolios.

If, instead, we select elements of f_t to be more basic macroeconomic
risk factors and, in particular, some elements of f_t are not portfolio returns,
then it seems necessary to parameterize the dependence of ϕ_{t-1} on $\mathcal{J}_{t-1}$,
say $\phi(z_{t-1})$, $z_{t-1} \in \mathcal{J}_{t-1}$. The reason is that excess returns conditioned on
$\mathcal{J}_{t-1}$ in this case are

$$E[r_t^x \mid \mathcal{J}_{t-1}] = r_{t-1}^f + \beta_{x,t-1}^{\mathcal{J}\prime} \lambda_{t-1},$$

(11.69)

$$\lambda_{t-1} = -r_{t-1}^f \operatorname{Cov}(\tilde{f}_t, f_t' \mid \mathcal{J}_{t-1}) \phi_{t-1}.$$

(11.70)

By parameterizing the conditional first and second moments of $(r_t^x, \tilde{f}_t')$ and
the dependence of ϕ_{t-1} on $\mathcal{J}_{t-1}$, the restrictions (11.69) and (11.70) on the
joint conditional distribution of returns and factors can be analyzed.

Part III

No-Arbitrage DAPMs

12
Models of the Term Structure
of Bond Yields

THIS CHAPTER SURVEYS models designed for pricing term structures of market yields on default-free bonds.[1] Our primary focus is on the interplay between the theoretical specification of dynamic term structure models (DTSMs) and their empirical fit to historical changes in the shapes of yield curves.[2] With this interplay in mind, we characterize DTSMs in terms of three primary ingredients: the *risk-neutral* distribution of the state variables or *risk factors*, the mapping between these risk factors and the short-term interest rate, and the factor risk premiums that (when combined with the first two) allow construction of the likelihood function of the historical bond yields. Particular attention is given to affine quadratic-Gaussian, and nonaffine stochastic volatility models, and models with "regime shifts." The goodness-of-fits of these DTSMs are assessed in Chapter 13.

There are several important segments of the fixed-income literature that we have chosen to omit from this chapter in order to keep its scope manageable. Specifically, we largely restrict our attention to dynamic pricing models that have examined features of the *joint* distribution of long- and short-term bond yields in estimation and testing. That is, we focus on models designed to explain the conditional distribution of yields on zero-coupon bonds with different maturities. This means that no attempt is made to systematically review the vast literature on descriptive, time-series models of interest rates (including the literature on short-term rates).[3] Nor do we address the vast literature on the "forward-rate" models developed in Heath

---

[1] This chapter is taken largely from Dai and Singleton (2003b). The pricing of defaultable fixed-income securities is taken up in Chapter 14.

[2] Recent, more mathematically oriented surveys of the theoretical term structure literature can be found in Back (1996), Sundaresan (2000), Gibson et al. (2001), and Yan (2001).

[3] See Chapman and Pearson (2001) for a survey with extensive coverage of empirical studies of short-rate models.

et al. (1992), Brace et al. (1997), and Miltersen et al. (1997). These models typically take the yield curve as given, and then use no-arbitrage relations to price fixed-income derivatives. As such, they abstract from modeling the time-series properties of yield curves. Their central role in the pricing of fixed-income derivatives is discussed in Chapter 16.

Recalling our notation, $D(t, T)$ denotes the price and y_t^{T-t} denotes the continuously compounded yield of a (default-free) zero-coupon bond issued at date t and with maturity date T. Similarly, the forward interest rate for a loan at date T of instantaneous duration that is contracted upon at date t is defined by $f(t, T) = -\partial \log D(t, T)/\partial T$, for any $T \geq t$. We let Y denote the vector of N state variables or "risk factors" that are hypothesized to determine the shape of the yield curve over time.

12.1. Key Ingredients of a DTSM

DTSMs are typically constructed from the following three ingredients:

$I_{\mathbb{Q}}$: The time-series process for Y under the risk-neutral measure $\mathbb{Q}$.
$I_{\mathbb{P}}$: The time-series process for Y under the historical measure $\mathbb{P}$.
I_r: The functional dependence of $r(t)$ on Y.

The ingredients $I_{\mathbb{Q}}$ and I_r underlie the computation of prices of fixed-income securities, and $I_{\mathbb{P}}$ and I_r are used to construct the moments of bond returns (under $\mathbb{P}$) used in estimation. Therefore, all three ingredients are essential for econometric analyses of DTSMs.

The set of specifications of $(I_{\mathbb{Q}}, I_{\mathbb{P}}, I_r)$ that are consistent with no arbitrage opportunities is enormous as a no-arbitrage requirement places relatively weak restrictions on a model. However, the computational demands of both pricing bonds and maximizing the estimation criterion function have typically led researchers to focus on specifications of $(I_{\mathbb{Q}}, I_r)$ that lead to closed-form or essentially closed-form solutions for zero-coupon bond prices. Additionally, with $(I_{\mathbb{Q}}, I_r)$ in hand, the specification of the risk premiums that link $I_{\mathbb{Q}}$ and $I_{\mathbb{P}}$ have often been chosen so that the resulting data-generating process ($\mathbb{P}$ distribution of bond yields) leads to computationally tractable criterion functions for estimation. We elaborate on these specification issues later.

As we will see, models vary in terms of their interpretation of the risk factors Y, whether they are observable variables or treated as latent factors, and how they parameterize the distribution of Y. Nevertheless, a common feature of most empirical DTSMs is that N, the dimension of Y, is taken to be quite small (say two or three) relative to the total number of available bonds to be priced. Therefore, prior to presenting some of the more popular specifications of DTSMs, it is helpful to provide some empirical motivation for the examination of low-dimensional factor models.

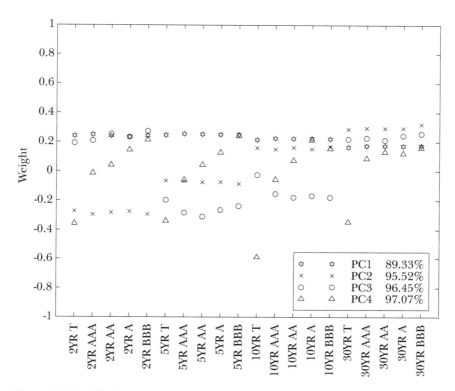

Figure 12.1. *Weights on principal components of changes in yields, by maturity. Bloomberg Data, 1991–1997.*

Figure 12.1 displays the weights associated with the first three principal components (PCs) of weekly changes in yields on twenty constant-maturity U.S. Treasury and corporate bonds.[4] A PC analysis decomposes the covariance matrix of yield changes into its eigenvalue-eigenvector representation $C\Lambda C'$, where C is the matrix of eigenvectors normalized to have unit lengths and Λ is the diagonal matrix of associated eigenvalues. The columns of C are the "factor weights" displayed in Figure 12.1. The cumulative proportions of variance explained by the PCs given in the legend to Figure 12.1 are $\sum_{j=1}^{k} \Lambda_{jj} / \sum_{j=1}^{20} \Lambda_{jj}$, for the first k PCs.

[4] The data were downloaded from Bloomberg. The Treasury yields are constant-maturity yields: approximate yields on newly issued Treasury bonds of the stated maturities. The corporate yields are Bloomberg's estimate of new-issue par-coupon yields, constructed from market prices on outstanding seasoned corporate bonds with the stated credit rating. Bloomberg uses a proprietary system for correcting these yields for the optionality inherent in many corporate bonds (e.g., the right of the issuer to call in the bonds).

Note first of all that the first three PCs explain over 96% of the variation in bond yields.[5] Thus, focusing on a small number of risk factors seems like a reasonable starting point.[6] Note further that the weights of the first PC lie approximately along a horizontal line. This implies that the changes in bond yields induced by a change in PC1 are all approximately equal. As such, we interpret PC1 as a parallel shift in the yield curve or a "level" factor.

PC2 has weights that are approximately equal for a given maturity but, with the credit rating held fixed, they tend to increase approximately linearly with maturity. Accordingly, changes in PC2 represent shifts in the *slope* of the yield curve, holding fixed the credit quality of the bonds. Finally, the weights on PC3, which again are approximately the same for all bonds of a given maturity, tend to have a parabolic shape. With a fixed credit rating, they start high, gradually decline, and then increase again for longer maturities. This pattern underlies the common label of "curvature" for factor PC3. Though these PCs are not literally risk factors of a DTSM—in particular, PCs are orthogonal by construction, whereas the Y's in a DTSM may be correlated—it is instructive to keep this decomposition in mind both in interpreting theoretical formulations and for our discussion of the empirical evidence.

Having chosen the dimension of Y, our next step is to select the numeraire used in pricing. Most studies of DTSMs that involve time series of bond yields focus on risk-neutral pricing, and we typically proceed in this manner as well. In contrast, the financial industry tends to have a cross-sectional, as opposed to a time-series, focus given the practical demands of "point-in-time" pricing systems. Accordingly, there is more focus on choosing a numeraire security price P and an associated measure $m(P)$ that give rise to convenient closed-form or numerical solutions for expectations of the form $E_t^{m(P)}[Z(T)]$, for terminal payoffs $Z(T)$. (See Chapter 8 for a discussion of the meaning of $E_t^{m(P)}[\cdot]$.) Particularly in the case of such LIBOR-based instruments as caps, floors, and swaptions, pricing has tended to focus on forward measures $\mathbb{Q}^T$, with the numeraire chosen to be either the price of a LIBOR-based zero-coupon bond or a swap price (see Chapter 16). Of course, if two derivatives based on the same underlying risk factors are

---

[5] This percentage is obtained by setting $k=3$ in the preceding expression for the proportion of variance explained by the PCs. That a small number of principal components explains well over 90% of the variation in yields across the maturity spectrum for bond yields has been widely documented in the literature; see, e.g., Litterman and Scheinkman (1991) for a discussion of U.S. markets, and Singleton (1995) and Driessen et al. (2000) for discussions of foreign bond markets.

[6] While letting N be small in empirical term structure analyses gives a reasonably accurate picture of the risk profile of bond yields, the residual 4% of yield variation may nevertheless be consequential for pricing fixed-income securities, particularly certain fixed-income options. See Chapter 16 for further discussion of these issues.

priced with different numeraires, then the resulting pricing models may be based implicitly on mutually inconsistent assumptions about the distributions of the risk factors (Brace et al., 1997; Jamshidian, 1997). This problem does not arise if $m(P) = \mathbb{Q}$ and the distribution of Y under $\mathbb{Q}$ is used in pricing all of the derivatives of interest. We revisit these issues in Chapter 16; for the remainder of this chapter we focus on risk-neutral pricing.

Another issue that arises in practice is that trading desks often require that a model correctly "price" an entire yield curve before it will be used for pricing derivatives based on this curve. This consideration in part underlies the widespread use of forward-rate based models, which prescribe the risk-neutral dynamics of the forward curve (as in Heath et al., 1992). In such models, the forward curve $f(t, \cdot)$ is an (observable) input into an arbitrage-free pricing model. As typically implemented in industry, forward-rate models are silent about the time-series behavior of yields under $\mathbb{P}$ and, therefore, are not within the family of DTSMs explored in depth here. We discuss the use of these models for the pricing of fixed-income derivatives in depth in Chapter 16.

Of course if, as is often the case, $\dim(Y) = N$ is small (say three or four), then N is likely much smaller than the number of securities to be priced, say K. As such, if the parameters of the model are held fixed, it may not be possible to price exactly all K securities using N risk factors. One means of circumventing this limitation of dimensionality in yield-based models [those based on $(I_{\mathbb{Q}}, I_r)$] is to introduce time-dependent parameters that allow for point-in-time calibration of a low-dimensional factor model to an entire yield curve of spot yields or volatilities. (This is an easy "add-on" in most of the DTSMs discussed subsequently.) This practice is not without controversy, since recalibrating the parameters as the shape of the underlying yield curve or option volatilities change amounts to "changing the model." Therefore, the resulting models are almost surely fraught with arbitrage opportunities from a dynamic perspective (Backus et al., 1998b; Buraschi and Corielli, 2000; Brandt and Yaron, 2001).

In principle, these issues disappear if the entire yield curve is viewed as the state vector and its dynamic properties are explicitly modeled under both $\mathbb{Q}$ and $\mathbb{P}$. Models of such high (possibly infinite) dimensions have been developed under the labels of "Brownian sheets" (Kennedy, 1994), "random fields" (Goldstein, 2000), and "stochastic string shocks" (Santa-Clara and Sornette, 2001). Bester (2004) explores the empirical fit of a particular parametric random field model.

An intermediate modeling strategy, one that has been widely pursued in academic studies, is to keep N small and fix the parameters of the conditional distribution of Y, but allow for the possibility that not all of the bonds are priced perfectly by the DTSM under investigation. Researchers typically consider one of two cases: all of the bonds are priced with errors by the model or N bonds are priced exactly by the model and the remaining $K-N$ bonds are priced with errors.

The central role of DTSMs in financial modeling has led to the development of an enormous number of models, many of which are not nested. Initially, we focus on the case where Y follows a diffusion process and discuss three of the most widely studied families of DTSMs: affine, quadratic-Gaussian (QG), and nonaffine stochastic volatility models. Then we step outside of the diffusion framework and discuss DTSMs with jumps and multiple "regimes."

12.2. Affine Term Structure Models

The ingredients of affine term structure models are:

$I_{\mathbb{Q}}(A)$: Under $\mathbb{Q}$, Y follows an affine process with

$$\mathrm{CCF}_t^{\mathbb{Q}} \ \text{ or } \ \mathrm{CMGF}_t^{\mathbb{Q}} = e^{\phi_{0t}^{\mathbb{Q}}+\phi_{Yt}^{\mathbb{Q}'}\,Y_t}, \tag{12.1}$$

where $\phi_{0t}^{\mathbb{Q}}$ and $\phi_{Yt}^{\mathbb{Q}}$ are complex (real) coefficients in the case of the CCF (CMGF).

$I_{\mathbb{P}}(A)$: Given $f^{\mathbb{Q}}(Y_{t+1}|Y_t)$ implied by (12.1), $f^{\mathbb{P}}(Y_{t+1}|Y_t)$ is determined once one specifies the Radon-Nykodym derivative $(d\mathbb{P}/d\mathbb{Q})_{t,t+1}$ $= d\mathbb{P}/d\mathbb{Q}(Y_t, Y_{t+1})$ of the measure $\mathbb{P}$ with respect to the $\mathbb{Q}$ measure:

$$f^{\mathbb{P}}(Y_{t+1}|Y_t) = f^{\mathbb{Q}}(Y_{t+1}|Y_t) \times (d\mathbb{P}/d\mathbb{Q})_{t,t+1}. \tag{12.2}$$

Implicit in the specification of $(d\mathbb{P}/d\mathbb{Q})_{t,t+1}$ is the specification of the market price of risk, Λ_t.

$I_r(A)$: The short rate is an affine function of Y:

$$r(t) = \delta_0 + \delta_Y' Y(t). \tag{12.3}$$

This DTSM is affine because of the assumptions $I_{\mathbb{Q}}(A)$ and $I_r(A)$. The former states that Y follows an affine diffusion, as defined in Section 5.1. For now we suppress a role for jumps.

If Y follows a discrete-time affine process, say a process in one of the families $DA_M(N)$ introduced in Chapter 5, then an immediate implication of Assumptions $\mathcal{A}(\mathbb{Q})$ and $\mathcal{A}(r)$ is that

$$D(t, T) = E_t^{\mathbb{Q}}\Big[e^{-\sum_{i=0}^{\tau-1} r_{t+i}}\Big] = e^{-r_t}E_t^{\mathbb{Q}}[D(t+1, \tau-1)] = e^{-\gamma_0(\tau)-\gamma_Y(\tau)Y_t},$$
$$\tag{12.4}$$

where $\tau \equiv (T - t)$ and γ_0 and γ_Y are determined by the recursions:

$$\gamma_0(\tau) = \delta_0 + \gamma_0(\tau - 1) - \phi_0^{\mathbb{Q}}\big(-\gamma^Y(\tau - 1)\big),$$

$$\gamma_Y(\tau) = \delta_Y - \phi_Y^{\mathbb{Q}}(-\gamma_Y(\tau - 1)),$$

with the initial condition $\gamma_0(0) = \gamma_Y(0) = 0$. As shown in Gourieroux et al. (2002) and Dai et al. (2005), this pricing relation follows from the fact that the CMGF$^{\mathbb{Q}}$ of Y is an exponential affine function of Y (see Chapter 5) and the law of iterated expectations.

Recall that for the family of continuous-time affine diffusions we have

$$\mu_Y^{\mathbb{Q}}(t) = \mathcal{K}^{\mathbb{Q}}\big(\theta^{\mathbb{Q}} - Y_t\big), \qquad (12.5)$$

and $\sigma_Y(t) = \Sigma\sqrt{S(t)}$, where

$$S_{ii}(t) = \alpha_i + \beta_i' Y(t), \quad S_{ij}(t) = 0, \ i \neq j, 1 \leq i, j \leq N, \qquad (12.6)$$

and Σ is an $N \times N$ matrix of constants. For this model, and under Assumption $I_r(A)$, Duffie and Kan (1996) show that the solution to the PDE (8.51) for $D(t, T)$ is exponential-affine:

$$D(t, T) = e^{\gamma_0(T-t) + \gamma_Y(T-t)' Y(t)}, \qquad (12.7)$$

where γ_0 and γ_Y satisfy known ordinary differential equations (ODEs).

Note that in deriving these pricing relations, we have been silent on the properties of Y under $\mathbb{P}$. To obtain (12.4) or (12.7), essentially any specification of $f^{\mathbb{Q}}(Y_{t+1}|Y_t)$, or equivalently any arbitrage-free specification of the pricing kernel, can be chosen so long as Y follows an affine process under $\mathbb{Q}$.

12.3. Continuous-Time Affine DTSMs

In Chapter 5 we discussed the concept of *admissibility* of an affine model. Families of benchmark, admissible models $\mathbb{A}_M(N)$ for the state vector Y were introduced, with sufficient structure imposed to ensure that $S_{ii}(t) \geq 0$. Using these concepts, we proceed to develop corresponding families of *canonical* affine DTSMs as follows. A canonical model is one that is admissible, econometrically identified, and "maximally flexible" within a specified family of models. Since we are focusing on pricing, we define our canonical models relative to the risk-neutral representation of the risk factors Y. We return subsequently to the specification and econometric identification of the $\mathbb{P}$ distribution of the risk factors and bond yields.

We start with ingredient $I_r(A)$ and a given benchmark model $\mathbb{A}_M(N)$ for Y, where, as before, the columns of the matrix $\mathcal{B}$ are the coefficients of the instantaneous conditional variances of Y and, therefore, $M = \text{rank}(\mathcal{B})$ indexes the degree of dependence of the conditional variances on the number of state variables. Using this index and applying the definition of a benchmark model $\mathbb{A}_M(N)$ from Chapter 5 to the risk-neutral representation of Y gives an admissible affine DTSM with N factors and M state variables driving volatilities. Not all admissible affine diffusions give rise to econometrically identified DTSMs, however, because Y is latent and enters the determination of r as $\delta'_Y Y_t$. We refer to models on which sufficient normalizations have been imposed to ensure identification as "canonical" $\mathbb{A}_M(N)$ DTSMs. As introduced by Dai and Singleton (2000) (hereafter DS), the canonical $\mathbb{A}_M(N)$ model is the most flexible econometrically identified affine DTSM on the state space $\mathbb{R}_+^M \times \mathbb{R}^{N-M}$; the first M state variables are volatility factors and so must have realizations in $\mathbb{R}_+^M$, the nonnegative region of $\mathbb{R}^M$, and the remaining factors can take on arbitrary values in $\mathbb{R}^{N-M}$. The subfamily $A_M(N)$ $(M=0, \ldots, N)$ of affine DTSMs is then defined, following DS, to be all models that are nested special cases of the Mth canonical model or of *invariant* transformations of this model.[7]

More formally, the canonical representation of $A_M(N)$ is defined as follows:

Definition 12.1 [Canonical Representation $\mathbb{A}_M(N)$]. *For each M, we partition $Y(t)$ as $Y' = (Y^{V'}, Y^{D'})$, where Y^V is $M \times 1$ and Y^D is $(N - M) \times 1$, and define the canonical model $\mathbb{A}_M(N)$ as the special case of (12.3), (12.5), and (12.6) with*

$$\mathcal{K}^{\mathbb{Q}} = \begin{bmatrix} \mathcal{K}^{VV}_{M \times M} & 0_{M \times (N-M)} \\ \mathcal{K}^{DV}_{(N-M) \times M} & \mathcal{K}^{DD}_{(N-M) \times (N-M)} \end{bmatrix}, \tag{12.8}$$

for $M > 0$, and $\mathcal{K}$ is either upper or lower triangular for $M = 0$,

$$\Theta^{\mathbb{Q}} = \begin{pmatrix} \Theta^V_{M \times 1} \\ 0_{(N-M) \times 1} \end{pmatrix}, \tag{12.9}$$

$$\Sigma = I, \tag{12.10}$$

---

[7] The union $\cup_{M=0}^N A_M(N)$ does not encompass all admissible N-factor affine models, however. The reason is that there are affine models defined on different state spaces that cannot be transformed to an observationally equivalent model defined on one of the state spaces $\mathbb{R}_+^M \times \mathbb{R}^{N-M}$, $M = 0, \ldots, N$.

$$\alpha = \begin{pmatrix} 0_{M \times 1} \\ 1_{(N-M) \times 1} \end{pmatrix}, \tag{12.11}$$

$$\mathcal{B} = \begin{bmatrix} I_{M \times M} & B^{\mathrm{VD}}_{M \times (N-M)} \\ 0_{(N-M) \times M} & 0_{(N-M) \times (N-M)} \end{bmatrix}, \tag{12.12}$$

with the following parametric restrictions imposed:

$$\delta_{Yi} \geq 0, \ M+1 \leq i \leq N, \tag{12.13}$$

$$\mathcal{K}_i^{\mathbb{Q}} \Theta^{\mathbb{Q}} \equiv \sum_{j=1}^{M} \mathcal{K}_{ij}^{\mathbb{Q}} \Theta_j^{\mathbb{Q}} > 0, \ 1 \leq i \leq M, \tag{12.14}$$

$$\mathcal{K}_{ij}^{\mathbb{Q}} \leq 0, \ 1 \leq j \leq M, \ j \neq i, \tag{12.15}$$

$$\Theta_i^{\mathbb{Q}} \geq 0, \ 1 \leq i \leq M, \tag{12.16}$$

$$\mathcal{B}_{ij} \geq 0, \ 1 \leq i \leq M, \ M+1 \leq j \leq N. \tag{12.17}$$

Equivalent affine models are obtained under invariant transformations that preserve admissibility and identification and leave the short rate (and hence bond prices) unchanged. Let $\psi_0 = (\delta_0, \delta_Y, \mathcal{K}^{\mathbb{Q}}, \Theta^{\mathbb{Q}}, \Sigma, \alpha_i, \beta_i : 1 \leq i \leq N)$ denote the vector of unknown parameters. One of the most widely applied transformations is[8]:

Definition 12.2 (Invariant Affine Transformation). *An invariant affine transformation $\mathcal{T}_A$ of an N-factor affine* DTSM *is an arbitrary combination of transformations of the form $\mathcal{T}_A Y_t = LY_t + \vartheta$,*

$$\mathcal{T}_A \psi_0 = \big(\delta_0 - \delta_Y' L^{-1} \vartheta, \ L'^{-1} \delta_Y, \ L\mathcal{K}^{\mathbb{Q}} L^{-1}, \ \vartheta + L\Theta^{\mathbb{Q}}, \ L\Sigma,$$
$$\big\{\alpha_i - \beta_i' L^{-1} \vartheta, \ L'^{-1} \beta_i : 1 \leq i \leq N\big\}\big),$$

where L is an $N \times N$ nonsingular matrix, and ϑ is an $N \times 1$ vector.

Invariant affine transformations $\mathcal{T}_A$ are generally possible because of the linear structure of affine DTSMs and the fact that the state variables are not observed. For instance, with r_t affine in Y_t as in (12.3), $\mathcal{T}_A$ could be any transformation of $Y_t \rightarrow LY_t$ and $\delta_Y \rightarrow L^{-1'} \delta_Y$ with L a nonsingular matrix.

---

[8] See Dai and Singleton (2000) for a discussion of other invariant transformations.

Implicit in our specification of a canonical model is a sufficient set of normalizations to guarantee that the resulting models are identified (in addition to being admissible) in the sense that one cannot find a "rotation" of the state Y that leaves r and, hence, bond prices unchanged, while changing the interpretations of the risk factors. Following is an itemized accounting of the normalizations along with a description of their roles in identifying the models. Throughout we presume that the instantaneous short rate is given by (12.3). For branch $\mathbb{A}_M(N)$, we have:

1. **Scale of the State Variables.** $\mathcal{B}_{ii} = 1, 1 \le i \le M, \alpha_i = 1, M+1 \le i \le N$, and $\Sigma_{ii} = 1, 1 \le i \le N$. Fixing the scale of Y_t in this way allows δ_Y to be treated as a free parameter vector.

2. **Level of the State Vector.** $\alpha_i = 0, 1 \le i \le M, \Theta_i^{\mathbb{Q}} = 0, M+1 \le i \le N$. Fixing the level of the state vector in this way allows δ_0 and Θ^{V} to be treated as free parameters.

3. **Interdependencies of the State Variables.** Three considerations arise:

   The upper-diagonal blocks of $\mathcal{K}^{\mathbb{Q}}$, Σ, and $\mathcal{B}$, which control the interdependencies among the elements of Y^V are not separately identified. This indeterminacy is eliminated by normalizing the upper-diagonal block of $\mathcal{B}$ to be diagonal.

   The lower-diagonal blocks of $\mathcal{K}^{\mathbb{Q}}$ and Σ, which determine the interdependencies among the elements of Y^D, are not separately identified. This indeterminacy is eliminated by normalizing the lower-diagonal block of Σ to be diagonal.

   The lower-left blocks of $\mathcal{K}^{\mathbb{Q}}$ and Σ, which determine the interdependencies between the elements of Y^V and Y^D, are not separately identified. We are free to normalize either $\mathcal{K}^{DV}$ or Σ^{DV} to zero. We choose to set $\Sigma^{DV} = 0$ in our canonical representation.[9]

4. **Signs.** The signs of δ_Y and Y_t are indeterminate if $\mathcal{B}$ is free. Normalizing the diagonal elements of the upper-diagonal block of $\mathcal{B}$ to 1 has the effect of fixing the sign of Y^V, and consequently $\Theta_i^{\mathbb{Q}}$ and $\delta_{Yi}, 1 \le i \le M$. The sign of Y^D is determined once we impose the normalization that $\delta_{Yi} \ge 0, M+1 \le i \le N$.

---

[9] Starting from a model with nonzero Σ^{DV}, the affine transformation with

$$L = \begin{bmatrix} I_{M \times M} & 0_{M \times (N-M)} \\ -\Sigma^{DV}_{(N-M) \times M} & I_{(N-M) \times (N-M)} \end{bmatrix}$$

transforms the model to an equivalent model with $\Sigma^{DV} = 0_{(N-M) \times M}$.

5. Brownian Motion Rotations. An orthogonal transformation of an affine diffusion Y, $T_A Y_t = OY_t$ with O satisfying $OO' = I$, gives

$$T_A \psi_0 = \left(\delta_0, \, O\delta_Y, \, O\mathcal{K}^{\mathbb{Q}}O', \, O\Theta^{\mathbb{Q}}, \, O\Sigma, \, \{\alpha_i, \, O\beta_i : 1 \le i \le N\} \right),$$

and has no observable effect on bond yields.

For the canonical model $\mathbb{A}_0(N)$, $\Sigma = I$ so the transformed covariance matrix becomes O. We are free to rotate the Brownian motion $dW^{\mathbb{Q}}(t)$ by O, thereby preserving the normalization $\Sigma = I$. Since there are $N(N-1)/2$ free parameters in O, we can choose O to "zero-out" $N(N-1)/2$ parameters in $\mathcal{K}^{\mathbb{Q}}$. Accordingly, we normalize $\mathcal{K}^{\mathbb{Q}}$ to be lower (or upper) triangular.

Even in cases with $M \neq 0$, if S_{ii} and S_{jj} are proportional for $i \neq j$, then the parameters $\mathcal{K}_{ij}^{\mathbb{Q}}$ and $\mathcal{K}_{ji}^{\mathbb{Q}}$ are not separately identified. One of them can be normalized to zero.

12.3.1. Illustrative Continuous-Time Affine DTSMs

For the case of $N = 1$, there are two families of affine DTSMs. The family $\mathbb{A}_0(1)$ (one-factor Gaussian), originally proposed by Vasicek (1977), has

$$dr(t) = \mathcal{K}^{\mathbb{Q}} \left(\theta^{\mathbb{Q}} - r(t) \right) dt + \Sigma_r \, dW^{\mathbb{Q}}(t). \tag{12.18}$$

The family $\mathbb{A}_1(1)$ (one-factor square-root diffusion), developed by Cox et al. (1985b) for pricing bonds with real (consumption-denominated) payoffs, has

$$dr(t) = \mathcal{K}^{\mathbb{Q}} \left(\theta^{\mathbb{Q}} - r(t) \right) dt + \Sigma_r \sqrt{r(t)} \, dW^{\mathbb{Q}}(t). \tag{12.19}$$

More recently, as the literature has moved beyond $N = 1$, two different tracks have been pursued. One branch has developed models with r being an affine function of a vector of state variables, as in our characterization of the families $A_M(N)$ using $(I_{\mathbb{Q}}(A), I_{\mathbb{P}}(A), I_r(A))$. The other has treated r as a state variable and introduced additional state variables to describe the dynamic properties of the mean and conditional variance of r. Though these two approaches are seemingly different, many of the models that have taken r to be a state variable are equivalent, after an invariant affine transformation, to a model in $A_M(N)$ with r defined as an affine function of Y.[10]

---

[10] Included in this set are those in Vasicek (1977), Langetieg (1980), Cox et al. (1985b), Brown and Dybvig (1986), Hull and White (1987, 1993), Longstaff and Schwartz (1992), Chen and Scott (1993), Brown and Schaefer (1994), Pearson and Sun (1994), Chen (1996), Balduzzi et al. (1996), and Backus et al. (2001).

For instance, consider the canonical DTSM based on the $A_1(2)$ affine process (5.16):

$$r_t = \delta_0 + \delta_1 Y_{1t} + \delta_2 Y_{2t}; \tag{12.20}$$

$$dY_1(t) = \kappa_{11}^{\mathbb{Q}}\left(\theta_1^{\mathbb{Q}} - Y_1(t)\right) dt + \sqrt{Y_1(t)}\, dW_1^{\mathbb{Q}}(t) \tag{12.21}$$

$$dY_2(t) = \left[\kappa_{21}^{\mathbb{Q}}\left(\theta_1^{\mathbb{Q}} - Y_1(t)\right) - \kappa_{22}^{\mathbb{Q}} Y_2(t)\right] dt + \sqrt{1 + \beta_2(1) Y_1(t)}\, dW_2^{\mathbb{Q}}(t), \tag{12.22}$$

with $\mathrm{Cov}(dW_1^{\mathbb{Q}}(t), dW_2^{\mathbb{Q}}(t)) = 0$. An equivalent model in which r is a state variable is obtained by applying the invariant affine transformation $(v_t, r_t)' = L Y_t + \vartheta$,

$$L = \begin{pmatrix} \beta_2(1) & 0 \\ \delta_{Y1} & \delta_{Y2} \end{pmatrix}, \qquad \vartheta = \begin{pmatrix} 0 \\ \delta_0 \end{pmatrix} \tag{12.23}$$

to Y to obtain

$$dv(t) = \kappa_{11}^{\mathbb{Q}}\left(\theta_v^{\mathbb{Q}} - v(t)\right) dt + \sigma_{vv}\sqrt{v(t)}\, dW_v^{\mathbb{Q}}(t), \tag{12.24}$$

$$dr(t) = \left[\kappa_{21}^{\mathbb{Q}}\left(\theta_v^{\mathbb{Q}} - v(t)\right) + \kappa_{22}^{\mathbb{Q}}\left(\theta_r^{\mathbb{Q}} - r(t)\right)\right] dt$$
$$+ \sigma_{rr}\sqrt{1 + v(t)}\, dW_r^{\mathbb{Q}}(t) + \sigma_{rv}\sqrt{v(t)}\, dW_v^{\mathbb{Q}}(t). \tag{12.25}$$

The first state variable serves as the "stochastic volatility" for $r(t)$, but note that it also enters the drift of $r(t)$ and is instantaneously correlated with $r(t)$.

Similarly, within the family $A_0(2)$, the most flexible (under $\mathbb{Q}$) version of the two-factor Gaussian ("Vasicek") model studied by Langetieg (1980), and its counterpart in which r is a state variable and the second state variable is a stochastic mean of r, are equivalent. The latter two-factor central-tendency model of r proposed by Beaglehole and Tenney (1991) and Balduzzi et al. (1998) is nested in our canonical model $\mathbb{A}_0(2)$.

Additional examples of equivalent models, within the families $A_M(3)$, are presented in Dai and Singleton (2000).

12.3.2. Unspanned Stochastic Volatility

All of the affine DTSMs that we have considered up to this point have the property (implicitly) that N bond yields span the risks underlying variation in the term structure. The continuously compounded yield on a $(T-t)$-period zero-coupon bond, $-\log D(t, T)/(T - t)$, is an affine function of Y, as seen from (12.7). Therefore, assuming that the matrix with rows $\gamma_Y(\tau_i)'$ for some set of maturities $i = 1, \ldots, N$ is invertible, we can express Y as an affine function of N bond yields.

An interesting question at this juncture is whether it is possible for a subset of M of the N risk factors (or M linear combinations of the N risk factors) to affect the conditional distribution of the factors, but have no effect on bond yields. Equivalently, is it possible for there to be N factors, but for the $\gamma_Y(T-t)$ to have zero entries for M factors *for all maturities* $(T-t)$? Collin-Dufresne and Goldstein (2002a) (hereafter CDG) explored this question for the case of unspanned stochastic volatility or USV; the presence of stochastic volatility that cannot be hedged away by taking positions in portfolios of bonds. Their motivation for examining USV was the empirical observation that there is substantial variation in the implied volatilities on bond options that appears to be independent of the risk factors in standard DTSMs—for example, level, slope, and curvature (see also Heidari and Wu, 2003). We explore this link to option pricing in more depth in Chapter 16. For now, we focus on an illustrative example of a model in which USV is possible. Since CDG show that N must be larger than two for USV to be present, we consider a case with $N=3$.

CDG show that any model with $N = 3$ in which bond markets are incomplete (i.e., not all of the risks can be hedged with positions in bonds) can be rotated so that the state variables are r_t, its drift $\mu_t^{\mathbb{Q}}$, and its volatility V_t. Moreover, if bond markets are incomplete, then bond prices are exponential-affine functions of r_t and $\mu_t^{\mathbb{Q}}$; that is, there is USV as V_t is independent of bond prices. To illustrate their ideas, we consider the canonical model $\mathbb{A}_1(3)$. This model can always be rotated so that the state variables are $(V_t, \mu_t^{\mathbb{Q}}, r_t)$, *whether or not there is USV*. Therefore, we first undertake this rotation, and then characterize the additional restrictions imposed by the assumption of USV.

The model $\mathbb{A}_1(3)$ can be rewritten as in DS with r as a state variable [see their equation (23)]:

$$dv_t = \kappa_{vv}(\bar{v} - v_t)dt + \sigma_{vv}\sqrt{v_t}\,dB_{vt}^{\mathbb{Q}}, \tag{12.26}$$

$$d\theta_t = \kappa_{\theta\theta}(\bar{\theta} - \theta_t)dt + \sqrt{\alpha_\theta + \beta_\theta v_t}\,dB_{\theta t}^{\mathbb{Q}} + \sigma_{\theta v}\sqrt{v_t}\,dB_{vt}^{\mathbb{Q}}$$
$$+ \sigma_{\theta r}\sqrt{\alpha_r + v_t}\,dB_{rt}^{\mathbb{Q}}, \tag{12.27}$$

$$dr_t = \kappa_{rv}(\bar{v} - v_t)dt + \kappa_{rr}(\theta_t - r_t)dt + \sqrt{\alpha_r + v_t}\,dB_{rt}^{\mathbb{Q}} + \sigma_{rv}\sqrt{v_t}\,dB_{vt}^{\mathbb{Q}}$$
$$+ \sigma_{r\theta}\sqrt{\alpha_\theta + \beta_\theta v_t}\,dB_{\theta t}^{\mathbb{Q}}, \tag{12.28}$$

where we assume that $\kappa_{rr} > 0$ (so that θ_t acts as a stochastic long-run mean of r_t). In order to apply the propositions of CDG, we first rewrite (12.26)–(12.28), through an invariant transformation, in terms of the state vector $(V_t, \mu_t^{\mathbb{Q}}, r_t)$. Noting that

$$\mu_t^{\mathbb{Q}} = \kappa_{rv}\bar{v} - \kappa_{rv}v_t + \kappa_{rr}\theta_t - \kappa_{rr}r_t, \tag{12.29}$$

$$V_t = \alpha_r + \sigma_{r\theta}^2\alpha_\theta + \left(1 + \sigma_{rv}^2 + \sigma_{r\theta}^2\beta_\theta\right)v_t, \tag{12.30}$$

we find the invariant transformation of interest to be

$$
T_A \begin{pmatrix} v_t \\ \theta_t \\ r_t \end{pmatrix} = \begin{pmatrix} L_{vv} & 0 & 0 \\ -\kappa_{rv} & \kappa_{rr} & -\kappa_{rr} \\ 0 & 0 & 1 \end{pmatrix} \begin{pmatrix} v_t \\ \theta_t \\ r_t \end{pmatrix} + \begin{pmatrix} \alpha_r + \sigma_{r\theta}^2 \alpha_\theta \\ \kappa_{rv}\bar{v} \\ 0 \end{pmatrix}, \quad (12.31)
$$

where $L_{vv} = 1 + \sigma_{rv}^2 + \sigma_{r\theta}^2 \beta_\theta$. The resulting equivalent maximal $A_1(3)$ model is given by

$$
d \begin{pmatrix} V_t \\ \mu_t^Q \\ r_t \end{pmatrix} = \begin{pmatrix} \kappa_{vv} & 0 & 0 \\ \frac{\kappa_{rv}(\kappa_{\theta\theta} - \kappa_{vv})}{L_{vv}} & (\kappa_{\theta\theta} + \kappa_{rr}) & \kappa_{rr}\kappa_{\theta\theta} \\ 0 & -1 & 0 \end{pmatrix} \left(\begin{pmatrix} \bar{V} \\ 0 \\ \bar{\theta} \end{pmatrix} - \begin{pmatrix} V_t \\ \mu_t^Q \\ r_t \end{pmatrix} \right) dt
$$

$$
+ \tilde{\Sigma} \begin{pmatrix} \sqrt{-\tilde{\alpha} + V_t/L_{vv}} & 0 & 0 \\ 0 & \sqrt{\alpha_\theta - \beta_\theta\tilde{\alpha} + \beta_\theta V_t/L_{vv}} & 0 \\ 0 & 0 & \sqrt{\alpha_r - \tilde{\alpha} + V_t/L_{vv}} \end{pmatrix} dB_t^Q,
$$

$$(12.32)$$

where $\bar{V} \equiv \sigma_{r\theta}\alpha_\theta + L_{vv}\bar{v}$, $\tilde{\alpha} \equiv (\sigma_{r\theta}^2\alpha_\theta + \alpha_r)/L_{vv}$, and

$$
\tilde{\Sigma} = \begin{pmatrix} L_{vv}\sigma_{vv} & 0 & 0 \\ \kappa_{rr}(\sigma_{\theta v} - \sigma_{rv}) - \kappa_{rv}\sigma_{vv} & \kappa_{rr}(1 - \sigma_{r\theta}) & -\kappa_{rr}(1 - \sigma_{\theta r}) \\ \sigma_{rv} & \sigma_{r\theta} & 1 \end{pmatrix}. \quad (12.33)
$$

Note that the linear combination of dB_t^Q in (12.32) that determines the instantaneous variance of r_t has the property that the constant terms sum to zero and the weights on V_t sum to one, thereby guaranteeing that V_t is the stochastic volatility of r_t.

Necessary and sufficient conditions for USV to obtain in this model, translated from Collin-Dufresne et al. (2004) into the notation of the preceding maximal model, are:

$$
\kappa_{rr}\kappa_{\theta\theta} = 2c_V^2; \quad (\kappa_{\theta\theta} + \kappa_{rr}) = -3c_V; \quad \frac{\kappa_{rv}(\kappa_{\theta\theta} - \kappa_{vv})}{L_{vv}} = -1; \quad (13.34)
$$

$$
(\kappa_{rr}(\sigma_{\theta v} - \sigma_{rv}) - \kappa_{rv}\sigma_{vv})^2 + (\kappa_{rr}(1 - \sigma_{r\theta}))^2\beta_\theta + (-\kappa_{rr}(1 - \sigma_{\theta r}))^2 = c_V^2, \quad (12.35)
$$

where

$$
c_V = \frac{\sigma_{rv}\left[\kappa_{rr}(\sigma_{\theta v} - \sigma_{rv}) - \kappa_{rv}\sigma_{vv}\right]}{L_{vv}} + \frac{\sigma_{r\theta}\kappa_{rr}(1 - \sigma_{r\theta})\beta_\theta}{L_{vv}} - \frac{\kappa_{rr}(1 - \sigma_{\theta r})}{L_{vv}}.
$$

$$(12.36)$$

Under these restrictions the entire yield curve does not depend on V_t, even though V_t affects the conditional distributions of r_t and $\mu_t^{\mathbb{Q}}$. Translated back to the original model in terms of (v_t, θ_t, r_t), with $\gamma_Y(\tau)' = (\gamma_v(\tau), \gamma_\theta(\tau), \gamma_r(\tau))$, USV implies

$$\gamma_v(T - t) = \frac{\kappa_{rv}}{\kappa_{r\theta}} \gamma_\theta(T - t), \tag{12.37}$$

and the state variables v and θ collapse to one state variable with regard to their effect on bond prices.

Under either rotation of the factors $(V_t, \mu_t^{\mathbb{Q}}, r_t)$ or (v_t, θ_t, r_t), when these constraints are imposed only two of the three factors affect bond yields. Moreover, the source of this phenomenon is volatility risk that cannot be perfectly hedged by only taking positions in bonds. We take up the empirical relevance of USV in Chapters 13 and 16.

12.3.3. Market Prices of Risk

Having specified the distribution of Y under $\mathbb{Q}$, the distribution of Y and the yields on bonds under $\mathbb{P}$ are fully determined upon specifying how the market prices of risk, Λ_t depend on Y. DS analyze the "completely affine" class of DTSMs with

$$\mu_Y^{\mathbb{P}}(t) = \mathcal{K}^{\mathbb{P}}(\theta^{\mathbb{P}} - Y(t)) \text{ and } \Lambda(t) = \sqrt{S(t)}\lambda_1, \tag{12.38}$$

where λ_1 is an $N \times 1$ vector of constants. In this case, both the $\mathbb{P}$-drift $\mu_Y^{\mathbb{P}}(t)$ and $\mathbb{Q}$-drift $\mu^{\mathbb{Q}} = \mu_Y^{\mathbb{P}}(t) - \sigma_Y(t)\Lambda(t)$ are affine in $Y(t)$. This specification encompasses virtually all of the econometric formulations of affine DTSMs studied in the literature prior to 2000. In particular, the Cox, Ingersoll, and Ross (CIR)–style models [the family $A_N(N)$] are obtained by setting $[S(t)]_{ii} = Y_i(t)$, and the Gaussian (Vasicek-style) models are obtained by setting $\Lambda(t)$ to a vector of constants.

A potentially important limitation of the specification (12.38) of Λ is that temporal variation in the instantaneous expected excess return on a $(T-t)$-period zero bond, $e_D(t, T) = \gamma_Y(T-t)'\Sigma S_t \lambda_1$ [see (8.52) and (12.7)], is determined entirely by the volatilities of the state variables through $S(t)$. Interpreting the market prices of risk as capturing the effect on security prices of agents' attitudes toward risk, this formulation forces the effects of changes in Y on these attitudes to be channeled entirely through factor volatilities. Moreover, the sign of each $\Lambda_i(t)$ is fixed over time by the sign of λ_{1i}. This does not preclude $e_D(t, T)$ from changing sign over time, but does represent a potentially strong limitation on the flexibility of excess returns to change sign. As stressed by Duffee (2002), this may be an important consideration in the empirical modeling of bond yields because excess returns on bonds tend to be small (near zero) and highly variable relative to their mean values.

To circumvent these limitations of specification (12.38), Duffee (2002) proposed the more flexible "essentially affine" specification of $\Lambda(t)$ that has

$$\Lambda_t = \sqrt{S_t}\lambda_1 + \sqrt{S_t^-}\lambda_2 Y_t, \tag{12.39}$$

where λ_1 is an $N \times 1$ vector and λ_2 is an $N \times N$ matrix, and $S_{ii,t}^- = (\alpha_i + \beta_i' Y_t)^{-1}$, if $\inf(\alpha_i + \beta_i' Y_t) > 0$, and zero otherwise. Within the canonical model for $A_M(N)$, the inf requirement allows us to normalize the first M rows of λ_2 to zero (corresponding to the M volatility factors). Thus, when $M = N$ (multifactor CIR models), the "completely" and "essentially" affine specifications are equivalent—excess returns vary over time only because of time variation in the factor volatilities.

However, when $M < N$, Duffee's essentially affine specification introduces the possibility that Y affects expected excess returns both indirectly through the $S_{ii}(t)$ and directly through the nonzero elements of $\lambda_2 Y_t$. Moreover, the signs of the $\Lambda_i(t)$ corresponding to the $N - M$ nonvolatility factors may switch signs over time. (The signs of the $\Lambda_i(t)$ corresponding to the first M volatility factors are fixed as in CIR-style models.) The smaller M, the more flexibility introduced by (12.39) over (12.38), though at the expense of less flexibility in matching stochastic volatility. The specification (12.39) preserves the property that the drifts of Y are affine under both $\mathbb{Q}$ and $\mathbb{P}$.

The requirement that the ith diagonal element of S_t^- be nonzero only if $\inf(\alpha_i + \beta_i' Y_t) > 0$ was imposed by Duffee to rule out arbitrage that might arise if elements of Λ_t approach infinity as $(\alpha_i + \beta_i' Y_t)$ approaches zero. Collin-Dufresne et al. (2004) and Cheridito et al. (2003) have shown that this condition imposes more structure than is necessary to ensure the absence of arbitrage. Specifically, Duffee imposed sufficient structure to ensure that the Novikov condition, a sufficient condition for the equivalence of the measures $\mathbb{P}$ and $\mathbb{Q}$ (Duffie, 2001), is satisfied. Even if the Novikov condition cannot be verified, so long as zero is not attainable by Y_t under both $\mathbb{P}$ and $\mathbb{Q}$, arbitrage is ruled out under some more flexible specifications of Λ_t.

To illustrate this point, consider the case of an $A_1(1)$ DTSM with

$$\Lambda_t = [\sigma(Y_t)]^{-1}\left[\mu_t^{\mathbb{P}} - \mu_t^{\mathbb{Q}}\right] = \frac{\lambda_0}{\sqrt{Y_t}} + \lambda_1\sqrt{Y_t}, \tag{12.40}$$

where $\lambda_0 = (\kappa^{\mathbb{P}}\theta^{\mathbb{P}} - \kappa^{\mathbb{Q}}\theta^{\mathbb{Q}})$. The essentially and completely affine models assume that $\lambda_0 = 0$. However, so long as $\lambda_0 \le (\kappa^{\mathbb{P}}\theta^{\mathbb{P}})/\sigma^2 - 0.5$, this $A_1(1)$ model is well-defined and admits no arbitrage opportunities. At a practical level, this extended model has both $\kappa\theta$ and κ changing with the measure change from $\mathbb{P}$ to $\mathbb{Q}$, whereas the essentially affine model allows only κ to change with the measure change.

Duarte (2004) proposed a complementary extension of the essentially affine models by specifying Λ to be

$$\Lambda(t) = \Sigma^{-1}\lambda_0 + \sqrt{S_t}\lambda_1 + \sqrt{S_t^-}\lambda_2 Y_t, \qquad (12.41)$$

where λ_0 is an $N \times 1$ vector of constants. With this extension, the market prices of risk of the M volatility factors in an $A_M(N)$ model may switch signs over time. Additionally, larger differences between the drifts of Y under the $\mathbb{P}$ and $\mathbb{Q}$ measures are accommodated because $\mu^\mathbb{P}(t)$ includes the term $\Sigma\sqrt{S(t)}\Sigma^{-1}\lambda_0$ in Duarte's model, as prescribed by (12.5). With this modification, Y follows a nonaffine process under $\mathbb{P}$—the drift involves both the level and square-root of the state variables—but one that is nevertheless affine under $\mathbb{Q}$ [so that the pricing relation (12.7) continues to hold].

A natural question at this juncture is whether the specification of Λ affects the econometric identification of a DTSM. We previously discussed normalizations on the parameters governing the $\mathbb{Q}$ distribution of Y to rule out observationally equivalent "rotations" of an affine DTSM. We defer discussion of the identification of the parameters governing $\Lambda(t)$ until Chapter 13.

The choice of affine model determines whether r remains strictly positive over the entire state space. Strictly speaking, negative values for r are not economically meaningful. However, the only family of affine diffusions that guarantees strictly positive r are those in the family $A_N(N)$. With $M = N$, negative correlations among the Y's are not easily generated (DS), and $\lambda_2 = 0$ in (12.39) thereby restricting the state dependence of $\Lambda(t)$ in essentially affine models. The generalized market price of risk (12.40) allows for nonlinear dependence of Λ_t on the volatility of Y, but not for a direct effect of Y on Λ_t. Therefore, by selecting models in $A_M(N)$, with $M < N$, one may well achieve greater flexibility at specifying factor correlations and market prices of risk, though at the expense of (typically small) positive probabilities of the realized r being negative.

12.4. Discrete-Time Affine DSTMs

Two conceptually distinct approaches to developing DTSMs in discrete time have been explored in the literature. One approach starts from a discrete-time approximation to the diffusions underlying a continuous-time DTSM. For example, following Sun (1992), several researchers have examined discrete-time counterparts to CIR-style affine DTSMs. Such models are approximate in that the conditional distribution of Y must be truncated to ensure nonnegativity of the conditional variance of Y. The second approach starts from a parametric, discrete-time specification of the pricing kernel q_t^*, as discussed in Chapter 8. We follow this second approach, as it yields exact discrete-time DTSMs.

Discrete-time versions of affine DTSMs are developed in Gourieroux et al. (2002), Ang and Piazzesi (2003), and Bekaert et al. (2004). The primary focus in these studies has been on Gaussian models. Gourieroux et al. (2002) develop the discrete-time counterpart to the one-factor square-root (CIR-style) model with a completely affine specification of the market price of risk. Dai et al. (2005) (hereafter DLS) extend these analyses by developing discrete-time counterparts to all $N+1$ families $A_M(N)$, $M=0, 1, \ldots, N$, of affine models. The subsequent discussion follows the analysis in DLS.

In Section 5.3 we developed the discrete-time counterparts, $DA_M(N)$, to the continuous-time affine processes $A_M(N)$. DLS adopt the process $DA_M(N)$ as the $\mathbb{Q}$ distribution of the risk factors Y. Since Y is $\mathbb{Q}$-affine, we know that bond prices are exponential-affine functions of Y. Moreover, as discussed in Chapter 5, the conditional $\mathbb{Q}$ densities of Y are known in closed form. In other words, these assumptions lead to a fully specified affine DTSM, one that is the discrete-time counterpart to the family $A_M(N)$.

To complete the specification of this discrete-time DTSM, it remains to specify the $\mathbb{P}$ distributions of Y and the bond yields. From the discussion of (8.26) in Section 8.3.1 we know that it is enough to specify the Radon-Nikodym derivative $(d\mathbb{P}/d\mathbb{Q})_{t,t+1}^{\mathcal{D}}$ in order to deduce $f^{\mathbb{P}}(Y_{t+1}|Y_t)$ from $f^{\mathbb{Q}}(Y_{t+1}|Y_t)$.[11] DLS assume that

$$(d\mathbb{P}/d\mathbb{Q})_{t,t+1}^{\mathcal{D}} = \frac{e^{\Lambda_t' Y_{t+1}}}{\phi^{\mathbb{Q}}(\Lambda_t^{\mathcal{D}}; Y_t)}, \tag{12.42}$$

where $\Lambda_t^{\mathcal{D}} = \Lambda^{\mathcal{D}}(Y_t)$ is closely related to market price of risk.[12] Since $\phi^{\mathbb{Q}}$, as the $\mathbb{Q}$-CMGF of Y, is known in closed form and $\Lambda_t^{\mathcal{D}}$ is given parameterically by the modeler, it follows that $f^{\mathbb{P}}$ is also known in closed form. Moreover, this is true for any specification of the state-dependence of the market prices of risk.

The motivation for this choice is DLS's desire to nest (the discrete-time version of) all $N+1$ families, $A_M(N)$, $M = 0, \ldots, N$, of affine models, for essentially arbitrary choices of the market price of risk Λ_t^C.[13] Recall from

---

[11] As noted in Chapter 8, $(d\mathbb{P}/d\mathbb{Q})_{t,t+1}^{\mathcal{D}} = 1/(e^{r_t} q_t^*)$, where q^* is the pricing kernel associated with this model. Therefore, we are effectively picking the pricing kernel q^*.

[12] $\Lambda^{\mathcal{D}}$ is the lead term in an expansion of the nonlinear expression for expected excess returns and in this sense is the dominant term in the true market price of risk. Furthermore, note that $(d\mathbb{P}/d\mathbb{Q})_{t,t+1}^{\mathcal{D}}$ is zero at $\Lambda^{\mathcal{D}} = 0$, consistent with our thinking of $\Lambda^{\mathcal{D}}$ as the market price of risk. See DLS for details.

[13] Here we add the superscript to Λ^c in order to differentiate it from the discrete-time counterpart.

the discussion in Section 8.3.2 that the change of measure from $\mathbb{P}$ to $\mathbb{Q}$ is accomplished by scaling the density under $\mathbb{P}$ by[14]

$$\frac{d\mathbb{Q}^C}{d\mathbb{H}}(t,T) = \frac{e^{-\frac{1}{2}\int_t^T \Lambda(s)'\Lambda(s)ds - \int_t^T \Lambda(s)'dW(s)}}{E_t^{\mathbb{P}}\left[e^{-\frac{1}{2}\int_t^T \Lambda(s)'\Lambda(s)ds - \int_t^T \Lambda(s)'dW(s)}\right]}. \tag{12.43}$$

Now, for a small time step Δ and approximate affine state process $Y_{t+\Delta} \approx \mu_Y^{\mathbb{P}}(Y_t)\Delta + \Sigma_Y\sqrt{S_{Yt}}\epsilon_{t+\Delta}^{\mathbb{P}}$, with $\epsilon_{t+\Delta}^{\mathbb{P}}|X_t \sim N(0, \Delta I)$,

$$(d\mathbb{Q}/d\mathbb{H})_{t,t+\Delta}^C \approx \frac{e^{-\Lambda_t^{C'}\epsilon_{t+\Delta}^{\mathbb{P}} - \frac{1}{2}\Lambda_t^{C'}\Lambda^C\Delta}}{E_t^{\mathbb{P}}\left[e^{\Lambda_t^{C'}\epsilon_{t+\Delta}^{\mathbb{P}} - \frac{1}{2}\Lambda_t^{C'}\Lambda^C\Delta}\right]} = \frac{e^{-\Lambda_t^{\mathcal{D}'}\Sigma_Y\sqrt{S_{Yt}}\epsilon_{t+\Delta}^{\mathbb{P}}}}{E_t^{\mathbb{P}}\left(e^{-\Lambda_t^{\mathcal{D}'}\Sigma_Y\sqrt{S_{Yt}}\epsilon_{t+\Delta}^{\mathbb{P}}}\right)}$$

$$= \frac{e^{-\Lambda_t^{\mathcal{D}'}Y_{t+\Delta}}}{E_t^{\mathbb{P}}\left[e^{-\Lambda_t^{\mathcal{D}'}Y_{t+\Delta}}\right]} = \frac{e^{-\Lambda_t^{\mathcal{D}'}Y_{t+\Delta}}}{\phi^{\mathbb{P}}\left(-\Lambda_t^{\mathcal{D}}; Y_t\right)}, \tag{12.44}$$

where $\Lambda_t^{\mathcal{D}} \equiv \left(\Sigma_Y\sqrt{S_{Yt}}\right)'^{-1}\Lambda_t^C$ is a transformation of the continuous-time market price of risk Λ_t^C. Thus, recognizing that $\phi^{\mathbb{P}}(-\Lambda_t^{\mathcal{D}}; Y_t) = \left[\phi^{\mathbb{Q}}(\Lambda_t^{\mathcal{D}}; Y_t)\right]^{-1}$, we see that this (approximate) continuous-time construction suggests that, for a small discrete interval of time Δ, the pricing kernel implied by (12.42) is approximately the same as the kernel for a continuous-time DTSM in $A_M(N)$.

Through this construction we see that DLS have developed a family of models that effectively replicates in discrete time the entire family of continuous-time pricing models in which Y follows an affine diffusion under $\mathbb{Q}$. By fixing a model $DA_M(N)$ for the $\mathbb{Q}$ distribution of Y and choosing $\Lambda_t^{\mathcal{D}}$ to be $\Lambda_t^{\mathcal{D}} = (\Sigma_Y\sqrt{S_{Yt}})'^{-1}\Lambda_t^C$, where Λ_t^C is any one of the widely studied specifications in continuous-time DTSMs [e.g., the specification (12.41)], we end up with the discrete-time counterpart $(DA_M(N), \Lambda^{\mathcal{D}})$ to the continuous-time model $(A_M(N), \Lambda^C)$. A key advantage of the discrete-time formulation is that the likelihood function is known for any state-dependent specification of $\Lambda^{\mathcal{D}}$. As such, one can construct (and estimate relatively easily) much richer discrete-time affine DTSMs than have heretofore been examined in the continuous-time literature.

12.5. Quadratic-Gaussian Models

The quadratic-Gaussian family of DTSMs includes the models studied by Longstaff (1989), Beaglehole and Tenney (1991), Constantinides (1992),

---

[14] To relate this expression to the Radon-Nikodym derivative that arises in the continuous-time model for the time interval $[0, T]$, recall that the latter is $\mathcal{D}_T \equiv e^{\frac{1}{2}\int_0^T \Lambda(s)'\Lambda(s)ds - \int_0^T \Lambda(s)'dW(s)}$. $\mathcal{D}$ follows the process $d\mathcal{D}_t = -\mathcal{D}_t\Lambda(t)'dW(t)$ and hence is a martingale: $E_t^{\mathbb{P}}[\mathcal{D}_T] = \mathcal{D}_t$. It follows that $(d\mathbb{Q}/d\mathbb{P})_{t,T}^C = \mathcal{D}_T/E_t^{\mathbb{P}}[\mathcal{D}_T]$ and, hence, $E_t^{\mathbb{P}}[\mathcal{D}_{t,T}] = 1$. This ensures that the induced conditional $\mathbb{Q}$ density integrates to unity.

Lu (2000), Ahn et al. (2002), and Leippold and Wu (2002) as special cases. The ingredients of QG models are:

$I_{\mathbb{Q}}(QG)$: Under $\mathbb{Q}$, the drift and volatility functions of the risk factors satisfy

$$\mu_Y^{\mathbb{Q}}(t) \;=\; \nu_0 + \nu_Y Y(t), \tag{12.45}$$

$$\sigma_Y \;=\; \Sigma, \text{ a constant matrix}, \tag{12.46}$$

where ν_0 is an $N \times 1$ vector and ν_Y is an $N \times N$ matrix of constants.

$I_{\mathbb{P}}(QG)$: Given $\sigma_Y(t)$ satisfying (12.46), the requirement (12.45) determines $\mu_Y^{\mathbb{P}}(t)$, once $\Lambda(t)$ is specified, and vice versa.

$I_r(QG)$: The short rate is a quadratic function of Y:

$$r(t) = a + Y(t)'b + Y(t)'cY(t), \tag{12.47}$$

where a is a scalar, b is an $N \times 1$ vector, and c is an $N \times N$ matrix of constants.

Ahn et al. (2002) and Leippold and Wu (2002) show that under these conditions the solution to the PDE (8.51) is an exponential quadratic function of Y:

$$D(t, T) = e^{\gamma_0(T-t) + \gamma_Y(T-t)'Y_t + Y_t'\gamma_Q(T-t)Y_t}, \tag{12.48}$$

where γ_0, γ_Y, and γ_Q can be computed from known ODEs or from the closed-form expressions presented in Kim (2004).

The drift condition (12.45) along with the assumption that the diffusion coefficient $\sigma_Y(t)$ is the constant matrix Σ imply that Y follows a Gaussian process under $\mathbb{Q}$. These assumptions do not restrict the drift of Y under $\mathbb{P}$, however. Subject to preserving no arbitrage, we are free to choose essentially any functional form for $\mu_Y^{\mathbb{P}}(t)$, so long as $\Lambda(t)$ is chosen so that $\mu^{\mathbb{Q}}(t) = (\mu_Y^{\mathbb{P}}(t) - \Sigma\Lambda(t))$ is affine in Y. The special case examined in Ahn et al. (2002) has $\Lambda(t) = \lambda_1 + \lambda_2 Y(t)$, which implies that Y is Gaussian under both $\mathbb{P}$ and $\mathbb{Q}$. This is the same functional form for Λ as in the essentially Gaussian affine model with $\Lambda(t)$ as in (12.39) since, in this case, $S(t) = I$. However, the effects of $\Lambda(t)$ on prices in the QG and this Gaussian affine model are not equivalent because the mappings between Y and zero-coupon bond prices are different.

The squared-autoregressive-independent-variable nominal term structure (SAINTS) model proposed by Constantinides (1992) is shown by Ahn et al. (2002) to be the special case of the QG model in which Σ is diagonal and $\mu_Y^{\mathbb{P}}(t) = -\mathcal{K}^{\mathbb{P}}Y(t)$ with $\mathcal{K}^{\mathbb{P}}$ diagonal (the N risk factors are mutually independent); and the coefficients λ_1 and λ_2 determining $\Lambda(t)$ are constrained to be specific functions of the parameters governing the Y process. These constraints potentially render the SAINTS model much less flexible than the general QG model in describing bond yields.

Analogously to our discussion of affine DTSMs, we can define a canonical QG model as follows. The normalization $\nu_0 = 0$ allows the coefficients b of the linear term in (12.47) to be unconstrained (Leippold and Wu, 2002). Alternatively, and equivalently, b can be normalized to zero, in which case ν_0 is a free parameter (Ahn et al., 2002). If one wants to ensure that r_t is nonnegative, then the admissible parameter regions for b and ν_0 can be constrained to $\mathbb{R}_+^N$ and $\mathbb{R}_+$, respectively. Additionally, Σ is normalized to be diagonal and ν_Y is normalized to be lower triangular. Finally, c is chosen to be symmetric and with diagonal elements that are normalized to unity. To ensure that r stays strictly positive, one can further impose the constraint that c is positive semidefinite.

12.6. Nonaffine Stochastic Volatility Models

Limited attention has been focused on DTSMs outside the affine and QG families, in large part because of the computational challenges that arise when bond prices are not known in closed form. One family that has received considerable attention in the financial industry (but relatively little attention in academic research), has $\log r(t)$ following a Gaussian process,

$$d \log r(t) = \mathcal{K}^{\mathbb{Q}}\big(\theta^{\mathbb{Q}} - \log r(t)\big)\, dt + \sigma_r\, dW^{\mathbb{Q}}(t). \tag{12.49}$$

Perhaps the most well-known version is the Black et al. (1990) model, along with its continuous-time counterpart studied in Black and Karasinski (1991). A two-factor (multinomial) extension was studied by Peterson et al. (1998). Zero-coupon bond prices are not known in closed form when r follows the process (12.49). However, approximate pricing formulas have been developed (e.g., Basu and Dassios, 1999). Further, for one-factor models, numerical solution of the PDE defining these prices is feasible. Since a lognormal process is strictly positive, it has been gaining favor in the context of modeling the arrival rate (intensity) of default (see Chapter 14).

Another nonaffine, one-factor DTSM is the "three-halves" model (Cox et al., 1980; Ahn and Gao, 1999)

$$dr(t) = \mathcal{K}^{\mathbb{Q}}\big(\theta^{\mathbb{Q}} - r(t)\big)r(t)\, dt + \sigma r(t)^{1.5} dW_r^{\mathbb{Q}}(t), \tag{12.50}$$

which is a stationary process, so long as $\mathcal{K}^{\mathbb{Q}}$ and σ are greater than zero. The conditional density $f(r_{t+1}|r_t)$ is known in closed form, which makes this a convenient alternative formulation to affine models. Ahn and Gao (1999) assumed that the market price of risk of r was $\Lambda(t) = \lambda_1/\sqrt{r(t)} + \lambda_2\sqrt{r(t)}$, which has exactly the same form as the extended specification (12.40) for CIR-style affine models. Thus, $\Lambda(t)$ may change signs over time if λ_1 and λ_2 have opposite signs. These positive features of the three-halves model must be balanced against the fact that correlated, multifactor extensions have yet to be worked out.

Outside of a pricing framework, Andersen and Lund (1997b, 1998) studied various special cases of the following nonaffine three-factor model:

$$
\begin{aligned}
d\log v(t) &= \mu(\bar{v} - \log v(t))dt + \eta\, dW_v(t), \\
d\theta(t) &= \nu(\bar{\theta} - \theta(t))dt + \sqrt{\alpha_\theta + \beta_\theta\theta(t)}\; dW_\theta(t), \qquad (12.51) \\
dr(t) &= \kappa(\theta(t) - r(t))dt + r(t)^\gamma v(t)dW_r(t),
\end{aligned}
$$

where (W_v, W_θ, W_r) are independent Brownian motions. In this model the volatility factor $v(t)$ follows a lognormal process and the instantaneous stochastic volatility of r, $r(t)^\gamma v(t)$, is affected both by v and r. These models do not have known closed-form solutions for bond prices. Largely for this reason this formulation of stochastic volatility has been studied primarily in the context of econometric modeling of the short rate and not as a DTSM.

As for nonaffine discrete-time models, Backus and Zin (1994) parameterize $-\log q_t^*$ as an infinite order, moving average process with i.i.d. normal innovations. This formulation accommodates richer dynamics than a Gaussian diffusion model and is easily extended to multiple factors, but it abstracts from time-varying volatility. More recently, Brandt and Yaron (2001) parameterize $-\log q_t^*$ as a Hermite polynomial function of (Y_t, Y_{t-1}), where Y_t is an observable state vector. Their model extends the Backus-Zin specification of q^* by allowing for nonnormality and time-varying conditional moments, but it is more restrictive in requiring that the pricing kernel depend only on (Y_t, Y_{t-1}) and that Y be observable. Similarly, Lu and Wu (2000) model q^* using a semi-nonparametric density based on Hermite polynomial expansions.

These semiparametric approaches, though flexible, often present their own challenges. Specifically, it may be difficult to verify that the parameters of the pricing kernel are identified from bond yield series. Moreover, if the state variables are taken to be functions of observable bond yields, then internal consistency requires that the same functions of the model-implied yields must recover the state vector. This consistency is not always easily imposed.

12.7. Bond Pricing with Jumps

There is growing evidence that jumps are an important ingredient in modeling the distribution of interest rates. For instance, Zhou (2001c), Das

(2002), and Johannes (2004) find that jump-diffusion models fit the conditional distribution of short-term interest rates better than the nested diffusion models they examine. Affine DTSMs are easily extended to allow Y to follow a jump diffusion

$$dY(t) = \mu_Y(Y)\,dt + \sigma_Y(Y)\,dW(t) + \Delta Y\,dZ(t), \qquad (12.52)$$

where Z is a Poisson counter, with state-dependent intensity $\{\lambda^{\mathbb{P}}(Y(t)) : t \geq 0\}$ that is a positive, affine function of Y, $\lambda^{\mathbb{P}}(Y) = l_0 + l'_Y Y$; and ΔY is the jump amplitude with distribution $\nu^{\mathbb{P}}$ on $\mathbb{R}^N$. If the jump risk is priced, then a compensated jump term also appears in the pricing kernel with a possibly state-dependent coefficient $\Gamma(\Delta Y, Y)$ representing the market price of jump risk:

$$\frac{d\mathcal{M}_t}{\mathcal{M}_t} = -r(Y)\,dt - \Lambda(Y)'\,dW^{\mathbb{P}}(t) - \left[\Gamma(\Delta Y, Y)\,dZ(t) - \gamma(Y)\lambda^{\mathbb{P}}(Y)\,dt\right],$$

$$(12.53)$$

where $\gamma(Y) = \int \Gamma(x, Y)\,d\nu^{\mathbb{P}}(x)$ is the conditional $\mathbb{P}$-mean of Γ. From (12.53), the risk-neutral distribution of the jump size and the risk-neutral jump arrival rate are given by

$$d\nu^{\mathbb{Q}}(x) = \frac{1 - \Gamma(x, Y)}{1 - \gamma(Y)}\,d\nu^{\mathbb{P}}(x), \quad \lambda^{\mathbb{Q}}(Y) = (1 - \gamma(Y))\lambda^{\mathbb{P}}(Y). \qquad (12.54)$$

Although in general $\Gamma(x, Y)$ may depend on both Y and the jump amplitude x, and therefore $\gamma(Y)$ may be state-dependent, in most implementations Γ is assumed to be a constant.

These expressions simplify further if we can write $\mathcal{M}_t = M(Y_t, t)$. This is possible, for example, in equilibrium pricing models, where M represents marginal utility that depends only on the current state. In this case, Ito's lemma implies that

$$r_t = -\frac{1}{\mathcal{M}_t}\left[\frac{\partial}{\partial t} + \mathcal{G}^{\mathbb{P}}\right]\mathcal{M}_t, \qquad (12.55)$$

$$\Lambda_t = -\sigma'_t \frac{\partial}{\partial Y_t} \log \mathcal{M}_t, \quad \Gamma_t(x) = 1 - \frac{M(Y_t + x, t)}{M(Y_t, t)}, \qquad (12.56)$$

where $\mathcal{G}^{\mathbb{P}}$ is the $\mathbb{P}$-infinitesimal generator [see (8.50)]. Note in particular the link between the market price of jump risk Γ and $\mathcal{M}$: the sign of $\mathcal{M}$ (read "marginal utility") depends on whether a jump in Y raises or lowers marginal utility relative to the prejump value. Moreover, the risk-neutral jump arrival rate and the risk-neutral distribution of the jump size are given by

$$\lambda^{\mathbb{Q}}(Y_t, t) = \frac{\int \mathcal{M}(Y_t + x, t) dv_t^{\mathbb{P}}(x)}{\mathcal{M}(Y_t, t)} \lambda^{\mathbb{P}}(Y_t, t), \tag{12.57}$$

$$dv_t^{\mathbb{Q}}(x) = \frac{\mathcal{M}(Y_t + x, t)}{\int \mathcal{M}(Y_t + x', t) dv_t^{\mathbb{P}}(x')} dv_t^{\mathbb{P}}(x). \tag{12.58}$$

If Y is an affine-jump diffusion under the risk-neutral measure, with the risk-neutral drift and volatility specifications being affine as in (12.5) and (12.6), and the "jump transform" $\varphi(c) = \int_{\mathbb{R}^N} \exp(c \cdot x) dv^{\mathbb{Q}}(x)$, for c an N-dimensional complex vector, is known in closed form, then the PDE defining the zero prices $D(t, T)$ admits a closed-form solution (up to ODEs) as an exponential-affine function of Y, just as in the case of affine diffusions (Duffie et al., 2000). Care must be taken in specifying $\varphi(c)$ to make sure that Y remains an admissible process. For instance, for those risk factors that follow square-root diffusions in the absence of jumps, it appears that an added jump must be positive to ensure that this factor never becomes negative. Das and Foresi (1996) and Chacko and Das (2001) present illustrative examples of affine bond and bond-option pricing models with jumps.

State variables with jumps have received relatively less attention in the empirical literature on DTSMs. One of the earliest affine models with jumps is that of Ahn and Thompson (1988), who extend the equilibrium framework of Cox et al. (1985b) to the case of Y following a square-root process with jumps. Brito and Flores (2001) develop an affine jump-diffusion model, and Piazzesi (2003) develops a mixed affine-QG model, in which the jumps are linked to the resetting of target interest rates by the Federal Reserve (see also Das, 2002).

12.8. DTSMs with Regime Shifts

None of the parametric models for Y considered so far are naturally suited to capturing *persistent* "turbulent" and "quiet" periods in bond markets. Such patterns have been documented in historical yields (e.g., Hamilton, 1988; Gray, 1996; Ang and Bekaert, 2002) using descriptive "switching regime" models (see Section 7.2.2). However, there has been much less work on incorporating switching regimes into dynamic pricing models. Following Dai and Singleton (2003b),[15] in this section we extend the family of affine DTSMs to allow for changes in economic regimes. In the presence of regime shifts, the parameters governing the distributions of the state variables (as well as possibly those of the market prices of risk) change as the economy

---

[15] Their analysis extends the complementary treatment in Landen (2000) by parameterizing the pricing kernel under the measure $\mathbb{P}$ (in addition to under $\mathbb{Q}$) and allowing for state-dependent probabilities of changing regimes.

transitions across regimes. If the state Y follows a diffusion in each regime, then the sample path of Y does not "jump" with a change in regime, only the conditional distribution from which Y is drawn changes.

The evolution of "regimes" is described by an $(S + 1)$-state continuous-time conditionally Markov chain $s_t : \Omega \to \{0, 1, \dots, S\}$ with a state-dependent $(S + 1) \times (S + 1)$ rate or generator matrix $R_t^{\mathbb{P}} = [R_{ij,t}^{\mathbb{P}}]$ in which all rows sum to zero. [See Bielecki and Rutkowski (2004) for formalities.] Intuitively, $R_{ij,t}^{\mathbb{P}} dt$, $i \neq j$ represents the probability of moving from regime i to regime j over the next short interval of time. The subsequent discussion is simplified notationally by introducing $(S + 1)$ regime indicator functions $z_t^j = 1_{\{s_t = j\}}$, $j = 0, 1, \dots, S$, with the property that $E[dz_t^j | s_t, Y_t] = R_t^{\mathbb{P}j} dt$, where $R_t^{\mathbb{P}j} \equiv R^{\mathbb{P}j}(s_t; Y_t, t) = \sum_{i=0}^{S} z_t^i R_{ij,t}^{\mathbb{P}}$.

To introduce regime-switching into a bond pricing model, we assume that the pricing kernel can be written as $\mathcal{M}_t \equiv M(s_t; Y_t, t) = \sum_{j=0}^{S} z_t^j M(s_t = j; Y_t, t)$. (As noted in the case of jumps, having $M(s_t; \cdot)$ depend only on Y implicitly constrains the state dependence of M.) Then, using Ito's lemma,

$$\frac{d\mathcal{M}_t}{\mathcal{M}_t} = -r_t dt - \Lambda_t' dW_t^{\mathbb{P}} - \sum_{j=0}^{S} \Gamma_t^j \left(dz_t^j - R_t^{\mathbb{P}j} dt \right), \tag{12.59}$$

where $\Lambda(s_t; Y_t, t)$ is the market price of diffusion risk and $\Gamma^j(s_t; Y_t, t)$ is the market price of a shift from the current regime s_t to regime j an instant later. Under this formulation of $\mathcal{M}_t$, $\Gamma^j(s_t = i; Y_t, t) = [1 - M(s_t = j; Y_t, t)/M(s_t = i; Y_t, t)]$. Therefore, $\Gamma^i(s_t = i; Y_t, t) = 0$ and

$$(1 - \Gamma^i(s_t = j; Y_t, t))(1 - \Gamma^j(s_t = i; Y_t, t)) = 1, \quad 0 \leq i, j \leq S. \tag{12.60}$$

Thus, there are only $\frac{1}{2}S(S + 1)$ free market prices of risk for regime shifts. In particular, for a two-regime model $(S = 1)$ there is only one free market price of regime-switching risk, representing the ratio of the pricing kernels for the two regimes.

The risk-neutral distribution of the short-rate is governed by the relations $r_t^i \equiv r(s_t = i; Y_t, t) = \delta_0^i + Y_t' \delta_Y^i$, and the assumption that (risk neutrally) Y follows an affine diffusion with regime-dependent drifts and volatilities:

$$\mu^{\mathbb{Q}}(s_t; Y_t, t) \equiv \sum_{j=0}^{S} z_t^j \kappa^{\mathbb{Q}j} \left(\theta^{\mathbb{Q}j} - Y_t \right),$$

$$\tag{12.61}$$

$$\sigma(s_t; Y_t, t) = \sum_{j=0}^{S} z_t^j \text{diag} \left(\alpha_k^j + Y_t' \beta_k^j \right)_{k=1,2,\dots,N},$$

where δ_0^i and α_k^i are constants, κ^{Qi} is a constant $N \times N$ matrix, and δ_Y^i, θ^{Qi}, and β_k^i are constant $N \times 1$ vectors. Under this formulation, when a regime shifts, the conditional moments of Y change, but its sample path remains continuous.

Letting $D(t, T) \equiv D(s_t, Y_t; t, T)$, we can write $D(t, T) \equiv \sum_{j=0}^{S} z_t^j D^j(t, T)$, where $D^j(t, T) \equiv D(s_t = j, Y_t; t, T)$. No arbitrage, which requires that $\mu^D(t, T) = r_t D(t, T)$ for all $0 \le s_t \le S$ and all admissible Y_t, implies that the $D^j(t, T)$ satisfy the $(S + 1)$ PDEs

$$\left[\frac{\partial}{\partial t} + \mathcal{G}^i \right] D^i(t, T) + \sum_{j=0}^{S} R_{ij,t}^Q D^j(t, T) - r^i(Y_t, t) D^i(t, T) = 0, \quad (12.62)$$

$0 \le i \le S$, where $\mathcal{G}^i$ is the counterpart to (8.50) for regime $s_t = i$, $R_{ij,t}^Q = (1 - \Gamma^j(s_t = i; Y_t, t)) R_{ij,t}^P$ if $j \ne i$, and $R_{ii,t}^Q = -\sum_{j \ne i} R_{ij,t}^Q$. ($R_t^Q$ is the rate matrix of the conditionally Markov chain under the risk-neutral measure $\mathbb{Q}$.) In general, the matrix R_t^Q is not diagonal. Therefore, these $S + 1$ PDEs are coupled, and the $(D^i(t, T) : 0 \le i \le S)$ must be solved for jointly. The boundary condition is $D(T, T) = 1$ for all s_T, which is equivalent to $(S + 1)$ boundary conditions: $(D^i(T, T) = 1 : 0 \le i \le S)$.

An affine regime-switching model with a closed-form solution for zero-coupon bond prices is obtained by specializing further to the case where R_t^Q is a constant matrix and κ^{Qi}, δ_Y^i, and β_k^i are independent of i. Under these assumptions,

$$D^i(t, T) = e^{\gamma_{0i}(T-t) + \gamma_Y(T-t)' Y_t}, \quad 0 \le i \le S, \quad (12.63)$$

where the $\gamma_{0i}(\cdot)$ and $\gamma_Y(\cdot)$ are explicitly known up to a set of ODEs. Note that in this specialized environment regime dependence under $\mathbb{Q}$ enters only through the "intercept" term $\gamma_{0i}(T - t)$; the derivative of zero-coupon bond yields with respect to Y does not depend on the regime. Though admittedly strong, these assumptions do allow for Y to follow a general affine diffusion and for the $\mathbb{P}$-rate matrix R^P to be state dependent.

In both respects, this formulation extends the one-factor, continuous-time formulation of Naik and Lee (1997) [as well as Proposition 3.2 of Landen (2000)]. Even with regime switching, it may be empirically more plausible to allow for multiple, correlated risk factors. Moreover, Naik and Lee assume constant market prices of regime-shift risk [the $\Gamma^j(t)$ are constants], and obtain regime independence of the risk-neutral feedback matrix κ^{Qj} under the stronger assumption that the actual matrix κ^{Pj} is independent of j.

In sorting out the added econometric flexibility of these models relative to single-regime, affine DTSMs, it is instructive to examine the implied excess returns on a $(T - t)$-period zero-coupon bond. Based on the pricing kernel (12.59), for current regime $s_t = i$, we have

$$\mu_{Dt}^i - r_t^i = \sigma_{Dt}^{i'}\Lambda_t^i - \sum_{j=0}^{S}\Gamma^j(s_t = i)\left[1 - \frac{D^j(t, T)}{D^i(t, T)}\right]R_t^{\mathbb{P}j}, \qquad (12.64)$$

where σ_{Dt}^i is the diffusion vector in regime i for $D^i(t, T)$. If $\Gamma^j(s_t = i) = 0$, for all $j = 0, 1, \ldots, S$, then excess returns may still be time varying for two reasons: (1) state dependence of Λ_t and/or $\sigma_Y(t)$ (as in single-regime models), and (2) the possibility that either of these constructs might shift across regimes. It is the latter added source of flexibility that the previous literature on DTSMs with regime shifts has relied on to improve goodness-of-fit over single-regime DTSMs.

By allowing for priced regime-shift risk ($\Gamma^j(s_t) \neq 0$), we see from (12.64) that Dai and Singleton introduce an additional source of variation in excess returns. This is true even if $R^{\mathbb{P}}$ is a constant (non-state-dependent) matrix. Of course, allowing $R^{\mathbb{P}}$ to be state dependent, while maintaining the assumption of constant $R^{\mathbb{Q}}$ for computational tractability, would add flexibility to this model.

Several researchers have developed discrete-time, regime-switching models. Bansal and Zhou (2002) examine regime-switching CIR-style models. They relax the assumptions that $\kappa^{\mathbb{Q}i}$ and β_t^i are regime independent, while maintaining the assumption that $R^{\mathbb{P}} = R^{\mathbb{Q}}$, a constant matrix [the $\Gamma^j(t) = 0$]. Their model does not admit a closed-form exponential-affine solution, so they proceed by linearizing the discrete-time Euler equations and solving the resulting linear relations for prices. In a related study, Wu and Zeng (2003) derive a general equilibrium, regime-switching model, building upon the one-factor CIR-style model of Naik and Lee (1997), with constant $R^{\mathbb{P}}$.

The model in Dai et al. (2003) has the risk factors following Gaussian processes with two regimes, so bond prices are obtained in closed form. It extends the Bansal-Zhou framework by allowing for state-dependent $R_t^{\mathbb{P}}$ and priced regime-shift risk (they assumed that the market price of regime-shift risk is zero). Ang and Bekaert (2003b) also examine a regime-switching Gaussian DTSM. They assume that regime-shift risk is not priced, $R^{\mathbb{P}}$ is constant, and the historical rates of mean reversion of the risk factors are the same across regimes. These assumptions can be relaxed, while preserving closed-form solutions for bond prices.

13

Empirical Analyses of Dynamic Term Structure Models

WE TURN NEXT to the estimation and assessments of fit of DTSMs. Focusing primarily on the parametric models just surveyed and drawing upon Chapter 5, we begin by reviewing alternative estimation strategies. The goodness-of-fit of DTSMs is then explored in two steps. First, we describe several notable empirical features of the historical behavior of bond yields that have been widely viewed as "puzzles." We present these as challenges that a successful DTSM should resolve, roughly speaking, by producing a match between certain moments of the model-implied and historical conditional distributions of bond yields.

13.1. Estimation of DTSMs

Chapter 5 introduced several estimation strategies for continuous-time models. Most of these methods are applicable to DTSMs, after making the requisite modifications to accommodate the fact that the state vector Y is observed only indirectly through the DTSM. We begin our discussion of estimation with affine models.

13.1.1. Affine DTSMs

Let ψ_0 denote the population parameters governing an affine DTSM and suppose that zero-coupon bond prices are to be used in estimation. If we let y_t denote an N-dimensional vector of yields on these bonds, it follows from (12.7) that $y_t = A(\psi_0) + B(\psi_0)Y_t$, where Y_t follows an affine diffusion, and the $N \times 1$ vector A and $N \times N$ matrix B are determined by an affine pricing model.[1] The parameter vector ψ_0 includes the parameters governing

---

[1] Recalling that the yield on a zero-coupon bond is defined as $-\log D(t, T)/\tau$, $\tau = (T-t)$, note that the components of A and B are $\gamma_0(\tau)$ and $\gamma_Y(\tau)$ from (12.7) scaled by $1/\tau$.

the affine diffusion Y_t under $\mathbb{Q}$, the parameters describing the functional dependence of r on Y, and the parameters governing the market prices of factor, jump, or regime-shift risks.

Assuming that $B(\psi_0)$ is invertible, we can solve for Y_t as an affine function of y_t,

$$Y_t = B(\psi_0)^{-1}(y_t - A(\psi_0)). \qquad (13.1)$$

Therefore, by the standard change-of-variable analysis, the conditional density function of y_t, f_y, is

$$f_y^{\mathbb{P}}(y_{t+1}|y_t; \psi) = f_Y^{\mathbb{P}}\big(B(\psi)^{-1}\big[y_{t+1} - A(\psi)\big]\,|\,y_t; \psi\big)\,\mathrm{abs}\,\big|B(\psi)^{-1}\big|. \qquad (13.2)$$

It follows that if the density of the state vector $f_Y^{\mathbb{P}}$ is known, then one can proceed directly with ML estimation of ψ_0. Within the family of continuous-time affine DTSMs, $f_Y^{\mathbb{P}}$ is known for the special cases of Gaussian models [models in $A_0(N)$] (Jegadeesh and Pennacchi, 1996) and independent square-root processes [models in $A_3(3)$ with $\mathcal{K}^{\mathbb{P}}$ diagonal] (Chen and Scott, 1993; Pearson and Sun, 1994), so long as the market price of risk Λ_t^c is chosen so that Y follows an affine process under $\mathbb{P}$.

For the case continuous-time affine models in the families $A_M(N)$ ($M \neq 0, N$), the unknown $f_y^{\mathbb{P}}$ can in principle be computed from knowledge of the conditional characteristic function (CCF). Since $B(\psi)$ is nonsingular, y_t and Y_t generate the same information set. Therefore, the CCF of y_{t+1} can be expressed in terms of the CCF of Y_{t+1}, which is known for affine diffusions (Chapter 5):

$$\phi_{yt}^{\mathbb{P}}(u, \psi) = e^{iu'A(\psi)}\phi_{Y_t}^{\mathbb{P}}(B(\psi)'u). \qquad (13.3)$$

Fourier inversion then gives $f_y^{\mathbb{P}}$ in terms of $\phi_Y^{\mathbb{P}}$,

$$f_y^{\mathbb{P}}(y_{t+1}|y_t; \psi) = \frac{1}{(2\pi)^N}\int_{\mathbb{R}^N} e^{-iu'y_{t+1}}\phi_{yt}^{\mathbb{P}}(u)\,du$$

$$= \frac{1}{(2\pi)^N}\int_{\mathbb{R}^N} e^{-iu'B(\psi)Y_{t+1}}\phi_{Y_t}^{\mathbb{P}}(B(\psi)'u)\,du, \qquad (13.4)$$

where it is understood that $\phi_Y^{\mathbb{P}}$ is evaluated at Y_t given by (13.1). When this Fourier inversion is computationally tractable, ML estimation of affine DTSMs can be implemented directly using (13.3). Fourier inversion is practical for scalar and perhaps low-dimensional problems, but it becomes increasingly numerically burdensome as N increases beyond one.

The computational burden of full information methods can be avoided, at the expense of some econometric efficiency, by using method-of-moments estimators. Knowledge of the CCF of Y leads directly to closed-form expressions for all of the conditional moments of Y and hence, owing to their affine dependence on Y, of zero-coupon bond yields y as well. Liu (1997) develops a GMM estimator based on this fact and shows that its efficiency approximates increasingly well that of the ML estimator as the set of moments included is expanded. A special case of the GMM estimator is the quasi-maximum likelihood estimator (Fisher and Gilles, 1996).

More tractability is achieved by shifting to discrete time. We saw in Chapter 12 that $f_Y^{\mathbb{P}}$ is known in closed form as long as the Radon-Nikodym derivative $(d\mathbb{P}/d\mathbb{Q})_{t,t+1}^{\mathcal{D}}$ is known in closed form. In particular, for the parameterization (12.42) adopted by Dai et al. (2005), $f_Y^{\mathbb{P}}$ is known for any admissible state-dependent market price of risk $\Lambda_t^{\mathcal{D}}$. This includes a wide class of nonlinear term structure models within the families $DA_M(N)$, $M = 0, 1, \ldots, N$, all of which can be estimated directly by the method of ML.

In the case of ML estimation, no additional complications are introduced for the case of coupon bond yields. However, since these yields are nonlinear functions $P(Y_t)$ of the state, their moments are typically not known. Therefore, GMM estimation based on knowledge of the moments of Y is generally not feasible. On the other hand, we can, as discussed in Chapter 6, use simulation to compute moments, so SME is feasible.

To compute the ML estimator using coupon bond yields, a change-of-variable argument can again be used to relate the distributions of the observed (coupon) yields y and the state Y. Assuming that the dimension of y_t is equal to that of Y_t gives

$$f_y^{\mathbb{P}}(y_{t+1}|y_t; \psi) = f_Y^{\mathbb{P}}\left(P^{-1}(y_{t+1}; \psi)\big| y_t; \psi\right) abs \left| \frac{\partial P^{-1}(y_{t+1}; \psi)}{\partial y} \right|. \quad (13.5)$$

This provides the likelihood function of the data up to knowledge of the conditional density of the state, $f_Y^{\mathbb{P}}$. It differs from the case for zero-coupon bonds in two respects: the mapping P is in general nonlinear so the fitted state Y must be obtained from y by numerical methods, and the Jacobian of this transformation is in general state dependent (in contrast to the constant $|B(\psi_0)^{-1}|$ for zero-coupon bonds). If the density $f_Y^{\mathbb{P}}$ is unknown, then one can in principle proceed to the likelihood function implied by (13.5) after substitution of an approximation for $f_y^{\mathbb{P}}$. For instance, one of the approximations proposed by Ait-Sahalia (2001) or Duffie et al. (2003b) (see Section 5.6) could be used.

Pursuing the example of coupon bonds, suppose that y is a vector of N yields on coupon bonds of various maturities. Letting y_t^n denote the coupon-yield on an n-year coupon-paying bond, we find that the coupon rate c_t^n for a newly issued n-year bond trading at par is

$$y_t^n = \frac{1 - D(t, t + n)}{\sum_{j=1}^{2n} D(t, t + 0.5j)},$$

where coupons are assumed to be paid semiannually. Though each zero price $D(t, t + j)$ is an exponential-affine function of the state, y_t^n is not. However, if $y_t = P(Y_t, \psi_0)$ and P is invertible so that $Y_t = P^{-1}(y_t; \psi_0)$, then (13.5) applies. Chen and Scott (1993), Pearson and Sun (1994), and Duffie and Singleton (1997) used this approach with the known conditional density of Y to compute ML estimators of multifactor CIR-style models.

A key premise of this estimation strategy is that the number of bonds to be used in estimation is equal to N, the dimension of Y. In practice, the number of bonds available for estimation, say K, is often much larger than N. A common strategy for addressing this situation is to assume that N of the K bonds are priced exactly by the model, whereas the remaining $K - N$ bonds are priced up to a vector of *additive* pricing errors, η_t (see Chen and Scott, 1993; Duffie and Singleton, 1997; Honore, 1998; Dai and Singleton, 2000; among others). More concretely, Chen and Scott (1993) and Duffie and Singleton (1997) assumed that η_t followed a first-order autoregressive process with normally distributed innovations,

$$\eta_{it} = \rho_{0i} + \rho_{1i}\eta_{it-1} + u_{it}, \quad u_{it} \sim N(0, \sigma_{ui}^2), \tag{13.6}$$

where the u_{it} could be mutually correlated, but were assumed to be independent of the state vector Y_t.

This approach allows the N bonds that are priced exactly to be used for inversion for Y in order to derive $f_y^{\mathbb{P}}$ from $f_Y^{\mathbb{P}}$. At the same time, there are K "shocks" driving the K yields being modeled and N factor risks plus $K - N$ pricing errors. The presence of the latter shocks ensures that there is no yield that is related deterministically to the other yields within the DTSM being estimated.

While this is a convenient means of using more bonds than risk factors in estimation, the interpretation of η remains somewhat problematic. One view is that these errors capture pricing errors in the market. The recorded prices in data sets may not be actual market transactions prices or the prices of bonds along the yield curve may not have been recorded at precisely the same time. Alternatively, some have included η_t as explicit recognition of the fact that the pricing model is an approximation and does not literally describe the prices in the market. Under either interpretation, one must make what are essentially ad hoc assumptions about the joint distribution of the η and y in order to complete the derivation of the likelihood function for the data on bond yields.

In some cases, an alternative to introducing additive errors is to introduce a bond-specific yield factor ℓ_t and to discount future cash flows for the bond in question using the adjusted short rate $r(t) + \ell(t)$. Duffie et al. (2003b) implement this approach in the context of an affine DTSM for pricing sovereign bonds.

If all K bonds are assumed to be priced with errors, then filtering methods must be used to obtain fitted states Y. Outside of the Gaussian case, the optimal filters are nonlinear so the Kalman filters typically used are only approximations (Duan and Simonato, 1999; Duffie and Stanton, 2001). Bobadilla (1999) found that estimates of ψ_0 in affine models were sensitive in some cases to the parameterization of the pricing errors.

These extraction issues do not arise if the state variables are observed economic time series (e.g., macroeconomic and yield curve variables). Critical in choosing yield curve variables as elements of Y is that the model maintain internal consistency—it must correctly "price" the state variables when they are known functions of the prices of traded securities. Duffie and Kan (1996) present a generic example of how this can be done in affine models. Imposing internal consistency in nonaffine settings can be challenging, so internal consistency is often ignored (e.g., Boudoukh et al., 1998). T. Wu (2000), S. Wu (2002), Ang and Piazzesi (2003), and Buraschi and Jiltsov (2004) incorporate macro factors (for which these consistency issues do not arise) directly into affine term structure models.

Up to this point we have said little about the specification of the market prices of risk, $\Lambda(t)$. In fact, we have implicitly been assuming that Λ is modeled as in (12.39) so that Y follows an affine diffusion under *both* $\mathbb{Q}$ and $\mathbb{P}$. This allowed us to use knowledge of the CCF under $\mathbb{P}$ to construct GMM or ML estimators of ψ_0. This estimation strategy would not be available for Duarte's formulation of $\Lambda(t)$ in (12.41), even though the $\mathbb{Q}$-drift of Y remains affine. In this case, as well as other situations where the estimators in the preceding paragraph are not applicable, efficient estimates are obtained using the Monte Carlo maximum likelihood estimator of Pedersen (1995) (see also Brandt and Santa-Clara, 2001), the approximate ML estimator of Ait-Sahalia (2001), or the efficient simulated method-of-moments estimator proposed by Gallant and Tauchen (1996).

Another important issue is whether or not all of the parameters governing $\Lambda(t)$ are econometrically identified. Some insight into whether there are new issues in identification arising from the choice of Λ comes from inspection of the case of an $A_0(1)$ model with the state-independent market price of risk $\Lambda = \lambda_1$, as in (12.38). For this one-factor model we can set $Y = r$ and $\mathcal{K}^{\mathbb{Q}} = \mathcal{K}^{\mathbb{P}} = \kappa$. With r following the risk-neutral process $dr_t = \kappa(\theta^{\mathbb{Q}} - r_t)\,dt + \sigma_r\,dB_t^{\mathbb{Q}}$, the coefficients in the exponential-affine representation of $D(t, T)$ in (12.7) are

$$\gamma_Y(\tau) = -\frac{(1 - e^{-\kappa \tau})}{\kappa}, \tag{13.7}$$

$$\gamma_0(\tau) = \left(\frac{\sigma_r^2}{2\kappa^2} + \frac{\sigma_r \lambda_1}{\kappa} - \theta^{\mathbb{P}} \right) (\tau + \gamma_Y(\tau)) - \frac{\sigma_r^2}{4\kappa} \gamma_Y(\tau)^2, \tag{13.8}$$

where $\tau = T - t$ and we have used the fact that $\theta^{\mathbb{Q}} = \theta^{\mathbb{P}} - \sigma_r \lambda_1 / \kappa$. Note that $\theta^{\mathbb{P}}$ and $\sigma_r \lambda_1 / \kappa$ enter (13.8) symmetrically. Additionally, the Jacobian of the transformation from r to observed bond yields y involves only the relevant $\gamma_Y(\tau)$, not $\gamma_0(\tau)$. Therefore, the parameters λ_1 and $\theta^{\mathbb{P}}$ are not separately identified from the first-order conditions to the likelihood function.

In a one-factor setting, there are two sources of identification of λ_1. One is the use of coupon bond yields instead of zero yields to estimate the model. The nonlinear mapping between the coupon yield and the underlying (Gaussian or otherwise) state variable implies that the Jacobian of the transformation from y to Y is state-dependent and the scores of the log-likelihood with respect to the parameters governing Λ and $\theta^{\mathbb{P}}$ are not collinear. Another source of identification is the assumption that the state variable follows a non-Gaussian process. In the case of a "completely affine" square-root model, $\Lambda(t) = \lambda_1 \sqrt{r_t}$ and there is no collinearity between the scores of the log-likelihood.

This intuition for one-factor models can easily be generalized to the case of N-factor affine models for $N > 1$. When zero yields are used to estimate a Gaussian model [in the $\mathbb{A}_0(N)$ branch] with market price of risk (12.38), one out of the N components of λ_1 is not identified. This is because δ_0 [the constant term in (12.3)] and the N components of λ_1 are not separately identified. By normalizing one of the elements of λ_1 to zero, the level of r, δ_0, and the other elements of λ_1 are identified. When zero yields are used to estimate non-Gaussian models [in the $\mathbb{A}_M(N)$ branch with $1 \leq M \leq N$], one out of N market prices of risk is not identified unless, at least for one k with $M + 1 \leq k \leq N$, β_k is not identically zero. When coupon yields are used to estimate affine models, λ_1 is fully identified.

These same considerations carry over to extended specifications of $\Lambda(t)$ such as (12.39). In this particular case, the first M rows of λ_2 would be normalized to zero.

13.1.2. QG Models

Estimation of QG models is complicated by the fact that there is not a one-to-one mapping from observed yields to the state vector Y, because of the quadratic dependence of r on Y. For example, in a one-factor QG model, the yield on an s-period, zero-coupon bond, y^s, is given by $y^s(t) =$

$a_s + b_s Y(t) + c_s Y(t)^2$. Given $y^s(t)$ and under suitable parameter values [so that $b_s^2 - 4c_s(a_s - y^s(t)) > 0$], there are two roots to the previous quadratic equation, corresponding to two possible values of the implied state variable:

$$Y(t) = \frac{-b_s \pm \sqrt{b_s^2 - 4c_s(a_s - y^s(t))}}{2c_\tau}. \tag{13.9}$$

Given this indeterminacy, filtering methods are called upon to estimate the model-implied Y. An efficient algorithm for extracting Y from observed yields is developed in Kim (2004). He uses this filter to obtain quasi-ML estimators for QG models.

Ahn et al. (2002) circumvent the need for filtering by using a SME (which effectively gives observable Y through simulation). Then they use the reprojection methods proposed by Gallant and Tauchen (1998) to estimate $E[Y(t)|y(t-1), \ldots, y(t-L)]$, with y being the vector of bond yields used in estimation. Lu (2000) uses the filtering density $f(Y(t)|y(t), y(t-1), \ldots, y(1))$ to compute the conditional expectation of $Y(t)$. Though the likelihood function for QG models can be written down in closed form, we are not aware of any studies that directly implement the ML estimator.

13.1.3. Other DTSMs

The one-factor three-halves model (12.50) for r gives a conditional density $f(r_{t+1}|r_t)$ that is known in closed form (Eom, 1998; Ahn and Gao, 1999). Therefore, ML estimation is feasible, again using standard transformation-of-variable techniques.

Outside of certain affine, QG, and the one-factor three-halves models, most of the DTSMs that have been studied empirically do not lead to known conditional densities for the state. For these cases, either GMM (simulated methods of moments) or an approximate ML method has been used in estimation.

13.2. Empirical Challenges for DTSMs

In evaluating the relative goodness-of-fits of DTSMs it is helpful to organize the findings in the literature around a few important empirical observations about bond yields. Following Dai and Singleton (2003b), we focus on the following features of the first and second moments of bond yields:

LPY: Letting $y^n \equiv -\log D(t, t+n)/n$ denote the yield on an n-period zero-coupon bond, linear projections of $y_{t+1}^{(n-1)} - y_t^n$ on to the slope of the yield curve, $(y_t^n - r_t)/(n-1)$ give fitted coefficients ϕ_{nT} that are negative, increasingly so for longer maturities (Campbell and Shiller, 1991).

CVY: Conditional volatilities of changes in yields are time-varying and typically highly persistent. Moreover, in recent years, the term structures of unconditional volatilities of swap and treasury yields have tended to be hump shaped, with the hump occurring within the 2- to 3-year maturity range.

13.2.1. Time-Varying Expected Returns on Bonds

In Section 9.6 we discussed expectations relations linking the changes in yield on an n-period bond and the slope of the yield curve [see (9.63)]. From this analysis we saw that the temporal variation in term premia play a central role in modeling time variation in expected excess returns on bonds. Further, the expectations theory—which asserts that yields on long-term bonds should adjust one-for-one with changes in the slope of the yield curve—was obtained only under the special assumption that term premiums are constant. Rather than testing the expectations theory, we view the conceptual and empirical observations drawn in Chapter 9 as underpinnings of goodness-of-fit tests of candidate DTSMs.

Specifically, the results from projections of $y_{t+1}^{n-1} - y_t^n$ onto $(y_t^n - r_t)/(n-1)$ shown in Table 9.7 are descriptive findings that a successful DTSM should match. This can be checked by simulating yields from a candidate DTSM and then computing the implied population projection coefficients and comparing them with those obtained in the data. A well-specified DTSM should replicate the failure of the expectations theory of the term structure.

Additionally, we noted that (9.63) implies that the projections of the "premium-adjusted" change in yields onto the (scaled) slopes of the yield curve, $(y_t^n - r_t)/(n-1)$,

$$\left[y_{t+1}^{n-1} - y_t^n - \left(c_{t+1}^{n-1} - c_t^{n-1} \right) + \frac{1}{n-1} p_t^{n-1} \right] = \phi_n^0 + \phi_n^{\mathcal{R}} \frac{(y_t^n - r_t)}{n-1} + v_{t+1}^n,$$

$$(13.10)$$

give $\phi_n^{\mathcal{R}} = 1$, for all n. That is, the term premiums implied by a candidate DTSM should be such that the violations of the expectations theory are fully corrected once the adjustments in (13.10) are made. There is also an analogous set of yield projections for the forward rates: $E_t[f_{t+1}^{n-1} - r_t] = (f_t^n - r_t) + (E_t[p_{t+1}^{n-1}] - p_t^n)$. So projections of the "premium-adjusted" forward rates $(f_{t+1}^{n-1} - r_t - (p_{t+1}^{n-1} - p_t^n))$ onto $(f_t^n - r_t)$ also give slope coefficients of one.

We stress that these projection results hold for *any* economic model; the content of (13.10) comes from the model-implied specification of the term premiums c_t^n and p_t^n. To check whether (13.10) is satisfied, we use *fitted* yields from a candidate DTSM to estimate these premium-adjusted projections and compare the resulting slope coefficients to unity.[2] Intuitively, these premium adjusted regressions check for the validity of the model-implied $\mathbb{Q}$ distribution of yields, whereas the unadjusted LPY projections check the validity of the implied $\mathbb{P}$ distribution of yields.

A related empirical pattern discussed in Chapter 9 is the high degree of predictability in excess returns over one-year holding periods documented in Cochrane and Piazzesi (2005). In the light of their findings, another question of interest is whether DTSMs, as conventionally specified with a small number N of risk factors, can replicate this predictability.

13.2.2. Volatility of Bond Yields

There is substantial evidence that bond yields exhibit time-varying conditional second moments (e.g., Ait-Sahalia, 1996; Brenner et al., 1996; Gallant and Tauchen, 1998). Other than in the case of the Gaussian affine and basic lognormal models, DTSMs typically build in time-varying volatility, a property that is naturally central to the reliable valuation of many fixed-income derivatives. Thus, the challenge CVY presents for DTSMs is not whether yields exhibit time-varying volatility, but rather whether there is *enough* model-implied variation in volatility (both in magnitude and persistence) to match historical experience.

Another important dimension of CVY is that the term structure of *unconditional* volatilities of (changes in) bond yields has tended to be hump shaped over the past 10 to 15 years (see, e.g., Litterman et al., 1991). Plotting the volatilities of zero-coupon treasury bond yields against maturity over the period 1983–1998 shows a hump that peaks around 2 to 3 years in maturity in both the swap and Treasury markets (Figure 13.1).[3] A very similar pattern of volatilities is obtained using U.S. dollar fixed-for-variable rate swap yields for the post-1987 period (for which data are available). Interestingly, it appears that this hump at 2 years was not a phenomenon observed for the entire post–World War II period in the United States. Figure 13.1 also displays the term structure of volatilities for the subperiod 1954–1978 (the period of the "monetary experiment" from 1979 to 1981 was omitted), during which the volatilities were both smaller and their term structure less humped.

Single-factor models, as traditionally formulated, are unlikely to be successful in matching these patterns. The most widely cited criticisms of one-factor models include: (1) they understate the volatility of long-term yields

---

[2] We do not use simulated data for this case because the resulting coefficients would be unity by construction.

[3] Annualized volatility is measured as the standard deviation of changes in the logarithms of bond yields, scaled up by the number of observations per year.

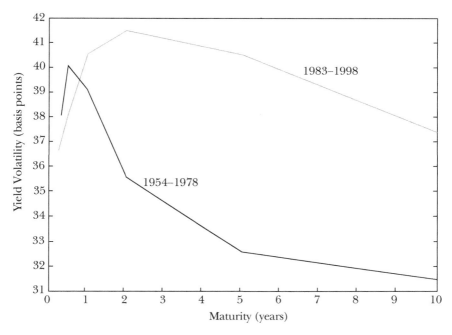

Figure 13.1. *Term structures of volatilities of yields on zero-coupon U.S. Treasury bonds based on monthly data from 1954 through 1998.*

(e.g., Brown and Dybvig, 1986) (fail to match CVY); (2) they overstate the correlation between yields at different maturities (see, e.g., Rebonato and Cooper, 1997, and Chapter 16); and (3) the mean reversion coefficient required to explain cross-maturity patterns at a point in time is inconsistent with the mean reversion coefficient that gives the best time-series fit (e.g., Brown and Schaefer, 1994). Additionally, Backus et al. (2001) show the impossibility of matching LPY with a one-factor affine DTSM.[4]

---

[4] A fourth issue is whether the linear drift specifications in one-factor models are appropriate. Evidence supporting a nonlinear conditional mean for the short rate is discussed in Ait-Sahalia (1996) and Stanton (1997). In principle, the finding of nonlinear drifts for one-factor models could be a consequence of misspecifying the number of factors. However, the nonparametric analyses in Boudoukh et al. (1998) and Balduzzi and Eom (2000) suggest that the drifts in both two- and three-factor models of Treasury yields are also nonlinear. In spite of this evidence, it does seem that having multiple factors in linear models is more important, at least for hedging purposes, than introducing nonlinearity into models with a smaller number of factors (see, e.g., Balduzzi and Eom, 2000). Perhaps for this reason, or because of the computational demands of pricing in the presence of nonlinear drifts, attention continues to focus primarily on DTSMs with linear drifts for the state variables.

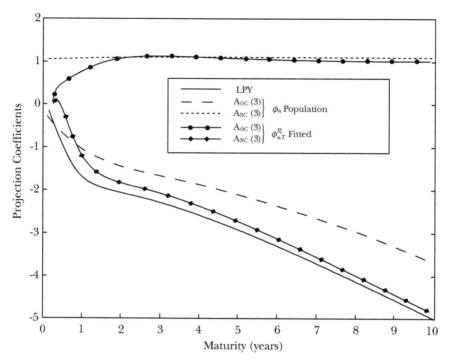

Figure 13.2. *Unadjusted sample and model-implied population projection coefficients ϕ_n. Risk-adjusted sample projection coefficients $\phi^{\mathcal{R}}$. Source: Dai and Singleton (2002).*

13.3. DTSMs of Swap and Treasury Yields

We begin our in-depth exploration of the empirical fit of DTSMs by reviewing their applications to the Treasury and swap yield curves.

13.3.1. DTSMs and Expected Returns

Roberds and Whiteman (1999), Backus et al. (2001), and Dai and Singleton (2002), among others, have examined whether implied yields from affine models match the patterns of "unadjusted" projection estimates ϕ_{nT} displayed in Figure 13.2 as LPY for the smoothed Fama-Bliss data set.[5] Drawing

---

[5] Dai (2003) and Wachter (2005) examine the puzzle LPY in the context of nonaffine macroeconomic models in which agents preferences exhibit habit formation. We revisit their analyses in Section 13.5. McCallum (1994) and Kugler (1997) propose resolutions of the puzzle LPY based on macroeconomic models with particular monetary policy rules.

upon the analysis in Dai and Singleton (2002),[6] Figure 13.2 also displays the population ϕ_n implied by canonical three-factor Gaussian $[A_{0C}(3)]$ and square-root or CIR-style $[A_{3C}(3)]$ models. Model $A_{0C}(3)$ was estimated using the extended risk-premium specification (12.39), whereas model $A_{3C}(3)$ was fit with the more restrictive specification (12.38).[7]

Model $A_{3C}(3)$ embeds the most flexible specification of factor volatilities (within the affine family), but requires the relatively restrictive risk premium specification (12.38). From Figure 13.2 we see that the fitted ϕ_{nT} form (approximately) a horizontal line at unity, implying that the multifactor CIR model fails to reproduce the downward sloping pattern LPY. The empirical analysis in Duffee and Stanton (2001) suggests that this failure of CIR-style models extends to the special case of (12.41) with $\lambda_2 = 0$. Thus, it seems that it is not enough to free up the mean of $\Lambda(t)$ in completely affine DTSMs to match LPY; the dynamics of Λ must also be changed as in (12.39). On the other hand, the Gaussian $A_{0C}(3)$ model, which gives maximum flexibility in both specifying the dynamic properties of the market prices of risk and the factor correlations, is successful at generating ϕ_n that closely resemble LPY.

Whether a DTSM matches LPY speaks to whether it matches the $\mathbb{P}$-dynamics of yields, but it does not directly address whether a DTSM matches the $\mathbb{Q}$-dynamics. To address the latter, Dai and Singleton (2002) suggest examining projections of the term-premium adjusted changes in yields (13.10) onto the scale slope $(y_t^n - r_t)/(n - 1)$. Under the null hypothesis that the DTSM is correctly specified, this projection should produce a coefficient $\phi_{nT}^{\mathcal{R}}$ of unity for all n. From Figure 13.2 it is seen that model $A_{3C}(3)$ gives $\phi_{nT}^{\mathcal{R}}$ that are virtually the same as the historical estimates LPY, instead of the theoretically predicted horizontal line at unity for a correctly specified model. In other words, it is as if model $A_{3C}(3)$ has constant risk premiums. In contrast, the $\phi_{nT}^{\mathcal{R}}$ implied by model $A_{0C}(3)$ are approximately unity, at least beyond maturities of about 2 years.[8] It turns out that the results for models $A_{MC}(3)$, $M = 1, 2$, lie in between these two extremes.

These findings highlight the demands placed on risk premiums in matching the first-moment properties of bond yields. The specification (12.38) appears to be grossly inconsistent with LPY, for any of the families $A_M(3)$. Since (12.38), or nested special cases of this specification, were used in most of the empirical literature on DTSMs up to around 2000, it follows

---

[6] As in their analysis, our canonical models $A_{MC}(N)$ assume that the first M factors are mutually independent. This allows us to use the ML estimator proposed by Duffie et al. (2003b).

[7] Based on the discussion around the specification (12.40) in Chapter 12, the specification of Λ_t in model $A_{3C}(3)$ could be relaxed further. An interesting question is whether this extension would improve the fit of this model relative to what Dai and Singleton report.

[8] See Dai and Singleton (2002) for a discussion of fitting the short end of the yield curve using a four-factor model.

that the models studied in this early literature were incapable of matching LPY. Even with Duffee's extended specification (12.39), only the Gaussian model appears to match both LPY and the requirement that $\phi^{\mathcal{R}} = 1$.

Turning to QG models, they share essentially the same market prices of risk as the extended Gaussian model. Therefore, we expect multifactor QG models to be equally successful at matching LPY. In fact, when we computed the $\phi_n^{\mathcal{R}}$ implied by one-factor Gaussian and QG models, calibrated to the moments of forward rates, we found that both models implied virtually identical $\phi_n^{\mathcal{R}}$ (that were approximately unity). Additionally, Lu (2000) [for multifactor versions of the SAINTS model of Constantinides (1992)] and Leippold and Wu (2003) (for a general two-factor QG model) generate patterns of unadjusted ϕ_n consistent with LPY in Figure 13.2.

The structure of risk premiums in regime-switching models also appears to be central to their flexibility in matching LPY. All of the empirical studies we are aware of adopt the relatively restrictive risk premium specification (12.38) within each regime, and assume that regime-shift risk is not priced. Naik and Lee (1997) and Evans (2000) have the market price of risk being proportional to volatility, with the same proportionality constant across regimes. In Naik and Lee, this implies that regime-dependence of the bond risk premium is driven entirely by the regime-dependence of volatility. Evans only allows the long-run means, and not the volatility, of the state variables to vary across regimes. In contrast, Bansal and Zhou (2002) allow the market price of risk to vary across regimes, through both the regime-dependence of volatility and the regime-dependence of the proportionality constant.

Interestingly, Evans's two-factor CIR-style model [an $A_2(2)$ model with two regimes] fails to reproduce the historical estimates of ϕ_n from U.K. data (see his Table 6). In contrast, Bansal and Zhou, who study a two-factor CIR model with two regimes using U.S. data, generate projection coefficients consistent with the pattern LPY in Figure 13.2. Taken together, these findings suggest that having multiple regimes may overcome the limitations of $A_N(N)$ models in matching LPY outlined above, so long as the factor volatilities and risk premiums vary independently of each other across regimes.

As noted previously, the key feature of bond yield data underlying the departures of the joint distribution of changes in bond yields from the implications of the expectations hypothesis (EH) is the high degree of predictability of excess holding-period returns. An interesting question then is whether DTSMs can replicate this predictability. Before addressing this question within the context of a formal DTSM, it is instructive to explore whether the predictive power of forward rates for excess returns is replicated using a small number of principal components of bond yields. The latent factors in many DTSMs are highly correlated with the low-order PCs. Therefore, high R^2's in predictive regressions using PCs would be an encouraging first step.

Table 13.1. *Contributions of the PCs to the R^2 from the Regressions of Excess Returns on All Five PCs*

Data	2-year bond	3-year bond	4-year bond	5-year bond
A. Total contribution of PC1–PC3				
UFB	0.838	0.774	0.762	0.827
SFB	0.974	0.953	0.946	0.947
B. Contribution of PC2				
UFB	0.555	0.580	0.610	0.672
SFB	0.624	0.670	0.708	0.737

To address this issue we regressed the excess 1-year holding-period returns on the PCs of the yields on bonds with maturities of 1 through 5 years (five yields).[9] Since there are five yields, the use of all five PCs would replicate the findings in Cochrane and Piazzesi (2005) (see Section 9.6) using five forward rates—these series embody precisely the same information. As we have seen, DTSMs are typically fit with N less than or equal to three and, therefore, we are particularly interested in whether the first three PCs have nearly as much predictive content as the five forward rates.

Table 13.1 shows that the first three PCs from data set SFB account for well over 90% of the predictive power of forward rates for excess returns. In contrast, for data set UFB the percentages range between 76 and 83%. These findings suggest that the fourth and fifth PCs and their relationships to excess returns in data set UFB are different than for data set SFB.

That the variation in yields associated with the fifth PC differs across data sets is seen from Table 13.2. The volatilities of the first three PCs are quite similar across data sets. However, the volatilities of PC4 and PC5 are larger in data set UFB than in the SFB data. It is this extra variation in data set UFB, which is not explained by the usual "level," "slope," and "curvature" factors, that underlies the differences in Table 13.1.A.

An interesting issue for future research is the nature of the extra variability in the UFB data: are there economic factors omitted from the SFB data, or is the extra variation in the UFB data an artifact of the particular spline used to construct them? If one concludes that there are key economic factors underlying the variation in yields in the UFB data that are not captured by the first three PCs, then it seems likely that three-factor DTSMs will also fail to incorporate this economic information.

To explore the forecasting power of DTSMs for excess holding-period returns, we estimate discrete-time, three-factor, Gaussian DTSMs [$DA_0(3)$

---

[9] These calculations discussed in the remainder of this section were undertaken in collaboration with Qiang Dai and Wei Yang.

Table 13.2.   Standard Deviations of PCs in Basis Points

Data	PC1	PC2	PC3	PC4	PC5
UFB	528	67.3	10.6	7.39	6.73
SFB	527	64.2	9.0	1.47	0.16

models] by the method of ML, using monthly data over the common period of 1970–2000. Then, treating the ML estimates as the true population parameters, we undertake two complementary exercises. First, from each model, we simulate time series of bond yields of length 10^5 and then, using the simulated data, we estimate the projections of excess returns onto the five forward rates. We interpret the resulting projection coefficients and R^2 as the population values implied by the models.

Second, to explore the small-sample properties of the model-implied R^2 in these projections, we simulated 10^4 time series of yields, each of length T, estimated the projections of excess returns onto forward rates for each simulation, and then computed the sample mean and standard deviation of the R^2 across simulations. In other words, we computed the means and standard deviations of the small-sample distributions of the R^2 statistic implied by the $DA_0(3)$ model. This exercise was undertaken for $T = 360$ and $T = 600$, corresponding to 30 and 50 years of data, respectively.

Given the linear dependence of excess returns on Y in affine DTSMs, the number of latent factors limits the number of noncollinear forward rates that can be used in these regressions. For our three-factor models, we choose to use the forward rates $f^{0 \to 1}$, $f^{2 \to 3}$, and $f^{4 \to 5}$, in addition to a constant term, as the regressors. For comparability, the reported sample R^2's are for projections of excess returns onto the same three forward rates.

The model-implied population R^2's ("Pop." in Table 13.3) are very similar across both data sets. This is surely a consequence of the fact that the fitted yields from the three-factor models share similar smoothness properties, even though the underlying data sets are not equally smooth. Furthermore, the sample R^2's are consistently larger than their population counterparts (compare columns "Samp." and "Pop."). The differences between these R^2's tend to be smaller for the relatively smooth SFB data.

The general tendency for population R^2's to be below their sample counterparts suggests that finite-sample R^2's are upward biased. To explore this possibility more systematically, we conducted a Monte Carlo analysis under the presumption that each DTSM, evaluated at the ML estimates, is the true data-generating model for the term structure data. The results confirm that, under the null hypotheses that our affine models accurately describe conditional first-moment properties of these bond yields, the actual (population) degree of predictability in excess returns is much less than what is indicated by the sample R^2's presented in Cochrane and Piazzesi (2005). The small-sample biases are large, on the order of 50% of Pop.

Table 13.3. **Monte Carlo Simulations for Model** $DA_0(3)$

Maturity	UFB				SFB			
	Samp.	360	600	Pop.	Samp.	360	600	Pop.
2	0.33	0.26	0.23	0.18	0.29	0.29	0.26	0.21
		(0.10)	(0.08)			(0.10)	(0.08)	
3	0.36	0.27	0.23	0.18	0.30	0.28	0.25	0.20
		(0.10)	(0.08)			(0.10)	(0.08)	
4	0.35	0.29	0.25	0.20	0.30	0.28	0.25	0.20
		(0.10)	(0.08)			(0.10)	(0.07)	
5	0.33	0.31	0.28	0.23	0.30	0.28	0.25	0.20
		(0.10)	(0.08)			(0.10)	(0.07)	

Note: For each data set and model, the first column reports the R^2's for regressions estimated from the observed data, the second and third columns report the small-sample means and standard errors (in parentheses) of the R^2's estimated from simulated samples of length 360 and 600 months, and the fourth column reports the model-implied population R^2.

Moreover, the means of the small-sample distributions of the R^2's are quite close to the realized values in the data sets (compare the column labeled "360" with the column "Samp."). The largest difference occurs for data set UFB. Thus, if one believes that UFB most accurately measures the zero and forward rates, then this finding constitutes mild evidence that model $DA_0(3)$ does not fully generate the degree of predictability in excess returns inherent in the historical data. However, the differences between the R^2's in the historical sample and the mean of the small-sample distribution of the model-implied R^2's are all within one standard deviation (of the small-sample distribution of the R^2) of each other.

Finally, an important question is whether the deviations from the EH—the high degree of predictability of excess returns—is economically important for optimal consumption and investment decisions. An interesting partial answer to this question is provided by Sangvinatsos and Wachter (2005), who examine the behavior of long-term investors in bond markets in the presence of the state-dependent market prices of risk that explain the failure of the EH. They find that these risk premiums induce substantial hedging demands and, consequently, the bond holdings of investors in their setting look very different than those of a mean-variance optimizer.

13.3.2. DTSMs and Bond-Yield Volatility

A hump-shaped term structure of yield volatilities is inconsistent with the theoretical implications of both one-factor affine and QG DTSMs. This is essentially a consequence of mean-reversion of the state.

In multifactor models, a humped-shaped volatility curve can be induced either by negative correlation among the state variables or hump-shaped loadings on the state variables Y in the mapping between zero coupon yields and Y. Fitted yields from both affine and QG DTSMs typically fit the volatility hump (e.g., Dai and Singleton, 2000; Leippold and Wu, 2003), so long as yields on bonds with maturities that span the humps are used in estimation.

The economic reasons for the different shapes in Figure 13.1 remain largely unexplored, though the differing patterns pre- and post-1979 are suggestive. In a study of U.S. Treasury yields over the period 1991–1995, Fleming and Remolona (1999) found that the term structure of "announcement effects"—the responses of Treasury yields to macroeconomic announcements—also have a hump-shaped pattern that peaks around 2 to 3 years. Moreover, they fit two-factor affine models in which r mean reverts to a stochastic long-run mean and found that the model-implied announcement impact curves were also humped shaped. Might it be that investors' attitudes toward macroeconomic surprises following the monetary experiment in the late 1970s changed, much like what happened in option markets following the "crash" of October 1987?

Piazzesi's (2003) analysis lends support to a monetary interpretation of the volatility hump. Her econometric model, which is essentially a four-factor mixed affine-QG model with jumps, not only matches the humped-shaped volatility pattern in Figure 13.1, but also the "snake" shape of volatility between 0 and 2 years (steeply declining volatility from 0 to 6 months and then rising volatility to 2 years). Her study provides a rich structural (monetary) interpretation of the need for a fourth factor to capture the very short end of the LIBOR curve (on the need for four factors, see also Liu et al., 2006).

The second aspect of CVY is the degree of model-implied time-varying volatility relative to what we find in the historical data. To set a historical benchmark for comparing models we estimated GARCH(1,1) (Bollerslev, 1986) models for the 5-year yields using historical data.[10] Next we computed ML estimates of the canonical $A_{1C}(N)$ models ($N = 2, 3$), based on the risk premium specification (12.39), with the 6-month and 2- and 10-year yields (2- and 10-year yields when $N = 2$) assumed to be fit perfectly by the model. Then we refit the same GARCH model using simulated yields from these models. In the case of swaps, we simulated 20 years of weekly data (1040 observations); whereas in the case of Treasury zero-coupon data, we simulated 20 years of monthly data (240 observations). We selected

---

[10] Clearly one could use a much richer parameterization of conditional volatility than a GARCH(1,1) model—the semi-non-parametric density proposed by Gallant and Tauchen (1996) is one such parameterization. Our goal here was to simply compute a descriptive measure of persistence in volatility that could be used to compare models. Going beyond this basic comparison is an interesting topic for future research.

Table 13.4.   ML Estimates of GARCH(1,1) Parameters Using Historical and Simulated Time Series of Swap and Treasury Yields

GARCH(1,1)	$\bar{\sigma}$	α	β
Swap sample	0.005 (0.001)	0.126 (0.038)	0.657 (0.062)
Model $A_{1C}(2)$	0.012 (0.003)	0.102 (0.040)	0.235 (0.209)
Model $A_{1C}(3)$	0.008 (0.000)	0.126 (0.027)	0.793 (0.024)
Treasury sample	0.016 (0.005)	0.165 (0.058)	0.749 (0.069)
Model $A_{1C}(3)$	0.000 (0.000)	0.146 (0.075)	0.605 (0.188)
Model $A_{1R}(3)$	0.000 (0.000)	0.164 (0.070)	NA

Note: The GARCH model has $\sigma_t^2 = \bar{\sigma} + \alpha u_t^2 + \beta \sigma_{t-1}^2$, where u_t is the innovation from an AR(1) representation of the level of the 5-year yield. Standard errors are given in parentheses.

the 5-year yield, because it lies between the 2- and 10-year yields that are matched perfectly at the implied state variables. The results are shown in Table 13.4.

The swap sample, 1987–2000, covers a period of relative tranquility in interest rates, compared to the period of the late 1970s and early 1980s. The 5-year yields implied by model $A_{1C}(3)$ exhibit comparable volatility characteristics to the historical data. In contrast, the model $A_{1C}(2)$ substantially understates the degree of volatility persistence in the 5-year swap yield. So moving from two to three factors makes a substantial difference in matching the persistence in stochastic volatility during this period, *even though in both cases only Y_1 drives the factor volatilities.*

The smoothed Fama-Bliss sample of Treasury zero-coupon bond yields covers a 25-year period that includes the monetary experiment in the late 1970s. Nevertheless, we see that the implied GARCH(1,1) estimates from model $A_{1C}(3)$ again match those in the sample quite closely. To see whether the specification $\Lambda(t)$ affects these results, we re-estimated model $A_{1C}(3)$ with $\Lambda(t)$ given by (12.38) instead of (12.39). The results for Treasury data—Model $A_{1R}(3)$ in Table 13.4—are striking, with the volatility in Model $A_{1R}(3)$ showing almost no persistence. The best-fitting model was an ARCH(1).[11]

The structure of conditional volatility in QG models has been explored extensively in Ahn et al. (2002, 2003) (see also Lu, 2000). They argue that there is a significant difference between three-factor QG and affine models along this dimension, with QG models doing a much better job of matching the conditional variation in the historical U.S. Treasury data as captured in their descriptive (semi-nonparametric auxiliary) model. However, their reference affine model was the preferred affine $A_1(3)$ model

---

[11] We repeated this calculation for several simulated time series 20 years long and obtained qualitatively similar results.

examined in Dai and Singleton (2000), which is based on specification
(12.38) of $\Lambda(t)$. As we have just seen, using the specification (12.39) instead
can have a significant effect on affine model-implied yield volatilities. Nevertheless, the analysis in Brandt and Chapman (2002) suggests that, even
with the extended specification of $\Lambda(t)$, the $A_1(3)$ model does not fit the historical distributions of bond yields as well as three-factor QG models. Kim
(2004) also provides evidence on the relatively good fit of QG models to
historical volatility.

In summary, affine- and quadratic-Gaussian DTSMs are evidently capable of resolving the puzzles associated with the rejections of the expectations
hypothesis. At the same time, for both families of models, there appears to
be a "tension" between matching properties of (1) the conditional mean,
(2) the conditional volatilities, and (3) the risk premiums (Duffee, 2002; Dai
and Singleton, 2002). Within the family of affine DTSMs, clearly we must
have $M > 0$ in order for there to be stochastic volatility. However, accommodating stochastic volatility in this manner seems to conflict with matching
the first-moment properties of yields. Duarte (2004) finds that his extended
market price of risk (12.41) does not contribute substantially to relaxing
this tension in matching first and second moments within the affine family.
Kim (2004) reaches a somewhat more optimistic conclusion for QG models
in that they seem to do a better job of generating substantial conditional
volatility, while having market prices of risk that address the expectations
puzzles.

13.4. Factor Interpretations in Affine DTSMs

Implicit in trying to meet the challenges of matching the conditional first-
and second-moment properties of bond yields are key trade-offs that are evidently being made by the likelihood functions associated with these models.
Introducing stochastic volatility, by moving from an $A_0(3)$ to an $A_3(3)$ model,
for example, necessarily improves a researcher's ability to match stochastic
volatility in the data. Moreover, the likelihood function for the $A_3(3)$ model
clearly weights matching this volatility more heavily than it weights matching the conditional first-moment properties of the zero-coupon bond yields,
under either $\mathbb{P}$ or $\mathbb{Q}$.

A complementary perspective on this tension is that it reflects the challenges in fitting the relative prices of bonds of different maturities and the
time-series properties of these yields at the same time. Collin-Dufresne et
al. (2004) have recently emphasized the dual role that the volatility factors
[the first M factors in an $A_M(N)$ model] play in affecting both the cross
section of bond yields and their time-varying volatilities. In particular, they
find that, in an unconstrained $A_1(3)$ DTSM, the volatility factor does not
match well with standard measures of the stochastic volatility of short-term

interest rates (e.g., GARCH or EGARCH models). This finding motivates their consideration of a constrained $A_1(3)$ model in which there is USV (see Section 12.3.2).

In assessing the importance of USV, Collin-Dufresne et al. use bond yield data alone, so not all of their parameters are identified.[12] Of particular interest is their findings for members of the family $A_1(3)$ with and without USV. In both cases, estimation proceeds assuming that the models price the first two principal components of swap yields (actually, the PCs of zero yields constructed from swap yields) perfectly. In their unconstrained $A_1(3)$ model, the third PC is assumed to be priced up to a normally distributed error. For the $A_1(3)$–USV model, the volatility factor that does not appear directly in bond prices is treated as the latent factor. An extended market price of risk specification is used that nests the specification (12.39) developed by Duffee (2002) by incorporating versions of the more flexible specification (12.40) for $A_1(N)$ models.

What they find is that the implied state variables filtered from the unconstrained $A_1(3)$ model match the first three PCs of the swap yields quite closely. The first two PCs are matched by construction and the third is an outcome of their estimation—the likelihood function chose the parameters so that one of the state variables roughly matched this PC. In contrast, whereas (again by construction) the first two state variables in the $A_1(3)$–USV model track the first two PCs, the third state variable looked much more like the volatility of the short-term bond yield than it did the third "curvature" PC from bond yields. The measures of volatility used were the fitted GARCH(1,1) and EGARCH(1,1) volatilities (see Chapter 7).

Since the $A_1(3)$–USV model is literally nested in the unconstrained $A_1(3)$ model, the finding that they imply different third factors must be a consequence of misspecification of the $A_1(3)$ family: nested models such as these cannot be built up from distinct risk factors. Indeed, when Collin-Dufresne et al. estimate a $A_1(4)$–USV model, they find that it fits the best of all of the models examined. This is to be expected, because three of the risk factors can capture the usual level, slope, and curvature factors, and one is free to capture USV.

That factor interpretations can change with the imposition of restrictions on the parameters of a DTSM may seem surprising at first, so some elaboration on this possibility seems warranted. Consider the analysis with U.S. Treasury data of the $A_1(3)$ family of models in Dai and Singleton (2002). Table 13.5 shows the mean reversion parameters under $\mathbb{P}$ of the

---

[12] This is because the bond prices do not depend on the unspanned volatility factors. All of the parameters would be identified if as many prices of derivatives as unspanned factors were included in the empirical analysis. We return to this point in Chapter 16 when discussing the empirical evidence on fitting to the implied volatilities of derivatives.

Table 13.5.   Mean Reversion Parameters from Various $A_1(3)$ Models

Parameter	$A_{1C}(3)$		$A_{1S}(3)$		$A_{1L}(3)$	
κ_{11}	0.002	(-0.005)	0.653	(0.574)	1.95	(1.94)
κ_{21}	0.204	(-0.107)	-5.45	(-6.33)	-0.44	(0.08)
κ_{31}	0.295	(-0.384)	0.029	(0.039)	1.01	(3.99)
κ_{22}	0.983	(0.062)	1.50	(1.80)	0.13	(0.002)
κ_{32}	-2.740	(-1.95)	-0.022	(-0.011)	0.25	(-0.03)
κ_{23}	-0.403	(0.471)	-16.6	(-38.2)	-0.26	(0.005)
κ_{33}	2.510	(2.340)	0.500	(0.244)	0.61	(0.58)
ML		33.54		33.54		33.42

Note: Parameters under $\mathbb{P}$ are presented with their associated $\mathbb{Q}$ counterparts in parentheses. Y_1 is the volatility factor.
Source: Dai and Singleton (2002).

three factors in three members of the family $A_1(3)$. The numbers in parentheses are the corresponding numbers under $\mathbb{Q}$. The first, model $A_{1C}(3)$, is a slightly constrained version of the canonical model for this family using Duffee's essentially affine specification of the market prices of risk (see Section 12.3.3). The volatility factor shows relatively little mean reversion under $\mathbb{P}$ ($\kappa_{11}^{\mathbb{P}} = 0.002$) and it is explosive under $\mathbb{Q}$ ($\kappa_{11}^{\mathbb{Q}} < 0$).

Model $A_{1S}(3)$ is the same model with the additional constraint that the volatility factor Y_1 be stationary under both $\mathbb{P}$ and $\mathbb{Q}$ measures. Though imposing $\mathbb{Q}$-stationarity has almost no effect on the value of the likelihood function (they are the same to two decimal places), it leads to a factor rotation. The volatility factor Y_1 now has an intermediate rate of mean reversion. Finally, model $A_{1L}(3)$ imposes the additional constraints that the second and third factors do not exhibit stochastic volatility. That is, they are correlated (through the drift) with Y_1, but Y_1 does not affect the instantaneous volatilities of factors Y_2 and Y_3 (which are constant). Again the factors are rotated and Y_1 now has the fastest rate of mean reversion among the volatility factors in these three models. Collin-Dufresne et al. (2004) found a similarly large change in the rate of mean reversion of the volatility factor in their $A_1(3)$ model when they imposed the constraints associated with USV. However, from (12.30) it follows that the volatility factors v_t and V_t are perfectly correlated and, hence, they should have the same degree of mean reversion.

Since all the models listed in Table 13.5 were estimated with the same data and with the same bonds being priced perfectly by the model, these rotations must be a consequence of model misspecification. Locally, the persistence in the volatility of r is determined only by the persistence in Y_1, the only factor with stochastic volatility. Each of these models leads to a different conclusion about the degree of this persistence. Something very similar appears to be happening in the analysis of Collin-Dufresne et al. Depending on the particular parametrization chosen, the likelihood function makes different trade-offs between fitting the cross-section and time-series properties of bond yields within the misspecified family $A_1(3)$. The consequences of this were striking in Dai and Singleton's (2002) analysis of expectations puzzles. Moving from model $A_{1C}(3)$ to $A_{1L}(3)$, they found that there was a substantial improvement in their models' abilities to fit correlations of bond yields and the slope of the yield curve historically. In particular, the risk-adjusted coefficients $\phi_{nT}^{\mathcal{R}}$ were much closer to unity. We relate these observations to the pricing of fixed-income derivatives in Chapter 16.

13.5. Macroeconomic Factors and DTSMs

Several complementary literatures have recently been exploring the linkages between interest rate behavior and the business cycle. Before examining these models, we note that there is substantial descriptive evidence that macroeconomic variables are highly correlated with the latent state variables in DTSMs. For instance, Wu (2000) and Evans and Marshall (2001) find that "aggregate demand" shocks are highly correlated with the first PC or "level" factor and that monetary policy shocks (at least under some identifying assumptions) affect the slope of the yield curve by having a disproportionately large effect on short-term rates.

To relate these descriptive studies to the properties of a DTSM, we proceed to decompose the responses of yields to factor "shocks" based on their contributions to expected future changes in short rates and to changes in term premiums. Recalling that

$$R_t^n = \frac{1}{n}\sum_{i=0}^{n-1} E_t[r_{t+i}] + \frac{1}{n}\sum_{i=0}^{n-1} p_t^i \equiv \mathrm{ES}_t(n) + \mathrm{TP}_t(n), \qquad (13.11)$$

we can decompose movements in zero yields into the "expected return" ($\mathrm{ES}_t(n)$) and "term premium" ($\mathrm{TP}_t(n)$) components. Focusing on the $A_0(3)$ model, with market price of risk specification (12.39), the factors have the following interpretations in terms of yield curve movements: Factor 1 is a "curvature" or "butterfly" factor, with a $\mathbb{P}$-half-life of about 2.2 months; Factor 2 is the "level" factor, with the longest $\mathbb{P}$-half-life of 2.65 years; and Factor 3 is the "slope" factor, with an intermediate $\mathbb{P}$-half-life of 1 year.

Figure 13.3 displays the responses of the Treasury zero curve to one-standard deviation shocks to the factors. Shocks to the level factor induce a roughly equal change in the yields of bonds of all maturities. At the short end, out to about 2.5 years, yields are affected almost entirely through $\mathrm{ES}_t(n)$. However, as the maturity of the bonds is increased, $\mathrm{TP}_t(n)$ grows while $\mathrm{ES}_t(n)$ declines to the point where they have roughly equal effects on the 10-year yield. It is precisely the growing importance (with maturity) of

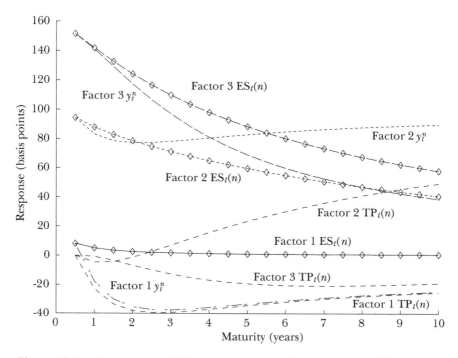

Figure 13.3. *Responses of yields, expected average short rates, and risk premiums to shocks to the factors in an $\mathbb{A}_0(3)$ model fit to U.S. Treasury bond yields.*

$\text{TP}_t(n)$ that underlies the success of model $\mathbb{A}_0(3)$ in replicating the failure of the expectations theory in the historical data. The responses of yields to level shocks are very similar to the responses to the aggregate demand shock in Evans and Marshall (2001).

The slope factor (Factor 3) moves short-term rates by three times as much as it moves the long-term rates (150 versus 50 basis points). It affects yields virtually entirely through $\text{ES}_t(n)$, having a near-zero effect on term premiums. This shock is very similar to one of the versions of the exogenous monetary policy shock used in the structural vector autoregression in Evans and Marshall (2001). Finally, the curvature shock (Factor 1) is a pure risk-premium phenomenon with a near-zero $\text{ES}_t(n)$ for all n. Previous descriptive studies have found that the curvature factor, as proxied by the third principal component, evidences little correlation with macroeconomic activity. As such, Duffee (2002) conjectured that it might represent a "flight to quality" shock.

While these descriptive studies are suggestive of the contributions of macroeconomic shocks to term structure movements, a deeper understanding of the roles of macro shocks requires the integration of term structure and business cycle models. The first generation of models along these lines introduced macro factors directly into DTSMs. For instance, Ang and Piazzesi (2003) estimate an $DA_0(5)$, a five-factor discrete-time Gaussian model, in which three of the factors are latent (as in standard DTSMs) and two are observed macroeconomic variables. One of the latter represents real economic activity and the other is related to inflation. While informative about the correlations between macro variables and yields, within a no-arbitrage setting, this formulation does not provide an economic interpretation of the latent shocks. Additionally, as specified, no feedback was allowed between the macro variables and the short-term interest rate. Such feedback is predicted by most formulations of monetary policy rules.

Another body of work introduces multiple regimes into affine DTSMs with latent risk factors. Common to all of these studies is the finding, consistent with the descriptive analyses of Ang and Bekaert (2002) and others, that the switches in regimes are closely matched with recessions and expansions in the U.S. economy. Ang and Bekaert (2003b) introduce inflation into a regime-switching model in order to extract measures of ex ante real interest rates within a DTSM. Dai et al. (2003) estimate a model with two regimes in which the risk of shifting across regimes is priced. They find that the market prices of regime-shift risk vary over time with the stage of the business cycle. Furthermore, the introduction of multiple regimes with state-dependent probabilities of switching regimes accommodates the asymmetric nature of business cycles: recoveries tend to take longer than contractions (see, e.g., Neftci, 1984, and Hamilton, 1989).

To develop more formal links between the risk factors in DTSMs and macroeconomic models of the business cycle Hordahl et al. (2003), Rudebusch and Wu (2003), and Bekaert et al. (2005) overlay an affine DTSM on an IS-LM-style macroeconomic model of the economies for Germany and the United States. They combine aggregate demand and aggregate supply equations with a monetary policy rule to determine the short-term interest rate. Then the absence of arbitrage opportunities is used to derive the implied model of long-term bond yields. These studies work within the $\mathbb{A}_0(N)$ framework, thereby ignoring macroeconomic links to conditional volatility. Time-varying conditional volatility could be introduced into these models within the discrete-time $\mathbb{A}_M(N)$ framework of Dai et al. (2005). Additionally, the literature has presumed that only the short-term interest rate enters into the aggregate demand equation. This facilitates model development, since long-term rates are then determined by an arbitrage-free DTSM. However, standard economic reasoning would support a role for long-term rates directly in the aggregate demand function.

Following Bekaert et al., a representative model has the monetary authority setting the short-term interest rate according to the rule

$$ i_t = \rho i_{t-1} + (1 - \rho) \left[\bar{i}_t + \beta E_t \big[\pi_{t+1} - \pi_t^* \big] + \gamma \left(y_t - y_t^n \right) \right] + \epsilon_{MP,t}, \quad (13.12) $$

where ρ is the interest rate smoothing parameter (see, e.g., Clarida et al., 1999), π denotes inflation and π^* is the central bank's inflation target, y is detrended output and y^n is the natural rate of output, and $\bar{i}$ is the desired level of i when $\pi = \pi^*$ and $y = y^n$.

Aggregate demand, incorporating adjustment costs, is given by

$$y_t = \alpha_{IS} + \mu_y E_t[y_{t+1}] + (1 - \mu_y)y_{t-1} - \phi\,(i_t - E_t[\pi_{t+1}]) + \epsilon_{IS,t}. \quad (13.13)$$

The leads and lags in (13.13) are sometimes increased to accommodate monthly data in a setting where expectations about the future or adjustment costs involve more periods (e.g., Fuhrer, 2000). The lagged y is motivated by the presence of external habit formation (see Section 10.5.2) in agents' preferences. Inflation is set according to a standard Phillips curve:

$$\pi_t = \delta E_t[\pi_{t+1}] + (1 - \delta)\pi_{t-1} + \kappa\left(y_- y_t^n\right) + \epsilon_{AS,t}. \quad (13.14)$$

To complete this model (as a model of the term structure), the market prices of risk must be specified. Since the IS curve (13.13) is derived from a linearization of the first-order conditions to a representative agent's intertemporal consumption/investment problem, the market prices of risk are not free parameters. All of the macroterm structure models that have been examined to date assume a linear structure to the aggregate demand and supply functions and the monetary policy rule, with Gaussian homoskedastic shocks. Under their assumption that marginal rates of substitution are lognormally distributed, this leads to the pricing kernel[13]

$$q_{t+1}^* = e^{-i_t - \frac{1}{2}\Lambda^{\mathcal{D}'}\Omega\Lambda^{\mathcal{D}} - \Lambda^{\mathcal{D}'}\epsilon_{t+1}}, \quad (13.15)$$

where $\epsilon_{t+1} \sim N(0, \Omega)$. That is, these models imply that the market prices of risk Λ are constant. This, in turn, implies that expected excess returns are constants and the EH holds.

Bekaert et al. (2005) impose this structure for internal consistency and, thereby, examine a macroeconomic model that, by construction, is not able to match the high degree of predictability in excess returns documented above. Hordahl et al. (2003) and Rudebusch and Wu (2003) adopt a specification of Λ_t that is an affine function of the macroeconomic and/or latent risk factors in their models. This allows their term structure models to better

---

[13] To relate this pricing kernel to the family considered by Dai et al. (2005), we write their pricing kernel [using (12.42)] as $q_{t+1}^* = e^{-i_t - \eta_t - \Lambda_t^{\mathcal{D}'}(Y_{t+1} - m_t^{\mathbb{P}})}$, where $\eta_t = \Lambda_t^{\mathcal{D}'} m_t^{\mathbb{P}} - a(\Lambda_t) - b(\Lambda_t)Y_t$ and $a(\Lambda^{\mathcal{D}}) = \Lambda^{\mathcal{D}'}\mu_0 + 1/2\Lambda^{\mathcal{D}'}\Omega_t\Lambda^{\mathcal{D}}$ and $b(\Lambda^{\mathcal{D}}) = \Lambda^{\mathcal{D}'}\mu_Y$ are the coefficients in the conditional $\mathbb{P}$-MGF for Y. It follows that $\eta_t = \frac{1}{2}\Lambda_t^{\mathcal{D}'}\Omega_t\Lambda_t^{\mathcal{D}}$ and we obtain (13.15) as the homoskedastic special case with $\epsilon_{t+1} \equiv Y_{t+1} - m_t^{\mathbb{P}}$.

fit the time-series properties of excess returns, but at the expense of introducing a logical inconsistency—their aggregate demand and market price of risk specifications are not mutually consistent.

Ang et al. (2005b) and Law (2005) pursue an intermediate strategy of emphasizing macro factors, without imposing the detailed structure outlined above. Instead they interpret their mappings between the short rate r and macroeconomic variables as variants of Taylor monetary policy rules. These formulations allow r to depend on its past and thereby allow for either policy inertia or interest rate smoothing. The implied DTSMs are assumed to be in the $DA_0(N)$ families but, unlike the more structured models just discussed, the market price of risk $\Lambda^{\mathcal{D}}$ is allowed to be an affine function of the state. This flexibility is allowed because the authors do not adopt a parametric model of aggregate demand. Upon estimating the models using MCMC methods (see Section 6.8), they find that the macro variables explain at least half of the variation in bond yields. Also of interest is their finding that the model-implied monetary policy shocks do not correspond closely to the policy shocks extracted using regression methods.

Finally, Dai (2003), Buraschi and Jiltsov (2004), and Wachter (2005) develop DTSMs directly from agents' intertemporal optimum problems. Buraschi and Jiltsov assume logarithmic preferences, Dai assumes that agents exhibit internal (stochastic) habit, and Wachter has agents exhibiting external habit. A primary focus of all three of these papers is on the abilities of preference-based models to resolve the expectations puzzles LPY outlined previously. To achieve their goals, Dai and Wachter assume exogenous inflation processes so that the pricing kernel for nominal bonds is agents' marginal rate of substitution scaled by the inverse of the inflation rate. Buraschi and Jiltsov, on the other hand, endogenize inflation by introducing money directly into agents' preferences. The latter model, as well as the related continuous-time model of Wu (2002), introduce Taylor-like monetary policy rules directly thereby incorporating a monetary policy shock.

14

Term Structures of Corporate
Bond Spreads

IF THE ISSUER of a fixed-income security might default prior to the maturity date T then, in addition to the risk of changes in r, both the magnitude and the timing of payoffs to investors may be uncertain. How these additional default risks affect pricing depends on how the default event is defined and how recovery in the event of a default is specified. This chapter presents several of the most widely studied models for pricing defaultable bonds and reviews the evidence on the empirical fits of these models.

14.1. DTSMs of Defaultable Bonds

At the broadest level, the two most commonly studied default processes are those of *reduced-form* and *structural* models. The former treat default as an unpredictable event, essentially the outcome of a jump process and its associated intensity or the arrival rate of default events. In contrast, the latter often provide an explicit characterization of the default event, like the first time that a firm's assets fall below the value of its liabilities. Hybrid models that combine aspects of both approaches have also been examined.

In the case where an issuer might default, we view a zero-coupon bond as a portfolio of two securities: (1) a security that pays \$1 at date T contingent on survival of the issuer to the maturity date T; and (2) a security that pays the (possibly random) recovery w received at default, if default occurs before maturity. More precisely, we let τ denote the random default time and $1_{\{\tau > t\}}$ be the indicator function for the event that $\tau > t$. The price of this defaultable zero-coupon bond, $B(t, T)$, is given by

$$B(t, T) = E_t^{\mathbb{Q}}\left[e^{-\int_t^T r_s\, ds}1_{\{\tau > T\}}\right] + E_t^{\mathbb{Q}}\left[e^{-\int_t^\tau r_s\, ds}w1_{\{\tau \leq T\}}\right]. \qquad (14.1)$$

The practical challenge in extending our pricing models to accommodate default is the evaluation of the two expectations in (14.1). The first involves a random payoff determined by the default process underlying the default time τ. The second involves the random recovery and discounting over an uncertain horizon also determined by the distribution of τ.

14.1.1. Reduced-Form Models

In reduced-form models the default time is determined by a counting (jump) process $Z(t)$ with associated state-dependent intensity process $\lambda^{\mathbb{P}}(t)$. Whether or not an issuer actually defaults is an *unpredictable* event because, conditional on the path of $\lambda^{\mathbb{P}}(t)$, survival is determined as the outcome of a random draw from a Poisson distribution. For pricing in this setting, we extend the formulation (8.32) of the pricing kernel to allow for a "jump" to the absorbing default state

$$\frac{d\mathcal{M}_t}{\mathcal{M}_t} = -r_t - \Lambda_t' dW_t^{\mathbb{P}} - \Gamma_t\left(dZ_t - \lambda_t^{\mathbb{P}} dt\right), \tag{14.2}$$

where $\Gamma_t = \Gamma(Y_t)$ is the market price of default risk, and $w(Y(t))$ denotes the recovery by holders of a fixed-income security in the event of default. For a defaultable zero-coupon bond with price $B(t, T)$, the absence of arbitrage opportunities implies that $B(t, T)\mathcal{M}_t$ is a martingale, which, in turn, implies that

$$\left[\frac{\partial}{\partial t} + \mathcal{G}\right] B(t, T) - \left(r_t + \lambda_t^{\mathbb{Q}}\right) B(t, T) + w_t^{\mathbb{Q}} \lambda_t^{\mathbb{Q}} = 0, \tag{14.3}$$

where $\lambda_t^{\mathbb{Q}} \equiv (1 - \Gamma_t)\lambda_t^{\mathbb{P}}$ is the risk-neutral intensity of arrival of default, $w^{\mathbb{Q}}$ is the risk-neutral recovery rate, and $\mathcal{G}$ is the infinitesimal generator discussed in Chapter 8 [see the discussion surrounding (8.50)].

Comparing (14.3) with (8.51) we see that the defaultable security is priced using the default-adjusted discount rate $r_t + \lambda_t^{\mathbb{Q}}$. To interpret this change in discounting, it is instructive to proceed in two steps. Consider first the role of survival in pricing. Suppose that Z is a Cox process (see Chapter 5 and Lando, 1998). Then the probabilities under $\mathbb{P}$ and $\mathbb{Q}$ that a firm survives from time t until time T are

$$p^{\mathbb{P}}(t, T) = E_t^{\mathbb{P}}\left[e^{-\int_t^T \lambda^{\mathbb{P}}(s)ds}\right] \text{ and } p^{\mathbb{Q}}(t, T) = E_t^{\mathbb{Q}}\left[e^{-\int_t^T \lambda^{\mathbb{Q}}(s)ds}\right], \tag{14.4}$$

respectively. These survival probabilities take the form of expected present value relations, with intensities in the place of interest rates. We exploit this analogy repeatedly in subsequent discussions. Note also that as we change the measure under which survival is computed, it is necessary to change both the distribution under which the expectation is computed and the underlying intensity.

Importantly, as discussed in Artzner and Delbaen (1995), Martellini and Karoui (2001), and Jarrow et al. (2005) the requirement of no arbitrage places only weak restrictions on the risk premium $\Gamma(t)$ and, hence, on the mapping between $\lambda^{\mathbb{Q}}$ and $\lambda^{\mathbb{P}}$. Not only may $\lambda^{\mathbb{P}}$ and $\lambda^{\mathbb{Q}}$ differ in their current levels, they may also have different degrees of persistence and time-varying volatility. Moreover, one might jump while the other follows a continuous sample path.[1] An important empirical issue is the magnitude of $\Gamma(t)$ or, equivalently, the degree to which $\lambda^{\mathbb{P}}$ and $\lambda^{\mathbb{Q}}$ differ. As we discuss later, this depends in part on the abilities of market participants to diversify away "jump-at-default" risk.

Next suppose that $w_t^{\mathbb{Q}} = 0$, so that there is no recovery in the event of default. In this case, an investor in a corporate zero-coupon bond receives the promised payoff of \$1 only if the firm survives to the maturity date T. That is, only if the random default time τ, should default occur, is after T. The price of this "survival contingent claim" is $B(t, T) = E_t^{\mathbb{Q}}[e^{-\int_t^T r(s)\,ds} 1_{\{\tau > T\}}]$. From (14.3), it follows that this bond price solves the PDE

$$\left[\frac{\partial}{\partial t} + \mathcal{G}\right] - \big(r(t) + \lambda^{\mathbb{Q}}(t)\big) B(t, T) = 0. \tag{14.5}$$

As shown by Lando (1998) and Madan and Unal (1998), the solution to this PDE is

$$B(t, T) = E_t^{\mathbb{Q}}\left[e^{-\int_t^T (r(s) + \lambda^{\mathbb{Q}}(s))\,ds}\right]. \tag{14.6}$$

It follows that the survival-contingent claim can be valued by treating the payoff as \$1 with certainty and simultaneously adjusting the rate of discounting. Intuitively, using $r_t + \lambda_t^{\mathbb{Q}}$ in discounting accounts for both the time value of money and mean rate of loss in the event of default, $\lambda^{\mathbb{Q}}(t) \times \$1$. Since there is no recovery, adjusting by the mean loss rate amounts to accounting for survival.

With nonzero recovery, the solution to (14.3) for $B(t, T)$ depends on what one assumes about recovery, $w_t^{\mathbb{Q}}$. Note the interesting parallel between the stochastic dividend h in (8.51) and the term $w_t^{\mathbb{Q}} \lambda_t^{\mathbb{Q}}$ in (14.3). The possibility of a recovery in the event of default effectively introduces a dividend that is received at the rate $w_t^{\mathbb{Q}} \lambda_t^{\mathbb{Q}}$. Since $\lambda_t^{\mathbb{Q}} dt$ is the probability of default over the next instant of time and $w_t^{\mathbb{Q}}$ is the recovery in the event of default, the dividend is the (risk-neutral) mean recovery rate owing to default.

Duffie and Singleton (1999) assume that investors lose an expected (risk-neutral) fraction $L_t^{\mathbb{Q}}$ of the market value of $B(t, T)$, measured just

---

[1] Thus, moving between $\lambda^{\mathbb{P}}$ and $\lambda^{\mathbb{Q}}$ is not analogous to the standard adjustment to the drift of r to obtain its risk-neutral representation.

prior to the default event (fractional recovery of market value). In this case, $w_t^Q = (1 - L_t^Q)B(t, T)$ and $B(t, T)$ solves the PDE

$$\left[\frac{\partial}{\partial t} + \mathcal{G}\right] - \left(r(t) + L^Q(t)\lambda^Q(t)\right)B(t, T) = 0. \tag{14.7}$$

It follows that $B(t, T) = E_t^Q[e^{-\int_t^T R_u\, du}]$, where $R_t \equiv r_t + \lambda_t^Q L_t^Q$ denotes the "default-adjusted" discount rate.

Lando (1998), Duffie (1998), and Duffie and Singleton (1999) consider the alternative assumption that a recovery amount of w_τ^Q is received at the time of default. With the face value of this bond normalized to unity, this recovery assumption is interpretable as fractional recovery of face value. As such, it is more closely aligned with the typical covenants of a bond, by which bondholders are entitled to the smaller of the face values of their bonds or to whatever portion of that value that remains after liquidation of the issuer's assets. By analogy to (8.33), the recovery-of-face value assumption leads to the pricing relation

$$B(t, T) = E_t^Q\left[e^{-\int_t^T (r_s + \lambda_s^Q)ds}\right] + E_t^Q\left[\int_t^T e^{-\int_t^u (r_s + \lambda_s^Q)\, ds} \lambda_u^Q w_u^Q\, du\right]. \tag{14.8}$$

Madan and Unal (1998) derive similar pricing relations for the case of junior and senior debts with different recovery ratios.

Finally, Jarrow and Turnbull (1995) assume a constant fractional recovery of an otherwise equivalent Treasury security with the remaining maturity of the defaultable instrument. This recovery assumption is natural for the case of default on a long-dated corporate zero-coupon bond, where it seems unlikely that a bankruptcy court would accelerate the bond holder to par (face value). Instead, one might expect the courts to consider the discounted values of comparable maturity default-free zero-coupon bonds. For coupon bonds, the recovery-of-treasury convention implies recovery of some portion of future coupon payments in addition to face value. This recovery assumption has been less widely applied in the empirical literature than the preceding two assumptions.

Throughout this discussion of pricing we have, naturally, focused on risk-neutral recovery w^Q. At the same time, we have followed standard practice and adopted the specification (14.2) of $\mathcal{M}$ that presumes that recovery risk is not priced: $w^Q = w^P$. Only the risk related to the timing of default is (possibly) priced with market price of risk Γ_t. Analogously to the treatment of jump amplitude risk in Chapter 12, we could introduce a risk premium associated with recovery risk. The practical consequence of such an extension for pricing would be that historical information about recovery would, in general, be an unreliable guide for parameterizing w^Q absent independent information about the risk premium associated with recovery risk. Since so little is known about the latter risk premium,[2] we focus on w^Q in pricing and assume that $w^Q = w^P$ in the few situations where w^P is the construct of interest.

14.1.2. Structural Models

Structural models, in their most basic form, assume default at the first time that some credit indicator falls below a specified threshold value. The conceptual foundations for this approach were laid by Merton (1970, 1974) and Black and Scholes (1973). They supposed that default occurs at the maturity date of debt provided that the issuer's assets are less than the face value of maturing debt at that time. (Default before maturity was not considered.) Black and Cox (1976) introduced the idea that default would occur at the first time that assets fall below a boundary D (which may or may not be the face value of debt), thereby turning the pricing problem into one of computing "first-passage" probabilities. For the case of exogenously given default boundary F and firm value A, if in the event of default bondholders lose the fraction L_T^Q of par *at maturity*, then the price $B(t, T)$ of a defaultable zero-coupon bond that matures at date T is

$$B(t, T) = E_t^Q \left[e^{-\int_t^T r_u \, du} \left(1 - L_T^Q 1_{\{\tau < T\}} \right) \right]$$

$$= D(t, T) \left[1 - L_T^Q H^T (A_t/F, r_t, T - t) \right], \tag{14.9}$$

where $H^T(A_t/F, r_t, T - t) \equiv E_t^T[1_{\{\tau < T\}}]$ is the first-passage probability of default between dates t and T under the *forward* measure induced by the default-free zero price $D(t, T)$ (see Chapter 8). Thus, $B(t, T)$ is the price of a riskless zero-coupon bond minus the value of a put option on the value of the firm.

Pricing in models with endogenous default thresholds has been explored by Geske (1977), Leland (1994), Leland and Toft (1996), Anderson and Sundaresan (1996), Mella-Barral and Perraudin (1997), and Ericsson and Reneby (2001), among others. The endogeneity of F arises (at least in part) because equity holders have an option as to whether to issue additional equity to service the promised coupon payments. With F determined by the actions of equity holders and debtors, it becomes a function of the underlying parameters of the structural model. The models of Anderson and

---

[2] It is also the case that little is known about the market price of default risk Γ_t. However, at least in the case of timing risk, there is relatively more information available from rating agencies on historical default rates.

Sundaresan (1996), Mella-Barral and Perraudin (1997), and Ericsson and Reneby (2001) accommodate violations of absolute priority rules (equity holders experience nonzero recoveries, even though bondholders recover less than the face value of their debt).

14.1.3. Pricing with Two-Sided Default Risk

For the cases of interest rate forward and swap contracts, default risk is "two-sided" in the sense that a financial contract may go "into the money" to either counterparty, depending on market conditions. As such, the relevant default processes for pricing change with market conditions. Duffie and Singleton (1999) show, in the context of reduced-form models, that this dependence of λ^{Q} and w_{τ}^{Q} on the price $P(t)$ of the contract being valued renders the preceding reduced-form pricing models inapplicable, at least in principle.[3] Fortunately, for at-the-money swaps (those used most widely in empirical studies of DTSMs), these considerations are negligible (Duffie and Huang, 1996; Duffie and Singleton, 1997). Hence, standard practice within academia and the financial industry is to treat such interest-rate swaps as if they are bonds trading at par (\$1), with the discount rate R chosen to reflect the credit/liquidity risk inherent in the swap market.

Using this approximate pricing framework, the resulting discount curve $-\log B(t, T)/(T - t)$ "passes through" short-term LIBOR rates. However, there is no presumption that long-term swap rates and LIBOR contracts reflect the same credit quality. They are in fact notably different (Sun et al., 1993; Collin-Dufresne and Solnik, 2000). Nor is there a presumption that $R_{t} - r_{t}$ reflects only credit risk; liquidity risk may be as, if not more, important [see Grinblatt (2001) and Liu et al. (2006) for discussions of liquidity factors in swap pricing].

14.2. Parametric Reduced-Form Models

The development of parametric reduced-form models of defaultable bond prices has largely paralleled the literature on DTSMs for default-free securities. Affine and quadratic-Gaussian models have received the most attention.

14.2.1. Affine Models

In the Duffie-Singleton framework with fractional recovery of market value, the default adjusted discount rate $R_{t} = r_{t} + \lambda_{t}^{Q} L_{t}^{Q}$ can be modeled as an

---

[3] Under fractional recovery of market value, one can still express $B(t, T)$ as the solution to (14.7). However, because of the dependence of R on P, $B(t, T)$ solves a quasi-linear equation, instead of a more standard linear PDE, and prices must be obtained by numerical methods.

affine function of the state Y_t. A researcher has the choice of modeling R directly or of building up a model of R from separate affine parameterizations of r and $\lambda^Q L^Q$. Importantly, since credit spreads on zero-coupon or coupon bonds depend only on the mean loss rate $\lambda_t^Q L_t^Q$, it is not possible to separately identify λ_t^Q and L_t^Q from bond data alone. Therefore, researchers who have wanted to draw conclusions about the default intensity λ_t^Q or the associated risk-neutral survival probability have typically fixed L_t^Q, which thereby allows them to back out λ_t^Q from the fitted mean loss rate.

The first steps toward an affine model under fractional recovery of face value are the modeling of $(r_t + \lambda_t^Q)$ and λ_t^Q as affine functions of Y. Then the price of \$1 contingent on survival to date T [the first term in (14.8)] is known in closed form. To price the recovery claim, we first observe that a random recovery w_t^Q can be replaced by its conditional mean $E^Q[w_t^Q|Y_{t-}]$ just prior to the date recovery is realized (see Duffie and Singleton, 1999). The model can then be completed by assuming a constant conditional mean recovery rate. Alternatively, though we are not aware of examples in the literature, one could assume that $\log w^Q(t)$ (or $\log E^Q[w_t^Q|Y_{t-}]$) are affine functions of the state. Under either of these generalizations, the recovery claim is priced using the extended transform of Duffie et al. (2000) (see Chapter 5) to evaluate

$$E^Q \left[e^{- \int_t^u (r_s + \lambda_s^Q) ds} \lambda_u^Q w_u^Q \right] du.$$

Only the one-dimensional integral in (14.8) is computed numerically.[4]

Note that λ^Q and L^Q do not enter the pricing equations symmetrically under fractional recovery of face value. As such, assuming that the market prices bonds according to this recovery convention, one can in principle separately identify recovery and default arrival rates from coupon bond data. This observation is developed in more depth, in the context of pricing sovereign debt, in Pan and Singleton (2005).

14.2.2. Quadratic-Gaussian Models

QG models are also easily adapted to the problem of pricing defaultable securities by having both r and λ^Q be quadratic functions of Y. In this setting, QG models offer the flexibility, relative to affine models, of having strictly positive (r, λ^Q) and negatively correlated state variables (see, e.g., Duffie and Liu, 2001).

---

[4] An equally tractable pricing model is obtained if the fractional loss L_τ^Q is incurred at T, the original maturity of the bond (the convention used in most structural models). In this case, $w_\tau^Q = (1 - L_\tau^Q)D(\tau, T)$ is the discounted recovery (from T to τ) and L_τ^Q must be chosen judiciously to facilitate computation of the relevant expectations.

14.3. Parametric Structural Models

Structural models of default combine an arbitrage-free specification of the default-free term structure with an explicit definition of default in terms of balance sheet information. The former is typically taken to be a standard affine DTSM. The new, nontrivial practical consideration that arises in implementing structural models is the computation of the forward, first-passage probability H^T.

A representative structural model has firm value A following a lognormal diffusion with constant variance and nonzero (constant) correlation between A and the instantaneous riskless rate r:

$$\frac{dA_t}{A_t} = (r - \gamma)\, dt + \sigma_A dW_{At}^{\mathbb{Q}}, \tag{4.10}$$

$$dr = \kappa(\mu - r)\, dt + \sigma_r dW_{rt}^{\mathbb{Q}}, \tag{4.11}$$

where $\text{Corr}(dW_A^{\mathbb{Q}}, dW_r^{\mathbb{Q}}) = \rho$ and γ is the payout rate. Kim et al. (1993) and Cathcart and El-Jahel (1998) adopt the same model for A, but assume that r follows a one-factor square-root $(A_1(1))$ process. Related structural models are studied by Nielsen et al. (1993) and Briys and de Varenne (1997).

The basic Merton model has: (1) the firm capitalized with common stock and one bond that matures at date T, (2) a constant net payout rate γ and a constant interest rate r, and (3) default occurs when $A_T < F$, where F is constant. (Firms default only at maturity of the bond.) In actual applications of this model, a coupon bond is typically assumed to be a portfolio of zero-coupon bonds, each of which is priced using the Merton model. Geske (1977) extended Merton's model to the case of multiple bonds maturing at different dates.

Building upon Black and Cox (1976), Longstaff and Schwartz (1995) allowed the issuer to default at any time prior to maturity of the bonds (not just at maturity) and replaced the assumption of constant r with the one-factor Vasicek (1977) model (4.11). Though the Longstaff-Schwartz model is in many respects more general than the Merton model, the latter is not nested in the former.[5]

In the Leland and Toft (1996) model, a firm continuously issues new debt with coupons that are paid from the firm's payout γA. The default boundary is endogenous, because equityholders can decide whether or not to issue new equity to service the debt in the event that the payout is not

---

[5] The Merton model gives a closed-form solution for defaultable zero-coupon bond prices. Longstaff and Schwartz provided an approximate numerical solution for H^T in their setting. Subsequently, Collin-Dufresne and Goldstein (2001a) provided an efficient numerical method for computing the $B(t, T)$.

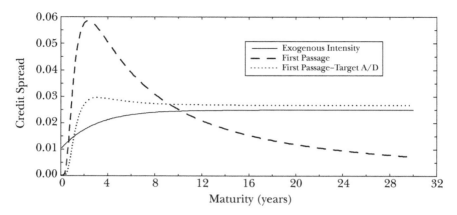

Figure 14.1. *Credit spreads implied by reduced-form and structural models.*

large enough to cover the dividends. Their model gives a closed-form expression for $B(t, T)$ under the assumption of constant r. Anderson and Sundaresan (1996) and Mella-Barral and Perraudin (1997) solve simplified bargaining games to obtain close-form expressions for their default boundaries.

A typical feature of structural pricing models is that the value of the firm diffuses continuously over time. This has the counterfactual implication that yield spreads on short-maturity, defaultable bonds will be near zero, since it is known with virtual certainty whether or not an issuer will default over the next short interval of time. This is illustrated in Figure 14.1 by the dashed line that shows spreads near zero for short-maturity bonds and then rising sharply over bonds with maturities in the 2- to 4-year range.[6] The notably spiked shape of the spreads is a consequence of the similar shape to the term structure of forward default probabilities induced by Merton-style structural models. As shown by Duffie and Lando (2001), more plausible levels of short-term spreads are obtained in structural models by making the assumption that bondholders measure firm's assets with error. Once measurement errors are introduced, this basic structural model becomes mathematically equivalent to an intensity-based, reduced-form model.

An alternative means of generating more plausible spreads for short-maturity bonds is to introduce a jump into the asset value process (14.10). Zhou (2001a) added the possibility of a jump in assets A with i.i.d. amplitudes at independent Poisson arrival times, thereby allowing for A to pass through the default threshold (F in our basic formulation) either through continuous fluctuations of the Brownian motion or by jumps. Given that

---

[6] We are grateful to Pierre Collin-Dufresne for providing this figure based on the work in Collin-Dufresne and Goldstein (2001a).

A can pass below F even when it is well away from F today, investors will demand a positive spread even at short maturities.

Another equally important feature of many structural models is that credit spreads tend to asymptote to zero with increasing maturity, again as illustrated by the dashed line in Figure 14.1. This is in contrast to the behavior of standard reduced-form models, which tend to asymptote to a constant long-term yield, as illustrated by the solid line in this figure. To see why, note that the zero-coupon bond yield spreads (under zero recovery) in reduced-form and structural models are given by their associated survival probabilities:

$$ -(T-t)\log\left(\frac{B(t,T)}{D(t,T)}\right) = \begin{cases} -\log p^{\mathbb{Q}}(t,T) & \text{reduced-form,} \\ -\log H^T(A_t/F, r_t, T-t) & \text{structural.} \end{cases} $$

In reduced-form models

$$ p^{\mathbb{Q}}(t,T) = E_t^{\mathbb{Q}}\left[e^{-\int_t^T \lambda^{\mathbb{Q}}(u)\,du}\right] = e^{-\int_t^T f^{\mathbb{Q}}(t,u)\,du}, $$

where $f^{\mathbb{Q}}(t,u)$ is the instantaneous, risk-neutral forward default probability for date u. Suppose that $\lambda^{\mathbb{Q}}(t)$ follows a square-root process with parameters $(\sigma, \theta^{\mathbb{Q}}, \kappa^{\mathbb{Q}})$. Then $f^{\mathbb{Q}}(t,T)$ converges to a positive constant as $T \to \infty$. As a consequence, $p^{\mathbb{Q}}(t,T) \to 0$ as $T \to \infty$; eventually, the issuer defaults with probability one. This behavior of the survival probability underlies the flattening out of the yield curve at the long end for the reduced-form model. On the other hand, in this structural model, the probability of never defaulting is $H(A_t/F, r_t, \infty) = 1 - e^{(-mX_t/\sigma^2)}$, where $m = r - \gamma - \sigma^2/2$. This is a consequence of the fact that (risk neutrally) A drifts away from the default boundary at the rate $r - \gamma$ (which is typically positive). This gives rise to the downward-sloping credit curve at long maturities.

To address this counterfactual implication of many structural models, Tauren (1999) and Collin-Dufresne and Goldstein (2001a) attribute a target debt/equity ratio to issuers, and Ericsson and Reneby (2001) assume a positive growth rate of total nominal debt. The term structure implied by a modified structural model with a target capital structure is given by the dotted line in Figure 14.1. With this modification, the term structures from these structural and reduced-form models are quite similar at the long end of the yield.

14.4. Empirical Studies of Corporate Bonds

As we set out to review the empirical fits of these pricing models, it is instructive to briefly step back and examine some of the descriptive properties of the term structures of credit spreads. Both the magnitudes and the time-series properties of spreads depend in part on the reference yield curve to which corporate bond yields are spread. Treasury, agency, interest rate swap, and high-grade corporate yields have all been used as reference yields for computing spreads.

Furthermore, spreads may reflect economic forces other than default risk. In cases where Treasury bonds are used for reference yields, spreads may reflect tax shields on Treasuries (Elton et al., 2001) and special repo rates for on-the-run Treasuries (Duffie, 1996). The liquidity effects may also be present for any of the other reference curves typically used in empirical studies.

For a given credit quality (typically measured by credit rating) Jones et al. (1984), Sarig and Warga (1989), and He et al. (2000) find that, historically, the term structures of credit spreads for high-grade issuers tend to be upward sloping, while those for lower-rated investment-grade issuers (such as Baa) are close to flat, or perhaps hump shaped. The shape of the term structure of credit spreads for low-grade bonds has been more controversial. Helwege and Turner (1999) argue that the findings in many previous studies of spreads reflect a selection bias associated with a tendency for better-quality speculative-grade issuers to issue longer-term bonds. By matching bonds by issuer and ratings, Helwege and Turner conclude that spread curves for B-rated U.S. industrial issues are upward sloping. Subsequently, He et al. (2000) refined this matching method and expanded the set of ratings examined. They found that spread curves for CCC and CC rated firms are downward sloping, but curves for more highly rated firms tend to be upward sloping.

Turning to the economic factors that drive credit spreads, Duffie and Singleton (1997) examined the correlations between interest rate swap spreads and various macroeconomic variables and proxies for market liquidity. They found that roughly 50% of the variation in swap spreads of various maturities was not explained by (observable) measures of credit or liquidity. Similarly, Neal et al. (2000) and Collin-Dufresne et al. (2001) examined the correlations of spreads on corporate bonds and various macroeconomic variables and proxies for credit and liquidity. The latter study also found that nearly half of the variation in spreads was unaccounted for by their regressors. Moreover, they found that upon computing principal components of the residuals from their projections, a single corporate-market specific factor explained most of the variation in their residuals. All of these studies point to substantial variability in spreads and co-movements among spreads. However, the latter co-movement is not necessarily related to our measured proxies for credit and liquidity risk or to macroeconomic activity.

Equally notable is the difference between the levels of spreads and the expected loss rates on the underlying bonds. Table 14.1 from Amato and Remolona (2003) displays the average historical spreads and the expected

Table 14.1. **Spreads and Expected Default Losses by Rating**

	Maturity					
	1–3 years		3–5 years		7–10 years	
Rating	Spread	Expected loss	Spread	Expected loss	Spread	Expected loss
AAA	49.5	0.06	63.9	0.18	74.0	0.61
AA	59.0	1.24	71.2	1.44	88.6	2.70
A	88.8	1.12	102.9	2.78	117.5	7.32
BBB	169.0	12.5	170.9	20.12	179.6	34.56
BB	421.2	103.1	364.6	126.7	322.3	148.1
B	760.8	426.2	691.8	400.5	512.4	329.4

Source: Amato and Remolona (2003).

loss rates (based on actual defaults) for U.S. corporate bonds, by rating over the period January 1997 to August 2003. What is striking about these calculations, which are based in part on the analysis in Altman and Kishore (1998), is how large the gap is between bond yield spreads and the average losses incurred from holding comparably rated defaultable bonds. The gap is particularly large for the more highly rated bonds. It seems unlikely that liquidity premia are sufficiently larger, proportionately, at higher ratings to explain these findings, because the universe of institutional investors who are eligible to hold investment-grade bonds is much larger than that of investors who can hold investment and speculative-grade bonds. Therefore, at first glance anyway, default risk premiums appear to be larger for high- than for low-grade corporate bonds.

Though descriptive studies of credit spreads often focus on the nature of the default process when interpreting results, we have seen that recovery may also play a central role. In fact, there is substantial evidence that recovery varies over the business cycle, with recovery rates being lower during recessions. Moreover, default rates also vary with the business cycle, being higher during recessions. Together, these patterns imply a quite strong negative correlation between speculative-grade default rates and recovery rates, at least in the aggregate and for corporate bonds. This is documented in Figure 14.2 for Moody's universe of rated bonds. While this pattern in $w^{\mathbb{P}}$ is now widely recognized, this correlation is rarely accommodated in econometric specifications of defaultable bond pricing models. Typically, for pricing, $w^{\mathbb{Q}}$ is assumed to be a known constant. While it is $w^{\mathbb{Q}}$, not $w^{\mathbb{P}}$, that is relevant for pricing (so a constant $w^{\mathbb{Q}}$ is not logically inconsistent with the evidence in Figure 14.2), further research into the empirical consequences of relaxing the assumption of constant $w^{\mathbb{Q}}$ seems warranted.

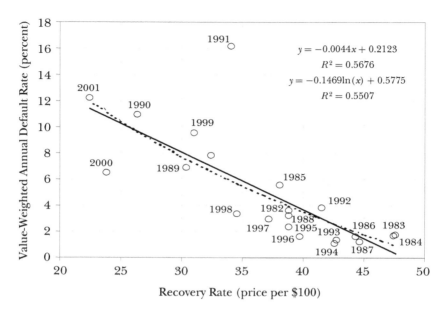

Figure 14.2. *Correlation of speculative-grade default and recovery rates. Source: Moody's Default and Recovery Report (2003).*

14.4.1. Reduced-Form Models

Within the family of reduced-form models with fractional recovery of market value, Duffee (1999) examined corporate spreads to the U.S. Treasury curve, with $D(t, T)$ described by an $A_2(2)$ affine model for independent (Y_1, Y_2) and the instantaneous credit spread $s_t = \lambda_t^Q L_t^Q$ given by an affine function of the independent $A_1(1)$ processes (Y_1, Y_2, Y_3). Correlation between s_t and r_t was induced by their common dependence on (Y_1, Y_2). This is not the most flexible affine model for s_t that could have been examined as there was no correlation among the Y's. Additionally, the market prices of risk were of the "completely" affine form, being proportional to the volatilities $\sqrt{Y_{it}}$. We now know that more flexible specifications along the lines of Cheridito et al. (2003) are possible without introducing arbitrage opportunities.

For Lehman Brothers data on trader quotes for noncallable corporate bonds, Duffee found a model-implied negative correlation between corporate yield spreads and U.S. Treasury rates, consistent with his earlier descriptive analysis. The average error in fitting noncallable corporate bond yields was less than 10 basis points. Similarly, Collin-Dufresne and Solnik

(2000) had r_t following a Gaussian $A_0(2)$ model and s_t following a Gaussian jump-diffusion model with constant jump intensity. Treating the U.S. Treasury curve as the reference curve and using yields on LIBOR contracts as the defaultable securities, they found that the correlation between r_t and s_t was also negative. The descriptive evidence in Duffie and Singleton (2003) suggests that the economic shocks underlying this negative correlation have short half-lives, dying out in 1 to 3 months.

Interestingly, for the 161 firms that Duffee examined, the median estimate of the mean reversion parameter $\kappa_3^{\mathbb{Q}}$ of the credit-spread specific factor Y_{3t} was less than zero. That is, this factor was explosive under the risk-neutral measure for more than 50% of the firms examined. There is nothing logically wrong with an explosive intensity $\lambda^{\mathbb{Q}}$ or mean loss rate $\lambda^{\mathbb{Q}} L^{\mathbb{Q}}$ under $\mathbb{Q}$. Evidence of such behavior may simply reflect the very pessimistic view about survival required to price bonds when treating investors as if they are neutral toward default risk. An explosive $\lambda^{\mathbb{Q}}$ leads, for fixed $L^{\mathbb{Q}}$ and horizon T, to a relatively small survival probability $p^{\mathbb{Q}}(t, T)$ compared to what would be obtained with $\kappa^{\mathbb{Q}} > 0$. Of course, an explosive mean loss rate could also be symptomatic of model misspecification. We revisit this issue later when we discuss the empirical evidence from other defaultable securities.

Though the preceding studies treated the spread s_t as a purely latent process, observable state variables are easily incorporated into reduced-form models by letting one or more of the Y's be an observable economic time series. In this manner, it is possible to capture part of the "spirit" of structural models within a reduced-form setting by having $\lambda^{\mathbb{Q}} L^{\mathbb{Q}}$ depend on information about the balance sheet of an issuer. For instance, Bakshi et al. (2004) examine a fractional recovery of market value, reduced-form model in which the default-adjusted discount rate R is an affine function of r and $Y_t = $ firm leverage, $R_t = \alpha_0 + \alpha_r r_t + \alpha_Y Y_t$. The reference rate r was determined by a Gaussian $A_0(2)$ model and the credit factor Y was assumed to follow a mean-reverting Gaussian diffusion. Upon estimating their models using Lehman Brothers data, they found that (after accommodating interest rate risk) higher leverage increases the default-adjusted discount rate, with leverage-related credit risk being more pronounced for long-dated than for short-dated corporate bonds. Bakshi et al. (2001) compare the relative fits of reduced-form models under various recovery timing conventions in a recovery of face value model. Janosi et al. (2002) also study a two-factor model for R in which r follows a one-factor Gaussian process and the credit factor is related to the level of the S&P500 equity index.

Affine models have also been used in the pricing of sovereign bonds. Merrick (2001) calibrates a discrete-time model (to Russian and Argentinean bonds) that can be reinterpreted as a model with a constant (state-independent) intensity. More generally, Pagès (2000) and Keswani (2002) apply special cases of the recovery of market value model to data on Latin

American Brady bonds, and Dullmann and Windfuhr (2000) apply a similar framework to price European government credit spreads under the EMU.

These models presume that holders of sovereign debt face a single credit event—default with liquidation upon default—and, in particular, do not allow for restructuring and the associated write-downs of face value. Among the types of credit events that may be relevant for a sovereign issuer are: obligation acceleration, failure to pay, restructuring, and repudiation/moratorium. In addition, there may be changes in political regimes that affect the credit quality of outstanding bonds. Following Duffie et al. (2003b) we can view each of these credit events as having its own associated arrival intensity λ_i^Q and loss rate L_i^Q. Then, under the assumption that the probability that any two of these credit events happen at the same time is zero, the effective λ_t^Q and L_t^Q for pricing sovereign bonds become:

$$\lambda_t^Q = \lambda_{acc,t}^Q + \lambda_{fail,t}^Q + \lambda_{rest,t}^Q + \lambda_{repud,t}^Q, \tag{14.12}$$

$$L_t^Q = \frac{\lambda_{acc,t}^Q}{\lambda_t^Q} L_{acc,t}^Q + \frac{\lambda_{fail,t}^Q}{\lambda_t^Q} L_{fail,t}^Q + \frac{\lambda_{rest,t}^Q}{\lambda_t^Q} L_{rest,t}^Q + \frac{\lambda_{repud,t}^Q}{\lambda_t^Q} L_{repud,t}^Q. \tag{14.13}$$

The λ_i^Q and L_i^Q may, of course, differ across countries. This model is equally appropriate for pricing corporate bonds in cases where multiple types of credit events are relevant.

Figure 14.3 displays the prices of Russian Ministry of Finance (MinFin) bonds, normalized to the value of $100 on July 31, 1998, just prior to the default on other Russian domestic securities in August 1998.[7] A striking feature of this graph is the substantial decline in market values experienced by the MinFin bonds during the week of the Russian default. Even though none of the outstanding MinFins were defaulted upon, these bonds lost approximately 80% of their market value during this one week. This episode illustrates how much the "surprise" of default was able to affect market values, even when investors were well aware of the increasing likelihood of a Russian default and, commensurately, the prices of MinFin bonds had fallen substantially. The yield on the MinFins had risen from a low of around 2–3% in November 1997 to around 10–11% in July 1998! Note also that all of the MinFin bonds lost approximately the same percentage of *market value* during the week of default, suggesting that in this case the assumption of recovery of market value is a reasonable pricing convention.

There is another feature of the prices of the MinFin3 bond that motivates a further extension of the standard defaultable bond pricing model developed in Duffie et al. (2003b). The MinFin3 bond was issued in May 1993 with a maturity of May 1999. From Figure 14.3 it is seen that the price

---

[7] These MinFin bonds are dollar denominated and issued under the jurisdiction of domestic Russian law; they are not Eurobonds. The data were obtained from Datastream.

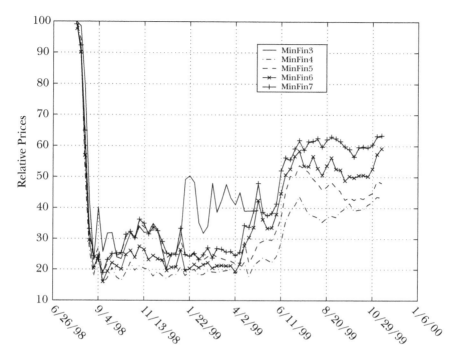

Figure 14.3. *Prices of the Russian MinFin3–7 bonds over the time period from 7/31/1998 (just prior to default) to 11/12/1999, normalized so that they all have a market value of 100 at 7/31/1998.*

of the MinFin3 gradually increased after the August default and then tended to settle down at about 40% of its predefault value. The reduced-form pricing models we have considered up to this point would imply that, in the absence of arbitrage opportunities, the price of this bond should approach $100 (face value) as the bond approaches maturity. The fact that this did not happen suggests that investors in Russian bonds had incorporated a "write-down" effect whereby investors treated a portion of the face value of the bond as effectively having been repudiated by the issuer. That is, for a risky payoff Z_T, the market price subsequent to a default event (assuming fractional recovery of market value) becomes

$$P_t = E_t^{\mathbb{Q}} \left[e^{-\int_t^T (r_s + \lambda_s^{\mathbb{Q}} L_s^{\mathbb{Q}}) ds} Z_T \right] E_t^{\mathbb{Q}} [X_\tau] , \qquad (14.14)$$

where X_τ is the proportional write-down of face value associated with the prior credit event at date τ. The expectation is included to allow for the possibility that the final resolution of the impact of the restructuring on the promised repayment of principal occurs only at the maturity of the bond.

Duffie et al. applied their model to data on Russian MinFin bonds around the Russian default in August 1998 and found substantial evidence for significant write-downs after the 1998 default. Moreover, the model-implied default intensity in their model was strongly correlated with various macroeconomic variables related to Russia's ability to repay bondholders at the maturity dates of their bonds.

14.4.2. Structural Models

Empirical implementation of structural models requires one to confront more directly the (often very) complex capital structures of issuers. Among the issues that must be addressed are: the components of the capital structure to be included in A and F; measurement of asset volatility σ_A and the correlation ρ between A and r; and the choice of recovery ratios. The empirical implementations of structural models have varied widely in their resolutions of these issues.

Jones et al. (1984) implemented the Merton model for a sample of callable coupon bonds for the sample period 1977–1981. They found absolute *pricing* errors of 8.5%: model prices were too high so spreads were too narrow. Ogden (1987) looked at primary market prices for bonds over the period 1973–1985. The Merton model underpredicted spreads by an average of 104 basis points. A major limitation of both of these studies was their use of callable bond prices.

More recently, Lyden and Sariniti (2000) used Bridge data, which provides actual transactions prices on noncallable bonds for both financial and nonfinancial firms. For the Merton model they found mean absolute errors in yield spreads of 80+ basis points. The model-implied spreads were particularly low (bond prices were high) for small firms and long maturities. For a two-factor Longstaff-Schwartz model, in which default occurs when A falls below the par value of outstanding bonds and any recovery is a constant fraction w of par value, they obtained roughly the same results. Moreover, the findings for the Longstaff-Schwartz model were largely insensitive to the assumed value of ρ. In interpreting these results, one should perhaps bear in mind that their sample included both financial and nonfinancial firms, with quite heterogeneous leverage ratios.

Ericsson and Reneby (2001) reach a more optimistic conclusion about the fit of a structural model with endogenous default and leverage ratios that reflect growth in both debt and equity values. Using maximum likelihood methods to estimate the parameters of their firm-value process, they obtain unbiased out-of-sample spread predictions of yield spreads for the noncallable debt of a small sample of 50 industrial firms.

The most comprehensive empirical comparison of structural models to date is provided by Eom et al. (2004), who examine versions of the

Merton (1974), Geske (1977), Longstaff and Schwartz (1995), Leland and
Toft (1996), and Collin-Dufresne and Goldstein (2001a) models. They restrict their sample to industrial firms with relatively simple capital structures, comprised largely of equity and noncallable debt. Consistent with
previous studies, the Merton model predicts spreads that are too small, as
does Geske's model, though to a lesser extent. Interestingly, the Leland-
Toft, Longstaff-Schwartz, and Collin-Dufresne-Goldstein models all tend
to *overpredict* spreads, though in different ways. The Leland-Toft model
overpredicts spreads for virtually all ratings and maturities; the Longstaff-
Schwartz model gives excessive spreads for relatively risky bonds, while yield-
ingspreads that are too small for relatively safe bonds; and the Collin-
Dufresne-Goldstein model with mean-reverting leverage ratios reduces the
underprediction of spreads on safe bonds, while still overpredicting spreads
on average.

   The difficulty in matching the levels of credit spreads within structural
models does not, by itself, imply that these models are incapable of predicting how changes in capital structure will affect spreads. Schaefer and
Strebulaev (2004) examine how the hedge ratios predicted by Merton-style
models perform empirically for corporate bonds in Merrill Lynch U.S. corporate bond indices. Letting $\overline{r}_{j,t}$ denote the excess return on the jth bond,
they estimate the regressions

$$\overline{r}_{j,t} = \alpha_{j,0} + \beta_{j,E} \, h_{E,j,t} \overline{r}_{E,t} + \alpha_{j,rf} \, \overline{rf}_{10y,t} + \epsilon_{j,t}, \qquad (14.15)$$

where $h_{E,j,t}$ is the hedge ratio for firm j at time t, as implied by the Merton
model; $\overline{r}_{E,t}$ is the excess return on the issuer's equity; and $\overline{rf}_{10y}$ is the excess
return on the 10-year constant maturity U.S. Treasury bond. Under the null
hypothesis that structural models imply the correct hedge ratios, $\beta_{j,E} = 1$.

   Table 14.2 shows their results for the case of $h_{E,j,t}$ calculated from the
basic Merton model. Their null hypothesis is not rejected at conventional
significance levels for the entire sample of bonds (column "All"). There

Table 14.2. *Estimates of the Coefficients in the Projection (14.15)*

	All	AA	A	BBB	BB	B	CCC
Constant	−0.001	−0.002	−0.002	−0.001	0.001	−0.001	−0.007
	(−4.5)	(−6.8)	(−8.6)	(−5.0)	(1.3)	(−1.2)	(−0.85)
β_E	1.206	0.552	1.173	0.787	2.498	1.540	0.415
	(1.2)	(−1.3)	(0.61)	(−0.63)	(3.0)	(1.8)	(−2.2)
$\overline{rf}_{10y,t}$	0.369	0.815	0.688	0.479	0.140	−0.116	−0.408
	(18)	(26)	(35)	(23)	(2.2)	(−2.2)	(−1.4)
$\bar{R}^2$	0.266	0.372	0.371	0.289	0.203	0.128	0.108

Source: Schaefer and Strebulaev (2004).

is more evidence against the Merton model for bonds below investment grade, particularly for ratings *BB* and *CCC*. Further, the R^2's are lower than what would be expected if the structural model fully explained the variation in spreads. However, overall, their results are suggestive of substantial predictive content of structural models for the effects of changes in capital structure on corporate bond spreads.

To achieve a deeper understanding of the limitations of structural pricing models researchers have looked beyond risk-neutral pricing models such as (14.10) to models in which agents' preferences are modeled explicitly and risk premia are calibrated to both bond and equity market information. Huang and Huang (2000) inquire whether the credit risk inherent in structural models is likely to account for the observed spreads in investment-grade bonds. Starting from the following $\mathbb{P}$-specification of firm value,

$$\frac{dA_t}{A_t} = \left(\pi_t^A + r - \gamma\right) dt + \sigma_A dW_{At}^{\mathbb{P}}, \qquad (14.16)$$

they explore the implications of alternative specifications of the asset risk premium π_t^A. Calibrating several structural models to both balance sheet information and historical default rates simultaneously, they conclude that, within their models, credit risk accounts for a small fraction of the observed spreads for investment-grade bonds. Their models are more successful at explaining the larger spreads for junk bonds.

Chen et al. (2005) extend the complexity of the risk premiums examined by Huang and Huang by developing models based on (1) habit formation (Campbell and Cochrane, 1999) and (2) the combination of long-run risks and Epstein-Zin preferences (Bansal and Yaron, 2004). The former model, for example, leads to the modified version of (14.16),

$$\frac{dA_t}{A_t} = \left(\pi^A(s_t) + r - \gamma(s_t)\right) dt + \sigma_A(s_t) dW_{At}^{\mathbb{P}}, \qquad (14.17)$$

in which the risk premium, payout rate, and volatility of firm value all depend on the habit shocks s_t (see Section 10.5.2 for a definition of s_t). While these models, with their larger time-varying risk premiums, are more successful at replicating historical credit spreads, in their basic forms they have the counterfactual implication that forward default rates are procyclical. The reason is that low expected returns when the economy is strong are associated with a higher probability of reaching the default boundary. To overcome this limitation of their structural models, Chen et al. introduce a countercyclical default boundary, one that is more countercyclical than the typical corporate leverage ratios. In this manner they replicate both credit spreads and the equity premium puzzle, while leaving open the issue of the economic forces that underlie the needed behavior of the default boundary.

A common feature of most structural models is that firm value does not depend directly on macroeconomic information. The interplay between the dependence of firm-value dynamics on macro information and credit spreads is explored by Hackbarth et al. (2004) and Tang and Yan (2005). The former paper develops a model of a firm's capital structure in which the cash flows of a firm depend on macroeconomic information as well as a firm-specific shock. The aggregate shock affecting firm value follows a regime-shifting model with transitions between regimes governed by a Poisson process. This generates countercyclical leverage ratios because the shifts across expansions and contractions affect the present values of future cash flows and, thereby, the optimal firm leverage ratios. Their calibrations suggest that these effects on leverage are quantitatively important. Thus, Hackbarth et al. have provided a potential explanation for the business cycle patterns in the default boundaries needed to match spreads in the preceding structural models.

Additionally, the regime-shift process in the model of Hackbarth et al. induces nonzero credit spreads at short maturities, thereby overcoming another limitation of structural models. However, this phenomenon arises primarily during recessions. An interesting question is whether these risks, at business cycle frequencies, are sufficient to sustain the large spreads observed historically on many short-term bonds.

14.5. Modeling Interest Rate Swap Spreads

In Chapter 13 we treated a plain-vanilla interest rate swap effectively as a coupon bond. As discussed in Duffie and Singleton (1997), this approach to pricing is justified under the special assumptions of symmetric credit qualities of the counterparties to the swap and that these parties are of "refreshed" LIBOR quality. That is, the parties remain roughly single- or double-A rated, firm at least up to the time of default by either counterparty. Relaxing these assumptions seems to have a small effect on the pricing of swaps (e.g., Duffie and Huang, 1996).

Nevertheless, the interest rate swap spreads—the spreads between the swap and Treasury rates—are often large and variable over time. If these spreads are not due to credit risk, then what economic forces underlie these spreads? Liu et al. (2006) try to quantify the relative contributions of credit and liquidity factors to swap spreads.[8] Treasury bond yields are discounted by a "riskless" rate $r(t)$. The liquidity component of the Treasury rate is captured by inclusion of the "repo" rate (the rate on a 3-month repurchase agreement): the relevant discount rate for pricing the repo

---

[8] Grinblatt (2001) argues that liquidity is an important factor in driving spreads, though he does not undertake a formal econometric analysis of this hypothesis.

contract is $r(t) + \gamma^Q(t)$, where γ^Q represents (risk-neutral) compensation holding a default-free illiquid bond. Finally, the discount rates implicit in the swap market are $r(t) + \gamma(t) + \lambda^Q(t)L^Q(t)$. This formulation extends the formulation in Duffie and Singleton (1997) by introducing the repo rate and defining liquidity in terms of the difference between the yields on on-the-run and off-the-run Treasury bonds. It does not address liquidity risk that is inherent in the swap market itself.

They find that a significant component of the swap spread is due to the mean loss rate $\lambda^Q(t)L^Q(t)$. However, no independent confirmation that this component is truly due to default is provided [i.e., the model-implied $\lambda^Q(t)L^Q(t)$ is not linked to observables]. In previous work Duffie and Single-ton (1997) found that much of their fitted (latent) mean-loss-rate for swaps was not explained by proxies for credit risk, even after controlling for repo specials. Thus, it seems that the nature of the economic forces underlying variation in swap spreads remains largely an open issue.

14.6. Pricing Credit Default Swaps

More recently, for the purpose of extracting information about λ^Q, re-searchers have been using credit default swap spreads.[9] In a plain-vanilla credit default swap (CDS) contract, the buyer is insuring against potential losses on an underlying loan or bond owing to a credit event. The buyer agrees to pay a default swap premium S_t^M for a period of up to M years (the maturity of the contract). The seller pays the buyer nothing, unless a relevant credit event occurs, where the relevant credit events are defined as part of the terms of the CDS contract. If a relevant credit event does occur, then the buyer receives the difference between the face value of the bond or loan being insured (say \$1) and the market value of the security subsequent to the event, say R^P. CDS contracts may be cash settled, in which case the insured receives the difference $(1 - R^P)$ in cash, or physical delivery, in which case the buyer delivers the bond to the seller in exchange for face value. In practice, when the contract specifies physical delivery, more than one reference bond may be selected for delivery to the seller. So physical delivery brings with it a "cheapest-to-deliver" option: the option to deliver the bond, among all admissible bonds for delivery, with the lowest market value at settlement.

The basic pricing relation for CDS contracts is much like that for the cash flows of a comparably risky corporate bond. Let R^Q denote the (con-stant) risk-neutral fractional recovery of face value on the underlying

---

[9] A partial list of the literature in this area includes Berndt et al. (2004), Hull and White (2004), Houweling and Vorst (2005), and Longstaff et al. (2005), for corporate contracts, and Pan and Singleton (2005) for sovereign contracts.

(cheapest-to-deliver) bond in the event of a credit event [with associated loss rate $L^Q \equiv (1 - R^Q)$], and λ^Q denote the risk-neutral arrival rate of a credit event. An M-year CDS contract with semiannual premium payments is priced at issue as (see, e.g., Duffie and Singleton, 2003):

$$S_t^M \sum_{j=1}^{2M} E_t^Q\left[e^{-\int_t^{t+.5j} (r_s + \lambda_s^Q) ds} \right] = L^Q \int_t^{t+M} E_t^Q\left[\lambda_u^Q e^{-\int_t^u (r_s + \lambda_s^Q) ds} \right] du, \quad (14.18)$$

where r_t is the riskless rate relevant for pricing CDS contracts and S_t^M is the annuity rate paid by the purchaser of default insurance. The left-hand side of (14.18) is the present value of the buyer's premiums, payable contingent upon a credit event not having occurred. Discounting by $r_t + \lambda_t^Q$ captures the survival-dependent nature of these payments. The right-hand side is the present value of the contingent payment by the protection seller upon a credit event. We have normalized the face value of the underlying bond to \$1 and assumed a constant expected contingent payment (loss relative to face value) of L^Q. In actual implementations, (14.18) is modified slightly to account for the buyer's obligation to pay an accrued premium if a credit event occurs between the premium payment dates.

For some CDS contracts, notably sovereign contracts, there is a menu of possible credit events that can trigger termination and settlement of the contract. Moreover, *default* is not a relevant event in the sense that sovereign issues are not governed by a bankruptcy court. In such cases, how should λ^Q and L^Q be interpreted? Once again we follow Duffie et al. (2003b) and view these constructs as composites as in (14.12). The same idea applies equally well to corporate CDS contracts when there are multiple relevant credit events.

Econometric studies of CDS spreads that have allowed for a stochastic intensity have typically assumed a one-factor model for λ^Q. The two most commonly studied models are the lognormal model ($\log \lambda_t^Q$ follows a Gaussian diffusion) and the square-root model (λ_t^Q follows a CIR-style diffusion). Evidence reported in Berndt et al. (2004) and Pan and Singleton (2005) suggests that the lognormal model better fits the fat-tailed feature of both corporate and sovereign CDS spreads.

Longstaff et al. (2005) use CDS and corporate bond data together to assess the role of credit risk in corporate bond spreads. The key premise underlying their analysis is that any liquidity premiums in the markets are in corporate, not CDS, markets. Under this premise, they follow Duffie and Singleton (1999) and discount corporate bond cash flows by a composite discount rate $r_t + \lambda_t^Q L_t^Q$ (fractional recovery of market value) plus a liquidity premium ℓ_t. On the other hand, CDS cash flows are discounted by $r_t + \lambda_t^Q$. The empirical evidence suggests that the default-related spread $\lambda_t^Q L_t^Q$, extracted from CDS data, explains roughly 50% of the variation in the corporate bond spreads. If in fact there are no liquidity premiums embedded in CDS spreads, then their findings suggest that large fractions of corporate bond spreads—including high-grade corporate bonds—are due to default-related risks.

A less restrictive interpretation of their analysis is that they are measuring the relative spread $s_t^{\text{Corp}} - s_t^{\text{CDS}}$, where s_t^i is the relevant spread over r for discounting the cash flows of security i. Under this interpretation, we conclude that the default and liquidity characteristics inherent in the CDS spread s_t^{CDS} are key factors in explaining the corporate bond spread s_t^{Corp}. Assessing the fraction that is default related relative to the fraction that is liquidity related must await more definitive measures of the liquidity factors in both markets.

Ericsson et al. (2004) relate the CDS spreads on individual corporate names to various potential determinants of spreads, motivated by structural models of default. They find that spreads: (1) widen with increases in firm-level measures of leverage; (2) widen with increases in firm-level equity volatility; and (3) narrow with increases in the 10-year bond yield. Approximately 60% of the variation in market quotes was explained by these three explanatory variables. Within the CDS market, then, a large fraction of spread variation is explained by precisely those factors that structural economic models rely on for modeling default. There is, however, also a sizable fraction of spread variation that is not explained by these factors. Just as with the corporate bond market, an interesting question for future research is whether the remaining variation is due to omitted default-related factors, state-dependent recoveries that are not modeled, or liquidity-related factors.

Zhang (2003) and Pan and Singleton (2005) investigate the pricing of sovereign CDS contracts. Zhang extracts the $\mathbb{Q}$-probability of default implicit in CDS spreads leading up to the default of Argentina. Pan and Singleton explore the goodness-of-fit of square-root, lognormal, and three-halves diffusion models for $\lambda^{\mathbb{Q}}$ using data on the term structure of spreads from Mexico, Russia, and Turkey. Initially, they assume that $L^{\mathbb{Q}} = 0.75$ consistent with industry practice of pricing sovereign contracts with a loss rate in the 75–80% range (Zhang makes a similar assumption for his study of Argentina). Upon estimating the mean reversion ($\kappa^{\mathbb{Q}}$), drift "intercept" ($\kappa^{\mathbb{Q}}\theta^{\mathbb{Q}}$), and volatility parameter (σ) by the method of ML, Pan and Singleton found that $\kappa^{\mathbb{Q}} < 0$ for both Mexico and Russia. That is, to fit this historical sovereign CDS data, the likelihood function called for a $\mathbb{Q}$-explosive credit intensity process. This is reminiscent of the findings in Duffee (1999) for corporate bonds.

Though it is standard practice in this literature to fix $L^{\mathbb{Q}}$ a priori, Pan and Singleton show, both theoretically and by Monte Carlo simulation, that (a constant) $L^{\mathbb{Q}}$ and the parameters governing $\lambda^{\mathbb{Q}}$ are separately identifiable using data on the term structure of CDS spreads. When their models were fitted with L^Q unconstrained, the ML estimates were closer to $L^Q = 0.25$. At the same time, the estimated value of $\kappa^Q \theta^Q$ was much larger than in the constrained case of $L^Q = 0.75$. These findings suggest that, at least for the sample periods and countries considered, the likelihood function trades off a lower (higher) value of L^Q against a higher (lower) intercept for the credit intensity process. This trade-off is intuitively sensible, because a less desirable loss rate is matched with a lower likelihood of experiencing a credit event, and vice versa. A likelihood ratio test favored the unconstrained estimate of $L^Q = 0.25$ at conventional significance levels, but various other descriptive measures showed that the fits were comparable.

14.7. Is Default Risk Priced?

One of the central issues in the area of modeling defaultable bond prices is whether or not the jump in price at the event of default is "priced" by investors in the markets. Equivalently, is Γ_t in (14.2) nonzero, in which case agents' pricing kernel jumps at the arrival date of a credit event? Since the term "price of default risk" has been used in a variety of nonequivalent ways in the literature, we introduce this issue by providing a precise description of the components of priced default risk.

Whatever one's assumption about recovery, the instantaneous excess return on a defaultable zero-coupon bond can be expressed as

$$e_{Bt} = \frac{1}{B(t, T)} \frac{\partial B(t, T)}{\partial Y'} \sigma_Y \Lambda_t + \frac{w_t - B(t, T)}{B(t, T)} \lambda_t^{\mathbb{P}} \Gamma_t. \qquad (14.19)$$

Compared to (8.52), e_{Bt} has an extra component, $[w_t - B(t, T)]\lambda_t^{\mathbb{P}} \Gamma_t / B(t, T)$, representing compensation for the expected loss owing to default. This component is the product of $[w_t - B(t, T)]/B(t, T)$, the percentage loss of value owing to default; $\lambda_t^{\mathbb{P}}$, the historical default arrival intensity; and Γ_t, the market price of default risk. Since bond prices reveal information only about λ^Q, to compute $\lambda^{\mathbb{P}}$ and e_{Bt} it is typically necessary to use additional information about the $\mathbb{P}$-likelihood of an issuer defaulting.

In expressing excess returns as in (14.19) we have assumed that the pricing kernel is given by (14.2) and, in particular, that recovery risk is not priced (i.e., $w_t = w_t^{\mathbb{P}} = w_t^Q$). If investors are risk averse toward the uncertainty about the recovery that they will receive at default, then an additional term needs to be added to (14.19) to reflect the price of recovery risk.

Even abstracting from recovery-magnitude risk, there are two default-related priced risks implicit in the excess return (14.19). One, just discussed, is the jump-at-default risk with the market price of risk Γ_t. It is this risk that we refer to in answering the question of whether default risk is priced in the markets.

In addition, investors are likely to be risk averse toward the unpredictable future variation in the risk-neutral intensity λ^Q. Where this shows up is in the first term of (14.19), $(\partial B(t, T)/\partial Y')\sigma_Y \Lambda_t$. Discounting, under either fractional recovery of market or face value, involves the constructs $r(t)$ and λ_t^Q. Both of these, in turn, are functions of the underlying state vector Y. Thus, the market price of factors risks, Λ_t, is linked directly to agents' concerns about variation in the risk-neutral mean arrival rate of default. As discussed in Duffie and Singleton (1997), in equilibrium, both r and λ^Q are functions of a common set of macro variables and the associated prices of risk are related to the covariation of these factors with agents' marginal rate of substitution. Therefore, it may be difficult to meaningfully associate some components of Λ_t with r and others with λ^Q. Whether or not specific components of Y are associated with variation in λ^Q, so long as λ^Q is not constant, Λ_t typically reflects risk aversion about the default process.

Whereas Λ_t is econometrically identifiable from information on defaultable bond prices, this is not true of Γ_t. Intuitively, the reason is that the solution to the PDE (14.3) holds only conditional on default not having occurred. [See Yu (2002) for a heuristic discussion of this point.] The last term in (14.19) enters only at the time of default. Accordingly, it is necessary to call upon information other than bond prices in order to estimate λ^P and, hence, Γ.

If jump-to-default risk is fully diversifiable, then Γ_t should be zero. Jarrow et al. (2005) provide formal conditions under which this risk is diversifiable and, hence, under which $\lambda^Q = \lambda^P$. They adopt the "doubly stochastic" model for default, which presumes that, conditional on the paths of the intensities of all issuers, the defaults of issuers are based on independent draws from Poisson processes. It follows that in a well-diversified portfolio, in the limit as the number of issuers represented in a portfolio gets large, default risk can be diversified away. Das et al. (2005) present evidence that the historical default experience of U.S. corporations is inconsistent with the doubly stochastic model: there is too much default clustering relative to that predicted by the doubly stochastic model. Additionally, Amato and Remolona (2005) challenge the presumption that one can effectively diversify away credit risk: given the highly skewed nature of return distributions, full diversification requires a very large portfolio, and this is difficult to achieve in practice. How these observations translate into the magnitude of λ^Q/λ^P is an empirical question to which we turn next.

Driessen (2005), using corporate bond data very similar to the data used by Duffee (1999), estimates (using quasi-ML methods) fractional recovery of market value models for the prices of bonds of several corporate issuers. This gives him model-implied estimates of λ_t^Q by issuer. Then, using information from Moody's and S&P about the default rates of corporate issuers by credit rating category, Driessen computes a constant factor of proportionality, $\mu \equiv \lambda_t^{\mathbb{Q}}/\lambda_t^{\mathbb{P}}$. His μ is $(1 - \Gamma)$ under the assumption that the market price of default risk, Γ, is not state dependent. Prior to computing μ, adjustments are made for the differential tax treatment of corporate and Treasury securities and for an illiquidity premium on corporate bonds. Within Driessen's affine term structure model with latent risk factors Y, he associates a subset of Y with the pricing of Treasury bonds and another subset with the determination of $\lambda_t^{\mathbb{Q}}L^{\mathbb{Q}}$. Thus, by construction, he associates a component of $(\partial B(t, T)/\partial Y')\sigma_Y\Lambda_t$ in (14.19) with variation in the mean loss rate that is independent of variation in the riskfree yield curve.

Driessen's estimate of μ is 2.3, suggesting that default event risk is priced with $\lambda^{\mathbb{Q}}$ being roughly twice as large as $\lambda^{\mathbb{P}}$. The contribution of priced jump-at-default risk to expected excess returns can be seen from Figure 14.4, which displays the model-implied decomposition of excess returns on BBB rated bonds. Default event risk accounts for roughly 20% of excess returns at the 10-year maturity and closer to a third of the excess returns on short-term bonds. Its absolute magnitude is roughly uniform across maturities. On the other hand, the priced uncertainty about future variation in $\lambda^{\mathbb{Q}}$, labeled "common factors risk," contributes an increasingly large amount to excess returns as maturity increases. At the 10-year maturity point, the latter risk is as large, or even slightly larger, a component of excess returns than default event risk. Critical to these results is Driessen's treatment of taxes, as the tax adjustment accounts for an even larger proportion of excess returns

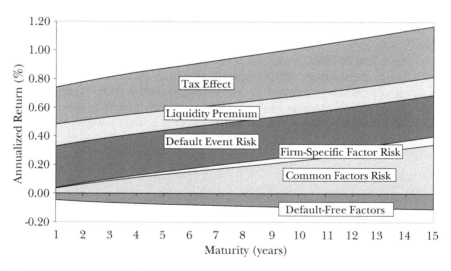

Figure 14.4. *Decomposition of expected excess returns on BBB-rated bonds. Source: Driessen (2005), by permission of the Society of Financial Studies.*

than does jump-at-default risk. Alternative treatments of taxation might lead
to a reallocation that increases the importance of default risk.

More direct evidence on the nature of default risk premiums is provided
by Berndt et al. (2004). They combine information about historical default
experience from Moody's/KMV with CDS spreads to infer both $\lambda^{\mathbb{Q}}$ and $\lambda^{\mathbb{P}}$
and, hence, default risk premiums. The risk-neutral arrival rate of default
$\lambda^{\mathbb{Q}}$ is extracted from CDS spreads, as outlined above, assuming no liquidity
factors for CDS spreads and a known constant loss rate $L^{\mathbb{Q}}$. Their loss rates
differed across industries, but were not company specific, since reliable
information about loss at the company level is not available.

To obtain $\lambda^{\mathbb{P}}$ they started with Moody's/KMV's EDF, an equity-based
measure of the probability that an issuer will default over the next year.
Placing this measure within the intensity framework, under the assumption
that $\lambda^{\mathbb{P}}$ follows a Markov process, EDF is related to survival according to

$$\text{EDF}_t = 1 - E^{\mathbb{P}}\left[e^{-\int_t^{t+1} \lambda^{\mathbb{P}}(s)\,ds}\big|\lambda_t^{\mathbb{P}}\right]. \tag{14.20}$$

Thus, given a model for $\lambda^{\mathbb{P}}$ and time-series data on EDF, one can invert
the relation (14.20) for the EDF-implied time series $\lambda_t^{\mathbb{P}}$. Berndt et al. parameterize $\log \lambda^{\mathbb{P}}$ as a Gaussian process and estimate the parameters of this
process by ML. From the implied $\lambda^{\mathbb{P}}$ they conclude that, on average, the
default risk premium $\mu = (1 - \Gamma)$ is between two and three, consistent with
what Driessen found for the corporate market. A key advantage of their
analysis over Driessen's is that, from the EDF data, Berndt et al. are able
to construct a time series of μ_t. For a representative oil and gas firm, for
example, they found that $\lambda_t^{\mathbb{Q}}/\lambda_t^{\mathbb{P}}$ starts out around one in the second half of
2001 ($\Gamma_t = 0$, so zero default risk premium), it peaks just over three during
the summer/fall of 2002, and then μ declines steadily thereafter through
2003. During the summer of 2002 speculative-grade default rates (as computed, e.g., by Moody's) peaked at over 10%. Hence the patterns found in
Berndt et al., which are premised on a constant risk-neutral recovery rate
$w^{\mathbb{Q}}$, suggest that the default risk premium $(1 - \Gamma_t)$ is increasing in the rate
of corporate defaults.

15
Equity Option Pricing Models

ACCORDING TO THE original Black-Scholes (1973) option pricing model, the implied volatilities on European options on common stocks should be the same for options of all maturities and all strike prices. This is an implication of their assumption that the stock price follows a lognormal diffusion with constant volatility. In fact, especially subsequent to the "crash" of October 1987, implied volatilities have exhibited a pronounced *smile* or *smirk*. A typical pattern of implied volatilities is displayed in Figure 15.1 for November 2, 1993. We see that call options that are deep in the money (put options that are deep out of the money) have higher implied volatilities than those that are nearer the money. Moreover, for a given degree of "out-of-the-moneyness," options with longer maturities tend to have lower implied volatilities. Neither of these patterns is consistent with the Black-Scholes model.

In this chapter we explore some of the models that have been put forth to explain these departures from the assumptions of the Black-Scholes model. Most of these models stay within the arbitrage-free framework of Black and Scholes and relax their strong assumptions about the distributions of stock prices, though a few examine equilibrium settings starting with specifications of agents' preferences. Furthermore, while much of the empirical work on equity option pricing has focused on S&P500 index options, recently several researchers have examined the pricing of options on individual common stocks. In both the study of options on individual stocks and stock indices, a key question that has been addressed is which risks are priced in the markets and what are the properties of the associated "market prices of risk."

We begin with an overview of no-arbitrage models that directly posit a pricing kernel with associated market prices of risk. This literature has focused on the relative contributions of priced volatility and jump risks in generating volatility smirks. Subsequently, we discuss the literature on preference-based models for option pricing.

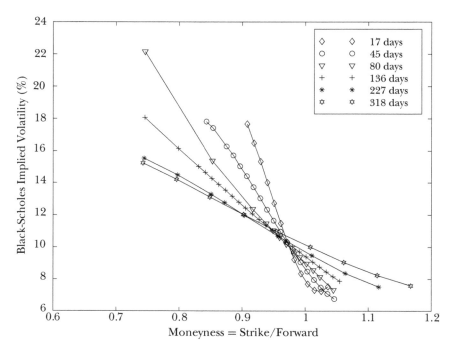

Figure 15.1. *"Smile curves" implied by S&P500 index options of six different maturities. Option prices are obtained from market data of November 2, 1993.*

15.1. No-Arbitrage Option Pricing Models

In an influential paper in the option-pricing literature, Heston (1993) showed that the risk-neutral exercise probabilities appearing in the call option pricing formulas for bonds, currencies, and equities can be computed by Fourier inversion of a conditional characteristic function, which is known in closed form under his assumption that stochastic volatility follows a square-root diffusion. Building on this insight,[1] researchers have developed a variety of option pricing models that can potentially explain these systematic deviations from the Black-Scholes model in the options data.

Initially, following the literature, we focus on the data-generating process:

$$dS_t = \mu_S^{\mathbb{P}}(S_t, v_t) S_t \, dt + \sqrt{v_t} S_t \, dW_{St} + dZ_{St}, \qquad (15.1)$$

---

[1] Early papers examining option prices for the case of state variables following square-root diffusions are Bates (1996, 2000), Scott (1996, 1997), and Bakshi et al. (1997).

$$dv_t = \kappa_v^{\mathbb{P}}\left(\bar{v}^{\mathbb{P}} - v_t\right) dt + \sigma_v \sqrt{v_t} \left(\rho dW_{St} + \sqrt{1 - \rho^2} dW_{vt}\right) + dZ_{vt}, \quad (15.2)$$

where $W = [W_S, W_v]'$ is a vector of independent Brownian motions in $\mathbb{R}^2$, $\rho \in (0, 1)$ is a constant coefficient controlling correlation between the Brownian shocks to S and v, and $\mu_S^{\mathbb{P}}(S_t, v_t)$ is a stock price and volatility dependent component of the drift of dS_t/S_t. The processes (Z_S, Z_v) are jumps with intensities (mean arrival rates) ζ_{St} and ζ_{vt}, respectively. The amplitudes of the jumps, when they occur, may be random.

Heston (1993) considered the special case of (15.1) and (15.2) in which $(\zeta_{St}, \zeta_{vt}) = 0$, so there were no jumps in either prices or volatility. Owing to his focus on pricing (as contrasted with estimation using time-series data), Heston assumed that the risk-neutral drift of S_t was $\mu_{St}^{\mathbb{Q}} = rS_t$ and $\mu_S^{\mathbb{P}}(S_t, v_t)$ was left unspecified. (The former is required by the assumption of no arbitrage opportunities—traded assets earn the riskfree rate when agents are risk neutral.) He allowed for a volatility risk premium that was proportional to $\sqrt{v(t)}$, giving

$$dv_t = \left[\kappa_v^{\mathbb{P}}\left(\bar{v}^{\mathbb{P}} - v_t\right) + \eta_v v_t\right] dt + \sigma_v \sqrt{v_t} \, dW_{vt}^{\mathbb{Q}} \quad (15.3)$$

under $\mathbb{Q}$. Consequently, the $\mathbb{P}$ and $\mathbb{Q}$ drifts of v_t were both affine functions of v. We refer to his model as model SV (with or without priced volatility risk).

Two recent studies that estimate models with stochastic volatility and a jump in stock returns (model SVJ) are Chernov and Ghysels (2000) and Pan (2002). To interpret their assumptions about the market prices of price and volatility risks, we let $\mu_t^{\mathbb{P}} = (\mu_{St}^{\mathbb{P}}, \mu_{vt}^{\mathbb{P}})'$ denote the drift of $(d S_t/S_t, d v_t)$ under the physical measure, and $\mu_t^{\mathbb{Q}}$ its counterpart under the risk-neutral measure. Recall that the relation between these two drifts (within this affine setting) is $\mu_t^{\mathbb{Q}} = \mu_t^{\mathbb{P}} - \Sigma \sqrt{\Omega_t} \Lambda_t$, where Λ_t is the vector of market prices of risk associated with return and volatility risk,

$$\Sigma = \begin{pmatrix} 1 & 0 \\ \sigma_v \rho & \sigma_v \sqrt{1 - \rho^2} \end{pmatrix}, \quad (15.4)$$

and Ω_t is the 2×2 diagonal matrix with v_t along the diagonal.

Chernov and Ghysels (2000) abstract from jumps (Z_t is omitted) and replace $\mu_{St}^{\mathbb{P}}$ in (15.13) with $\bar{\mu}_S^{\mathbb{P}}$, a constant. They also treat the riskless interest rate as a constant r. Straightforward calculation then shows that for the drift of S_t to be r under the risk-neutral measure,

$$\Lambda_t^S = \frac{\bar{\mu}_s^{\mathbb{P}} - r}{\sqrt{v_t}}. \quad (15.5)$$

For the volatility process, Chernov and Ghysels assume that the drift under $\mathbb{Q}$ is $\kappa_v^{\mathbb{Q}}(\bar{v}^{\mathbb{Q}} - v_t)$, from which it follows that

$$\kappa_v^{\mathbb{P}}\big(\bar{v}^{\mathbb{P}} - v_t\big) - \sigma_v\rho\sqrt{v_t}\Lambda_t^S - \sigma_v\sqrt{1-\rho^2}\sqrt{v_t}\Lambda_t^v = \kappa_v^{\mathbb{Q}}\big(\bar{v}^{\mathbb{Q}} - v_t\big). \quad (15.6)$$

Substituting in (15.5) and solving for Λ_t^v gives

$$\Lambda_t^v = \frac{C_1}{\sqrt{v_t}} - C_2\sqrt{v_t}, \quad (15.7)$$

where

$$C_1 = \frac{\kappa_v^{\mathbb{P}}\bar{v}^{\mathbb{P}} - \kappa_v^{\mathbb{Q}}\bar{v}^{\mathbb{Q}} - \big(\bar{\mu}_S^{\mathbb{P}} - r\big)\sigma_v\rho}{\sigma_v\sqrt{1-\rho^2}}, \quad (15.8)$$

$$C_2 = \frac{\kappa_v^{\mathbb{P}} - \kappa_v^{\mathbb{Q}}}{\sigma_v\sqrt{1-\rho^2}}. \quad (15.9)$$

Note that neither component of Λ_t in the Chernov-Ghysels model has a "completely affine" form, which would have the risk premiums proportional to $\sqrt{v_t}$. Instead, they involve multiples of $1/\sqrt{v_t}$.

An implication of their formulation is that as v_t approaches its lower bound of zero, Λ_t approaches infinity. As such, their model potentially admits arbitrage opportunities. This is precisely the same issue that arose in our discussions of the risk premiums in "essentially" affine DTSMs. There we constrained the parameters of the market prices of risk to rule out such arbitrage opportunities (see Chapter 12). Perhaps similar constraints on the parameters determining (C_1, C_2) could be derived to rule out arbitrage opportunities in this setting.

Pan (2002) uses a variant of the model in Bates (2000) in which there are no jumps in volatility ($\zeta_{vt} = 0$) and the intensity of the jump process Z_S is an affine function of volatility $\{\zeta_{vt} = \zeta_1 v_t : t \geq 0\}$, for a nonnegative constant ζ_1. At the ith jump time τ_i, the stock price is assumed to jump from $S(\tau_i-)$ to $S(\tau_i-)\exp(U_i^s)$, where U_i^s is normally distributed with mean $\mu_J^{\mathbb{P}}$ and variance δ_J^2, independent of W, of interjump times, and of U_j^s for $j \neq i$. The *mean relative jump size* is $m_{SJ}^{\mathbb{P}} = E(\exp(U^s) - 1) = \exp(\mu_J^{\mathbb{P}} + \delta_J^2/2) - 1$.

She assumes that the representation of (S, v) under $\mathbb{Q}$ is

$$dS_t = \Big[r_t - q_t - \zeta_1 v_t m_{SJ}^{\mathbb{Q}}\Big] S_t\, dt + \sqrt{v_t}\, S_t\, dW_{St}^{\mathbb{Q}} + dZ_{St}^{\mathbb{Q}}, \quad (15.10)$$

$$dv_t = \Big[\kappa_v^{\mathbb{P}}\big(\bar{v}^{\mathbb{P}} - v_t\big) + \eta_v v_t\Big]dt + \sigma_v\sqrt{v_t}\Big(\rho\, dW_{St}^{\mathbb{Q}} + \sqrt{1-\rho^2}dW_{vt}^{\mathbb{Q}}\Big), \quad (15.11)$$

where r is the riskless interest rate, q is the dividend payout rate, and $m_{SJ}^{\mathbb{Q}}$ is the risk-neutral mean of the relative jump size of the stock price. $W^{\mathbb{Q}} = (W_S^{\mathbb{Q}}, W_v^{\mathbb{Q}})$ is a standard Brownian motion under $\mathbb{Q}$ defined by

$$W_t^{\mathbb{Q}} = W_t + \int_0^t \Lambda_u \, du, \quad 0 \le t \le T, \tag{15.12}$$

with $\Lambda_t = (\Lambda_t^S, \Lambda_t^v)'$ being the market prices of risk associated with the Brownian motions W_S and W_v. Additionally, she assumes that

$$\mu_{St}^{\mathbb{P}} = \begin{pmatrix} r_t - q_t + \eta_s v_t - \zeta_1 v_t m_{SJ}^{\mathbb{Q}} \\ \kappa_v^{\mathbb{P}}(\bar{v}^{\mathbb{P}} - v_t) \end{pmatrix}. \tag{15.13}$$

From these expressions we infer that Pan assumes the market price of risk Λ_t to be given by

$$\Lambda_t^S = \eta_s \sqrt{v_t}, \tag{15.14}$$

$$\Lambda_t^v = -\frac{1}{\sqrt{1-\rho^2}} \left(\rho \eta_s + \frac{\eta_v}{\sigma_v} \right) \sqrt{v_t}, \tag{15.15}$$

with η_s and η_v being constant coefficients.

The risk-neutral mean relative jump size $m_{SJ}^{\mathbb{Q}}$ differs from its physical counterpart $m_{SJ}^{\mathbb{P}}$ in order to accommodate a premium for jump-size risk. Pan assumes that there is no risk premium associated with jump-timing risk (there is no distinction between ζ_{St} under $\mathbb{P}$ and $\mathbb{Q}$). Such a premium could be added by allowing the coefficient $\zeta_1^{\mathbb{Q}}$ for the risk-neutral jump-arrival intensity to be different from $\zeta_1^{\mathbb{P}}$. The motivation for assuming no premium on jump timing risk seemed to be largely practical: it might be difficult to econometrically identify separate timing and amplitude premiums. Of course, by making this assumption, any risk premium in jump timing that is in fact present is being absorbed into one of the risk premiums that is allowed.

Two models with jumps in both returns and volatility were introduced by Duffie et al. (2000). In Chapter 7 we discussed the empirical properties of these models as descriptions of the historical behavior of returns. In this chapter we explore some of their implications for the pricing of options. Recall that model SVIJ assumes that the jump amplitude processes J_S and J_v are independent with respective amplitude distributions

$$J_{vt} \sim \exp(m_{Jv}) \text{ and } J_{St} \sim N(m_{JS}, \delta_{JS}^2). \tag{15.16}$$

Since J_v follows an exponential distribution, volatility can only jump up. Further, since J_v and J_S are independent, any "leverage" effects must be induced by the correlation among the diffusive shocks. A critical ingredient added by the jumps in volatility is the clustering of large return movements. Following an upward jump in v_t, the higher level of volatility persists owing to its slow reversion to its mean.

Alternatively, model SVCJ has the jumps in returns and volatility driven by the same jump process (simultaneous jumps, $Z_v = Z_S$) and their amplitudes are correlated:

$$J_{vt} \sim \exp(m_{Jv}) \text{ and } J_{St}| J_{vt} \sim N\big(m_{JS} + \rho_J J_{vt}, \delta_{JS}^2\big). \qquad (15.17)$$

This formulation introduces an additional leverage effect owing to jumps when $\rho_J < 0$ (see Chapter 7 for an introduction to the leverage effect). A jump in volatility with a large amplitude J_{vt} (with $\rho_J < 0$), lowers the mean of the price jump amplitude thereby amplifying the leverage effect. At the same time, the positive jumps in volatility contribute to the right skewness of the distribution of volatility. Both features of this model tend to fatten the tails of the return distribution.

These models are easily extended to allow for state-dependent jump intensities as in Bates (2000) and Pan (2002). Such a model SVSCJ with correlated jumps and stochastic arrival rate for jumps in stock prices,

$$\zeta_{St} = \zeta_0 + \zeta_1 v_t, \qquad (15.18)$$

is explored in Eraker (2004). With $\zeta_1 > 0$, jumps tend to occur more frequently in high-volatility regimes. Furthermore, as with model SVJ, one can introduce risk premiums associated with both the jump amplitudes and the timing of jumps. Like Pan, Eraker assumed the former, but not the latter, risk was priced.

15.2. Option Pricing

If we let C_t denote the time-t price of a European-style call option on S, struck at K_t and expiring at T, and $X'_t = (r_t, q_t, v_t)$,

$$C_t = E^{\mathbb{Q}} \left[\exp \left(- \int_t^T r_u \, du \right) (S_T - K)^+ \, \Big| \, S_t, X_t \right]. \qquad (15.19)$$

We can price this option using the time-t conditional transform of $\ln S_T$,

$$\psi(u, X_t, T - t) = E^{\mathbb{Q}} \left[\exp \left(- \int_t^T r_s \, ds \right) e^{u \ln S_T} \, \Big| \, X_t, S_t \right], \qquad (15.20)$$

for any $u \in \mathbb{C}$, introduced in Chapter 5. Letting $k_t = K_t/S_t$ be the time-t "strike-to-spot" ratio gives

$$C_t = S_t \, O(X_t, T - t, k_t), \qquad (15.21)$$

where $O : \mathbb{R}_+^3 \times \mathbb{R}_+ \times \mathbb{R}_+ \to [0, 1]$ is defined by

$$O(x, T - t, k) = \Pi_1 - k \, \Pi_2, \tag{15.22}$$

with

$$\Pi_1 = \frac{\psi(1, x, T - t)}{2} - \frac{1}{\pi} \int_0^\infty \frac{\text{Im}\left(\psi(1 - iu, x, T - t)e^{i \, u(\ln k)}\right)}{u} \, du,$$

$$\tag{15.23}$$

$$\Pi_2 = \frac{\psi(0, x, T - t)}{2} - \frac{1}{\pi} \int_0^\infty \frac{\text{Im}\left(\psi(-iu, x, T - t)e^{i \, u(\ln k)}\right)}{u} \, du,$$

where $\text{Im}(\cdot)$ denotes the imaginary component of a complex number. The transform ψ is a known exponential-affine function of X_t.

15.3. Estimation of Option Pricing Models

One easy to implement estimation strategy is to minimize the squared deviations between the market and model-implied option prices. That is, letting

$$\epsilon_{it} \equiv \frac{C_{it}}{S_t} - O(X_t, T_i - t, k_{it}), \tag{15.24}$$

where i indexes options of possibly different strike prices and maturities, one minimizes the squared deviations ϵ_{it}^2 by choice of the parameter values of the model. Bakshi et al. (1997) estimate the parameters using a cross section of strikes and maturities for a given day. (In this case, S_t cancels from the optimization problem.) Conceptually, this approach amounts to changing the model every period, because different parameter values are obtained for each date in the sample. As discussed in Chapter 12, such recalibration may well introduce dynamic arbitrage opportunities when viewed through the lens of the correct pricing model. Further, though it is common when using this approach to report the average values of the parameters across the days in a sample, such averages are often not directly interpretable in terms of the parameters of a "true" pricing model.

In contrast, Bates (2000) holds the parameters fixed over time and adopts an error components structure. He groups options according to their moneyness and maturity and allows the group pricing errors to be serially correlated with normally distributed, group-specific shocks. In addition, he allows for an idiosyncratic shock for each option with a variance that is common to the group. That is, he assumed that for group I

$$\epsilon_{it} = \epsilon_{It} + \sigma_I \eta_{it}, \quad \text{for } i \in G(I, t), \tag{15.25}$$

$$\epsilon_{It} = \rho_I \epsilon_{I,t-1} + v_{It}, \tag{15.26}$$

where $G(I, t)$ is the set of observations for group I at date t, v_{It} is a mean zero normally distributed shock that is common to all options in group I

and the v_{It} may be correlated across groups, and $\eta_{it} \sim N(0, 1)$ and is un-correlated with v_{It}. He uses Kalman filtering methods to estimate the error components and a generalized least-squares fitting criterion to estimate the parameters.

Chernov and Ghysels (2000) use the SME approach to estimation with an auxiliary model of the type suggested by Gallant and Tauchen (1996) (see Chapter 6). They focus on short-term ATM call prices, with ATM defined as $k_t \in [0.97, 1.03]$, for the sample period November 1985 until October 1994. The resulting series of call prices reflects variation over time in both the strike price, as ATM changes with market levels, and maturity, as the maturity of the short-term option that is closest to being ATM changes.

In constructing simulated series, with the simulation length $\mathcal{T}$ larger than the sample size T, one has to make assumptions about the changing nature of the strike prices and contract maturities of the ATM calls. Chernov and Ghysels address this issue by cycling through both the set of option maturities and the degree of moneyness in the data set. The latter was chosen, instead of strike prices, because the simulated cash prices may be very different than what was experienced in the historical sample.

A third estimation strategy, implied-state method-of-moments (IS-GMM), was pursued by Pan (2002).[2] Letting $y_t = \ln S_t - \ln S_{t-1} - (r - q)$ and $(\vec{y}_t^\ell, \vec{v}_t^\ell)$ denote ℓ-histories of y and v, Pan constructs $M \geq K$ moment conditions of the form $E[h(\vec{y}_t^\ell, \vec{v}_t^\ell, \theta_0)] = 0$, where $\theta_0 \in \mathbb{R}^K$ is the population parameter for her model and $h : \mathbb{R}^\ell \times \mathbb{R}_+^\ell \times \Theta \to \mathbb{R}^M$ is the function defining the moments to be used in estimation. Key to her analysis is the fact that h is constructed using moments of the underlying state vector, the stock price and volatility in her case, and not moments of the option prices. The reason is that, since (S_t, v_t) follows an affine diffusion, its conditional moments are all known in closed form (see Chapter 5). In contrast, option prices are nonlinear functions of the state and, in general, their moments are not known.

What makes it feasible for Pan to focus on moments of the underlying state vector rather than observed option prices is that she evaluates the moments with model-implied volatilities in place of the unobserved v_t. Specifically, let $c_t = C_t/S_t$ denote the price-to-spot ratio of the option observed on date t, with time τ_t to expiration and strike-to-spot ratio k_t. Given this option price, S_t and a value of the parameter vector θ, we invert the option

---

[2] Pan allows for stochastic interest rates and dividend yields in her empirical analysis. The processes for interest rates and dividends were estimated first and then the parameters from these processes were input into the option pricing analysis as if they were the population parameter values (no adjustment to the standard errors of the option pricing model were made for two-stage estimation). We abstract from this first stage and discuss estimation as if r and q are constant or follow known processes.

pricing model (15.24) for v_t^θ. Then, for any $\theta \in \Theta$, the date-t option-implied volatility is defined by $v_t^\theta = g(c_t, \theta, \tau_t, k_t)$. At $\theta = \theta_0$, $v_t^{\theta_0}$ is the true market-observed (according to this model) volatility. Using these model-implied volatilities in the construction of h, and the associated sample moments

$$G_T(\theta) = \frac{1}{T} \sum_{t \leq T} h\left(\vec{y}_t^\ell, \vec{v}_t^{\ell\theta}, \theta\right), \qquad (15.27)$$

the IS-GMM estimator is defined as

$$\theta_T = \underset{\theta \in \Theta}{\text{argmin}}\ G_T(\theta)'\, \mathcal{W}_T\, G_T(\theta), \qquad (15.28)$$

where $\{\mathcal{W}_T\}$ is a $M \times M$ positive semidefinite distance matrix.

The moment function h was constructed using the moments $E^\theta[\epsilon_t|\mathcal{F}_{t-1}]$ $= 0$ with the elements of ϵ_t taking the form $g(y_t) - E_{t-1}^\theta[g(y_t)]$, where $g(\cdot)$ raised its argument to various integer powers and $\mathcal{F}_t$ was the information set generated by the history of (S_t, v_t). All of the conditional expectations are known functions of θ and v_{t-1}.[3] For this set of conditional moment restrictions based on ϵ_t, the optimal set of instruments can be constructed following Hansen (1985) and the discussions in Chapters 3 and 5. In the case of IS-GMM estimation, one cannot literally use Hansen's optimal instruments, as they involve terms of the form $E\left[\partial \epsilon_t/\partial \theta|\mathcal{F}_{t-1}\right]$. The error term ϵ_t depends on θ in two ways: directly through the functional dependence of the expectations $E[\cdot|\mathcal{F}_{t-1}]$ on θ and indirectly through the parameter dependence of v_t^θ. The contribution of the former term resides in $\mathcal{F}_{t-1}$ so the conditioning can be dropped. However, in general, the contribution of the second term is not in $\mathcal{F}_{t-1}$ and the conditional expectation of this term enters the optimal instruments. This expectation is unknown and therefore implementation of the optimal instruments would, at a minimum, be computationally demanding. Pan circumvented this problem by omitting the second term; that is, she computed the optimal instruments as if v_t^θ was known (did not depend on θ). The resulting computational simplicity is traded off against the loss in efficiency from omitting a component of the truly optimal instruments.

Whether one pursues an estimation strategy based on GMM or ML, the asymptotic theory from Chapter 3 is often not directly applicable to the estimation of option pricing models because, for exchange-traded options in particular, a time series of fixed-maturity options is not generally available. Therefore, it has become common practice to choose the maturity τ_t of the option whose price is observed at date t to be as close as possible to

---

[3] The fact that the conditional characteristic function of y_t depends only on v_{t-1} was seen in Chapters 5 and 7. This is a feature of this particular formulation of the stochastic volatility model.

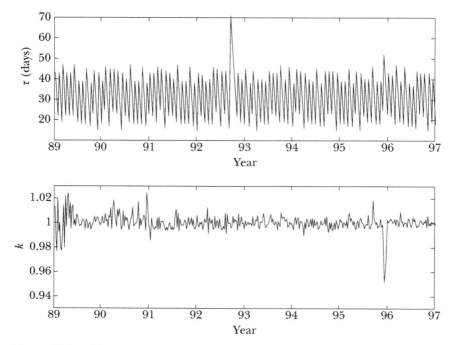

Figure 15.2.   *Time series of contract variables: time-to-expiration τ and strike-to-spot ratios k. Source: Pan (2002: p. 18), with permission from Elsevier.*

a given maturity (say 30 days), subject to the requirement that the option price is not too far out of the money. Typically, this selection rule implies a repetitive, nearly deterministic time path for $\{\tau_t\}$. A representative example of this problem is displayed in Figure 15.2 from Pan (2002).

To accommodate this problem, following Pan, we let $X_t^{\theta\ell}$ denote the ℓ-history of $X_t = (y_t, v_t^\theta, k_t)$ and $\vec{Y}_t^\ell$ denote the ℓ-history of τ_t. Suppose that $\{Y_t\}$ has finitely many outcomes, denoted $\{1, 2, \ldots, I\}$. For each outcome i and each positive integer T, we let $A_T^{(i)} = \{t \le T : Y_t = i\}$ be the dates, up to T, on which Y has outcome i. Then, for each i, we assume that there is some $w_i \in [0, 1]$, such that

$$\lim_T \frac{\#A_T^{(i)}}{T} = w_i \quad \text{a.s.,} \tag{15.29}$$

where $\#(\cdot)$ denotes cardinality.

If X_t^θ is geometrically ergodic for given $\theta \in \Theta$, we know that functions of $X_t^{\theta\ell}$ satisfy a strong law of large numbers. For consistency we assume in addition that a uniform strong law of large numbers is satisfied under the preceding sampling assumption. That is, for each outcome i of Y, if we let

$$G_T^{(i)}(\theta) = \frac{1}{\#A_T^{(i)}} \sum_{t \in A_T^{(i)}} h(\vec{X}_t^{\ell\theta}, \theta, i),$$

$G_\infty^{(i)}(\theta) = \lim_T G_T^{(i)}(\theta)$ exists and the convergence is uniform over the parameter space Θ. To develop more primitive assumptions that would imply a uniform strong law, we would need to impose some type of Lipschitz condition on $h(x, \theta, i)$ as a function of θ as in Chapter 6. See Pan (2000) for further discussion of these issues.

Finally, MCMC estimation (see Section 6.8) is a potentially attractive approach when one or more of the state variables are latent. This situation arises in the analysis of option pricing models when the parameters of the SVJ model are fit to stock return data alone (volatility is latent) or, more generally, volatility follows a multifactor process and a smaller number of asset prices than state variables are used in estimation. The MCMC estimator is used in Eraker et al. (2003) and Eraker (2004).

15.4. Econometric Analysis of Option Prices

Comparing the results from the estimation of no-arbitrage option pricing models is complicated by the fact that some authors have estimated their models using both options and spot market data, whereas others have used only options data[4]; various estimation methods have been used; and different sample periods for the data are often used. Eraker (2004) uses both returns and options data (daily) on the S&P500 index over the period January 1987 to December 1990, and then out-of-sample tests are based on the period January 1991 to December 1996. Pan (2002) uses both returns and option data (weekly) on the S&P500 index from January 1989 to December 1996. Bakshi et al. (1997) use only options data on the S&P500 index from June 1988 to May 1991. Bates (2000) uses S&P500 index options data from January 1988 to December 1993. Finally, Broadie et al. (2004) use data on S&P futures options from 1987 through 2003.

Representative estimates of the parameters of models with jumps, estimated using options or both options and return data, are shown in Tables 15.1 and 15.2.[5] Focusing first on the parameters of the diffusion part of the models (Table 15.1), there is a notable similarity across these studies even though they used different sample periods and very different methods of estimation. The rate of mean reversion of the volatility, κ_v, is low under both

---

[4] In this chapter we focus primarily on studies that have used options prices directly in the estimation. Studies of the distribution of the underlying stock price processes were reviewed in Chapter 7.

[5] We follow the convention in Eraker (2004) and present the results for a daily time interval. Annualized numbers referenced in the subsequent discussions are obtained by multiplying by 252 (approximate number of trading days per year). We are grateful to Bjorn Eraker for assistance with the conversions of the annualized estimates reported in other papers.

Table 15.1. **Estimates of the Diffusion Parameters**
Using Data on S&P500 Index Options Prices

Author	Model	$\kappa_v^{\mathbb{Q}}$	$\bar{v}$	σ_v	ρ	η_v
				Diffusion parameter estimates		
Bakshi et al.	SVJ	0.008	1.60	0.15	−0.57	NA
Pan	SVJ	0.013	0.61	0.12	−0.53	0.012
Eraker	SVJ	0.011	1.65	0.20	−0.59	0.009
	SVCJ	0.011	1.35	0.16	−0.58	0.013
	SVSCJ	0.006	0.94	0.14	−0.54	0.017

Table 15.2. **Estimates of the Jump Parameters Using Data on the S&P500 Index**

Author	Model	ζ_v	$E[\zeta_S]$	$m_{SJ}^{\mathbb{Q}}(\%)$	$m_{SJ}^{\mathbb{P}}(\%)$	$\delta_J\,(\%)$	ρ_J	m_{vJ}
				Jump parameter estimates				
Bakshi et al.	SVJ	NA	0.002	−5.00	NA	7.00	NA	NA
Pan	SVJ	NA	0.001	−19.2	−0.80	3.87	NA	NA
Eraker	SVJ	NA	0.002	−2.00	−0.39	6.63	NA	NA
	SVCJ	$=\zeta_S$	0.002	−7.51	−6.06	3.36	−0.69	1.64
	SVSCJ	$=\zeta_S$	0.002	−7.90	−1.54	2.07	−2.24	1.50

$\mathbb{Q}$ and $\mathbb{P}$ consistent with a high degree of persistence in volatility, which was documented in Chapter 7.[6] These studies also consistently find evidence for a substantial "leverage" effect in that the estimates of ρ are all roughly −0.5. The most notable difference is Pan's relatively lower estimate of the long-run mean of the volatility process, $\bar{v}$.

All three studies also show a positive volatility risk premium ($\eta_v > 0$)— investors tend to be adverse to increases in volatility. Thus when volatility is high, option prices are higher than what would be obtained by using historical volatility in pricing. Eraker reports that η_v is statistically significant (at conventional levels) in model SVCJ, but not in model SVJ. Precise estimation of the risk premium parameters is difficult, partly because of the limited history of options data available for estimation and (in some cases) limited availability or use of prices on options far out of the money. Moreover, as illustrated by the calculations in Das and Sundaram (1999), the drift of the volatility process (and hence the volatility risk premium) has a very small impact on the pricing of OTM puts and calls. Analogous to the case of dynamic term structure models for bond yields, an analysis of the term structure of implied volatilities would likely lead to more precision in the

---

[6] The mean reversion under $\mathbb{P}$, $\kappa_v^{\mathbb{P}}$, is obtained as $\kappa^{\mathbb{P}} = \kappa^{\mathbb{Q}} + \eta_v$. What is new here, relative to the insights learned from the study of stock returns alone (see Chapter 7), is that volatility remains persistent under $\mathbb{Q}$, after adjusting for the volatility risk premium.

estimation of η_v. However, options with long maturities are relatively illiquid, so they are typically not included in these empirical studies.

Where these studies differ is in their implications for the role of jumps in option pricing. The model-implied average arrival rates of jumps $E[\zeta_S]$ (which is just the estimated stock price jump intensity when ζ_S is state independent) suggest that jumps in returns occur about 0.002 times per day, or once every 2 years. Interestingly, this is a different picture than the one that emerged from the studies of stock return data alone. For example, Eraker et al. (2003), in their study of jump diffusions estimated with stock returns alone, obtained an arrival rate closer to two jumps per year. Eraker re-estimated model SVCJ for the sample period underlying Table 15.2 using return data alone and obtained an arrival rate of about one jump per year. While the estimates clearly differ with sample period, these patterns do suggest that inclusion of the options data tends to reduce the predicted frequency of jumps over what is obtained from return data alone. One possible explanation for this pattern is that when only return data are studied, the jump parameters are used by the likelihood function to provide a better fit to the time-varying volatility of returns. An extreme version of this was seen in Chapter 7, where a pure-jump diffusion model (with no stochastic volatility) gave rise to nearly 200 jumps per year! With the inclusion of options data, much more weight in the likelihood function is given to the role of jumps matching the volatility skew in this market. The estimated jump frequency also depends on the actual incidence of jumplike behavior during the sample period.

Table 15.2 reveals differences across studies in the average size of jumps in returns when they do occur, particularly under $\mathbb{Q}$. Whereas the mean jump sizes range between -5 to -10% for most studies, Pan obtains a mean of -19%. Thus her analysis gives somewhat less frequent jumps, with much more severe (under $\mathbb{Q}$) amplitudes for those that do occur. Using a similar model, but a different data set, Bates (2000) also finds evidence for somewhat more severe jump amplitudes. These larger (in absolute value) amplitudes generate a more pronounced volatility skew in model-implied Black-Scholes volatilities. Perhaps Pan's inclusion of an in-the-money call in her empirical analysis of model SVJ underlies her larger estimate of $m_{SJ}^{\mathbb{Q}}$.

Note that, comparing Pan's results for model SVJ with Eraker's results for model SVSCJ (the two models share a stochastic arrival rate for return jumps), quite similar estimates of $m_{SJ}^{\mathbb{P}}$ are obtained. As stressed by Eraker, $m_{SJ}^{\mathbb{P}}$ is difficult to estimate precisely, because it affects the distribution of stock returns but not option prices. Nevertheless, these findings suggest that differences in $m_{SJ}^{\mathbb{Q}}$ across studies arise owing to very different estimates of the jump-amplitude risk premiums.

In order to preserve positivity of the volatility process, jumps in volatility in models SVCJ and SVSCJ are constrained to have (constant) positive amplitudes. As such, these models are by construction incapable of capturing abrupt declines in volatility, such as occurred after the period of high volatility during the 1987 crash. Similar observations have led some authors to examine multifactor models for volatility; see, for example, Bates (2000) and Chernov et al. (2000). Pan (2002) and Eraker (2004) find evidence in support of such an extension, but we are not aware of any systematic studies of option prices using a two-factor model for volatility.

How much does the enrichment of these models through additions of jumps to returns and volatility improve their fits to options prices and volatility skews? Bakshi et al. (1997) find a substantial improvement in model SV's usefulness in hedging options positions, over the Black-Scholes model with constant volatility. However, adding jumps in returns (extending to model SVJ) does not lead to a further improvement in hedging performance. Though the pricing errors are on average smaller with than without jumps, Bates (2000) and Pan (2002) also find substantial improvements in fit for model SVJ over model SV to the volatility smirks, over a wide range of market conditions. These findings are in contrast to those of Eraker (2004), who finds that jumps in returns or volatility lead to quite small improvements in pricing errors. Similar results were obtained in his out-of-sample analysis. Finally, using a much longer time series of (futures) options prices than these other studies, Broadie et al. (2004) find that jumps in returns and volatility both contribute substantially to the improved pricing performance of their models. Their findings also suggest that jump risk premiums are time varying.

The differences across these studies may be partly attributable to the different estimation strategies used. Some studies choose the parameter estimates to minimize squared pricing errors, whereas others use estimation methods that do not minimize pricing errors (e.g., MCMC). Differences in conclusions could also arise from the ways pricing errors are measured, though most studies adopted the convention of measuring errors in terms of dollars and cents. Alternative measures, such as pricing errors as a percentage of the price of the underlying option, would effectively change the weights given to contracts by maturity and degree of moneyness.

Overall it seems that to explain the presence and temporal behavior of implied-volatility smirks, jumps in returns or volatility, or some other non-diffusing behavior of returns, are necessary. We also found in Chapter 7 that such extensions of the basic lognormal diffusion model with stochastic volatility are necessary to model conditional distributions of stock returns.

15.5. Options and Revealed Preferences

Two complementary approaches to linking preferences and option prices have been pursued in the literature. Ait-Sahalia and Lo (2000), Jackwerth

(2000), and Rosenberg and Engle (2002) use nonparametric and semi-parametric estimates of the marginal rate of substitution (or alternatively the pricing kernel) to back out the implied risk aversion of the representative agent. Alternatively, Garcia et al. (2003) and Liu et al. (2005) explore specific parametric specifications of preferences and state variables with the goal of generating the empirical characteristics observed in option pricing data.

15.5.1. Nonparametric/Semiparametric Approaches

The objective of this literature is to back out from option prices information about the risk aversion of market participants. In Chapter 8 we saw that the pricing kernel transforms the historical to the risk-neutral distribution of the state vector Y underlying risk in an economy. Suppose that we are in an economic environment where the pricing kernel q^* is a representative agent's marginal rate of substitution,

$$q^*_{t+1} = m_{t+1} \equiv \frac{U'_{t+1}}{U'_t}, \tag{15.30}$$

where U denotes the period utility function including agents' subjective discount factor. Then, using (8.25), we can write

$$m_{t+1} = e^{-r_t} \frac{f^{\mathbb{Q}}(Y_{t+1}|Y_t)}{f^{\mathbb{P}}(Y_{t+1}|Y_t)}. \tag{15.31}$$

It follows that from knowledge of the historical and risk-neutral distributions of the state, we can infer agents' marginal rate of substitution.

Using results from Leland (1980), we can use this observation to construct a measure of agents' coefficient of absolute risk aversion (CRA). Specifically, assume markets are economically complete, there is one traded risky asset, and that the representative agent's consumption (C_t) is equal to her wealth, which, in turn, is equal to the value of the risky asset (S_t), $C_t = S_t$. In this setting, agents' coefficient of relative risk aversion,

$$\mathrm{CRA}_{t+1} = -\frac{U''_{t+1}}{U'_{t+1}} = -\frac{\partial m_{t+1}/\partial C_{t+1}}{m_{t+1}}, \tag{15.32}$$

can be expressed in terms of the densities $f^{\mathbb{P}}$ and $f^{\mathbb{Q}}$:

$$\mathrm{CRA}_{t+1} = \frac{\partial f^{\mathbb{P}}(S_{t+1}|S_t)/\partial S_{t+1}}{f^{\mathbb{P}}(S_{t+1}|S_t)} - \frac{\partial f^{\mathbb{Q}}(S_{t+1}|S_t)/\partial S_{t+1}}{f^{\mathbb{Q}}(S_{t+1}|S_t)}. \tag{15.33}$$

It follows that, if the density functions $f^{\mathbb{P}}$ and $f^{\mathbb{Q}}$ can be estimated non-parameterically, then the risk aversion implicit in security prices can be computed without having to specify $U(\cdot)$ explicitly.

Ait-Sahalia and Lo (2000) and Jackwerth (2000) pursue this idea by using kernel density estimators of $f^{\mathbb{P}}$ constructed from historical return data. To compute $f^{\mathbb{Q}}$, Ait-Sahalia and Lo (2000) exploit the insight of Banz and Miller (1978) and Breeden and Litzenberger (1978) that the state-price density can be computed from the second derivative of an option price with respect to the strike price of the option. That is, letting $\mathcal{O}(S_t, K)$ denote the price of an option on the market index S struck at K and maturing at date $t + 1$. They obtain

$$f^{\mathbb{Q}}(S_{t+1} = K|S_t) = e^{r_{t+1}} \frac{\partial^2 \mathcal{O}(S_t, K)}{\partial K^2}. \tag{15.34}$$

Next, following Ait-Sahalia and Lo (1998), market option prices and kernel regression techniques are used to estimate the function $\mathcal{O}(S_t, K)$ nonparametrically. This estimate is then differentiated with respect to K to estimate $f^{\mathbb{Q}}(S_{t+1}|S_t)$.

Alternatively, Jackwerth (2000) follows the approach of Jackwerth and Rubenstein (1996) in estimating $f^{\mathbb{Q}}$. The risk-neutral density is chosen nonparametrically to fit a cross section of option-implied volatilities, subject to exogenously given smoothness constraints on the shape of the conditional density. Rosenberg and Engle (2002) pursue a third approach by working with a parametric model of the pricing kernel and modeling the equity index return process using an asymmetric GARCH process (see Chapter 7).

Depending on the model and choice of nonparametric estimator, the resulting pricing kernel is not always monotonically decreasing in the wealth level of investors. Consequently, in the studies of Jackwerth (2000) and Rosenberg and Engle (2002) there are regions of negative risk aversion. Ait-Sahalia and Lo (2000) find that relative risk aversion is positive, but nonmonotonic, and varies greatly (from 1 to 60 in the specified range, with the weighted average being 12.7). These authors also find that the marginal rate of substitution is nonmonotonic in wealth levels. Together these studies suggest that the CRRA model of preferences (see Chapter 10) is not consistent with the options data. Jackwerth (2000) finds that before the 1987 crash, the physical and the risk-neutral distributions for the S&P500 were more "lognormal"-like than after the crash. Additionally, after the crash, the risk-neutral distribution is more left skewed and more peaked (leptokurtic).

A natural question is: how robust are these findings to assumptions being made about the underlying economic environment and the dimensionality of the state vector? These studies presume that stock prices follow a univariate process and, in particular, rule out stochastic volatility. Preferences are also defined over this single state variable, wealth. Garcia et al. (2004) illustrate how the approach taken by Rosenberg and Engle (2002) can lead to incorrect inferences about risk aversion, essentially because of a missing factor in the pricing kernel. It seems plausible that their concerns about nonparametric estimates of risk aversion are equally applicable to the other fitting methods applied to date. If agents' pricing kernels are state dependent—depend on more than the price of the security underlying the option being priced—then conclusions drawn about agents' preferences may well be misleading.

15.5.2. Preference-Based Models of Option Prices

With these cautionary observations in mind, we turn next to the literature that has used parametric specifications of preferences in an attempt to generate volatility smirks like those observed historically. Two specifications that are natural candidates for exploration in this setting are the recursive preferences of Epstein and Zin (1989) and preferences that accommodate habit formation.

Garcia et al. (2003) explore the properties of options prices implied by a model in which preferences are given by the recursive form (8.21) and (8.22). Consumption and dividend growths are assumed to follow a joint i.i.d. process conditional on a latent state variable that follows a Markov switching process. Three different models are compared: their most general option pricing model implied by the Epstein-Zin-style preferences, the special case of expected utility (the CRRA is equal to the inverse of the intertemporal elasticity of substitution), and a preference-free model that amounts to a discrete-time version of the model examined in Hull and White (1987). The latter model adjusts the basic Black-Scholes model to accommodate stochastic volatility that is *not priced*. They find that, on average, their most general model has the smallest pricing errors and the preference-free model has the largest errors.

In a complementary study, these authors also examine the implications of their model for volatility smiles. Several features of their results suggest that Epstein-Zin preferences, along with their Markov switching model for the state, cannot generate the smirklike patterns observed in index options markets. Most notably, from Garcia et al. (2001: fig. 10), one sees that, holding the CRRA constant across models, the added flexibility of Epstein-Zin preferences over the nested expected utility model shifts the Black-Scholes implied volatility surface horizontally to the right. This is approximately true in both of their regimes. Given their quoting convention, moving to the right highlights call options that are more in the money and put options that are deeper out of the money. The pronounced volatility smirk in actual markets implies that these options should be more expensive (have higher implied volatilities). However, for the parameters chosen, the graphs suggest that the model with recursive Epstein-Zin preferences generates cheaper, rather than more expensive, out-of-the money put option prices than the nested expected utility model. In other words, it appears that Epstein-Zin preferences generate even less of a volatility smirk than the expected utility model.

Interestingly, relatively less attention has been given to investigating the properties of option prices in models of habit formation. Bansal et al. (2004) price options on an aggregate consumption claim using a model with habit formation that is calibrated to U.S. aggregate data. However, they do not explore the implications of their model for volatility smiles in depth.

Driessen and Maenhout (2004) take the complementary route of examining, in a partial equilibrium setting, the question of who would optimally want to buy puts and straddles in the face of the risk premiums documented in the empirical literature. They find that investors with CRRA preferences always hold economically short positions in OTM puts and ATM straddles (among other things, this implies that portfolio insurance is never optimal). Moreover, the desire to hold short positions in options also extends to loss-averse and disappointment-averse investors. This is true even though these investors avoid stock market risk entirely in the absence of derivatives. Driessen and Maenhout argue that their findings are robust to various frictions, including transaction costs, margin requirements, crash-neutral derivatives strategies, and time-varying portfolio weights. Within the contexts of the families of preferences that they consider, it appears that the jump and volatility risk premia documented empirically are economically substantial.

The premise of the general equilibrium analysis of Liu et al. (2005) is that standard recursive formulations of preferences are unlikely to be able to generate volatility smirks like those observed in the data because of "rare event" premia implicit in the options prices. These authors consider a representative agent model in which the representative agent's aggregate endowment is affected by a diffusion component and a jump component, with the latter being the source of rare and unpredictable events. The agent is risk averse over both components.

More precisely, in the reference model, the agent's endowment process under $\mathbb{P}$ is given by the following special case of (15.1):

$$dY_t = \mu Y_t dt + \sigma Y_t dW_t + \left(e^{J_t} - 1\right) Y_{t-} dZ_t, \qquad (15.35)$$

where the Poisson jump process Z (with intensity λ) has been scaled by its random amplitude and $J_t \sim N(m_J, \delta_J^2)$. The mean percentage jump in the endowment is $k \equiv \exp\{m_j + \delta_j^2/2\} - 1$.

A special feature of the jump component is that the agent is not fully informed about the parameters of the distribution of this component. That is, with regard to the jump (but not the return) component there is uncertainty of the type formalized by Knight (1921). To capture this uncertainty, the agent is presumed to consider alternative models for the jump process that are characterized by their Radon-Nikodym derivatives ξ_T with respect to the reference model:

$$d\xi_t = \left(e^{a+bJ_t - bm_J - \frac{1}{2}b^2\delta_J^2} - 1\right)\xi_{t-}dZ_t - (e^a - 1)\lambda\xi_t dt, \quad \xi_0 = 1. \quad (15.36)$$

Relative to the reference model with jump arrival intensity λ and mean jump size k, agents examine alternative models with arrival intensities and mean jump sizes (k) in the set

$$\lambda^\xi = \lambda e^a \text{ and } 1 + k^\xi = (1+k)e^{b\sigma_J^2}, \quad (15.37)$$

for predictable processes a and b. As agents roam over different choices of a and b, they are effectively considering alternative models of the underlying economy with $a = 0$ and $b = 0$ giving the reference economy.

Finally, the representative agent is assumed to solve a "robust control" problem (see Anderson et al., 2000) with preferences defined over the admissible a and b as

$$U_t = \inf_{a,b} E_t^\xi\left[\int_t^T e^{-\rho(s-t)}\left(\frac{1}{\phi}\psi(U_s)H(a_s, b_s) + \frac{c_s^{1-\gamma}}{1-\gamma}\right)ds\right], \quad (15.38)$$

where H is the cost of deviating from the reference model:

$$H(a, b) = \lambda\left[1 + \left(a + \frac{1}{2}b^2\delta_J^2 - 1\right)e^a + \beta\left(1 + e^a\left(e^{a+b^2\delta_J^2} - 2\right)\right)\right]. \quad (15.39)$$

Since out of the money options are more sensitive to large movements (jumps), they are able to separately identify the risk premia associated with risk aversion and uncertainty aversion. Introducing uncertainty aversion over the jump component increases the implied volatility for ATM options and also adds flexibility in fitting the OTM option prices so as to allow them to match the implied volatility smile/smirk patterns observed in the data. Absent this uncertainty aversion, their model (with what amounts to standard CRRA preferences) generates a relatively small smile. The authors argue further that extending the benchmark model to allow for habit formation (without uncertainty aversion) would probably not produce the required smirk in implied volatilities.

Ultimately, whether or not models with standard recursive preferences are able to replicate the volatility smiles observed historically depends on how preferences are matched with the underlying uncertainty in the economy. Benzoni et al. (2005) reach a more optimistic conclusion about our ability to explain the high implied volatilities of OTM put options. Following Bansal and Yaron (2004), they combine Epstein-Zin preferences with a dividend process driven by a persistent stochastic growth variable that can jump. Their model is calibrated so that it simultaneously matches the equity premium and the prices of ATM and deep OTM puts, while at the same time matching the level of the riskfree rate. An important question in this literature going forward is: To what degree are volatility smiles induced by investors' attitudes toward risk and uncertainty versus fat-tailed or skewed shocks that agents face in making their investment/consumption decisions?

15.6. Options on Individual Common Stocks

Bakshi and Kapadia (2003) and Bakshi et al. (2003) document a number of empirical observations about individual stock options, especially in comparison to index options, offer intuition for these differences, and discuss some of their implications for pricing. Among the empirical observations they highlight are: (1) index volatility smiles are more negatively sloped than individual volatility smiles; (2) individual stocks are mildly negatively skewed (and sometimes positively skewed) and are generally less negatively skewed than the index (which is never observed to be positively skewed); (3) implied volatilities for individual options are higher than the corresponding historical return volatilities, but the differences are smaller than for index returns; and (4) volatility risk premiums are smaller for individual stock options than for the index options.

Underlying these empirical observations is the proposition that any payoff function with bounded expectation is spanned by a continuum of option prices (Bakshi and Madan, 2000). Drawing upon this result, Bakshi et al. (2003) introduce payoffs that are powers of the return $R(t, \tau) = \log(S(t + \tau)) - \log(S(t))$, and show that the particular prices $V(t, \tau) = E^{\mathbb{Q}}[e^{-r\tau}R(t, \tau)^2]$, $W(t, \tau) = E^{\mathbb{Q}}[e^{-r\tau}R(t, \tau)^3]$, and $X(t, \tau) = E^{\mathbb{Q}}[e^{-r\tau}R(t, \tau)^4]$, determine $\text{Skew}^{\mathbb{Q}}(t, \tau)$ and $\text{Kurt}^{\mathbb{Q}}(t, \tau)$. Furthermore, the prices (V, W, X) can be computed directly from call and put prices.

These authors also show that for a model with power utility with CRRA γ, up to first order in γ, the risk-neutral skewness and the physical moments of the index are related by[7]:

$$\text{Skew}^{\mathbb{Q}}(t, \tau) \approx \text{Skew}^{\mathbb{P}}(t, \tau) - \gamma \left(\text{Kurt}^{\mathbb{P}}(t, \tau) - 3\right)\text{STD}^{\mathbb{P}}(t, \tau). \qquad (15.40)$$

From (15.40) it is seen that skewness under $\mathbb{P}$ induces skewness under $\mathbb{Q}$. At the same time, even if $\text{Skew}^{\mathbb{P}} = 0$, the risk-neutral distribution tends to be skewed if the stock return exhibits excess kurtosis under $\mathbb{P}$. In general, these expressions for risk-neutral skews do not aggregate linearly across time if the $\mathbb{P}$ distribution of stock returns exhibits serial correlation. Interestingly, a

---

[7] This approximation actually holds somewhat more generally, to first order, and in particular applies to certain models with time-varying γ.

positive autocorrelation tends to induce a U-shaped term structure of skewness, whereas negative autocorrelation gives skews of short-term returns that are more negative than their counterparts for long-term returns.

With moneyness denoted by $y = S/K$, these calculations also suggest that the Black-Scholes implied volatility $\sigma_i(y; t, \tau)$ is related to the higher-order moments of the $\mathbb{Q}$ distribution according to

$$\sigma_i(y; t, \tau) \approx \alpha_i[y] + \beta_i[y]\mathrm{Skew}_i^{\mathbb{Q}}(t, \tau) + \theta_i[y]\mathrm{Kurt}_i^{\mathbb{Q}}(t, \tau). \qquad (15.41)$$

This expression is useful for its direct linkage of $\mathrm{Skew}^{\mathbb{Q}}$ and $\mathrm{Kurt}^{\mathbb{Q}}$ to the shape of the volatility skew. Bakshi et al. show that firms with more negative skewness have larger implied volatilities at low levels of moneyness, and firms with larger kurtoses have larger implied volatilities for both OTM and ITM put options. Further, whereas skewness is a first-order effect on the shape of the volatility smile, making it steeper, kurtosis is a second-order effect on the smile and affects out-of-the money call and put prices symmetrically.

To explore the higher-moment properties of stock returns implicit in options data, Bakshi et al. (2003) use daily spot and options prices of the thirty largest stocks (by market capitalization) and the S&P500. Though the options on individual stocks are "American" options, the authors found that their results were largely insensitive to ignoring the early exercise premium. So they treated these options as "European" in their analysis. They found that the slope of the volatility curve tends to be much steeper for the index than for the individual stocks. Additionally, the at-the-money implied volatility for the index is lower than that of most individual stocks. The relatively high volatilities of returns on individual stocks imply that large $\mathbb{P}$-moves are possible even with relatively small $\mathbb{P}$ skewnesses and kurtoses. These patterns are naturally manifested in relatively flat implied volatility surfaces for options on individual stocks. Consistent with (15.41), individual stocks that exhibit more negative risk-neutral skewness also exhibited steeper volatility smile.

In a complementary study, Bakshi and Kapadia (2003) estimate the gains or losses on delta-hedged positions in individual stock options in order to assess the magnitude of the volatility risk premium in the markets for options on individual common stocks. They find that the premiums are negative, but less so on average than for the index option market.

16
Pricing Fixed-Income Derivatives

Two QUITE DISTINCT approaches to the pricing of fixed-income derivatives have been pursued in the literature. One approach takes the yield curve as given—essentially the entire yield curve is the current state vector. Then, assuming no arbitrage opportunities, prices for derivative claims with payoffs that depend on the yield curve are derived. Examples of models in this first group are the widely studied "forward-rate" models of Heath et al. (1992), Brace et al. (1997), and Miltersen et al. (1997). Since the yield curve is an input, there is typically no associated DTSM; the model used to price derivatives does not price the underlying bonds. The second approach starts with a DTSM, often in one of the families discussed in Chapter 12, which is used to simultaneously price the underlying fixed-income securities and the derivatives written against those securities, all under the assumption that there are no arbitrage opportunities. With the growing availability of time-series data on the implied volatilities of fixed-income derivatives, both approaches have been pursued in exploring the fits of pricing models to the historical implied volatilities of fixed-income derivatives.

In discussing the pricing of fixed-income derivatives, we place particular emphasis on the formulations of the pricing models underlying recent empirical studies of derivatives pricing models. We begin with a review of pricing with affine DTSMs.[1] This is followed by an introduction to pricing with forward-rate-based models. Since these models are being introduced for the first time, we deal with the various pricing measures that have been used to price derivatives in some depth. We then turn to a discussion of some of the more striking empirical challenges that have been raised based

---

[1] See Leippold and Wu (2002) for a discussion of the pricing of fixed-income derivatives in the class of quadratic-Gaussian DTSMs. Many of the solutions discussed subsequently to the pricing problems faced with affine DTSMs carry over, in suitably modified forms, to the QG class of models.

on examination of the historical data on implied volatilities in the LIBOR-based derivatives markets. We conclude this chapter with a discussion of how well various models address these challenges.

16.1. Pricing with Affine DTSMs

Particular attention has been given to the pricing of caps/floors and swaptions in the LIBOR/swap markets, no doubt in part because of the size and importance of these markets. To fix the notation for the tenor structure, let us suppose that, at time $t = 0$, there are N consecutive interest rate reset dates T_n, $n = 1, 2, \ldots, N$. The relevant rate for the time interval δ_n, $\delta_n = T_{n+1} - T_n$, is the Eurodollar deposit rate with tenor δ_n, $n = 1, 2, \ldots, N$ (with $T_{N+1} \equiv T_N + \delta_N$). For t greater than zero and less than or equal to T_N, we let $n(t) = \inf_{n \leq N} \{n : T_n \geq t\}$ denote the next delivery date on forward contracts.

Let $B(t, T)$ be the LIBOR discount factor at time t with maturity date T. Then, since LIBOR rates are set on a simple-interest basis,

$$B(T_n, T_{n+1}) = \frac{1}{1 + \delta_n \mathcal{R}(T_n)}, \qquad (16.1)$$

where $\mathcal{R}$ is the quoted LIBOR rate for tenor δ_n at date T_n. The time-t forward LIBOR rate for a loan spanning the period $[T_n, T_{n+1}]$ is therefore given by

$$L_n(t) = \frac{1}{\delta_n} \left[\frac{B(t, T_n)}{B(t, T_{n+1})} - 1 \right]. \qquad (16.2)$$

Note that $L_n(T_n) = \mathcal{R}(T_n)$, the LIBOR rate at date T_n.

A cap is a loan at a variable interest rate that is capped at some prespecified level. To price a cap, it is convenient to break up the cash flows into a series of "caplets" that capture the value of the interest rate cap in each period. Specifically, a caplet is a security with payoff $\delta_n [L_n(T_n) - k]^+$, determined at the reset date T_n and paid at the settlement date T_{n+1} (payment in arrears), where $L_n(T_n)$ is the spot LIBOR rate at T_n and k is the strike rate. The market value at time 0 of the caplet paying at date T_{n+1} is

$$\text{Caplet}_0(n) = E^{\mathbb{Q}} \left[\exp \left(- \int_0^{T_{n+1}} r_u \, du \right) \delta_n \left(L_n(T_n) - k \right)^+ \right]$$

$$= E^{\mathbb{Q}} \left[\exp \left(- \int_0^{T_{n+1}} r_u \, du \right) \left(\frac{1}{B(T_n, T_{n+1})} - (1 + \delta_n k) \right)^+ \right]. \qquad (16.3)$$

Within an affine DTSM, $1/B(T_n, T_{n+1}) = e^{-\gamma_0(\delta_n) - \gamma_Y(\delta_n)'Y_{T_n}}$ [see (12.7)].[2]
Therefore, valuing a caplet in this setting is equivalent to pricing a call
option with contingent payoff $e^{-\gamma_0(\delta_n) - \gamma_Y(\delta_n)'Y_{T_n}}$ at date T_n and strike price
$(1 + \delta_n k)$. Referring back to the transform analysis for affine processes of
Duffie et al. (2000) discussed in Section 5.4, we see that the transform
(5.39) can be applied directly to (16.3) to price the caplets and, hence,
a cap.

Looking ahead to the case of coupon bonds, we find it instructive to
elaborate briefly on the pricing of an option on a zero-coupon bond. If we
use the S-forward measure $\mathbb{Q}_t^S$ induced on $\mathbb{Q}$ by the price of a zero-coupon
bond issued at date t and maturing at time S, $B(t, S)$ (see Section 8.3.2 for
a discussion of the forward measure), the price $C(t, Y_t; S, T, K)$ of a call
option with strike K and maturity S written on a zero-coupon bond with
maturity T is

$$
\begin{aligned}
C(t, Y_t; S, T, K) &= E_t^{\mathbb{Q}}\left[e^{-\int_t^S r_u du}(B(S, T) - K)^+\right] \\
&= B(t, T)E_t^{\mathbb{Q}^T}\left[1_{\{B(S,T) > K\}}\right] - KB(t, S)E_t^{\mathbb{Q}^S}\left[1_{\{B(S,T) > K\}}\right] \\
&= B(t, T)\mathrm{Pr}_t^T\{B(S, T) > K\} - KB(t, S)\mathrm{Pr}_t^S\{B(S, T) > K\},
\end{aligned}
$$

where $\mathrm{Pr}_t^S\{X > K\}$ is the conditional probability of the event $\{X > K\}$,
based on the S-forward measure $\mathbb{Q}_t^S$. For the entire family of affine term
structure models, these forward probabilities are easily computed using the
known conditional characteristic functions of affine diffusions and Levý
inversion (Bakshi and Madan, 2000; Duffie et al., 2000). That is, since
$\{B(S, T) > K\} \equiv \{\gamma_0(T - S) + \gamma_Y(T - S)'Y_S > \ln K\}$ and the characteristic
function of $\gamma_Y(T - S)'Y_S$ conditional on Y_t is known in closed form, two
one-dimensional Fourier transforms give the requisite probabilities under
the two forward measures. Note that only one-dimensional transforms are
needed, even though the dimension of Y might be much larger.

The difficulty that arises in extending these ideas to the case of coupon
bond options is that the exercise region is defined implicitly and, therefore, its probability is often difficult to compute. To illustrate the nature
of the problem, let $V_t = V(t, Y_t; \{c_i\}_{i=1}^N, \{T_i\}_{i=1}^N)$ be the price of a fixed-
income instrument with certain cash flows $c_1, c_2, \ldots, c_N$ payable at dates
$T_1, T_2, \ldots, T_N$. Then the price of a European option on this bond with strike
K and maturity S is given by

---

[2] See Duffie et al. (2000) for a discussion of pricing caps when the payoff is expressed
directly in terms of the floating rate $\mathcal{R}(T_n)$. Also, see Jarrow et al. (2004) for a discussion of
pricing the payoff $(L_n(T_n) - k)^+$ using the transform methods in Duffie et al. (2000) applied
to the forward measure when $\log L_n(t)$ follows a square-root diffusion.

$$C\left(t, Y_t; S, K, \{c_i\}_{i=1}^N, \{T_i\}_{i=1}^N\right) = E_t^Q\left[e^{-\int_t^S r_u du}(V_S - K)^+\right]$$

$$= \sum_{i=0}^N c_i B(t, T_i)\mathrm{Pr}_t^{T_i}\{V_S > K\} - KB(t, S)\mathrm{Pr}_t^S\{V_S > K\}. \qquad (16.4)$$

The exercise region of this call option is

$$\{V_S > K\} \equiv \left\{\sum_{i=1}^N c_i B(S, T_i) > K\right\} \equiv \left\{\sum_{i=1}^N c_i e^{\gamma_0(T_i - S)} e^{\gamma_Y(T_i - S) \cdot Y_S} > K\right\},$$

where we are assuming that there are N remaining cash flows after the expiration date of the option.

If all the future cash flows c_i are positive, then this exercise boundary is a concave surface. Figure 16.1 illustrates these observations by plotting exercise boundaries for 5-year at-the-money calls on 30-year 10% coupon and discount bonds implied by the two-factor square-root model [an $A_2(2)$ model], with parameter values taken from Duffie and Singleton (1997) and the state variables evaluated at their long-run means.

Various approximations to the option price (16.4) have been proposed in the literature. Singleton and Umantsev (2002) exploit properties of the conditional distribution of the state variables in typical affine DTSMs to locally approximate the exercise boundaries in Figure 16.1 with straight-line segments. This leads to a very accurate approximate pricing formula in terms of the values of options on zero-coupon bonds. Alternatively, Collin-Dufresne and Goldstein (2002b) propose another accurate approximation strategy based on an Edgeworth expansion of the probability distribution of the future value of the underlying bond.

Turning to the specific case of a swaption,[3] we see that the value of a (settled in arrears) swap today (date t) that matures at date T_n is given by

$$V_t = c\sum_{i=i_t}^n B(t, T_i) + B(t, T_n) - \frac{B(t, T_{i_t})}{B(T_{i_t-1}, T_{i_t})}, \qquad (16.5)$$

where the T_i are the cash-flow dates and i_t is the index of the next cash-flow date at time t. The last term in (16.5) appears because the LIBOR floating side of the contract is settled in arrears using the LIBOR rate at the preceding cash-flow date. An important consequence of this settlement convention is that V_t depends not only on the current state, but also on the value of the state on the previous cash-flow date. Only on cash-flow dates

---

[3] This discussion follows Singleton and Umantsev (2002) where a more detailed discussion of the implementation of the pricing formulas can be found.

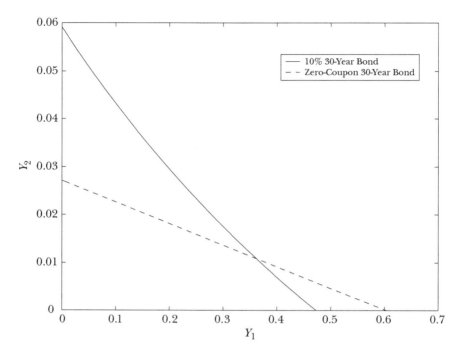

Figure 16.1.   *Exercise boundaries for 5-year ATM calls on 30-year 10% coupon and zero-coupon bonds implied by an $A_2(2)$ affine term structure model. Source: Singleton and Umantsev (2002).*

when the last term simplifies to unity does the direct parallel between a swap and a coupon bond emerge.

On cash-flow dates, the floating side of a swap is at par so the swaption price is equal to the price of a call of the same maturity and strike of one written on a coupon bond with maturity and coupon rate equal to those of the swap. Specifically, with $T = T_N - S$ at the inception of a "T-in-S" swaption—the right to enter into a T-period swap at some future date S— the swaption price is

$$E_t^{\mathbb{Q}}\left[e^{-\int_t^S r_u du}\left(c\sum_{i=i_S}^N B(S, T_i) + B(S, T_N) - 1\right)^+\right], \qquad (16.6)$$

where r_t is being set to the discount rate implicit in the pricing of swaps. We could easily extend this valuation approach to the case where the counterparties in the swaption contract had different ratings than those (say AA) underlying the pricing of generic swaps by introducing a different discount rate for pricing swaptions versus pricing swaps.

The pricing of both swaps and swaptions recognizes the two-sided nature of the credit risk of swaps. However, following Duffie and Singleton (1997), we are assuming that the counterparties have symmetric credit risks. (See Chapter 14 for further discussion of one- versus two-sided default risk.) Within this framework, the pricing of newly issued swaptions proceeds as in the case of a coupon-bond option.

16.2. Pricing Using Forward-Rate Models

A significant part of the literature on the pricing of fixed-income derivatives[4] has focused on forward-rate models in which the terminal payoff $Z(T)$ is assumed to be completely determined by the discount function $(B(t, T) : T \geq t)$ (as in Ho and Lee, 1986), or equivalently, the forward curve $(f(t, T) : T \geq t)$ (as in Heath et al., 1992) defined by

$$f(t, T) = -\frac{\partial \log B(t, T)}{\partial T}, \quad \text{for any } T \geq t. \tag{16.7}$$

The time-t price of a fixed-income derivative with terminal payoff $Z(T) = Z(f(T, T + x) : x \geq 0)$ is then given by

$$Z(t) = E^{\mathbb{Q}}\left[e^{-\int_t^T f(u, u) du} Z(f(T, T + x) : x \geq 0) \,\middle|\, f(t, t + x) : x \geq 0 \right]. \tag{16.8}$$

For this model to be free of arbitrage opportunities, Heath et al. (1992) show that the risk-neutral dynamics of the forward curve must be given by

$$df(t, T) = \left[\sigma(t, T) \int_t^T \sigma(t, u) \, du \right] dt + \sigma(t, T) \, dW(t), \quad \text{for any } T \geq t, \tag{16.9}$$

and for a suitably chosen volatility function $\sigma(t, T)$. This forward-rate representation of prices is particularly convenient in practice because the forward curve can be taken as an input for pricing derivatives and once the functions $\sigma(t, T)$, for all $T \geq t$, are specified, then so are the processes $f(t, T)$ under $\mathbb{Q}$. This approach, as typically used in practice, allows the implied r_t and Λ_t to follow general Ito processes (up to mild regularity conditions); there is no presumption that the underlying state is Markov in this forward-rate formulation. Additionally, taking $(f(t, T) : T \geq t)$ as an input for pricing means that a forward-rate-based model can be completely agnostic about the behavior of yields under the actual data-generating process.

---

[4] This section draws extensively from Dai and Singleton (2003a).

Building on the original insights of Heath, Jarrow, and Morton (HJM), a variety of different forward-rate-based models have been developed and used in practice. The finite dimensionality of $W^\mathbb{Q}$ was relaxed by Musiela (1994), who models the forward curve as a solution to an infinite-dimensional stochastic partial differential equation (SPDE) (see Da Prato and Zabczyk, 1992, and Pardoux, 1993) for some mathematical characterizations of the SPDE). Specific formulations of infinite-dimensional SPDEs have been developed under the labels of "Brownian sheets" (Kennedy, 1994), "random fields" (Goldstein, 2000), and "stochastic string shocks" (Santa-Clara and Sornette, 2001). The high dimensionality of these models gives a better fit to the correlation structure, particularly at high frequencies. Since solutions to SPDEs can be expanded in terms of a countable basis (cylindrical Brownian motions—see, e.g., Da Prato and Zabczyk, 1992, and Cont, 2005), the SPDE models can also be viewed as infinite-dimensional factor models. Though these formulations are mathematically rich, in practice they often add little generality beyond finite-state forward-rate models, because practical considerations tend to lead modelers to work with a finite-dimensional Brownian motions $W^\mathbb{Q}$.

Key to all of these formulations is the specification of the volatility function, since this determines the drift of the relevant forward rates under $\mathbb{Q}$ (as in Heath et al., 1992). Amin and Morton (1994) examine a class of one-factor models with the volatility function given by

$$\sigma(t, T) = [\sigma_0 + \sigma_1(T - t)]\, e^{-\lambda(T-t)} f(t, T)^\gamma. \tag{16.10}$$

This specification nests many widely used volatility functions, including the continuous-time version of Ho and Lee (1986) ($\sigma(t, T) = \sigma_0$), the lognormal model ($\sigma(t, T) = \sigma_0 f(t, T)$), and the Gaussian model with time-dependent parameters as in Hull and White (1993). When $\gamma \neq 0$, (16.10) is a special case of the "separable specification" $\sigma(t, T) = \xi(t, T)\eta(t)$ with $\xi(t, T)$ a deterministic function of time and $\eta(t)$ a possibly stochastic function of Y. The state vector may include the current spot rate $r(t)$ (see, e.g., Jeffrey, 1995), a set of forward rates with fixed time-to-maturity, or an autonomous Markovian vector of latent state variables (Brace and Musiela, 1994; Cheyette, 1994; Andersen et al., 1999b). In practice, the specification of $\eta(t)$ has been kept simple to preserve computational tractability, often simpler than the specifications of stochastic volatility in yield-based models. On the other hand, Y often has a large dimension (many forward rates are used) and $\xi(t, T)$ is given a flexible functional form. Thus, there is the risk with forward-rate models of misspecifying the dynamics through restrictive specifications of $\eta(t)$, while "overfitting" to current market information through the specification of $\xi(t, T)$.

More discipline, as well as added computational tractability, is obtained by imposing a Markovian structure on the forward-rate processes. Two logically distinct approaches to deriving Markov HJM models have been explored in the literature. Ritchken and Sankarasubramanian (1995), Bhar and Chiarella (1997), and Inui and Kijima (1998) ask under what conditions, taking as given the current forward-rate curve, the evolution of future forward rates can be described by a Markov process in an HJM model. These papers show that an N-factor HJM model can be represented, under certain restrictions, as a Markov system in $2N$ state variables. While these results lead to simplifications in the computation of the prices of fixed-income derivatives, they do not build a natural bridge to Markov spot-rate-based DTSMs. The distributions of both spot and forward rates depend on the date and shape of the initial forward rate curve.

Carverhill (1994), Jeffrey (1995), and Bjork and Svensson (2001) explore conditions under which an N-factor HJM model implies an N-factor Markov representation of the short rate r. In the case of $N = 1$, the question can be posed as: Under what conditions does a one-factor HJM model—which by construction matches the current forward curve—imply a diffusion model for r with drift and volatility functions that depend only on r and t? Under the assumption that the instantaneous variance of the T-period forward rate is a function only of (r, t, T), $\sigma_f^2(r, t, T)$, Jeffrey proved the remarkable result that $\sigma_f^2(r, t, T)$ must be an affine function of r (with time-dependent coefficients) in order for r to follow a Markov process. Put differently, his result essentially says that the only family of "internally consistent" one-factor HJM models (see also Bjork and Christensen, 1999) that match the current forward curve and imply a Markov model for r is the family of affine DTSMs with time-dependent coefficients. Bjork and Svensson discuss the multifactor counterpart to Jeffrey's result.

An important recent development in the HJM modeling approach, based on the work of Brace et al. (1997), Jamshidian (1997), Miltersen et al. (1997), and Musiela and Rutkowski (1997), is the construction of arbitrage-free models for forward LIBOR rates at an observed discrete tenor structure. Besides the practical benefit of working with observable forward rates (in contrast to the unobservable instantaneous forward rates), this shift overcomes a significant conceptual limitation of continuous-rate formulations. Namely, as shown by Morton (1988) and Sandmann and Sondremann (1997), a lognormal volatility structure for $f(t, T)$ is inadmissible, because it may imply zero prices for positive-payoff claims and, hence, arbitrage opportunities. With the use of discrete-tenor forwards, the lognormal assumption becomes admissible. The resulting *LIBOR market model* (LMM) is consistent with the industry-standard Black model for pricing interest rate caps.

In addition to taking full account of the observed discrete-tenor structure, the LMM framework also facilitates tailoring the choice of "pricing measures" to the specific derivative products. (See Section 8.3.2 for a discussion of the pricing measures $m(P)$ based on the numeraire P.) The LIBOR market model is based on either one of the following two pricing measures: the *terminal (forward) measure* proposed by Musiela and Rutkowski (1997) and the *spot LIBOR measure* proposed by Jamshidian (1997).

Letting $C_n(t)$ denote the price of the caplet, Brace et al. (1997) show that, in the absence of arbitrage, both $B(t, T_n)/B(t, T_{n+1})$ [and hence $L_n(t)$] and $C_n(t)/B(t, T_{n+1})$ are martingales under the forward measure, $\mathbb{Q}^{n+1} \equiv m(B(t, T_{n+1}))$, induced by the LIBOR discount factor $B(t, T_{n+1})$. Furthermore, under the assumption that $L_n(t)$ is lognormally distributed,[5] the Black model for caplet pricing obtains:

$$C_n(t) = \delta_n B(t, T_{n+1}) \left[L_n(t) N(d_1) - k N(d_2) \right], \tag{16.11}$$

$$d_1 \equiv \frac{\log(L_n(t)/k) + v_n/2}{\sqrt{v_n}}, \quad d_2 \equiv \frac{\log(L_n(t)/k) - v_n/2}{\sqrt{v_n}}, \tag{16.12}$$

where $N(\cdot)$ is the cumulative normal distribution function and v_n is the cumulative volatility of the forward LIBOR rate from the trade date to the delivery date: $v_n \equiv \int_t^{T_n} \sigma_n(u)' \sigma_n(u)\, du$. The price of a cap is simply the sum of all unsettled caplet prices (including the value of the caplet paid at settlement date $T_{n(t)}$, which is known at t).

The Black-Scholes type pricing formula (16.11) and (16.12) for caps is commonly referred to as the *cap market model*. Its simplicity derives from the facts that: (1) each caplet with reset date T_n and payment date T_{n+1} is priced under its own forward measure $\mathbb{Q}^{n+1}$; (2) we can be completely agnostic about the exact nature of the forward measures and their relationship with each other; and (3) we can be completely agnostic about the factor structure: the caplet price C_n does not depend on how the total cumulative volatility v_n is distributed across different shocks W^n.

The simplicity of the cap market model does not immediately extend to the pricing of securities whose payoffs depend on two or more spot LIBOR rates with different maturities, or equivalently two or more forward LIBOR rates with different reset dates. A typical example is a European swaption with expiration date $n \geq n(t)$, final settlement date T_{N+1}, and strike k. Let

---

[5] That is,

$$\frac{dL_n(t)}{L_n(t)} = \sigma_n(t)' \, dW^n(t),$$

where W^n is a vector of standard and independent Brownian motions under $\mathbb{Q}^n$, and $\sigma_n(t)$ is a deterministic vector commensurate with W^n.

$$S_{n,N}(t) = \frac{B(t, T_n) - B(t, T_{N+1})}{\sum_{j=n}^{N} \delta_j B(t, T_{j+1})}$$

be the forward swap rate, with delivery date T_n and final settlement date T_{N+1}; the payoff of the payer swaption at T_n is a stream of cash flows paid at T_{j+1} and in the amount $\delta_j [S_{n,N}(T_n) - k]^+$, $n \leq j \leq N$, where the spot swap rates $S_n(T_n)$ are completely determined by the forward LIBOR rates $L_j(T_n)$, $n \leq j \leq N$. The market value of these payments, as of T_n, is given by

$$\sum_{j=n}^{N} \delta_j B(T_n, T_{j+1})[S_n(T_n) - k]^+ = \left[1 - B(T_n, T_{N+1}) - k \sum_{j=n}^{N} \delta_j B(T_n, T_{j+1})\right]^+.$$

In order to price instruments of this kind, we need the joint distribution of the forward LIBOR rates $\{L_j(t) : n \leq j \leq N, 0 \leq t \leq T_n\}$, under a *single* measure. The LMM arises precisely in order to meet this requirement.

Musiela and Rutkowski (1997) show that under the *terminal measure* $\mathbb{Q}^* \equiv \mathbb{Q}^{N+1}$, that is, the probability measure induced by the LIBOR discount factor $B(t, T_{N+1})$, the forward LIBOR rates can be modeled as a joint solution to the following stochastic differential equations (SDEs): for $n(t) \leq \forall n \leq N$,

$$\frac{dL_n(t)}{L_n(t)} = \sigma_n(t)' \left[-\sum_{j=n+1}^{N} \frac{\delta_j L_j(t)}{1 + \delta_j L_j(t)} \sigma_j(t) \, dt + dW^*(t) \right], \qquad (16.13)$$

where W^* is a vector of standard and independent Brownian motions under $\mathbb{Q}^*$. These SDEs have a recursive structure that can be exploited in simulating the LIBOR forward rates: first, the drift of $L_N(t)$ is identically zero, because it is a martingale under $\mathbb{Q}^*$; second, for $n < N$, the drift of $L_n(t)$ is determined by $L_j(t)$, $n < j \leq N$.

Jamshidian (1997) proposes an alternative construction of the LIBOR market model based on the so-called *spot LIBOR measure*, $\mathbb{Q}^B$, induced by the price of a "rolling zero-coupon bond" or "rolling CD" (rather than a continuously compounded bank deposit account that induces the risk-neutral measure):

$$B(t) \equiv \frac{B(t, T_{n(t)})}{B(0, T_1)} \prod_{j=1}^{n(t)-1} \left[1 + \delta_j L_j(T_j)\right].$$

He shows that, under this measure, the set of LIBOR forward rates can be modeled as a joint solution to the following set of SDEs: for $n(t) \leq \forall n \leq N$,

$$\frac{dL_n(t)}{L_{n(t)}(t)} = \sigma_n(L_{n(t)}(t), t)' \left[\sum_{j=n(t)}^{n} \frac{\delta_j L_j(t)}{1 + \delta_j L_j(t)} \sigma_i(L_i(t), t) dt + dW^B(t) \right], (16.14)$$

where W^B is a vector of standard and independent Brownian motions under $\mathbb{Q}^B$ and the possible state dependence of the volatility function is also made explicit. These SDEs also have a recursive structure: starting at $n = n(t)$, $L_{n(t)}(t)$ solves an autonomous SDE; for $n > n(t)$, the drift of $L_n(t)$ is determined by $L_j(t)$, $n(t) \leq j \leq n$.

Under the LMM, the time-t price of a security with payoff $g(\{L_j(T_n) : n \leq j \leq N\})$ at T_n is given by

$$\begin{aligned} P_t &= B(t, T_{N+1}) E_t^* \left[\frac{g\left(\{L_j(T_n) : n \leq j \leq N\}\right)}{B(T_n, T_{N+1})} \right] \\ &= B(t, T_{n(t)}) E_t^B \left[\frac{g\left(\{L_j(T_n) : n \leq j \leq N\}\right)}{\prod_{j=n(t)}^{n-1}\left(1 + \delta_j L_j(T_j)\right)} \right], \end{aligned} \tag{16.15}$$

where $E_t^*[\cdot]$ denotes the conditional expectation operator under the terminal measure $\mathbb{Q}^*$ and $E_t^B[\cdot]$ denotes the conditional expectation operator under the spot LIBOR measure $\mathbb{Q}^B$. The Black model for caplet pricing or the cap market model is recovered under the assumption that the proportional volatility functions $\sigma_j(t)$ are deterministic.[6]

According to (16.15), the price of a payer swaption with expiration date T_n and final maturity date T_{N+1} is given by

$$\begin{aligned} P_{n,N}(t) &= B(t, T_{N+1}) E_t^* \left[\frac{\left(1 - B(T_n, T_{N+1}) - k \sum_{j=n}^{N} \delta_j B(T_n, T_{j+1})\right)^+}{B(T_n, T_{N+1})} \right] \\ &= B(t, T_{n(t)}) E_t^B \left[\frac{\left(1 - B(T_n, T_{N+1}) - k \sum_{j=n}^{N} \delta_j B(T_n, T_{j+1})\right)^+}{\prod_{j=n(t)}^{n-1}(1 + \delta_j L_j(T_j))} \right]. \end{aligned}$$

Under the assumption of deterministic proportional volatility for forward LIBOR rates, the above expression cannot be evaluated analytically. In order to calibrate theoretical swaption prices directly to market quoted Black

---

[6] The pricing equation (16.15) holds even when the proportional volatility of the forward LIBOR rates are stochastic. Narrowly defined, the LMM refers to the pricing model based on the assumption that the proportional volatilities of the forward LIBOR rates are deterministic. Broadly defined, the LMM refers to the pricing model based on any specification of state-dependent proportional volatilities (as long as appropriate Lipschitz and growth conditions are satisfied).

volatilities for swaptions, a more tractable model for pricing European swaptions is desirable. Jamshidian (1997) shows that such a model can be obtained by assuming that the proportional volatilities of forward swap rates, rather than those of forward LIBOR rates, are deterministic. The resulting model is referred to as the *swaption market model*.

The swap market model is based on the *forward swap measure*, $\mathbb{Q}^{n,N}$, induced by the price of a set of fixed cash flows paid at T_{j+1}, $n \leq j \leq N$, namely,

$$B_{n,N}(t) \equiv \sum_{j=n}^{N} \delta_j B(t, T_{j+1}), \quad t \leq T_{n+1}.$$

Under $\mathbb{Q}^{n,N}$, the forward swap rate $S_{n,N}(t)$ is a martingale:

$$\frac{dS_{n,N}(t)}{S_{n,N}(t)} = \sigma_{n,N}(t)' dW^{n,N},$$

where $W^{n,N}$ is a vector of standard and independent Brownian motions under $\mathbb{Q}^{n,N}$. Thus, the price of a European payer swaption with expiration date T_n and final settlement date T_{N+1} is given by

$$P_{n,N}(t) = B_{n,N}(t) E_t^{n,N} \left[\left(S_{n,N}(T_n) - k \right)^+ \right], \quad t \leq T_n. \tag{16.16}$$

Under the assumption that the proportional volatility of the forward swap rate is deterministic, the swaption is priced by a Black-Scholes type formula:

$$P_{n,N}(t) = B_{n,N}(t) \left[S_{n,N} N(d_1) - k N(d_2) \right],$$

$$d_1 \equiv \frac{\log(S_{n,N}/k) + v_{n,N}/2}{\sqrt{v_{n,N}}}, \quad d_2 \equiv \frac{\log(S_{n,N}/k) - v_{n,N}/2}{\sqrt{v_{n,N}}},$$

where $v_{n,N} \equiv \int_t^{T_n} \sigma_{n,N}(u)' \sigma_{n,N}(u) \, du$ is the cumulative volatility of the forward swap rate from the trade date to the expiration date of the swaption.

Several approaches have been taken to translate these ideas into econometrically tractable models for the analysis of time-series data on derivatives prices. Longstaff et al. (2001a) use a version of the LMM to price caps and swaptions.[7] They take the LIBOR forward rates $F_i = F(t, T_i, T_i + 1/2)$ to be

---

[7] Though these authors refer to their model as a "string" model, they construct their pricing model using a finite number of forward rates with discrete tenors. Therefore, the resulting framework is usefully thought of as an LMM. See Kerkhof and Pelsser (2002) for a formal discussion of the equivalence of the LMM and discrete string models.

the fundamental variables driving the term structure, and assume that their $\mathbb{Q}$ dynamics are

$$dF_i = \alpha_i F_i dt + \sigma_i F_i dW_i^{\mathbb{Q}}. \tag{16.17}$$

The shocks $dW_i^{\mathbb{Q}}$ are correlated across forward rates with the time-homogeneous covariance matrix Σ. To obtain the model-implied representation of zero-coupon bond prices, Longstaff et al. note that $F_i = (360/a)$ $(B(t, T_i)/B(t, T_i + 1/2) - 1)$, where a is the actual number of days between T_i and $T_i + 1/2$, and then they use Ito's lemma to obtain

$$dB = rBdt + J^{-1}\sigma F \, dW^{\mathbb{Q}}, \tag{16.18}$$

where $\sigma F dW^{\mathbb{Q}}$ is formed by stacking the $\sigma_i F_i dW_i$ and the Jacobian matrix J, obtained from the mapping from bond prices to forwards, has a banded diagonal form.

As noted above, the LMM does not lead to closed-form expressions for the prices of European swaptions. Longstaff et al. (2001a) proceed using simulation methods, based on their full characterization of the joint distribution of forward rates, to compute prices. Calibration then amounts to choosing Σ to match the market data on derivatives prices. They proceed from the spectral decomposition of the historical correlation matrix of changes in forward rates, $H = U \Lambda U'$. The relevant covariance matrix for the forward rates is assumed to be of the form $\Sigma = U \Phi U'$. In other words, the eigenvectors of H are assumed to be those of Σ in the pricing model, and all that remains is to select the eigenvalues of Σ, diag$[\Phi]$, to match the historical swaption prices. The assumption that H and Σ share the same eigenvectors amounts to imposing a special structure on the $\mathbb{P}$ drifts of the forward rates.

Han (2004) extends the LMM model in Longstaff et al. (2001a) to allow for stochastic volatility. Starting directly with bond prices, he assumes that

$$\frac{dB(t, T)}{B(t, T)} = r(t)dt - \sum_{k=1}^{N} \beta_k (T - t)\sqrt{v_k(t)} \, dZ_k^{\mathbb{Q}}(t), \tag{16.19}$$

where the volatility factors $v_k(t)$ are assumed to follow square-root diffusions $[A_1(1)$ processes]. Rather than using simulation methods to price caps and swaptions, Han depends on certain approximate analytic pricing formulas.

More recently, Jarrow et al. (2004) develop a model in which

$$\frac{dL_n(t)}{L_n(t)} = \alpha_n(t)dt + \sigma_n(t)dW_{L,n+1}^{\mathbb{P}}(t) + dZ_n^{\mathbb{P}}(t) \tag{16.20}$$

where $W_{L,n+1}^{\mathbb{P}}$ is a standard Brownian motion and $Z^{\mathbb{P}}$ is an independent jump process under $\mathbb{P}$. To reduce the dimensionality of the parameter space, Jarrow et al. follow Longstaff et al. (2001a) and Han (2004) and assume that the instantaneous covariance matrix of changes in LIBOR rates takes the form $\Sigma_t = U\Phi_t U'$, where U is the $N \times 3$ (N is the number of forward LIBOR rates included) matrix of the first three eigenvectors of the historical covariance matrix of LIBOR rates. In other words, they assume that there are three factors underlying the temporal variation in the instantaneous variances and covariances of LIBOR rates. The ith diagonal element of Φ_t, $v_i(t)$, is the instantaneous variance of the ith common factor and it is assumed to follow a square-root diffusion. The jump is assumed to take the same form as that in Pan's (2002) study of equity options, including her assumption that the jump timing risk is not priced (see Chapter 15).

To complete their model, Jarrow et al. (2004) assume that the risk premiums associated with both the jump amplitude and stochastic volatilities are linear functions of time to maturity. A richer parameterization is not identified econometrically because they are not studying both the cash and derivatives prices simultaneously. Finally, cap prices are obtained using the transforms in Duffie et al. (2000) applied under various forward measures. The model is estimated using cap data and a variant of the implied-state GMM methods proposed by Pan (2002) (see Section 15.3).

16.3. Risk Factors and Derivatives Pricing

Much of the recent literature applying DTSMs to the pricing of derivatives has focused on two features of the distributions of swap rates and implied volatilities on LIBOR-based derivatives. First, a substantial portion of the variation in the prices of options on fixed-income securities is uncorrelated with the variation in the prices of the underlying bonds on which the options are based. Second, developing a model that prices various types of options written on the same underlying securities has been challenging, particularly for the case of caps and swaptions. We briefly review each of these puzzles prior to discussing the econometric studies of derivative pricing models.

16.3.1. Unspanned Stochastic Volatility

Heidari and Wu (2003) document that the common interest rate factors that explain more than 99% of the variation in the yield curve can explain less than 60% of the variation in swaption implied volatilities. These results come from examining yields on LIBOR contracts with maturities ranging between 1 and 12 months; interest rate swaps with maturities ranging between 2 and 30 years; and at-the-money (ATM) swaptions on 1- up to 10-year swap contracts with maturities of 1, 3, and 6 months. Their sample period was from October 1995 to July 2001.

The interest rate factors—the first three principal components of LIBOR and swap yields—have the familiar interpretation of "level," "slope," and "curvature" factors (see Chapter 12). To these three factors they add three volatility-related factors extracted from the swaptions data. Adding these sequentially to the interest rate factors increases the average variation of implied volatilities explained to 85, 96, and almost 98%, respectively. Thus, their findings suggest that a large fraction of the variation in implied volatilities on swaption contracts is largely uncorrelated with the sources of variation in the underlying swap rates.

Similarly, Collin-Dufresne and Goldstein (2002a) explore how much of the variation in straddles (of ATM caps and floors) can be explained by the variation in swap rates. These authors focus on straddles because they are relatively insensitive to small changes in the level of yields while being highly sensitive to changes in bond-price volatility. The data for their analysis were the 6-month LIBOR rate and swap rates for 1 through 10 years to maturity from the United States, United Kingdom, and Japan; and straddles ranging in maturity from 6 months to 10 years for the United States, and 6 months to 11 years for the United Kingdom and Japan. Their sample period was February 1995 through December 2000.

When they regressed the changes in straddle prices on changes in swap rates, they obtained relatively low (adjusted) R^2's: 0.085–0.391% for the United States, -0.071–0.134% for the United Kingdom, and 0.044–0.254% for Japan. To put these low numbers in perspective, the authors simulated data from an estimated $A_1(3)$ affine DTSM and used these data to rerun the regressions. They obtained R^2 of roughly 90%, clearly well above those observed in the historical data. Based on this evidence, the authors conclude that bonds do not span the fixed-income markets, and specifically floors and caps seem to be sensitive to stochastic volatility, which cannot be hedged by a position solely in bonds.

To better understand the nature of this unspanned stochastic volatility (USV), Collin-Dufresne and Goldstein (2002a) construct the principal components of the covariance matrix of the residuals from their historical regressions of straddle prices on swap yields. The first PC explained more than 80% of this residual variation and the second explained an additional 10% or more for all three countries. Thus, the portions of the option prices that are not spanned by the bond yields appear to have a common factor that accounts for most of their variations. Of course, this USV puzzle, though striking, is not logically inconsistent with arbitrage-free pricing. We saw in Section 12.3.2 that factors can affect the distribution of the short rate r, but not the yields on bonds of all maturities.

Fan et al. (2003) raise several caveats about interpreting the empirical evidence in the studies by Collin-Dufresne and Goldstein (2002a) and Heidari and Wu (2003) as indicative of USV or, more generally, economically incomplete markets. First, an ATM straddle has a highly convex payout structure while at the same time being nearly delta neutral with respect to changes in the underlying bond yields. The latter property implies that shocks (at least small ones) to the PCs of swap rates should have small effects on the prices of straddles. Large shocks to bond yields, on the other hand, will have an effect through the nonlinear (highly convex) dependence of straddles on their underlying risk factors. Second, in assessing the degree of economic incompleteness of a market, one is interested in how changes in the prices of straddles are related to changes in the prices of traded securities. Changes in swap rates do not correspond to the changes in prices of relevant replicating portfolios of bonds. It remains an empirical question then as to whether DTSMs with low-dimensional factor structures are capable of describing the time-series behavior of derivatives prices.

16.3.2. Relative Pricing of Caps and Swaptions

Though financial theory predicts a close link between the prices of caps and swaptions (as they are both LIBOR-based derivatives), developing a model that simultaneously prices both contracts has proved challenging. Explanations for this "swaption/cap puzzle" often focus on the nature of the model-implied factor volatilities and/or correlations and their roles in determining prices. For instance, Rebonato and Cooper (1997) and Longstaff et al. (2001b) compare the correlations among forward swap rates with those implied by low-dimensional factor models and find that the correlations implied by the models are much larger than those in the data. Brown and Schaefer (1999) and Carverhill (2002) find similar results using Treasury strip yields.

We can anticipate the difficulty standard DTSMs have in matching yield correlations by comparing historical and model-implied correlations among weekly changes in the yield spreads for nonoverlapping segments of the U.S. dollar swap yield curve. The correlation 3–2/4–3, for example, in Table 16.1 represents the correlation of daily changes in the 3-year–2-year swap spread with changes in the 4-year–3-year spread. The rows labeled 2 PC and 4 PC

Table 16.1. Correlations of Changes in Swap Yield Spreads for Various Yield-Curve Segments

Segment	3–2/4–3	4–3/5–4	5–4/7–5	7–5/10–7
Historical	0.34	0.09	0.13	0.14
2 PC	0.99	0.99	0.99	0.99
4 PC	0.81	0.96	0.84	0.32

Note: 3–2/4–3, for example, indicates the correlation between changes in the 3-year–2-year yield spread and the 4-year–3-year yield spread.

present the corresponding correlations for fitted spreads from projections onto the first two and four principal components (PCs), respectively. Notably, even using four PCs the segment correlations are larger than their sample counterparts, and the match is much worse using only two PCs (in the spirit of a two-factor DTSM).

Not surprisingly, when we compute model-implied segment correlations from the affine $A_M(N)$ models with $N \leq 3$, using swap data, they are all substantially larger than their historical counterparts. The same is true for the fitted, relative to the historical, treasury yields from the study of QG models by Ahn et al. (2002).

Closely related to this swaptions/caps pricing puzzle, many have found that model-implied volatilities extracted from cap prices tend to be larger than those backed out from swaption prices. One interpretation of this puzzle is based on the observation that a cap can be viewed as a portfolio of options on forward LIBOR rates, whereas a swaption can be viewed as an option on a portfolio of forward LIBOR rates. As such, cap prices are relatively insensitive to the correlation structure of forward LIBOR rates, whereas the swaption prices depend crucially on the correlation structure. Indeed, a one-factor model can be calibrated exactly to all ATM cap prices, but it will likely misprice swaptions because forward rates are perfectly correlated in such a model. If swaptions and caps have different sensitivities to a model's (in)ability to match yield curve segments or forward-rate correlations, then this could resolve the pricing puzzles. However, the literature is not fully in agreement about the relative responses of the prices of caps and swaptions to changes in factor volatilities or correlations.

16.4. Affine Models of Derivatives Prices

Empirical work addressing the fit of DTSMs to the joint distributions of swap and swaption prices has been limited. Upon fitting an $A_3(3)$ model (with independent factors) to historical swap yields, Jagannathan et al. (2003) find that their model is incapable of accurately pricing caps and swaptions.[8] However, in the light of the preceding discussion, reliable pricing of swaptions would seem to depend on using swaption data in estimation in order to "pick up" the effectively unspanned factors. That is, if one fits an $A_M(3)$ model, for example, to swap rates alone, then the likelihood function tends to select factors that (suitably rotated) are highly correlated with the first three PCs of swap rates. Including option prices directly changes the "weight" given by the likelihood function to matching the structure of volatility and will likely lead to a different factor structure.

---

[8] To value the swaptions, Jagannathan et al. (2003) use a method developed by Chen and Scott (1995) that is specific to multifactor $A_N(N)$ (CIR) models.

This is confirmed by Umantsev (2001), who estimated $A_M(3)$ models using data on swap rates and swaption volatilities simultaneously over the sample period 1997 though 2001. He finds that $A_M(3)$ models, for $M = 1, 2$, fit the data notably better than an $A_3(3)$ model. Moreover, as anticipated by the descriptive findings of Heidari and Wu (2003), the third factor is related more to volatility in the swaption market than to "curvature" in the swap curve (the more typical third factor in DTSMs fit to yield data alone). Relating Umantsev's findings back to those of Collin-Dufresne et al. (2004), the latter study found that the third factor (beyond the first two PCs of bond yields) in $A_1(3)$ models was either the curvature factor or a proxy for the volatility of the short rate. However, with only three factors, an $A_1(3)$ model was not capable of matching both the curvature factor and the volatility factor. By explicitly including the implied volatilities of options into his ML estimation, Umantsev effectively forced selection of a volatility factor as the third factor. The results of Collin-Dufresne et al. suggest that adding a fourth factor may allow a match to both the curvature factor and the common volatility factor that Heidari and Wu found in swaption volatilities.

16.5. Forward-Rate-Based Pricing Models

Longstaff et al. (2001a) examined data on swap rates between July 1992 and July 1999, and a cross section of thirty-four swaptions and cap prices from January 1997 to July 1999. Working with a four-factor ($N = 4$) model, the first three eigenvectors, constructed from the $\mathbb{P}$-covariance matrix of the forwards, were the familiar level, slope, and curvature factors, and the fourth factor affected the very short end of the yield curve.[9] In this regard, they extended the complementary analysis in Hull and White (2000), where a three-factor LMM was examined.

The probability model for forward rates was obtained by solving for the eigenvalues in Φ (from the decomposition $\Sigma = U\Phi U'$ of the covariance matrix of forward rates) that minimized the pricing errors for the swaptions. This minimization was done cross sectionally so Φ was updated every week. The temporal variation in the elements of Φ suggests the presence of time-varying conditional second moments of the forward rates, a feature of the data that was not formally taken into account in the pricing of swaptions or caps. The presence of such stochastic volatility/correlation motivates the analyses of Collin-Dufresne and Goldstein (2001b) and Han (2004).

Longstaff et al. found that their four-factor model did a quite good job of matching the cross section of thirty-four swaption prices, except during the fall of 1998 period, when Russia defaulted on its domestic debt.

---

[9] See Chapter 13 for a discussion of the role of this factor in explaining the properties of the very short end (under 1 year) of the yield curve.

However, when they used the model calibrated to swaption prices to price
ATM caps, they found mean pricing errors ranging from 23% for 2-year caps
to 5% for 5-year caps, with caps being undervalued relative to swaptions.

In a more systematic study of forward-rate and LIBOR market models
Driessen et al. (2003) examine the effect of the number of factors on the
pricing and hedging of caps and swaptions. Their HJM-style models have

$$df(t, T) = \mu_f(t, T, \omega)dt + \sum_{i=1}^{K} \sigma_{f,i}(t, T, \omega) \, dW_i(t). \tag{16.21}$$

For their LMM, LIBOR rates are assumed to follow the processes

$$dL_n(t) = \ldots dt + \sum_{i=1}^{K} \sigma_{L,i}(t, n, \omega)L_n(t)dW_i(t). \tag{16.22}$$

Up to three-factor models are considered with the time-homogeneous vola-
tility specifications: a parametric HJM model in which $\sigma_{f,i}(T-t) = \sigma_i e^{\kappa_i(T-t)}$;
and an LMM in which $\sigma_{L,i}(T-t) = h_i(T-t)$, where the h_i are deterministic
functions. The data set for this analysis covers money market and swap rates,
swaptions, and caps for the period January 1995 to June 1999. In both the
HJM and LIBOR market models, the three factors resemble the standard
PCs of swap yields, level, slope, and curvature, which together explain more
than 96% of the variation in yields.

The smallest pricing errors are obtained for the models estimated over
rolling windows, so that parameters are allowed to change over time. Further, incorporation of the options data directly into the estimation improves
the fit of both the cap and swaption pricing models. Consistent with previous studies, the three-factor model of Driessen et al. (the largest number of
factors considered) fits the best.

Jarrow et al. (2004) use cap price data from SwapPX to examine volatility smiles in fixed-income derivatives markets. The smile is asymmetric with
ITM caps having a stronger skew than OTM caps. Furthermore, the smile
is more pronounced after September 2001. Particular attention is given to
the relative performance of alternative LMMs in explaining these smiles.
Toward this end, the authors used data on caps of maturities from 1 to 10
years and ten different strike prices, and they divide their sample period
into four subsamples: September 2000 to March 2001, March 2001 to August
2001, November 2001 to May 2002, and May 2002 to November 2002.

Consistent with previous studies using similar models, the first three
principal components underlying the construction of Σ_t corresponded to
the level, slope, and curvature of the LIBOR yield curve. Based on cap
data for the sample period June 1997 through July 2000, the level factor

had the most volatile stochastic volatility (v_{it}), and the slope factor was the least volatile. Allowing all three factors to have stochastic volatilities led to notably smaller pricing errors for caps than when a subset of the three factors had constant volatilities. However, even in their most flexible model with stochastic volatility, they found significant underpricing of ITM and overpricing of OTM caps. These patterns suggest a potentially important role for jumps and are indicative of misspecification of previous LMMs with constant or stochastic volatility and no jumps (e.g., Longstaff et al., 2001a, and Han, 2004).

The model in Jarrow et al. with stochastic volatility is not capable of capturing a volatility smile because the volatility factors underlying Φ_t and the Brownian motions $W_n^{\mathbb{P}}(t)$ driving forward rates are mutually independent. We saw in Sections 7.7 and 15.4 that negative correlation between volatility and price shocks is a potentially important contributor to skewness in returns and smile in equity options markets. However, in equity markets, this "leverage" effect does not generate sufficient skewness to match the observed smile in implied volatilities of options.

Introducing jumps in LIBOR rates (while preserving the independence between LIBOR and volatility shocks) substantially improves the fit of the LMM. Analogously to prior findings for equity markets, introducing jumps lowers volatilities of the factors v_i. At the same time, there is evidence of large negative jumps in LIBOR rates under the forward measure. The estimated arrival intensities of jumps were between 2 and 6% per year with very large mean relative jumps sizes (between -50 and -90%).

16.6. On Model-Based Hedging

An alternative, informative means of assessing model performance, apart from the magnitudes of pricing errors, is the effectiveness of hedge positions based on an estimated model. This approach to model assessment seems particularly relevant in this literature because of the ongoing debates about the importance of unspanned risk factors in the bond markets. The low correlations between the PCs of bond yields and implied option volatilities suggest, at first glance, that hedges of option positions constructed from bond positions should be ineffective against key sources of risk in the options markets.

Longstaff et al. (2001a) used their four-factor model and the nested Black model to compute hedge ratios for each of the swaptions in their data base. From these ratios, they computed hedging errors, defined to be the change in swaption price less the change in value of the hedge portfolio. For the Black model, each swaption has its own hedge instrument (the underlying swap rate), whereas in the four-factor model there are only four common instruments. Nevertheless, the performance of the two models

Table 16.2.   *Root-Mean-Squared Errors (in Basis Points) of the Hedged and Unhedged*
Portfolios 1 Week Out-of-Sample, with and without recalibration of the Models

| | | | Number of factors in the model | | | | | | | |
| | | | With recalibration | | | | Without recalibration | | | |
Expiry (years)	Swap maturity (years)	Unhedged swaption	1	2	3	4	1	2	3	4
1	2	13.1	5.5	3.3	3.3	3.2	6.1	3.9	3.9	3.8
	3	18.9	6.6	4.4	4.1	4.6	7.1	4.8	4.7	4.8
	4	24.1	7.8	5.7	5.4	5.7	8.5	6.4	6.3	6.3
	5	28.9	8.4	6.5	6.3	6.2	8.8	7.0	6.8	6.7
5	2	10.8	5.5	4.0	3.9	4.5	5.9	4.3	4.3	4.5
	3	16.4	7.9	5.7	5.8	5.7	8.4	6.2	6.2	6.2
	4	21.5	10.1	7.2	7.2	7.1	10.7	7.9	7.9	7.9
	5	26.3	12.0	8.6	8.6	9.5	12.6	9.3	9.3	11.2
R^2, 1 week out-of-sample			0.83	0.92	0.92	0.91	0.80	0.90	0.90	0.90
R^2, 4 weeks out-of-sample			0.67	0.86	0.92	0.91	0.62	0.80	0.86	0.86

Source: Fan et al. (2003).

was almost indistinguishable (89.28 versus 89.35% of variability explained). Notably, a large percentage of the variation in changes in swaption prices was explained by the hedge portfolios.

The question of whether a small number of hedge instruments might lead to effective hedges for swaptions is the primary focus of the analysis in Fan et al. (2003). Table 16.2 shows the absolute hedging errors (in basis points)[10] for biweekly swaption data from March 1, 1998, to October 31, 2000. The number of factors N is the number of factors underlying the covariation in forward LIBOR rates, and it determines the number of instruments used to construct the hedge portfolios. The difference between the columns with and without "recalibration" is that in the former case the parameters are recalibrated every week, whereas in the latter case they are fixed for 4 weeks at the values used for the first week of hedging.

The results show a substantial decline in the root mean-squared errors of the hedged positions with the addition of factors out to $N = 3$. The improvement in hedging performance with the addition of one more factor ($N = 4$) is economically small and statistically insignificant. Furthermore, the (unadjusted) R^2 show that, for a 1-week horizon, the hedges account for more than 90% of the variation in the unhedged positions. Even over horizons of 4 weeks, the percentage of the variation in the unhedged positions explained by the hedges remains large.

[10] The authors multiply the root mean square of the hedging errors for a contract by 10,000 so that it becomes interpretable as a basis point error.

Fan et al. (2003) repeat their hedging analysis with straddles, motivated in large part by the earlier findings by Collin-Dufresne and Goldstein (2002a) that a significant fraction of the variation of changes in the prices of straddles was unrelated to variation in swap rates. Again they find that large percentages (over 80%) of the variation of the unhedged straddle positions were explained by the bond-based hedge portfolios. Fan et al. argue that a primary reason for the difference between their findings and those of Collin-Dufresne and Goldstein is that they are using actual traded bonds to construct hedges rather than running regressions of straddle prices on swap yields. Indeed, when Fan et al. regressed the corresponding straddle volatilities (computed from swaption contracts as opposed to cap contracts) onto swap yields, they obtained low R^2's, comparable to those reported in Collin-Dufresne and Goldstein (2002a) for their analysis of straddle prices. Overall Fan et al. (2003) conclude that the role of USV in understanding the prices of LIBOR-based derivatives is likely to be economically small.

Driessen et al. (2003) undertake a similar analysis of hedging, examining both caps and swaptions and a wider variety of models and methods for computing hedge ratios. They also find that a large percentage of the variation in prices of unhedged positions in derivatives is explained by changes in the prices of hedge portfolios constructed from bonds. However, these percentages are smaller than those documented by Fan et al. As a result, the authors reach a more measured conclusion regarding the potential importance of USV, noting a potentially important role for stochastic volatility and jumps in understanding the behavior of cap and swaption prices.

16.7. Pricing Eurodollar Futures Options

A different perspective on the pricing of fixed-income derivatives is offered by the study of Bikbov and Chernov (2004) of options on Eurodollar futures contracts. These authors examine $A_0(3)$, $A_1(3)$, and $A_1(3)$–USV affine DTSMs estimated using weekly data on Eurodollar futures and options over the sample period January 1994 through June 2001. The model with USV is obtained by imposing the constraints on the canonical $A_1(3)$ model that lead to the volatility factor having no effect on bond prices for all maturities (see Collin-Dufresne and Goldstein, 2002a, and Section 12.3.2). The market prices of risk were of the form proposed by Cheridito et al. (2003) as an extension of Duffee's (2002) essentially affine formulation (see Chapter 12). Call prices were computed using the transform results in Duffie et al. (2000). All of the futures and options contracts were allowed to be priced with errors (no contracts were priced perfectly by the models), and estimation was accomplished using QML and Kalman filtering.

When only futures data were used in estimation, signified by the superscript "f," Bikbov and Chernov found that the volatility factor is highly correlated with a "butterfly" Eurodollar futures position (long the 6-month and 10-year futures and short two times the 2-year futures) for model $A_1(3)^f$, while in model $A_1(3)^f$–USV it was most highly correlated with the long end of the futures curve. Thus, imposing the USV constraint seems to effect a factor rotation, a feature of constraints that we discussed in Chapter 13. When both options and futures data were used in estimation, signified by the superscript "fo," the volatility factor was most highly correlated with the slope of the futures curve (10-year minus 6-month futures) in model $A_1(3)^{fo}$, while it was highly correlated with the implied variance from the options market in model $A_1(3)^{fo}$–USV. Thus, only in this final model did the authors find that the volatility factor is closely matched to the implied volatility in the options market. Perhaps the most surprising aspect of these results is the labeling of the factors for model $A_1(3)^{fo}$. One might have expected, as for example in Umantsev (2001), that inclusion of options prices in the estimation would lead to at least one of the factors matching up closely with the implied volatilities in this market.

Of particular interest to the issues raised in this chapter about risk factors in cash and options markets is Bikbov and Chernov's formal analysis of the USV restrictions on model $A_1(3)$. Comparing models $A_1(3)^{fo}$ to model $A_1(3)^{fo}$–USV, they find a notable deterioration in the fit (measured by pricing errors) for *both* the futures and the options data. The percentage errors in options prices are more than twice as large at the 6-month expiration and more than six times as large at the 1-year expiration. Formal likelihood ratio tests of the USV constraints also indicate rejection at conventional significance levels.

Furthermore, a familiar tension arises: the models are able to fit certain moments at the expense of others. The $A_1(3)$ models "fo" without USV match the kurtosis in the data quite well, but fail to match the historical volatilities. Imposing the USV constraints increases this tension relative to that in the canonical $A_1(3)$ model.

References

Abel, A. (1990). Asset Prices under Habit Formation and Catching Up with the Jones. *American Economic Review Paper and Proceedings* **80**, 38–42.

Ahn, C., and H. Thompson (1988). Jump Diffusion Processes and Term Structure of Interest Rates. *Journal of Finance* **43**, 155–174.

Ahn, D., and B. Gao (1999). A Parametric Nonlinear Model of Term Structure Dynamics. *Review of Financial Studies* **12**, 721–762.

Ahn, D., R. Dittmar, and A. Gallant (2002). Quadratic Term Structure Models: Theory and Evidence. *Review of Financial Studies* **15**, 243–288.

Ahn, D., R. Dittmar, B. Gao, and A. Gallant (2003). Purebred or Hybrid? Reproducing the Volatility in Term Structure Dynamics. *Journal of Econometrics* **116**, 147–180.

Ait-Sahalia, Y. (1996). Testing Continuous-Time Models of the Spot Interest Rate. *Review of Financial Studies* **9**(2), 385–426.

——— (2001). Closed-Form Likelihood Expansions for Multivariate Diffusions. Working Paper, Princeton University.

——— (2002). Maximum-Likelihood Estimation of Discretely-Sampled Diffusions: A Closed-Form Approximation Approach. *Econometrica* **70**, 223–262.

Ait-Sahalia, Y., and A. W. Lo (1998). Nonparametric Estimation of State-Price Densities Implicit in Financial Asset Prices. *Journal of Finance* **53**, 499–547.

——— (2000). Nonparametric Risk Management and Implied Risk Aversion. *Journal of Econometrics* **94**, 9–51.

Akaike, H. (1973). Information Theory and an Extension of the Likelihood Principle. In B. Petrov and F. Csaki (Eds.), *Proceedings of the Second International Symposium of Information Theory*. Budapest: Akademiai Kiado.

Altman, E., and V. Kishore (1998). Defaults and Returns on High Yield Bonds: Analysis through 1997. Working Paper, New York University Salomon Center.

Alvarez, F., and U. Jermann (2001). Quantitative Asset Pricing Implications of Endogenous Solvency Constraints. *Review of Financial Studies* **14**, 1117–1151.

Amato, J., and E. Remolona (2003). The Credit Spread Puzzle. *BIS Quarterly Review December*, 51–63.

———— (2005). The Pricing of Unexpected Credit Losses. Working Paper, Bank for International Settlements.

Amemiya, T. (1974). The Nonlinear Two-Stage Least-Squares Estimator. *Journal of Econometrics* 2, 105–110.

———— (1985). *Advanced Econometrics.* Cambridge: Harvard University Press.

Amin, K. I., and A. J. Morton (1994). Implied Volatility Function in Arbitrage-Free Term Structure Models. *Journal of Financial Economics* 35, 141–180.

Andersen, T., and J. Lund (1997a). Estimating Continuous Time Stochastic Volatility Models of the Short Term Interest Rate. *Journal of Econometrics* 72, 343–337.

———— (1997b). Estimating Continuous-Time Stochastic Volatility Models of the Short-Term Interest Rate. *Journal of Econometrics* 72, 343–377.

———— (1998). Stochastic Volatility and Mean Drift in the Short Term Interest Rate Diffusion: Sources of Steepness, Level and Curvature in the Yield Curve. Working Paper, Northwestern University.

Andersen, T., H. Chung, and B. Sorensen (1999a). Efficient Method of Moments Estimation of a Stochastic Volatility Model: A Monte Carlo Study. *Journal of Econometrics* 91, 61–87.

Andersen, T. G., H.-J. Chung, and B. E. Sorensen (1999b). Efficient Method of Moments Estimation of a Stochastic Volatility Model: A Monte Carlo Study. *Journal of Econometrics* 91, 61–87.

Andersen, T., L. Benzoni, and J. Lund (2002). An Empirical Investigation of Continuous-Time Equity Return Models. *Journal of Finance* 57, 1239–1284.

Anderson, E., L. Hansen, and T. Sargent (2000). Robustness, Detection and the Price of Risk. Working Paper, University of North Carolina.

Anderson, R. W., and S. M. Sundaresan (1996). The Design and Valuation of Debt Contracts. *Review of Financial Studies* 9, 37–68.

Andrews, D. W. (1991). Heteroskedasticity and Autocorrelation Consistent Covariance Matrix Estimation. *Econometrica* 59, 817–858.

Ang, A., and G. Bekaert (2002). Regime Switches in Interest Rates. *Journal of Business and Economic Statistics* 20, 163–182.

———— (2003a). Stock Return Predictability: Is It There? Working Paper, Columbia University.

———— (2003b). The Term Structure of Real Rates and Expected Inflation. Working Paper, Columbia University.

Ang, A., and M. Piazzesi (2003). A No-Arbitrage Vector Autoregression of Term Structure Dynamics with Macroeconomic and Latent Variables. *Journal of Monetary Economics* 50, 745–787.

Ang, A., G. Bekaert, and J. Liu (2005a). Why Stocks May Disappoint. *Journal of Financial Economics* **76**, 471–508.

Ang, A., S. Dong, and M. Piazzesi (2005b). No-Arbitrage Taylor Rules. Working Paper, Columbia University.

Artzner, P., and F. Delbaen (1995). Default Risk Insurance and Incomplete Markets. *Mathematical Finance* **5**, 187–195.

Back, K. (1996). Yield Curve Models: A Mathematical Review. In I. Nelkin (Ed.), *Option Embedded Bonds: Price Analysis, Credit Risk, and Investment Strategies*. Chicago: Irwin.

Backus, D. K., and S. E. Zin (1994). Reverse Engineering the Yield Curve. NBER Working Paper 4676.

Backus, D., S. Foresi, and C. Telmer (1998a). Discrete-Time Models of Bond Pricing. Working Paper, New York University.

Backus, D., S. Foresi, and S. Zin (1998b). Arbitrage Opportunities in Arbitrage-Free Models of Bond Pricing. *Journal of Business and Economic Statistics* **16**, 13–26.

Backus, D., S. Foresi, A. Mozumdar, and L. Wu (2001). Predictable Changes in Yields and Forward Rates. *Journal of Financial Economics* **59**, 281–311.

Backus, D., B. Routledge, and S. Zin (2004). Exotic Preferences for Macro-economists. NBER Working Paper 10597.

Baille, R., and T. Bollerslev (1989). The Message in Daily Exchange Rates: A Conditional Variance Tale. *Journal of Business and Econmic Statistics* **7**, 297–305.

Bakshi, G., and Z. Chen (1996). The Spirit of Capitalism and Stock Market Prices. *American Economic Review* **86**, 133–157.

Bakshi, G., and N. Kapadia (2003). Volatility Risk Premium Embedded in Individual Equity Options: Some New Insights. *The Journal of Derivatives* Fall, 45–54.

Bakshi, G., and D. Madan (2000). Spanning and Derivative-Security Valuation. *Journal of Financial Economics* **55**, 205–238.

Bakshi, G., C. Cao, and Z. Chen (1997). Empirical Performance of Alternative Option Pricing Models. *Journal of Finance* **52**, 2003–2049.

Bakshi, G., D. Madan, and F. Zhang (2001). Understanding the Role of Recovery in Default Risk Models: Empirical Comparisons and Implied Recovery Rates. Working Paper, Federal Reserve Board.

Bakshi, G., N. Kapadia, and D. Madan (2003). Stock Return Characteristics, Skew Laws, and the Differential Pricing of Individual Equity Options. *Review Of Financial Studies* **16**, 101–143.

Bakshi, G., D. Madan, and F. Zhang (2004). Investigating the Sources of Default Risk: Lessons from Empirically Evaluating Credit Risk Models. Working Paper, University of Maryland.

Balduzzi, P., and Y. Eom (2000). Non-linearities in U.S. Treasury Rates: A Semi-Nonparametric Approach. Working Paper, Boston College.

Balduzzi, P., S. R. Das, S. Foresi, and R. K. Sundaram (1996). A Simple Approach to Three Factor Affine Term Structure Models. *Journal of Fixed Income* **6**, 43–53.

Balduzzi, P., S. R. Das, and S. Foresi (1998). The Central Tendency: A Second Factor in Bond Yields. *Review of Economics and Statistics* **80**, 62–72.

Bansal, R., and A. Yaron (2004). Risks for the Long Run: A Potential Resolution of Asset Pricing Puzzles. *Journal of Finance* **59**, 1481–1509.

Bansal, R., and H. Zhou (2002). Term Structure of Interest Rates with Regime Shifts. *Journal of Finance* **57**, 1997–2043.

Bansal, R., R. Gallant, and G. Tauchen (2004). Rational Pessimism, Rational Exuberance, and Markets for Macro Risks. Working Paper, Duke University.

Banz, R. (1981). The Relationship Between Return and Market Value of Common Stocks. *Journal of Financial Economics* **9**, 3–18.

Banz, R., and M. Miller (1978). Prices for State-Contingent Claims: Some Estimates and Applications. *Journal of Business* **51**, 653–672.

Barberis, N., and M. Huang (2001). Mental Accounting, Loss Aversion, and Individual Stock Returns. *Journal of Finance* **61**, 1247–1292.

Basu, S. (1983). The Relationship Between Earning Yield, Market Value, and Return for NYSE Common Stocks: Further Evidence. *Journal of Financial Economics* **12**, 129–156.

Basu, S., and A. Dassios (1999). Approximating Prices of Bonds with Log-Normal Interest Rate. Working Paper, London School of Economics.

Bates, D. (1996). Jumps and Stochastic Volatility: Exchange Rate Processes Implicit in PHLX Deutschemake Options. *Review of Financial Studies* **9**, 69–107.

——— (2000). Post-'87 Crash Fears in the S&P500 Futures Option Market. *Journal Of Econometrics* **94**, 181–238.

Beaglehole, D. R., and M. S. Tenney (1991). General Solutions of Some Interest Rate–Contingent Claim Pricing Equations. *Journal of Fixed Income* September, 69–83.

Bekaert, G., and R. Hodrick (2001). Expectations Hypotheses Tests. *Journal of Finance* **56**, 1357–1394.

Bekaert, G., and J. Liu (2004). Conditioning Bounds Information and Variance on Pricing Kernels. *Review of Financial Studies* **17**, 339–378.

Bekaert, G., R. Hodrick, and D. Marshall (1997). On Biases in Tests of the Expectations Hypothesis of the Term Structure of Interest Rates. *Journal of Financial Economics* **44**, 309–348.

Bekaert, G., E. Engstrom, and S. Grenadier (2004). Stock and Bond Returns with Moody Investors. Working Paper, Stanford University.

Bekaert, G., S. Cho, and A. Moreno (2005). New-Keynesian Macroeconomics and the Term Structure. Working Paper, Columbia University.

Benzoni, L., P. Collin-Dufresne, and R. Goldstein (2005). Can Standard

Preferences Explain the Prices of Out-of-the-Money S&P500 Put Options? Working Paper, University of Minnesota.

Bernanke, B. (1990). On the Predictive Power of Interest Rates and Interest Rate Spreads. *New England Economic Review* Nov/Dec, 51–68.

Berndt, A., R. Douglas, D. Duffie, M. Ferguson, and D. Schranzk (2004). Measuring Default Risk Premia from Default Swap Rates and EDFs. Working Paper, Stanford University.

Berndt, E., and N. Savin (1977). Conflict among Criteria for Testing in the Multivariate Linear Regression Model. *Econometrica* **45**, 1263–1278.

Bester, C. (2004). Random Field and Affine Models for Interest Rates: An Empirical Comparison. Working Paper, University of Chicago.

Bhar, R., and C. Chiarella (1997). Transformation of Heath-Jarrow-Morton Models to Markovian Systems. *European Journal of Finance* **3**, 1–26.

Bielecki, T., and M. Rutkowski (2004). Modeling of the Defaultable Term Structure: Conditionally Markov Approach. *IEEE Transactions on Automatic Control* **49**, 361–373.

Bikbov, R., and M. Chernov (2004). Term Structure and Volatility: Lessons from the Eurodollar Markets. Working Paper, Columbia Business School.

Billingsley, P. (1968). *Convergence of Probability Measures*. New York: Wiley.

Billingsley, P. (1979). *Probability and Measure*. New York: Wiley.

Bjork, T., and B. J. Christensen (1999). Interest Rate Dynamics and Consistent Forward Rates Curves. *Mathematical Finance* **9**(4), 323–348.

Bjork, T., and L. Svensson (2001). On the Existence of Finite-Dimensional Realizations for Nonlinear Forward Rate Models. *Mathematical Finance* **11**(2), 205–243.

Black, F. (1972). Capital Market Equilibrium with Restricted Borrowing. *Journal of Business* **45**, 444–454.

——— (1976). Studies in Stock Price Volatility Changes. In *Proceedings of the 1976 Meetings of the Business and Economic Statistics Section*, pp. 177–181. American Statistical Association.

Black, F., and J. Cox (1976). Valuing Corporate Securities: Liabilities: Some Effects of Bond Indenture Provisions. *Journal of Finance* **31**, 351–367.

Black, F., and P. Karasinski (1991). Bond and Option Pricing when Short Rates are Lognormal. *Financial Analysts Journal* **47**, 52–59.

Black, F., and M. Scholes (1973). The Pricing of Options and Corporate Liabilities. *Journal of Political Economy* **81**, 637–654.

Black, F., E. Derman, and W. Toy (1990). A One-Factor Model of Interest Rates and Its Application to Treasury Bond Options. *Financial Analysts Journal* **46**, 33–39.

Blume, M., and R. Stambaugh (1983). Biases in Computed Returns: An Application of the Size Effect. *Journal of Financial Economics* **12**, 387–404.

Bobadilla, G. (1999). Choose the Right Error in Term Structure Models. Working Paper, CEMFI.

Bollerslev, T. (1986). Generalized Autoregressive Conditional Heteroskedasticity. *Journal of Econometrics* **31**, 307–327.

——— (1987). A Conditionally Heteroskedastic Time Series Model for Speculative Prices and Rates of Return. *Review of Economics and Statistics* **69**, 542–547.

Bollerslev, T., and J. Wooldridge (1992). Quasi-Maximum Likelihood Estimation in Dynamic Models with Time-Varying Covariances. *Econometric Reviews* **11**, 143–172.

Bollerslev, T., R. Chou, and K. Kroner (1992). ARCH Modeling in Finance: A Review of Theory and Empirical Evidence. *Journal of Econometrics* **52**, 5–59.

Bollerslev, T., R. Engle, and D. Nelson (1994). ARCH Models. In R. Engle and D. McFadden (Eds.), *Handbook of Econometrics*, Volume IV. Amsterdam: Elsevier Science B.V.

Boudoukh, K., and M. Richardson (1993). The Statistics of Long-Horizon Regressions. *Mathematical Finance* **4**, 103–120.

Boudoukh, J., M. Richardson, and R. Whitelaw (1994). A Tale of Three Schools: Insights on Autocorrelations of Short-Horizon Stock Returns. *Review of Financial Studies* **7**, 539–573.

Boudoukh, J., M. Richardson, R. Stanton, and R. F. Whitelaw (1998). The Stochastic Behavior of Interest Rates: Implications from a Multifactor, Nonlinear Continuous-Time Model. Working Paper, New York University.

Brace, A., and M. Musiela (1994). A Multifactor Gauss Markov Implementation of Heath, Jarrow, and Morton. *Mathematical Finance* **4**, 259–283.

Brace, A., D. Gatarek, and M. Musiela (1997). The Market Model of Interest Rate Dynamics. *Mathematical Finance* **7**, 127–154.

Brandt, M., and D. Chapman (2002). Comparing Multifactor Models of the Term Structure. Working Paper, Duke University.

Brandt, M., and P. Santa-Clara (2001). Simulated Likelihood Estimation of Diffusions with an Application to Exchange Rate Dynamics in Incomplete Markets. Working Paper, Wharton School.

Brandt, M., and A. Yaron (2001). Time-Consistent, No-Arbitrage Models of the Term Structure. Working Paper, Wharton School.

Breeden, D. (1979). An Intertemporal Asset Pricing Model with Stochastic Consumption and Investment Opportunities. *Journal of Financial Economics* **7**, 265–296.

——— (1986). Consumption, Production, and Interest Rates: A Synthesis. *Journal of Financial Economics* **16**, 3–39.

Breeden, D., and R. Litzenberger (1978). Prices of State-Contingent Claims Implicit in Option Prices. *Journal of Finance* **51**, 621–651.

Breiman, L. (1968). *Probability*. Reading, Mass.: Addison-Wesley.

Brenner, R. J., R. H. Harjes, and K. F. Kroner (1996). Another Look at Models of the Short Term Interest Rate. *Journal of Financial & Quantitative Analysis* **31**(1), 85–107.

Breusch, T., and A. Pagan (1980). The Lagrange Multiplier Test and Its Application to Model Specification in Econometrics. *Review of Economic Studies* **47**, 239–254.

Brito, R., and R. Flores (2001). A Jump-Diffusion Yield-Factor Model of Interest Rates. Working Paper, EPGE/FGV.

Briys, E., and F. de Varenne (1997). Valuing Risky Fixed Rate Debt: An Extension. *Journal of Financial and Quantitative Analysis* **32**, 239–248.

Broadie, M., M. Chernov, and M. Johannes (2004). Model Specification and Risk Premiums: The Evidence from the Futures Options. Working Paper, Columbia University.

Brock, W. (1980). Asset Prices in a Production Economy. In J. J. McCall (Ed.), *The Economics of Uncertainty*. Chicago: University of Chicago Press.

Brown, D., and M. Gibbons (1985). A Simple Econometric Approach for Utility-Based Asset Pricing Models. *Journal of Finance* **40**, 359–381.

Brown, R. H., and S. M. Schaefer (1994). The Term Structure of Real Interest Rates and the Cox, Ingersoll and Ross Model. *Journal of Financial Economics* **35**, 3–42.

———— (1999). Why Long Forward Interest Rates (Almost) Always Slope Downwards. Working Paper, London Business School.

Brown, S. J., and P. H. Dybvig (1986). Empirical Implications of the Cox, Ingersoll, Ross Theory of the Term Structure of Interest Rates. *Journal of Finance* **41**, 143–172.

Buraschi, A., and F. Corielli (2000). Staying Ahead of the Curve: Model Risk and the Term Structure. Working Paper, London Business School.

Buraschi, A., and A. Jiltsov (2004). Time-Varying Inflation Risk Premia and the Expectations Hypothesis: A Monetary Model of the Treasury Yield Curve. *Journal of Financial Economics,* **75**, 429–490.

Cai, J. (1994). A Markov Model of Unconditional Variance in ARCH. *Journal of Business and Economic Statistics* **12**, 309–316.

Campbell, J. (1991). A Variance Decomposition for Stock Returns. *Economic Journal* **101**, 157–179.

———— (1993). Intertemporal Asset Pricing without Consumption Data. *American Economic Review* **83**, 487–512.

———— (1999). Asset Prices, Consumption, and the Business Cycle. In *Handbook of Macroeconomics*, Chapter 19, pp. 1–72. Amsterdam: Elsevier Science B.V.

Campbell, J., and J. Cochrane (1999). By Force of Habit: A Consumption-Based Explanation of Aggregate Stock Market Behavior. *Journal of Political Economy* **107**, 205–251.

Campbell, J., and J. Cochrane (2000). Explaining the Poor Performance of Consumption-Based Asset Pricing Models. *Journal of Finance* **55**, 2863–2878.

Campbell, J., and R. Shiller (1988). Stock Prices, Earnings, and Expected Dividends. *Journal of Finance* **43**, 661–676.

——— (1989). The Dividend-Price Ratio and Expectations of Future Dividends and Discount Factors. *Review of Financial Studies* **1**, 195–228.

——— (1991). Yield Spreads and Interest Rate Movements: A Bird's Eye View. *Review of Economic Studies* **58**, 495–514.

Carrasco, M., M. Chernov, J. Florens, and E. Ghysels (2005). Efficient Estimation of Jump Diffusions and General Dynamic Models with a Continuum of Moment Conditions. Working Paper, University of North Carolina.

Carverhill, A. (1994). When Is the Short Rate Markovian. *Mathematical Finance* **4**, 305–312.

——— (2002). Predictability and the Dynamics of Long Forward Rates. Working Paper, University of Hong Kong.

Cathcart, L., and L. El-Jahel (1998). Valuation of Defaultable Bonds. *The Journal of Fixed Income* June, 66–78.

Chacko, G. (1999). Continuous-Time Estimation of Exponential Separable Term Structure Models: A General Approach. Working Paper, Harvard University.

Chacko, G., and S. Das (2001). Pricing Interest Rate Derivatives: A General Approach. *Review of Financial Studies* **15**, 195–241.

Chacko, G., and L. Viceira (2005). Dynamic Consumption and Portfolio Choice with Stochastic Volatility. *Review of Financial Studies* **18**, 1369–1402.

Chan, L., Y. Hamao, and J. Lakonishok (1991). Fundamentals and Stock Returns in Japan. *Journal of Finance* **46**, 1739–1789.

Chapman, D., and N. Pearson (2001). What Can be Learned From Recent Advances in Estimating Models of the Term Structure? *Financial Analysts Journal* **57**, 77–95.

Chen, L. (1996). *Stochastic Mean and Stochastic Volatility—A Three-Factor Model of the Term Structure of Interest Rates and Its Application to the Pricing of Interest Rate Derivatives.* Oxford: Blackwell.

Chen, L., P. Collin-Dufresne, and R. Goldstein (2005). On the Relation Betwen Credit Spread Puzzles and the Equity Premium Puzzle. Working Paper, University of California, Berkeley.

Chen, R., and L. Scott (1993). Maximum Likelihood Estimation for a Multifactor Equilibrium Model of the Term Structure of Interest Rates. *Journal of Fixed Income* **3**, 14–31.

Chen, R., and L. Scott (1995). Interest Rate Options in Multifactor Cox-

Ingersoll-Ross Models of the Term Structure. *Journal of Fixed Income* Winter, 53–72.

Cheridito, R., D. Filipovic, and R. Kimmel (2003). Market Price of Risk in Affine Models: Theory and Evidence. Working Paper, Princeton University.

Chernov, M., and E. Ghysels (2000). A Study towards a Unified Approach to the Joint Estimation of the Objective and Risk Neutral Measures for the Purpose of Option Valuation. *Journal of Financial Economics* **56**, 407–458.

Chernov, M., R. Gallant, E. Ghysels, and G. Tauchen (2000). A New Class of Stochastic Volatility Models with Jumps: Theory and Estimation. Working Paper, Columbia University.

Cheyette, O. (1994). Markov Representation of the Heath-Jarrow-Morton Model. Working Paper, BARRA Inc.

Christoffersen, P., F. Diebold, and T. Schuermann (1998). Horizon Problems and Extreme Events in Financial Risk Management. *Economic Policy Review, FRB New York* November, 109–118.

Chumacero, R. (1997). Finite Sample Properties of the Efficient Method of Moments. *Studies in Nonlinear Dynamics and Econometrics* **2**, 35–51.

Chung, K. (1974). *A Course in Probability Theory* (2nd edition). New York: Academic.

Clarida, R., J. Galí, and M. Gertler (1999). The Science of Monetary Policy: A New Keynesian Perspective. *Journal of Economic Literature* **37**, 1661–1707.

Cochrane, J. (1988). How Big is the Random Walk in GNP? *Journal of Political Economy* **96**, 893–920.

——— (1996). A Cross-Sectional Test of an Investment-Based Asset Pricing Model. *Journal of Political Economy* **104**, 572–621.

Cochrane, J., and L. Hansen (1992). Asset Pricing Explorations for Macroeconomics. In *NBER Macroeconomics Annual 1992*. Cambridge, MIT Press.

Cochrane, J., and M. Piazzesi (2005). Bond Risk Premia. *American Economic Review* **95**, 138–160.

Collin-Dufresne, P., and R. Goldstein (2001a). Do Credit Spreads Reflect Stationary Leverage Ratios? *Journal of Finance* **56**, 1929–1958.

——— (2001b). Stochastic Correlation and the Relative Pricing of Caps and Swaptions in a Generalized Affine Framework. Working Paper, Carnegie Mellon University.

——— (2002a). Do Bonds Span the Fixed Income Markets? Theory and Evidence for "Unspanned" Stochastic Volatility. *Journal of Finance* **57**, 1685–1730.

——— (2002b). Pricing Swaptions within an Affine Framework. *Journal of Derivatives* **10**, 1–18.

Collin-Dufresne, P., and B. Solnik (2000). On the Term Structure of Default Permia in the Swap and LIBOR Markets. *Journal of Finance* **56**, 1095–1115.

Collin-Dufresne, P., R. Goldstein, and C. Jones (2004). Can Interest Rate Volatility Be Extracted from the Cross Section of Bond Yields? An Investigation of Unspanned Stochastic Volatility. Working Paper, NBER 10756.

Collin-Dufresne, P., R. S. Goldstein, and J. Martin (2001). The Determinants of Credit Spread Changes. *Journal of Finance* **56**, 2177–2208.

Constantinides, G. (1990). Habit Formation: A Resolution of the Equity Premium Puzzle. *Journal of Political Economy* **98**, 519–543.

———— (1992). A Theory of the Nominal Term Structure of Interest Rates. *Review of Financial Studies* **5**, 531–552.

Cont, R. (2005). Modeling Term Structure Dynamics: An Infinite Dimensional Approach. *International Journal of Theoretical and Applied Finance* **8**, 357–380.

Corradi, V. (2000). Reconsidering the Continuous Time Limit of the GARCH(1,1) Process. *Journal of Econometrics* **96**, 145–153.

Cox, J., J. Ingersoll, and S. Ross (1980). An Analysis of Variable Loan Contracts. *Journal of Finance* **35**, 389–403.

———— (1985a). An Intertemporal General Equilibrium Model of Asset Prices. *Econometrica* **53**, 363–384.

———— (1985b). A Theory of the Term Structure of Interest Rates. *Econometrica* **53**, 385–407.

Dai, Q. (2001). Asset Pricing in a Neoclassical Model with Limited Participation. Working Paper, New York University.

———— (2003). Term Structure Dynamics in a Model with Stochastic Internal Habit. Working Paper, University of North Carolina.

Dai, Q., and K. Singleton (2000). Specification Analysis of Affine Term Structure Models. *Journal of Finance* **55**, 1943–1978.

———— (2002). Expectations Puzzles, Time-Varying Risk Premia, and Affine Models of the Term Structure. *Journal of Financial Economics* **63**, 415–441.

———— (2003a). Fixed-Income Pricing. In C. Constantinides, M. Harris, and R. Stulz (Eds.), *Handbook of Economics and Finance*. Amsterdam: North-Holland.

———— (2003b). Term Structure Dynamics in Theory and Reality. *Review of Financial Studies* **16**, 631–678.

Dai, Q., K. Singleton, and W. Yang (2003). Regime Shifts in a Dynamic Term Structure Model of U.S. Treasury Bond Yields. Working Paper, Stanford University.

Dai, Q., A. Le, and K. Singleton (2005). Nonlinear Dynamic Term Structure Models. Working Paper, New York University.

Daniel, K., and S. Titman (1997). Evidence on the Characteristics of Cross Sectional Variation in Stock Returns. *Journal of Finance* **52**, 1–33.

Da Prato, G., and Z. Zabczyk (1992). *Stochastic Equations in Infinite Dimensions.* New York: Cambridge University Press.

Darolles, S., C. Gourieroux, and J. Jasiak (2001). Compound Autoregressive Processes. Working Paper, CREST.

Das, S. (2002). The Surprise Element: Jumps in Interest Rates. *Journal of Econometrics* **106**, 27–65.

Das, S., and S. Foresi (1996). Exact Solutions for Bond and Option Prices with Systematic Jump Risk. *Review of Derivatives Research* **1**, 7–24.

Das, S., and R. Sundaram (1999). Of Smiles and Smirks: A Term Structure Perspective. *Journal of Financial and Quantitative Analysis* **34**, 211–239.

Das, S., D. Duffie, N. Kapadia, and L. Saita (2005). Common Failings: How Corporate Defaults Are Correlated. Working Paper, Stanford University.

Davis, J., E. Fama, and K. French (2000). Characteristics, Covariances, and Average Returns: 1929 to 1997. *Journal of Finance* **55**, 389–406.

DeGroot, M. (1970). *Optimal Statistical Decisions.* New York: McGraw-Hill.

Dickey, D., and W. Fuller (1979). Distribution of the Estimators for Autoregressive Time Series with a Unit Root. *Journal of the American Statistical Association* **74**, 427–431.

——— (1981). Likelihood Ratio Statistics for Autoregressive Time Series with a Unit Root. *Econometrica* **49**, 1057–1072.

Diebold, F., A. Inoue, A. Hickman, and T. Schuermann (1998). Scale Models. *Risk* **11**, 104–107.

Doob, J. (1953). *Stochastic Processes.* New York: Wiley.

Driessen, J. (2005). Is Default Event Risk Priced in Corporate Bonds? *Review of Financial Studies* **18**, 165–195.

Driessen, J., and P. Maenhout (2004). A Portfolio Perspective on Option Pricing Anomalies. Working Paper, University of Amsterdam.

Driessen, J., B. Melenberg, and T. Nijman (2000). Common Factors in International Bond Returns. Working Paper, Tilburg University.

Driessen, J., P. Klaassen, and B. Meleberg (2003). The Performance of Multi-Factor Term Structure Models for Pricing and Hedging Caps and Swaptions. *Journal of Financial and Quantitative Analysis* **38**, 635–672.

Drost, F., and T. Nijman (1993). Temporal Aggregation of GARCH Processes. *Econometrica* **61**, 909–927.

Duan, J. (1997). Augmented GARCH(p, q) Process and its Diffusion Limit. *Journal of Econometrics* **79**, 97–127.

Duan, J., and J. Simonato (1999). Estimating and Testing Exponential-Affine Term Structure Models by Kalman Filter. *Review of Quantitative Finance and Accounting* **13**, 111–135.

Duarte, J. (2004). Evaluating an Alternative Risk Preference in Affine Term Structure Models. *Review of Financial Studies* **17**, 379–404.

Duffee, G. (1999). Estimating the Price of Default Risk. *The Review of Financial Studies* **12**, 197–226.

——— (2002). Term Premia and Interest Rate Forecasts in Affine Models. *Journal of Finance* **57**, 405–443.

Duffee, G., and R. Stanton (2001). Estimation of Dynamic Term Structure Models. Working Paper, University of California, Berkeley.

Duffie, D. (1996). Special Repo Rates. *Journal of Finance* **51**, 493–526.

——— (1998). Defaultable Term Structure Models with Fractional Recovery of Par. Working Paper, Graduate School of Business, Stanford University.

——— (2001). *Dynamic Asset Pricing Theory* (3rd edition). Princeton: Princeton University Press.

Duffie, D., and P. Glynn (2004). Estimation of Continuous-Time Markov Processes Sampled at Random Times. *Econometrica* **72**, 1773–1808.

Duffie, D., and M. Huang (1996). Swap Rates and Credit Quality. *Journal of Finance* **51**, 921–949.

Duffie, D., and R. Kan (1996). A Yield-Factor Model of Interest Rates. *Mathematical Finance* **6**, 379–406.

Duffie, D., and D. Lando (2001). Term Structures of Credit Spreads with Incomplete Accounting Information. *Econometrica* **69**, 633–664.

Duffie, D., and J. Liu (2001). Floating-Fixed Credit Spreads. *Financial Analysts Journal* **57**, 76–88.

Duffie, D., and K. Singleton (1993). Simulated Moments Estimation of Markov Models of Asset Prices. *Econometrica* **61**, 929–952.

——— (1997). An Econometric Model of the Term Structure of Interest Rate Swap Yields. *Journal of Finance* **52**, 1287–1321.

——— (1999). Modeling Term Structures of Defaultable Bonds. *Review of Financial Studies* **12**, 687–720.

——— (2003). *Credit Risk*. Princeton: Princeton University Press.

Duffie, D., J. Pan, and K. Singleton (2000). Transform Analysis and Asset Pricing for Affine Jump-Diffusions. *Econometrica* **68**, 1343–1376.

Duffie, D., D. Filipovic, and W. Schachermayer (2003a). Affine Processes and Applications in Finance. *Annals of Applied Probability* **13**, 984–1053.

Duffie, D., L. Pedersen, and K. Singleton (2003b). Modeling Credit Spreads on Sovereign Debt: A Case Study of Russian Bonds. *Journal of Finance* **55**, 119–159.

Dullmann, K., and M. Windfuhr (2000). Credit Spreads between German and Italian Sovereign Bonds—Do One-Factor Affine Models Work? *Canadian Journal of Administrative Sciences* **17**, 166–181.

Dunn, K., and K. Singleton (1983). An Empirical Analysis of the Pricing of Mortgage Backed Securities. *Journal of Finance* **36**, 769–799.

——— (1986). Modeling the Term Structure of Interest Rates under Nonseparable Utility and Durability of Goods. *Journal of Financial Economics* **17**, 27–55.

Dybvig, P., and J. Ingersoll (1982). Mean-Variance Theory in Complete Markets. *Journal of Business* **55**, 233–251.

Eichenbaum, M., and L. Hansen (1990). Estimating Models with Intertemporal Substitution Using Aggregate Time Series Data. *Journal of Business and Economic Statistics* **8**, 53–69.

Eichenbaum, M., L. Hansen, and S. Richard (1987). The Dynamic Equilibrium Pricing of Durable Consumption Goods. Working Paper, Carnegie Mellon University.

Eichenbaum, M., L. Hansen, and K. Singleton (1988). A Time Series Analysis of Representative Agent Models of Consumption and Leisure Choice under Uncertainty. *Quarterly Journal of Economics* **103**, 51–78.

Elton, E., M. Gruber, D. Agrawal, and C. Mann (2001). Explaining the Rate Spread on Corporate Bonds. *Journal of Finance* **56**, 247–277.

Engle, R. (1982). Autoregressive Conditional Heteroskedasticity with Estimates of the Variance of U.K. Inflation. *Econometrica* **50**, 987–1008.

———— (1984). Wald, Likelihood Ratio, and Lagrange Multiplier Tests in Econometrics. In Z. Griliches and M. Intriligator (Eds.), *Handbook of Econometrics*, Volume II, pp. 776–826. Elsevier Science Publishers.

Eom, Y. (1998). An Efficient GMM Estimation of Continuous-Time Asset Dynamics: Implications for the Term Structure of Interest Rates. Working Paper, Yonsei University.

Eom, Y., J. Helwege, and J.-Z. Huang (2004). Structural Models of Corporate Bond Pricing: An Empirical Analysis. *Review of Financial Studies* **17**, 499–544.

Epstein, L., and S. Zin (1989). Substitution, Risk Aversion, and the Temporal Behavior of Consumption and Asset Returns: An Theoretical Framework. *Econometrica* **57**, 937–969.

———— (1991). Substitution, Risk Aversion, and the Temporal Behavior of Consumption and Asset Returns: An Empirical Investigation. *Journal of Political Economy* **99**, 263–286.

Eraker, B. (2004). Do Stock Prices and Volatility Jump? Reconciling Evidence from Spot and Option Prices. *Journal of Finance* **59**, 1367–1403.

Eraker, B., J. Johannes, and N. Polson (2003). The Impact of Jumps in Volatility and Returns. *Journal of Finance* **53**, 1269–1300.

Ericsson, J., and J. Reneby (2001). The Valuation of Corporate Liabilities: Theory and Tests. Working Paper, McGill University.

Ericsson, J., K. Jacobs, and R. Oviedo-Helfenberger (2004). The Determinants of Credit Default Swap Premia. Working Paper, McGill University.

Evans, C., and D. Marshall (2001). Economic Determinants of the Nominal Treasury Yield Curve. WP2001-16, Federal Reserve Bank of Chicago.

Evans, M. (2000). Regime Shifts, Risk and the Term Structure. Working Paper, Georgetown University.

Fama, E. (1965). The Behavior of Stock Market Prices. *Journal of Business* **38**, 34–105.

———— (1970). Efficient Capital Markets: A Review of Theory and Empirical Work. *Journal of Finance* **25**, 383–417.

———— (1984a). The Information in the Term Structure. *Journal of Financial Economics* **13**, 509–528.

———— (1984b). Term Premiums in Bond Returns. *Journal of Financial Economics* **13**, 529–546.

Fama, E. F., and R. R. Bliss (1987). The Information in Long-Maturity Forward Rates. *American Economic Review* **77**(4), 680–692.

Fama, E., and K. French (1988). Permanent and Temporary Components of Stock Prices. *Journal of Political Economy* **96**, 246–273.

———— (1989). Business Conditions and Expected Returns on Stocks and Bonds. *Journal of Financial Economics* **25**, 23–49.

———— (1992). The Cross-Section of Expected Stock Returns. *Journal of Finance* **47**, 427–465.

———— (1993). Common Risk Factors in the Returns on Stocks and Bonds. *Journal of Financial Economics* **33**, 23–49.

Fama, E., and J. MacBeth (1973). Risk, Return, and Equilibrium: Empirical Tests. *Journal of Political Economy* **81**, 607–636.

Fan, R., A. Gupta, and R. Ritchken (2003). Hedging in the Possible Presence of Unspanned Stochastic Volatility: Evidence from Swaption Markets. *Journal of Finance* **58**, 2219–2248.

Feller, W. (1951). Two Singular Diffusion Problems. *Annals of Mathematics* **54**, 173–182.

Ferson, W. (1983). Expectations of Real Interest Rates and Aggregate Consumption: Empirical Tests. *Journal of Financial and Quantitative Analysis* **18**, 477–497.

Ferson, W., and G. Constantinides (1991). Habit Formation and Durability in Aggregate Consumption: Empirical Tests. *Journal of Financial Economics* **28**, 199–240.

Ferson, W., and C. Harvey (1999). Conditioning Variables and the Cross-section of Stock Returns. *Journal of Finance* **54**, 1325–1360.

Ferson, W., and A. Siegel (2003). Stochastic Discount Factor Bounds with Conditioning Information. *Review of Financial Studies* **16**, 567–595.

Feuerverger, A. (1990). An Efficiency Result for the Empirical Characteristic Function in Stationary Time Series Models. *Canadian Journal of Statistics* **18**, 155–161.

Feuerverger, A., and P. McDunnough (1981). On the Efficiency of Empirical Characteristic Function Procedures. *Journal of the Royal Statistical Society, Series B* **43**, 20–27.

Fisher, L. (1966). Some New Stock Market Indices. *Journal of Business* **39**, 191–225.

Fisher, M., and C. Gilles (1996). Estimating Exponential Affine Models of the Term Structure. Working Paper, Federal Reserve Bank of Atlanta.

Fleming, M. J., and E. Remolona (1999). The Term Structure of Announcement Effects. FRB New York Staff Report No. 76.

Fuhrer, J. (2000). Habit Formation in Consumption and Its Implications for Monetary-Policy Models. *American Economic Review* **90**, 367–390.

Fuller, W. (1976). *Introduction to Statistical Time Series*. New York: Wiley.

Gallant, A. R., and D. W. Jorgenson (1979). Statistical Inference for a System of Simultaneous, Nonlinear, Implicit Equations in the Context of Instrumental Variables Estimation. *Journal of Econometrics* **11**, 275–302.

Gallant, A. R., and J. R. Long (1997). Estimating Stochastic Differential Equations Efficiently by Minimum Chi-Square. *Biometrika* **84**, 125–141.

Gallant, A. R., and G. Tauchen (1989). Seminonparametric Estimation of Conditionally Constrained Heterogeneous Processes: Asset Pricing Implications. *Econometrica* **57**, 1091–1120.

——— (1996). Which Moments to Match? *Econometric Theory* **12**, 657–681.

——— (1997). Estimation of Continuous Time Models for Stock Returns and Interest Rates. *Macroeconomic Dynamics* **1**, 135–168.

——— (1998). Reprojecting Partially Observed Systems with Application to Interest Rate Diffusions. *Journal of American Statistical Association* **93**, 10–24.

Gallant, R., and H. White (1988). *A Unified Theory of Estimation and Inference for Nonlinear Dynamic Models*. Oxford: Blackwell.

Gallant, A., L. Hansen, and G. Tauchen (1990). Using Conditional Moments of Asset Payoffs to Infer the Volatility of Intertemporal Marginal Rates of Substitution. *Journal of Econometrics* **45**, 141–179.

Garcia, R., R. Lugar, and E. Renault (2001). Asymmetric Smiles, Leverage Effects and Structural Parameters. Working Paper, Cirano, University of Montreal.

——— (2003). Empirical Assessment of an Intertemporal Option Pricing Model with Latent Variables. *Journal of Econometrics* **116**, 49–83.

Garcia, R., E. Ghysels, and E. Renault (2004). The Econometrics of Option Pricing. In Y. Aït-Sahalia and L. Hansen (Eds.), *Handbook of Financial Econometrics*. Amsterdam: Elsevier-North Holland.

Gerlach, S., and F. Smets (1997). The Term Structure of Euro-Rates: Some Evidence in Support of the Expectations Hypothesis. *Journal of International Money and Finance* **16**, 305–321.

Geske, R. (1977). The Valuation of Corporate Securities as Compound Options. *Journal of Financial and Quantitative Analysis* **12**, 541–552.

Gibbons, M. (1982). Multivariate Tests of Financial Models: A New Approach. *Journal of Financial Economics* **10**, 3–27.

Gibbons, M., S. Ross, and J. Shanken (1989). A Test of the Efficiency of a Given Portfolio. *Econometrica* **57**, 1121–1152.

Gibson, R., F. Lhabitant, and D. Talay (2001). Modeling the Term Structure of Interest Rates: A Review of the Literature. Working Paper, HEC.

Glosten, L., R. Jagannathan, and D. Runkle (1993). On the Relation between the Expected Value and the Volatility of the Nominal Excess Returns on Stocks. *Journal of Finance* **48**, 1779–1801.

Goldstein, R. (2000). The Term Structure of Interest Rates as a Random Field. *Review of Financial Studies* **13**, 365–384.

Gordon, S., and P. St-Amour (2004). Asset Returns and State-Dependent Risk Preferences. *Journal of Business and Economic Statistics* **22**, 241–252.

Gourieroux, C., and J. Jasiak (2001). Autoregressive Gamma Processes. Working Paper, CREST.

Gourieroux, C., A. Monfort, and V. Polimenis (2002). Affine Term Structure Models. Working Paper, University of Toronto.

Grauer, F., L. Litzenberger, and R. Stehle (1976). Sharing Rules and Equilibrium in an International Capital Market under Uncertainty. *Journal of Financial Economics* **3**, 233–256.

Gray, S. (1996). Modeling the Conditional Distribution of Interest Rates as a Regime Switching Process. *Journal of Financial Economics* **42**, 27–62.

Grinblatt, M. (2001). An Analytic Solution for Interest Rate Swap Spreads. *Review of International Finance* **2**, 113–149.

Grossman, S., and R. Shiller (1981). The Determinants of the Variability of Stock Market Prices. *American Economic Review* **71**, 222–227.

Gul, F. (1991). A Theory of Disappointment Aversion. *Econometrica* **59**, 667–686.

Hackbarth, D., J. Miao, and E. Morellec (2004). Capital Structure, Credit Risk, and Macroeconomic Conditions. Working Paper, Indiana University.

Hall, R. (1988). Intertemporal Substitution and Consumption. *Journal of Political Economy* **96**, 339–357.

Hamilton, J. (1988). Rational-Expectations Econometric Analysis of Changes in Regime: An Investigation of the Term Structure of Interest Rates. *Journal of Economic Dynamics and Control* **12**, 385–423.

——— (1989). A New Approach to the Economic Analysis of Nonstationary Time Series and the Business Cycle. *Econometrica* **57**, 357–384.

——— (1994). *Time Series Analysis.* Princeton: Princeton University Press.

Hamilton, J., and R. Susmel (1994). Autoregressive Conditional Heteroskedasticity and Changes in Regime. *Journal of Econometrics* **64**, 307–333.

Han, B. (2004). Stochastic Volatilities and Correlations of Bond Yields. Working Paper, Ohio State University.

Hannan, E. J. (1973). Central Limit Theorems for Time Series Regressions. *Zeitschrift fur Wahrscheinlichkeitstheorie und Verwandte Gebeite* **26**, 157–170.

Hansen, B. (1992). The Likelihood Ratio Test under Nonstandard Conditions: Testing the Markov Switching Model of GNP. *Journal of Applied Econometrics* **7**, S61–S82.

Hansen, L. (1982a). Consumption, Asset Markets, and Macroeconomic Activity: A Comment. *Carnegie-Rochester Conference Series on Public Policy* **17**, 239–250.

——— (1982b). Large Sample Properties of Generalized Method of Moments Estimators. *Econometrica* **50**, 1029–1054.

——— (1985). A Method for Calculating Bounds on the Asymptotic Covariance Matrices of Generalized Method of Moments Estimators. *Journal of Econometrics* **30**, 203–238.

——— (2005). Law of Large Numbers for Random Functions. Working Paper, University of Chicago.

Hansen, L., and R. Hodrick (1980). Forward Exchange Rates as Optimal Predictors of Future Spot Rates: An Economic Analysis. *Journal of Political Economy* **88**, 829–854.

Hansen, L., and R. Jagannathan (1991). Implications of Security Market Data for Models of Dynamic Economies. *Journal of Political Economy* **99**, 225–262.

——— (1997). Assessing Specification Errors in Stochastic Discount Factor Models. *Journal of Finance* **52**, 557–590.

Hansen, L., and S. Richard (1987). The Role of Conditioning Information in Deducing Testable Restrictions Implied by Dynamic Asset Pricing Models. *Econometrica* **55**, 587–613.

Hansen, L., and J. Scheinkman (1995). Back to the Future: Generating Moment Implications for Continuous-Time Markov Processes. *Econometrica* **63**, 767–804.

Hansen, L., and K. Singleton (1982). Generalized Instrumental Variables Estimation of Nonlinear Rational Expectations Models. *Econometrica* **50**, 1269–1286.

——— (1983). Stochastic Consumption, Risk Aversion, and the Temporal Behavior of Asset Returns. *Journal of Political Economy* **91**, 249–265.

——— (1984). Errata. *Econometrica* **52**, 267–268.

——— (1990). Computing Semiparametric Efficiency Bounds for Linear Time Series Models with Moving Average Errors. In W. Barnett, J. Powell, and G. Tauchen (Eds.), *Nonparametric and Seminonparametric Methods in Econometrics and Statistics.* Cambridge: Cambridge University Press.

——— (1996). Efficient Estimation of Linear Asset Pricing Models with Moving Average Errors. *Journal of Business and Economic Statistics* **14**, 53–68.

Hansen, L., S. Richard, and K. Singleton (1982). Testable Implications of the Intertemporal Capital Asset Pricing Model. Working Paper, Carnegie Mellon University.

Hansen, L., J. Heaton, and M. Ogaki (1988). Efficiency Bounds Implied by Multiperiod Conditional Moment Restrictions. *Journal of the American Statistical Association* **83**, 863–871.

Hansen, L., J. Heaton, and E. Luttmer (1995). Econometric Evaluation of Asset Pricing Models. *Review of Financial Studies* **8**, 237–274.

Hardouvelis, G. (1994). The Term Structure Spread and Future Changes in Long and Short Rates in the G7 Countries. *Journal of Monetary Economics* **33**, 255–283.

Harrison, M., and D. Kreps (1979). Martingales and Arbitrage in Multiperiod Securities Markets. *Journal of Economic Theory* **20**, 381–408.

Hayashi, F., and C. Sims (1983). Nearly Efficient Estimation of Time Series Models with Predetermined, but not Exogenous, Instruments. *Econometrica* **51**, 783–789.

He, J., W. Hu, and L. Lang (2000). Credit Spread Curves and Credit Ratings. Working Paper, Chinese University of Hong Kong.

Heath, D., R. Jarrow, and A. Morton (1992). Bond Pricing and the Term Structure of Interest Rates: A New Methodology. *Econometrica* **60**, 77–105.

Heaton, J. (1995). An Empirical Specification of Asset Pricing with Temporally Dependent Preference Specifications. *Econometrica* **63**, 681–717.

Heaton, J., and D. Lucas (1995). The Importance of Investor Heterogeneity and Financial Market Imperfections for the Behavior of Asset Prices. *Carnegie Rochester Conference Series on Public Policy* **42**, 1–32.

Heidari, M., and L. Wu (2003). Are Interest Rate Derivatives Spanned by the Term Structure of Interest Rates? *Journal of Fixed Income* **13**, 75–86.

Helwege, J., and C. Turner (1999). The Slope of the Credit Yield Curve for Speculative-Grade Issuers. *Journal of Finance* **54**, 1869–1884.

Heston, S. (1993). A Closed-Form Solution for Options with Stochastic Volatility, with Applications to Bond and Currency Options. *Review of Financial Studies* **6**, 327–344.

Heston, S. L., and S. Nandi (2000). A Closed-form *GARCH* Option Pricing Model. *Review of Financial Studies* **13**, 585–625.

Ho, T. S., and S. Lee (1986). Term Structure Movements and Pricing Interest Rate Contingent Claims. *Journal of Finance* **41**, 1011–1028.

Hodrick, R. (1992). Dividend Yields and Expected Stock Returns: Alternative Procedures for Inference and Measurement. *Review of Financial Studies* **5**, 357–386.

Hodrick, R., and X. Zhang (2001). Evaluating the Specification Errors of Asset Pricing Models. *Journal of Financial Economics* **62**, 327–376.

Honore, P. (1998). Five Essays on Financial Econometrics in Continuous-Time Models. Ph.D. Dissertation, Aarhus School of Business.

Hordahl, P., O. Tristani, and D. Vestin (2003). A Joint Econometric Model of Macroeconomic and Term Structure Dynamics. Working Paper, European Central Bank.

Houweling, P., and T. Vorst (2005). Pricing Default Swaps: Empirical Evidence. *Journal of International Money and Finance* **24**, 1200–1225.

Hsieh, D. (1989). Modeling Heteroskedasticity in Daily Foreign-Exchange Rates. *Journal of Business and Economic Statistics* **7**, 307–317.

Huang, J., and M. Huang (2000). How Much of the Corporate-Treasury Yield Spread is Due to Credit Risk? A New Calibration Approach. Working Paper, Stanford University.

Hull, J., and A. White (1987). The Pricing of Options on Assets with Stochastic Volatilities. *Journal of Finance* **52**, 281–300.

———— (1993). One-Factor Interest-Rate Models and the Valuation of Interest-Rate Derivative Securities. *Journal of Financial and Quantitative Analysis* **28**, 235–254.

———— (2000). Forward Rate Volatilities, Swap Rate Volatilities, and the Implementation of the LIBOR Market Model. *Journal of Fixed Income* **10**, 46–62.

———— (2004). The Relationship Between Credit Default Swap Spreads, Bond Yields, and Credit Rating Announcements. Working Paper, University of Toronto.

Ikeda, N., and S. Watanabe (1981). *Stochastic Differential Equations and Diffusion Processes.* Amsterdam: North-Holland.

Inui, K., and M. Kijima (1998). A Markovian Framework in Multi-factor Heath-Jarrow-Morton Models. *Journal of Financial and Quantitative Analysis* **33**(3), 423–440.

Jackwerth, J. C. (2000). Recovering Risk Aversion from Option Prices and Realized Returns. *Review of Financial Studies* **13**, 433–451.

Jackwerth, J., and M. Rubinstein (1996). Recovering Probability Distributions from Option Prices. *Journal of Finance* **51**, 1611–1631.

Jacquier, E., N. Polson, and P. Rossi (1994). Bayesian Analysis of Stochastic Volatility Models. *Journal of Business and Economic Statistics* **12**, 70–87.

Jagannathan, R., and Wang, Z. (1996). The Conditional CAPM and the Cross-section of Expected Returns. *Journal of Finance* **51**, 3–54.

Jagannathan, R., A. Kaplan, and S. Sun (2003). An Evaluation of Multifactor CIR Models Using LIBOR, Swap Rates, and Swaption Prices. *Journal of Econometrics* **116**, 113–146.

Jamshidian, F. (1997). Libor and Swap Market Models and Measures. *Finance Stochastics* **1**, 293–330.

Janosi, T., R. Jarrow, and Y. Yildirim (2002). Estimated Expected Losses and Liquidity Discounts Implicit in Debt Prices. *Journal of Risk* **5**, 1–38.

Jarrow, R., and S. Turnbull (1995). Pricing Options on Financial Securities Subject to Default Risk. *Journal of Finance* **50**, 53–86.

Jarrow, R., H. Li, and F. Zhao (2004). Interest Rate Caps Smile Too! But Can the LIBOR Market Models Capture It? Working Paper, Cornell University.

Jarrow, R. A., D. Lando, and F. Yu (2005). Default Risk and Diversification: Theory and Empirical Implications. *Mathematical Finance* **15**, 1–26.

Jeffrey, A. (1995). Single Factor Heath-Jarrow-Morton Term Structure Models Based on Markov Spot Interest Rate Dynamics. *Journal of Financial and Quantitative Analysis* **30**, 619–642.

Jegadeesh, N. (1991). Seasonality in Stock Price Mean Reversion: Evidence from the U.S. and U.K. *Journal of Finance* **46**, 1427–1444.

Jegadeesh, N., and G. Pennacchi (1996). The Behavior of Interest Rates Implied by the Term Structure of Eurodollar Futures. *Journal of Money, Credit, and Banking* **28**, 426–446.

Jennrich, R. (1969). Asymptotic Properties of Non-Linear Least Squares Estimators. *Annals of Mathematical Statistics* **40**, 633–643.

Jiang, G., and J. Knight (1997). A Non-Parametric Approach to the Estimation of Diffusion Processes, with an Application to a Short-Term Interest Rate Model. *Econometric Theory* **13**, 615–645.

——— (1999). Efficient Estimation of the Continuous Time Stochastic Volatility Model via the Empirical Characteristic Function. Working Paper, University of Western Ontario.

Johannes, M. (2004). The Statistical and Economic Role of Jumps in Interest Rates. *Journal of Finance* **59**, 227–260.

Johannes, M., and N. Polson (2005). MCMC for Financial Econometrics. In Y. Aït-Sahalia and L. Hansen (Eds.), *Handbook of Financial Econometrics*. Amsterdam: Elsevier-North-Holland.

Johnsen, T., and J. Donaldson (1985). The Structure of Intertemporal Preferences under Uncertainty and Time Consistent Plans. *Econometrica* **53**, 1451–1458.

Jones, E., S. Mason, and E. Rosenfeld (1984). Contingent Claims Analysis of Corporate Capital Structures: An Empirical Investigation. *Journal of Finance* **39**, 611–625.

Jorgenson, D., and J. Laffont (1974). Efficient Estimation of Nonlinear Simultaneous Equations with Additive Errors. *Annals of Economic and Social Measurement* **3**, 615–640.

Jorion, P. (1988). On Jump Processes in the Foreign Exchange and Stock Markets. *Review of Financial Studies* **1**, 427–445.

Kahneman, D., and A. Tversky (1979). Prospect Theory: An Analysis of Decision under Risk. *Econometrica* **49**, 263–291.

Keim, D., and R. Stambaugh (1986). Predicting Returns in the Stock and Bond Markets. *Journal of Financial Economics* **17**, 357–390.

Kendall, M. (1954). Note on Bias in the Estimation of Autocorrelation. *Biometrika* **41**, 403–404.

Kennedy, D. P. (1994). The Term Structure of Interest Rates as a Gaussian Random Field. *Mathematical Finance* **4**, 247–258.

Kerkhof, J., and A. Pelsser (2002). Observational Equivalence of Discrete String Models and Market Models. *Journal of Derivatives* **10**, 55–61.

Keswani, A. (2002). Estimating a Risky Term Structure of Brady Bonds. Working Paper, Lancaster University.

Kiefer, N. (1978). Discrete Parameter Variation: Efficient Estimation of a Switching Regression Model. *Econometrica* **46**, 427–434.

Kim, D. (2004). Time-Varying Risk and Return in the Quadratic-Gaussian Model of the Term Structure. Working Paper, Federal Reserve Board.

Kim, J., K. Ramaswamy, and S. Sundaresan (1993). Does Default Risk in Coupons Affect the Valuation of Corporate Bonds? A Contingent Claims Model. *Financial Management* **22**, 117–131.

Kim, S., N. Shephard, and S. Chib (1998). Stochastic Volatility: Likelihood Inference and Comparison with ARCH Models. *Review of Economic Studies* **65**, 361–394.

Kloeden, P., and E. Platen (1992). *Numerical Solutions of Stochastic Differential Equations.* Berlin: Springer-Verlag.

Knight, F. (1921). *Risk, Uncertainty and Profit.* Boston: Houghton, Mifflin.

Knight, J., and J. Yu (2002). Empirical Characteristic Function in Time Series Estimation. *Econometric Theory* **18**, 691–721.

Kogan, L., S. Ross, J. Wang, and M. Westerfield (2006). The Price Impact of Survival of Irrational Traders. *Journal of Finance* **61**.

Kraus, A., and J. Sagi (2004). Asset Pricing with Unforeseen Contingencies. Working Paper, University of California, Berkeley.

Kreps, D., and E. Porteus (1978). Temporal Resolution of Uncertainty and Dynamic Choice Theory. *Econometrica* **46**, 185–200.

Kugler, P. (1997). Central Bank Policy Reaction and Expectations Hypothesis of the Term Structure. *International Journal of Financial Economics* **2**, 217–224.

Lamont, O. (2001). Economic Tracking Portfolios. *Journal of Econometrics* **105**, 164–181.

Landen, C. (2000). Bond Pricing in a Hidden Markov Model of the Short Rate. *Finance and Stochastics* **4**, 371–389.

Lando, D. (1998). On Cox Processes and Credit Risky Securities. *Review of Derivatives Research* **2**, 99–120.

Langetieg, T. (1980). A Multivariate Model of the Term Structure. *Journal of Finance* **35**, 71–97.

Law, P. (2005). Macro Factors and the Yield Curve. Ph.D. Dissertation, Stanford University.

Lee, B., and B. Ingram (1991). Simulation Estimation of Time Series Models. *Journal of Econometrics* **47**, 197–205.

Leippold, M., and L. Wu (2002). Asset Pricing under the Quadratic Class. *Journal of Financial and Quantitative Analysis* **37**, 271–295.

——— (2003). Design and Estimation of Quadratic Term Structure Models. *European Finance Review* **7**, 47–73.

Leland, H. (1980). Who Should Buy Portfolio Insurance? *Journal of Finance* **35**, 581–594.

Leland, H. E. (1994). Corporate Debt Value, Bond Covenants, and Optimal Capital Structure. *Journal of Finance* **49**, 1213–1252.

Leland, H., and K. Toft (1996). Optimal Capital Structure, Endogenous Bankruptcy, and the Term Structure of Credit Spreads. *Journal of Finance* **51**, 987–1019.

Lettau, M., and S. Ludvigson (2001a). Consumption, Aggregate Wealth, and Expected Stock Returns. *Journal of Finance* **56**, 815–849.

———— (2001b). Resurrecting the (C)CAPM: A Cross-Sectional Test When Risk Premia Are Time-Varying. *Journal of Political Economy* **109**, 1238–1287.

Lewellen, J. (2004). Predicting Returns with Financial Ratios. *Journal of Financial Economics* **74**, 209–235.

Lewellen, J., and S. Nagel (2005). The Conditional CAPM Does Not Explain Asset Pricing Anomalies. Forthcoming, *Journal of Financial Economics*.

Lintner, J. (1965). Valuation of Risk Assets and the Selection of Risky Investments in Stock Portfolios and Capital Budgets. *Review of Economics and Statistics* **47**, 13–37.

Litterman, R., and J. Scheinkman (1991). Common Factors Affecting Bond Returns. *Journal of Fixed Income* **1**, 54–61.

Litterman, R., and K. Winkelmann (1998). Estimating Covariance Matrices. Working Paper, Goldman-Sachs, Risk Management Series.

Litterman, R., J. Scheinkman, and L. Weiss (1991). Volatility and the Yield Curve. *Journal of Fixed Income* **1**, 49–53.

Liu, J. (1997). Generalized Method of Moments Estimation of Affine Diffusion Processes. Working Paper, Graduate School of Business, Stanford Unversity.

Liu, J., J. Pan, and T. Wang (2005). An Equilibrium Model of Rare-Event Premia and Its Implication for Option Smirks. *Review of Financial Studies* **18**, 131–164.

Liu, J., F. Longstaff, and R. Mandell (2006). The Market Price of Credit Risk: An Empirical Analysis of Interest Rate Swap Spreads. *Journal of Business* **79**.

Lo, A., and C. MacKinlay (1988). Stock Market Prices Do Not Follow Random Walks: Evidence from Simple Specification Tests. *Review of Financial Studies* **1**, 41–66.

———— (1989). The Size and Power of the Variance Ratio Test in Finite Samples: A Monte Carlo Investigation. *Journal of Econometrics* **40**, 203–238.

———— (1990). An Econometric Analysis of Nonsynchronous Trading. *Journal of Econometrics* **45**, 181–212.

Long, J. (1974). Stock Prices, Inflation, and the Term Structure of Interest Rates. *Journal of Financial Economics* **1**, 131–170.

Longstaff, F. A. (1989). A Nonlinear General Equilibrium Model of the Term Structure of Interest Rates. *Journal of Financial Economics* **2**, 195–224.

Longstaff, F. A., and E. S. Schwartz (1992). Interest Rate Volatility and the Term Structure: A Two-Factor General Equilibrium Model. *Journal of Finance* **47**, 1259–1282.

———— (1995). A Simple Approach to Valuing Risky Fixed- and Floating-Rate Debt. *Journal of Finance* **50**, 789–819.

Longstaff, F., P. Santa-Clara, and E. Schwartz (2001a). The Relative Valuation of Caps and Swaptions: Theory and Empirical Evidence. *Journal of Finance* **56**, 2067–2109.

———— (2001b). Throwing Away a Billion Dollars: The Cost of Suboptimal Exercise Strategies in the Swaptions Market. *Journal of Financial Economics* **62**, 39–66.

Longstaff, F., S. Mithal, and E. Neis (2005). Corporate Yield Spreads: Default Risk or Liquidity? New Evidence from the Credit-Default Swap Market. *Journal of Finance* **60**, 2213–2253.

Lu, B. (2000). An Empirical Analysis of the Constantinides Model of the Term Structure. Working Paper, University of Michigan.

Lu, B., and G. Wu (2000). Implied Bivariate State Price Density. Working Paper, University of Michigan.

Lucas, R. (1978). Asset Prices in an Exchange Economy. *Econometrica* **46**, 1429–1445.

Luenberger, D. (1969). *Optimization by Vector Space Methods*. New York: Wiley.

Lustig, H., and S. V. Nieuwerburgh (2005). Housing Collateral, Consumption Insurance, and Risk Premia: An Empirical Perspective. Forthcoming, *Journal of Finance*.

Lyden, S., and D. Sariniti (2000). An Empirical Examination of the Classical Theory of Corporate Security Valuation. Working Paper, Barclays Global Investors.

Madan, D., and H. Unal (1998). Pricing the Risks of Default. *Review of Derivatives Research* **2**, 121–160.

Maddala, G., and I. Kim (1998). *Unit Roots, Cointegration, and Structural Change*. Cambridge: Cambridge University Press.

Mankiw, G., J. Rotemberg, and L. Summers (1985). Intertemporal Substitution in Macroeconomics. *Quarterly Journal of Economics* **100**, 225–251.

Marcet, A., and K. Singleton (1999). Equilibrium Asset Prices and Savings of Heterogeneous Agents in the Presence of Portfolio Constraints. *Macroeconomic Dynamics* **3**, 243–277.

Martellini, L., and N. E. Karoui (2001). A Theoretical Inspection of the Market Price for Default Risk. Working Paper, University of Southern California.

McCallum, B. T. (1994). Monetary Policy and the Term Structure of Interest Rates. NBER Working Paper No. 4938.

McFadden, D. (1987). A Method of Simulated Moments for Estimation of Discrete Response Models without Numerical Integration. *Econometrica* **57**, 995–1026.

Mehra, R., and E. Prescott (1985). The Equity Premium Puzzle. *Journal of Monetary Economics* **15**, 145–161.

Melino, A., and S. Turnbull (1990). Pricing Foreign Currency Options with Stochastic Volatility. *Journal of Econometrics* **45**, 239–265.

Mella-Barral, P., and W. Perraudin (1997). Strategic Debt Service. *Journal of Finance* **52**, 531–556.

Merrick, J. J. (2001). Crisis Dynamics of Implied Default Recovery Ratios: Evidence from Russia and Argentina. *Journal of Banking and Finance* **25**, 1921–1939.

Merton, R. (1970). A Dynamic General Equilibrium Model of the Asset Market and Its Application to the Pricing of the Capital Structure of the Firm. Working Paper, Sloan School of Management, Massachusetts Institute of Technology.

——— (1973). Theory of Rational Option Pricing. *Bell Journal of Economics and Management Science* **4**, 141–183.

——— (1974). On the Pricing of Corporate Debt: The Risk Structure of Interest Rates. *Journal of Finance* **29**, 449–470.

——— (1980). On Estimating the Expected Return on the Market. *Journal of Financial Economics* **8**, 323–361.

Michner, R. (1984). Permanent Income in General Equilibrium. *Journal of Monetary Economics* **14**, 297–305.

Miltersen, K. R., K. Sandmann, and D. Sondermann (1997). Closed Form Solutions for Term Structure Derivatives with Log-Normal Interest Rates. *Journal of Finance* **52**(1), 409–430.

Mokkadem, A. (1985). Le Modele Non Lineaire AR(1) General. Ergodicite et Ergodicite Geometrique. *Comptes Rendues Academie Scientifique Paris* **301** Serie I, 889–892.

Morton, A. (1988). Arbitrage and Martingales. Technical Report 821, Cornell University.

Moskowitz, T. (2003). An Analysis of Covariance Risk and Pricing Anomalies. *Review of Financial Studies* **16**, 417–457.

Mossin, J. (1968). Equilibrium in a Capital Asset Market. *Econometrica* **34**, 768–783.

Mulligan, C. (2004). Robust Aggregate Implications of Stochastic Discount Factor Volatility. NBER Working Paper 10210.

Musiela, M. (1994). Stochastic PDEs and Term Structure Models. Working Paper, University of New South Wales, Sydney.

Musiela, M., and M. Rutkowski (1997). Continuous-time Term Structure

Models: A Forward Measure Approach. *Finance and Stochastics* **1**, 261–291.

Naik, V., and M. H. Lee (1997). Yield Curve Dynamics with Discrete Shifts in Economic Regimes: Theory and Estimation. Working Paper, Faculty of Commerce, University of British Columbia.

Neal, R., D. Rolph, and C. Morris (2000). Interest Rates and Credit Spreads. Working Paper, Kelley School of Business, Indiana University.

Neftci, S. (1984). Are Economic Time Series Asymmetric Over the Business Cycle? *Journal of Political Economy* **92**, 307–328.

Nelson, C., and A. Siegel (1987). Parsimonious Modelling of Yield Curves. *Journal of Business* **60**, 473–489.

Nelson, D. (1990). ARCH Models as Diffusion Approximations. *Journal of Econometrics* **45**, 7–38.

——— (1991). Conditional Heteroskedasticity in Asset Returns: A New Approach. *Econometrica* **59**, 347–370.

Newey, W. K. (1984). A Method of Moments Interpretation of Sequential Estimators. *Economics Letters* **14**, 201–206.

——— (1991). Uniform Convergence in Probability and Stochastic Equicontinuity. *Econometrica* **59**, 703–708.

Newey, W., and K. D. West (1987a). Hypothesis Testing with Efficient Method of Moment Estimation. *International Economic Review* **28**, 777–787.

——— (1987b). A Simple Positive Semi-Definite, Heteroskedasticity and Autocorrelation Consistent Covariance Matrix. *Econometrica* **55**, 703–708.

Niederhoffer, V., and M. Osborne (1966). Market Making and Reversal of the Stock Exchange. *Journal of the American Statistical Association* **61**, 897–916.

Nielsen, L. T., J. SaaRequejo, and P. Santa-Clara (1993). Default Risk and Interest Rate Risk: The Term Structure of Default Spreads. Working Paper, INSEAD, Fontainebleau, France.

Nummelin, E., and P. Tuominen (1982). Geometric Ergodicity of Harris Recurrent Markov Chains with Applications to Renewel Theory. *Stochastic Processes and Their Applications* **12**, 187–202.

Ogden, J. (1987). Determinants of the Relative Interest Rate Sensitivities of Corporate Bonds. *Financial Management* **10**, 22–30.

Pagès, H. (2000). Estimating Brazilian Sovereign Risk from Brady Bond Prices. Working Paper, Bank of France.

Pakes, A., and D. Pollard (1987). The Asymptotics of Simulation Estimators. *Econometrica* **57**, 1027–1058.

Pan, J. (2000). Jump-Diffusion Models of Asset Prices: Theory and Empirical Evidence. Ph.D. Thesis, Stanford University.

——— (2002). The Jump-Risk Premia Implicit in Options: Evidence from an Integrated Time-Series Study. *Journal of Financial Economics* **63**, 3–50.

Pan, J., and K. Singleton (2005). Default and Recovery Implicit in the Term Structure of Sovereign CDS Spreads. Working Paper, Stanford University.

Pardoux, E. (1993). Stochastic Partial Differential Equations: A Review. *Bulletin des Sciences Mathématiques* **117**, 29–47.

Pearson, N. D., and T. Sun (1994). Exploiting the Conditional Density in Estimating the Term Structure: An Application to the Cox, Ingersoll, and Ross Model. *Journal of Finance* **49**, 1279–1304.

Pedersen, A. (1995). A New Approach to Maximum Likelihood Estimation for Stochastic Differential Equations Based on Discrete Observations. *Scandinavian Journal of Statistics* **22**, 55–71.

Perron, P. (1988). Trends and Random Walks in Macroeconomic Time Series: Further Evidence from a New Approach. *Journal of Economic Dynamics and Control* **12**, 297–332.

Peterson, S., R. Stapleton, and M. Subrahmanyam (1998). An Arbitrage-Free Two-factor Model of the Term Structure of Interest Rates: A Multivariate Binomial Approach. Working Paper, New York University.

Phelan, M. J. (1995). Probability and Statistics Applied to the Practice of Financial Risk Management: The Case of JP Morgan's RiskMetrics. Working Paper, The Wharton Financial Institution Center.

Phillips, P. (1987). Time Series Regression with a Unit Root. *Econometrica* **55**, 277–301.

Piazzesi, M. (2003). Bond Yields and the Federal Reserve. *Journal of Political Economy* **113**, 311–344.

Plosser, C., and W. Schwert (1978). Money, Income and Sunspots: Measuring Economic Relationships and the Effects of Differencing. *Journal of Monetary Economics* **4**, 637–660.

Poterba, J., and L. Summers (1988). Mean Reversion in Stock Prices: Evidence and Implications. *Journal of Financial Economics* **22**, 27–59.

Quandt, R., and J. Ramsey (1978). Estimating Mixtures of Normal Distributions and Switching Regressions. *Journal of the American Statistical Association* **73**, 730–738.

Rebonato, R., and I. Cooper (1997). The Limitations of Simple Two-Factor Interest Rate Models. *Journal of Financial Engineering* **5**, 1–16.

Richardson, M. (1993). Temporary Components of Stock Prices: A Skeptic's View. *Journal of Business and Economics Statistics* **11**, 199–207.

Richardson, M., and T. Smith (1991). Tests of Financial Models in the Presence of Overlapping Observations. *Review of Financial Studies* **4**, 227–254.

——— (1994). A Unified Approach to Testing for Serial Correlation in Stock Returns. *Journal of Business* **67**, 371–399.

Richardson, M., and J. Stock (1989). Drawing Inferences from Statistics Based on Multiyear Asset Returns. *Journal of Financial Economics* **25**, 323–348.

Ritchken, P., and L. Sankarasubramanian (1995). Volatility Structure of Forward Rates and the Dynamics of the Term Structure. *Mathematical Finance* **5**, 55–72.

Roberds, W., and C. Whiteman (1999). Endogenous Term Premia and Anomalies in the Term Structure of Interest Rates: Explaining the Predictability Smile. *Journal of Monetary Economics* **44**, 555–580.

Roll, R. (1977). A Critique of the Asset Pricing Theory's Tests: Part I. *Journal of Financial Economics* **4**, 129–176.

——— (1984). A Simple Implicit Measure of the Effective Bid-Ask Spread in an Efficient Market. *Journal of Finance* **39**, 1127–1140.

Rosenberg, B. (1972). The Behavior of Random Variables with Nonstationary Variance and the Distribution of Security Prices. Working Paper, University of California, Berkeley.

Rosenberg, B., K. Reid, and R. Lanstein (1985). Persuasive Evidence of Market Inefficiency. *Journal of Portfolio Management* **11**, 9–17.

Rosenberg, J. V., and R. F. Engle (2002). Empirical Pricing Kernels. *Journal of Financial Economics* **64**, 341–372.

Rosenblatt, M. (1971). *Markov Processes: Structure and Asymptotic Behavior.* Berlin: Springer-Verlag.

Ross, S. A. (1978). A Simple Approach to the Valuation of Risky Streams. *Journal of Business* **3**, 453–476.

Rubinstein, M. (1976). The Valuation of Uncertain Income Streams and the Pricing of Options. *Bell Journal of Economics* **7**, 407–425.

Rudebusch, G., and T. Wu (2003). A No-Arbitrage Model of the Term Structure and the Macroeconomy. Working Paper, Federal Reserve Bank of San Francisco.

Said, S., and D. Dickey (1984). Testing for Unit Roots in Autoregressive-Moving Average Models of Unknown Order. *Biometrika* **71**, 599–607.

Sandmann, G., and S. Koopman (1998). Estimation of Stochastic Volatility Models via Monte Carlo Maximum Likelihood. *Journal of Econometrics* **87**(2), 271–302.

Sandmann, K., and D. Sondermann (1997). A Note on the Stability of Lognormal Interest Rate Models and the Pricing of Eurodollar Futures. *Mathematical Finance* **7**, 119–125.

Sangvinatsos, A., and J. Wachter (2005). Does the Failure of the Expectations Hypothesis Matter for Long-Term Investors? *Journal of Finance* **60**, 179–230.

Santa-Clara, P., and D. Sornette (2001). The Dynamics of the Forward Interest Rate Curve with Stochastic String Shocks. *Review of Financial Studies* **14**, 149–185.

Santos, T., and P. Veronesi (2005). Labor Income and Predictable Stock Returns. Forthcoming, *Review of Financial Studies.*

Sarig, O., and A. Warga (1989). Some Empirical Estimates of the Risk Structure of Interest Rates. *The Journal of Finance* **44**, 1351–1360.

Savin, N. (1976). Conflicts among Testing Procedures in a Linear Regression Model with Autoregressive Disturbances. *Econometrica* **44**, 1303–1313.

Schaefer, S., and I. Strebulaev (2004). Structural Models of Credit Risk Are Useful: Evidence from Hedge Ratios on Corporate Bonds. Working Paper, Graduate School of Business, Stanford University.

Scholes, M., and J. Williams (1977). Estimating Betas from Nonsynchronous Data. *Journal of Financial Economics* **5**, 309–327.

Schroder, M., and C. Skiadas (2002). An Isomorphism Between Asset Pricing Models with and without Linear Habit Formation. *Review of Financial Studies* **15**, 1189–1221.

Scott, L. (1996). The Valuation of Interest Rate Derivatives in a Multi-Factor Cox-Ingersoll-Ross Model that Matches the Initial Term Structure. Working Paper, University of Georgia.

——— (1997). Pricing Stock Options in a Jump-Diffusion Model with Stochastic Volatility and Interest Rates: Application of Fourier Inversion Methods. *Mathematical Finance* **7**, 345–358.

Shanken, J. (1992). On the Estimation of Beta-Pricing Models. *Review of Financial Studies* **5**, 1–33.

Sharpe, W. F. (1964). Capital Asset Prices: A Theory of Market Equilibrium under Conditions of Risk. *Journal of Finance* **19**, 429–442.

Shiller, R. (1979). The Volatility of Long-Term Interest Rates and Expectations Models of the Term Structure. *Journal of Political Economy* **87**, 1190–1219.

——— (1982). Consumption, Asset Markets, and Macroeconomic Activity. *Carnegie-Rochester Conference Series on Public Policy* **17**, 203–238.

Singleton, K. (1980). Expectations Models of the Term Structure and Implied Variance Bounds. *Journal of Political Economy* **88**, 1159–1176.

——— (1985). Testing Specifications of Economic Agents' Intertemporal Optimum Problems against Non-Nested Alternatives. *Journal of Econometrics* **30**, 391–413.

——— (1990). Specification and Estimation of Intertemporal Asset Pricing Models. In B. Friedman and F. Hahn (Eds.), *Handbook of Monetary Economics*, Volume 1, pp. 5–32. Amsterdam: Elsevier Science.

——— (1993). Econometric Implications of Consumption-Based Asset Pricing Models. In *Advances in Econometrics, Sixth World Congress*. New York: Cambridge University Press.

——— (1995). Yield Curve Risk Management for Government Bond Portfolios: An International Comparison. In W. Beaver and G. Parker (Eds.), *Risk Management Problems and Solutions*, pp. 295–322. New York: McGraw-Hill.

——— (2001). Estimation of Affine Asset Pricing Models Using the Empirical Characteristic Function. *Journal of Econometrics* **102**, 111–141.

Singleton, K., and L. Umantsev (2002). Pricing Coupon-Bond Options and Swaptions in Affine Term Structure Models. *Mathematical Finance* **12**, 427–446.

Stambaugh, R. F. (1997). Analyzing Investments Whose Histories Differ in Length. *Journal of Financial Economics* **45**, 285–331.

Stanton, R. (1997). A Nonparametric Model of Term Structure Dynamics and the Market Price of Interest Rate Risk. *Journal of Finance* **52**, 1973–2002.

Stock, J., and M. Watson (1989). New Indexes of Coincident and Leading Economic Indicators. *NBER Macro Annual* **4**, 351–395.

Stockman, A. (1978). Risk, Information, and Forward Exchange Rates. In J. Frenkel and H. Johnson (Eds.), *The Economics of Exchange Rates: Selected Studies*. Reading, Mass.: Addison Wesley.

Summers, L. (1986). Does the Stock Market Rationally Reflect Fundamental Values? *Journal of Finance* **41**, 591–601.

Sun, T. (1992). Real and Nominal Interest Rates: A Discrete-Time Model and Its Continuous-Time Limit. *Review of Financial Studies* **5**(4), 581–611.

Sun, T., S. Sundaresan, and C. Wang (1993). Interest Rate Swaps—An Empirical Investigation. *Journal of Financial Economics* **34**, 77–99.

Sundaresan, S. (1989). Intertemporally Dependent Preferences and the Volatility of Consumption and Wealth. *Review of Financial Studies* **2**, 73–88.

——— (2000). Continuous-Time Methods in Finance: A Review and an Assessment. *Journal of Finance* **55**, 1569–1622.

Tang, D., and H. Yan (2005). Macroeononomic Conditions, Firm Characteristics, and Credit Spreads. Working Paper, University of Texas, Austin.

Tauren, M. (1999). A Model of Corporate Bond Prices with Dynamic Capital Structure. Working Paper, Indiana University.

Taylor, S. (1986). *Modeling Financial Time Series*. Chichester, UK: Wiley.

——— (1994). Modeling Stochastic Volatility: A Review and Comparative Study. *Mathematical Finance* **4**, 183–204.

Telmer, C. (1993). Asset Pricing Puzzles and Incomplete Markets. *Journal of Finance* **48**, 1803–1832.

Tweedie, R. (1982). Criteria for Rates of Convergence of Markov Chains, with Applications to Queuing and Storage Theory. In J. Kingman and G. Reuter (Eds.), *Probability, Statistics, and Analysis*. Cambridge: Cambridge University Press.

Umantsev, L. (2001). Econometric Analysis of European LIBOR-based Options with Affine Term Structure Models. Ph.D. Dissertation, Stanford University.

Vasicek, O. (1977). An Equilibrium Characterization of the Term Structure. *Journal of Financial Economics* **5**, 177–188.

Vassalou, M. (2003). News Related to Future GDP Growth as a Risk Factor in Equity Returns. *Journal of Financial Economics* **68**, 47–73.

Wachter, J. (2005). A Consumption-Based Model of the Term Structure of Interest Rates. Forthcoming, *Journal of Financial Economics*.

Weil, P. (1989). The Equity Premium Puzzle and the Risk-free Rate Puzzle. *Journal of Monetary Economics* **24**, 401–421.

West, K. (1988). Asymptotic Normality, When Regressors Have a Unit Root. *Econometrica* **56**, 1397–1417.

White, H. (1982). Maximum Likelihood Estimation of Misspecified Models. *Econometrica* **50**, 1–16.

——— (1984). *Asymptotic Theory for Econometricians*. New York: Academic.

Wu, S. (2002). How Do Changes In Monetary Policy Affect the Term Structure of Interest Rates? Working Paper, University of Kansas.

Wu, S., and Y. Zeng (2003). A General Equilibrium Model of the Term Structure of Interest Rates under Regime-Switching Risk. Working Paper, University of Kansas.

Wu, T. (2000). Macro Factors and the Affine Term Structure of Interest Rates. Working Paper, Yale University.

Yamada, T., and S. Watanabe (1971). On the Uniqueness of Solutions of Stochastic Differential Equations. *Journal of Mathematics Kyoto University* **11**, 155–167.

Yan, H. (2001). Dynamic Models of the Term Structure. *Financial Analysts Journal* **57**, 60–75.

Yu, F. (2002). Modeling Expected Return on Defaultable Bonds. *Journal of Fixed Income* **12**, 69–81.

Zhang, F. (2003). What Did the Credit Market Expect of Argentina Default? Evidence from Default Swap Data. Working Paper, Federal Reserve Board.

Zhou, C. (2001a). The Term Structure of Credit Spreads with Jump Risk. *Journal of Banking and Finance* **25**, 2015–2040.

——— (2001b). Finite Sample Properties of EMM, GMM, QMLE, and MLE for a Square-Root Interest Rate Diffusion Model. *Journal of Computational Finance* **5**, 89–122.

——— (2001c). Jump-Diffusion Term Structure and Ito Conditional Moment Generator. Working Paper, Federal Reserve Board.

Index

Page numbers followed by n indicate notes; those followed by f indicate figures; those followed by t indicate tables.

9 780691 122977